Novels
for Students

National Advisory Board

Novels for Students

Presenting Analysis, Context, and Criticism on
Commonly Studied Novels

Volume 25

Ira Mark Milne
Project Editor

Foreword by Anne Devereaux Jordan

THOMSON

GALE

Detroit • New York • San Francisco • New Haven, Conn. • Waterville, Maine • London

Novels for Students, Volume 25

Project Editor
Ira Mark Milne

Editorial
Jennifer Greve

Rights Acquisition and Management
Lori Hines, Aja Perales, Lista Person, Sue Rudolph

Manufacturing
Drew Kalasky

Imaging
Leitha Etheridge-Sims, Lezlie Light, Mike Logusz, Dan Newell

Product Design
Pamela A. E. Galbreath

Vendor Administration
Civie Green

Product Manager
Meggin Condino

ISBN-13: 978-0-7876-8682-6
ISBN-10: 0-7876-8682-4
ISSN 1094-3552

Printed in the United States of America
10 9 8 7 6 5 4 3 2 1

Table of Contents

The Informed Dialogue: Interacting with Literature

When we pick up a book, we usually do so with the anticipation of pleasure. We hope that by entering the time and place of the novel and sharing the thoughts and actions of the characters, we will find enjoyment. Unfortunately, this is often not the case; we are disappointed. But we should ask, has the author failed us, or have we failed the author?

We establish a dialogue with the author, the book, and with ourselves when we read. Consciously and unconsciously, we ask questions: "Why did the author write this book?" "Why did the author choose that time, place, or character?" "How did the author achieve that effect?" "Why did the character act that way?" "Would I act in the same way?" The answers we receive depend upon how much information about literature in general and about that book specifically we ourselves bring to our reading.

Young children have limited life and literary experiences. Being young, children frequently do not know how to go about exploring a book, nor sometimes, even know the questions to ask of a book. The books they read help them answer questions, the author often coming right out and *telling* young readers the things they are learning or are expected to learn. The perennial classic, *The Little Engine That Could, tells* its readers that, among other things, it is good to help others and brings happiness:

"Hurray, hurray," cried the funny little clown and all the dolls and toys. "The good little boys and girls in

the city will be happy because you helped us, kind, Little Blue Engine."

In picture books, messages are often blatant and simple, the dialogue between the author and reader one-sided. Young children are concerned with the end result of a book—the enjoyment gained, the lesson learned—rather than with how that result was obtained. As we grow older and read further, however, we question more. We come to expect that the world within the book will closely mirror the concerns of our world, and that the author will *show* these through the events, descriptions, and conversations within the story, rather than *telling* of them. We are now expected to do the interpreting, carry on our share of the dialogue with the book and author, and glean not only the author's message, but comprehend how that message and the overall affect of the book were achieved. Sometimes, however, we need help to do these things. *Novels for Students* provides that help.

A novel is made up of many parts interacting to create a coherent whole. In reading a novel, the more obvious features can be easily spotted—theme, characters, plot—but we may overlook the more subtle elements that greatly influence how the novel is perceived by the reader: viewpoint, mood and tone, symbolism, or the use of humor. By focusing on both the obvious and more subtle literary elements within a novel, *Novels for Students* aids readers in both analyzing for message and in determining how and why that message is communicated. In the discussion on Harper Lee's *To*

Kill a Mockingbird (Vol. 2), for example, the mockingbird as a symbol of innocence is dealt with, among other things, as is the importance of Lee's use of humor which "enlivens a serious plot, adds depth to the characterization, and creates a sense of familiarity and universality." The reader comes to understand the internal elements of each novel discussed—as well as the external influences that help shape it.

"The desire to write greatly," Harold Bloom of Yale University says, "is the desire to be elsewhere, in a time and place of one's own, in an originality that must compound with inheritance, with an anxiety of influence." A writer seeks to create a unique world within a story, but although it is unique, it is not disconnected from our own world. It speaks to us *because* of what the writer brings to the writing from our world: how he or she was raised and educated; his or her likes and dislikes; the events occurring in the real world at the time of the writing, and while the author was growing up. When we know what an author has brought to his or her work, we gain a greater insight into both the "originality" (the world of the book), and the things that "compound" it. This insight enables us to question that created world and find answers more readily. By informing ourselves, we are able to establish a more effective dialogue with both book and author.

Novels for Students, in addition to providing a plot summary and descriptive list of characters—to remind readers of what they have read—also explores the external influences that shaped each book. Each entry includes a discussion of the author's background, and the historical context in which the novel was written. It is vital to know, for instance, that when Ray Bradbury was writing *Fahrenheit 451* (Vol. 1), the threat of Nazi domination had recently ended in Europe, and the McCarthy hearings were taking place in Washington, D.C. This information goes far in answering the question, "Why did he write a story of oppressive government control and book burning?" Similarly, it is important to know that Harper Lee, author of *To Kill a Mockingbird,* was born and raised in Monroeville, Alabama, and that her father was a lawyer.

Readers can now see why she chose the south as a setting for her novel—it is the place with which she was most familiar—and start to comprehend her characters and their actions.

Novels for Students helps readers find the answers they seek when they establish a dialogue with a particular novel. It also aids in the posing of questions by providing the opinions and interpretations of various critics and reviewers, broadening that dialogue. Some reviewers of *To Kill A Mockingbird,* for example, "faulted the novel's climax as melodramatic." This statement leads readers to ask, "Is it, indeed, melodramatic?" "If not, why did some reviewers see it as such?" "If it is, why did Lee choose to make it melodramatic?" "Is melodrama ever justified?" By being spurred to ask these questions, readers not only learn more about the book and its writer, but about the nature of writing itself.

The literature included for discussion in *Novels for Students* has been chosen because it has something vital to say to us. *Of Mice and Men, Catch-22, The Joy Luck Club, My Antonia, A Separate Peace* and the other novels here speak of life and modern sensibility. In addition to their individual, specific messages of prejudice, power, love or hate, living and dying, however, they and all great literature also share a common intent. They force us to *think*—about life, literature, and about others, not just about ourselves. They pry us from the narrow confines of our minds and thrust us outward to confront the world of books and the larger, real world we all share. *Novels for Students* helps us in this confrontation by providing the means of enriching our conversation with literature and the world, by creating an *informed* dialogue, one that brings true pleasure to the personal act of reading.

Sources

Harold Bloom, *The Western Canon, The Books and School of the Ages,* Riverhead Books, 1994.

Watty Piper, *The Little Engine That Could,* Platt & Munk, 1930.

Anne Devereaux Jordan
Senior Editor, TALL
(Teaching and Learning Literature)

Introduction

Purpose of the Book

The purpose of *Novels for Students (NfS)* is to provide readers with a guide to understanding, enjoying, and studying novels by giving them easy access to information about the work. Part of Gale's "For Students" Literature line, *NfS* is specifically designed to meet the curricular needs of high school and undergraduate college students and their teachers, as well as the interests of general readers and researchers considering specific novels. While each volume contains entries on "classic" novels frequently studied in classrooms, there are also entries containing hard-to-find information on contemporary novels, including works by multicultural, international, and women novelists.

The information covered in each entry includes an introduction to the novel and the novel's author; a plot summary, to help readers unravel and understand the events in a novel; descriptions of important characters, including explanation of a given character's role in the novel as well as discussion about that character's relationship to other characters in the novel; analysis of important themes in the novel; and an explanation of important literary techniques and movements as they are demonstrated in the novel.

In addition to this material, which helps the readers analyze the novel itself, students are also provided with important information on the literary and historical background informing each work. This includes a historical context essay, a box comparing the time or place the novel was written to modern Western culture, a critical essay, and excerpts from critical essays on the novel. A unique feature of *NfS* is a specially commissioned critical essay on each novel, targeted toward the student reader.

To further aid the student in studying and enjoying each novel, information on media adaptations is provided, as well as reading suggestions for works of fiction and nonfiction on similar themes and topics. Classroom aids include ideas for research papers and lists of critical sources that provide additional material on the novel.

Selection Criteria

The titles for each volume of *NfS* were selected by surveying numerous sources on teaching literature and analyzing course curricula for various school districts. Some of the sources surveyed included: literature anthologies; *Reading Lists for College-Bound Students: The Books Most Recommended by America's Top Colleges;* textbooks on teaching the novel; a College Board survey of novels commonly studied in high schools; a National Council of Teachers of English (NCTE) survey of novels commonly studied in high schools; the NCTE's *Teaching Literature in High School: The Novel;* and the Young Adult Library Services Association (YALSA) list of best books for young adults of the past twenty-five years.

Input was also solicited from our advisory board, as well as from educators from various areas.

From these discussions, it was determined that each volume should have a mix of "classic" novels (those works commonly taught in literature classes) and contemporary novels for which information is often hard to find. Because of the interest in expanding the canon of literature, an emphasis was also placed on including works by international, multicultural, and women authors. Our advisory board members—educational professionals—helped pare down the list for each volume. If a work was not selected for the present volume, it was often noted as a possibility for a future volume. As always, the editor welcomes suggestions for titles to be included in future volumes.

How Each Entry Is Organized

Each entry, or chapter, in *NfS* focuses on one novel. Each entry heading lists the full name of the novel, the author's name, and the date of the novel's publication. The following elements are contained in each entry:

- **Introduction:** a brief overview of the novel which provides information about its first appearance, its literary standing, any controversies surrounding the work, and major conflicts or themes within the work.

- **Author Biography:** this section includes basic facts about the author's life, and focuses on events and times in the author's life that inspired the novel in question.

- **Plot Summary:** a factual description of the major events in the novel. Lengthy summaries are broken down with subheads.

- **Characters:** an alphabetical listing of major characters in the novel. Each character name is followed by a brief to an extensive description of the character's role in the novel, as well as discussion of the character's actions, relationships, and possible motivation.

  Characters are listed alphabetically by last name. If a character is unnamed—for instance, the narrator in *Invisible Man*—the character is listed as "The Narrator" and alphabetized as "Narrator." If a character's first name is the only one given, the name will appear alphabetically by that name.

  Variant names are also included for each character. Thus, the full name "Jean Louise Finch" would head the listing for the narrator of *To Kill a Mockingbird,* but listed in a separate cross-reference would be the nickname "Scout Finch."

- **Themes:** a thorough overview of how the major topics, themes, and issues are addressed within

the novel. Each theme discussed appears in a separate subhead and is easily accessed through the boldface entries in the Subject/Theme Index.

- **Style:** this section addresses important style elements of the novel, such as setting, point of view, and narration; important literary devices used, such as imagery, foreshadowing, symbolism; and, if applicable, genres to which the work might have belonged, such as Gothicism or Romanticism. Literary terms are explained within the entry but can also be found in the Glossary.

- **Historical Context:** This section outlines the social, political, and cultural climate *in which the author lived and the novel was created.* This section may include descriptions of related historical events, pertinent aspects of daily life in the culture, and the artistic and literary sensibilities of the time in which the work was written. If the novel is a historical work, information regarding the time in which the novel is set is also included. Each section is broken down with helpful subheads.

- **Critical Overview:** this section provides background on the critical reputation of the novel, including bannings or any other public controversies surrounding the work. For older works, this section includes a history of how the novel was first received and how perceptions of it may have changed over the years; for more recent novels, direct quotes from early reviews may also be included.

- **Criticism:** an essay commissioned by *NfS* which specifically deals with the novel and is written specifically for the student audience, as well as excerpts from previously published criticism on the work (if available).

- **Sources:** an alphabetical list of critical material used in compiling the entry, with full bibliographical information.

- **Further Reading:** an alphabetical list of other critical sources which may prove useful for the student. It includes full bibliographical information and a brief annotation.

In addition, each entry contains the following highlighted sections, set apart from the main text as sidebars:

- **Media Adaptations:** a list of important film and television adaptations of the novel, including source information. The list also includes stage adaptations, audio recordings, musical adaptations, etc.

- **Topics for Further Study:** a list of potential study questions or research topics dealing with the novel. This section includes questions related to other disciplines the student may be studying, such as American history, world history, science, math, government, business, geography, economics, psychology, etc.

- **Compare and Contrast Box:** an "at-a-glance" comparison of the cultural and historical differences between the author's time and culture and late twentieth century/early twenty-first century Western culture. This box includes pertinent parallels between the major scientific, political, and cultural movements of the time or place the novel was written, the time or place the novel was set (if a historical work), and modern Western culture. Works written after 1990 may not have this box.

- **What Do I Read Next?:** a list of works that might complement the featured novel or serve as a contrast to it. This includes works by the same author and others, works of fiction and nonfiction, and works from various genres, cultures, and eras.

Other Features

NfS includes "The Informed Dialogue: Interacting with Literature," a foreword by Anne Devereaux Jordan, Senior Editor for *Teaching and Learning Literature* (*TALL*), and a founder of the Children's Literature Association. This essay provides an enlightening look at how readers interact with literature and how *Novels for Students* can help teachers show students how to enrich their own reading experiences.

A Cumulative Author/Title Index lists the authors and titles covered in each volume of the *NfS* series.

A Cumulative Nationality/Ethnicity Index breaks down the authors and titles covered in each volume of the *NfS* series by nationality and ethnicity.

A Subject/Theme Index, specific to each volume, provides easy reference for users who may be studying a particular subject or theme rather than a single work. Significant subjects from events to broad themes are included, and the entries pointing to the specific theme discussions in each entry are indicated in **boldface.**

Each entry may have several illustrations, including photos of the author, stills from film adaptations, maps, and/or photos of key historical events, if available.

Citing Novels for Students

When writing papers, students who quote directly from any volume of *Novels for Students* may use the following general forms. These examples are based on MLA style; teachers may request that students adhere to a different style, so the following examples may be adapted as needed.

When citing text from *NfS* that is not attributed to a particular author (i.e., the Themes, Style, Historical Context sections, etc.), the following format should be used in the bibliography section:

"Night." Novels for Students. Ed. Marie Rose Napierkowski. Vol. 4. Detroit: Gale, 1998. 234–35.

When quoting the specially commissioned essay from *NfS* (usually the first piece under the "Criticism" subhead), the following format should be used:

Miller, Tyrus. Critical Essay on *Winesburg, Ohio. Novels for Students.* Ed. Marie Rose Napierkowski. Vol. 4. Detroit: Gale, 1998. 335–39.

When quoting a journal or newspaper essay that is reprinted in a volume of *NfS,* the following form may be used:

Malak, Amin. "Margaret Atwood's *The Handmaid's Tale* and the Dystopian Tradition," *Canadian Literature* No. 112 (Spring, 1987), 9–16; excerpted and reprinted in *Novels for Students,* Vol. 4, ed. Marie Rose Napierkowski (Detroit: Gale, 1998), pp. 133–36.

When quoting material reprinted from a book that appears in a volume of *NfS,* the following form may be used:

Adams, Timothy Dow. "Richard Wright: Wearing the Mask," in *Telling Lies in Modern American Autobiography* (University of North Carolina Press, 1990), 69–83; excerpted and reprinted in *Novels for Students,* Vol. 1, ed. Diane Telgen (Detroit: Gale, 1997), pp. 59–61.

We Welcome Your Suggestions

The editor of *Novels for Students* welcomes your comments and ideas. Readers who wish to suggest novels to appear in future volumes, or who have other suggestions, are cordially invited to contact the editor. You may contact the editor via e-mail at: **ForStudentsEditors@thomson.com.** Or write to the editor at:

Editor, *Novels for Students*
Thomson Gale
27500 Drake Road
Farmington Hills, MI 48331–3535

Literary Chronology

1789: James Fenimore Cooper (the middle name Fenimore is added in 1826) is born the twelfth of thirteen children on September 15 in Burlington, New Jersey.

1812: Charles Dickens, one of eight children, is born on February 7 in Portsmouth, England.

1841: James Fenimore Cooper's *The Deerslayer* is published.

1850: Charles Dickens's *David Copperfield* is published.

1851: James Fenimore Cooper dies on September 14 and is buried in the cemetery of Cooperstown.

1870: Charles Dickens dies of a stroke on June 8 and his body is buried at Westminster Abbey in London.

1892: Pearl S. Buck is born on June 26 in Hillsboro, West Virginia to Christian missionaries, who take her to China when she is three months old.

1923: John Okada is born in September in Seattle, Washington to Japanese American parents.

1931: Pearl S. Buck's *The Good Earth* is published.

1932: Pearl S. Buck is awarded the Pulitzer Prize for her novel *The Good Earth.*

1933: Philip Roth is born on March 19 in Newark, New Jersey to Herman and Bess Roth, who are Jewish immigrants from Europe.

1938: Pearl S. Buck is awarded the Nobel Prize in literature "for her rich and truly epic descriptions of peasant life in China and for her biographical masterpieces."

1944: Richard Ford is born on February 16 in Jackson, Mississippi.

1946: Ursula Hegi is born on May 23 in Düsseldorf, Germany.

1949: Richard Russo is born James Richard Russo on July 15 in Johnstown, New York.

1950: Charles Frazier is born on November 4 in Asheville, North Carolina.

1956: Ha Jin is born on February 21 in a small rural town in Liaoning province, China.

1957: Marcel Möring is born in Enschede, Holland, near the Dutch-German border to a Dutch Reformed father and a Jewish mother.

1957: John Okada's *No-No Boy* is published.

1963: Michael Chabon (pronounced shay-bon) is born May 24 in Washington, D.C.

1971: John Okada dies of a heart attack on February 20 at the age of forty-seven.

1973: Pearl S. Buck dies on March 6 at the age of eighty.

1994: Ursula Hegi's *Stones from the River* is published.

1995: Richard Ford's *Independence Day* is published.

1996: Richard Ford is awarded the Pulitzer Prize for his novel *Independence Day.*

1997: Philip Roth's *American Pastoral* is published.

1997: Charles Frazier's *Cold Mountain* is published.

1997: Marcel Möring's *In Babylon* is published.

1998: Philip Roth is awarded the Pulitzer prize for his novel *American Pastoral.*

1999: Ha Jin's *Waiting* is published.

2000: Michael Chabon's *The Amazing Adventures of Kavalier & Clay* is published.

2001: Michael Chabon is awarded the Pulitzer prize for his novel *The Amazing Adventures of Kavalier & Clay.*

2001: Richard Russo's *Empire Falls* is published.

2002: Richard Russo is awarded the Pulitzer prize for his novel *Empire Falls.*

Acknowledgments

The editors wish to thank the copyright holders of the excerpted criticism included in this volume and the permissions managers of many book and magazine publishing companies for assisting us in securing reproduction rights. We are also grateful to the staffs of the Detroit Public Library, the Library of Congress, the University of Detroit Mercy Library, Wayne State University Purdy/Kresge Library Complex, and the University of Michigan Libraries for making their resources available to us. Following is a list of the copyright holders who have granted us permission to reproduce material in this volume of *NFS*. Every effort has been made to trace copyright, but if omissions have been made, please let us know.

COPYRIGHTED EXCERPTS IN *NFS*, VOLUME 25, WERE REPRODUCED FROM THE FOLLOWING PERIODICALS:

The Christian Century, v. 111, August 10, 1994. Copyright © 1994 by the Christian Century Foundation. All rights reserved. Reproduced by permission.—*Commentary*, v. 113, January, 2002 for "Surfing the Novel," by Joseph Epstein. Copyright © 2002 by the American Jewish Committee. All rights reserved. Reproduced by permission of the publisher and the author.—*Commonwealth Club*, October 9, 2001. © The Commonwealth Club of California, 2001. www.commonwealthclub.org, the website of The Commonwealth Club of California. Reproduced by permission.—*failbetter.com*, v. II, summer–fall, 2001. Reproduced by permission.—*Mississippi Quarterly*, v. 55, winter, 2001–2002. Copyright © 2001-2002 Mississippi State University. Reproduced by permission.—*The Nation*, May 12, 1997. Copyright © 1997 by The Nation Magazine/The Nation Company, Inc. Reproduced by permission.—*The New Republic*, v. 217, July, 1997. Copyright © 1997 by The New Republic, Inc. Edited and translated by Michael Kelly. Reproduced by permission of *The New Republic*.—*The New York Times Magazine*, February 6, 2000. Copyright © 2000 by The New York Times Company. Reprinted with permission.—*Publishers Weekly*, v. 241, March 14, 1994; January 31, 2000. Copyright © 1994, 2000 by Reed Publishing USA. Reproduced from *Publishers Weekly*, published by the Bowker Magazine Group of Cahners Publishing Co., a division of Reed Publishing USA, by permission.—*SHOFAR*, v. 22, spring, 2004. Reproduced by permission.—*The Southern Quarterly*, v. 37, 1999. Copyright © 1999 by the University of Southern Mississippi. Reproduced by permission.—*Times Literary Supplement*, July 2, 1999. Copyright © 1999 by The Times Supplements Limited. Translated by Stacey Knecht. Reproduced from *The Times Literary Supplement* by permission.—*World and I*, v. 15, May, 2000; v. 16, February, 2001. Copyright 2000, 2001 News World Communications, Inc. Both reproduced by permission.

COPYRIGHTED EXCERPTS IN *NFS*, VOLUME 25, WERE REPRODUCED FROM THE FOLLOWING BOOKS:

Chauhan, Pradyumna S. From "Pearl S. Buck's 'The Good Earth': The Novel As Epic," in *The*

Several Worlds of Pearl S. Buck: Essays Presented at a Centennial Symposium, Randolph-Macon Woman's College, March 26–28, 1992. Edited and translated by Elizabeth J. Lipscomb, Frances E. Webb, and Peter Conn. Greenwood Press, 1994. Copyright © 1994 by Elizabeth J. Lipscomb, Frances E. Webb, and Peter Conn. All rights reserved. Reproduced by permission of Greenwood Publishing Group, Inc., Westport, CT.—Darnell, Donald. From *James Fenimore Cooper: Novelist of Manners.* Associated University Presses, Inc., 1993. Copyright © 1993 by Associated University Presses, Inc. All rights reserved. Reproduced by permission.—Gao, Xiongya. From *Pearl S. Buck's Chinese Women Characters.* Associated University Presses, 2000. Copyright © 2000 by Associated University Presses, Inc. All rights reserved. Reproduced by permission.—Kim, Elaine H. From *Asian American Literature: An Introduction to the Writings and Their Social Context.* Temple University Press, 1982. Copyright © 1982 by Temple University. All rights reserved. Used by permission of Temple University Press.—Russo, Richard. From "Interview with Richard Russo," in *HBO*, 2006. Copyright © 2006 Home Box Office, Inc. All rights reserved. Reproduced by permission of the publisher and the author.

Contributors

Bryan Aubrey: Aubrey holds a Ph.D. in English and has published many articles on twentieth century literature. Entries on *American Pastoral*, *The Deerslayer*, *The Good Earth*, *Independence Day*, *No-No Boy*, and *Waiting*. Critical essays on *American Pastoral*, *The Deerslayer*, *The Good Earth*, *Independence Day*, *No-No Boy*, and *Waiting*.

Melodie Monahan: Monahan has a Ph.D. in English and operates an editing service, The Inkwell Works. Entry on *Stones from the River*. Critical essay on *Stones from the River*.

Wendy Perkins: Perkins is a professor of American and English literature and film. Entries on *Cold Mountain*, *David Copperfield*, and *In Babylon*. Critical essays on *Cold Mountain*, *David Copperfield*, and *In Babylon*.

Laura Pryor: Pryor has a B.A. from University of Michigan and over twenty years experience in professional and creative writing with special interest in fiction. Entry on *Empire Falls*. Critical essay on *Empire Falls*.

Carol Ullmann: Ullmann is a freelance writer and editor. Entry on *The Amazing Adventures of Kavalier & Clay*. Critical essay on *The Amazing Adventures of Kavalier & Clay*.

The Amazing Adventures of Kavalier & Clay

Michael Chabon

2000

The Amazing Adventures of Kavalier & Clay, by Michael Chabon, was published in 2000 to critical and popular acclaim. Some critics found Chabon's novel overly long, but all agreed that it is stylistically sound and well written. *Kavalier & Clay* took the Pulitzer Prize for Fiction in 2001 and has drawn as much notice as Chabon's previous book, *Wonder Boys*, which was made into a feature film. *Kavalier & Clay* is an epic tale that is topically unique within Chabon's body of work but stylistically consistent with his distinctive, graceful use of language.

Drawing on his own love of comic books for *Kavalier & Clay*, Chabon deftly weaves historical facts and figures together with light touches of fantasy. The author's inspiration in part came from Superman's creators: two Midwestern Jewish boys, Joe Shuster and Jerry Siegel, who sold their nascent superhero to the publisher of *Detective Comics* (DC Comics) for a hundred and thirty dollars. *Kavalier & Clay* follows two Jewish cousins in New York City, Joe Kavalier and Sammy Clay, who grow into adulthood during the onset of World War II. They experience fame, tragedy, love, and a little bit of magic. With its clever mix of literary self-consciousness and shameless adventure, *Kavalier & Clay* is one of those rare books which appeal to readers of both serious and popular fiction.

Michael Chabon Photograph by Paul Sakuma. AP Images

Author Biography

Michael Chabon (pronounced shay-bon) was born May 24, 1963, in Washington, D.C., to Robert and Sharon Chabon. His father worked as a lawyer, physician, and a hospital manager; his mother as a lawyer. His parents divorced when he was eleven years old. Chabon grew up in Columbia, Maryland, while most of that planned city was still being constructed. He was introduced to comic books as a child by his grandfather, who brought them home from the plant where he worked. Chabon earned a Bachelor of Arts in philosophy from the University of Pittsburgh in 1984 and a Master of Fine Arts in creative writing at the University of California at Irving.

Chabon has been a successful writer since the publication of his first novel, *The Mysteries of Pittsburgh* (1988), which was his master's thesis and became a bestseller. His second novel, *Wonder Boys* (1995), was made into a feature film in 2000, starring Michael Douglas. *The Amazing Adventures of Kavalier & Clay* (2000) won Chabon the 2001 Pulitzer Prize for Fiction. As of 2006, a film adaptation was reportedly in the works. With *Summerland* (2002), Chabon dabbled in the

young adult market and won the 2003 Mythopoeic Fantasy Award. *The Final Solution*, a short novel about Sherlock Holmes, was published in 2004.

As of 2006, Dark Horse Comics, in conjunction with Chabon, was publishing a quarterly comic book edition of *The Amazing Adventures of the Escapist*, drawing on the fictional history of this superhero. *The Amazing Adventures of the Escapist* won the 2005 Eisner Award for Best Anthology. Chabon has also published two volumes of short stories and a number of screenplays, including part of the popular movie *Spider-Man 2* (2004).

Chabon often writes about Jewish identity, homosexuality, and single parenthood.

Plot Summary

Part I: The Escape Artist

Chapter 1

The Amazing Adventures of Kavalier & Clay begins in October 1939. Josef Kavalier has just arrived in New York City after escaping Nazi-occupied Prague. He hopes that his cousin Sammy Klayman can help him find a job because he needs money to free his family.

Chapter 2

In trying to leave Czechoslovakia, Josef is sent back to Prague on a paperwork technicality. Too ashamed to face his family, he asks his former mentor Bernhard Kornblum for help. Kornblum agrees so long as Josef will go by way of Lithuania.

Chapter 3

It is 1935 and fourteen-year-old Josef attempts a dangerous escape feat that results in his near drowning and that of his brother Thomas. They are saved by Kornblum. Thereafter, Kornblum ceases his escape artist instruction of Josef.

Chapter 4

Kornblum and Josef find where the Golem has been hidden and prepare it for travel disguised as the corpse of a giant. Josef smuggles himself inside the casket. Once in Lithuania, he secures papers to get him to San Francisco.

Part II: A Couple of Boy Geniuses

Chapters 1–3

Sammy and Josef pick grown-up, American names: Sam Clay and Joe Kavalier. Inspired by Joe's artistic skill, Sammy pitches a comic book idea to his boss Sheldon Anapol, who reluctantly accepts it. They have to develop a superhero character and a twelve-page story in three days. Joe and Sammy start planning right away. They run into Julius Glovsky, called Julie, and hire him on the spot. Julie takes them to his brother's apartment to work.

Chapter 4

Sammy remembers his father, the Mighty Molecule, a traveling circus performer. Four years before, Sammy hoped to travel with his father, but the Molecule left home without Sammy. He died in a performance accident the previous year.

Chapters 5–7

When no one answers the door, Joe breaks into Jerry's apartment and surprises a beautiful sleeping woman who runs out the door, crying. Sammy searches through her forgotten satchel—her name is Rosa Luxemburg Saks. Sammy settles in and Joe tells him about his training as an escape artist. Sammy in turn tells Joe about his father, the "World's Strongest Jew." From this discussion, the Escapist is born.

Chapter 8

This chapter tells the history of Tom Mayflower, also known as the Escapist, and provides the Escapist's inaugural story in *Amazing Midget Radio Comics*.

Chapters 9–11

Sammy declares that they are going to be very successful with this superhero and Joe's family will be freed with the money they make. Julie's brother Jerry returns home with his friends. Sammy talks up their comic book project, and the other boys get involved in the development as well. Sammy writes the scripts while the others either draw or ink. Joe paints a beautiful and violent cover of the Escapist punching out Adolf Hitler. Before they fall asleep early Monday morning, Joe tells Sammy that he wants to see Rosa again.

Chapter 12

Sammy and Joe deliver their comic book to Anapol. He calls in Ashkenazy and Deasey to consult, and they make a ridiculously modest offer to Joe and Sammy. Sammy tries to haggle with them, but the cover is the deal breaker. Anapol is uneasy with such a political cover, but Joe says they have to use that cover or the deal is off. Anapol tries to offer more money in lieu of the Hitler cover, and Joe and Sammy walk out of his office.

Part III: The Funny-Book War
Chapters 1–3

It is October 1940, a year later. *The Escapist* is a success, and Anapol and Ashkenazy are making ten times the income of Joe and Sammy. On his way to the German consulate, Joe detours to Hoboken to see a ship from Holland disembark. For a moment, he believes he sees his father. Later, Adjutant Milde tells Joe that his father has died from pneumonia. Shocked and angry, Joe gets on a train bound for Canada so that he can enlist in the Royal Air Force and fight Germans, but he realizes he still has family who need his help, and he turns back at Albany.

Chapter 4

Joe breaks into an office calling itself the Aryan-American League. It is just a one-man operation, but he trashes the place. Ebling, the owner, returns, and Joe says he is Tom Mayflower. They grapple until Ebling hits his head and is knocked out.

Chapter 5

Empire Comics receives a phony bomb threat from Ebling. When everyone returns, James Love and Anapol talk about doing an Escapist radio play. Deasey advises Joe and Sammy on how to bargain for a piece of the radio play.

Chapters 6–10

Deasey takes them to a party for Salvadore Dalí thrown by Longman Harkoo. After Deasey introduces them to Harkoo, the host takes the young men around the room. Eventually they come to Rosa Luxemburg Saks, Harkoo's daughter. Joe recognizes her but pretends he does not know her as he charms her.

A cry for help brings everyone to the ballroom where the breathing apparatus on Dalí's diving suit has failed and the wing nut of his helmet is stuck. Joe wrenches the nut free with the penknife Thomas gave him and becomes the hero of the party. He and Rosa go up to her studio/bedroom to look at her artwork. Rosa's room is a mess, and there are moths everywhere. They talk about art for a while before Rosa knocks Joe over and kisses him. Sammy appears just then and says he is leaving; he does not tell them, but he is disturbed to have come upon two men kissing in the kitchen pantry. Rosa makes Joe go after his cousin. Joe and Rosa plan to meet the next day at the agency where she is a volunteer, helping rescue Jewish children from Europe.

Chapters 11–12

At the Transatlantic Rescue Agency (TRA) offices, Joe convinces the owner, Hermann Hoffman, to put Thomas on board his ship by paying for Thomas and several other children. Joe also agrees to do a magic show at Hoffman's son's bar mitzvah celebration. Elated, Joe makes a dinner date with Rosa. When he leaves the TRA office and crosses Union Square, Joe sees a large iridescent green moth on the trunk of a tree. The luna moth reminds Joe of Rosa.

Chapter 13

This chapter introduces the story of the comic book character Luna Moth.

Chapters 14–15

Joe and Sammy convince Anapol to use their new character, Luna Moth. She is very sexy, but Anapol knows she will make a lot of money. The cousins bargain for a better contract, but Anapol wants them to stop Nazi-bashing. Joe and Sammy walk out on the deal. Deasey follows and shows them a letter: Anapol and Ashkenazy are being sued for copying Superman. Sammy decides he will offer to perjure himself to get what he and Joe want.

Part IV: The Golden Age

Chapters 1–2

It is 1941 and Sammy and Joe meet the cast of the *Escapist* radio show. Tracy Bacon plays Tom Mayflower/the Escapist; he looks exactly like Joe and Sammy have imagined their character. Bacon and Sammy go out for drinks and then Sammy takes him to Ethel's apartment for dinner. Sammy is aware he is bringing home "the world's largest piece of trayf," but Bacon and Ethel hit it off well. ("Trayf" is a Yiddish word which means a food item is unclean and forbidden, the opposite of kosher. Bacon is a pork product and therefore forbidden by kosher law.) Sammy tells his mother that he wants to meet someone and she gives him a strange look.

Chapters 3–4

The next day Joe is practicing for his evening magic performance. Rosa's father gives Joe a gift of a midnight blue suit with a gold skeleton key lapel pin. Joe is carrying around an unopened letter from his mother. In it she tells Joe to get on with his life and forget about her and his grandfather. At the reception, Joe ties on his mask and a waiter cries out and runs from the ballroom.

Chapters 5–6

The waiter is Ebling. He thinks he is a super-villain and Joe is the Escapist. Ebling plants a bomb, and Joe tries to prevent it from going off, but Ebling attacks him, and they are both slightly injured in the blast. That night Joe wakes up in a panic looking for his mother's unopened letter, but it is gone. "The true magic of this broken world lay in the ability of the things it contained to vanish, to become so thoroughly lost, that they might never have existed in the first place."

Chapter 7

In April 1941, Sammy is on the eighty-sixth floor of the Empire State Building as a volunteer sky watcher for the military. Bacon shows up unexpectedly, and he and Sammy share their first kiss as thunder and lightning occur outside the building.

Chapters 8–10

On May 1, 1941, Joe, Sammy, Rosa, and Bacon go to the cinema to see *Citizen Kane*. Sammy talks about going to Los Angeles to write for movies. *Citizen Kane* has a huge artistic impact on Joe who wants to pursue a new approach in his work, which Anapol interprets as comics for adults. Joe finally agrees with Anapol to stop fighting Nazis. The stories published by Empire Comics thereafter shift from warfare to everyday heroics and employ a radical new use of layout. Circulation for Kavalier and Clay titles continues to soar.

Chapter 11

In September 1941, Bacon is pushing Sammy to move to Los Angeles with him, but Sammy is not sure he wants to go. Sammy will not admit that he is in love with Bacon, but he believes his affection to be reciprocated. They visit the abandoned site of the World's Fair and break into the Perisphere and make love.

Chapter 12

The *Ark of Miriam* sails on December 3, 1941. Joe rents a nice apartment for Thomas and himself. Rosa gives Joe a painting she made of him, and Joe gives her a key to the apartment. She is touched but had secretly hoped for an engagement ring.

Chapters 13–14

On December 6, 1941, Joe has a performance and is planning to ask Rosa to marry him. Rosa is painting a mural for Thomas and learns that his ship has been lost at sea when she walks to the corner store. She rushes to the hotel and finds out that Joe attempted to drown himself during an escape and then fled the hotel when he was fished out the fountain.

Chapter 15

Sammy and Bacon are guests at Love's beach house. Ruth Ebling calls the police on them all when she finds a copy of the *The Escapist*. Sammy evades arrest but is found later by an FBI agent who sexually abuses him.

Chapters 16–17

Joe lands on Ethel's doorstep, frozen and drunk. She takes care of him until Rosa picks him up. When Rosa wakes in the morning, Pearl Harbor has been attacked and Joe has left to enlist in the navy. Sammy comes over and tells Rosa he is not going to Los Angeles; "he would rather not love at all than be punished for loving." Rosa tells Sammy that she is pregnant. Joe is the father, but he does not know—and they cannot tell him now.

Part V: Radioman

Chapters 1–2

Joe is stationed in Antarctica. On April 10, 1944, he and his dog companion Oyster barely survive carbon monoxide poisoning. The pilot, Shannenhouse, also survives. Joe and Shannenhouse recognize that they have more than enough supplies, but the real danger is the unnamable menace that lurks out on the Ice. "Antarctica was beautiful. . . . But it was trying, at every moment you remained on it, to kill you."

Chapter 3

Joe and Shannenhouse cannot leave Antarctica until September. Joe spends every waking hour monitoring radio waves. In July, he learns about a German station, Jotunheim, which is occupied by a lone geologist named Klaus Mecklenburg. In September, Joe and Shannenhouse decide to kill the German.

Chapter 4

Joe reads Rosa's letters and learns about her marriage to Sammy and about Tommy. Joe believes that he will not survive this mission, but if he does he does not want to ruin the happy life that they have. He burns Rosa's letters.

Chapters 5–6

Joe transmits a warning to Jotunheim before leaving. Shannenhouse's appendix bursts en route and he dies. Joe finishes the mission alone, crash landing near Jotunheim. Joe no longer wants to kill the German, but Klaus is scared and shoots at Joe. They grapple over the gun, and Klaus is fatally shot. "In seeking revenge, he had allied himself with the Ice." Klaus's death is more heartbreaking to Joe than anything else that has ever happened to him.

Chapter 7

Joe survives Antarctica by accident. He holes up at Augustaberg ten miles away and subsists on

Media Adaptations

- *The Amazing Website of Kavalier & Clay* at http://www.sugarbombs.com/kavalier/ is a fan site for Chabon's book created and maintained by Nate Raymond. It collects reviews, historical information, artwork, news, and more.

- *The Amazing Adventures of Kavalier & Clay* has been adapted as an abridged audio book narrated by David Colacci. It was produced by Brilliance Audio in 2005 and was, as of 2006, available on both compact disc and cassette tape.

thirty-year-old rations and morphine until the navy picks him up. Joe leaves behind Thomas's drawing of Houdini. He recuperates at Guantánamo Bay until the war is over in 1945.

Part VI: The League of the Golden Key

Chapters 1–3

In April 1954, Sammy stops at the Excelsior Cafeteria and learns from his colleagues that someone claiming to be the Escapist is going to jump off the Empire State Building. Many people think that the jumper is Joe. In his office, Sammy pulls out the box with Bacon's Escapist costume and finds it empty.

Detective Lieber comes around, asking Sammy about Joe. Sammy has not seen Joe since he sailed for basic training in December 1941. Lieber wonders why Joe would not come home. Sam thinks Joe feels he has no home to return to with his family dead in Europe. Harkoo appears with Tommy, who has been caught playing hooky again.

Chapter 4

When the Escapist does not appear at the Empire State Building, people think it is a hoax. Lieber figures out that Tommy wrote the jumper's letter. Sammy is disappointed that he will not see Joe, but Tommy insists that Joe *is* here. He takes them into the elevator.

Chapters 5–6

In July 1953, Sammy takes Tommy to Louis Tannen's for a birthday gift. Tommy sees Joe in Tannen's back room. Days later, Tommy spots Joe at Spiegelman's Drugs, and they finally meet—as cousins. Tommy asks Joe to come to dinner. Joe will not, but he helps Tommy with his card tricks. They meet every Thursday for seven months in Joe's office/apartment in the Empire State Building. Tommy realizes that Joe cannot figure out *how* to return home. Based on something Joe said, Tommy writes the infamous letter.

Chapters 7–9

Tommy leads Sammy, Lieber, Anapol, and Harkoo to Joe's office, but he is not there. He is on the observation deck, dressed in Bacon's old Escapist costume and wearing a harness of rubber bands. When Joe sees Tommy he realizes that he has failed to escape his own trap of fear and habit, which has kept him from returning to his family. He steps backward into thin air, but the rubber bands fail to hold him and he lands on a ledge two floors down. He assures everyone that he is all right. Sam rides with Joe to the hospital and the long-lost cousins reunite at last.

Chapters 10–12

In Joe's office/apartment, Lieber, Harkoo, Tommy, and Sammy find a vast amount of comic books and four to five thousand pages of a comic book Joe is drawing about the Golem of Prague. A man comes to the office and delivers a congressional subpoena to Sammy. Sammy, Joe, and Tommy return home. Rosa and Joe talk to each other as if nothing has happened. In bed that night, Sammy tells Rosa he convinced Lieber to drop charges against Joe. He and Lieber are going to have lunch together—a euphemism for a date. They talk about the Senate subcommittee hearing. Wertham's book has indirectly labeled Sammy a homosexual, and he believes this is why is been summonsed.

Chapter 13

Joe still loves Rosa and finds her attractive. He feels guilty because he does not want to be a home-wrecker. Joe apologizes to her and they kiss briefly.

Chapters 14–16

Sammy looks through the epic Joe has drawn after Joe packs up his office. Sammy loves the book and wants to publish it. Anapol stops by to tell them that he has retired the Escapist character because he lost the Superman lawsuit. After Anapol leaves, Sammy and Joe talk about buying Empire Comics.

Joe has nearly one million dollars in his old bank account. He stays up all night thinking about it, borrowing the Studebaker to drive around in the early morning. Joe winds up at Houdini's tomb where he takes a nap and dreams of Kornblum telling him to go home. While Joe is gone, a large, heavy pine box arrives at the Clay house from Nova Scotia. Joe returns and recognizes the Golem's casket but is dumbfounded as to how it found its way to him. The box is filled with silky silt from the banks of the Moldau. The Golem's soul has departed.

Chapters 17–18

Later that same day of April 22, 1954, Sam testifies before the Senate Subcommittee to Investigate Juvenile Delinquency. Senator Hendrickson all but accuses Sammy of homosexuality and promoting pedophilia through his use of sidekicks. Later, Sammy realizes that he feels liberated by his public outing and regrets his cowardice regarding his relationship with Bacon. He is ready to make a change and maybe go to Los Angeles and work in television.

Chapters 19–20

At the bottom of a crate of memorabilia, Tommy finds a strip of photos showing Joe and Rosa from when they were younger. They finally explain to him that Joe is his biological father. Tommy understands but is concerned about Sammy. Sammy returns home late at night with train tickets to Los Angeles. Rosa and Joe ask him to stay; Joe has bought Empire Comics and wants to work with Sammy again. Sammy says he can send his stories from Los Angeles, but he is definitely going this time. When they wake up in the morning, Sammy is gone.

Characters

Sheldon Anapol

Sheldon Anapol, an owner of Empire Comics and Joe and Sam's boss for several years, is a businessman first and foremost and plays his historic role in cheating two naïve young men out of their multi-million dollar idea. But he is not without a conscience, having worked hard more than a decade at his own, less-successful novelty business. As co-owner of Empire Comics (with his brother-in-law Jack Ashkenazy), Anapol is subject to both its successes and its troubles. Even as Anapol is settling into a life made comfortable by lots of money, he is also receiving death threats from

Nazi-sympathizers and a major law suit from the owners of Superman. While making deals for radio plays and movie shorts, Anapol tries to convince Sammy and Joe to stop beating up Nazis so that he can get a decent night's rest. His relationship to the Escapist is purely business.

Jack Ashkenazy

Jack Ashkenazy, the brother of Sheldon Anapol's wife as well as Anapol's business partner in Empire Comics, has bad taste in everything from literature to clothing. Ashkenazy's success results from the intelligence and talent of the people around him, namely Anapol, Deasey, Joe, and Sammy. When he left Empire Comics in 1943, Ashkenazy tried out several other business ventures but they all failed.

Tracy Bacon

Tracy Bacon, Sammy's true love, lives life vigorously, working as an actor and rarely taking no for an answer. He has a mysterious, unpleasant history shrouded in a confusion of conflicting facts. Whatever has come before, he is undeniably happy with Sammy. He is handsome and charismatic—everything Sammy never thought he could have. Bacon's name is a joke that plays upon the idea of forbidden fruit: as a Jew, Sammy is not supposed to eat pork. He knows famous people all over town, such as Orson Welles and Ed Sullivan, but he is guileless and does not seek fame so much as acceptance. Bacon knows he is gay and is not ashamed of it, but he cannot convince Sammy to feel the same way about himself. Bacon ultimately leaves for Los Angeles alone, just as the United States is entering World War II. He joins the Air Force and is shot down over the Solomon Islands in 1943.

Eugene Begelman

Eugene Begelman is Tommy's best friend. Tommy discovers his love of magic when playing with a set of magic tricks belonging to Eugene.

Bubbie

Bubbie, Sam and Joe's grandmother, lives with her daughter Ethel and her grandson Sammy in Brooklyn. Bubbie dies peacefully in her sleep at age ninety-six.

Rosa Clay

See Rosa Luxemburg Saks

Sammy Clay

Sammy Clay, the everyday hero of Chabon's novel, is a quiet Jewish boy from Brooklyn who

chases his dreams—to publish comic books—and catches them. Sammy's bravery and pluck are seen in his initial pitch to Anapol and later in how he stands up to Anapol, Ashkenazy, and Deasey to get what he feels he and Joe deserve for their talent. Some argue that Sammy is Joe's sidekick, but that interpretation does not work. Joe and Sammy's relationship is not that of a mentor and his student or a father and his son. They are fully partners, sharing in the creation of characters, the development of stories, and the negotiation of payment. Despite Sammy's courage in the office, his real struggle is in seeking to accept his homosexuality. Sammy spends most of the novel in denial, even though nearly every other character seems to know he is gay just from meeting him. Tracy Bacon is Sammy's great love, but Sammy turns his back on that relationship after he is sexually abused by another man. This denial nearly destroys Sammy's spirit; when he and Joe are reunited after twelve years, Joe describes Sammy as haggard. But he is also tough and resilient. When he is publicly outed by Senator Hendrickson, Sammy realizes he has nothing to lose, and he finally buys his ticket to Los Angeles and gets on that westbound train he was supposed to be on with Bacon twelve years earlier.

Tommy Clay

Tommy is the son of Joe Kavalier and Rosa Saks, but Sammy Clay is father to him for the first twelve years of his life. He takes after Joe in looks and his interest in magic. Tommy successfully schemes to bring Joe back to his family when Joe has lost his way.

Salvador Dalí

Surrealist painter Salvador Dalí is the guest of honor at Longman Harkoo's party where Joe and Rosa are formally introduced. Joe saves Dalí's life when Dalí's diving suit malfunctions.

George Deasey

George Deasey, the editor of Empire Comics and a mentor to Sammy, is harsh but sincere. Although Deasey is management, several times he gives Joe and Sammy hints on how to effectively negotiate their contracts so they will not get shortchanged by Anapol and Ashkenazy. He also introduces them to Harkoo.

Carl Henry Ebling

Carl Ebling is a mentally unstable Nazi-sympathizer whom Joe runs afoul of. Joe's attack on Ebling's office pushes Ebling over the edge. Ebling decides he is a super-villain named the Saboteur and Joe is the Escapist. Ebling plants a phony bomb at the Empire Comics office and later tries to blow up Joe and a roomful of guests at a bar mitzvah. People are spared because his incompetence far outweighs his enthusiasm for anti-Semitic activity. To the horror of his family who know he is mentally ill, Ebling is found guilty of terrorism and attempted murder and put away in Sing Sing.

Ruth Ebling

Ruth Ebling, Carl's older sister, is a housekeeper at James Love's beach house estate in Pawtaw, New Jersey. Angered about her brother's imprisonment, she calls the police to raid Love's house after she finds a copy of the *Escapist* in Sammy's room.

FBI Agent

The second, unnamed FBI agent is the one who sexually assaults Dave Fellowes at Love's Pawtaw estate.

Dave Fellowes

Dave Fellowes hides with Sammy when the police raid Love's house in Pawtaw. Dave is sexually abused by the unnamed FBI agent. Dave is John Pye's lover.

Jerry Glovsky

Jerry Glovsky, Julie's older brother, shares a house with Marty and Davy. Jerry is a comic book illustrator and calls his place Palooka Studios. He lets Sammy and Joe use their place to work on the first issue of their Escapist comic book.

Julie Glovsky

Julius Glovsky, called Julie, is a childhood friend of Sammy's and also a comic book illustrator. Julie is the first artist Joe and Sammy hire to help them create the inaugural issue of the *Escapist*.

Marty Gold

Marty Gold, Jerry's housemate and an inker for comic books, works with Sammy and Joe on the first issue of the Escapist comic book.

Longman Harkoo

Longman Harkoo is Rosa's father and a wealthy surrealist art dealer living in an odd house in Greenwich Village. He renamed himself after he had a reoccurring dream about a Long Man of Harkoo. Harkoo is cheerful, quirky, and supportive of his daughter and her friends. He is very well-connected and enjoys using his connections to help people.

Joe's Grandfather

Joe's grandfather is a renowned operatic Czech tenor. He survives the war with Joe's mother until they are both sent to a death camp.

Dr. Anna Kavalier

Anna Kavalier is Joe's mother. She and Joe keep up a faithful communication until he enlists in the navy. She dies in a death camp along with Joe's grandfather.

Dr. Emil Kavalier

Emil Kavalier, Joe's father, dies from pneumonia less than a year after Joe leaves his family.

Joe Kavalier

Joe Kavalier is the central character of Chabon's book. The plot follows his life, recounting his late childhood in Prague, his arrival in New York City as a young man, his naval assignment in Antarctica, and eventually his return to his family in New York. Trained as an escape artist by one of the profession's unsung masters, Joe is incredibly adept at any task he takes on, making him somewhat larger than life. He is also a gifted artist and half of the genius behind the book's popular comic book superhero, the Escapist. Joe works closely with his cousin Sammy to create this superhero, which is inspired in equal parts by the unique backgrounds of these cousins. Despite Joe's repeated ability to escape and survive, he is incapable of saving even one of his family members from the war in Europe. The loss of his brother Thomas, en route to New York, nearly destroys Joe, but he cannot die, even when he wants to (this is repeated again in Antarctica, when he goes to Jotunheim). Joe's great love is Rosa Saks, and their affection for each other is not diminished though time, guilt, shame, and anger must separate them for twelve years. Joe tries to stay away from Rosa, Sammy, and Tommy after the war out of a misdirected sense of forfeiture, but the night that he at last reads Rosa's letters and learns about the birth of Tommy is a turning point for Joe, who at last stops fighting.

Josef Kavalier

See Joe Kavalier

Thomas Masaryk Kavalier

Thomas Kavalier is Joe's younger brother. Joe arranges to have Thomas transported to New York

City on a ship carrying Jewish children refugees, but the ship is overcome by a U-boat and a sudden storm and all the children drown.

Alter Klayman

See The Mighty Molecule

Ethel Klayman

Ethel Klayman (née Kavalier), Sammy's mother and Joe's aunt, works as a nurse and is a very practical, no-nonsense woman. She thinks Sammy's dream of drawing comic books is ridiculous—even in the midst of his success, she considers it to be ephemeral. Her love is tough but not meager, and she gladly embraces Joe, Rosa, and even Bacon into her home. Ethel saves most of the money Sammy gives her. She dies of a brain aneurysm in the mid-1940s, shortly after retiring to Miami Beach.

Samuel Klayman

See Sammy Clay

Bernhard Kornblum

Bernhard Kornblum, a retired performing illusionist who mentors the teenage Joe in escape tricks, helps smuggle Joe out of Prague when Nazi restrictions threaten to trap the boy. Thereafter Kornblum only appears to Joe in visions, offering advice.

Detective Lieber

Detective Lieber is assigned to the case of the Empire State Building jumper. He figures out that Tommy was the one who wrote the jumper's letter.

James Haworth Love

James Love is chairman of the board for Oneonta Mills and instrumental in getting the Escapist on the radio through his sock company's sponsorship. He invites Bacon and Sammy to his beach house in Pawtaw with a group of other gay men.

Klaus Mecklenburg

Klaus Mecklenburg, a German geologist stationed at Jotunheim, Antarctica, dies from a gunshot wound after struggling with Joe for control of the weapon.

The Mighty Molecule

The Mighty Molecule is Ethel's husband and Sammy's father. He is a traveling strong man who survived hardship and imprisonment in Eastern Europe. After Sammy is afflicted with polio as a child, his father takes him walking to keep his legs strong. Although he does not live at home, he and Ethel love each other. The Molecule dies in 1938, crushed beneath a tractor he was attempting to lift.

Herr Milde

Milde is the adjutant at the German consulate in New York City. Joe visits him weekly, trying to find a way to get his family out of Prague. Milde is polite but unhelpful. He is the one who delivers the news to Joe that his father has died.

Davy O'Dowd

Davy O'Dowd is Jerry's housemate and one of the illustrators who work on the inaugural issues of the *Escapist*.

Frank Pantaleone

Frank Pantaleone is friends with Jerry, Marty, and Davy. He is a more experienced illustrator and also works on the inaugural issue of the *Escapist*.

John Pye

John Pye, Dave Fellowes's lover, is considered one of the most beautiful men in New York City.

Rosa Luxemburg Saks

Rosa Saks is salvation and muse. She and Joe fall madly in love in the way young people do. Rosa becomes indispensable to the cousins as she helps them with domestic affairs and with rescuing Thomas Kavalier from Prague. Rosa also inspires Joe to create the sexy superhero, Luna Moth. When Joe unknowingly leaves Rosa in the lurch, she and Sammy get married, thus saving each other from a world that does not yet accept deviance. Their marriage of convenience is not at all romantic, but it is not awkward because they have always been close, like siblings. Over time, Rosa and Sammy develop a strong partnership, churning out comic books the way Joe and Sammy did. Although Rosa is not directly responsible for Thomas's death, she feels guilty because of the role she played in placing Thomas on the doomed ship. She names her son after Joe's brother to honor Thomas's memory and possibly to keep a connection with the love of her life, from whom she is separated for twelve years. When Rosa and Joe are reunited, they easily pick up where they left off, happy and in love.

Siegfried Saks

See Longman Harkoo

Hal Spiegelman

Spiegelman is the proprietor of Spiegelman's Drugs in Bloomtown, New York. Tommy introduces Joe to him as his magic teacher.

Agent Frank Wyche

Agent Frank Wyche finds Sammy hiding at Love's house and sexually abuses him.

Themes

Escapism

Chabon's overarching theme in *The Amazing Adventures of Kavalier & Clay* is escapism: escape from tyranny, escape from reality, escape from death. Joe Kavalier, trained as an escape artist by a master *Ausbrecher* has an ability to escape and survive that pushes the limits of reality, even a fictional reality. In the day-to-day grind, Joe escapes the painful reality of the growing war in Europe by battling Nazis on paper. His more dramatic escapes include the River Moldau, Nazis in Prague, the fountain of the Hotel Trevi, a happy life with Rosa, carbon monoxide poisoning, Antarctica and madness, Sammy and the rest of his family, and finally—the most difficult of all—his self-imposed exile. Joe is the novel's real-life escapist.

Sammy Clay, although much more grounded and practical than his cousin Joe, finds escape from his life in daydreams: traveling with his father; providing for his mother and grandmother; being a famous and respected publisher. Sammy's master feat of escape is from his own homophobia. After a few happy, clandestine months with his first and only love, Tracey Bacon, Sammy turns his back on romantic love and spends the next thirteen years in proverbial chains. These chains of shame burden Sammy. When Senator Hendrickson effectively springs the last lock and exposes Sammy's homosexuality in public forum, he is not humiliated but relieved. Bacon is gone from this world, but Sammy is finally ready to pick up where he left off and move to Hollywood.

Escapism is a precarious indulgence—too much and one is beyond rational judgment; too little and one is mired in real world minutia. Comic books from their inception were understood to offer a fantastical escape, generally geared toward young boys and girls full of hope to change their situation in some way. Joe and Sammy's superhero, the Escapist, is thus a metafictional device for comic books in general.

Guilt

Guilt is a feeling of responsibility for wrongdoing. Sammy, reserved about spending money after growing up on modest means, feels guilty about indulging in the luxuries he and Joe can afford when they are at the height of their success. The excess money itself is a physical representation of guilt which must be experienced any time money is spent. Sammy buys a beloved and costly phonograph over which he never stops feeling guilt. Despite his weak legs, he rarely takes a taxi. More devastating is the guilt Sammy feels regarding his homosexuality. In the world of this novel, there is a strong taboo against homosexuality, which makes it even more difficult for Sammy to come to terms with his sexual orientation. The raid in Pawtaw and sexual abuse at the hands of the FBI agent only serve to justify Sammy's shame. But there is no denying human nature, and Sammy is fortunate to survive Wertham's trial by fire and thus free himself of this crippling guilt.

Joe suffers from survivor guilt during the three years he is first living and working in New York City. For two years he does not even allow himself to have fun or to spend any more money than is necessary. Joe spends all his spare time trying to safely extricate his father, mother, brother, and grandfather from Prague. One by one his immediate family is taken away from him even as he is building a new family in the United States. He finds love and happiness with Rosa, but his guilt over the accidental death of his brother Thomas drives Joe first to attempt suicide and then to run away from everyone who loves him. Having failed to protect his brother, Joe denies himself comfort and pleasure by leaving Rosa and Sammy. The war eventually ends, but Joe's guilt over abandoning them and fear of rejection obscure the way back to the only family he has left. It takes Joe ten years and the love of his son to overcome that last, difficult hurdle.

Family

What makes up a family is a question explored throughout *Kavalier & Clay*. The most unusual arrangement occurs when Sammy and Rosa marry to raise Rosa and Joe's son, Tommy, as well as to hide Sammy's homosexuality. In Prague, Joe lives in an extended, or complex, family including his parents, his brother, and his grandfather. In New York City, Joe first lives with Sammy, his aunt Ethel, and his grandmother Bubbie; later Joe and Sammy move into their own apartment and Rosa unofficially lives with them part-time. When Joe leaves to enlist in the navy, Rosa and Sammy find themselves both in vulnerable situations with only each other to look to for security. What Chabon expresses through these

Topics For Further Study

- Individually or in groups, create a superhero and write a story featuring him or her. Include a weakness along with a superpower, a villain, a secret identity, and sidekick or other supporters. For extra credit, illustrate your tale.

- Science has traditionally been important to superheroes and their villains, either as a source of superpower or inventions to aid in fighting or causing crime. What area of science interests you? For example, biology, nuclear physics, astronomy, chemistry, geology, etc. Dream up an invention or application of technology within your field of interest that would be an aid to a superhero or villain. Create an illustrated poster demonstrating your idea.

- Research a heroic figure from legend or history. Does this figure fit any of the superhero criteria such as a secret identity, superpowers, and an idealistic mission? Write a brief report to share with your classmates.

- One of Rosa's artistic expressions is a dreambook. In her dreambook, Rosa uses collage, illustration, and text to tell the stories she experiences when she is dreaming. Find or make a blank journal and create your own dreambook based on a dream you have had.

- The Holocaust took a terrible toll of loss and displacement on the groups targeted by the Nazis. Unfortunately, genocide still happens to this day. Research an incident of genocide that has happened in the recent past, examining why it was carried out and what can be done to stop future genocides.

- Letter writing was an important form of communication before widespread use of email in the 1990s. Write a letter by hand (not computer) to a friend or family member whom you do not see often. Tell the person what is new in your life and any interesting stories that have happened to you. Enclose relevant photographs, drawings, or article clippings. After your teacher has checked that you have completed the assignment, mail your letter.

- Joe spends most of a year stationed on Antarctica, monitoring radio waves for the U.S. Navy. Research current political and scientific activity relating to this unusual continent. Also look up information about Antarctica's climate and geography. Which countries have laid claim to portions of Antarctica? What scientific studies are being conducted there and why? Are there parts of Antarctica that have yet to be explored? How does the size of the land mass today compare to one hundred years ago? Write an essay about the current importance of Antarctica.

- Under Judaic law, a boy reaches maturity when he turns thirteen and is made a bar mitzvah ("son of the commandment"). Girls are made bat mitzvahs ("daughters of the commandment") at twelve years of age. They are then responsible for following and upholding Jewish traditions, which is expressly a religious aspect of Judaism. Secular or ethnic Jews do not always choose to become a bar or bat mitzvah. What other rites of passage do you know? What time of life do they typically occur? Are they cultural, religious, or related to some other aspect of life? What are the components of the ritual? What are the conferred rewards and responsibilities? Prepare a presentation for your class using PowerPoint, slides, overheads, or other visual aids.

- Prague is the capital of the Czech Republic and Joe's childhood home. What foods are particular to the Czech people? Research authentic Czech recipes, assemble a cookbook to distribute to each student in the class, have everyone select a different recipe to prepare, and then host a Czech food day. What are your favorite dishes? What flavors are unusual to you? Is there anything you would like to make again? Share your answers with your classmates as you enjoy this new cuisine.

unusual family assemblages is that family is a matter of what is in people's hearts and cannot and should not be limited to the group determined by blood relatives and marriage. Rosa, Joe, and Sammy struggle with this subtly when Joe finally returns to his family. They keep asking each other what they should do now that Joe has returned. They are wondering, without vocalizing it, how their unusual family fits together, with Joe as biological father and Sammy as surrogate father to Tommy. Tommy puts it best when, after Joe and Rosa explain that Joe is his real father, he asks them, "Only what about *Dad*?" This question succinctly expresses how a young child easily accepts two men as his fathers; one does not replace the other in Tommy's heart.

Joe struggles with the love and identity of his family throughout the novel: his cool farewell to his tearful parents, brother, and grandfather in Prague; his rebuff of Harkoo and Rosa the night Harkoo gives him the suit; coping with the deaths of his father, brother, mother, and grandfather; and the years spent coming to the realization that he has family in Rosa, Sammy, and Tommy and how important they are to him. Sammy's family identity is both more simple and more complex. He and his mother, Ethel, have a tough love sort of relationship in which they bicker affectionately almost all the time. In marrying Rosa and raising Tommy, Sammy is both expressing family love and slowly killing himself through the repression of his homosexuality. At the end of the novel, Sammy leaves for Los Angeles to discover a part of himself in both his career and personal life which he has denied for thirteen years. As his family, Rosa and Joe are sad to see him leave but support Sammy fully in what he feels he needs to do.

Style

Allusion

Allusion occurs when an author refers to people, events, symbols, or stories external to his or her story. Allusions may be only hinted or implied as the author assumes the reader understands the connection and what it means. Allusions are an economical device, permitting an author to introduce new ideas without a long explanation. Usually comprehension of an allusion is not critical to a basic understanding of a story, but the reader's experience is enhanced if he or she does recognize what the author is trying to say. The title of *The*

Amazing Adventures of Kavalier & Clay is an allusion to common comic book titles. Joe Kavalier and Sammy Clay are an allusion to Joe Shuster and Jerry Siegel, the creators of Superman. Tracey Bacon's name is an allusion to kosher law because he and his love is forbidden to Sammy, a good Jewish boy.

Chabon alludes to mythology when he compares Joe's leaving Prague with the legendary Jewish hero Golem. According to folklore, Golem, a larger-than-life automaton, was sculpted by Rabbi Loew in the sixteenth century from river mud pulled from the banks of the Moldau. Golem was created to protect the Jews of Prague and was awakened when need arose. Sammy Clay's name is an allusion to the Golem; when he is no longer essential at the end of the story, he leaves, having accomplished his task of helping Rosa, Joe, and Tommy.

Foreshadowing

Foreshadowing occurs when an image or event in a story gives information about what is going to happen later in the text. In *Kavalier & Clay*, the smuggling of the Golem out of Prague foreshadows doom for the Jews in Prague because the Golem, the legendary hero, is made unavailable when they need help the most. Joe and Thomas's near drowning in the River Moldau foreshadows Thomas's death by drowning six years later. Sammy's view of Joe at the top of the fire escape of Jerry's building, with the light slanting down on him out of a grey sky foreshadows the success of the Escapist, whom they create later that day. Joe's sighting of a man he mistakes for his father at the docking of the *Rotterdam* foreshadows his father's death. Joe's first attempt to leave New York City foreshadows his later, dramatic departure to the U.S. Navy when the United States finally enters World War II. Foreshadowing is an important literary device which adds cohesion to the plot and allows the reader to anticipate the future event without knowing exactly when it will happen.

Title Significance

The title of *The Amazing Adventures of Kavalier & Clay* is meant to evoke the excitement and glamour of an old pulp comic book. The title promises action on an epic level because "Adventures" is plural. "Amazing" and "Adventures" and "Kavalier" and "Clay" are alliterative words, which mean the initial sounds are the same within each word pair. Alliteration makes the title flow neatly off the tongue, adding to its energy and sense of smooth composition. The title introduces, from the front cover, the two main characters of the story, Joe Kavalier and Sammy Clay. The placement of Joe's last name before Sammy's subtly hints that Joe is a more important than Sammy.

Historical Context

Conflict in the Middle East

In the 1990s, tensions increased in Middle Eastern countries such as Israel and Iraq. Palestinian dissidents stepped up their efforts to separate from the State of Israel, and some of these protests escalated to terrorism, including bombing public places and shooting innocent people if they crossed into the wrong territory. On November 4, 1995, Israeli prime minister Yitzhak Rabin was assassinated by an Israeli extremist because of Rabin's role in negotiating peace between Israel and the Palestinians.

Following the Gulf War in 1991, worldwide concern grew that Iraq was stockpiling weapons and possibly attempting to build nuclear weapons. The United States has historically taken a hard-line approach to dealing with Saddam Hussein, who was president of Iraq from 1979 until 2003. Hostility between Hussein and the United States threatened to escalate the problem of Iraq disarmament in the late 1990s, forcing United Nations secretary-general Kofi Annan to step in and negotiate new arrangements, including U.N. inspectors to search Iraq for weapons of mass destruction. These arrangements did not last long. Paul Wolfowitz, a U.S. military analyst, called for more aggressive action, which presidents Clinton and Bush tempered with less hostile philosophies such as those proposed by then secretary of state Colin Powell.

Although there is no evidence connecting the terrorist attacks of September 11, 2001 (the 9/11 terrorists were citizens of Saudi Arabia, Lebanon, the United Arab Emirates, and Egypt) and Iraq or Hussein, the Bush administration linked them. Overnight opinions in Washington changed in regard to the disarmament of Iraq and arguments were made for a U.S.-led invasion of Iraq. Hundreds of thousands took to streets in the United States and in other countries to protest the aggression, to no avail.

Gaming

Comic books have maintained a presence into the 1990s in the United States, but computers and video game consoles have replaced books and magazines as the major source of solitary entertainment available to young people. The wildly popular Sony PlayStation game console was first released in 1995, using more advanced technology than was previously available for similar systems. Other companies moved quickly to keep up with PlayStation, including the Nintendo 64 in 1996, Sega Dreamcast in 1999, PlayStation 2 in 2000, and the Microsoft Xbox in 2001.

Computer games for use on personal computers became more technologically advanced in the 1990s. First-person, three-dimensional shooter games were particularly popular, games such as Doom (five separate games released from 1993–1996), Quake (1996), and Half-Life (1998). Controversy over the violent content of these games and their connection to juvenile delinquency echoes arguments made about television and movie content—or Dr. Fredric Wertham's opinions about comic books in his book *Seduction of the Innocents* (1954).

Gay Rights

A decade after AIDS and HIV first appeared in the United States in 1981, this virus was still a major topic within gay and lesbian communities of the 1990s. In the early 2000s, much more was understood as to how AIDS is transmitted and can be treated, helping to reduce fear and give hope to living with the disease. Gay rights activists in the 1990s were increasingly concerned with marginalized groups such as those who are transgender or intersexual. Transgender individuals identify with a gender other than their birth gender and may undergo hormone therapy or surgery. An intersexual person is born with genitalia or secondary sexual characteristic that combine genders or are otherwise ambiguous. As with other minority groups, gay and lesbian activists seek social equality.

Y2K

Y2K is an abbreviation for the year 2000. In the late 1990s, many people became increasingly concerned about the approaching millennium change. Businesses had to check their software to make sure that it was compliant with a rollover to the year 2000, resulting in costly upgrades and overhauls. Some people were worried about sudden shortages of energy, water, or other necessities (as a result of businesses not being prepared) and chose to stock up on supplies. Cults proclaiming the end of the world and other dramatic prophesies gained

Compare & Contrast

- **1940s:** World War II begins in 1939. The United States becomes directly involved in 1941. By the time the war ends in 1945, over 62 million soldiers and civilians are dead, marking this as the world's deadliest war to date.

  1990s: A series of civil wars and armed conflicts break out in the former Yugoslav republic in 1991 and lasts until 2001. Reported numbers of deaths vary but range between 100,000 and 200,000 civilians and soldiers on all sides.

  Today: The United States invades Iraq in 2003, beginning the Second Gulf War (also known as the Iraq War). As of 2006, approximately 3,000 Americans and perhaps as many as 500,000 Iraqis have been killed.

- **1940s:** In this Golden Age of comic books, the most popular superheroes are Superman, Batman, and Captain America.

  1990s: The Modern Age of comic books is sometimes also called the Gimmick Age, the Dark Age, or the Diamond Age, for a variety of reasons. The X-men team of superheroes enjoys resurgence in popularity. Anti-heroes such as Spawn and Venom also become trendy.

  Today: Japanese comic books called *manga* are extremely popular with readership comprising 60 percent women, a sharp contrast to the male-dominated readership of comic books. Popular series include *Chobits* and *Doraemon*.

- **1940s:** Levitt & Sons builds the first planned suburban community, named Levittown, on Long Island in New York, starting in 1947. Over 17,000 single-family dwellings are built in five years.

  1990s: In the United States, economic prosperity and cost-effective construction lead to suburban communities with exceptionally large, mass-produced houses on small plots of land. These look-alike houses are sometimes referred to as McMansions.

Today: People are more interested in higher density living for the first time in over fifty years due to environmental concerns (pollution and destruction of wildlife habitat), rising gas prices, and health concerns (people in urban areas walk more). The majority of Americans still live in suburban areas.

- **1940s:** Letter writing and the telegraph are major forms of long-distance personal communication. The telephone is used primarily to communicate within a local area.

  1990s: Electronic mail, called email, grows in popularity, thanks in part to ubiquitous usage on college campuses and within businesses.

  Today: Cellular phones are a popular way for people to keep in touch as well as to express personal style. Email remains important as well.

- **1940s:** Prior to World War II, Jews in Prague number 50,000.

  1990s: Following the Holocaust and the establishment of the State of Israel, Jews in Prague number about 800.

  Today: With the fall of communism in Czechoslovakia in 1989, known as the Velvet Revolution, the population of Jews in Prague rises to 1,600.

- **1940s:** Reinhard Heydrich, the Nazi governor of the region and possible successor to Hitler, is assassinated by Czech soldiers in 1942. In 1945–1946, Czech citizens expel 3,000,000 Germans from their country in an effort to revolt against the Nazis. The Soviet Army invades in 1948 and establishes communist rule in Czechoslovakia.

  1990s: Czechoslovakia divides into the Czech Republic and Slovakia in 1993. The Czech Republic becomes part of the North Atlantic Treaty Organization (NATO) in 1999.

  Today: The Czech Republic is part of the European Union. Prague is a popular city with tourists, businesses, and the film industry. The Czech economy grows but has a reputation for corruption.

some attention. The world celebrated a momentous and peaceful event the evening of December 31, 1999. Even though the millennial rollover affected businesses when moving from the year 1999 to 2000 and many people around the world believed the new millennium arrived then, others maintained that the new millennium did not arrive until January 1, 2001. The year 2000 was also the beginning of a mild recession in the United States, following a decade of strong economic growth. Thus the new millennium, for many, seemed to mark the passing of a golden age—much as Sammy feels in 1941, just before the United States enters World War II.

Rwandan Genocide

The Rwandan genocide involved two ethnic groups, the displaced Tutsis and the government-leading Hutus. Over the course of only four months in 1994, extremist Hutu militia murdered approximately one million Tutsis and Hutus. The genocide ended when Tutsi rebels finally overthrew the Hutu-led government and the Hutus fled the country. The number of people killed and how quickly they were killed was shocking. The Rwandan genocide is also significant because of the meager response of the United Nations, which failed to intervene to help prevent the genocide when mounting tensions in the region foreshadowed such an outcome. While in the early 2000s, Rwanda was still recovering from this brutal period in its history, ethnic wars continued to rage across Africa (particularly in the Democratic Congo, Burundi, and the Sudan), some motivated by continued aggression between Tutsi and Hutus.

Critical Overview

Chabon has been popular with readers and favored by critics since the publication of his first novel, *The Mysteries of Pittsburgh*, in 1988. His novels are distinct and imaginative. Tom Deignan and other critics have observed that, with *The Amazing Adventures of Kavalier & Clay*, Chabon has finally come into his own as a writer. Stewart O'Nan, writing for the *Pittsburgh Post-Gazette*, compliments Chabon's larger-than-life comic book style of writing but feels that the length makes this grandiose language exhausting for the reader: "At its best, *Kavalier and Clay* is a heady, frothy concoction, finely drawn and broadly comic, but in its own baroqueness ... runs the risk of

Book cover from Michael Chabon's The Amazing Adventures of Kavalier & Clay

collapsing of its own weight." In a review for the *New York Times*, Janet Maslin describes Chabon's third novel as "excitingly imaginative" with "loving if sometimes windy detail." Ken Kalfus, also writing for the *New York Times*, celebrates Chabon's "passionate, expressive language." He observes that this novel is "generously optimistic about the human struggle for personal liberation." John Podhoretz, in an article for *Commentary*, echoes the novel's sentiment that so much of what defines the American way sprang from the hearts and minds of recent immigrants. Podhoretz writes that *Kavalier & Clay* is an ambitious book, but it "does not have all that much of interest to say.... A wonderful book but, despite its scope, a small one."

Criticism

Carol Ullmann

Ullmann is a freelance writer and editor. In the following essay, Ullmann applies Joseph

Campbell's model of an archetypical hero journey to Joe Kavalier's experience in The Amazing Adventures of Kavalier & Clay.

The Amazing Adventures of Kavalier and Clay, by Michael Chabon, is a sweeping tale of grand proportions that uses some of the bold, over-the-top stylistic devices of comic books, such as archetypes. Critics have noted that Joe Kavalier, although quiet and hardworking, is also suave, competent, talented, and indestructible. Joe's uncanny abilities are not overstated to the point of magic realism, but he is as supernatural and heroic as the characters he illustrates for his comic books. The work of Joseph Campbell, an expert in the fields of comparative mythology and comparative religion, was heavily influenced by psychologist Carl Jung. Campbell's seminal text, *The Hero with a Thousand Faces* (1949), provides the following outline for the journey of the archetypical hero, a hero just like Joe Kavalier.

DEPARTURE
The Call to Adventure
Refusal of the Call
Supernatural Aid
The Crossing of the First Threshold
The Belly of the Whale or Rebirth

INITIATION
The Road of Trials
The Meeting with the Goddess or the Attainment
    of Knowledge
Woman as the Temptress or Fear of Failure
Atonement with the Father
Apotheosis or Glorification
The Ultimate Boon

RETURN
The Refusal of Return
The Magic Flight
Rescue from Without
The Crossing of the Return Threshold
Master of the Two Worlds, Supernatural and
    Human
Freedom to Live

The first part of Joe's journey is simply getting out the door, that is, departure. Joe's call to adventure is the encroaching Nazi presence in Czechoslovakia and his family's decision to send him to his aunt in the United States. Joe's mother sells her favorite emerald to help pay for Joe to leave. Saying good-bye at the train station, Joe blithely refuses the call with his foolish stoicism when faced with the heartbreak of his family who weep while he is impatient to leave. This is a refusal because Joe's attention is on the enjoyment of travel rather than the seriousness of his family's

situation. When the authorities send him back to Prague, Joe cannot pretend he is having fun anymore. He goes to his former mentor, the retired performing escapist Bernhard Kornblum, for help. Kornblum, here and throughout Chabon's novel, is Joe's supernatural aid. Ever after, Joe has dream-like visions of Kornblum whenever he needs guidance.

The guardian of the first threshold is the Golem. (Golem is a creature from Jewish legend, created by Rabbi ben Loeb to protect the Jews of Prague from persecution.) With Kornblum's aid, Joe passes this threshold by finding the Golem and preparing it for their passage to Lithuania. Joe enters the proverbial belly of the whale, a place of rebirth, when he hides inside the Golem's casket and travels toward freedom. Emerging safe in Lithuania nearly two days later, Joe is reborn from the Golem's dusty chamber. He can never return to the home he once knew because it no longer exists. Literally speaking, Joe's family has been forced by the Nazis to move from their comfortable apartment. Figuratively, Joe is not a boy anymore. He has successfully completed the first part of his journey, and he is now a man, although still young.

The next stage is initiation. On the road of trials, Joe encounters many tests as well as helpers. In this part of his story, Joe successfully creates and establishes the Escapist, with the help of Sammy and against those who would hinder, redirect, or hold them back, i.e., Anapol, Ashkenazy, and Deasey. He survives numerous fights with various German people and struggles with Carl Ebling (including a bomb attack). Joe perseveres despite set backs such as his father's death, difficulties with the German adjutant, and strident negotiations with his boss about money and artistic freedom.

In the meeting with the goddess, also sometimes called a marriage, the hero attains knowledge of life. Rosa is Joe's goddess and his muse. Her influence in his life and their deep love for each other quell much of Joe's anger and frustration that his family is still trapped in Prague. Rosa delivers hope that he may at least be able to rescue his brother. From within this new peace, Joe creates Luna Moth and stops fighting Nazis so that he can focus on his creative expression. He has chosen life/birth over death. He is less aware of worrying as his loved ones are absorbed into the chaos of war, beyond Joe's reach. But when Thomas drowns at sea, Joe has a crisis of faith, and he is engulfed by his own fear of failure. He knows he can no longer reach his mother and grandfather, and now his father and brother are dead. This means Joe has failed in his original purpose in

New York City, and he cannot forgive himself for being the one in his family who survives.

Joe flees Rosa and Sammy and takes his pain to Antarctica, where he is stationed by the navy and thus denied a chance to express his anger directly to Nazis. This exile leads to Joe's atonement. He casts off ignorance and at last opens Rosa's letters from the past three years. From them he discovers his love for her as well as a new opportunity for love: his son Tommy. Joe forgives Rosa and himself for his brother's death. Just before leaving on his sworn mission to finally kill a German, Joe sends his victim a warning. This is his apotheosis or glorification because Joe, having forgiven himself, can return to life. Face to face with the German geologist, Joe desires only to make a human connection, for now he is grasping his ultimate boon, what Joseph Campbell in *The Hero with a Thousand Faces* calls his "life-transmuting trophy" of love. When the geologist dies anyway, Joe, under the influence of his boon, is more heartbroken than he has ever been, even over the deaths of his family members.

Returning home is the final stage of Joe's adventure and by far the hardest. He imagines Sammy, Rosa, and Tommy living happily ever after, and against the wishes of his own lonely heart, he forbids himself to return. At this critical point in the journey, the hero may opt to never complete his or her quest. The magic flight is Joe's attempt to return, by degrees, to the life he once knew. It is, by definition, somewhat ridiculous. Joe takes up residence in an office near the top of the Empire State Building because he likes to be near the Escapist. He becomes a hermit and carries on a clandestine friendship with his son Tommy, who thinks Joe is his cousin.

Tommy senses Joe's dilemma, senses that he wants to return but has forgotten how. Tommy is the one who rescues Joe by forcing him out into public where he can reunite with Sammy. Joe crosses the return threshold in his quiet homecoming to Sammy and Rosa's house. He accepts their love and acknowledges that things are not as he thought they were. Sammy and Rosa have created a family that offers space for Joe; indeed, their strange marriage has been waiting for Joe's return for a long time. He is needed; he is home.

The last two phases of the archetypical hero journey demonstrate the hero's new powers. As master of two worlds (the supernatural and the human), Joe uses his million dollars to purchase the failing Empire Comics, enflamed by love of

> **"** Joe enters the proverbial belly of the whale, a place of rebirth, when he hides inside the Golem's casket and travels toward freedom."

his character, the Escapist, and full of vigor for new work. Joe has no fear of failure or success because of the boon he brings with him, love, which now gains strength through reciprocation. In rediscovering Rosa's love for him and his relationship with Tommy, Joe has the freedom to live. His strange quest is over, and he returns to ordinary life, older and wiser. Thus is a hero made. Sammy, at the end of the novel, departs for Los Angeles—but that is a different hero's story for a different day.

Campbell's thesis, as a Jungian mythographer, is that the hero journey lives within every human being and is an essential story for all humankind. People experience the hero journey in their dreams, which are transformed into stories; it is a pattern of timeless meaning. The hero, unlike the king and other roles which are merely assigned, is made through self-achievement. Joe Kavalier is a quietly fantastical character, but he is also, more importantly, a real-life hero: a performing magician, a brilliant illustrator of a popular comic book, a soldier, a father, and a man dedicated to the rescue of his family from Nazi-occupied Czechoslovakia. Joe's qualities add up to larger-than-life proportions and distance him from readers as a sympathetic character—but like any celebrity, he is no less appealing to observe.

Source: Carol Ullmann, Critical Essay on *The Amazing Adventures of Kavalier & Clay*, in *Novels for Students*, Thomson Gale, 2007.

Barbara Lane

In the following interview, Chabon discusses the golem folklore and the various themes in his book, the process involved in his writing, the relation between World War II and comics, and the comic book creators who inspired him.

[Barbara Lane:] Talk a little bit about the story of the golem, which is central to this novel.

[Michael Chabon:] The golem is a character out of Jewish folklore, a myth that dates back thousands of years, before the time of Christ. The most famous legend is the one that deals with the golem of Prague, who was made by Rabbi Judah Loew ben Bezalel. There were lots of other stories about different rabbis making golems, but for some reason, this is the one that caught the imagination, not just of Jewish listeners over the centuries, but of novelists.

A lot has been written about the golem of Prague; films have been made about this artificial man, formed from river clay, who is brought to life by spells and incantations. In some stories, he's made merely to be a servant, to help clean up around the synagogue on Friday nights, to do menial jobs that somebody with a soul and brain would not want to do. In others, he's made to be a protector of the Jews of the Prague ghetto. That is the version I'm most interested in, because I see those stories of creating a defender as a possible antecedent for the idea of the superhero. It was that aspect of it that first excited me.

Comic books fought the Second World War. I knew the Jewishness of the two characters was going to be important. Somehow, I decided to have Joe Kavalier be a refugee from a country that was occupied by the Nazis. In 1939, there was the annexation of Austria and then Czechoslovakia. Then, in September, we got the invasion of Poland that started the war. I'd been to Prague, so I chose Prague. He just gets off the boat, more or less. He shows up in New York, and the day he gets there, his crazy cousin says, "We're going into the comic book business, and since you can draw, you can draw my Superman." Joe has no idea what Superman is, what a superhero is, or even what a comic book is. So when he's asked to draw a superhero, the only thing he can think of is a golem. When I was writing that, I began to feel that there was going to be more to this book than just superheroes, that somehow it was going to tie into a lot of other stuff having to do with Jewish folklore.

Did you ever discover why so many of the early comic book creators were Jewish?

That was one of my main questions when I started writing, one of the things that I thought I might answer for myself. It's very striking; it's an inescapable thing to notice, once you start doing research. Just to cite the most famous examples: Superman was created by Jerry Siegel and Joe Schuster, two Jewish kids from Cleveland; Batman was created mostly by Bob Kane, with help from Bill Finger and Jerry Robinson, who were Jewish; Captain America was created by Joe Simon and Jack Kirby. So it was very apparent to me that something was happening.

I had a very key experience early on in the writing of the book. I was living in Los Angeles and flew up to Oakland to attend WonderCon, a big comic book convention held every year. One of the guests was going to be Will Eisner, one of the greatest comic book artists ever. He's in his early or mid-80s and still working. One of the first questions I asked him was the question you just asked me: Why do you think, along with yourself, so many of the early comic book creators were Jews? He gave me what I think is the right answer. New York was the center of the publishing business and also the comic book and pulp magazine business.

The population of New York was fairly heavily Jewish. If you were a young, Jewish kid and wanted to make your living drawing, if you had an artistic ability and wanted to try to make money with your pen, you didn't have that many options available to you. The really well-paying, prestigious fields of commercial art, illustration, and advertising art were closed. You wouldn't get hired at the advertising agencies, but you could get hired by the comic book business. All these kids who thought they could draw, many of whom were somewhat mistaken in that judgment, were taken here. A lot of the comic book companies and pulp publishers were Jewish-owned businesses. In many cases, it was a familial thing.

Stan Lee, the famous Marvel Comics impresario whose name was originally Stanley Lieber, was the nephew of Martin Goodman, the owner of what later became Marvel Comics. It was an economic, demographic thing. But Eisner paused after he gave me that answer and said, "You know, I've often wondered if there wasn't something else at work, if there wasn't some other explanation. We have this history of impossible solutions to insoluble problems," which became the epigraph for this novel. He said that we have this narrative history of trying to come up with ways of solving the problems of the world through various kinds of mystical means, such as the golem.

Another person who inspired him—and you mention him in the afterwards to the book—is Jack Kirby, who did Spiderman and The Incredible Hulk. Can you talk about his influence?

Jack Kirby revolutionized comics twice in his career—first, in the 1940s by creating Captain

America with his partner Joe Simon. Kirby was young when he started in comics—about 17. He was poorly educated—self-educated in the way that a lot of New York kids tended to be in this period, and the way that Sam Clay is in my book. He had this bursting, dynamic drawing style; it looked like his characters were barely contained by the panels. When someone got punched in a Jack Kirby comic, they came flying out of the panel. A lot of violence, but an almost pugnacious, New York kind of violence. Then, he did it all over again in the 1960s, participating in the Marvel Comics revolution with Stan Lee.

The idea of collaboration was always at the heart of comics—another thing I really wanted to write about in this novel. The best-known characters are probably the Fantastic Four, taking comics into a completely different realm. They aimed them at a much older readership—college students—and it was very successful. Kirby's imagination was allowed to roam completely wild, creating these incredible pantheons of cosmic superheroes the size of planets.

I'm always fascinated by the image of an artist who lives this very mundane existence. Jack Kirby lived most of his life first on Long Island, then out in Thousand Oaks in the San Fernando Valley. He was this small, drab looking man. You never would have looked at him twice, but every night he went out to his studio and sent his imagination voyaging out into the universe and created characters like Galactus, the big devourer of worlds. The image of this person voyaging through the cosmos of his own imagination while everyone else is asleep is a potent one for me.

You mentioned that comic books have always played a role in war. In the Second World War, didn't they have a jingoistic nature?

Absolutely. Comic books went to war before the United States did. Captain America dates from, I believe, May 1941. No villain was up to Superman. Kryptonite, in a way, is a substitute for Hitler, because Hitler was the ultimate villain. They fought the Japanese and demonized them, but this was what superheroes were made for. Comic book covers from the period are superheroes punching out U-boats, and tying anti-aircraft guns into knots. You have to remember that for the first several years of the war, it wasn't going that well; it looked as though there was a good chance that the Allies might not win. There was a lot of very violent, potent, wish fulfillment going on there, and it did get expressed in very unattractive jingoistic, racially-offensive ways.

> Comic books went to war before the United States did."

The flip side of that is that the comics were actually investigated by the feds; you have a scene about that towards the end of the book.

Comic books never pleased adults. Even when they were fighting in the Second World War, that didn't get anywhere with the teachers and parents of America. It was still this forbidden, trashy kind of literature. The comics of the time—for all that they were toeing the standard line about being a good American and turning in your neighbors if you thought they might be Nazi spies—were being burned and banned.

The other thing that emerges as a theme in this book, and you've alluded to it already, is the idea of escape. Your comic book character is named The Escapist. We have the escape out of Prague. Everybody in this novel needs to escape from something.

Well, it was accidental. Theme is the last thing I worry about when I'm writing. I start with character and setting, and I try to figure out my story as quickly as I can. I actually pay no attention to theme at all during the first full draft of the novel. I had at some point decided to make Joe study escape artistry, and there were other little bits about the theme of escape, but I wasn't aware of them at all. I didn't notice them until I sat down with a first draft and read through it. At that point, I said to myself, What is this book about, besides being about Sammy, Joe, and comics?

If you're paying attention, as a writer, to language and your characters and trying to see them in your imagination and know what they would be doing at a given moment, theme just emerges organically. At some point, you have to stop and gather up that residue. That's the point at which I noticed that there was a lot to do with escape in the book. Comics have always been condemned as escapism. I wondered if there was some connection between escapism and literature, and it all just clicked into place. That's when you know it's working well, when that stuff starts happening and you didn't really try to make it happen.

What Do I Read Next?

- *Tales to Astonish: Jack Kirby, Stan Lee and the American Comic Book Revolution* (2004), by Ronin Ro, covers the life and career of influential comic book artist, Jack Kirby.

- *Superman Chronicles, Volume 1* (2006) is a collection by the original Superman creators, Jerry Siegel and Joe Shuster. In this graphic novel, they reprint all of Superman's early appearances, beginning in 1938.

- *The Final Solution: A Story of Detection* is Michael Chabon's 2004 novel about an aged Sherlock Holmes engaged in solving one last mystery.

- *Houdini!!! The Career of Ehrich Weiss* (1996), by Kenneth Silverman, is an acclaimed biography of the world's most famous escape artist. It contains more than a hundred photos, many of them rare and previously unseen.

- *Maus: A Survivor's Tale* (Volume I, 1986; Volume II, 1991), by Art Spiegelman, is a graphic novel memoir with comic-like drawings about Spiegelman's father and how he survived World War II and the Holocaust. *Maus* won many awards, including the 1992 Pulitzer Prize Special Award.

- *A Heartbreaking Work of Staggering Genius* (2001), by Dave Eggers, is a critically acclaimed memoir about Eggers's life as a single-parent to his younger brother after the death of both of their parents. Eggers is the editor of *McSweeney's*, a publishing house to which Chabon has strong ties.

- *A Model World and Other Stories* (1991), by Michael Chabon, is the author's first collection of short stories. These stories are about quirky individuals in ironic situations.

People look at you, publishing your first novel, The Mysteries of Pittsburgh, *which was actually a master's thesis, at the age of 24, and think you've never failed. In fact, you did have a huge failure of a sort, although you turned it into a success. Tell us about the experience of* Fountain City.

I suppose that's an example of this method I just described not working. I started to write this novel around the time the first book was published. I thought it was going to be about architecture and an architect. There was a movement just beginning then in architecture called the "new urbanist" movement—the idea of restoring identity to the American city. If you're building a new housing unit, it dictates that you shouldn't try to build a suburban tract house, but actually craft a city with a downtown, a place where people can live and work.

That was in the air in the late '80s; it interested me because I grew up in Columbia, Maryland, which had very much a utopian urban design scheme of the late 1960s—the idea of creating a perfect community, one that would be racially integrated. So, I just started to write about a guy that was doing something like this. I thought it was going to be this little, slender book, maybe 225 pages. Five and a half years later, I found myself with an 800-plus page monster—to use Spalding Gray's phrase, a monster in a box—and somehow or another, baseball, French cooking, eco-terrorism, the plan that some religious Jews have to rebuild the temple in Jerusalem, and a lot of other things had all worked themselves into this thing. I allowed that organic process of just seeing what happens. Maybe one problem was that I never sat down and asked myself what this book was about. You might think that was sort of an obvious question that a writer would want to ask himself, but I think it eluded me.

You dumped Fountain City *on the sly when your wife told you that she was going to take some days off to study for her bar exam. You snuck down to the basement and started a new book.*

I was about to start the ninth draft of this novel. I was so sick and tired of it. I didn't know how I was going to fix it or even what was really wrong with it. My then-fiancée said that she was going to take the bar six months earlier than she originally thought, so she wasn't going to see me for six weeks. That night I made this decision. I decided to keep it a secret. The first night I think I wrote 12 pages. I had 25 pages in three days. I had 75 pages in two weeks. I hit on the voice of Grady Tripp, the narrator of that novel, instantly, as if he was waiting there for me to get to him. I never went back.

But you did use the experience of the novel that you couldn't finish for Wonder Boys.

Grady Tripp had a very different experience than mine in that I did finish *Fountain City* a number of times, over and over. I never had that thing that Grady did where you're endlessly adding, and when you think you're getting close to the end, you're only a quarter of the way done. What I did draw on from my own experience was the deep mortification and embarrassment of working on the same project for that long a period of time. By the fifth Thanksgiving that rolls around, you're sitting with your family, and they ask about the book almost with dread.

Many people loved the movie, "Wonder Boys," which had a strange marketing campaign. Aren't you working with the same producer for the screenplay of "Kavalier and Clay"?

Yes, Scott Rudin and Paramount Pictures. When they first told me that they were going to make a movie of *Wonder Boys,* I asked why. Who do they think will go and see it? I trusted that they knew what they were doing, and they made what I think was a really good movie. It's very well acted and directed, and the script is great. I really enjoyed it, and so did 17 other people. But it was tough; it's hard to sell a movie about a pot-smoking, overweight English professor who carries a dead dog in his trunk and cheats on his wife. They did this great thing of re-marketing it six months after the initial release. They re-released it with a new poster and a new series of commercials on television. It still didn't quite work. I thought they did a fair enough job the first time. It seemed like a tough sell. I hope that's not going to be the same case with this novel.

Armistead Maupin was here recently and we were talking about, with a lot of laughter, how when The Mysteries of Pittsburgh, *first came out,*

Newsweek *came out with a story on the new generation of gay writers, among whom you were listed. Armistead was laughing about how it had finally become marketable to be a young, gay writer, because you brought a whole audience with you.*

That was part of the problem, in a way. There was no real attempt by my publishers to define me as anything. There was nothing in the marketing of the book or the press kit that referred to my own sexuality. But, because of the subject, a lot of the readers, and especially the owners of some of the gay and lesbian bookstores around the country, assumed that I was gay, and that's how I was being sold by my publisher. When they found out that I wasn't gay, there was some resentment. It's ironic that being a gay writer can be a marketable thing. The proof of it was that these booksellers actually imagined that my publishers would have passed me off as gay in order to sell more books. That was not the case.

At the time of writing Kavalier and Clay, *did you realize that you would become the hero of comic book fans worldwide? How does it feel to have put this marvelous and unsung medium on the historical map?*

I was skeptical that anybody would be interested in hearing about these guys and this world at all. Comic book fans, for all that we love the medium, go cringing into every situation where you talk about comic books. You try to be proud, but it's hard, because the prejudice against them is still so strong. I love the superhero comic books. I think what Jack Kirby did qualifies as genuine art.

Did you see "Chasing Amy"?

Yes, I love that film. I never thought that I would be viewed as championing an art form, because I had that ambivalence myself. In the course of writing the novel, I came to this inescapable conclusion that some of these guys in the 1940s, and many artists since then, who were genuinely deserving of the name "artist," put as much of their soul and ability into their comic book work as I put into writing novels. I hope that conviction permeates the novel enough to possibly begin to persuade other people, including some who have always been prejudiced against comic books, to take another look and reconsider the art form. We're really behind the curve here in America on comic books. In Europe, comic books are given the status of art without any hesitation whatsoever. It's silly and arbitrary to deny them that status.

You've written two collections of short stories, A Model World and Other Stories *and* Werewolves

> " But as Chabon makes clear, comic books, in a lot of ways, are playing with kiddie dynamite, in the psychological sense."

in Their Youth. *I read somewhere that you got nervous when you wrote short stories. Why is that?*

Failure. It's so easy to blow a short story. It's much harder to blow a novel. Novels I find are a much more forgiving form. You can write a great novel, and it can still have slow parts; look at *Anna Karenina*. Or, let's talk about the little essay on Napoleon that closes *War and Peace*. Again, it's not what you want to be reading at that point, but a novel can encompass that stuff. Short stories can't. You start a short story with this sense that you have this pure, simple idea that you're going to sketch out quickly and neatly, and from the first sentence you begin to go awry. You lose that purity. By the time you're five or six pages into it, you often feel like you're writing something totally different from what you thought you started out with. The consciousness of going wrong is always with me when I write short stories.

I've grown dissatisfied with my own short stories, to some degree, and with the short stories that I read in magazines. I just feel like I don't know why I'm writing short stories. It's not the form; it's me. I need to find my way back to something. I am germinating a new approach to the short story for myself, but so far not much has come of it, except for one very strange story about a clown-murdering cult that was in *The New Yorker*.

To me, the roots of the short story come out of that kind of fiction. They go back to Edgar Allen Poe, to Balzac, to Kipling. These are writers that wrote what we would now tend to call more genre fiction—horror, detective, mystery, adventure. At the time they were writing, that is what a short story was. There was no genre; that was the genre. I guess I'm trying to work my way back towards that a little bit, and then hopefully toward a more contemporary, modern approach.

Source: Barbara Lane, "Interview with Michael Chabon," in *Commonwealth Club*, October 9, 2001.

Tom Deignan

In the following review, Deignan explores Chabon's characters, the various themes—especially escapism, the comic book empire and the legitimacy of comics, and puzzles over the identity of the narrator in The Amazing Adventures of Kavalier & Clay.

It's not hard to imagine the great works of American literature as comic books. Think of Huck and Jim diving into the Mississippi, in a colorful explosion of white foam and splintered wood, just as their raft is destroyed by a steamboat. Or think of Gatsby, a soft-focus silhouette at dusk, staring out at the harbor with its flashing lights. Such imagery is easy to imagine, not only because these are memorable and vivid archetypes, but because there have already been countless versions of "classic" comic book lit. In fact, as American as the comic book is, foreigners such as raging King Lear, or even suffering Job, have found their anguished words floating above their heads in white balloons.

The purpose of comic book "classics" is obvious: to make literature more accessible to kids. It's the literary version of sneaking vitamins into Yoo-Hoo or Hi-C. But there's an unquestioned assumption here, that the comic book form is inherently "low." The best we can seem to do, since the kids are hopelessly hooked, is use this "low" form for positive ends. That is, to feed the kids what's ultimately good for them.

Don't try any of this on best-selling author Michael Chabon. Captain America, Superman, Spiderman, Wonder Woman—all those literally cartoonish figures who've been devoured by generations of American boys are doing just fine, he says, when it comes to challenging the youthful intellect and imparting wisdom.

"He's truly the Shakespeare or Cervantes of comic books," Chabon told the *New York Times Book Review* recently, referring to Marvel comics legend Jack Kirby, who created the Incredible Hulk and many others. If there's any doubt regarding the sincerity of Chabon's comparisons, pick up his new novel, *The Amazing Adventures of Kavalier and Clay*. At nearly seven hundred pages, it is an epic treatment of the "golden age" of American comics—and America itself, from the 1930s to the 1950s. The novel has many aspirations: historical, political, sexual. One aim is to show that precisely because the best comics appeal to kids, they are on par with great literature in several ways.

As the very elusive third-person narrator in *Amazing Adventures* puts it, comic books are to be appreciated

for their pictures and stories they contained, the inspirations and lubrications of five hundred aging boys dreaming as hard as they could for fifteen years, transfiguring their insecurities and delusions, their wishes and their doubts, their public educations and their sexual perversions, into something that only the most purblind of societies would have denied the status of art.

High and low

The book (Chabon's fifth, after two novels and two story collections) is the latest skirmish in the ongoing battle between "high" and "low" culture. To some, Chabon may seem particularly baby boomerish (though he's only 37) in his need to intellectualize comic books, a topic laden with nostalgia.

Maybe there's some merit to this killjoy view of things. But *The Amazing Adventures of Kavalier and Clay* is still a slam-bang accomplishment, dazzling and profound, cerebral and yet wonderfully touching. Always a stunning stylist, Chabon has come up with some of his most impressive prose yet in this book. But first, a minor question—is this novel, at least in some respects, roughly a decade too late?

The Brooklyn-born Sammy Clay, one of the two Jewish male protagonists, wonders at one point: "What if . . . they tried to do stories about costumed heroes who were more complicated, less childish, as fallible as angels." Who can't help but think of Tim Burton's fantastic Batman movie from 1989—or even the blockbuster X-Men, released just a few months after Chabon's novel. Both departed from the Superman comic book movie of the 1970s, which played up the special effects and damsels in distress and played down the dark psychology evident in Burton's film. Meanwhile, these days, so-called graphic novels like Chris Ware's *Jimmy Corrigan: The Smartest Kid on Earth* and Daniel Clowes' *David Boring* literally combine comic book art with literary narratives.

One reason this is more than a quibble is Chabon's mysterious narrator, who—in scattered footnotes or the main text—discusses present-day events, from a 1990s, ultra-omniscient perspective. Since the novel presents a brief but learned history of the American comic book as both art and commerce, one would expect some commentary on how the comic book hero, at the mass level, has attained the semiserious stature that Chabon's characters seem to covet.

Again, taking such things so seriously may be just another sign of the "devolution of American culture," as one jaded, self-loathing comic book executive puts it. Either way, the narrator problem could be the only off-key note in this otherwise brilliant symphony of a novel.

Hitler's rise

The Amazing Adventures of Kavalier and Clay begins with Hitler's ascendancy in Europe. It concludes with America's postwar era, when unprecedented comfort and wealth combined with a latent paranoia that surfaced in bizarre Senate hearings on the potentially harmful effects of comic books on America's youth.

All these global doings—as well as parental neglect, corporate ruthlessness, cinema, sex (gay and straight), memory, magic, and suicide—find their way, in suffused form, into the Technicolor pages churned out by Empire Comics. This fictional company rises (and falls) thanks to the diligent work of the novel's title characters.

"Houdini was a hero to little men, city boys, and Jews," Chabon writes. "Sammy Louis Klayman was all three." ("My professional name is Clay," he later explains.) A talented, ambitious teen fond of Houdini (and Jack London), Sammy Clay "dreamed the usual Brooklyn dreams of flight and transformation and escape." Which is to say, Sammy's problems are those of many American boys, especially of modest backgrounds—distant parents, a limited worldview, a certain claustrophobia.

But Sammy also has a fierce, highly American optimism, one that makes the reader inevitably think of him as an undersized Augie March. Sammy "dreamed with fierce contrivance, transmuting himself into a major American novelist, or a famous smart person . . . or perhaps into a heroic doctor," Chabon writes.

All this is in stark contrast to Josef Kavalier, Sammy's cousin from Prague, who has made a long, dark journey from a Europe slowly yielding to fascism. Josef's dreams of escape are haunted by persecution and death. Though he fled Europe, his family is not so lucky. The specter of the Holocaust will haunt him his entire life.

But Joe is in America now. And he and Sammy can draw. And when spilled onto the comic book pages, the traumas and contrasting personalities of this dreaming American and brooding exile will captivate a generation of American youth.

Magic and escape

"Forget about [what] you are escaping from. . . . Reserve your anxiety for what you are escaping to."

Josef recalls this nugget of wisdom from his Czech mentor in magic, Bernard Kornblum—an "Ausbrecher, a performing illusionist who specialized in tricks with straitjackets and handcuffs—the sort of act made famous by Harry Houdini."

Needless to say, escape and imprisonment are crucial themes in this book. In Prague, Kornblum, Joe, and the rest of the middle-class, educated Kavalier family are profoundly aware of the Nazi threat. Yet they must also go about the daily business of work—and play. "Josef had become interested in stage magic right around the time his hands had grown large enough to handle a deck of playing cards," Chabon writes. Yet even the seemingly innocent business of cultivating magic skills exposes vulnerability. To Kornblum, "Josef was one of those unfortunate boys who become escape artists not to prove the superior machinery of their bodies against outlandish contrivances and the laws of physics, but for dangerously metaphorical reasons."

Joe nearly kills himself trying to impress Kornblum with a perilous escape. Later, both pupil and teacher must combine their talents to pull off two tricks: relocating the legendary Golem of Prague (a protective giant out of Jewish lore) and making Josef disappear to America. That they accomplish the former feat by posing as undertakers and the latter by stowing Josef in a coffin suggests the grim brutality hovering over these scenes.

The Czech scenes are impressive but wordy. There are informative but lengthy digressions on how Josef met Kornblaum and Prague's rich tradition of illusionists and sleight-of-hand artists. Generally, though, Chabon bails himself out with shrewd plot twists, such as when Josef, concealed in his escape coffin, is nearly discovered by Nazis.

The big money

When Sammy discovers that Josef is a brilliant artist who spent two years at Prague's Academy of Fine Arts, he does what any enterprising American boy would do: "Josef, I tell you what. I'm going to do better than just get you a job. . . . I'm going to get us into the big money." Josef has just one question: "What is a comic book?"

It's a multilayered question, though, not just a joke about Josef's ignorance of American culture. The narrator gives a historical answer of sorts, in a discursive essay. At one point, we read: "Then, in June 1938, Superman appeared. He had been mailed to the offices of National Periodical publications from Cleveland, by a couple of Jewish boys." Fittingly, that's what Sammy's bosses want

when he pitches them a comic book idea—another wildly popular superhero to help sell their novelty trinkets to kids.

But the bosses are ultimately skeptical of Josef's ideas. "To me, this Superman is . . . maybe . . . only an American Golem," Josef says. Even Sammy comments: "Joe, the Golem is . . . well . . . Jewish." It's the classic story of ethnic assimilation—the fear that (in this case) you'll appear too Jewish. So imagine how the bosses feel when Sammy and Joe come up with their first cover, on which their hero—the Escapist—is punching Adolf Hitler in the face. (Also consider Sammy's last name, and that he, like the Golem, is a "clay man.")

As The Escapist evolves—enriching Sammy and Joe but their bosses much more so—each creator dumps his emotional baggage into the storyline. With Josef, of course, it's his family's doom in Europe. With Sammy, it's his dead father, who spent long stretches of time on the road as a performer. For Chabon, however, the true magic happens when these ingredients are savored by thousands of frightened, lonely, and passionate young readers. Josef is more skeptical. Hell-bent on using the comics as propaganda to ultimately crush Hitler, he at times wonders if "all they were doing . . . was indulging their own worst impulses and assuring the creation of another generation of men who revered only strength and domination."

But later, looking back, Joe concludes:

> Having lost his mother, father and brother, and grandfather, the friends and foes of his youth, his beloved teacher Bernard Kornblum, his city, his history—his home—the usual charge leveled against comic books, that they offered merely an escape from reality, seemed to Joe actually to be a powerful argument on their behalf. . . . The escape from reality was, he felt—especially right after the war—a worthy challenge.

The next generation

Somewhere in the middle of *Amazing Adventures*—the 1940s, basically, recorded in parts 4 and 5—the focus drifts. To be fair, tackling this decade would have required an additional 150 pages. Important things do happen: Josef leaves his lover Rosa and joins the military to fight the Nazis; Sammy has a love affair with a man. But at 200 pages, these sections feel baggy. Only when a child appears (who may either be Sammy's or Josef's) does Chabon recapture the intimacy and intensity that mark the book's most impressive sections.

Comfortable in suburbia, with Josef seemingly lost to the world, Rosa and Sammy have gotten married. They are also raising a son—one who loves comics and skips school too often, despite his guardians' best efforts. "Another escape artist," quips a detective, aware that the once-famous, now vanished Josef Kavalier is a relative.

Quite a few people are interested when Josef—or at least his most famous creation, the Escapist—is ready to leap back into the public consciousness. Literally. From the Empire State Building perhaps, according to a letter that appears in a 1954 edition of the *Herald-Tribune*. The letter also notes that Sammy and Josef were vastly underpaid by their bosses.

It's still a best-seller, but Kavalier and Clay have ceased their affiliation with The Escapist. The quality of the product has declined. So when fans and family alike gather at the Empire State Building for a supposed Escapist appearance, it touches a nostalgic chord. For Sammy, though, it could mean that his troubled cousin has finally lost it.

First Chabon spirals back in time (by page 500 we're used to this) and outlines how Josef came to know the young boy who is his nephew . . . or son. All the principal characters and their dilemmas are drawn into this slightly absurd hoax, which, as it turns out, must be taken seriously. And yet, when the episode is resolved, the troubles have only begun for Sammy, Josef, and Rosa, now under the same roof.

Chabon is a deft chronicler of love and other domestic troubles who manages to explore politics and the nature of art. Familial problems hold the later sections of *Amazing Adventures* together as the rise of Sammy and Josef does the earlier parts. With neither sentimentality nor cynicism, Chabon allows his characters to confront their past, present, and future.

Seduction of the innocent

And what prose! Here's Josef exploring his regrets, as he stays under the same roof as his one-time lover Rosa, now married to Sammy.

> After their initial conversation in the kitchen, he and Rosa seemed to find it hard to get a second one started . . . he attributed her silence to animosity. For days, he stood in the cold shower of her imagined anger, which he felt entirely deserved. Not only for having left her pregnant and in the lurch, so that he might go off in a failed pursuit of an impossible revenge; but for having never returned, never telephoned or dropped a line, never once thought of her—so he imagined that she imagined—in all those years away. The expanding gas of silence between them only excited his shame and lust the more. In the absence of verbal intercourse, he became hyperaware

of other signs of her—the jumble of her makeups and creams and lotions in the bathroom, the Spanish moss of her lingerie dangling from the shower curtain rod, the irritable tinkle of her spoon against her teacup.

Before this knot of regret and sex can be untangled, politics will intervene. Sammy Clay is called before the Senate Subcommittee to Investigate Juvenile Delinquency, prompted by Dr. Frederic Wertham's classic anticomic study *The Seduction of the Innocent*.

In Chabon's fictional re-creation, a reactionary senator goes for Sammy's secret.

> "Isn't it true," an unnerved Sammy is asked during televised hearings, "that you have a reputation in the comic book field for being particularly partial to boy sidekicks." And that, "[T]he relationship between Batman and [Robin] is actually a thinly veiled allegory of pedophilic inversion?"

But to Sammy—humiliated, now determined to make a fresh start (out in the new world of California, of course)—his comic book work was indeed worthy of psychoanalysis. Just not on a predatory level. "Dr. Wertham was an idiot; it was obvious that Batman was not intended, consciously or unconsciously, to play Robin's corrupter: he was meant to stand in for his father, and by extension for the absent, indifferent, vanishing fathers of the comic-book-reading boys of America."

This is fitting, of course, given Sammy's troubles with his own dad. In exploring the comic book hearings, however, the novel is on more sensitive turf, as it's far too easy to critique the concerned senators. After all (like Chabon), they knew there was something deep going on with comics, didn't they? In one insightful scene, Josef is offered money to draw a nude—indicating that whatever "escapist" wonders comics are capable of, they can also be used to indulge baser fantasies of sex, violence, or whatever. It's not that the senators should have pursued the comic book "threat" with more vigor. But as Chabon makes clear, comic books, in a lot of ways, are playing with kiddie dynamite, in the psychological sense. Unfortunately, we can't all expect to see the ignition here as a strictly positive one. Anyway, Chabon doesn't linger very long on the senators. The episode is mainly used to prod Sammy to an epiphany—an "escapist" one at that.

The narrator

What finally remains is the book's narrator question. Who's telling this story in (roughly) the year 2001? "In later years, holding forth to an interviewer or to an audience of aging fans at a comic book convention" are the novel's first words. Off the bat, we know this is a narrator who can see it all. Knowledgeable factoids pretty much rule out an aged Sammy or Josef, since we learn things they do not know. Perhaps the narrator is the boy who, at different times, was their son. Why Chabon has chosen to sprinkle the text with contemporary insight is ultimately unclear. It's entertaining and enlightening but also distracting. It sets off alarms, given the many narrative experiments we've seen in recent novels.

Is the storyteller simply Michael Chabon, comic book lover? Maybe—but the narrator is hardly authoritative. (Recall that the recent Batman movies are never mentioned, nor for that matter are the many 1930s and '40s artifacts of antifascist pop culture that Sammy and Joe could have used to defend their leanings.) Readers can be forgiven for questioning why things are handled this way.

One other minor flaw here: Though it's intriguing to consider "Citizen Kane"'s influence on all forms of popular art, a cameo by Orson Welles (as well as Salvador Dali) feels unnecessary. But on the whole Chabon has produced a great and very American novel, which feels both intimate and worldly. It is funny and dramatic, deeply researched yet freewheeling. Some could even say that *Amazing Adventures* is downright patriotic, despite its jabs at comic-burning senators. It defends polyglot American pop culture on both an aesthetic and political level. Comic books, with all their crudities, also seem to be symbols of freedom.

When Josef Kavalier, the Holocaust-haunted immigrant, realizes he is about to be paid handsomely to draw comics, he thinks:

> All this has conformed so closely to Joe's movie-derived notions of life in America that if an airplane were now to land on Twenty-fifth Street and disgorge a dozen bathing suit clad Fairies of Democracy come to award him the presidency of General Motors, a contract with Warner Bros., and a penthouse on Fifth Avenue with a swimming pool in the living room, he would have greeted this, too, with the same dream-like unsurprise.

This is, of course, just a moment of euphoria. But not for nothing does one character later say: "I wasn't aware that Nazis read comic books."

That's just it—they don't.

Source: Tom Deignan, "Playing with Kiddie Dynamite," in *World and I*, Vol. 16, No. 2, February 2001, p. 220.

Lee Behlman

In the following excerpt, Behlman explains how comics offered escapism and an effective distraction from memory for Jewish immigrants to the United States in the 1930s and 1940s, some of whom entered the comics industry and prospered.

Michael Chabon's Comic Book Americans and the Golem of Prague

Near the end of *Everything is Illuminated*, Alex, the fledgling Ukrainian writer, composes a letter in his own inimitable, thesaurusized English, in which he tells his friend Jonathan about a precious fantasy:

> [I]f we are to be such nomads with the truth, why do we not make the story more premium than life? It seems to me that we are making the story even inferior. We often make ourselves appear as though we are foolish people, and we make our voyage, which was an ennobled voyage, appear very normal and second rate. We could give your grandfather two arms, and could make him high-fidelity. . . . [I]t could be perfect and beautiful and funny, and usefully said, as you say. . . . I do not think there are any limits to how excellent we could make life seem. (pp. 179–180; emphasis in original])

Alex fantasizes about eluding the terms of his own history and healing the physical and emotional wounds of both his and Jonathan's families. The new fiction that could result might well be fantastical itself, with a miraculous set of happy reversals and revisions of the past. Alex expresses this wish for an escape from an uncomfortable reality, if only for a few moments, near the end of the story, and his perspective is not clearly endorsed by a narrative that more typically uses fantasy to give shape to ugly truths.

While in *Everything is Illuminated* this wish to escape through fiction appears only briefly and as a subterranean desire, it is very much the main subject of Michael Chabon's Pulitzer Prize-winning novel, *The Amazing Adventures of Kavalier & Clay* (2000). Through its sweeping narrative about two young Jewish comic book artists making their careers in New York during the "Golden Age" comics era of the late 1930s and 1940s, *Kavalier & Clay* explores the use of fantasy not as a means of giving shape to the documentary facticity of the Holocaust, not as a set of stage properties surrounding the real, but as a potential means of "escape" from the past. Chabon's novel explores a major moral and aesthetic issue which is only partially addressed in the Holocaust fictions I have discussed thus far: the fact that fantasy itself, no matter how disruptive, no matter how "unsentimental" it may be, can give pleasure to an artist and an audience, and that pleasure may be a distraction from the past. What's more, and this is where Chabon is most surprising, his novel guardedly presents the idea that

that distraction may be itself be a valid response. *Kavalier & Clay* is an extended meditation, with comic books as its central subject, on the value of fantasy as a deflective resource rather than a reflective one.

Escapism is a prominent characteristic of American popular art forms, and this quality, when it is found in Hollywood entertainment, episodic television, or mass-market fiction, is often dismissed by critics as essentially shallow or trivial. Without denying the trashiness of much American popular culture, Chabon issues an aesthetic and ultimately moral defense of escapism as it is found in one of America's only original contributions to world culture (along with jazz music), superhero comic books. Through its exploration of this form, the novel is remarkable for the intimate ways it shows how much pleasure and value may be found in producing and reading fantasy. Chabon's intent in exploring superhero comics is not to issue a postmodern critique of the "real" and realistic art forms, nor a populist anti-intellectual assault on "elites" and their art, but to show, in a phenomenological way, how fantasy feels, and how it may assuage pain. With this comforting gesture may come the admittedly problematic, quintessentially American phenomenon of forgetting.

Kavalier & Clay announces from its beginning a fracture between the distanced American experience of the Holocaust and the events of the Holocaust themselves. In what is in some respects a classic Jewish immigrant narrative, Josef Kavalier, a teenage art student from Prague, travels to America and makes his way in this new world at the side of his American cousin and partner in comics, Sam Clay (formerly Klayman) of Brooklyn. The novel begins almost immediately with the meeting of these two characters and then flashes back in a series of episodes to Josef's early life in Prague, where we learn of his secular, upper-middle-class Jewish family's increasing difficulties under the Nazi regime in the late 1930s, and of his eventual lonely escape to America. As an adolescent, Josef had learned the skills of escape artistry under the guidance of Kornblum, an *ausbrecher* [escape artist] of Eastern European origin, and Josef comes to use these skills in his escape from Prague. The rest of the novel takes place in America and follows Josef and Sam's career as they invent and further develop their character "The Escapist," a superhero who, like Houdini, can escape from any restraint and, like Captain America and the Human Torch, can fight whole divisions of Nazi soldiers

> "... *Kavalier & Clay* explores the use of fantasy not as a means of giving shape to the documentary facticity of the Holocaust, not as a set of stage properties surrounding the real, but as a potential means of 'escape' from the past."

single-handedly. The comic book itself becomes the key means of imaginative escape for Josef, who works constantly to effect the physical escape of his brother, Thomas, from occupied Prague to America.

The recent history of comic books—particularly the longer-form "graphic novels" produced by such artists as Will Eisner, Daniel Clowes, and Chris Ware—has demonstrated the vast storytelling potential of the form beyond the limitations of the superhero genre. Many critics and "serious" comic book artists alike seek to draw aesthetic distinctions between such recent work and the now sixty-year history of stories about men and women in tights. Art Spiegelman has confronted the connotations of triviality often associated with both artists and fans of superhero comics by popularizing an alternate term, "comix," which stands for a "co-mix" of images and words. Yet in *Kavalier & Clay*, Chabon embraces the superhero comic book in its earliest incarnation, with its crude drawing style, monotone dialogue, and unlikely plots, as a rough but vivid and fertile form. Unlike Clowes and Ware, who in some ways embrace the form but also tend to put ironic quotes around their referencing of superheroes, Chabon is notable for his enthusiastic endorsement of this by now rather "square" art form. In a bravura section beginning on page 74, Chabon's narrator describes the early history and aesthetics of comic books with a kind of learned enthusiasm not unlike that found in Melville's discussion of whale facts and statistics in the "cetology" chapter of *Moby Dick*. Chabon's narrator does such things as compare the relative artistic merits of superhero comics covers and their inside material, and in doing so he can also be quite critical, with the wonkish air of any enthusiast, about the limitations of the form:

> In 1939 the American comic book, like the beavers and cockroaches of prehistory, was larger and, in its cumbersome way, more splendid than its modern descendant. . . . [Yet] as with all mongrel art forms and pidgin languages, there was, in the beginning, a necessary, highly fertile period of genetic and grammatical confusion. . . . [T]he men tended to stand around in wrinkleless suits that looked stamped from stovepipe tin and in hats that appeared to weigh more than the automobiles, ill at ease, big-chinned, punching one another in their check-mark noses. . . . Consequently, the comic book, almost immediately upon its invention, or soon thereafter, began to languish, lacking purpose or distinction. There was nothing here one could not find done better, or cheaper, somewhere else (and on the radio one could have it for free).

Then, in June 1938, Superman appeared.

Inspired by the extraordinary success of the Man of Steel, Siegel and Schuster's crude but portentous invention, Sam (with Josef in tow as his artist) proposes a new superhero comics line for Sheldon Anapol's Empire Novelties Company. Anapol agrees to let them produce a sample issue, which leaves them in the position of having to come up with a hero to build their comic book around over a single weekend. In a witty scene that follows, complete with in-jokes about later comic book inventions, we witness Sam and Josef struggle to come up with a new comic book hero, and we are told that many such conversations were simultaneously blooming in New York in the post-Superman year of 1939. Sam argues that the problem involved in creating a new superhero is not centrally about what powers he will have, but about his motivation.

> "This is not the question," he said. "If he's like a cat or a spider or a f—— wolverine, if he's huge, if he's tiny, if he can shoot flames or ice or death rays or Vat 69, if he turns into fire or water or stone or India rubber. He could be a Martian, he could be a ghost, he could be a god or a demon or a wizard or monster. Okay? It doesn't *matter*, because right now, see, at this very moment, we have a bandwagon rolling, I'm telling you. Every little skinny guy like me in New York who believes there's life on Alpha Centauri and got the s—— kicked out of him in school and can smell a dollar is out there right this minute trying to jump onto it, walking around with a pencil in his shirt pocket, saying, "He's like a falcon, no, he's like a tornado, no, he's like a g——d—— wiener dog." Okay?
>
> . . . The question is *why*."

Over the next 48 hours, Sam and Josef toil with a group of young fellow artists to create a set of superheroes for a new series called Masked Man

Comics, and among the heroes will be their main creation, the Escapist, a figure who combines the *ausbrecher* talents of Houdini with the dark, secret history of the Shadow, along with the prodigious but limited physical strength of the early Superman. In the time before America enters the Second World War, the Escapist fights the Nazis—even, on the cover of the first issue, putting the kibosh on Hitler himself. But Chabon does not just describe Sam and Josef's co-creation of the character— he inserts a full chapter in which the origin tale of the Escapist is told as a short story, in prose that manages to combine sophisticated narrative and descriptive material with the gee-whiz dialogue of Sam Klay's comic book. The comic book story, then, is transmuted in the narrator's hands into a kind of literary hybrid. It becomes a purely textual short story that includes a level of physical detail and even psychological sophistication that would never appear in a comic book of this era; yet it is also clearly a comic book story, with all the trappings of its fantasy world: a lame boy who can suddenly walk, secret evil societies, men from the East with arcane knowledge. With this "origin" tale, as well as that of a later character Sam and Josef create—the mousy-librarian-turned-superheroine "Luna Moth"—Chabon gives life to the pulpy energy, excitement, and crude imaginative power of superhero comics without a trace of condescension.

In telling the story of Sam and Josef's creative career, Chabon sets them within a larger story of the development of "Golden Age" superhero comics, a story populated largely by Jewish men. Most of Sam and Josef's fellow artists are New York Jews, and real-life Jewish comic creators such as Jack Kirby and Siegel and Schuster are referenced (Stan Lee even makes a cameo appearance). Perhaps the most important influence on the novel's conception of Jewish comic book artists in this period is the life and autobiographical comic book fiction of Will Eisner, an innovative early comic artist and, more recently, theorist and inventor of the graphic novel form. The connection between Jewish artists and their comic book creations is frequently alluded to in the novel, as when Sam says, "What, they're all Jewish, superheroes. Superman, you don't think he's Jewish? Coming over from the old country, changing his name like that. Clark Kent, only a Jew would pick a name like that for himself."

In some respects, *Kavalier & Clay* aims to be a novel of social realism, capturing the working environments of late depression-era New York, but despite its attempts at a hard-edged depiction, the novel more often slips into a sentimental view of this period and setting. For much of the middle section of the novel, Chabon describes in loving detail several different New York milieus, including the lower-middle-class home of Sam's mother in Flatbush, Brooklyn, and the Greenwich Village intellectual set of Josef's girlfriend, Rosa Saks Luxemborg. But the main emphasis is on the workplace, Sheldon Anapol's "Empire," where the Jewish comic book artists are usually underpaid and overworked under their Jewish boss. In its representation of the rough world of commerce of the time, Chabon doesn't approach the gruff realism of Saul Bellow's Chicago in *The Adventures af Augie March*. For example, in an unlikely development, Sam and Joe manage to leverage from their employer a percentage of profits on certain Escapist-related products (including the Escapist radio show)—this during a period in which comic book artists were almost always cut out of a share of any profits that accrued from their creations.

It is understandable that Sam and Josef's New York lives are told in a somewhat broad and even sentimental manner, for these two characters must carry a great symbolic weight in *Kavalier & Clay*. They represent the divided experience that is the story of Jewish American life at this time and in our time, for they are both American and Other, native-born and refugee, newly-formed and unsettlingly old. Josef stands, in many respects, for a particular Jewish American notion of the dark but romantic Mittel-european past, with his serious intellectual bearing, his background of suffering and stoicism, and his masculine and slightly mysterious aura; Sam, on the other hand, is the short, clever, fast, funny, and ambitious New York Jew, a man who "[l]ike all of his friends . . . considered it a compliment when somebody called him a wiseass." Neither character conforms perfectly to these archetypal roles—for example, Sam's closeted homosexuality adds considerable complexity to his portrayal—but instead, like Dickens' greatest creations, each is both a finely delineated, idiosyncratic human figure and a caricature or type.

In Sam and Josef's story, Chabon represents a familiar Jewish American conception of America as the place of Jewish creativity and hope, the place to escape *to*, and of Europe as the place of Jewish history and death, the place to escape *from*. The Jewish story, in this telling, seems at first to end in the Holocaust but is, at least to an extent, revived in America, and this is nowhere so evident as in Chabon's use of the Golem legend. In the early chapters of the novel, Chabon describes how Josef's escape is made possible by the rediscovery of the body of Rabbi Loew's famous Golem of Prague. This giant immobile figure, formed from the clay of the River Moldau, has long been kept hidden in an unmarked, sealed-off room in an apartment house near the *Alneuschul* (the Old-New Synagogue), but it is eventually retrieved by Josef and Kornblum (his *ausbrecher* tutor) and becomes the literal vehicle for Josef's escape out of Europe. Josef and Kornblum disguise the Golem as a "dead *goyische* giant", secret Josef away in its casket, and send it eastward, out of Nazi-controlled territory and into Lithuania. Once he escapes from the confines of the Golem's casket, Josef manages to make his way halfway around the world through the Soviet Union and Japan, and finally to America and (physical) salvation.

The Golem in this story represents both the dead hope of Jewish life in Europe and the ever-living promise of Jewish creativity, which can be transferred to the new world. It is a predecessor, then, as an artifact of Jewish fantasy, to the new Jewish fantasy-creation, the comic book hero. Chabon makes this connection between Golems and comic books clear early in the novel, when Josef sketches a Golem in his first effort at representing a superhero. (Upon seeing it, his future boss, Sheldon Anapol, is confused and exclaims, "'Is that the *Golem*? . . . My new Superman is the Golem?'") The connection is made even more explicit late in the novel, in a fascinating passage:

> The shaping of a Golem, to [Josef], was a gesture of hope, offered against hope, in a time of desperation. It was the expression of a yearning that a few magic words and an artful hand might produce something— one poor, dumb, powerful thing—exempt from the crushing strictures, from the ills, cruelties, and inevitable failures of the greater Creation. It was the voicing of a vain wish, when you get down to it, to escape. To slip, *like the Escapist,* free of the entangling chain of reality and the straitjacket of physical laws. (emphasis added)

The Golem represents the dream of "escape," which in this passage involves a flight from both the physical bondage of the Nazis and the imaginative bondage that may limit the expression of any artist. As such, the Golem is commensurate with comic book superheroes and with comic books themselves as artifacts of "escapist" Jewish creativity in the fecund commercial world of American pop culture.

The Ethics of Escapism

We arrive, through the figure of the Golem, at comic books as the central signifier and singular fetish of *Kavalier & Clay*, and with it the central issue of this essay, which is the question of how these young Jewish American writers understand the nature and efficacy of fantasy in the context of the Holocaust. Comic books, in Chabon's hands, represent a form of Jewish fantasy markedly different from Englander's Chelm legends and Foer's magical-realist shtetl, Trachimbrod: while these two authors indirectly give shape to the reality of the Holocaust through these fantastical devices, to an unusual degree Chabon uses comic books as a recourse or alternative to shaping that reality. The Escapist, like America itself, is always set in contrast to the Holocaust experiences of Josef, and is never used as vehicle for the depiction of those experiences, indirect or otherwise.

Through their deliberately broad, even crude vocabulary, the Escapist storylines and layouts provide an opportunity for Josef to mobilize anti-Nazi sentiment in the period before America would enter the war, and to provide for himself a dose of short-lived imaginative revenge. Josef furiously wants to believe that if he and Sam "could not move Americans to anger against Hitler, then Joe's existence, the mysterious freedom that had been granted to him and denied to so many others, had no meaning," and yet he is also aware that his persuasive powers will always be limited, for "[t]he Escapist was an impossible champion, ludicrous and above all *imaginary*, fighting a war that could never be won." While the Escapist fulfills the fantasy of protecting the persecuted (much like Rabbi Loew's Golem patrolling the streets of Prague) and even goes further to visit active retribution upon Hitler and his cronies, still, the effectiveness and the satisfactions of such a creative consolation are seriously curtailed by an awareness of what is actually happening in Europe. Josef also realizes the fact that superhero comics may promote dangerous fantasies of the kind of violent revenge that fuel the Nazi assault on Jews. Chabon thus acknowledges through Josef's experiences the problem of the extreme incommensurateness between fantasy and reality, most intensely in the scene where Josef discovers that, despite his great efforts to save his brother, Thomas, the boy has been killed along with a ship full of other Jewish refugee children by a German U-Boat.

Near the end of the novel, Chabon does make some efforts to reconcile the American impulse to escape through fantasy with the memory of the European Jewish past and of the Holocaust itself. He seeks to achieve this reconciliation by bringing the Golem, and its evocation of the lost, pre-Holocaust Jewish European past, into the present, so that it no longer just prefigures American comic books but becomes their subject. After finding out about Thomas's death, Josef leaves to become a U.S. serviceman and cuts off contact from Sam and his pregnant girlfriend, but years later. he returns to their lives and reveals that he has been spending time secretly writing a 2,256-page comic book based loosely on the Golem legend. It is both a superhero story and a Golem story, a "long and hallucinatory tale of a wayward, unnatural child, Josef Golem, that sacrificed itself to save and redeem the little lamplit world whose safety had been entrusted to it." For Josef, it seems that this new, breakthrough work is "helping to heal him" of his wounds, not by erasing his memory of the pre-American Jewish past, but by recasting them in comic book form, and having European Jewish fantasy mingle with the American variety. In a similar gesture at acknowledging the "pastness" of the European Jewish past and yet seeking to recall it into memory, Chabon has the long-lost casket of the Golem reappear in Josef's life at the very end of the novel. Whereas before the Golem was fully formed but nearly weightless, now it is but a heap of dust; yet it is heavy now, perhaps with the souls of the lost European Jews.

But despite Chabon's efforts in applying a kind of thematic reconciliation to match the characters' scenes of reconciliation at the end of the novel, the reincursions of the Golem into the conclusion of the novel seem a sudden and therefore somewhat clumsy and unconvincing narrative device, particularly for a writer who is usually so consummately in command of his plot. While this device seeks to place the burden of the Jewish European past—the burden of the Holocaust itself—into an American narrative, and therefore to give more heft and relevance to the superhero comic book dream of escape, it's not clear that the concept of escapism itself can properly assume such a weight. What is assumed, in any case, is not the memory of the past, nor the direct experience of the Holocaust, but an idea of it, one that is, in Chabon's account, necessarily abstracted by American distance. James E. Young discusses this phenomenon in the context of distinguishing U.S. Holocaust memorials from their European counterparts:

> Where European memorials located *in situ* often suggest themselves rhetorically as the extension of the events they would commemorate, those in America

must gesture abstractly to a past removed in time and space. If memorials in Germany and Poland composed of camp ruins invite visitors to mistake them for the events they represent, those in America inevitably call attention to the great distance between themselves and the destruction. . . . In this sense, American memorials seem not to be anchored in history so much as in the ideals that generated them in the first place.

According to Young's description, American engagements with the Holocaust never gain full purchase on its history because they tend to turn facts into abstracted "ideals," a practice characteristic of American distance (as well as a Protestant-influenced messianic optimism). Chabon's novel struggles with explaining this impulse to abstract the Holocaust from an American-Jewish present, and with describing the very real pleasures to be gained from submitting those abstractions to a fantastic set of reversals and escapes. The novel is most vivid and ultimately most convincing in its defense of fantasy not as a device that gives shape to the real but as one that is inevitably, hopelessly, and yet somehow hopefully distant from it. As the narrator says of Josef in the novel's strongest defense of escapism,

> Having lost his mother, father, brother, and grandfather, the friends and foes of his youth, his beloved teacher Bernard Kornblum, his city, his history—his home—the usual charge leveled against comic books, that they offered *merely an easy escape* from reality, seemed to Joe actually to be a powerful argument on their behalf. He had escaped, in his life, from ropes, chains, boxes, bags, and crates, from handcuffs and shackles, and regimes. . . . The escape from reality was, he felt—especially right after the war—a worthy challenge.

By noting that escapism is "especially" worthy for survivors immediately after the war, Chabon is careful to mark out escapism's limitations, but the fact remains that even in the short term, escapism is a turn away from history. It is a safe refuge from the memory of the Nazi genocide and not a sufficient means of representing it directly—something that, to its credit, the novel never attempts. Though Englander and Foer use fantastic elements of Jewish folklore as a vehicle for memorial, Chabon shows, through his meditation on the thoroughly Jewish-American medium of early superhero comics, how fantasy may also act as an interruption to memory, a holding action against the incursions of the past.

Source: Lee Behlman, "The Escapist: Fantasy, Folklore, and the Pleasures of the Comic Book in Recent Jewish American

Holocaust Fiction: Michael Chabon's Comic Book Americans and the Golem of Prague," in *SHOFAR*, Vol. 22, No. 3, Spring 2004, pp. 61–71.

Sources

Campbell, Joseph, *The Hero with a Thousand Faces*, Princeton University Press, 1968, p. 193.

Chabon, Michael, *The Amazing Adventures of Kavalier & Clay*, Picador, 2000.

Kalfus, Ken, "The Golem Knows," in *New York Times Book Review*, September 24, 2000, p. 8.

Maslin, Janet, "A Life and Death Story Set in Comic Book Land," in *New York Times*, September 21, 2000, pp. B10, E10.

O'Nan, Stewart, Review of *The Amazing Adventures of Kavalier & Clay*, in *Pittsburgh Post-Gazette*, September 17, 2000, p. G8.

Podhoretz, John, Review of *The Amazing Adventures of Kavalier & Clay*, in *Commentary*, Vol. 3, No. 6, pp. 68–72.

Further Reading

Amundsen, Roald, *The South Pole*, Cooper Square Press, 2001.

> This book gives a first-hand account of Amundsen's 1911 expedition to the South Pole.

Chabon, Michael, and others, *Michael Chabon Presents: The Amazing Adventures of the Escapist*, Vol. 1–3, Dark Horse Comics, 2004–2006.

> This series of graphic novels reprint the Escapist comic books along with original content. Dark Horse Comics launched *The Amazing Adventures of the Escapist* following the popularity of Chabon's novel.

McCloud, Scott, *Reinventing Comics: How Imagination and Technology Are Revolutionizing an Art Form*, Harper, 2000.

> This book, told in McCloud's boldly black and white comic style, examines the Internet as the next frontier for the comic book industry.

———, *Understanding Comics: The Invisible Art*, Kitchen Sink Press, 1993.

> McCloud examines comics as art and as communication media. Although his arguments are rigorous, the content is laid out as a black and white comic book.

Singer, Isaac Bashevis, *The Golem*, illustrated by Uri Shulevitz, Farrar, Straus, and Giroux, 1982.

> Nobel laureate Isaac Singer retells the story of the legendary Golem of Prague. This is one of Singer's most famous short stories.

American Pastoral

Philip Roth

1997

American Pastoral (1997) is the twenty-second book by Philip Roth, one of the leading twentieth-century American writers. This long novel, which is almost mythic in scope, explores the course of American history from the late 1940s, which Roth's narrator and alter ego, Nathan Zuckerman, regards as a golden period, to the social upheavals that marked the 1960s and early 1970s. The focal point of the story is a Jewish character called Swede Levov, an outstanding man in every respect—brilliant athlete, successful businessman, devoted husband and father—whose only goal is to live a tranquil, pastoral life in rural Old Rimrock, New Jersey. But his rebellious sixteen-year-old daughter, Merry, gets caught up in the anti-Vietnam War movement and plants a bomb at the local post office, killing one person. Swede's idyllic life is shattered forever, and for the rest of his life, as the novel zigzags its way back and forth in time, Swede tries without success to understand what went wrong. How could such a thing have happened? In his searching examination of how confident, post-World War II America gave way to the violence and disorder of the 1960s, Roth explores, with depth, understanding, and compassion, issues such as the nature of community and belonging, Jewish assimilation, father-daughter relations, familial loyalty and betrayal, and political fanaticism.

Author Biography

One of America's leading novelists of the twentieth century and into the twenty-first century, Philip Roth explores the conflicts and tensions in American Jewish life. Roth was born in Newark, New Jersey, on March 19, 1933, the eldest son of Herman and Bess Roth, who were Jewish immigrants from Europe. Roth was raised in the Weequahic area of Newark, during the Depression. He graduated from high school at the age of sixteen and then earned a bachelor's degree in English from Bucknell University in 1954 and a master of arts degree, also in English, from the University of Chicago in 1955.

Roth served in the U.S. Army from 1955 to 1956 and married Margaret Martinson in 1959; they separated in 1963. His first book, *Goodbye, Columbus, and Five Short Stories* (1959), won the National Book Award in 1960. After two novels that received comparatively little attention, Roth wrote one of his best known novels, *Portnoy's Complaint* (1969). Its portrayal of the overbearing Jewish mother and her repressed son, Alex Portnoy, gave thousands of readers a hilarious picture of growing up Jewish in America in the 1940s and 1950s.

Through the 1970s Roth published a number of successful novels. In 1979, Roth published *The Ghost Writer*, the first novel in which Nathan Zuckerman appeared. Zuckerman, a writer, is Roth's alter ego, a semi-autobiographical figure, although not everything that happens to Zuckerman also happened to Roth. Throughout the 1980s and 1990s, Roth used Zuckerman repeatedly as a protagonist. Among the novels in which Zuckerman appears is *American Pastoral* (1997), which won the Pulitzer Prize. *I Married a Communist* (1998) may have been inspired by Roth's stormy relationship with his ex-wife, the actress Claire Bloom. They had married in 1990 and divorced in 1994, and Bloom wrote a memoir in which she portrayed Roth in an unflattering light. In the novel, a radio actor's life is ruined by a memoir written by his ex-wife.

Roth continued to write through the 1990s, winning awards repeatedly for his work. As of 2006, Roth's most recent novel was *The Plot Against America* (2004), an exploration of the anti-Semitism that might have developed in the United States had Charles A. Lindbergh defeated Franklin Roosevelt for the presidency in 1940.

Roth has also written a number of nonfiction works. Probably the best known is *Patrimony: A True Story* (1991), about the relationship between Roth and his father during the last five months of

Philip Roth   © AP Images

his father's life. The book won the National Book Critics Circle Award. As of 2006, Roth lived in Connecticut and continued to write prolifically.

Plot Summary

Part 1: Paradise Remembered
Chapter 1

American Pastoral begins in Weequahic, a middle-class area of Newark, New Jersey. The narrator, Philip Roth's alter ego Nathan Zuckerman, recalls his high school years during the late 1940s. In particular, he recalls Seymour Levov, a Jewish boy seven years his senior, who was Weequahic High School's star athlete during the early years of World War II. Everyone called Seymour, "the Swede" or "Swede," and he was widely loved and admired. Swede joined the Marines in 1945 and became a drill instructor. After college graduation, he married Dawn Dwyer, a Catholic woman and former Miss New Jersey.

Zuckerman recalls that in 1985 he went to New York to watch the Mets and happened to see Swede. He introduced him to his companions as the greatest athlete in the history of Weequahic High School. Ten years later, Zuckerman received a letter from the Swede in which Swede said he wanted to meet Zuckerman for dinner in New York. He wanted to talk about his father, who recently died at the age of ninety-six and had "suffered because of the shocks that befell his loved ones." Flattered, Zuckerman agreed, and they met at an Italian restaurant. But the Swede talked mostly about his three sons and did not mention his father. Zuckerman was frustrated at being unable to penetrate the Swede's bland exterior. He wanted to know what lay behind the man's polite, smooth manner.

Chapter 2

Zuckerman reports on an enjoyable forty-fifth high school reunion, for which he drove three hours from his home in western Massachusetts. He meets his old friend Mendy Gurlik, and they discuss the fact that twenty members of their class are now dead, two of them from prostate cancer, which Gurlik fears, and which Zuckerman has already had. Zuckerman also meets Ira Posner and Alan Meisner, and they recall their high school days. Then Jerry Levov, Zuckerman's old classmate and Swede's younger brother, unexpectedly arrives at the reunion.

Chapter 3

Jerry informs Zuckerman that Swede died of prostate cancer only a few days earlier. Jerry speaks appreciatively of his brother's generous nature and his skill at running his business manufacturing ladies' gloves. But the Swede's life was destroyed, according to Jerry, by his daughter, Meredith, known as Merry. Merry was sixteen years old when in a protest against the Vietnam War in 1968, she planted a bomb in the post office at Old Rimrock, the village five miles from where the Levovs lived. The explosion killed a doctor who happened to be there. After that, Merry was known as the Rimrock Bomber. Jerry says that the Swede brought her up in a permissive way, in keeping with the times, but she resented it. The bomb put an end to the charmed life the Swede had led up to that point.

Jerry recalls a moment two years earlier when he found the Swede, who always maintained his placid exterior, sobbing in his car outside a restaurant. Swede told him that Merry, who had gone into hiding after planting the bomb, was dead. Jerry believed that Swede had always known where she was and had been going to see her. Jerry hated Merry and told his brother he was better off without her.

Jerry tells Zuckerman more about Swede's life. Dawn, in Jerry's view, was never satisfied with what Swede provided for her, and Merry was

afflicted with a stutter. Swede took her to speech therapists and psychiatrists, but nothing seemed to help. His reward was that his own daughter started to hate him. Jerry wonders why such a thing would happen to a man like Swede.

Intrigued by Swede's life, Zuckerman decides to write a book with Swede as the main character. He wants to delve into the man's character and discover what he was really like.

As the narrative returns to the reunion, Zuckerman meets Joy Helpern, and they recall a hayride they took together when they were in high school. As they talk, Zuckerman continues to think about Swede. He guesses that what Swede had really wanted to tell him about in the restaurant was not his father but his daughter. This was the great wound in his life that the Swede could not get out of his mind despite the fact that he had rebuilt his life with a second wife and three sons.

Joy tells Zuckerman details of her life as a girl that he had not known about, but then Zuckerman continues his speculations about what went wrong in Swede's life and how his desire to live a utopian, "American pastoral" life had turned into its antithesis, the "violence, and the desperation of the counterpastoral." As he dances with Joy, he contemplates the wider historical question of how Swede had become "history's plaything." Zuckerman thinks of the transition in U.S. society from World War II to the 1960s and the chaos created by the Vietnam War.

He begins in his mind to write the book about the Swede, imagining himself into the other man's life. He first creates a scene in Deal, New Jersey, at a seaside cottage when Merry is eleven. Driving back from the beach, Merry asks Swede to kiss her the way he kisses her mother. After an initial refusal, her father kisses her passionately on the mouth. He later wonders whether this one lapse is the cause of their subsequent suffering.

Zuckerman then reconstructs Merry's early life. When attempts to cure her stutter fail, Merry starts eating junk food, and by the time she is sixteen, she is very overweight. She becomes politically minded, opposing the Vietnam War and renouncing her family's middle-class values. She starts to fight with her parents. Swede argues with her about her Saturday afternoon trips to New York, where she sometimes stays overnight. After Merry rebels against the conditions he imposes on her, Swede bans her from leaving the house on Saturdays. He tells her she can demonstrate against the war locally. She does not go to New York again, but one day she blows up a nearby post office.

Part 2: The Fall

Chapter 4

Four months after the bombing and Merry's disappearance, a young woman named Rita Cohen comes to Swede's factory, claiming to be a graduate student doing a thesis on the leather industry in Newark. Swede gives her a tour of the factory. As she is about to leave, Rita tells him that "she," meaning Merry, wants the scrapbook she made about Audrey Hepburn. Swede then knows that Merry has sent her. He meets Rita the next day at the Newark airport parking lot and gives her the scrapbook. The following week he hands over her ballet slippers, her leotard, and a diary she kept about her stuttering. But Rita refuses to tell him where Merry is, and she denounces him as a capitalist who abuses his workers. He tells her she does not know what she is talking about and demands to know where Merry is. He arranges to meet Rita at a room in the New York Hilton and takes five thousand dollars in cash that she has requested, plus five thousand more. When he arrives at the room, Rita taunts him and asks him to have sex with her, after which, she says, she will take him to see Merry. Disgusted, Swede runs from the room and calls the FBI, but by the time they arrive she is gone.

Five years pass. Across the United States, more bombs are being set off by anti-war radicals. Two years after Merry's disappearance, a house in Greenwich Village, New York, is destroyed by a bomb. Swede is convinced that the young woman seen staggering from the building was Merry, and he believes she will show up at their house. Then the woman is identified and is not Merry. After that, Swede thinks that the corpse of a young woman discovered in the house must be Merry, but again, this proves false.

In trying to work out what went wrong with Merry, Swede thinks back to an incident in 1963, when she was eleven. She watched on television as a Buddhist monk immolated himself in South Vietnam. The image frightened her, but when more monks were shown doing the same thing, she became fascinated by it, less horrified than curious.

Desperate to find Merry, Swede becomes convinced that Angela Davis, a political radical on trial for kidnapping, murder, and conspiracy, knows where Merry is. He carries on imaginary conversations with Davis in his kitchen. To her charges that wealthy whites exploit black workers, he tells her of his loyal black employee Vicky, who stayed with him in the building during the Newark riots in June 1967. After the riots, he refused to move his factory from Newark, despite his father's

urging. One reason was that he did not want Merry to think that he had employed black people and then deserted them at the first sign of trouble.

Over time, the Swede's torment, of which he is reminded every time he goes to Old Rimrock, increases; his mind is full of "tyrannical obsessions, stifled inclinations, superstitious expectations, horrible imaginings, fantasy conversations, unanswerable questions."

Chapter 5

In September of 1973, Swede receives a letter from Rita Cohen, informing him that Merry is working under the name of Mary Stolz at a dog and cat hospital in Newark. Rita tells him how he may contact Merry. The letter comes at a time when Dawn Levov seems finally to be getting over the tragedy. Since it happened, she has been hospitalized twice for suicidal depression, and Swede had thought she would never fully recover. But her recovery dates from the previous year, when she went to a clinic in Geneva for a facelift. She was delighted with the results. She also managed to persuade Swede to agree to sell their old stone house and have a new house built.

The dog and cat hospital is located in a decrepit old building only ten minutes' car drive from Swede's Newark Maid glove factory. He waits for his daughter on the sidewalk. When she sees him, she races across the street, and they embrace.

Chapter 6

Merry tells her father that she has become a Jain (the Jains are a small Indian religious sect) and has adopted an extreme philosophy of renunciation. She wears a mask over her mouth because she does not want to harm the microscopic organisms in the air. She cultivates asceticism and self-denial because she does not want to commit violence against any living thing.

Merry has been living for six months in squalor in a tiny room in a wreck of a house on a narrow street where there are only two other houses left. Swede asks her whether she bombed the post office, and she admits that she did, but she also claims that she does not know Rita Cohen and did not send her, or anyone, to her father. Swede starts to think that Rita was nothing but a criminal who tricked him.

Merry then explains what she has been doing for the last five years. For seventy-two hours after the bombing she had been hidden in the home of Sheila Salzman, her speech therapist. Then she left and moved around every few days, taking on fifteen aliases in two months. In Indianapolis, she was taken in by an antiwar minister and assumed the name Mary Stolz. For nearly a year, she washed dishes in an old people's home until the minister told her she must leave immediately and go to a commune in Portland, Oregon. On the way, she was raped and robbed in Chicago. In Oregon, she planted two bombs which killed three people. Assembling bombs had become her specialty. After Portland, she worked in the potato fields in Idaho and planned to go to Cuba. She moved to Miami, Florida, where she only just managed to escape capture by the FBI. Swede asks her to go home with him, but she refuses.

After he leaves all he can think of is the fact that his daughter was raped. Distressed, he calls his brother Jerry, who tells him to go back and get Merry and bring her home. Jerry then criticizes Swede for all his faults, especially for not showing his true feelings about anything, always wanting to be diplomatic and not hurt anyone. He urges Swede to either assert his will and get his daughter or forget about her altogether. He even offers to come and get her himself if that is what Swede wants. Swede says no and is convinced that Jerry's explanations for what went wrong are false, but he can find no reason himself that would explain the tragedy that befell Merry.

Part 3: Paradise Lost

Chapter 7

Swede returns home from his meeting with Merry. He, Dawn, and Swede's parents, who are visiting from Florida, watch the Watergate hearings on television. (Watergate was the scandal that led to the resignation of President Richard M. Nixon in 1974.) Lou Levov rails against Nixon and his cohorts. The talk gets round to Merry, but Swede tells them there is no news. He cannot bring himself to tell them the truth because he wants to protect his family.

That evening, the Levovs hold a dinner party. The guests include Bill and Jessie Orcutt, their neighbors. Bill, who is designing the Levovs' new home, comes from a family that has been in the area since the eighteenth century, and he is an expert on local history. Orcutt once took Swede on a tour of the area, and Swede realized that he could never match Orcutt in terms of the latter's illustrious family history. Orcutt belonged to the area in a way that the Jewish Swede never could.

During dinner, Jessie Orcutt drinks too much, but Lou Levov tries to get along with her and

engage her in conversation, even though he has no respect for the Orcutts. Dawn has always claimed not to like Bill Orcutt, either, but when Swede catches sight of her and Orcutt in the kitchen, it is obvious from the way that Orcutt touches her that they are having an affair.

Chapter 8

Swede is stunned by the revelation of his wife's infidelity, and he thinks about it as the dinner conversation centers on the Watergate scandal and the X-rated movie, *Deep Throat*. Swede is also disturbed by the fact that one of his dinner guests is Sheila Salzman, who, he has that afternoon learned, sheltered Merry after the bombing. The narrative also reveals that for four months following Merry's disappearance, Sheila was Swede's mistress.

Other guests at the dinner are Barry and Marcia Umanoff, Columbia University professors with whom Merry stayed in New York a couple of times before the bombing. Marcia is an argumentative person; she and Dawn loathe each other. As the conversation continues, Lou Levov protests against *Deep Throat*, asserting that such things should be kept out of the general culture. Orcutt argues that doing so is impossible because permissiveness is a part of the times in which they live. When Dr. Shelly Salzman speaks, all Swede can think of is that the Salzmans had harbored Merry and never told him. Swede had once visited Salzman's office intending to confess his affair with the doctor's wife, but once he was there he remained silent about it. Swede now feels extremely hostile toward Sheila and Orcutt.

As Marcia provokes everyone, especially Lou Levov, into arguing, Swede suddenly realizes that the house that Orcutt is supposedly designing for the Levovs will, in fact, be occupied by Dawn and Orcutt, after Dawn leaves Swede and Orcutt deserts his drunken wife, Jessie.

Chapter 9

Swede takes a phone call in his study from Rita Cohen. She accuses him of telling Merry that he had refused to have sex with her at the hotel. Swede had, in fact, not mentioned this to Merry. He is confused, not knowing what the relationship is between Rita and Merry and not knowing what to believe. When Rita get abusive, Swede hangs up, after which Sheila enters the study, inquiring whether he is all right. He confronts her with the fact that she gave Merry refuge and did not tell him; she replies that she had no choice. Her first obligation was to

Merry. Swede insults her, pulls a picture off the wall and throws it at her feet. She leaves the room quietly, still in control of herself. He returns to the terrace, where he talks to Orcutt, full of hatred of him. He is also momentarily overwhelmed by the thought that he should never have left Merry; he thinks he should go back to her and bring her back, but he does not act on the thought. He is also distressed at the thought of life without Dawn, and for a moment he thinks he should not have married her.

The narrative then loops back to the time when Swede and Dawn first got married. Lou Levov wanted to know how they would bring their children up, as Catholics or Jews. Lou summoned Dawn to his factory and interrogated her, and they worked out a compromise in the child's upbringing that would permit limited exposure to Catholicism, although Dawn later had Merry secretly baptized.

Back at the dinner, Dawn tells the Salzmans about the trip she and Swede made to Switzerland when Merry was six. Swede holds her hand and recalls it, also. After a digression about Dawn's days as a beauty queen, the narrative returns to the dinner party, but all Swede can think about is Merry. He convinces himself that Jerry has informed the FBI about Merry's whereabouts. The dinner party ends in disarray when the drunken Jessie Orcutt, who has been talking to Lou Levov in the kitchen, stabs him near the eye with a fork. This action shows how far the rampant disorder of the times has spread.

Characters

Rita Cohen

Rita Cohen is a young woman who comes to Swede's factory, claiming to be a graduate student needing information about the leather industry in Newark. She is tiny and looks younger than Merry but claims to be twenty-two years old. She is polite and interested as Swede gives her a tour of the factory, but as she is about to leave it becomes apparent that Merry has sent her. After Swede gives her some of Merry's personal belongings, Rita asks him to bring cash to a hotel room. When he arrives, she demands that he have sex with her and also roundly abuses him as a capitalist who exploits his workers. Rita then disappears for five years until Swede receives a letter from her in which she tells him where to find Merry. She claims to love and admire Merry as an "incredible spirit" and writes

that she never did anything other than what Merry told her to do. But Merry denies even knowing Rita, which makes Swede feel that Rita is a criminal who tricked him and stole money from him. Who Rita really is and what relationship, if any, she has or has had with Merry is never explained.

Angela Davis

Angela Davis was a real-life African American left-wing political activist during the 1960s.

Dorothy Dwyer

Dorothy Dwyer is Dawn Levov's mother. Her life appears to revolve around the Catholic Church.

Jim Dwyer

Jim Dwyer was Dawn Levov's father. He was a plumber who died of a heart attack in 1959. He was also a staunch Catholic, but to everyone's surprise he and Lou Levov used to get on very well, swapping stories about their boyhood.

Mendy Gurlik

Mendy Gurlik is an old high school friend of Zuckerman. In high school, Gurlik was the closest the school had to a delinquent, and he used to take Zuckerman to music events in town. Zuckerman meets Gurlik at the reunion and finds out that he is now a retired restaurateur.

Joy Helpern

Joy Helpern is a former high school sweetheart of Zuckerman; they meet again at the reunion.

Dawn Levov

Dawn Levov is Swede's first wife. As Dawn Dwyer, daughter of Irish immigrants, she was crowned Miss New Jersey in 1949, at the age of twenty-two. She later claimed that winning the beauty title ruined her life. She only entered the contest to win money that would enable her brother to go to college. At the time, she wanted to teach music, and she did not want to marry. But Swede pursued and won her, and for years the marriage of the handsome athlete and the beauty queen looked picture-perfect. Dawn wanted to be more than a wife and mother, so Swede set her up in business raising beef cattle. She worked hard at it, running the business almost by herself and developing an interest in cross-breeding. She showed her strength and determination in other aspects of her life, too. Even at twenty-two, she maintained her poise when she was interrogated by Swede's overbearing father about her Christian faith.

Dawn was devastated by Merry's rebellion and her act of terrorism, and for several years, Dawn suffered from suicidal depression. She sold the cattle business in 1969 since it had become too much for her to handle. However, she managed to pull out of her depression after she went to Geneva for a facelift. It later transpires that she is having an affair with Bill Orcutt, with whom she is helping to design a new house, and it becomes clear that she will soon leave Swede and live in the new house with Orcutt.

Jerry Levov

Jerry Levov is Swede's younger brother, a contemporary of Zuckerman. In high school, Zuckerman was as close as anyone ever got to being a friend of Jerry. Jerry was aggressive and self-assertive and at the age of fifteen would angrily confront his strong-minded father. Jerry was also unusual. In his junior year of high school, he tried to win the heart of a girl by presenting her with a Valentine gift, a coat which he had made out of hamster skins that he cured in the sun and sewed together himself. The girl was horrified. Jerry became very successful and is a cardiac surgeon in Miami who makes a million dollars a year. He has been married four times, each time to a nurse, and has six children, five girls and one boy. Jerry is very self-confident and something of a bully. He always believes he is right. In Zuckerman's view, Jerry "had a special talent for rage and another special talent for not looking back." Jerry berates Swede for his diplomatic nature and thinks he should have been firmer in the way he raised Merry.

Lou Levov

Lou Levov is the Swede's father, a second-generation Jewish immigrant. Physically, he is a small man, but he has a strong character with a firm sense of right and wrong. He left school at fourteen to help support the family of nine by working in a tannery. He later founded Newark Maid Leatherware, a business manufacturing ladies' gloves. He worked prodigiously hard to build the business, and he eventually became rich. Proud of what he had achieved, he handed over the business to the Swede. After the riots in Newark in 1967, he urged Swede to move the business from New Jersey.

Lou Levov is a man of strong views who expresses himself forcefully. He spends much of his life "in a transitional state between compassion and antagonism, between comprehension and blindness, between gentle intimacy and violent irritation." In the 1970s, he rails passionately against President Nixon during the Watergate scandal, and he is also indignant about the permissiveness of American culture, wondering where it will all end.

Meredith Levov

See Merry Levov

Merry Levov

Merry Levov is the daughter of Swede and Dawn Levov. Intelligent and gifted, she was a normal, affectionate child, with the usual childish enthusiasms. For a while, she kept a scrapbook about Audrey Hepburn and then went through a Catholic phase, keeping religious trinkets in her room. Her only problem was that she stuttered. No amount of treatment by psychiatrist or speech therapist cured the problem.

When she was in her mid-teens, a change came over Merry. She became politically aware, developed a violent opposition to the war in Vietnam, and adopted a left-wing philosophy. She developed a hatred for her father, becoming rude and abusive towards him despite his patient attempts to reason with her.

When Merry was sixteen, she planted a bomb that destroyed the post office in Old Rimrock, killing a doctor there. No one could explain why she did it. A newspaper article at the time said that her teachers regarded her as "a multi-talented child, an excellent student and somebody who never challenged authority," although others remembered her "stubborn streak."

Merry then went into hiding, depending on the help of the underground antiwar network. She washed dishes in an old people's home in Indianapolis and then lived in Portland, Oregon, where she developed expertise in assembling bombs. She planted bombs that killed three more people. She moved to Idaho and then to Miami, Florida, where she planned to go to Cuba. After almost being caught by the FBI in Miami, she went to live with a blind woman and took care of her until she died of cancer. She studied religion in libraries and became a Jain. Then she moved back to Newark to work in a dog and cat hospital, living in a tiny, dirty room in a decrepit old house, where she met her father again for the first time in five years. He found that she had adopted an extreme form of renunciation, a position that espouses reverence for all life. She did not wash because she did not want, as she put it, to harm the water, and she did not walk about after dark for fear of crushing tiny creatures beneath her feet.

While Jerry Levov loathes Merry and calls her a "monster," Swede still deeply cares for her.

It appears that he may have gone on visiting Merry regularly until she died in her forties, in about 1993.

Seymour Levov

See Swede Levov

Swede Levov

Swede is the nickname given to Seymour Levov because of his fair complexion and blond hair. He is the principal character in the novel. During his years at Weequahic High School, the handsome Jewish Swede was a star performer in baseball, basketball, and football. Everyone in the Jewish community idolized him. During the uncertain days of World War II, Swede became a symbol of strength and hope. He was also modest, polite, and responsible, with a strong sense of duty. Sailing through life without any apparent difficulty, he seemed in his youth to be perfection itself, Newark's Jewish version of John F. Kennedy. Swede joined the Marines in 1945, too late to see combat, but he became a very effective drill instructor. In 1947, he enrolled in nearby Upsala College, and after graduation he married Dawn Dwyer. Swede went to work for his father at Newark Maid and learned the business from the bottom up. After a while, he took over the company and proved to be an astute businessman. According to his brother, Jerry, Swede was "an absolute, unequivocal success. Charmed a lot of people into giving their all for Newark Maid."

All Swede ever wanted was to live a quiet, unexceptional pastoral life in the countryside of Old Rimrock, devoted to his wife and family. He was always kind and generous, thinking only of the welfare of the family. But trouble comes into his life through his daughter, Merry, who inexplicably turns against him and becomes a terrorist. This change devastates Swede. He is never the same again, although he covers his anguish with his usual calm outward demeanor. He spends the rest of his life trying to understand what went wrong with Merry. His life, formerly so perfect and orderly, becomes a mental hell in which he agonizes over whether it was some failure of his own that caused Merry's rebellion and rejection of everything he stands for. But he never comes to an understanding of why such a thing could happen. According to Jerry, after the bombing he was "plagued with shame and uncertainty and pain for the rest of his life."

Sylvia Levov

Sylvia Levov is Lou's husband and Swede's mother. Zuckerman describes her, when she was still a youngish woman, as "a tidy housekeeper, impeccably well mannered, a nice-looking woman tremendously considerate of everyone's feelings." She manages to quietly endure her husband's cantankerous personality, and the wellbeing of her sons means everything to her. After 1968, she is devastated by Merry's act of terrorism and ages rapidly.

Alan Meisner

Alan Meisner was a high school friend of Zuckerman. His father was a dry cleaner, but Alan grew up to be a superior court judge in Pasadena.

Bill Orcutt

Bill Orcutt comes from a prominent legal family in Morris County, New Jersey, and is a neighbor of the Levovs. He can trace his ancestry in the area back to the time of the revolution. After graduating from Princeton, he broke with family tradition by moving to a studio in Manhattan and becoming an abstract painter. After three years, he moved back to Jersey to begin architecture studies at Princeton. Since then he has made his living as an artist, but he also mounts exhibitions of new paintings from time to time. Orcutt, a smoothly confident man with all the social graces, is married to Jessie, and they have five children. In the 1970s, Orcutt has an affair with Dawn, Swede's wife.

Jessie Orcutt

Jessie Orcutt is a Philadelphia heiress and the wife of Bill Orcutt. As a young woman, she was lively, sociable, and attractive. But later she became an alcoholic, and when she first appears in the novel in 1973, she looks much older than her fifty-four years. At Levovs's dinner party, she is drunk and makes a fool of herself and then stabs Lou Levov with a fork.

Ira Posner

Ira Posner is one of Zuckerman's former high school acquaintances. He came from what he calls a benighted family, and his father's best idea for a graduation present was to buy Ira a shoeshine kit, so he could shine shoes at the newsstand. Posner later became a psychiatrist.

Bucky Robinson

Bucky Robinson is an optician who joins Orcutt and Swede for weekly touch-football games. He remembers and admires Swede for his athletic prowess in high school. He tries to persuade him to become part of the Morristown Jewish community, but Swede is not interested.

Sheila Salzman

Sheila Salzman is a speech therapist who tried to cure Merry of her stutter and who harbored Merry after the bombing. Not knowing this, Swede had a four-month affair with her following Merry's disappearance. Sheila is a dignified, refined woman who always appears in control of her emotions.

Shelly Salzman

Shelly Salzman is a physician and wife of Sheila. A polite, inoffensive man, he is described as a "hardworking family doctor who could not keep the kindness out of his voice." When Swede had an affair with Dr. Salzman's wife, he felt sorry for the man, but when he finds out that the Salzmans harbored Merry for several days after the bombing, he is less sympathetic toward the doctor.

Barry Umanoff

Barry Umanoff is the husband of Marcia. He is a law professor at Columbia and was once the Swede's teammate and closest high school friend. After Merry's disappearance, Swede consults him for legal advice.

Marcia Umanoff

Marcia Umanoff is a professor of literature in New York. She is an argumentative person who likes to provoke and shock people. She is described as "a militant nonconformist of staggering self-certainty much given to sarcasm and calculatedly apocalyptic pronouncements designed to bring discomfort to the lords of the earth." On a couple of occasions before the bombing, Merry stayed with the Umanoffs in New York.

Vicky

Vicky is a black, thirty-year employee at the glove factory in Newark. She showed great loyalty to Swede during the Newark riots of 1967, staying with him in the building round the clock.

Nathan Zuckerman

Nathan Zuckerman is the narrator. He is the alter-ego of Philip Roth, the author, and has appeared in a number of other books by Roth. Zuckerman is a sixty-two-year-old writer living alone and isolated in a hamlet in western Massachusetts. He had surgery for prostate cancer a year earlier, and the treatment left him impotent and incontinent. When he attends the forty-fifth reunion of Weequahic High School, he is intrigued by what he hears from Jerry Levov about the life story of Jerry's brother, Swede Levov, who has just died.

As a boy, Zuckerman idolized Swede, his senior by seven years, because of the Swede's athletic prowess. He decides to research and write a book about Swede that will try to explain the tragedy that befell him.

Themes

From Glorious Forties to Turbulent Sixties

The main portion of the narrative covers a period of just over two decades, from the 1940s to the late 1960s, a period that saw huge changes in American society, which Zuckerman refers to as "that mysterious, troubling, extraordinary historical transition." For Zuckerman, this period represents a fall from innocence into a confusing, chaotic world in which all the rules of life have changed. He idealizes the immediate post-World War II era, as the title of Book I, "Paradise Remembered," demonstrates, and he looks back on it nostalgically. This attitude is strongly conveyed in the chapters about the forty-fifth high school reunion, in which Zuckerman and his old friends reminisce about times long past. Many of the people at the reunion have emerged from humble backgrounds and difficult childhoods to become successful professionals. There was a work ethic in place then in Newark's Jewish community, as well as a sense of shared purpose and goals. Zuckerman refers to "the common experience that had joined us as kids. . . . something powerful united us." People in Zuckerman's Jewish neighborhood at that time knew where they were going and how they would get there. They were determined to rise above poverty and hardship and make something of their lives. Everyone knew their role and played by the rules. This newfound confidence was present in the wider society as well. At a time of unprecedented U.S. hegemony throughout the world, there was a release of pent-up energy in the United States. As Zuckerman puts it in the speech he wrote, but did not give, at the high school reunion: "Everything was in motion. The lid was off. Americans were to start over again, en masse, everyone in it together." It was an exuberant time when Americans marched forward, "inflated with every illusion born of hope."

Then Zuckerman asks the key question, through the story of Swede, of how the unity, order, and clear sense of purpose of this period gave way so quickly to the disorder, violence, and chaos of the 1960s, embodied in the story of Merry, the

Topics For Further Study

- At the heart of *American Pastoral* is the conflict created within the United States by the Vietnam War. Write an essay explaining how the United States got involved in the war, why the war created such opposition at home, and what the eventual outcome was. In what ways does the Vietnam War still affect the United States today?

- Roth is sometimes accused of misogyny. What roles do the women play in *American Pastoral*? Are they presented sympathetically or with hostility? Examine the roles of Merry, Dawn, and Jessie Orcutt. Are they positive or negative figures? Does Merry have any redeeming qualities? Write an essay on the topic.

- Form a group with three other students. Discuss why teenagers sometimes rebel against their parents. What values do you not share with those of your parents' generation? Make a class presentation that shows the issues underlying generational conflicts such as the ones you have discussed in your small group.

- Investigate race relations in the United States. What conditions produced the riots in the Watts area of Los Angeles; in Newark, New Jersey; and in Detroit during the 1960s? How were those issues addressed by the authorities? Have race relations in this country improved since the 1960s? What issues remain and how should they be approached? Make a class presentation on your findings.

---

nice-little-girl-turned terrorist. In the 1960s, in the discord that accompanied the Vietnam War, the old rules and values were overturned. Children turned against their parents, and urban violence broke out in places such as Newark (the riots of 1967), and even pastoral retreats like Old Rimrock became subject to bombings and violent death. It was a different America altogether, what Zuckerman calls "the counterpastoral . . . the indigenous American berserk."

Swede spends the rest of his life tortured by the need to find out why this terrible thing happened to his family, but he never finds a satisfactory answer. At first, he assumes that he must have been responsible in some way for it because he believes he lives in an orderly, rational world in which cause and effect can be analyzed and known. But when he finally talks to Merry in 1973, he is forced to recognize that nothing he has ever done could explain what happened. His assumption that if he acted according to his sense of duty and responsibility, everything would work out smoothly, turns out to have been wrong. Merry went her own way, and that was all that could be said. She was never in his power to begin with, he realizes. No one is responsible, not Merry, not the Swede himself, and the same applies to the violence that disrupted society as a whole. He decides that everyone is in the power of "something demented" that cannot be understood. Later that day, he vehemently rejects Jerry's notion that as a parent, he was too permissive, and it was this that caused Merry's rebellion. Jerry believes that things can be connected in a cause and effect way, but Swede rejects such thinking: "But there are no reasons. She [Merry] is obliged to be as she is. We all are. Reasons are in books." The conclusion must be that life is unjust and incomprehensible and must be accepted as such.

Jewish Separatism or Assimilation

Although the book deals with broad issues in American history and culture, it is also focused on narrowly specific Jewish issues. It asks the questions, To what extent should Jews assimilate themselves to mainstream (Gentile) American culture? If they do this, how will they maintain their distinctive characteristics? Zuckerman writes of "the contradiction in Jews who want to fit in and want to stand out, who insist they are different and insist they are no different." He comments also on the "generalized mistrust of the Gentile world" felt by the Jews of Newark in the 1940s.

The issue of assimilation is embodied in Swede. To begin with, because of his blond hair and blue eyes, he does not look like a Jew. He also has an "unconscious oneness with America" and seems to lack any of the traits that Zuckerman identifies as Jewish. "Where was the Jew in him? You couldn't find it and yet you knew it was there," Zuckerman writes. For his part, Swede has no interest in Jewish religion or customs; he does not attend services in a synagogue and is astonished when his mother asks him if Dawn is going to convert to Judaism. When Bucky Robinson tries to get Swede to be a part of the Morristown Jewish community, Swede expresses no interest. The ideal life envisaged by this second-generation Jewish immigrant is quintessentially American rather than Jewish. In spite of his position, however, there are frequent allusions to the fact that Swede, his all-American attitudes notwithstanding, does not quite belong to the United States in the way that Gentiles do. This point is made clear to him when Orcutt takes him on a tour of the local area, where there are traces of Orcutt's ancestors everywhere. Swede realizes that "Every rung into America for the Levovs there was another rung to attain." He is well aware that Ivy League universities, such as the one Orcutt attended, "Didn't admit Jews, didn't know Jews, probably didn't like Jews all that much." When Swede first decides to move to Old Rimrock, his father warns him that he will encounter prejudice there, but Swede takes no notice. He feels none of the "Jewish resentment" that his father feels. But the issue of Jewishness lurks in the background for him. At one point, Swede wonders whether the problem with Merry had been foreseen by his father, who had expressed his concern about Swede's marriage to a Catholic because any children of theirs would be raised half Catholic, half Jewish, without a clear sense of who they were. For her part, Merry appears to show no interest at all in her Jewish heritage.

Style

Mythic Framework

This narrative about post-World War II American society is given a mythic and Biblical framework in the titles for the three sections into which the book is divided: "Paradise Remembered," "The Fall," and "Paradise Lost." These are allusions to the book of Genesis, in which Adam and Eve disobey God and are thrust out of paradise, and to the epic poem by John Milton entitled *Paradise Lost*, in which the fall and the expulsion from Eden are

presented. In the novel, paradise corresponds to Zuckerman's recollections of the 1940s and to the Swede's pastoral life in Old Rimrock before the bombing, which is the act that precipitated the fall and the expulsion, in mind and spirit, of the Levov family from the peace and tranquility they had known up to that point. Just as Christian theologians have debated why the fall of Adam and Eve happened and what its consequences have been, so too *American Pastoral* is an attempt to understand this traumatic period in American history by framing it in mythological terms. This framework gives the story a broader relevance, suggesting not only that something happened in particular decades in American history and to a particular family, but some reversal occurred in the universal experience of collective humanity.

The biblical fall is mentioned late in the novel, at the dinner party at the Levovs's house in chapter 9, when the provocative Marcia alludes to the point made in Genesis that Adam and Eve ate of the tree of knowledge. She implies that this was ultimately a positive act, since "Without transgression there is no knowledge," she says. However, it is hard to see what knowledge emerges from the Swede's transgression. All along, Swede has assumed that it must be some transgression of his that caused the tragedy—unless it is the knowledge that life is suffering, cause or causes unknown.

Point of View

The point of view from which the story is told changes during the course of the novel. It begins in the first-person, as Zuckerman introduces the Jewish community of Newark in the 1940s. It continues this angle as Zuckerman attends the high school reunion. But at the same time, the author prepares his reader for the switch to an omniscient third-person point of view, with heavy emphasis on the mind of the Swede, that will apply to the final three-fourths of the book. In doing so, Roth carefully draws attention to the way the book is constructed as a work of fiction. He explains how Zuckerman conceived the idea for the book through his memories of Swede and his later conversations with Swede and his brother. Imagining himself into the mind of the Swede, Zuckerman (as Roth's mouthpiece) writes, "I dreamed a realistic chronicle." At the same time, further drawing attention to the way the story has been created, Zuckerman freely entertains the idea that he may be quite wrong in his conclusions about how Swede's mind worked. He spends two long paragraphs imagining how Jerry will pick his manuscript apart and say that Zuckerman's portrayals of Swede, Dawn, and Lou Levov are all wrong. In rumination, Zuckerman makes much of the notion that no one can know another person accurately:

> The fact remains that getting people right is not what living is all about anyway. It's getting them wrong that is living, getting them wrong and wrong and wrong and then, after careful consideration, getting them wrong again. That's how we know we're alive: we're wrong.

This authorial notion of the unknowability of others and the impossibility of arriving at truth parallels the struggle and the failure of Swede to arrive at a satisfactory understanding of why such tragedy befell his family.

Narrative Structure and Flashbacks

The novel has a kind of looping back structure, in which the telling of the central story is frequently interrupted by digressions and flashbacks. The novel begins with Zuckerman in the present, reminiscing about the 1940s. Then it flashes briefly forward to 1985 and the chance meeting with Swede, then forward again to Zuckerman's dinner with Swede in 1995 and his high school reunion, then flashes back, as Zuckerman begins to create his narrative of the Swede, to Merry and Swede on the beach when Merry was eleven (about 1963). Chapter 4 begins four months after the bombing in 1968, and the narrative then moves slowly, with flashbacks and long introspective sections in which Swede examines himself and the dire situation in which he has been placed. More than half the book, from the final few pages of Chapter 5 to the end, takes place on a single afternoon and evening in September 1973 and is filled out by extensive flashbacks. The non-linear structure of the book seems to imitate the endless back and forth of Swede's own mind as he struggles to understand but gets nowhere.

Historical Context

Race Riots in the Sixties

The 1960s was a period of great upheaval in American society. The civil rights movement made solid gains and forced people in the United States to confront centuries of racism and discrimination against African Americans. The landmark Civil Rights Act was passed in 1964. In the later part of the decade, the nonviolence advocated by Dr. Martin Luther King Jr. gave way to more militant approaches to confronting racism favored by groups such as the Black Panthers. In 1966, there were race riots in the Watts area of Los Angeles, and in June 1967, serious riots broke out in Newark, New Jersey, as described in *American Pastoral*. At the time, Newark was a city in which the white population had shrunk by more than one-third since the 1950s. By 1966, blacks found themselves in the majority, but power and influence in the city remained in white hands. In 1967, for example, there were only 150 black police officers in a police force of 1,400. Rioting began on the night of July 12, 1967, after a black taxi driver was arrested and beaten by police. The next day the riots spread across the city. Twenty-six people were killed and 1,500 injured. Arrests numbered 1,600, and there was $10 million in property damage, much of it by fire. Over a thousand businesses were burned or were looted. Most of these businesses did not reopen after the riots, and thousands of whites moved out the city permanently. Whole neighborhoods, including Weequahic, were rapidly transformed from majority white to majority black, with a corresponding drop in economic status. This is the background against which Swede's decision in the novel to keep his factory in Newark should be measured.

Newark continued to decline during the 1970s. In 1975, it was ranked according to twenty-four categories by *Harper's* magazine as the worst of fifty major American cities. In *American Pastoral*, Lou Levov's comments made at the dinner party in 1973 sum up the drastic decline of the city:

> Streets aren't cleaned. Burned-out cars nobody takes away. People in abandoned buildings. *Fires* in abandoned buildings. Unemployment. Filth. Poverty. More filth. More poverty. Schooling nonexistent. Schools a disaster. On every street corner dropouts. Dropouts doing nothing. Dropouts dealing drugs. Dropouts looking for trouble. . . . Police on the take. Every kind of disease known to man.

Violent Protest Against Vietnam War

As the war in Vietnam escalated and the United States committed hundreds of thousands of troops to South Vietnam in an attempt to prevent a takeover of the country by communist North Vietnam, protests within the United States against the war also escalated. Many of the protests were conducted by university students and were focused on resistance to the military draft. Anti-war protesters rioted at the Democratic Convention in Chicago in 1968. The decade also saw the rise of the New Left, a movement that was more radical and more militant than the Communist Party of the 1950s. One radical group, which was a splinter group of the

Compare & Contrast

- **1960s:** Affirmative action programs begin during the Kennedy administration (1961–1963). Such programs are designed to redress historic disadvantages suffered by minority groups.

  Today: Affirmative action programs remain in place, although conservatives generally oppose them and even some liberals question their desirability in their present form.

- **1960s:** In 1969, American troop strength in Vietnam reaches its peak, with 543,000 troops stationed in South Vietnam. Anti-war demonstrations in the United States also peak. In November 1969, some 250,000 demonstrators march in Washington, D.C.

  Today: The United States enjoys normal trade and diplomatic relations with Vietnam, even though Vietnam is one of the few remaining communist countries in the world.

- **1960s:** The feminist movement becomes a force in American society. Thousands of women no longer see their roles solely as wives and mothers and demand equal opportunities in employment, as well as equal pay for equal work.

  Today: Women find employment in a range of occupations that were formerly dominated by men. On average, however, women still earn less than men, even when they are in the same profession and performing comparable work.

organization, Students for a Democratic Society, was called the Weathermen. The Weathermen was a terrorist organization dedicated to fomenting revolution within the United States, destroying capitalism and bringing an end to what it called U.S. imperialism abroad. The Weathermen was made up of young people, male and female, many of whom came from middle and upper middle-class families. They were, as Todd Gitlin writes in *The Sixties*, "the children of cornucopia par excellence . . . they came from wealth; they were used to getting what they demanded, stamping their feet if they had to, wriggling away without punishment." According to Gitlin, one of the Weathermen slogans, alluded to in *American Pastoral*, was "Bring the war home," which was a call to bring the same death and mayhem to the United States as was happening in Saigon, capital of South Vietnam. (Not surprisingly, then, in *American Pastoral*, it is Merry, a spoiled child of privilege, who brings the war home by bombing the local post office.)

In October of 1969, the so-called Days of Rage riots occurred in Chicago, in which there was extensive property damage, and 250 Weathermen were arrested. On March 16, 1970, three Weathermen died in an explosion in a Greenwich Village, New York, townhouse while they were manufacturing pipe bombs and bombs studded with roofing nails. This incident is mentioned in chapter 4 of *American Pastoral*. The police later reported that there was enough undetonated dynamite in the house to blow up an entire city block. Gitlin reports that between September 1969 and May 1970 there were at least 250 bombings in the United States, and the figure may have been much more. The main targets were ROTC buildings, draft boards, induction centers, and other federal buildings. The Weathermen was only one of the groups responsible for these bombings.

Critical Overview

There was near unanimous agreement among reviewers that *American Pastoral* represented another formidable achievement by one of America's leading writers. Writing in the *New York Times*, Michiko Kakutani describes the novel as "a resonant parable of American innocence and disillusion . . . a big, rough-hewn work built on a grand design . . . that is . . . moving, generous and ambitious." Kakutani interprets the novel in terms of how Roth presents "two contradictory impulses in American

Members of the "Women's Strike for Peace" push their way to the doors of the Pentagon Building. February 1967 © Bettmann/Corbis

history." The first impulse was the "optimistic strain of Emersonian self-reliance, predicated upon a belief in hard work and progress" that is seen in Swede; the second impulse, embodied in Merry, represents "the darker side of American individualism."

Michael Wood, in the *New York Times Book Review*, is one of a few critics who have some complaint about the slow pace of the novel, but his overall assessment is enthusiastic nonetheless: "the mixture of rage and elegy in the book is remarkable, and you have only to pause over the prose to feel how beautifully it is elaborated."

In *Washington Post Book World*, Donna Rifkind praises the novel as "possibly the finest work of [Roth's] career." She particularly admires "the thoroughness and intensity with which he plumbs the souls of his characters. One senses he's not so much writing about them as feeling them, probing every inch of their pain."

Rifkind's praise of Roth's characterization is echoed by R. Z. Sheppard in *Time*, who comments that "Never before has Roth written fiction with such clear conviction. Never before has he assembled so many fully formed characters or shuttled so authoritatively through time."

Criticism

Bryan Aubrey

Aubrey holds a Ph.D. in English and has published many articles on twentieth century literature. In this essay, he discusses how the character Swede Levov develops the view that life is chaotic and cannot be understood rationally.

American Pastoral, Philip Roth's long lament for an unobtainable pastoral ideal, ends with a scream, a laugh, and a question mark. Each in its own way is significant.

The scream is uttered at the dinner party by Lou Levov, who has been in the kitchen of Swede's home doing his clumsy and inadequate best to stop the drunken Jessie Orcutt from making a fool of herself. Upset at his condescension, she stabs him with a fork, aiming for his eye and missing only by an inch. In wounding the family patriarch, Jessie is symbolically stabbing at the entirety of the old order that is collapsing as a result of the turbulence of the 1960s and 1970s. Lou Levov is the character who stands most firmly for the established order, whose uncompromising approach to right and wrong—people must obey God's laws or the consequences will follow them the rest of their lives— is implacably opposed to all the cultural forces that are undermining the values with which he grew up. The scream represents not only the dying of those values, but also the anguish of incomprehension at the passing of the familiar and the trusted. For Lou Levov and what he represents, it is as if a tsunami has obliterated all the landmarks that give life meaning:

> We grew up in an era when it was a different place, when the feeling for community, home, family, parents, work . . . well, it was different. The changes are beyond conception. I sometimes think that more has changed since 1945 than in all the years of history there have ever been.

Lou Levov's scream, then, is the scream of dissolution, and it is followed very quickly, on the last page of the novel, by the laugh that mocks the scream. This is the laughter of Marcia Umanoff, the quarrelsome professor of literature who dismisses all moral absolutes and takes pleasure in watching the edifices of certainty, on which people less enlightened than she base their lives, come crumbling down. For Marcia Umanoff, such edifices were never what they appeared to be anyway, and it is almost a duty to expose them. She revels in a fashionable postmodern ambiguity that disrupts any attempt to reach out for a firm moral ground on which life can be based.

But the laughter that mocks everything explains nothing, and this long, question-filled novel ends appropriately enough with a question, two questions, in fact. One is about why events have turned out so tragically for the Levov family, and the other is about why everything seems so set against their happiness and what they stand for: "And what is wrong with their life? What on earth is less reprehensible than the life of the Levovs?"

These are the questions that throughout the novel, the Swede struggles so hard to answer. He entertains one possibility after another but never arrives at a clear understanding. Reviewers and critics of the novel have been quick to offer the explanations that Swede has supposedly missed. Some regard *American Pastoral* as an indictment of the culture of permissiveness that dominated the 1960s. This view is expressed most forcefully by Jerry Levov: Swede was too accommodating, too indulgent of his errant daughter, and he allowed her to get out of control. An opposing view that has been expressed is that Swede is himself to blame for what happens. He tries to rigidly control his world and shape the women in his life according to his own beliefs and ideals, and he also fails to confront the sources of social discontent: the evils of capitalism and the exploitation of workers. Still other critics have suggested that Roth's target is the violence and shallowness of the New Left that emerged in the 1960s—they are the ones to blame for the disaster that befalls Swede. Others have seized on Lou Levov's opposition to his son's marrying a non-Jew. In this view, the novel becomes a critique of Jewish assimilation.

Swede thinks about many of these explanations, but he rejects Jerry's position absolutely, and although at one point he entertains the possibility that his father may have been correct about the consequences of marrying the Catholic Dawn, this explanation does not satisfy him for long. His mind scurries one way and then another as he seeks to understand the causes of the sequence of events that led him to where he is. But the implications of his search are not easy for him to accept. Humans like to believe that they live in an intelligible, orderly world, but this is a conclusion Swede finds impossible to reach.

Early in the novel, when Zuckerman describes the series of baseball novels by John R. Tunis he used to read in the 1940s, Roth provides a foreshadowing of the view of the world that Swede is forced to develop. One of the baseball novels was called *The Kid from Tomkinsville*. The Kid is a young pitcher from rural Connecticut who overcomes an impoverished background to become a star of the Brooklyn Dodgers. He also overcomes a career-threatening injury and then, in a moment of glory, makes a running catch that sends the Dodgers to the World Series. But in doing so, he smashes up against a wall and is carried off inert on a stretcher. At that point the novel ends. Ten-year-old Zuckerman wonders whether the Kid is dead and chafes at the implications of what he has just read: "The cruelty of life. The injustice of it."

It is Swede's fate to suffer not only the cruelty and injustice of life but something perhaps even worse, the feeling that there is no order in the universe. Life is chaos; nothing seems connected to anything else; there are no discernible cause-and-effect relationships that would explain why Merry rejected her upbringing, turned into a terrorist, and brought endless misery to her family. Poor Swede is like Job in the Old Testament, the man to whom misfortune comes for no reason known to him. Job is eventually consoled by his vision of the totality of God's power and mastery of the universe; he is reconciled to his fate, and his fortunes are restored. Not so Swede, who is Roth's Job, without a trace of redemption or hope. Again and again, Swede comes back to this point. "He had learned the worse lesson that life can teach—that it makes no sense," explains Zuckerman just before he plunges into relating Swede's story. The very idea that there could be a "rational existence" is eventually seen by Swede as a "utopia," an unrealistic fantasy. After Jerry has assailed him on the telephone with a list of his faults and failings that in Jerry's view caused the tragedy, Swede expresses the idea that the causes of anything in life are unknowable:

> His [Jerry's] idea that things are connected. But there *is* no connection. How we lived and what she did? Where she was raised and what she did? It's as disconnected as everything else—it's all a part of the same mess!

There are therefore no reasons for anything that happens: "It is not rational. It is chaos. It is chaos from start to finish."

Even as the tale advances, Swede's understanding does not. As the drama intensifies in the final pages, his sense of the randomness of life, its lack of connectedness, increases. As he thinks about Merry, he decides that there is not even a connection between members of the same family. He muses about "how improbable it is that we do come from one another," and decides "that we *don't* come from one another, that it only

> ## " It is Swede's fate to suffer not only the cruelty and injustice of life but something perhaps even worse, the feeling that there is no order in the universe. Life is chaos; nothing seems connected to anything else...."

appears that we come from one another." Then he reaffirms to himself that he had been wrong when he thought that life was orderly and that only a little part of it was disorderly. "He'd had it backwards," he realizes.

This moment is all the more poignant because it is immediately followed by one of the most moving passages in the entire novel, when Swede recalls how he and Merry, when she was still a fine little girl, would walk the hilly roads in the countryside around their home, observing the wild flowers and the trees in their delightful American pastoral—a pastoral that for them can be no more and will never return.

It might be objected that in his failure to find connectedness in anything or to fathom why things turned out the way they did, Swede is merely being obtuse. As many critics of the novel have implied, perhaps Swede is simply blind to the larger picture of cause and effect. But the more likely possibility, as well as the more alarming one, is that Swede, in his painful awareness of the chaos and randomness at the heart of things, is right and that this is, in fact, the theme of the novel. Life is unknowable and unfathomable, and people who think they have it right are always wrong. Indeed, in an amusing, although also deeply serious passage early in the novel, Zuckerman takes up this very idea as it applies to personal interactions. When two people meet, he says, they try hard to understand each other, but they always get the other person wrong. The interior of another person's mind cannot be known:

> You get them wrong before you meet them, while you're anticipating meeting them; you get them wrong while you're with them; and then you go home to tell somebody else about the meeting and you get them all wrong again.

So it is also when people try to figure out the endless, unknowable stream of causation. The Swede's continuous effort to find answers to his questions is doomed because it is at root an attempt to control life, to make it conform to his expectations and understanding. Superior to understanding, which always eludes one's grasp, is the wisdom of acceptance, but this is something the Swede never manages to find. He lives and dies as Job unredeemed.

Source: Bryan Aubrey, Critical Essay on *American Pastoral*, in *Novels for Students*, Thomson Gale, 2007.

Robert Boyers

In the following review, Boyers discusses Roth's interest in the "ordinary and the virtuous" that is "embodied in a good-hearted man."

In Philip Roth's new novel, his alter ego, Nathan Zuckerman, alludes in passing to a once famous writer now largely forgotten, whose "sense of virtue is too narrow" for contemporary readers. The writer, no doubt about it, is Bernard Malamud. And what is it that passes for virtue in Malamud? In *The Assistant,* a grim and slender novel, the Jewish groceryman is eulogized as "a man that never stopped working . . . to make a living for his family," a man who "worked so hard and bitter," so that for his family there was "always something to eat." Morris Bober was "a good provider," the rabbi says, and, "besides," he was "honest." He assumed responsibilities. He showed up. He is to be venerated, without exaggeration or ceremony.

It is a narrow sense of virtue, to be sure, and not at all peculiar to Malamud among American Jewish writers. Saul Bellow, too, a provocateur who writers in a racy, unstable idiom and sometimes expresses a venomous antipathy toward the milder emotions, nonetheless swells with admiration for those who show and claim affection, who know, as we used to say, how to behave. "I saw now what I had done," says the narrator in Bellow's novella "Cousins": "treated him with respect, observed his birthdays, extended to him the love I had felt for my own parents. By such actions, I had rejected certain revolutionary developments of the past centuries, the advanced views of the enlightened, the contempt for parents illustrated with such charm and sharpness by Samuel Butler . . ." Susceptible to the allure of subversive ironies and modern ideas, the Bellow protagonist is still responsive to what he calls "the old thoughtfulness."

The narrow virtues have often seemed narrow precisely because they were thought to require little thought. Often they have seemed feeble and gray because they were believed to entail no struggle, no weighing of choices. Habit, it is often felt, is the paralysis of spirit. Ordinariness is the negation of virtue. What is dull and dutiful and comes more or less naturally is not to be prized. But Malamud and Bellow (and in this they were not altogether alone) hoped to identify in the ordinary activities available to any decent and thoughtful person, in social ritual and mundane interaction, a stay against the inhuman, against the brutality that ensures in the absence of the quotidian ideals and restraints.

Now Philip Roth engages this possibility. In his new novel, he examines decency, as it is embodied in a good-hearted man whose life seems for a while *"most simple and most ordinary and therefore just great."* No reader will be surprised to find that such a life turns out to be neither simple nor just great. No one will wonder at Roth's ability to show what can become of "ordinary" when an orderly life takes an unexpected turn, or the repressed rears its head, or the good and measured life seems suddenly tedious and intolerable. Roth has for a long time, through many books, developed a powerful and unanswerable subversion of the rock-solid assurances around which many people attempt to organize their lives. He has taught his readers to hold their noses when confronted by pious reflections on "the human condition." An expert in apostasy and distortion, he has made of his own occasional attraction to moralizing rhetoric an opportunity for savage contradictoriness and wit. His present interest in the ordinary and the virtuous is new in the sense that they now hold him, tempt him, transfixed and bewildered, on a degree not generally discernible in his earlier fiction.

The ordinary man in *American Pastoral* is an assimilated Jew with an unlikely "steep-jawed, insentient Viking mask" and the youthful attributes of a demi-god. The young Seymour "Swede" Levov is a star athlete worshiped by everyone in his neighborhood in Newark, a large "household Apollo" of an adolescent who goes on from schoolboy fame to marry a Catholic beauty queen, inherit a thriving business, and move his family to a prosperous farm in rural New Jersey. The Swede is ordinary only in the sense that he shapes his life to the measure of the American dream, aspiring to no more and no less than his share of perfection, which is to say, an existence largely without misgiving or menace.

There is nothing ordinary, of course, about the superb physical grace, or the country estate, or the ravishingly beautiful wife, or indeed the temperament of a man who can seem both mild and confident, resourceful and contained. But Roth is most taken with his character's desire to be ordinary, at ease in his place, without great ambition, without any desire to tear through appearances or to rage against his own limitations. He draws a character who, for all of his success, may be easily condescended to as well-meaning, naïve, blandly idealistic, without force—an average man, disappointing, pleasant, natural, displaying no capacity for irony or wit. Surely such a person—some will feel—deserves whatever can happen to him.

The Nathan Zuckerman who narrates *American Pastoral,* for whom Seymour Levov is an ostensibly remembered person and a character whose life needs to be imagined, is sorely tempted by the prospect of blasting such a life, stripping away every vestige of attractiveness from the character in all of his impeccable generosity and highly-mindedness. An early reviewer of Roth's novel describes Seymour as a puppet, "mounted precisely for the purpose of being ripped," a figure who exists "to be punished": for his idealism, his grace and his credulous embrace of the good life. Not exactly. Zuckerman is more than a little bit in love with this fellow. Recently recovered from prostate surgery, impotent and in every way more subdued and more thoughtful than we remember him in previous Roth novels, Zuckerman wonders at the Swede the way one wonders at something moving and peculiar, something that defies explanation.

Still, explanations are advanced. Seymour's brother Jerry, a cardiac surgeon in Miami, has no trouble summing him up as the man with "a false image of everything," a man committed to tolerance and decorum, to "appearances" and the pathetic desire "to belong like everybody else to the United States of America." But this diatribe, it is clear, doesn't begin to explain Seymour, and the more he is assaulted by explanations and denunciations, and hears himself maligned and diminished, the more securely he remains a wonder, a man astonished to the end at the continuously unfolding spectacle "of wantonness and betrayal and deception, of treachery and disunity" and "cruelty." Zuckerman wants, like the others, to have done with the crummy goodness of this common man, to dismiss him as a man unable "to understand anyone," a man without a shit detector, a fraud. But he remains

> But Malamud and Bellow (and in this they were not altogether alone) hoped to identify in the ordinary activities available to any decent and thoughtful person, in social ritual and mundane interaction, a stay against the inhuman, against the brutality that ensures in the absence of the quotidian ideals and restraints."

transfixed, somehow admiring and exasperated. Against his better judgment, he makes the man so much more appealing than anyone else he can invent.

Not until very late in the novel does Swede Levov understand what Roth insists that he grasp. "He's had it backwards. He had thought most of it was order and only a little of it was disorder." But reality is otherwise. Nothing follows clearly from anything else. Where once there was thought to be cause there is now only chance. A secure home environment can bring forth anything at all. A person blessed with every good fortune may despise her life as surely as a person blasted by fate may remain an optimist. A man with a beautiful wife may be attracted for no apparent reason to a mousy woman deficient in every quality. Those who don't know these things may be virtuous in one degree or another, but they will not know what life is. That is what Zuckerman would have us accept. That is what Roth would seem also to support. But Seymour's capacity to arrive at this knowledge in his own way, his capacity for reluctance and suffering, is a part of what makes him a man we can admire.

But *American Pastoral* is more than an examination of virtue, more than an attack on the delusoriness of liberal good intentions. Roth means it also to be a portrait of America. It moves gracefully from one quintessential American setting to another, from factory floor to rolling hills, from beauty pageant to high-school reunion. Conversations turn on standard American themes, from assimilation to athleticism, from business ethics to sexual fidelity. Characters correspond to familiar American types, including WASP gentry, old-style Jewish liberals, and therapeutic intellectuals armed with fashionably advanced views. Historical markers—the Second Worlds War, Vietnam, Joseph McCarthy, race riots, Weathermen, and so on—routinely identify the public landscape within which Americans of the pertinent generations move. The novel is eloquent in its evocation of vanished American neighborhoods such as Jewish Newark, and it allows characters to be sweetly or fiercely defensive about "what this county's all about."

The story line takes many turns, but in essence it is a fairly simple narrative. Zuckerman remembers the Swede, meets up with him late in life, learns what he can about him, and constructs a narrative of the Swede's life that occupies most of the novel. Seymour is the son of Lou, a prosperous glove manufacturer who looms large in his son's life until his death at the age of 96. Seymour tries to live the good life in an expensive WASP suburb, but he has to contend with a teenage daughter who develops from elfin companion to tormented stutterer, from antiwar protester to underground terrorist and bomb-throwing killer of innocent civilians.

Merry Levov remains, throughout the novel, a source of enormous agitation and distress for both of her parents. Seymour thinks about her incessantly, rehearsing various episodes in her life and reliving in his imagination all that she does and suffers. He recalls their acrimonious debates and her withering New Left invective. Most especially, he thinks about her setting off a bomb at a local post office and thereby killing an elderly man. He is contacted by a young companion of his daughter, who grotesquely exposes herself to him and offers to lead him to Merry if he will sleep with her. When he learns that Merry has been raped by someone in the terrorist underground, he cannot drive the fact from his mind, he seems almost mad with grieving and pity for his savage little lost girl. Though there are numerous opportunities for the novel to move in for a closer look at the terrorist operation, Roth is satisfied to focus on Merry and her revolting companion, emblems of the ravening ferocity of their kind.

In Merry's final incarnation, she is a fanatic of non-violence, a Jain who wears a mask over her face to avoid doing damage to delicate micro-organisms in the air. Her father cannot bring himself to turn her in when he has the chance, and he torments himself about what has happened to her, about his responsibility for having produced a monster. Though he cannot abandon his attachment to America and all that it has represented to him, he is sorely tried in his relations with his wife, his brother, and his father—particularly his father, a powerful man who periodically erupts in outbursts of colorful invective against degradation and indecency.

The dust jacket of Roth's novel promises a work that will take us back "to the conflicts and violent transitions of the 1960s." It invokes, in Roth's language, "the indigenous American berserk," "the sweep of history," "the forces of social disorder." It describes, in short, a novel with large ambitions. The narrow virtues celebrated by earlier American Jewish writers were often played out in settings do circumscribed that one could feel the pressure to forget the world and to refine the perspective to a metaphysical essence. But Roth's novel is absorbed in worldly matters, in history. He wants to know how things happen, how places and events leave their mark on people.

There are instances, here and there, of the profligate extravagance that consumes so much of our attention in novels like *Sabbath's Theather* and *Operation Shylock,* with their verbal energy and their compulsive recourse to every variant of shtick and artifice. But *American Pastoral* strives mightily to situate its characters in a more classical manner, to insist that their passions are shaped, constrained, and exacerbated by circumstance. It worries about probability and verisimilitude, and it asks, again and again, how this can be and how that can be when reality so manifestly declares what is and what is not allowable. Questions of virtue and responsibility are complicated in this novel by what Henry James called the "swarming facts." It is not simply that nothing Roth imagines quite adds up; it is that he does not expect the facts to add up, that he supposes reality to lie in their multiplicity, their thickness of texture, their bewildering resistance to dreams of order.

So what is Philip Roth's America? It is a place where some people work and build and thrive while others fail and destroy and suffer. It is a place where everyone is increasingly aware of vast differences in wealth, and where those who feel guilty about their own successes are increasingly made to feel foolish and irrelevant. It is a place in which radical ideas about fundamental change are held almost exclusively by lunatics and by intellectuals so divorced from fellow-feeling that they can only

What Do I Read Next?

- Roth's novel *The Plot Against America* (2004) is an alternative history that imagines what the United States would have been like, especially for Jews, if the Nazi sympathizer, Charles A. Lindbergh, who became a national hero after flying solo across the Atlantic Ocean in 1927, had defeated Franklin D. Roosevelt in the 1940 presidential election.

- Doris Lessing's short novel *The Fifth Child* (1988) presents a situation that in some respects is not unlike what happens to Swede and Dawn in *American Pastoral*. In this novel set in England in the 1960s, Harriet and David Lovatt raise a large family. Their lives are perfect until the birth of their fifth child, who is altogether strange and brings anxiety and confusion into their lives as they try to cope with him through childhood and adolescence.

- *Bringing the War Home: The Weather Underground, the Red Army Faction, and Revolutionary Violence in the Sixties and Seventies* (2004),

by Jeremy Veron, is an analysis of left-wing violence in the United States and West Germany during the period in part covered by *American Pastoral*. Veron attempts to answer the question of why so many young middle-class people took to violence and attempted to overthrow their democratic governments.

- *Fugitive Days: A Memoir* (2001), by Bill Ayers, is a memoir by a former member of the Weather Underground. Ayers went underground following the accidental bombing of a house in Greenwich Village in 1970. Ayers describes his New Left involvement as a result of the Vietnam War, inner-city race relations, and police brutality, especially in Chicago during demonstrations at the 1968 Democratic convention. After going underground, Ayers traveled continuously under different aliases to avoid police and FBI. He gave himself up in 1981; most of the charges against him were dropped. As of 2006 Ayers was a professor of education at the University of Illinois.

laugh at deterioration and disaster, "enjoying enormously the assailability, the frailty, the enfeeblement of supposedly robust things."

There is a side of Roth that likewise revels in the tendency of things to fall apart and to expose the illusoriness of order and optimism. But he is also susceptible to fellow-feeling. Roth appreciates, however reluctantly, the satisfactions that are sometimes generated by those who believe literally in the American dream. When Seymour Levov mourns the Newark destroyed by riots and decay, the Newark "entombed there," its "pyramids . . . huge and dark and hideously impermeable as a great dynasty's burial edifice has very historical right to be," Roth invests with weight and dignity the sense of loss for things hard-won and precious. His America, after all, is the place where immigrants not only make fortunes as a result of often despised virtues such as hard work and persistence, but in which those

same immigrants often bring forth children endowed with vision and compassion.

It is possible, of course, to suppose that what Roth calls "the indigenous American berserk" has more to tell us about the country than the stories of immigrant success and the building of viable political institutions. Or at least it may tell us what Roth himself regards as fundamental to the American spirit: a propensity to violence, conspiracy, and irrationality. This propensity is not at all times and places obvious. Americans are adept at convincing themselves that it is a limited propensity, that it belongs to lunatic fringes that cannot in the long term threaten our collective commitment to reasonableness and tolerance. Yet Roth seems to believe that violence and irrationality are never very far from the surface of American life, that we deny it at our peril, and that our optimism is purchased in the way the individual purchases tranquility, through repression and willful blindness. The daughter of Seymour Levov is not simply a lunatic. She is to be understood, insofar as we may presume to understand her, as an important expression of our collective unconscious. If this is not easy to accept, any more than we would find it easy to accept, say, that the Bader Meinhof gang in Germany or the Red Brigades in Italy expressed the deeper selves of the societies they terrorized, well, as the novelist would seem to say, there it is.

Merry Levov is Roth's exemplification of our impatience with limits, our hatred of the gradualism and the decorum that we profess to prize. As an adolescent growing up in the first days of the Vietnam War, she finds her opinions confirmed by her parents and her grandfather, but she grows impatient with their support. Like other young people involved in antiwar activities in the '60s, she finds a way to turn the epithet "extreme" against her own family, as in: "No, I think extreme is to continue on with life as usual when this kind of craziness is going on . . . as if nothing is happening." Those who are opposed to America's involvement in Vietnam must bear witness—so she insists—by turning against their own comfortable lives, if necessary by throwing bombs. Just so, those who profess concern black people going to pieces in urban ghettos must refuse to persist in business as usual, must refuse to insist upon profits, even if their refusal should cause their factories to fail and jobs to disappear. The worst is not to be feared if it may be a prelude to drastic change. The American berserk, as embodied in the figure of Merry Levov, is associated with ideas that were pervasive in the '60s and it is in part the burden of *American Pastoral* to suggest that these views really do express an important feature of American life.

The strangest thing about all of this is that Merry Levov never emerges in this novel as anything but a pathetic figure. as a child she is appropriately lovable and childish, but she rapidly grows into a fearful thing, twisted and angry, a caricature of herself. She becomes a type. She is, in fact, precisely the type pilloried by those critics for whom opposition to the Vietnam War and participation in the civil rights movement were mainly psychological expressions, the work of rebellious adolescents acting out their mostly impotent rage against authority. This tendency to reduce the movements of the '60s to an undifferentiated cartoon of adolescent rebellion is given new life in Roth's novel. By contrast, writers such as James, Conrad and Vargas Llosa, in their novels of politics and society, mounted a savage attack on bomb-throwers and ideologues while permitting them their misguided idealism and a sometimes adult grasp of power and injustice. To place Vargas Llosa's wild-eyed Alejandro Mayta alongside Merry Levov is to appreciate at once the dignified passion for radical renovation that the Peruvian novelist permits his character and the utter puerility and one-dimensionality of the American novelist's radical figures.

That Merry Levov is depicted as something of a lunatic is not especially objectionable, for it is surely true that there were lunatics and obsessives in the radical movements of the '60s. But she and her more luridly drawn companion are, in Roth's novel, the primary exponents of oppositionist and critical views. The conditions that aroused so many mature adults to participate in the antiwar and civil rights movements are barely mentioned in a book committed to examining the period. For *American Pastoral,* recent American radicalism is to be associated with irrationality and the unconscious. In fact, it was both more dangerous and less dangerous than that. There is no effort in Roth's novel to link it to the genuine tradition of American radicalism that goes back at least to Emerson and Thoreau and, in this century, to Randolph Bourne, Paul Goodman and Bayard Rustin. Merry Levov and her companions in extremism are all we need to know, apparently, when we come to consider what blasted the social order.

The failure of Roth's novel, in this respect, is quite considerable, however unmistakably particular passages are the work of a master. If there is such a thing as the indigenous American berserk, then surely it must entail a good deal more than a lunatic fringe largely limited to deranged adolescents acting out fantasies of retributive violence. And if these adolescents, who usually grow up into pinstripes, tweeds and cappuccino bars, can be so readily dismissed and condescended to by their elders, including Nathan Zuckerman, then how can they be said to represent an enduring and significant feature of American life, a tendency to which even the best of us are regularly susceptible? This novel wants to have it both ways. It wishes to develop an apocalyptic vision of the real America, the underside of our characteristic optimism and bland goodwill, but it wants also to propose that what we refuse to acknowledge in our pusillanimous American selves is pathetic, adolescent, laughable, and decidedly marginal, however terrible the occasional consequences associated with this "other," truer reality.

Consider Roth's presentation of the facts involved in the destruction of Newark. The dominant perspective belongs, more or less equally, to

Zuckerman, to the Swede, and to his father. According to them, there was once a "country-that-used-to-be, when everyone knew his role and took the rules dead seriously, the acculturating back-and-forth that all of us here grew up with." Of course there were conflicts in that one-upon-a-time land, but they were usually manageable, they conformed to something about which you could make some sense. And Newark was very much a part of the "country-that-used-to-be," a place where pastoral visions may not always have been easy to come by, but where "the desperation of the counterpastoral" was also not much in evidence.

In Roth's reasonable Newark of Jewish and other immigrants, there are factories and businesses that produce well-made goods and turn reasonable profits. They employ people "who know what they're doing," who are pleased to do good work and more or less content with what they are paid. At least they do not complain. They are loyal to their employers, and they may well remember gratefully how things have changed for the better since the bad old times 100 years earlier when factories were places "where people . . . lost fingers and arms and got their feet crushed and their faces scalded, where children once labored in the heat and the cold . . ." The factory owners are also apt to have a vivid sense of their own origins, to remember working "day and night" and living in intimate contact with working people at all levels of manufacturing and selling. Their stubborn celebration of everything American has much to do with how well things can go when people believe in the system and rely on each other.

Given this account of reality, it is no wonder that the eruption of civil strife in the '60s should seem so incredible not only to the Levovs but, apparently, also to Zuckerman. The nostalgia for the "country-that-used-to-be" is so palpable in this novel that it virtually immobilizes the imagination of reality and leaves the reader susceptible to a rhetoric for which the deteriorating urban landscape is a "shadow world of hell" and predatory blacks roaming the Newark streets are part of a "surreal vision." Once, not long ago, according to this narrative, everybody had it good, or good enough. But many Americans suddenly went unaccountably crazy, and what "everyone craves" came to pass, "a wanton free-for-all" in which what was released felt "redemptive, . . . purifying, . . . spiritual and revolutionary." However "gruesome" and "monstrous" what followed, something real happened in Newark, something irresistible and deeply implicated in the American grain.

So we are to believe. Though the Levovs watched with horror, and deplored, and most other Americans presumably recoiled as well, we are asked to accept that somehow "America" spoke its deep, revealing truths in the intoxication of riot and mayhem. We are also asked to accept, as befits this pattern, that those who set the cities on fire, who beat on "bongo drums" while their neighbors looted and sniped and left behind a "smoldering rubble," were actually in flight from the good life. We are to accept—so the logic of the novel dictates—that the blacks of the inner city must have been incomprehensibly dissatisfied with their wonderful jobs and turned on by the prospect of liberating something vital and long buried in their otherwise admirable lives.

The problem is, Roth's book offers us no way to think about such a view of things. Its elegy for the dead city and its old ways is affecting, but it is also disconnected from anything like a serious account of what the old ways actually entailed, and what were the varied motives and desires of the inner-city residents who were caught up in the destruction of their own communities. To read Roth on the Newark riots is to suppose that just about everyone participated in the looting and the carnage, and that no one can have had good, concrete reasons for loathing the conditions in which they lived. To understand the '60s is, again, to invoke individual and group psychology, to refer to something deep and peculiarly American, to deplore what happened while at the same time suggesting that it had to happen and cannot be accounted for by citing social, political or economic factors.

Roth's novel is finally not an adequate study of social disorder. It does not tell us what we need to know about America, what a novel can tell us about the complex attitudes and allegiances of a time and a place. It laments the denial of reality on the part of middle-class suburbanites such as Seymour Levov, while offering as the alternative to illusion "surreal" and "grotesque" eruptions such as few Americans are likely to encounter. It sets up as representative figures of disorder and "reality" persons who are mad, and whose attachment to disorder is so pathological that they make it impossible for us to consider seriously the actual sources of discontent in American society. When violence breaks out in this novel, it seems more like an inexplicable convulsion than an expression of feelings shaped by complicated individuals responding to the actual conditions of their lives.

And yet Roth's interest in an idea of simple virtue is an impressive achievement. For if the world, as he understands it, is a place of chaos and

Bayonet-wielding National Guardsmen face residents of Newark, New Jersey during a riot on July 14, 1967 © Bettmann/Corbis

contradiction, in which order is fragile or even illusory, then virtue, too, may seem like a figment of someone's wishful thinking, a willed fantasy with nothing to sustain it. But Roth finally suggests that it is not. Like the rest of us, he wonders what virtue can be worth when it is rarely effectual in worldly terms. And he refuses to allow goodness to sweeten anything, to distract him from what we are and what we do. Yet his triumph in *American Pastoral* is the portrayal of persons who are unmistakably good and genuine. They understand no better than he does what to make of events that astonish and assault them, but they do not give up on their sense of how to behave.

Seymour Levov is no paragon of perfect virtue, and his father can seem shrill and forbidding in his vehemences. But these are men who continue to display thoughtfulness, however much reason they have to be disappointed and to flee in bitterness from the decencies that make them seem irrelevant to their contemporaries. The father may have absurd ideas about how to deal with disorder—"I say lock [the kids] in their rooms"—but he is strangely appealing in his insistence that "degrading things should not be taken in their stride." That is right. And the son, who suffers greatly, who does not know enough, who takes "to be good" everyone

"who flashed the signs of goodness," retains in Roth's hands the capacity to be appalled—not thrilled, but appalled—by transgression, to be tormented by the spectacle of needless suffering, and to think, ever to think, about "justification" and "what he should do and . . . what he shouldn't do." His humanity is intact. And it is, Roth seems to be saying, the only thing we can rely on.

Source: Robert Boyers, "The Indigenous Berserk," in the *New Republic*, Vol. 217, No. 1, July 7, 1997, pp. 36–41.

Todd Gitlin

In the following review, Gitlin comments on Roth's attempt to bring the sixties to life as well as his endeavor to paint the "large social canvas."

You have to admire Philip Roth for refusing to repeat himself in his twenty-second book. *American Pastoral* is a family epic about social breakdown and freakout—Thomas Mann goes Jersey. Roth puts on a straightforward disposition. He goes pre-postmodern. His antics and fantasies are minimal, as if Roth the shtickmeister-magician is just keeping his hand in. The dead stay dead. The protagonists are winners who, after long free rides, can't win for losing. Roth treats these uncomprehending scramblers with a certain troubled distance and intermittent compassion. He's aiming to bag the big saga about the doom in the heart of the American dream—in particular about what John Murray Cuddihy called the ordeal of assimilation.

American Pastoral opens awkwardly, as if a new script had been badly dubbed into the mouth of the familiar bitching god-child Nathan Zuckerman. Nathan exudes lyric nostalgia for his childhood hero, Swede Levov of Newark. Swede was born Seymour Irving Levov, "a boy as close to a goy as we were going to get," blond and blue-eyed, his face a "steep-jawed, insentient Viking mask." This "household Apollo of the Weequahic Jews" starred in football, basketball and baseball. Cheerleaders rendered him special tribute—and then this triple-threat embodiment of conventional responsibility went off to the Marines in 1945.

> The contradiction in Jews who want to fit in and want to stand out, who insist they are different and insist they are no different, resolved itself in the triumphant spectacle of this Swede who was actually only another of our neighborhood Seymours whose forebears had been Solomons and Sauls and who would themselves beget Stephens who would in turn beget Shawns.

Swede's glove-manufacturing father, Lou, had worked himself up from a tannery job he took after leaving school at 14 to help support a family of nine. Lou Levov

> was one of those slum-reared Jewish fathers whose rough-hewn, undereducated perspective goaded a whole generation of striving, college-educated Jewish sons: a father for whom everything is an unshakable duty, for whom there is a right way and a wrong way and nothing in between, a father whose compound of ambitions, biases, and beliefs is so unruffled by careful thinking that he isn't as easy to escape from as he seems. Limited men with limitless energy; men quick to be friendly and quick to be fed up; men for whom the most serious thing in life is *to keep going despite everything.* And we were their sons. It was our job to love them.

Thus Roth at his best, with his gift for miniatures in broad strokes.

But what Nathan is doing here, besides delaying the action for some ninety pages, isn't clear. After the false start, Roth resigns the first-person narratorship, whereupon plot moves and chaos mounts. Swede marries shiksa goddess Dawn, petite and Catholic Miss New Jersey of 1949, and they move to the pastures of bucolic Old Rimrock, there to raise the bright child Merry, while Swede settles into the manufacturing pleasures of the postwar

> " Merry, he writes late in the game, 'entered the world screaming and the screaming did not stop.' Long before the Vietnam War and the counterwar, she was an infant out of control. Her darkness was presumably bred in the bone. The Levovs' journey toward light is cursed by fate, not history."

boom. Gloves are a good business in an age of decorum, when a well-dressed woman would own twenty-five pair, one for each of her dress-up colors. And thus into the sixties, when the achieving, believing Levovs, Who Had It All, lose it. The family blows up because Merry, a stutterer who beams heavy sexual vibes at her father, finds herself in 1968 a not-so-sweet 16 who falls in among antiwar terrorists in New York. Although he opposes the war, Swede cannot fathom the depth of his daughter's fury against everything in America that certifies his success. He forbids her to hang out with her radical friends and gets her to a therapist. Surprise! Merry blows up the community store that houses the rural post office—the only federal facility around—killing a local doctor whose specialty is good works.

Merry goes underground, and the family trouble really begins. An emissary from Merry's underground cell offers Swede a sexual invitation. Dawn goes crazy and Swede goes philandering. Merry goes from bad to worse. Swede proves helpless. Events of suburban angst and entanglement follow. Family intrigue smolders. Things fall apart.

The settings are rich enough, the characters vivid enough, that the result ought to be more moving, more propulsive, than it is. The novel is not devoid of rewards but it is bloated, the prose frequently flat, with motion more sideways than forward. The characters flash ahead and back, but we don't feel them in motion. The plot pauses for stretches so long you can hear the grass grow and brown. A long excursus into the workings of the

Levov glove factory is so sluggish it reminds the reader that Roth is no Melville. The prose brightens when Roth larks around (when Swede, trying to figure out his daughter, argues with a phantasmagorical Angela Davis) or when family acrimony ignites.

Here is Roth's real subject: how people horrify the ones they love. The writing comes to life when Swede inveighs against the ungrateful blacks who riot in Newark in 1967. It rises to the quivering point when he encounters his broken daughter, and when his lurid imagination goes to work on the disasters that have befallen her. It rises yet again when he calls up his brother Jerry, a multiply divorced surgeon, to ask advice about what to do with Merry, and Jerry keeps an office of patients waiting while screaming at Swede about everything that he has botched about his life. What Roth catches most convincingly are Jewish males ranting against a whole world that spits in their half-closed eyes.

Mark Twain said about Wagner's music that it was better than it sounded. The cruel thing to say about Roth would be that *American Pastoral* is better than it reads. Inside this long, viscous book, a solid, serious allegory struggles to get out. Roth has hung his family anti-romance on the varieties of sixties experience, so his story depends on whether he can bring the wildness of that time of life and make his characters live their doom. Mainly, he doesn't. The family arguments feel forced and sometimes clunky. The reader never penetrates Merry's radical circle but comes to it by hearsay, through her fights with her father, when she says things like, "They were students. Now they organize people for the betterment of the Vietnamese." Merry has gone from golden-haired maiden of ballet class and speech therapy to avenging angel of the Third World in fifteen minutes, and not only does Swede not seem to grasp what has happened to her, Roth doesn't either. The writer who would bring Merry to life would have to bring to life more than Merry, would have to re-create the milieu that reached out and snared the Merries out of their Old Rimrocks—the movements, media, raptures, hopes, rages, entitlements, moral defaults.

Given all his effort to get social details right, from family histories to Watergate hearings, Roth's sixties are chronologically odd. Merry bombs the store on February 3, 1968—before the Columbia occupation, before the Chicago Götterdämmerung and during the Tet offensive, when the antiwar movement was only just turning (in a phrase of that time) "from protest to resistance." The militant vanguard wasn't anywhere near bombing. Two years would pass before the Weather Underground's 11th

Street townhouse in New York City blew up, killing three of their own. Two and a half would pass before a cell bombed the army math research center in Madison, Wisconsin, costing the life of a graduate student working late. Merry explodes prematurely.

Moreover, her mother, who obsesses about the Miss America pageant of 1949, doesn't notice its successor of 1968, when feminists organized their first visible demonstration. Six months after their daughter had gone underground in a cloud of ranting against her sellout liberal bourgeois parents, you might have thought the Levovs would be paying closer attention to the upheaval going off around them.

But then Roth offers a clue that the sixties might be only a backdrop to his private plot and not its dynamic at all. Merry, he writes late in the game, "entered the world screaming and the screaming did not stop." Long before the Vietnam War and the counterwar, she was an infant out of control. Her darkness was presumably bred in the bone. The Levovs' journey toward light is cursed by fate, not history. If so, then the moral point of the family saga grows dim, and Roth's Levovs come to resemble the hapless parents of Doris Lessing's *The Fifth Child*, whose grotesque son is a Neanderthal throwback, not so much evil as clueless. This piece of fatalism makes Roth's anachronisms less consequential, but also renders much of the story's atmospherics redundant.

Could it be that Roth's failure to bring the sixties to life is more than Roth's? Is there some larger cultural blockage, a case of clogged cognitive arteries? Precious little realistic fiction has brought the movements of the sixties to light. There are exceptions: the early chapters of Rosellen Brown's *Civil Wars* invoking the civil rights movement; the flashback chapter in Marge Piercy's *Vida* on the organizing of a demonstration in 1967; the Boston commune sequence in John Sayles's *Union Dues*; Sol Yurick's *The Bag*; and, in a more lurid vein, sections of Updike's *Rabbit Redux*, Malamud's *The Tenants* and John Gardner's *Sunlight Dialogues*. Why, with all the scribbling through and after this period, with so much cultural baggage riding on this freight, is there so little fictional invention to show?

Roth saw the problem coming even before the self-inventions of Richard Nixon and Lee Harvey Oswald: Reality puts fictionists to bashful shrugs and shame. And it's not only the first-magnitude stars who make Jay Gatz look banal. In the second tier of the famous, consider only the true-life confidence men and women Timothy Leary, Eldridge Cleaver, Jerry Rubin, Abbie Hoffman and Bernardine Dohrn.

Norman Mailer once observed that a novelist needs a sense of the real. And that sense is exactly what shook, rattled, rolled and eventually blew up in the sixties. The ground of what was taken for granted liquefied. Feelings were volcanic, and the lava rolled all over the land. The recognizable stopped being recognized. Plausibility? Cause and effect? By the standards of normality, means were peeling away from ends. Vietcong winning territory? Drop napalm. Suburbia dull? Drop acid. Demonstrations don't stop the war? Declare fealty to Albania and build antipersonnel weapons. When ordinary people think extraordinary thoughts, realistic imagination runs aground.

Even most of the great social novelists were best in, and on, the interval between revolutions. Balzac avoided the 1789 revolution itself. Dicken's French Revolution is most evocative when it tracks the course of wine through the cobblestoned Paris streets, not the course of ideas through the synapses. Raskolnikov is an emblematic schemer of the run-up to revolution, not a cadre. Malraux's China and Spain were overheated inventions—great in moments, but mainly abstract. There remain, of course, the achievements of the Dostoyevsky of *The Possessed*, of Babel and Silone, the Rebecca West of *The Birds Fall Down*, Lessing of *The Golden Notebook* and the Martha Quest books—a short list for a long history of radical politics. Many a critic has rightly observed that the large social canvas is not the forte of American writers in the first place. Then Philip Roth's failure looks overdetermined, and the odds against the realistic novel of American radicalism may be insuperable.

Source: Todd Gitlin, "Weather Girl," in the *Nation*, May 12, 1997, pp. 63–64.

Sources

Gitlin, Todd, *The Sixties: Years of Hope, Days of Rage*, Bantam Books, 1987, pp. 385, 403.

Kakutani, Michiko, "A Postwar Paradise Shattered from Within," in *New York Times*, April 15, 1997, pp. C11, C14.

Rifkind, Donna, "The End of Innocence," in *Washington Post Book World*, Vol. 27, No. 23, June 8, 1997, pp. 1, 14.

Roth, Philip, *American Pastoral*, Houghton Mifflin, 1997.

Sheppard. R. Z., Review of *American Pastoral*, in *Time*, Vol. 149, No. 17, April 28, 1997, p. 74.

Wood, Michael, "The Trouble with Swede Levov," in *New York Times Book Review*, April 20, 1997, p. 8.

Further Reading

Alexander, Edward, "Philip Roth at Century's End," in *New England Review*, Vol. 20, No. 2, Spring 1999, pp. 183–90.
 Alexander, a neoconservative, regards the novel as a critique of the radical New Left of the 1960s, which became fascinated by violence. Merry is an embodiment of their naïve political creed.

Gentry, Marshall Bruce, "Newark Maid Feminism in Philip Roth's *American Pastoral*," in *Turning Up the Flame: Philip Roth's Later Novels*, edited by Jay L. Halio and Ben Siegel, University of Delaware Press, 2005, pp. 160–71; originally published in *Shofar*, Vol. 19, No. 1, Fall 2000, pp. 74–83.
 Gentry argues that far from being the wronged, innocent man, Swede is himself responsible for his own troubles. He accepts the injustices of capitalism, he tries to mold Dawn and Merry into conventional gender roles, and he does not think for himself.

Gordon, Andrew, "The Critique of Utopia in Philip Roth's *The Counterlife* and *American Pastoral*," in *Turning Up the Flame: Philip Roth's Later Novels*, edited by Jay L. Halio and Ben Siegel, University of Delaware Press, 2005, pp. 151–59.
 Gordon regards Roth as an anti-utopian and anti-pastoralist, but in *American Pastoral*, although he demolishes the American dream, he clings to certain pastoral ideals, as shown in his nostalgia for the 1940s.

Stanley, Sandra Kumamoto, "Mourning the 'Greatest Generation': Myth and History in Philip Roth's *American Pastoral*," in *Twentieth Century Literature*, Vol. 51, No. 1, Spring 2005, pp. 1–24.
 Stanley reviews the conflicting interpretations of Alexander and Gentry and argues that the novel supports both readings. Roth portrays the 1940s "greatest generation" sympathetically but also critiques the myths by which they lived, which helped to create the rebellions of the 1960s.

Cold Mountain

Charles Frazier

1997

When Charles Frazier's *Cold Mountain* was published in 1997, it gained immediate critical and popular success, lasting sixty-one weeks on the *New York Times* bestseller list and gaining the National Book Award along with other accolades that year. Readers responded to the stirring tale of a Confederate soldier named Inman, his long journey home from the horrors of the Civil War, and his bittersweet reunion with the woman who waited for him. The novel cuts back and forth between Inman's difficult journey that tests his physical as well as his emotional strength and Ada's tale of her own struggles to survive in a harsh landscape and violent time.

Stories of Frazier's ancestors along with those of the North Carolina mountaineers who were caught up in the frenzy of the war years became the inspiration for the novel. Frazier explains in an interview with *Salon*, "The story seemed like an American odyssey and it also seemed to offer itself as a form of elegy for that lost world I had been thinking about." Serving as a model for the fictional Inman was Frazier's great-great-uncle W. P. Inman, who also turned his back on the war and met a similar fate. *Cold Mountain* is a moving tribute to those who were lost in the war and those who survived it, as well as a celebration of an indomitable sense of hopeful readiness in confronting the possibilities life holds.

Author Biography

Charles Frazier was born on November 4, 1950, in Asheville, North Carolina, to Charles, a high-school principal, and Betty, a librarian and school administrator. He grew up in small neighboring towns and graduated from Franklin High School in 1969 with a vague aspiration to teach literature. He did his undergraduate work at the University of North Carolina at Chapel Hill where his favorite authors were Edith Wharton, Ernest Hemingway, and Edgar Allan Poe. After earning a B.A. there in 1973, Frazier completed an M.A. program at Appalachian State University in Boone, North Carolina, graduating the following year.

Frasier tried his hand at writing fiction but was disappointed with the results and so turned his attention to teaching and academic writing. While he was pursuing a Ph.D. at the University of South Carolina in Columbia, where he specialized in twentieth-century American literature, he completed his first book, *Developing Communications Skills for the Accounting Profession* (1980), a practical business manual.

After earning his Ph.D., Frazier accepted a teaching position at the University of Colorado. His next book, based on his travels to South America, *Adventuring in the Andes: The Sierra Club Travel Guide to Ecuador, Peru, Bolivia, the Amazon Basin, and the Galapagos Islands*, was published in 1985.

In 1986, Frazier and his wife moved back to North Carolina when he accepted a teaching position at North Carolina State University. A year later his first fictional work, a short story titled "Licit Pursuits," was published in the *Kansas Quarterly*. The North Carolina landscape is an important element in this story, as it was to be in his first novel, *Cold Mountain*. This novel sprang from his extensive research of the culture and history of his home state, including studies of its folklore, music, travel guides, and historical diaries.

His father's story of his great-great-uncle, W. P. Inman, a Confederate soldier who had deserted during the war and walked back to his home at Cold Mountain, became the inspiration for Frazier's fictional treatment of the area and its history. Encouraged by his wife, Frazier quit his teaching position to devote himself to writing his novel, which took seven years to complete. *Cold Mountain* appeared in 1997.

As of 2006, Frazier lived on a horse farm in North Carolina, where he continued to write.

Charles Frazier   AP Images. Reproduced by permission

Plot Summary

the shadow of a crow

Cold Mountain opens in late summer as Inman, a Confederate soldier, lies wounded in a hospital after being hit in the neck during a battle near Petersburg, Virginia. As he does each morning when he wakes, Inman stares out a large open window in front of his bed, imagining scenes from home.

Inman watches a blind man who sells peanuts and newspapers from a cart outside the window. He is surprised to find out that the man has been blind since birth and not through "some desperate and bloody dispute." When Inman comments on the man's accepting attitude toward his disability, the man says, "it might have been worse had [he] ever been given a glimpse of the world and then lost it" for this would have turned him "hateful." Inman insists that is what the war has done to him.

Inman describes the battle that had the greatest effect on him: Fredericksburg. Thousands of Federals were shot down as they charged the wall behind which he and other Confederates had amassed. Inman recalls, "The Federals kept on coming long past the point where all the pleasure of whipping them vanished." That night, Inman and his fellow soldiers climbed over the wall and took

Media Adaptations

- Anthony Minghella directed and wrote the screenplay for the critically acclaimed and commercially successful film version of the novel. Jude Law, Renee Zellweger, and Nicole Kidman starred in this 2003 production. As of 2006, the film was available on DVD.

boots off of the dead Federals. He was stunned by the carnage, which included a man killing wounded Federals by hitting them in the head with a hammer. The blind man tells him, "You need to put that away from you," but Inman cannot prevent the nightmares from returning.

While in the hospital, Inman reads *Travels* (1791), by naturalist William Bartram, and thinks about the topography of his home in the Blue Ridge Mountains, remembering as many details as he can. He walks into town from the hospital to buy clothes and supplies in preparation for escape, for he knows that when he gets better, he will be shipped back to the front lines. He reads in the paper that the government has been hunting down deserters and outliers, men who have evaded Confederate Army service.

Inman thinks about one summer when he was sixteen and herding cattle in the mountains. He met Swimmer there, a sixteen-year-old Cherokee who was also herding in the mountain with a group from his tribe. The two boys spent long hours fishing as Swimmer told stories of "how the world came about and where it is heading." Swimmer determined the spirit to be "a frail thing, constantly under attack and in need of strength, always threatening to die inside you." He insisted that one could go to a great forest above heaven where "the dead spirit could be reborn." Inman decides that Cold Mountain could be such a place, a "healing realm . . . where all his scattered forces might gather."

Inman starts to write a letter to Ada about his war experiences but tears it up, afraid of what her

response would be to what he has seen and done. That night he awakens and steps out of the window.

the ground beneath her hands

During the same period, Ada sits on the porch of her Black Cove home in the shadow of Cold Mountain, trying to write to Inman. She had come here with her father, Monroe, six years earlier when he was asked to preach at the local chapel. Since her father died, she has been alone on their farm with no knowledge about how to run it. Her education has not prepared her for the daily rigors of farm work and the struggle just to survive. As a result, there is little sustenance left. She often seeks out a space inside the boxwoods near the house where she feels safe and cut off from the realities of her new life. That day, after seeking the solace of the hidden space, the farm's only remaining rooster attacks her there. After she escapes, an overwhelming feeling of helplessness fills her with despair.

She has had little will to improve her situation during the three months since her father died, spending most of her days reading. This day, after placing flowers on Monroe's grave, she walks to the farm of Sally and Esco Swanger who took her in for a few days after Monroe's funeral. They talk on the front porch about the war and their growing fear of a man named Teague, the leader of the Home Guard, a cruel band that has been setting its own rules for handling suspected deserters and northern sympathizers. Esco, who has been recording omens, insists that a hard winter is coming.

After Sally and Esco convince Ada to look into their well to see her future, Ada makes out the vague figure of a man, but she cannot tell if he is walking toward or away from her and is confused by its intended significance for her. She soon leaves after receiving a gift of preserves from Sally.

She and Monroe had come to the area to find relief for his consumption. Ada was apprehensive about adapting to the new environment since she had grown up in the genteel atmosphere of Charleston. Ada found little common ground with the mountaineers, whom she found "touchy and distant, largely unreadable" and frequently acting as if she and her father had insulted them.

Deciding to teach Monroe a lesson about judging others too quickly, Esco pretended a complete ignorance of the Bible and acted the part of the country bumpkin. Monroe made it his mission to educate the poor man until Sally took pity on him and told him that he had been the butt of her husband's and the town's humor. After Monroe humbly accepted the ironic etiquette lesson, he and Ada began to be more accepted in the community. As a result, Monroe decided to buy the working farm at Black Cove, but since they lived off his Charleston investments, he soon neglected it to the point that after he died, the farm was no longer self-sufficient. Ada's bleak situation was further compounded by the news that the war had wiped out her father's investments.

The next morning as Ada is considering her limited options, Ruby appears, sent by Sally to help her. Ruby, a young woman who has basically raised herself on the land surrounding Cold Mountain, insists that she can help Ada get the farm running again but demands to be treated as an equal partner, which Ada accepts. Ruby proves her capabilities when she pulls off the head of the rooster who attacked Ada and cooks him up for dinner.

the color of despair

Days after his escape from the hospital, Inman is bone weary, partially lost, and in constant fear of dog attacks and capture by the Home Guard. One afternoon, he arrives in a crossroads settlement where three men jump him. As Inman defends himself, his growing anger causes him to beat them savagely. As he walks away, he repeats a spell Swimmer had taught him "aiming it out against the world at large, all his enemies." Yet his stance soon troubles him as he remembers Monroe quoting Ralph Waldo Emerson during one of his sermons on the necessity of expressing God within oneself.

Inman's path ends at Cape Fear River where a girl offers to pilot him across for cash. While they are half way across, men on the opposite bank begin to fire at them, sinking the canoe. They are swept downstream and eventually pull themselves out of the river, battered and bruised.

verbs, all of them tiring

Ruby and Ada spend their first several days together, taking inventory of what needs to be done at the farm to make it self-sufficient. Ruby insists that they must work "to require every yard of land do its duty." She finds some hope in the extensive apple orchard, a neglected tobacco patch, bags of coffee beans in the cellar, and Ada's piano, all of which she will use to barter for the goods they need.

Ada remembers a party that she and Monroe gave for their neighbors during which she came upon Inman in the kitchen, drying himself. After an awkward beginning, the two shared a tender moment as Ada leaned her head against his chest and declared "that she never wished to leave this place."

Ruby soon arranges a work schedule for both of them that keeps them busy with hard, physical labor for the entire day. She teaches Ada "the rudeness of eating, of living" as she refuses "to tackle all the unpleasant work herself." After supper, they sit on the porch as Ada reads Homer to Ruby or the latter recounts her life story. Ruby admits that she never knew her mother, and her father, Stobrod Thewes, made her fend for herself by the time she was old enough to walk. She has not heard from him since he enlisted in the army.

like any other thing, a gift

Inman continues to follow the river until he sees a man ready to hurl a woman into it. The man, named Veasey, is a preacher who has gotten the woman pregnant. Inman intervenes and forces Veasey with the aid of his pistol to return to his town. Veasey explains that if he had been found out, he would have been run out. When Inman tells him that there would have been better ways to handle the situation, including marriage, Veasey admits that he is already betrothed.

After they reach the town, Inman ties Veasey to a tree and carries the woman back to her bed, warning her that Veasey is no good. When he returns, Inman writes a note explaining what Veasey has done and secures it to the tree. He continues his journey until he comes to a camp of gypsies, show folk, and outliers along the river. After they feed him, he watches some rehearse a medicine show and listens to others tell stories. That night he dreams of Ada, and the image of her stays with him when he wakes.

ashes of roses

At the beginning of fall, Ruby and Ada work on their winter garden. They take in for a night and feed a group of women and children fleeing the Federals. Ada is growing increasingly satisfied with the knowledge she is gaining about the farm.

exile and brute wandering

As he continues his journey, Inman meets Veasey, who has been banished from his town and is now on his way to Texas to "start fresh." Inman tells him about the battle of Petersburg when Federals blew up Confederate trenches and the two sides engaged in gruesome hand-to-hand combat. They soon reach a roadside inn where Veasey goes off into a backroom with a prostitute. Inman shares a bed with a peddler who tells him how he lost his inheritance after he fell in love with one of his father's slaves and of the cruel treatment blacks receive in the South.

source and root

Ruby and Ada walk to town where they hear a prisoner tell the story of his capture by the Home Guard. Like Inman, this man decided to walk home after becoming disillusioned by the war. The Guard, led by a ruthless man named Teague, discovered him and a group of other outliers on a farm and brutally slaughtered all but him.

to live like a gamecock

Inman and Veasey help out a man named Junior whose water supply is threatened by a dead bull. In payment, Junior invites the two to his home for dinner. Junior complains that his wife and two sisters are harlots as the three get drunk. Later, as Junior's wife tries to seduce Inman, Junior bursts in and pulls a gun on him. Junior admits that he sells outliers to the men in the Home Guard who are waiting outside. The Guard tie up Inman and Veasey and get drunk with the women and Junior, who decides that Inman should marry his wife.

After the ceremony, the Guard tie Inman to a string of other captured men and head east, back over the land Inman has traveled. That night, the Guard decides the men are not worth turning in and begin to shoot them. A bullet grazes Inman, but he survives. A slave he meets brings him to his master's farm and feeds and shelters him for a few days. He warns Inman to stay off the main roads that the Guard are patrolling and draws him a map. Before he continues on his journey, Inman returns to Junior's home and beats him senseless, perhaps killing him.

in place of the truth

Ada receives a letter from Inman, the first in four months. He tells her not to look at the picture of him he gave her four years ago when he left for the war, fearing that he bears no resemblance to it now, "in either form or spirit." She remembers when he came to say goodbye to her and her cool response to him, which prompted her to go to him the next day and make amends. After she apologized, he kissed her and they expressed their desire to reunite soon.

the doing of it

Inman meets an old woman who herds goats in the mountains. She feeds him and tends his wounds. They discuss the war, the consequences of slavery, and the benefits of living a solitary life.

freewill savages

Ruby catches her father Stobrod, who has been living with a band of outliers in a mountain cave, in the corncrib trap. She agrees to feed him and then determines to "send him on his way." That night Stobrod returns and Ruby grudgingly feeds him again. He talks to Ada about the war and plays tunes on a fiddle with a masterful touch.

bride bed full of blood

Inman comes across a cabin in the woods where Sara, a young woman whose husband was killed in the war, lives with their child. She feeds him and invites him to sleep next to her that night for comfort. She tells him of her happy but difficult life with her husband.

The next morning, Federal raiders appear at the cabin and Inman hides in the woods. The men set the baby on the cold ground in an effort to get Sara to give them anything she has, but when they realize that she has nothing, they release her. When they leave with her hog, her only means of sustenance for herself and her baby, Inman follows and kills them. After he returns to the cabin, Inman slaughters the hog for Sara and leaves the next day.

a satisfied mind

Stobrod returns to the farm with a comrade, a mentally disabled man named Pangle. The two had been living in a cave community of outliers who had been raiding wealthy farmers. After Stobrod taught Pangle how to play the banjo, the two became a duo. They play for Ruby and Ada, who are moved by it. Stobrod tells Ruby he wants to leave the outliers who have become militant in their opposition to the war and needs shelter and help. Ruby refuses, still bitter over his treatment of her as a child. When Ada tries to intervene, Ruby reminds him of the time he left her alone for three months when she was seven. That night Ada writes Inman a line from one of Stobrod's songs: "Come back to me is my request."

a vow to bear

Inman stops to help a woman bury her child. Later, a bear charges him and plunges over a cliff. Inman kills its cub and eats it, knowing that it could not survive without its mother. As he gets closer to home, his heart fills with joy.

naught and grief

Stobrod, Pangle, and Reid, a boy from the cave, camp on the mountain. After the boy goes off to relieve himself, the Home Guard, led by Teague, find the remaining two and after listening to them play, shoot them.

black bark in winter

After Reid runs back to the farm, Ruby and Ada go up the mountain to find the bodies. When they discover Pangle, they bury him and soon find Stobrod barely alive. Ruby tends his wounds and decides to find shelter, knowing that her father could not survive the trip home. They find an old Cherokee village and clean out two of the cabins.

footsteps in the snow

Inman determines to declare his love for Ada and heads for Black Cove. There Reid tells him Ruby and Ada have left for Cold Mountain, and he follows them. When Ada kills some wild turkeys, Inman hears the shot and finds her, but it takes her a while to recognize him.

the far side of trouble

Stobrod and Inman sleep in one cabin, Ada and Ruby the other. When Ruby leaves to tend to Stobrod, Ada and Inman are left alone. After he shares his fears and feelings, the two embrace. The next day she and Inman go hunting and she tells him about herself and how she has changed. That night, Ruby stays with her father and Ada and Inman consummate their love and talk about their future together.

spirits of crows, dancing

Inman and Ada decide that his best option would be to go North and surrender to the Federals. In the morning of their fourth day on the mountain, they decide Stobrod is well enough to travel. Inman insists that Ruby and Ada walk ahead while he follows with Stobrod on horseback.

Soon Teague and his men come up behind them. Inman is able to kill all but one, the boy, Birch. Inman tells him, "I'm looking for a way not to kill you," but his hesitation costs him his life when the boy shoots him. He dies in Ada's arms.

epilogue

In October 1874, Ruby is married to Reid and they have three children. Ada has Inman's child, a girl now nine years old. All, including Stobrod, live on the farm. The novel closes with a depiction of the children playing together.

Characters

Birch

Birch is the youngest member of Teague's Home Guard. He appears to have some measure of

humanity when after he listens to Pangle and Stobrod play, he is so moved that he calls them holy men. Yet he does not hesitate to help kill the two and Inman, too, at the end of the novel.

Goatwoman

Inman meets an elderly mountain woman who is later referred to as "the goatwoman" on his journey home. Her humanity is evident as she cares for his wounds and feeds him. On the surface, she appears hardened, due to the difficult life that she has lived, but her eyes "were wells of kindness despite all her hard talk." She has been able to retain an optimistic perspective. She insists: "our minds aren't made to hold on to the particulars of pain the way we do bliss. It's a gift God gives us, a sign of His care for us." At this point, Inman is not able to agree, but her kindness toward him does help provide him with the spirit to continue his journey.

Inman

Inman, one of the novel's two main characters, initially thinks of himself as a peaceful man, but once he faces the battlefield, he discovers "fighting had come easy to him," which he considers "a gift." Yet this gift plagues him throughout his journey home, prompting him to wonder if after so much application of this gift, he has lost his soul.

Even though he tries to harden himself to others in an effort to ensure his own survival, his large heart cannot allow him to ignore those who are suffering, which often puts him in harm's way. He also has a strong sense of justice, evident when he saves the woman Veasey tries to drown and forces the preacher to return to the town and face his punishment. Toward the end of this journey, Inman feels tremendous guilt over the accidental death of a bear that charges him and his subsequent killing of her cub, which he knows will not survive without her. He forces himself to eat the cub, following the laws of nature, but it tastes "like sin" and "regret."

Inman had a great desire for freedom, as evident in his story about being bored in the classroom and his constant desire to walk out the hospital window. He enlists in the war not to uphold slavery but to stave off the influence of the North, which he sees as a threat to his way of life. He also values solitude and self-reliance, dreaming of the time when he can live up on Cold Mountain with Ada. He shows his resourcefulness when he repeatedly finds a way out of a predicament, as when he determines how to best get a dead bull out of a stream before it poisons it.

Junior

Junior lures Inman and Veasey to his home in order to entrap and sell them to the Home Guard. He and Teague exhibit more depravity than other characters in the novel. Junior is able to convey a sense of normalcy, however, long enough to make Inman trust him. Soon after the three arrive at Junior's home, his true character emerges in his harsh treatment of his wife and her sisters. He shows no remorse after turning over Inman and Veasey to the Guard and reveals a sick sense of humor when he forces Inman to marry his wife.

Monroe

Monroe is devoted to his daughter, Ada, but has no foresight and so leaves her completely unprepared to take care of herself after he dies. His romantic nature prompted him to buy the farm, but he was never interested in the daily running of it. Initially, he feels superior to those in his new community, and he patronizes them, which earns him ridicule. Yet his good nature and dedication to his church eventually win others over. His congregation also comes to admire his stubbornness in refusing to follow tradition.

Ada Monroe

When Ada first comes to Black Cove, she is, according to Inman, "somewhat thistleish in comportment," having little patience with and making quick, often harsh judgments of all she meets. Inman tells her that speaking to her is "like grabbing up a chestnut burr, at least thus far." She had not been satisfied with Charleston society either, finding all of her suitors defective in some way.

Yet, she begins to recognize this quality in herself and is willing to change it. When Inman comes to say goodbye, he tells her a Cherokee story about Cold Mountain that she dismisses, calling it folkloric. She later recognizes that she "had been glib. Or flinty and pinched. None of which she really wished to be," and "she feared that without some act of atonement," these qualities "would take hold and harden within her and that one day she would find herself clenched tight as a dogwood bud in January."

She fits in neither city nor country, until Ruby shows her how to make real connections. Through Ruby's tutelage, Ada learns to live fully in her world by paying attention to its smallest details. Even though "simply living had never struck Ada as such a tiresome business," she soon comes to envy Ruby's "knowledge of how the world runs." Monroe had insisted that she gain a good education, but that did not prepare her for the rigors of life on the farm. She gains a sense of independence through her work with Ruby as the latter teaches her how to be self-sufficient.

Ada soon feels a sense of pride in her accomplishments, acknowledging that her friends in Charleston would no longer recognize her, that "all such rough work" that she has done on the farm "has changed" her. She recognizes that her thoughts have changed, too; she no longer sees things as a metaphor for something but as the thing itself, and this fills her with contentment. This paring down of things to their essence prompts her to write to Inman, determined to say "what [her] heart felt, straight and simple and unguarded" and to accept him fully when he returns to Cold Mountain.

Pangle

Pangle is a mentally challenged thirty-year-old who attaches himself to Stobrod. His love of music is evident by his devotion to learning how to play the banjo, which he does quite well. The narrator describes Pangle this way: "He was gentle and kind and looked on everything that passed before him with soft wide eyes." His innocence is also revealed by his attitude toward the world: "Everything he saw was new-minted, and thus every day was a parade of wonders." His trusting nature causes him to smile at the Home Guard, even as they prepare to execute him.

Sara

Inman meets eighteen-year-old Sara during his journey home. Her husband has been killed in the war, leaving her with the care of their newborn. She becomes a symbol of the profound sense of loss experienced by families whose relatives are killed in military action. The narrator notes that "etched in every angle of her body [are] all the lineaments of despair." Her desperation and fear that she will not be able to save her child emerges in her song, which speaks of "resentment, [and] an undertone of panic."

Esco Swanger

Like his wife, Esco Swanger is open-minded and kind-hearted. He shows his penchant for humor when he plays a trick on Monroe after the later underestimates his knowledge of the world. He had been generally sympathetic with the Federals, which was common among those living in the mountains, but had grown angry with both sides after the killing wore on. The war has made him bitter.

Sally Swanger

Sally Swanger, Ada's neighbor, shows her kindness and concern for Ada when she invites her to stay with them after Monroe's funeral. Like her husband, Esco, Sally is quiet and gentle. She literally saves Ada's life when she sends Ruby to Black Cove. She also took pity on Ruby when she was a child, often providing her with food and shelter.

Teague

The brutal leader of the Home Guard, Teague looks like a traveling preacher in his black coat. He and his men "moved as a partnership of wolves will hunt, in wordless coordination of effort toward a shared purpose," which is the joy of the kill rather than any sense of justice. His total lack of humanity emerges when he refuses to help speed the death of one of his victims and sounds "festive" after the murder of others.

Ruby Thewes

Ruby is an example of the mountain people researched by Frazier for the novel. In an article published in *Salon*, Frazier explains that the people who lived in the mountains of North Carolina exhibited a "limitation of desire, stability, [a capacity for] making do, a healthy suspicion of change for its own sake, extreme independence of thought and action, reluctance to acknowledge authority." He also found "beneath it all, a hint of deep earth spirituality."

Ruby is unsure how old she is since her father never celebrated her birthday. Even though she had a difficult childhood, she has "a willing heart" as she proves when she teaches Ada to be as self-reliant as she is, and she accepts Stobrod after he has deserted her. She determines not to let Ada fail. Ruby also has seemingly boundless energy. Even though she is uneducated, she has gained confidence in her abilities and refuses to allow anyone, including Ada, to treat her as less than an equal. She is self-sufficient, learning how to live off the land when she was a child, and "she had whipped men single-handed."

She appreciates the world around her with an almost spiritual sense, gained from a night that she spent outside alone when she was a child. Ada marvels at how she can blow in the nostrils of her skittish horse and calm him, creating "an understanding between them." Her connection with the natural world causes her to regard "money with a great deal of suspicion . . . especially when she contrasted it in her mind with the solidity of hunting and gathering, planting and harvesting."

Stobrod Thewes

When Ruby's forty-five-year-old father, Stobrod Thewes, appears at Ada's farm asking for a handout, Ruby rejects him, citing his appalling treatment of her when she was a child. Stobrod was not well-suited for this task. He had simple needs, evinced by his lack of care for the cabin where they lived: "If not for the inconvenience of his having a daughter, he might happily have taken up dwelling in a hollow tree." He was also averse to hard work, which made it difficult for him to provide food or shelter for Ruby. He had been "a man so sorry he got his nickname from being beat half to death with a stob after he was caught stealing a ham."

When he arrives at Ada's, however, he has found a calling that appears to have transformed him. His musical prowess on the fiddle is "proof positive that no matter what a waste one has made of one's life, it is ever possible to find some path to redemption, however partial," which becomes evident when Pangle notes to Ada after she has listened to one of his tunes, "he's done you some good there." When Stobrod plays, Ada and Ruby see "a saint's blithesome face, loose and half a-smile with the generosity of his gift and with a becoming neutrality toward his own abilities." His music has also provided him with an "appetite to live," which helps him survive after he is shot by the Home Guard.

Solomon Veasey

Solomon Veasey, the young preacher whom Inman meets on his journey, becomes an apt illustration of hypocrisy, reinforcing Inman's disgust with humanity. Veasey is "overly charmed by the peculiarities of the female anatomy," which often gets him in compromising situations, most notably when he tries to drown a woman whom he has impregnated. His greed becomes apparent when he tries to rob a shopkeeper. He continually tries to excuse his actions by either declaring that he has seen the light and will become a better person or waxing philosophic in an effort to confuse the issue. An example of the later occurs when Inman notes that he is "mighty free and easy with the property of others," and Veasey responds that "such things distract you from the grand view."

Themes

The Meaninglessness of War

Inman determines that the men of the mountain areas in North Carolina went to war "to drive

Topics For Further Study

- Choose one of the themes discussed in the fiction section and write a poem or a short story that explores that theme in a different way.

- Read Stephen Crane's *The Red Badge of Courage* and prepare a PowerPoint presentation comparing and contrasting each main character's view on the social and political aspects of the war and their participation in it.

- Read Shelby Foote's *The Civil War: A Narrative* and/or watch Ken Burns PBS mini-series on the Civil War and conduct imaginary interviews with some of the people presented in the book/film on their experiences during the war.

- Watch the film version of the novel. In what ways does the film follow correctly the novel? Does the film have the same thematic focus as the novel? Are the characterizations similar? Note the scenes in the film that have been altered or added and think about why those changes might have been made. Write an essay that compares and contrasts the book and the film.

---

off invaders" whom they felt would threaten their way of life. Ruby had thought that the North "was a godless land, or rather a land of only one god, and that was money." The people of Cold Mountain, however, soon discover that they are fighting someone else's war—those who want to protect a system that requires the subjugation of an entire race to another. Many men in the South, like Inman "had been fighting battles for such men as lived in [the grand plantations], and it made him sick." The goatwoman insists: "N———-owning makes the rich man proud and ugly and it makes the poor man mean. It's a curse laid on the land. We've lit a fire and now it's burning us down."

Inman also finds no clear purpose for the aggression from the North, insisting that "anyone [who thinks] the Federals are willing to die to set loose slaves has got an overly merciful view of mankind." His cynical view of the motives on both sides causes him to experience an overwhelming sense of waste: "every man that died in that war on either side might just as soon have put a pistol against the soft of his palate and blown out the back of his head for all the meaning it had." Ada makes a similar judgment when she declares the war to be "brutal and benighted on both sides about equally" and "degrading to all."

In the early days of the war, Inman, along with other mountaineers, got caught up in "war frenzy . . . the powerful draw of new faces, new places, new

lives. And new laws whereunder you might kill all you wanted and not be jailed, but rather be decorated." Inman now determines that "it was boredom with the repetition of the daily rounds that had made them take up weapons." Yet his first assumption proves to be correct as well. One of the deadly consequences of war is its ability to bring out the worst in human nature.

His battle experience shows him that men enjoy the killing: "the more terrible it is the better." He sees evidence of this continually. One of the worst incidents occurs after Inman and Veasey have been captured by the Home Guard. Determining that taking their prisoners back to face justice is a waste of time, one of the guards decides to kill them. When one of the prisoners, a twelve-year-old boy begins to cry, one Guard member recoils, declaring, "I didn't sign on to kill grandpaws and little boys." But when the leader of the Guard warns him, "Cock back to fire or get down there with them," he complies, and all but Inman are slaughtered.

Inman also finds that the war brings out the worst in him. He has been hardened by all of the violence he has witnessed, which has caused him to act with similar brutality. After beating Junior most likely to death, he "feared that the minds of all men share the same nature with little true variance." As a result of what he has seen and experienced, Inman wants to "be hid and safe from the wolfish gaze of the world at large."

Recognition of Randomness and the Search for Order

Disorder permeates war, concerning who wins and who loses, who lives and who dies. Inman "had seen so much death it had come to seem a random thing entirely." In an effort to find some sort of order, he looks in the bottom of his coffee cup before he starts out on his journey, "as if pattern told something worth knowing," but he determines that "anyone could be oracle for the random ways things fall against each other." This sense is reinforced by a Homeric quotation he reads in the hospital: "the comeliest order on earth is but a heap of random sweepings."

Ada too finds this sense of disorder after she and Ruby bury Pangle. Ruby has taught her that nature contains a certain order, that logical patterns can be found in the flights of birds or the growing of crops. When she discovers what has happened to Stobrod and Pangle, however, Ada's belief in order is shaken. She had found a clear cause and effect relationship in the burying of winter cabbages to help ensure their survival during the winter, but she can find no such pattern in Pangle's murder, no reason that an innocent man should have died in such a way. Inman has a similar reaction when he looks at Stobrod's wounds, thinking "much in life offered little access to logic."

Yet both Inman and Ada find clear patterns in nature that comfort them, Inman as he reads Bartram's descriptions of the North Carolina landscape, which help him focus on home, and Ada as she learns how to work her farm. At first, Ada rejects Ruby's superstitions about nature:

> the crops were growing well, largely . . . because they had been planted, at her insistence, in strict accordance with the signs. In Ruby's mind, everything . . . fell under the rule of the heavens.

Yet as Ada's desire to forge a connection with the land grows, she comes to view Ruby's signs as "an expression of stewardship, a means of taking care, a discipline." In this way, Ada can accept paying attention to natural patterns as a "way of being alert."

Another sense of order that comforts the characters comes from listening to Stobrod's fiddle playing. After he plays for a dying girl, he recognizes the power of music when "the tune had become a thing unto itself, a habit that served to give order and meaning to a day's end." His own playing speaks to "the rule of creation . . . that there is a right way for things to be ordered so that life might not always be just tangle and drift but have a shape, an aim." Those who listen to Stobrod's playing find "a powerful argument against the notion that things just happen."

Literary Allusions and Connections

A literary allusion is a brief, sometimes indirect reference to a literary character, event, place, or work that encourages readers to make connections between literary works that will enrich their understanding of the present work. Many critics have noted the similarities between the novel and Homer's *Odyssey*, focusing on plot and character details: a warrior must make a long and difficult journey back home where he hopes to be reunited with the woman he loves. He must rely on his cunning and intelligence as he continually faces severe impediments to his goal. The woman at home who waits for him confronts her own troubles. Both face internal as well as external struggles that present physical as well as spiritual tests. Frazier also makes two specific allusions to Homer, one in the initial hospital scene in which the man in the bed next to Inman translates Greek passages from the epic and the second when Ada reads the *Odyssey* to Ruby.

Both the novel and the epic are structured episodically, which heightens the focus on the importance of the journey itself. Inman recognizes that "this journey will be the axle of [his] life." Ada keeps the cabriolet when Ruby comes to the farm because of "the promise in its tall wheels that if things got bad enough she could just climb in and ride away." She held "the attitude that there was no burden that couldn't be lightened, no wreckful life that couldn't be set right by heading off down the road." The Gypsies that offer Inman aid during his journey regard the road as "a place apart, a country of its own ruled by no government but natural law" and consider that "its one characteristic was freedom."

Frazier uses traditional elements found in literature about journeys. He describes the idealistic beginning of Inman's trek: "all the elements that composed [the scene] suggested the legendary freedom of the open road: the dawn of day, sunlight golden . . . a tall man in a slouch hat, a knapsack on his back, walking west." But Inman soon faces the reality of his time and place when Frazier includes wasteland imagery. The Civil War landscape here appears to echo the modern landscapes of T. S. Eliot's epic poem *The Waste Land*, which was written post–World War I. Inman's "first true vision" during his journey is of a fence that appears as "some foul variety of brown flatland viper" slithering through the "trash trees" and later of broad ditches that were "smear[s] on the landscape" along side streams clogged with "balls of yellow scud collected in drifted foamy heaps upstream of grounded logs." In response to this desolation, he wonders how he ever thought this was "his country and worth fighting for." Here the real landscape of his journey echoes his own internal wasteland as he feels "all his life adding up to no more than catfish droppings on the bottom of this swill trough of a river." When Frazier makes these connections between the novel and other literary works, his characterizations gain more depth and complexity and he gives readers another vantage point from which to discover meaning.

Historical Context

The Civil War and the Battle of Petersburg

The U.S. Civil War, lasting from 1861 to 1865, broke out between the northern states (the Union) and the southern states (the Confederacy that seceded from the Union). The causes of the war were complex and involved political, economic, and social forces. The South had increasingly tried to separate itself from the North since the Revolutionary War, a movement that escalated sharply after 1820 when the newly formed western territories began to consider the question of slavery. This coupled with the rise of the abolitionists in the North caused the South to worry about maintaining equal status in the national governance of the country.

Abraham Lincoln's election in 1860 prompted South Carolina to secede immediately from the Union, a move soon repeated by Mississippi, Florida, Alabama, Georgia, Louisiana, and Texas. The war began on April 12, 1861, when P. G. I. Beauregard led an attack on Fort Sumter, South Carolina. Soon after Arkansas, North Carolina, Virginia, and Tennessee joined the other Confederate states. Robert E. Lee (1807–1870) became commander of the Confederate Army and Ulysses S. Grant (1822–1885) led the North.

Inman is wounded during the battle of Petersburg, one of the most protracted and bloody of the war. Petersburg is located on the Appomattox River in southeast Virginia, near Richmond, which became the Confederate capital during the war. Confederates and Union soldiers fought each other at Petersburg from June 15, 1864 to April 3, 1865. Entrenching his troops there for months, General Lee refused to give up Petersburg since it offered protection for Richmond. Each side continually tried to break the other's lines. On July 30, 1864, Union soldiers exploded a mine under a portion of the Confederate encampment, an incident depicted in the novel. Union soldiers swarmed into the crater and were mowed down by the Confederates. Grant's army, however, was better supplied and so was able to outlast Lee's. The city finally fell on April 3, 1865, one week before Lee surrendered at the Appomattox courthouse, officially ending the war although combat continued in remote areas of the southwest.

The Home Guard

Captain Albert Teague and his Confederate Home Guard, officially organized in 1863, terrorized outliers, deserters, and families who lived in the North Carolina mountain area. Frazier's research led him to the story of the Home Guard and the ruthless Teague who killed a fiddle player and a mentally handicapped boy. The Guard had asked the fiddler to play a song before his execution. The two, the inspiration for Stobrod and Pangle in the novel, were found buried together on Mt. Sterling in the Smoky Mountains in North Carolina.

Another story involved a retaliatory strike by the Confederates after a Union raid in 1863. One woman, who would become Sara in the novel, was tied to a tree while her baby was placed naked on the cold ground in an effort to get information from her about the raid. In another incident, the Home Guard executed a group of fifteen men and boys, only five of whom belonged to the raiders. Frazier fictionalized different pieces of the story in his descriptions of the executions carried out by the Home Guard in the novel.

Frazier explains in an essay he wrote for *Salon* that the stories of these dead men intrigued him, understanding that none of them "could have had much to do with either of the warring sides, no strong ties to slave agriculture or industrial capitalism." He assumes that they were Scots whose ancestors had immigrated in the eighteenth century, "existing in the seams between the two great incompatible powers."

Frazier's Connection to the Novel

Frazier's great-great-uncle, W. P. Inman, enlisted at the beginning of the Civil War and was engaged in some of its fiercest fighting in Virginia. After suffering a serious wound, Inman decided to

Jude Law and Nicole Kidman in the 2003 film version of Charles Frazier's Cold Mountain
Miramax/The Kobal Collection

desert and walk home, back to the North Carolina mountains. He was subsequently shot and killed by the Home Guard at the close of the war. Frazier knew very little about his relative, and in the course of his research about him and the era, he began to imagine what he and his journey might have been like. The fictionalized Inman evolved from that research and his imaginings.

Karen C. Holt, in an article on the legends behind the novel, concludes: "By superimposing the life of his great-great-uncle on the life of the fictional Inman, Frazier has united them in a single grave, the stories inseparable from the landscape where the victims are buried." In this sense, then, "the graves of North Carolina have become the graves of *Cold Mountain*, entombing a sense of place, and the setting, for which Frazier searched."

Critical Overview

Cold Mountain has been praised for its historic detail, its rich characterizations, and its compelling themes. In a review for *Salon*, Laura Miller notes that *Cold Mountain* "has been greeted with some

of the most impressive accolades we've ever seen for a first novel." David A. Beronä, in his review for *Library Journal*, highly recommends this "monumental novel," considering it to be "a remarkable effort that opens up a historical past that will enrich readers not only with its story but with its strong characters." In his essay on the novel for *Southern Review*, David Heddendorf praises the way Frazier "lovingly describes" and "painstakingly depicts . . . nineteenth-century rural life." Heddendorf also points out the novel's "fully imagined characters," who "can make compelling claims on us, for in their strangeness they grip our attention as our own problems do."

Offering one of the few notes of criticism, James Gardner, in his piece on the novel in the *National Review*, complains that at times, Frazier expresses a "desire to sound novelistic" in the development of his characters. Gardner insists that "one feels, his characters are infused with a *faux* complexity, a host of 'issues' to make them seem heavier than they otherwise would," and he finds some of the details implausible. Yet, he concludes, "such missteps are surely not fatal to the success of *Cold Mountain*," finding that overall, it can be judged as "an ambitious example of the historical novel . . . and very much to its credit—the book treats the past as if it were, in a way, *present*."

Gardner explains that "though Frazier has acquired a scholar's feel for the period's idioms, costumes, and mores, these become for him merely the conduits through which passes the fluent essence of life lived *now*." He also finds "in certain details . . . a genuine novelistic talent and tact which simply cannot be faked." Gardner adds that "Frazier clearly takes pleasure in the English language," revealing himself to be "self-consciously literate without being opaque."

A review in *Publishers Weekly* claims the novel to be "rich in evocative physical detail and timeless human insight" in its consideration of "themes both grand (humanity's place in nature) and intimate (a love affair transformed by the war)." The reviewer finds: "The sweeping cycle of Inman's homeward journey is deftly balanced by Ada's growing sense of herself and her connection to the natural world around the farm." Frazier has constructed "a leisurely, literate narrative" that becomes a "quiet drama in the tensions that unfold as Inman and Ada come ever closer to reunion, yet farther from their former selves." The review concludes with praise for the deft intertwining of character and theme, insisting that "Frazier shows how lives of soldiers and of civilians alike deepen and are transformed as a direct consequence of the war's tragedy."

Criticism

Wendy Perkins

Perkins is a professor of American and English literature and film. In this essay, she examines the characters' struggle for physical and emotional survival.

When Inman decides to desert the Confederate Army and walk back to Ada and his home on Cold Mountain, he faces serious impediments to his safety, almost as grave as those he encountered on the Civil War battlefield. Physical survival, though, is not his most challenging task. He must also survive the emotional damage wrought by the war, which he fears has made him "so lost in bitterness and anger that [he] could not find [his] way back." Ada faces her own physical and emotional trials while Inman is gone. Although hers are not as severe as Inman's, they also ultimately require strength of character as well as a hopeful readiness

and openness to the world, qualities that become fully realized during Inman's and Ada's bittersweet reunion at the end of their difficult journeys.

As Inman lies in the hospital after experiencing the horrors of the war, he suffers from a profound lack of hope for his future and for that of humanity. He now agrees with his Native American friend Swimmer, who believes in the vulnerability of the spirit, which "could be torn apart and cease" while the body kept living. Inman knows this has happened to him. His wound becomes symbolic of his spirit, damaged and appearing unlikely to heal. Inman feels an overwhelming sense of emptiness, as if his spirit "had been blasted away so that he had become lonesome and estranged from all around him." This spiritual numbness has become a survival mechanism for him. He has kept his fears of death at bay by setting himself "apart as if dead already, with nothing much left of [himself] but a hut of bones."

As he sits "brooding and pining for his lost self," he fixates on the large window in front of him, through which he envisions scenes from home. These scenes become a respite from the harsh reality that surrounds him. He allows himself to replace the present with the past "for he had seen the metal face of the age and had been so stunned by it that when he thought into the future, all he could vision was a world from which everything he counted important had been banished or had willingly fled." This recognition prompts him to make a bold decision.

After imagining "many times that it would open onto some other place and let him walk through and be there," Inman decides to make fantasy reality, and he begins his journey away from the war and toward home and Ada. He determines that if he can just get home and build a cabin on Cold Mountain and so isolate himself from the rest of the world, he can survive. "And if Ada would go with him, there might be the hope . . . that in time his despair might be honed off to a point so fine and thin that it would be nearly the same as vanishing." Swimmer had told him that there are high places where "the dead spirit could be reborn." Inman thus envisions Cold Mountain as such a place, a "healing realm . . . where all his scattered forces might gather." During his journey, he reads Bartram's account of his own travels in the region, which helps sustain him.

The violence he witnesses, however, as he makes his way home compounds his spiritual emptiness. As he observes Veasey's cruelty toward the young woman he has impregnated, the Home Guard's slaughtering of innocent men and children, the Federals' emotional torture of Sara by placing her unwrapped baby on the frozen ground, and Junior's betrayal of him, Inman develops what David Heddendorf, in his essay on the novel, calls "a self-protective irony that sees him home from the outermost reaches of danger." Heddendorf claims that this irony, revealed "in the laconic, guarded tones of one accustomed to ambush and betrayal," helps him detach himself from the misery he observes and experiences. An example of this detachment occurs in Inman's understated response to Veasey's declaration, "when I took to preaching I answered a false call." Inman tells him, "Yes . . . I'd say you're ill suited for that business."

This misery also causes him to develop another self-protective measure—a hardness toward others. He regards each person he meets during his journey as "another stone in his passway" and determines "not to be smirched with the mess of other people. A part of him wanted to hide" while "another part yearned to wear the big pistol openly on his hip . . . , letting rage be his guide against anything that ran counter to his will." Two incidents show him in danger of losing the last remnants of his humanity: his savage beating of the men who attack him in a town he is passing through, and his beating, perhaps to death, of Junior after the man betrays him to the Home Guard.

Inman ultimately, however, does not lose his humanity, due in part to his inability to steel himself against the suffering of others. He feels compelled to save the woman Veasey tries to drown and to help Sara get back her hog, the only means of sustenance for her and her child. He recognizes Sara's need for comfort and so listens to her tell about her life with her husband. After he kills the men who harassed her and stole her hog, he reveals that even after all he has experienced, he still cannot get used to killing. He tries to rationalize his actions, deciding that on the battlefield, "he had probably killed any number of men more satisfactory in all their attributes than" these. Yet, he cannot quite separate himself from his act, admitting that "this might be a story he would never tell."

He also experiences acts of kindness on the road that help mend his spirit. Several people offer him food and shelter without accepting payment, such as the slave who feeds him at his own peril and warns him of the dangerous roads to avoid, and the goatwoman, who helps heal his physical and psychic wounds. His movement toward healing is

> When the two finally meet on Cold Mountain, it becomes evident that the emotional damage they both have endured has not been fully healed."

a slow one, however: "he would like to love the world as it was, and he felt a great deal of accomplishment for the occasions when he did, since the other was so easy. Hate took no effort other than to look about."

At times, the struggle between hope and despair causes him to want to "sprout wings and fly," to live separate "among the tree limbs and cliff rocks," high above "the society of people . . . observing the bright light of common day." The goatwoman becomes a symbol of the kind of solitary life for which Inman thinks he is suited, but after being with her for a time, he realizes the unbearable sadness of such a life. Her kindness, coupled with Sara's tenderness toward him, strengthens his resolve to continue his journey and get back to Ada.

After her father dies, Ada also must struggle to survive physically and emotionally; however, she has no knowledge about running a farm or about supporting herself. Her loneliness and inability to adapt to her surroundings fill her with a sense of helplessness and despair. At this point, nature appears to echo her emotional state as she looks toward Cold Mountain after her father dies: "The prospect from the reading chair confronted her with all the major shapes and colors of her current position. Through the summer, the landscape's most frequent mood had been dim and gloomy," in sharp contrast to her world in Charleston. Yet, Ada soon learns that "survival had such a sharp way of focusing one's attentions elsewhere," from her past life to the realities of her present.

Ada recognizes that she will not survive the coming hard winter unless she learns to be self-sufficient, but she has no idea where to start. Fortunately, in much the same way as strangers help Inman, kind and resourceful others help Ada

What Do I Read Next?

- William Bartram's *Travels and Other Writings* (Library of America edition, 1996) contains the book read by Inman during his journey home that chronicled the author's own travels through the Carolinas. Bartram, one of the earliest American nature writers, carefully gathered details of the landscape that he supplemented with his own drawings.

- Stephen Crane's naturalistic novel, *The Red Badge of Courage*, originally published in 1894, provides a fictional account of the Civil War and examines the complex ways that the participants responded to it. In his characterization of Henry Fleming, a young Union soldier, Crane explores the disillusionment soldiers feel from military action and questions concerning the nature of honor and courage.

- Frazier's *Adventuring in the Andes: The Sierra Club Travel Guide to Ecuador, Peru, Bolivia, the Amazon Basin, and the Galapagos Islands* (1985) is based on his travels to South America.

- While doing research for his novel, Frazier consulted Phillip Shaw Paludan's *Victims: A True Story of the Civil War* (1981), which focuses on the North Carolina mountaineers who were unsuccessful in their attempts to avoid involvement in the conflict between the North and the South.

---

find physical as well as emotional security. The Swangers provide aid when they give Ada food and, later, when they send Ruby to Black Cove.

Ruby is instrumental in teaching Ada how to make the farm operational as well as in helping her foster a deep awareness and comforting connection to the world around her. Before Ruby came, Ada had exhibited an openness to Black Cove, determining that she could find "a satisfactory life of common things" there along with "the promise of a more content and expansive life." Ruby helps her realize that promise as she teaches her to shed the superficial world of Charleston society for the natural world of the farm.

Ada at first balks at the backbreaking work necessary for survival, but with Ruby's insistence that the two share duties equally, she slowly gains physical and emotional strength. While she learns the "tiresome business" of "simply living," she also comes to appreciate the beauty of her surroundings. Ada discovers that one of the benefits of rising early to begin chores, besides the obvious one of having enough time to complete one's work, is to see a sunrise: she watches as "the light from outside would rise and fill the room. It seemed a thing of such wonder to Ada, who had not witnessed many dawns." Ruby teaches Ada

that "to live fully in a place all your life, you kept aiming smaller and smaller in attention to detail," appreciating and caring for customs and natural laws. Ada is not fully content, however, until she is reunited with Inman.

When the two finally meet on Cold Mountain, it becomes evident that the emotional damage they both have endured has not been fully healed. At first, Ada does not recognize the "blasted and ravaged" figure before her, "yearning for food, warmth, kindness. . . . his mind scoured and his heart jailed within the bars of his ribs." Although Ada has learned to be self-sufficient and independent, she acknowledges that her world has been "such an incredibly lonely place." Their coming together on the mountain, however, provides each finally with the fulfillment for which they have been searching. Ada finds that lying beside Inman is the "only cure" for her loneliness, while Inman, who "had been living like a dead man" finds "life [suddenly] before him, an offering within his reach." The two spend their last evening together contentedly envisioning their future on the farm at Black Cove.

Ironically, it is Inman's renewed sense of humanity that ultimately destroys him. After he is able to defend himself against Teague and his men, he faces the one last member of the Home Guard—Birch. When Inman hesitates, reluctant to kill a boy, Birch kills him.

Frazier suggests that Inman, however, has achieved his goal—the restoration of his soul at the end of his journey home. His ability to find his way back physically and emotionally to Ada provides a sense of closure to the novel, which is reinforced by the focus in the final pages on the strong sense of community shared by the rest of the characters. Inman is also there with Ada through their nine-year-old daughter, who becomes their testament to the endurance of the human spirit.

Source: Wendy Perkins, Critical Essay on *Cold Mountain*, in *Novels for Students*, Thomson Gale, 2007.

Ed Piacentino

In the following essay, Piacentino comments on "cross-racial bonding," unity beyond race, and a sense of home in Frazier's novel.

Charles Frazier's *Cold Mountain*, a book about Civil War Appalachia and the writer's first novel, has enjoyed a phenomenal popular and critical success since its publication in 1997. A best seller, *Cold Mountain* won the National Book Award, the Book Critics' Circle Award, and the Pulitzer Prize for fiction; in addition, a film version of the novel, directed by Anthony Minghella, is under production.

Its merits widely acclaimed by contemporary reviewers, *Cold Mountain* has been perceived in many contexts. While James Polk has called it an "American Odyssey," John C. Inscoe regards Inman, the novel's co-protagonist, as an "Appalachian Odyseus." To Malcolm Jones, *Cold Mountain* is veritably a "page turner that attains the status of literature," and John B. Breslin, who likewise considers the book's literary merit, accurately praises it as an "exquisite diptych: in Inman's story, an unstinting epic of war and its ravages, on and off the battlefield; and in Ada's, an account of life's stubborn refusal to surrender to either man or nature's relentless onslaught." William R. Trotter, who has written about guerilla warfare in Civil War North Carolina, celebrates *Cold Mountain* as "great and haunting novel, almost mythic in the depth of its power to evoke people, landscapes, and the mood of the time in which it is set." And Jane Tompkins, who calls *Cold Mountain* a "story of a search for love and healing," sees the book as sharing affinities with the popular Western, its "hero stoic, reticent, and lonely, a lovingly portrayed landscape, disaffection with institutions and

> **" It is relationship, forming human connections outside one's self, that Inman desperately needs before he can be restored to some semblance of wholeness, of a healthy and balanced life, which, in his mind, he comes to associate with home."**

dogmas . . . ; and a spirituality expressed through the worship of nature."

Among academic critics, many of whom often have an aversion to books that achieve popular status, *Cold Mountain* has received scant attention, but the few academics who have written about Frazier's novel have recognized its artistic dimensions. Kathryn Stripling Byer perceives the book as exhibiting a "poetic vision," which, she notes, contributes to "its luminous texture, illuminating its wealth of history, local detail and character," and, in drawing on Ursula Le Guin, like a "medicine bundle, holding things in a particular, powerful relation to one another and to us." Paul D. Knoke, who briefly examines the novel's crow symbolism, also explores, in a collaborative essay with Bill McCarron, some of the structural interrelationships provided "through a . . . combination of parallelism (where characters, scenes, and symbols 'double,' prefigure, and are reduplicated by other characters, scenes, and symbols) and antithesis (where events and symbols demand dual antithetical interpretation)." And finally Knoke, the critic who has written about *Cold Mountain* most prolifically, perceptively and meticulously charts the precise time frame and identifies the places in North Carolina through which Inman, Frazier's physically and spiritually maimed Confederate soldier, journeyed in his effort to return home after deserting the war.

Many readers of Civil War novels authored by Southerners would agree with Mel Gussow that *Cold Mountain* is a "Civil War novel with a difference," since many facets of the book show that Frazier elected not to showcase the familiar stereotypes and repeat the scenarios commonly featured in earlier best sellers such as Margaret Mitchell's *Gone with the Wind* (1936). Rather than glorifying the heroism of men fighting in war, Frazier followed a different path. In his words, "when you grow up in the South, you get this concept of the war as this noble, tragic thing, and when I think of my own family's experience, it doesn't seem so noble in any direction. To go off and fight for a cause they had not much relation to: that's the part I see as tragic" (qtd. in Gussow, F1). In describing the key differences between *Cold Mountain* and books of earlier chroniclers of historical fiction about the Civil War in the South, historian John C. Inscoe points out:

> The war depicted here is indeed very different from the war . . . which Robert E. Lee experienced. There are few if any plantations, slaveholders, or slaves on this home front. The many characters who people Frazier's saga are far removed from those who made up Margaret Mitchell's or John Jakes's fictionalized Confederacy. With very few exceptions, these people are poor; leading lives of quiet—and often not so quiet—desperation. For all participants, the war has become one of disillusionment, of resentment, of desolation, and of brutality as they engage in a primal quest for sheer survival. ("Appalachian Odyssey," p. 333)

In a recent essay "A War Like All Wars," Tom Wicker, who does not regard *Cold Mountain* as being exclusively about the Civil War, notes rather that Frazier's book is a novel of war—"any war in any time—and what it does to men and society." Nor does Wicker regard Inman as a deserter, seeing him instead as resembling the character in Ernest Hemingway's "A Very Short Story" who "made a separate peace." Moreover, Wicker perceptively observes that Frazier's principal interests, "are with a world nearing the end of a calamitous war, with a society in devastation, and with people who seem mostly to want the battle to be over so that their men can come back and rebuilding can begin."

Yet there is another important aspect of *Cold Mountain* that makes it a different variety of Southern Civil War novel: Frazier's portrayal of race relations. In his portrayal Frazier features cross-racial bonding with some frequency and in doing so reflects a sentiment that similarly echoes Dr. Martin Luther King, Jr.'s emotional appeal for human rights, racial equality and social harmony, which he expressed in his 1963 "I Have a Dream" speech, delivered at the Lincoln Memorial on the one-hundredth anniversary of the signing of the Emancipation Proclamation. In contrast to the situation that existed in the years before the Civil War when slavery and a constant fear of the eruption of slave rebellion provided the white Southern writer with the impetus for what Leonard Cassuto describes as the "manufacture of bucolic Southern fantasies . . . , peopled with Sambos because they can easily fit within its parameters," Frazier, in *Cold Mountain*, presents a perspective more reflective of the attitudes of the post-Civil Rights era. During this time, the hopes expressed in Dr. King's widely influential speech were beginning to be realized in American society. While it can be claimed that Frazier's novel seems directed to a contemporary readership whose views on race relation were more liberal and more humane than those of many readers of the pre-Civil Rights era whose attitudes had been conditioned to accept segregation and racial prejudice, Frazier was not violating historical plausibility in his handling of race. Admittedly, he cautiously avoids populating his book with dehumanizing racial stereotypes or resonating a bigoted bias that many Southerners of the Civil War period would likely have felt toward African Americans. But in choosing to follow what may at first seem an ahistorical course, Frazier featured in *Cold Mountain* a viewpoint toward race common among Southern Appalachian inhabitants who typically did not own slaves and who did not readily support slavery, an attitude, as will be noted later in this essay, that is consonant with historical plausibility. Moreover, the book, as we will see, celebrates the need for humanity, connection, togetherness, and harmony, values that Inman, the co-protagonist, finds in William Bartram's *Travels through North and South Carolina, Georgia, East and West Florida, the Cherokee Country, the Extensive Territories of the Muscogulges, or Creek Confederacy, and the Country of the Choctaws* (1791) and that he likewise associates with his southwestern North Carolina home, Cold Mountain.

Some of the basic socio-historical facts about Civil War western North Carolina that Frazier seemed to be aware of and that provided the context for influencing his development of the storyline in *Cold Mountain* were the relatively fewer slave owners and slaves in this region than in other parts of the South, the lack of widespread popular support for North Carolina's secession from the Union in the state's mountain regions in 1861, the loss of enthusiasm by mountain residents for the war when realizing it would last much longer than they had anticipated, the shortages of food and male labor, and the threats of Federal military raids.

In attempt to establish a rationale for the cross-racial bonding that pervades and recurs in *Cold*

Mountain, we must take into account the novel's historical context. Inman, the novel's co-protagonist and a Confederate deserter, resides in the southwestern North Carolina mountains, a region where there were few slaves, and in his life there prior to his enlistment in the Confederacy, slavery was never a part of his experience. Such an attitude is consistent with Inman's upbringing and with the principal historical Carolina, Georgia, East and West Florida, the Cherokee Country, the Extensive accounts of the pre-Civil War and Civil War eras in the Southern Appalachians. Moreover, as Inman makes clear, in the chapter titled "the doing of it," in a frank conversation with a goat woman—a hard but kind woman in whom he feels comfortable confiding—neither the perpetuation of the "peculiar institution" nor persons whose way of life depended upon slave labor was ever his motivation for joining the Confederate cause. As the goat woman observes Inman's wounds, she asks him: "What I want to know is, was it worth it, all that fighting for the big man's n——?" He responds, "That's not the way I saw it" and then goes on to tell her that he neither owned slaves nor did he know anyone who did. When the goat woman inquires further, "Then what stirred you up enough for fighting and dying?" Inman candidly explains why he and other North Carolina highlanders fought in the war:

> I reckon many of us fought to drive off the invaders. One man I knew had been north to the big cities, and he said it was every feature of such places that we were fighting to prevent. All I know is anyone thinking the Federals are willing to die to set lose slaves has got an overly merciful view of mankind.

It is cynicism such as this that Inman, while still convalescing in the hospital in Raleigh, North Carolina, displays in Chapter One as he reminisces about his home region—in particular, the summer when he and Swimmer, a Cherokee friend, were sixteen, wondering now if Swimmer too is fighting against the Federals, a common link that they possibly share as adults. In this, the first instance of cross-racial bonding in *Cold Mountain*, Inman does not show the condescension and prejudice one might expect to see in a society comprised primarily of a low-class white racial majority in an encounter with a minority other. Instead, in his recollection, Inman exhibits compassion for and understanding of a person of color, actually seeing Swimmer, not as an anachronism, a recycled noble savage figure, but, as McCarron and Knoke point out, as a "spiritual guide." In recalling his initial meeting with Swimmer and a band of Cherokees

from Cove Creek, who had come to Balsam Mountain with a herd of cows to find available grazing land, Inman and a group of white men from Catalooch, whose cows are also grazing these same lands, regard and treat the Native Americans respectfully as equals. In describing the activities that Inman and the Catalooch whites engage in while in the company of Swimmer and his fellow Cherokees, Frazier emphasizes that discrimination is nonexistent, that no color barriers separate the two races to prevent them from interacting:

> The two groups camped side by side for two weeks, the younger men playing the ball game [lacrosse] most of the day, gambling heavily on the outcomes. It was a contest with no fixed time of play and few rules so that they just ran about slamming into each other and hacking with the racquets as if with clubs until one team reached a set number of points scored by striking the goalposts with the ball. They'd play most of the day and then spend half the night drinking and telling tales at fireside, eating great heaps of little speckled trout, fried crisp, bones and all.

As McCarron and Knoke insightfully note, the competitors' "slamming" and "hacking" in the lacrosse game is "never with malicious intent" and "what might have looked like a 'war' to an outsider was instead, and paradoxically, a casualty-less vehicle for 'peace,' the bonding of a friendship between whites and Indians." Interestingly, in the gambling activity, which the lacrosse matches has prompted, the Cherokees win the spoils, "the Catalooch party [losing] to the Indians everything they could do without and things they couldn't—fry pans and dutch ovens, sacks of meal, fishing poles, rifles and pistols."

When viewed on the basis of the one-to-one relationship that develops between Inman and Swimmer during this brief summer interlude in the "high balds" on Balsam Mountain, the shared home country of both young men, the so-called "bonding of friendship" between a white and a red man is thematically significant. This is especially true if we consider this friendship within the context of Inman's subsequent experiences (either direct, observed, or heard about) in cross-racial bonding later in the novel. Even though Inman considers some of Swimmer's folk explanations "dismal," he comes to hold him in high esteem and to regard his new Cherokee friend as possessing intuition and insight superior to his own. In fact, Swimmer's keen knowledge of the mysteries of the spiritual world attests to this. Convalescing in a Raleigh military hospital, existing in a physical and spiritual void at the time, Inman remembers a folktale Swimmer had once related to him, a story about a place of refuge and renewal, a "far and inaccessible region," where human beings could retreat temporarily to escape the foulness of this world, and "in that high land the dead spirit could be reborn." This "healing realm . . . , a place where all his scattered forces might gather," but a place Inman has never seen, he comes to associate with Cold Mountain, his home. Though one would be inclined to think that Inman might readily dismiss Swimmer's story about a "world invisible," a "better place" as spurious, as a superstitious folk tale of a primitive culture, he accepts his friend's beliefs about this "healing realm" as authentic, as worthy of consideration. Because of his high regard for Swimmer, Inman subsequently comes to perceive the Cherokee's beliefs as relevant to his own immediate needs of restoring wholeness to his "lost self," both to his war-ravaged body and to his disillusioned, "blasted away" spirit, the latter causing him to feel "lonesome and estranged from all around him." The common link between Swimmer and Inman, then, is one formulated on distinctly human grounds. Inman's malaise, his wounded body and his traumatized spirit, which contribute significantly to his loneliness, disenchantment, and despair, is a basic one that may be experienced by any human being, regardless of racial, ethnic, socio-economic, or cultural differences. Moreover, Swimmer's remedy to find a "healing realm," where one can find a comfort zone by restoring contact with the friendly community of his home, offers a workable anodyne for Inman's malady.

Inman's recollection of this instance of cross-racial bonding seems to provide the main impetus for his decision to desert the war and to return home to Cold Mountain. But even more importantly, his reflections on his friendship with Swimmer make Inman a different kind of hero. As Kathryn Stripling Byer explains, "unlike the classic hero, Inman is not at the solitary center of the story, nor would he wish to be. *Relationship* is what he desires, not heroism" (p. 116, my emphasis). It is relationship, forming human connections outside one's self, that Inman desperately needs before he can be restored to some semblance of wholeness, of a healthy and balanced life, which, in his mind, he comes to associate with home. In his friendship with Swimmer, Inman discovers the importance of acknowledging otherness by crossing the barriers of racial discrimination. And as a resident of Southern Appalachia and of the yeoman class, Inman is somewhat marginalized himself, a factor that likely enables him to accept and to connect with Swimmer who, as a Native American, has been similarly marginalized. Inman's experience in

cross-racial understanding and friendship with Swimmer may suggest by association a feeling akin to being in a safe place, removed from those things that destroy the body as well as the spirit. In addition, the memory of their bonding, coupled with Swimmer's tale about the existence of a "better place," a "healing realm," offers Inman the same kind the security and consolation that he had formerly associated with home.

In the chapter titled "like any other thing, a gift," Inman, after he has actually begun his homeward journey, encounters a racially mixed group of gypsies, who also help him to see the kind of re-socialization and re-orientation process that will best serve him as he attempts to reintegrate into the society of his home. In initially observing these gypsies, a "jumble of people wearing about every thing of skin there is," he speculates that they are "outlaws and Ishmaelite as himself. Show folk, outliers, a tribe of Irish gypsy horse traders all thrown in together." Yet Inman feels a common bond with these multi-racial vagabonds, despised outcasts like himself, who similarly do whatever expediency demands for survival. As Inman notices, these gypsies use deception, transforming old horses so as to disguise their real features and defects, making them to appear young and vibrant. A veritable clinic in applied racial and ethnic equality, they engage in these and other duplicities for the benefit of *all* the members of their society. Discounting the morality of their actions, Inman, who neither narrow-mindedly condemns the gypsy clan's fraudulent behavior nor their social practices, bonds with them almost immediately. Moreover, they accept him without condition or suspicion, and "they [take] him in with apparent generosity," feeding and entertaining him, taking care of his basic needs and otherwise making him feel "at home." Interestingly, Inman observes and is attracted to a young, beautiful gypsy woman, and "something in the darkness of her hair or the way she moved or the thinness of her fingers reminded him momentarily of Ada." While apparently inconsequential, this encounter shows that the connection that Inman perceives between Ada, the woman he loves and to whom he wishes to return, and this gypsy woman functions to accentuate for him the principal reason he desires to return home to Cold Mountain.

Yet Inman learns another vital lesson from his interlude with the gypsies—one that reinforces and reverberates his earlier relationship with Swimmer—their acceptance and practice of racial equality. These societal outcasts, an anomaly in their humane ethic and liberal racial attitudes, are comprised, Frazier writes, of a "big, grey-bearded Ethiopian who had a regal bearing" and "a little menagerie of Indians of several makes, a Seminole from Florida, a Creek, a Cherokee from Echota, and a Yemassee woman." Both the Ethiopian and the Native Americans are showmen. As performers, the Ethiopian was "dressed in purple robes . . . , [and] was portrayed to have been in his youth the king of Africa" and the Indians were drummers, dancers, and chanters. The ritualistic act of eating, which brings Inman and the multi-racial gypsies together, reaffirms their observance of the equality that they advocate: "The Ethiopians and the Indians joined in the meal as if they were all of a color and equals. They took their turns speaking, and permission to talk was neither sought nor given." In a gesture of unity, indicative of their bonding, these gypsy showmen take a drink from the same bottle and likewise share in recounting stories about their life on the road, the road, as they see it, being a "place apart, a country of its own ruled by no government but natural law, its one characteristic [being] freedom." In one sense, then, the way of life the gypsies follow represents their own sense of home, a communal domicile predicated on unequivocal acceptance and an egalitarian ethic. For Inman, his experience with the gypsies provides an important lesson in integration with a different culture and the mutual benefits derived from the acceptance of diversity in favor of singularity.

Cross-racial bonding in *Cold Mountain* also involves an encounter between Ada, the novel's co-protagonist and the woman Inman loves, and Ruby, her companion in equal living who teaches Ada "self-confidence . . . , compassion, 'other-centeredness'" (McCarron and Knoke, p. 278), and a group of war refugees from neighboring Tennessee whom they befriend. Their husbands away from home and engaged in the war, the three white women refugees, who between them have half a dozen children in their care and two dutiful slaves to assist them, desire to re-connect with family in South Carolina. Collectively, these refugees, regardless of racial, class, or age differences, share the common plight of victimization and homelessness, a predicament forced upon them by self-serving Federal marauders, who, one of them asserts, "make women and children atone for the deaths of soldiers." In graphically detailing the atrocities of the Federal troops, one of the women reports: "The Federals rode down on us and robbed even the n——— . . . . They took every bit of food we had been able to raise this year. I even saw one man filling his coat pockets with our lard. Dipping

by the handful." The Federals also steal their jewelry and burn their home. The reunion with their South Carolina relatives will provide, these refugees undoubtedly hope, some semblance of family identity, order, and peaceful accord, in short, the home feeling that the war has despoiled. Yet in the course of their journey through the mountains, when these war-ravaged travelers become lost, Ruby and Ada, moved by compassion, offer *all* their visitors, including the slaves, food and shelter, providing for them a safe and temporary home and place for renewal. "When supper was ready," Frazier writes, "they called in the visitors and sat them at the dining-room table. The slaves had the same fare, but ate out under the pear tree."

While long-standing social custom may account for the slaves eating separately from the white women and children, Frazier does not belabor this point. Still, he is consistent in mentioning it, for, in his initial description of the refugee group, he does casually interject a horrifying possibility, saying that the "pair of kind slaves, who hovered about the women as close as shadows, might just as easily have cut every throat in the family any night as they slept." Even so, this does not appear to be a prominent fear in the minds of the white women refugees, who, out of the necessity of survival, appear to have cultivated a bond of mutual trust with their slaves and seem comfortable in their company. Moreover, the women's minds seem focused not on the potential eruption of racial violence or perhaps massacre at the hands of their slaves but rather on reaching their relatives in South Carolina safely. Their intended destination with family will, they hope, provide for them a new home, offering the sense of security and comfort which presumably they had formerly associated with their home in Tennessee before the war displaced them. In raising the notion of the possible insidious intentions of the refugees' slaves, Frazier may only be offhandedly acknowledging the unsettled feelings of Ada and Ruby, neither of whom is accustomed to seeing strangers of any color in and around Black Cove. Perhaps too, Ada and Ruby may privately feel that their own isolation has been violated by the sudden appearance of outsiders. With the arrival of the refugees, whether Ada and Ruby admit it or not, they have been forced to confront, albeit vicariously, the reality of the disruption of home life and the kinds of losses concomitant with it that can and do occur when the activities of war directly affect people's lives. While such thoughts may be disturbing, Frazier presents no further indication that any hostile act on the part of these women's slaves, such as the one he casually mentions, would ever occur.

Despite this one discomfiting conjecture, which, I repeat, never materializes before the refugees depart for South Carolina, nor as far as we know during the reminder of their journey (which Frazier chooses not to develop), he quickly restores the same sense of comfort and trust, features of genuine and healthy relationship, manifested in Ada and Ruby's earlier hospitality in their first encounter with these homeless travelers:

> Ada and Ruby saw the travelers off to bed, and the next morning they cooked nearly all the eggs they had and made a pot of grits and more biscuits. After breakfast, they drew a map of the way to the gap and set them on the next leg of their journey.

This final hospitable act simultaneously foreshadows and parallels the novel's next instance of crossracial bonding when a slave befriends Inman, who has miraculously survived the home guard's mass execution of Confederate deserters.

The scene of Inman's bonding with the yellow slave, a man of a hospitable and humane disposition, occurs soon after wild boars uproot the wounded Inman, whom the home guard executioners have buried in a shallow grave and have left for dead. Weak and disoriented and trying to decide the best route to follow in continuing his westward journey to Cold Mountain, Inman sees a yellow slave coming down the road toward him on a steer-drawn sled loaded with watermelons. Inman's encounter with the yellow man begins on a note of surprise and comic relief when the slave, upon first seeing Inman, colloquially exclaims: "They Lord God amighty, . . . You look like a dirt man." Yet the slave, who quickly perceives Inman's weakened condition, tosses him a melon, which he ravenously devours. Further, the slave gives Inman a ride on his sled, taking him to the farm of his owner and hiding him in a barn on the premises.

During Inman's recuperation, this slave and other slaves make Inman "feel at home," offering him safe refuge and showing him many kindnesses in much the same manner as Ada and Ruby did in assisting the war refugees from Tennessee. They feed him, helping to renew his strength, clean his clothes, provide a secure domicile for him, and otherwise protect him from disclosure. Yet the hospitality of the slaves does not end here. Once Inman's health is restored and he seems ready to travel again, the yellow slave, cognizant that dangers await Inman, alerts him that Confederate patrols are on the roads, searching for Federals who have escaped from the nearby Salisbury prison. As he warns Inman, "You try to go through there, they'll sure catch you up, you're not careful. Probably catch you even if you are." The slave's unsolicited and gratuitous words of warning not only attest to his compassionate character but also affirm Inman's trust in him, prompting Inman to rely exclusively on the slave for accurate information regarding the safest route to follow in resuming his homeward journey. According to the yellow slave's keen knowledge of the lurking dangers in the vicinity and special advantages that may be of benefit to Inman during his westward trek, he cautiously advises Inman to "cut north. Go toward Wilkes. Taking that heading, there's Moravians and Quakers all the way that will help. Hit the bottom of the Blue Ridge and then cut south again following the foothills. Or go on into the mountains and follow the ridges back down to your course." Added to all that he has already done for Inman, the yellow man, again in a demonstration of his admirable humanity and other-directedness, equips Inman with substantial food. In addition, the slave even spends considerable time, as Ada and Ruby had done for the Tennessee refugees, patiently and meticulously drawing a map with useful notations to direct him safely in his travels. This map, "all detailed with little houses and odd-shaped barns and crooked trees with faces in their trunks and limbs like arms and hair [with] a fancy compass . . . in one corner . . . , and notes in a precise script to say who could be trusted and who could not," serves as a first-hand, reliable rendering of what the yellow slave experientially knows about the region to the west that extends to the edge of the mountains. When Inman, who is noticeably appreciative of the slave's genuine humanity and assistance, tries to offer him money for his many kind services and discovers that he has none, the yellow man, in keeping with his consistently admirable character, tells Inman: "I might not have took it anyway." It appears that both Inman and the slave accept and understand each other on a basic human level. In doing so, they recognize the commonality of their human connection and therefore bond unconditionally without apparent preconceived bias or suspicion. In the slave's eyes, Inman, regardless of his color or affiliation, is a human being in need. In this instance, the more advantaged of the parties—the yellow slave, likely at some past time a victim of dehumanization himself as a member of an oppressed race—freely aids the disadvantaged Confederate fugitive.

While one might be inclined to wonder if the yellow slave represents an updated version of docile and faithful retainers such as those Thomas Nelson Page portrayed in some of the stories of *In Ole Virginia* (1887), this is not the case. In no way whatsoever does Frazier's slave resemble Page's fawning black retainers. Instead, the yellow slave exhibits a personal identity of his own. In Inman, the slave recognizes a fellow outcast (rather than an enemy), and he assists Inman without compromising his personal interests and feelings in the process. Nor does Frazier insinuate that the yellow slave represses resentment that he may feel toward the Confederate deserter. In short, in emphasizing this black man's gratuitous behavior toward a Southern white man, Frazier shows no interest in resurrecting the "lost cause" ideology, popularized by Page, with its emphasis on African-American stereotypes favoring inferiority, subservience, complacency, and absolute loyalty to the white man. Instead Frazier's apparent intent was to mold his slave character into a likable human being of genuine and endearing sensitivity.

After all, the yellow slave's kindnesses to a Confederate deserter, a fugitive from justice, are beyond the call of duty and actually pose a potential danger to his personal security should his master, other slaveholding Confederates in the area, or the home guard find out about them. Moreover, the slave could have shown indifference to Inman's plight and could have ignored the wounded soldier entirely, leaving him to die on the road where he found him. By being his brother's keeper, however, the slave becomes an agent in helping Frazier advance the novel's thematic intent by reawakening the war-conditioned Inman to a valuable life-affirming lesson: the importance of living in harmony with other human beings and helping them when they are need. This same lesson Inman carries out himself when he subsequently elects to assist Sarah, the widow of a Confederate soldier, the mother of an infant child, and a victim of Federal thieves, whom he encounters later in the novel. Importantly, during his brief sojourn with Sarah, Inman gains a clear sense of what a marital relationship actually involves. Adopting the role of Sarah's surrogate husband, Inman becomes her sympathetic confidant and sounding board (listening to and communicating with her), sleeping companion (though not sexual partner), and protector—all of which anticipate the principal functions that he would be expected to perform in his eventual return home and subsequent marriage to Ada Monroe.

The final instance of cross-racial bonding in *Cold Mountain*, found in the chapter "exile and brute wandering," is not a part of either Inman's or Ada's direct experience. Instead, it concerns a former relationship between Odell, a young white man and a rich planter's son from south Georgia, and Lucinda, an octoroon house slave with whom he had fallen in love. Odell tells Inman, who sympathetically listens to his sorrowful story of illicit and thwarted love, that though he was married himself at the time when he fell in love with Lucinda, he "loved her far past the point of lunacy, for as everyone knew, just to have loved her at all was a mark of an unsound mind." Then when Odell informs his father, Lucinda's owner, of his love for the octoroon, his father immediately sends her away to the nearby farm of a non-slave-owning white man, who works Lucinda as a field hand. Despite this setback that the separation causes, Odell remains unwavering in his love for the slave woman and even undermines his father's intentions to keep him and the slave apart. In retaliation, Odell resorts to lies and deception so as to continue to see Lucinda. Consummating his love with her and eventually getting her pregnant strengthen the bond between the two. Yet in accordance with the statutes regarding interracial marriage that would have prohibited a legal union between Odell and an African-American slave, Odell's father adamantly refuses to sell Lucinda to his son, and in an effort to terminate the relationship between two lovers permanently, he sells Lucinda, apparently sending her to Mississippi. Physically separated from the woman he loves and their child that she may still be carrying, Odell repudiates his family, home, inheritance, and community. And he leaves his home never to return again. Furthermore, publicly dishonored through his attempts to transgress racial boundaries, Odell takes to the open road, becoming an itinerate peddler, whose main objective is to find Lucinda and to reunite with her. This reunion, as he apparently sees it, will alleviate his personal loneliness and sense of homelessness, restoring some semblance of wholeness to his shattered existence. While his efforts to accomplish this goal have proven futile, he remains steadfast in his quest to reinstate a bond with this woman of color, yet a bond that society considers illicit and forbidden. Even so, Frazier leaves us with the impression that Odell will not relinquish his search, that he will continue to look for Lucinda, indefinitely if need be. For Odell it seems that Lucinda has become an unattainable ideal. On the one hand to find and marry her would surely destroy any possibility for him ever to regain his former birthright and status and the good favor of his privileged family; but on the other, a union with Lucinda would initiate for him the possibility of renewing what he once possessed with his estranged family—a viable relationship and its benefits—in short, the values essential to creating the security associated with home. Though at this time, women of mixed racial heritage were victims of prejudice and racism and were often regarded as sexual objects, Lucinda, an octoroon, could have, if she so chose, passed for white; and she and Odell could conceivably have lived together as husband and wife, finding a new home where no one had knowledge of her racial composition.

While it appears that in his search for Lucinda, Odell will persist and as a consequence will continue to remain alienated and homeless, he does experience another opportunity for cross-racial bonding, but of another kind and on another level. This unanticipated bonding experience is precipitated by Odell's compassion for another human being in need. In his travels, he observes first hand many atrocities against slaves, the most thematically significant being a suffering and helpless slave woman who has been incarcerated in a cage of beanpoles, likely as a punishment for some undisclosed transgression, her exposed flesh and body parts becoming carrion to ravenous buzzards. In a scene somewhat paralleling that of the wounded Inman being assisted by the yellow slave who saves his life, Odell, overcome by pity for this slave woman, wondering perhaps if she might be his beloved Lucinda, desperately but unsuccessfully attempts to rescue her. Though he frees her from the cage and gives her water, Odell, during his indecisiveness about what to do for her next, vacillates; and the slave "vomited blood and died." Her death, which the well-intentioned Odell could probably not have prevented, even had he acted more quickly and decisively to give her further care, echoes his unsuccessful attempt to cross the color line, to break down the seemingly impenetrable barriers segregating races, and to marry Lucinda. In both cases, Odell's failure to act in a timely manner, the consequence perhaps of having been raised in a society that considered African-American slaves as chattel, may have in part prohibited him from carrying out his intentions successfully.

Odell's story of cross-racial love and compassion for the oppressed and afflicted seems to have significant impact on Inman. Odell's unwavering desire, persistence and determination to reunite with Lucinda, the woman he loves, teaches Inman that the power of love surpasses all fear and danger

and seems to provide an impetus for Inman to continue his own journey home to reconnect with Ada Monroe. Moreover, Odell's unrelenting quest to find Lucinda parallels Inman's own tireless dedication to returning home to Ada. And their respective quests encourage in both men the practice of other-directed sensitivity. The ultimate significance of the encounter between these two men, however, is that Odell's attempts to follow the dictates of his heart rather than to conform to the racial politics and social customs of the South's patriarchal culture seem to rekindle and reinforce in Inman, if only indirectly, his own difficult pursuit of recovering the values of home, humanity, harmony, love, and togetherness—all of which he seems to associate with his return to Cold Mountain.

Inman, of course, does eventually reach Cold Mountain and does reunite with Ada Monroe. And while the time that they spend together in their reunion is relatively short, Inman, as McCarron and Knoke state, does nevertheless "consummate the healing of his wounded spirit in a sexual liaison with Ada which will result in the birth of a daughter who will insure his legacy." Thus Inman's death, as McCarron and Knoke further note, is due "not to the meaningless violence of a politically motivated war hundreds of miles away, but [results from his desire] to protect his 'family' on the homefront." Functioning in this role as a man who has been restored to a way of thinking and acting consonant with being at home, of feeling one with his Appalachian culture and achieving a sense of unity with the woman he loves and plans to marry and with whom he will share his future, Inman is killed. He dies simply because he cannot, when the situation demands it, readily and quickly revert to the mindless savagery to which his war experience had previously conditioned him. Now with a renewed and strengthened sensitivity, which the bonding experiences of his journey home have rejuvenated in him, Inman cannot become again the person that he once was. With the sudden appearance of the home guard, even though Inman "recognized himself back in the familiar terrain of violence," he refrains from reacting instinctively and therefore violently, as he has often done earlier in his journey, hoping, Frazier tells us, "not to have to shoot" a young Confederate home guardsman who challenges him. As a consequence of his sensitivity, Inman lets down his guard, and the youthful guardsman fatally wounds him. It seems understandable that Inman, a new Inman, who has begun to be restored to a sense of comfort and security derived from being on home ground again, appropriately dreams, as he lies

Soldiers lined up for battle in the 2003 film version of Cold Mountain   Miramax/The Kobal Collection

dying in Ada's arms, "a bright dream of a home." His dream, which has an enticing and solacing serenity about it, suggestive of the charm of pastoral ambiance, conveys a sense of unified cohesion, of all things interfusing into what appears a perfect harmonic whole:

> It had coldwater rising spring rising out of rock, black dirt fields, old trees. In his dream the year seemed to be happening all at one time, all the seasons blending together. Apple trees hanging heavy with fruit but yet unaccountably blossoming, ice rimming the spring, okra plants blooming yellow and maroon, maple leaves red as October, corn tops tasseling, a stuffed chair pulled up to the glowing parlor hearth, pumpkins shining in the fields, laurels blooming on the hillsides, ditch banks full of orange jewelweed, white blossoms on dogwood, purple on redbud. Everything coming around at once. And there were white oaks, and a great number of crows, or at least the spirits of crows, dancing and singing in the upper limbs.

The vision that the dying Inman sees in his dream, then, becomes not one of divisiveness, disparity, and meaningless violence but of the reconciliation of opposites, coalescing into what seems a perfect harmonious whole. In describing how this tranquil moment might appear to a passing observer, Frazier clearly conveys that the scene affirms togetherness and exudes tranquility: "A scene of such quiet and peace that the observer on the ridge could avouch to it later in such a way as might lead those of glad temperaments to imagine some conceivable history where long decades of happy union stretched before the two on the ground."

While Inman's dream may be interpreted as his discovery of a "heaven on earth" (McCarron and Knoke, p. 383), of the kind he remembered that his Cherokee friend Swimmer once told him about, it also seems analogous to the kind of hope for togetherness, community, understanding, and ultimately racial accord that Dr. Martin Luther King proclaimed in his "I Have a Dream" speech. King closes his speech with a prophetic vision commemorating liberation, solidarity and unification, and equality, which he predicts will occur "when *all* of God's children, black men and white men, Jews and Gentiles, Protestants and Catholics, will be able to join hands" (my emphasis). Inman's dream too resonates with images connoting merger, the synthesis of disparate and contradictory elements, such as "all the seasons *blending* together [and] apple trees hanging heavy with fruit but yet unaccountably blossoming, ice rimming the spring . . . , [with] everything coming around at once."

Cold Mountain reverberates some of the same ideals of King's speech by featuring situations involving cross-racial bonding and the values of a peaceful loving home concomitant with it, both of which are predicated on the notions of the acceptance of differences and togetherness, that seem generally analogous to King's optimistic vision of the coalition of different races, religious denominations, and the like. After all, Inman has been exposed, directly or indirectly, and Ada, to a lesser extent, to situations that afforded them the opportunities to cross barriers, especially racial barriers, and to learn and/or participate first hand in such experiences. As we have seen, in addition to his bonding with the Cherokee Swimmer, Inman also attentively observed and has been affected by the practice of harmonic communal living among a racially diverse gypsy band; the sensitivity and other-directedness of the yellow slave who fed, sheltered, and assisted him to find a safe route home; and finally Odell, whose persistent dedication to finding and to reconnecting with an octoroon slave woman is followed, upon his failure to accomplish that goal, by his discovering another sense of bonding in his willing display of compassion for the "other" in his efforts to help a suffering slave woman. And Ada and her companion, Ruby, who seem to harbor no racial prejudice, bonded with, helped to renew, and otherwise assisted the homeless war refugees and their slaves from Tennessee, whose intent was to connect with relatives in South Carolina. Underlying all these events, one may discover the key to understanding the broader ramifications of *Cold Mountain.* In the context of King's "I Have a Dream" speech, the trope of cross-racial bonding, which occurs with some frequency in *Cold Mountain,* underscores one of the novel's central themes: the need for cohesive community, social stability, and togetherness, a need most frequently actuated in the willingness of the central characters and those who guide and assist them to accept, to embrace, and ultimately to emulate behavior that encourages human bonding and that correspondingly promotes the sense of the values conducive to harmonic home life.

Source: Ed Piacentino, "Searching for Home: Cross-Racial Bonding in Charles Frazier's *Cold Mountain*," in *Mississippi Quarterly*, Vol. 55, No. 1, Winter 2001–2002, pp. 97–116.

Sources

Beronä, David A., Review of *Cold Mountain*, in *Library Journal*, May 15, 1997, p. 100.

Frazier, Charles, *Cold Mountain*, Vintage Books, 1998.

————, "How the Author Found the Inspiration for His Civil War-Era Novel among the Secrets Buried in the Backwoods of the Smoky Mountains," in salon.com, http://www.salon.com/july97/colddiary970709.html (accessed May 28, 2006).

Gardner, James, "Common 'Cold?'" in *National Review*, December 31, 1997, pp. 54–55.

Heddendorf, David, "Closing the Distance to *Cold Mountain*," in *Southern Review*, Vol. 36, No. 1, Winter 2000, pp. 188–95.

Holt, Karen C., "Frazier's *Cold Mountain*," in *Explicator*, Vol. 63, No. 2, Winter 2005, pp. 118–21.

Miller, Laura, "Charles Frazier's Majestic Civil War Novel, *Cold Mountain*, Evokes a Harrowing Odyssey and a Lost Way of Life in the Blue Ridge Mountains," in salon.com, http://www.salon.com/july97/coldintro970709.html (accessed May 28, 2006).

Review of *Cold Mountain*, in *Publishers Weekly*, May 5, 1997, pp. 196–97.

Further Reading

Foote, Shelby, *The Civil War: A Narrative*, Vintage, 1986.
In this trilogy that was adapted by Foote and Ken Burns into a popular PBS mini-series, Foote chronicles not only the historical facts of the war, but brings a novelist's sensibility to his characterization of many of those who were affected by it, which makes them come alive on the page.

Knoke, Paul, and Bill McCarron, "Images of War and Peace: Parallelism and Antithesis in the Beginning and Ending of *Cold Mountain*," in *Mississippi Quarterly*, Vol. 52, Spring 1999, pp. 273–85.
In this article, the authors show how the novel's main themes are illustrated by the design of the opening and closing chapters. This design, they claim, contrasts images of war and peace and so establishes the main characters' struggle to move away from the first and toward the latter.

Ross, John, *The Smithsonian Guides to Natural America: Atlantic Coast & the Blue Ridge Mountains: Delaware, Maryland, District of Columbia, Virginia, North Carolina*, Random House, 1995.
Updating and expanding Bartram's guide through this region, Ross presents a comprehensive view of the natural landscape of the Blue Ridge Mountains.

Wagner, Margaret E., and Gary Gallagher, *The American Civil War: 365 Days*, Harry N. Abrams, 2006.
This book gathers together over five hundred photographs, lithographs, drawings, cartoons, posters, maps, and letters from the war, covering a wide range of subjects, including politics, battles, slavery, and the treatment of women and civilians during this period.

David Copperfield

Charles Dickens
1850

Charles Dickens's autobiographical novel, *David Copperfield*, published in 1850, was the author's favorite and has remained a favorite for generations of readers. In fact, Dickens is arguably England's most beloved, read, and critically acclaimed novelist. Noted scholar Harold Bloom, in his study of Dickens, praises the author's "astonishing universality, in which he nearly rivals Shakespeare and the Bible." This universality is one of the novel's celebrated qualities.

The novel is a *bildungsroman*, a story of growing up, that takes the protagonist from early childhood to early middle age. It is a story of the development of a writer, but it is also a portrait of Victorian England at mid-century with a host of characters designed to show various social features, for example, class structure, the penal system, the education available for poorer children, and the sundry forms of child labor and abuse. A novel of social protest, *David Copperfield* examines social problems while in certain particulars it relates the story of Dickens's own development into adulthood and into his life's work as a writer.

Author Biography

Many scholars have noted that Charles Dickens incorporated autobiographical details in *David Copperfield* (1850). George H. Ford, in his article on Dickens in the *Dictionary of Literary Biography*,

Charles Dickens AP Images

notes the similarities in manner between the author's father, John, and Mr. Micawber. His mother, Elizabeth Barrow, would become, according to Ford, the model for a character in another of her son's novels, *Nicholas Nickleby*.

Charles, one of eight children, was born in Portsmouth, England, on February 7, 1812. His early years were spent quite contentedly in small coastal towns in southern England. His life changed radically, however, when the family moved to London, where his father was soon sent to debtors' prison. As a result, twelve-year-old Charles was forced to go to work at a boot-blacking warehouse and to live on his own in the city slums. He fictionalized this harrowing and grim existence in his descriptions of David's similar experiences in London after his mother dies. Eventually Dickens's father regained some financial stability, but Dickens never completely lost the feeling that he had been abandoned and neglected by his parents. His experiences prompted him to develop a life-long concern for the welfare of children and of the poor.

Dickens excelled at school and graduated at the top of his class, but his parents never considered sending him to university. He read voraciously and gained work as an apprentice in a law office. In 1834, he was employed as a reporter for the

Morning Chronicle. These two jobs taught him a great deal about the legal profession, a subject that figures in many of his novels.

While he worked as a reported, Dickens began to write sketches of London scenes and of its picturesque citizens. His first, "A Dinner at Poplar Walk," was published by the *Monthly Magazine* in 1833 when he was twenty-one. He had several more published by the magazine and later collected them into two volumes, *Sketches by Boz* (1836), which publicized his pen name. The volumes sold well and earned favorable reviews. That same year he married Catherine Hogarth, with whom he had ten children. But his marriage was not a happy one. He fell in love with the eighteen-year-old actress Ellen Ternan. Dickens caused a public scandal when he set up his wife at a separate London residence and lived and traveled with Ellen Ternan.

His first book, *The Posthumous Papers of the Pickwick Club* (1837), later known as *The Pickwick Papers*, became an immediate success on both sides of the Atlantic. More celebrated novels followed, including *Oliver Twist* (1838) and *Nicholas Nickleby* (1839). For the next two decades, Dickens produced an astonishing number of novels, including *David Copperfield* (1850) and *Bleak House* (1853). The serialization of his novels, along with his work as an editor for *Household Words*, a successful weekly magazine, made Dickens a wealthy man. Along with his novels, he gained fame for public readings of his works, directed and acted in amateur plays, traveled widely in Canada, the United States, and Italy, and called for international copyright laws after many of his works were pirated.

On June 8, 1870, Charles Dickens died of a stroke, and his body was buried at Westminster Abbey in London. As of 2006, his novels have never been out of print.

Plot Summary

Chapters 1–3

After a digression about the predictions concerning his future at the time of his birth, David, the adult narrator of *David Copperfield*, notes that he was born at Blunderstone, in Suffolk, England, six months after his father had died. David's great-aunt, Betsey Trotwood, appeared at the Copperfield home just prior to David's birth, insisting that Clara, David's mother, would have a daughter and that Betsey would become her godmother. When

Clara remembered her husband's kindness to her, she became upset, which started her labor. When Betsey discovered that she had delivered a boy, she said nothing, immediately walked out and never returned, vanishing "like a discontented fairy."

One day Clara brings home Edward Murdstone, whom, David later discovers, has been courting her. David and his beloved nanny, Peggotty, immediately dislike him, and David becomes jealous of his mother's attentions toward him. Peggotty insists that Clara should not marry a man that her husband would not like, which brings Clara to tears. Murdstone brings David into town with him in an effort to try to win him over, but David, who admits that his observational powers are keen, finds the man "clever and cold" in his dealings with his business acquaintances and later, "stern and silent."

One evening, Peggotty asks David if he would like to go with her to stay with her brother and his family for two weeks at Yarmouth, a seaside village. David worries about who will take care of his mother while they are gone, but after Peggotty's assurances that she has found someone to help Clara, David agrees to go.

David and Peggotty arrive at the beached, black barge that is the Peggotty family home, and David "could not have been more charmed with the romantic idea of living in it." There he meets all of Peggotty's family: her brother Dan Peggotty; Mrs. Gummidge, the widow of Mr. Peggotty's partner; and Little Em'ly and Ham, her niece and nephew. The family warmly receives David, and he spends an idyllic two weeks playing on the beach with Em'ly, with whom he falls in love. He is quite reluctant to leave them at the end of his stay but looks forward to being reunited with his mother.

When David arrives home, he discovers that his mother has married Mr. Murdstone, which fills him with trepidation. He immediately sees a change in her as she approaches him timidly. David soon discovers that Mr. Murdstone has taken control of her as well as the household, and he is unable to look at either of them.

Chapters 4–11

David is despondent about the radical changes in his home. When Clara tries to comfort her son, who feels as if no one wants him in this new family, Murdstone insists that she be firm with him. When the two are alone, Murdstone tells David that if he had an obstinate horse or dog, he would "conquer" him by beating him into submission. David recognizes this as a threat to him.

Jane Murdstone, Edward's sister, soon arrives and proves herself to be as harsh and unfeeling as her brother. In an effort to protect him, Clara tells David to try to love his new father and to obey him. Miss Murdstone begins to take control of the house just as her brother has taken control of Clara and David. When Clara tries to protest, insisting that she has never previously had any trouble running the house, Murdstone rebukes her sternly, for "everybody was to be bent to his firmness." Clara gives in, resigning herself to her loss of control.

Murdstone and his sister determine that they will educate David, forcing him to complete difficult and long daily lessons. Yet, under their stern and unforgiving eyes, he fails miserably. Miss Murdstone admonishes Clara every time she tries to slip David answers. One day, after David is unable to make any progress on his lessons, Murdstone determines that a beating will encourage him to perform more satisfactorily. When, in an effort to stop him, David bites his hand, Murdstone beats him brutally as Clara and Peggotty cry outside the door. David is then locked in his room for five days, forbidden to see anyone except Miss Murdstone.

On the fifth night, Peggotty informs him that he will be sent away to Salem House, a boarding school near London the next day. As David travels by coach to school, crying inconsolably, Peggotty appears along the side of the road and climbs in. She hugs him and crams food and money into his pockets before leaving. David determines to be brave like Roderick Random or the captain in the Royal British Navy, heroes of his father's adventure novels. He discovers a note from his mother folded around some money among the things that Peggotty has given him.

After David shares some of Peggotty's cakes with the driver, Mr. Barkis, the later inquires whether she is married and asks David to inform her that "Barkis was willin,'" his way of proposing to her, which David eventually passes on to her in a letter. David and Barkis soon stop at an inn where a waiter swindles David out of his dinner and a good portion of his money as a tip. David continues with an empty stomach to school on a new coach full of passengers who have assumed that he has eaten the large meal all by himself and so make fun of him.

David's excitement over seeing London, the city where many of his literary heroes experienced their most exciting adventures, is soon overcome by a feeling of abandonment and uncertainty about his future. Eventually, Mr. Mell, one of the teachers

Media Adaptations

- There have been several television and film versions of the novel dating from 1911. One version, available as of 2006 on DVD, was a television series produced in 2000, starring Hugh Dancy as David.

- Several abridged and unabridged audio versions are also available. Books on Tape put out a popular, full-length cassette audio version in 1977.

from the school, picks him up and takes him to his mother's house for breakfast before continuing onto Salem House.

David arrives at school, deeming it, "the most forlorn and desolate place [he] had ever seen" and finds the boys, along with Mr. Creakle, the proprietor, all gone for the holidays. Mr. Mell has been instructed to tell David that he must wear a sign on his back that reads: *Take care of him. He bites.* The sign causes him great suffering during his early days at school, but he gains some support from Mr. Mell who speaks only a little but provides some company for him.

David meets the proprietor of Salem House, Mr. Creakle, a cruel man who beats the children for the slightest infraction or just to exercise his power. He then meets Tommy Traddles, a good-natured boy who, much to David's relief, makes a game of the sign on his back. David is brought before the most powerful boy at the school, James Steerforth, who declares the sign "'a jolly shame,'" sparking David's undying devotion to him. The older boy convinces David to give him all of his money, claiming that he can get what ever he wants from the outside and that he will take care of him.

On the first day of school, Mr. Creakle chides David about the sign and strikes him with his cane, as he does eventually with most of the other boys, except Steerforth, due to his family's social status and wealth. David is extremely flattered by the protection and attention Steerforth offers him, yet he fails to recognize that the older boy is taking

advantage of him, insisting that David hand over Peggotty's food baskets and spend half the night telling stories from his father's books. He also fails to recognize his friend's class prejudices when Steerforth tries to humiliate Mr. Mell and eventually engineers his dismissal. David's devotion to him is instead redoubled after Steerforth charms Mr. Peggotty and Ham during a visit.

David returns home during school break and finds that his mother has given birth to a boy. They all have a warm reunion since Murdstone and his sister have gone out for a visit that day. Yet, David notes that his mother looks much more tired and worn. The next morning, David apologizes to Murdstone for biting him, but while the man accepts it, it does not remove the "sinister expression in his face." David's days at home are filled with melancholy and discomfort under the Murdstones' domination. As a result of his ill treatment there, David is happy to return to school.

Two months later, he learns that his mother and brother have died and that he is now an orphan. David returns for the funerals where he is comforted by Peggotty. After Miss Murdstone fires Peggotty, she invites David to Yarmouth for a visit with her family. David is reunited with Little Em'ly who has grown more pretty and "both sly and shy at once," which captivates him "more than ever." He feels, however, a distance between them. After David and Em'ly attend Peggotty's wedding to Barkis, he swears his undying devotion to her and she allows him to kiss her.

When he returns home, he is neglected but is allowed to visit Peggotty occasionally. In an effort to get rid of him, Murdstone sends ten-year-old David to London to work in his wine bottling warehouse where he finds decayed floors, rats, and general "rottenness." David is despondent over his situation, especially since he now sees no hope of regaining his status in the world. His introduction to Mr. Micawber, however, with whom he is offered lodging, provides him with some relief from his gloom. Micawber takes him to his rather shabby home where he meets his wife and children. Although Mrs. Micawber complains that the creditors will not leave them alone, she and her husband have full confidence that their situation will soon change for the better.

While David is happy to live with the Micawbers, his feelings of abandonment and lack of support cause him much misery. He gradually, however, learns how to fend for himself in the city and to master the work at the warehouse, and his loneliness is eased by his growing attachment to the Micawbers. After his numerous attempts to raise money fail, Micawber is sent to debtors' prison where his family eventually joins him, leaving David, once again, on his own.

Chapters 12–15

After Micawber is discharged, he decides to move out of London in an effort to improve his fortunes. David, despondent over losing the only friends he has, determines to run away from the warehouse and find his aunt, Betsey Trotwood, who lives in Devon. On the road, his trunk and money are stolen, so he must walk the entire way. He sells his coat to earn some money for food but must sleep out in the open, sometimes near rough travelers, who threaten his physical safety. By the time he arrives in Devon, he is dirty and disheveled and thoroughly exhausted.

David pours his heart out to his aunt, telling her how he has suffered and been mistreated since his mother died and begging her to take him in. After listening to his story, Aunt Betsey asks Mr. Dick, an eccentric elderly man who has been living with her, what they should do with him. They decide at that point to give him a bath and put him to bed. The next morning, Aunt Betsey tells David that she has written to Mr. Murdstone, informing him that David is with her. Upon hearing the news, David's heart sinks.

Mr. Murdstone arrives with his sister on donkeys, which Aunt Betsey tries to shoo off, not knowing who they are. When they all eventually sit down to discuss David's situation, Aunt Betsey upbraids Murdstone for treating David's mother so badly. Murdstone ignores her and offers instead an extremely negative assessment of David's character, concluding that he "is the worst boy." When Aunt Betsey asks David if he wants to return with the Murdstones, he pleads with her to not let him go, reminding her of their ill-treatment of him and his mother. After consulting with Mr. Dick, Aunt Betsey tells Murdstone that she will keep David, insisting that she does not believe a word of what he has said about the boy and rebuking him for breaking Clara's heart. After she quickly dismisses the man and his sister, David thanks her and Mr. Dick heartily. Aunt Betsey determines that she will call David, Trotwood Copperfield.

David, and Mr. Dick, who have become good friends, often fly a kite together. Aunt Betsey, who now calls him Trot, decides to send David to school in nearby Canterbury, which pleases him. They

stop first at the home of Mr. Wickfield, Aunt Betsey's friend and lawyer, who advises them about the best schools in the area. There, David meets Uriah Heep, a strange young man with a "cadaverous face" who works as a clerk for Mr. Wickfield, and Wickfield's lovely daughter, Agnes. Wickfield chooses a school and suggests that David stay with him until he can find other lodgings. Aunt Betsey leaves him at the Wickfields, confident that he is in good hands. After she leaves, David offers his hand to Uriah but finds it so clammy and ghostly that he is repelled by it.

Chapters 16–18

David begins at the Canterbury school, which is run by Dr. Strong, although it takes him a while to adjust since he has been out for so long. David is happy to stay with the Wickfields, especially since he is quite close with Agnes, whom he trusts and respects. Uriah tells David that he is studying law and insists, "I'm a very umble person," as is, he claims, his mother.

David adapts well to Dr. Strong's school, which he finds is an excellent one, and to life at the Wickfields. One evening a party is given at the Strongs for the doctor's birthday and for Jack Maldon, who is leaving for India. Annie, Dr. Strong's young wife, appears nervous and pale during the evening, and after Jack leaves, she collapses. The guests assume that she was overcome by saying goodbye to her childhood friend.

During a visit, Mr. Dick talks to David about a mysterious man whom he has seen lurking around Aunt Betsey's house, frightening her. He has seen her give money to the man and wonders why. David goes to Uriah's home for tea, not wanting him to think that he is too proud, where he meets Uriah's mother, who has a striking similarity to her son in appearance and mannerisms. She also continually calls attention to their humbleness. During the evening, David sees Mr. Micawber pass by and invites him in but is eager for his friend to keep private many details of his past life. They soon leave to find Mrs. Micawber, who greets David warmly. David is surprised by a letter the next morning from Micawber, noting their destitute situation and the probability that they will never see each other again.

David recalls incidents during his school years, including his falling in love with first a girl and then an older woman, and fistfights with a local butcher. The love affairs turn out badly for him, but he is eventually able to best the butcher, and he is proud that he has become the top boy at school.

Chapters 19–30

David is sorry to leave his school since he feels distinguished there. He tells Agnes how important she has become to him, and she informs David of her concerns about her father's welfare. Observing a tension between Annie and Mr. Wickfield, David becomes bothered by Agnes's friendship with Annie. On a trip to London, David runs into Steerforth, who has been attending school at Oxford, and accompanies him home to meet his mother and her companion, Rosa Dartle. He and Steerforth make plans to meet later at Yarmouth, where they find Em'ly engaged to Ham. David notices that Em'ly sits far away from Ham during the evening. After they leave, Steerforth criticizes Ham to David, which shocks him, but David maintains his faith in his friend.

When David finds Steerforth brooding one night in front of the fire, the latter declares, "you come upon me . . . like a reproachful ghost." Steerforth's mood soon passes and he admits that he sometimes suffers from depression. Later David runs into Ham, Em'ily, and a friend of hers who has been disgraced and has come for help. After the friend leaves, Em'ly breaks down, crying, "I am not as good a girl as I ought to be," and asks Ham and her aunt to help her be more thankful for what she has.

David tells his aunt that he has decided to make law his profession, which pleases her. As they are walking in town, David sees a shabbily dressed man watching them. Aunt Betsey insists that she must talk to him alone and refuses to explain who he is. David soon takes a position with Spenlow and Jorkins, and his aunt provides him with lodgings. He runs into Steerforth in the city and the two go out and get drunk. Agnes spots them and later warns David about Steerforth's character and influence. David contradicts her but listens to her judgment, which he values highly. Agnes expresses her fears that her father is in financial trouble and that Uriah has made himself indispensable to him. She concludes that Uriah's goal is to use her father to gain power and position and blames herself for putting her father in this dire position. She persuades David not to confront Uriah since she is not sure of her judgment of him and she does not want any more trouble for her father.

David sees Traddles at a dinner party and the two get reacquainted. Uriah tells David that Mr. Wickfield is facing disgrace and that Uriah is trying to help him. He also admits that he is in love with Agnes and hopes to marry her, which disgusts David. When Uriah subtly warns David not to divulge his secret or he will cause problems for her father, David determines that he has no choice but to comply.

David is invited to Mr. Spenlow's home where he meets his daughter Dora, with whom he immediately falls in love. He discovers that Dora's guardian is Miss Murdstone, who informs David that she will not bring up the past. David visits Traddles who is studying for the bar and trying to earn enough money to get married. At his rather shabby lodgings, he runs into the Micawbers. During a dinner party David gives for Traddles and the Micawbers, Steerforth's servant appears looking for his master. Later the Micawbers assure David that they are doing well financially, but David discovers that they have used Traddles' name to obtain credit.

After David's guests leave, Steerforth appears and tells David that he has been to Yarmouth and that Mr. Barkis is near death. Steerforth convinces him to spend a day with him at his mother's home before he goes to see Peggotty. At the end of the evening, he finds a letter Micawber has left behind, informing David that he does not have the money to repay Traddles. The next day, after David arrives at Mrs. Steerforth's home, Miss Dartle watches him and Steerforth intensely. She asks David why he has kept Steerforth away for so long, but David denies having spent any time with him lately and insists that he does not know where he has been. Later, Steerforth gets David to swear that he will always think the best of Steerforth.

Chapters 31–42

When David arrives at Peggotty's, he greets Em'ly, who appears quite unsettled and cannot look at him. He and Peggotty go up to Barkis's room and stay with him until he dies. David later discovers that Barkis has left Peggotty and her brother a large inheritance. At Mr. Peggotty's, David discovers that Em'ly has run away with Steerforth, which has broken Ham's heart. She left a note, expressing her hope that Steerforth will marry her and so make her a lady, and her deep love for her uncle. Mr. Peggotty insists, "I'm going to seek her. That's my dooty evermore," and bring her back home. David blames himself and curses Steerforth.

David accompanies Mr. Peggotty to Mrs. Steerforth's home. Mrs. Steerforth insists that her son cannot marry Em'ly since she is "far below him . . . uneducated and ignorant." Later, Miss Dartle explodes with rage against David, blaming him for

Steerforth's relationship with Em'ly and calling the Peggottys a "depraved worthless set." After they leave, Mr. Peggotty reaffirms his commitment to finding Em'ly and asks David to tell her that he forgives her, if anything should happen to him.

David turns to Dora for relief from this troubled situation, and the two soon become engaged. He learns from Traddles that Mr. Micawber has changed his name to Mortimer to avoid his creditors and that all of his possessions, along with Traddles's, have been taken by the authorities. Later, Aunt Betsey, along with Mr. Dick, appears at David's lodgings with all of her things, explaining that she is financially ruined.

David is quite depressed because he thinks that his turn in fortunes will prevent him from buying Dora presents. He and his aunt visit the Wickfields where Agnes tells them that Uriah and her father are now partners and that he and his mother have moved in with them. She fears the control that Uriah has over her father and how much he has changed under it. David later accepts a position as secretary to Dr. Strong and Traddles finds transcription work for Mr. Dick. Later, David runs into Mr. Micawber, who informs him that he is now working for Uriah.

David tries to explain his financial situation to Dora, but she refuses to listen to him. She claims that she still loves him, but whenever David talks of how they will have to economize, she becomes frightened and tells him to go away. Mr. Spenlow discovers the engagement and tries to break it off, but that evening he is killed in a carriage accident. Overcome by grief, Dora refuses to see David.

Mrs. Heep hovers over David and Agnes all evening, preventing them from talking about her father. After Uriah admits later that he was afraid that David was his rival, David insists that Agnes is too far above him for him to consider marrying her. When Uriah declares his intentions in front of Mr. Wickfield, the latter becomes hysterical, blaming himself for his daughter's predicament. Later, Agnes reassures David that she will never marry Uriah.

The next day David runs into Mr. Peggotty, who has been traveling around Europe looking for Em'ly. The only contact he has had are a few letters from her, which tell him how much she loves him. Recognizing Dora's changed financial position, her aunts encourage David to see her but to proceed slowly. That evening, David finds Dr. Strong despondent in his study after Uriah has told him that Annie has feelings for Mr. Maldon. Uriah tricks Mr. Wickfield and

David into admitting that they had suspected these feelings. Dr. Strong blames himself for marrying Annie when she was so young. When they are alone, David strikes Uriah for what he has done to Dr. Strong, and Uriah makes him feel guilty for doing so. David receives a letter from Mrs. Micawber complaining that her husband has changed while working for Uriah, becoming morose, severe, and estranged from his children.

Chapters 43–52

David, now twenty-one, marries Dora and reports parliamentary debates and writes stories for a local newspaper. Mr. Dick discovers what Dr. Strong has been told about Annie and brings the two together to talk. Annie admits that she had feelings for Maldon in the past but realized that they were not right for each other and that she is completely devoted to her husband.

A year later, Steerforth's servant tells David that he had been with his master and Em'ly in different countries in Europe. After Steerforth grew restless and suggested that she marry his servant, she became hysterical and left the house. No one knows what has happened to her. David passes this information on to Mr. Peggotty. That evening, he finds the strange man who had been following his aunt in her house. After the man leaves, Aunt Betsey admits that he is her husband and that she has been giving him money since they separated because he has been destitute.

Six months later, David realizes that he will never be able to expand Dora's mind and resigns himself to a less than happy marriage. In the meantime, Dora's health has declined, and David has to carry her up and down the stairs. Em'ly's friend Martha contacts David and Mr. Peggotty and asks them to meet her at her home. When David arrives, he witnesses Miss Dartle's vicious, verbal attack on Em'ly before Mr. Peggotty rescues her. Later, Em'ly tells her uncle how she made her way back to London and Martha's home. Mr. Peggotty decides to take her and Mrs. Gummidge to Australia where Em'ly can start a new life.

Micawber arranges a meeting with Traddles, Aunt Betsey, Mr. Dick, and David at the Wickfields, where he insists that he will expose Uriah as a villain and a fraud. With great theatrics, Micawber confronts Uriah there with evidence of the latter's illegal activities during his partnership with Mr. Wickfield, including those that caused Aunt Betsey's financial ruin. Uriah responds violently to the accusations, immediately dropping his "umble" persona, but he calms down when Traddles threatens to call the authorities. After the confrontation, Mr. Micawber insists, "The cloud is past from my mind," and he feels restored to his old self again. Aunt Betsey suggests that he emigrate to Australia with Mr. Peggotty, which he agrees to do.

Chapters 53–64

As Dora's health worsens, she tells David that he would have grown tired of "his child-wife," and so "it is better as it is." One evening soon after, Jip, Dora's beloved dog, dies at David's feet at the same time that Dora dies upstairs. Traddles has been able to recover Aunt Betsey's and Mr. Wickfield's money, and Uriah and his mother have disappeared. Mr. Peggotty and Aunt Betsey, whose husband has recently died, provide Mr. Micawber with funds to pay off his debts and to relocate to Australia.

David leaves for Yarmouth to see Ham and finds that a storm on the channel has wrecked a ship from Spain. David sees a lone man hanging on the mast that looks like Steerforth. Ham goes out to rescue him, but they both drown. When David goes to Mrs. Steerforth's to tell her that her son has died, the news strikes her dumb. Miss Dartle then launches invectives at her, insisting that she corrupted him through her "pampering of his pride and passion." She admits that she loved him and that he loved her and curses David, declaring, "It was in an evil hour that you ever came here!"

The Micawbers, Mr. Peggotty, Em'ly, and her friend Martha leave for Australia, and David leaves for Switzerland, where he will spend the next few years mourning his losses and thinking about his future. At the end of this time, he realizes that he loves Agnes. After he returns, he finds that Traddles has become a successful lawyer and is happily married and that Peggotty lives with Aunt Betsey and Mr. Dick in Dover. After some misunderstandings, David and Agnes profess their love for each other and are soon married. Traddles discovers that Uriah is in prison for bank robbery and that Mr. Creakle is the warden. When he and David visit the prison, Mr. Creakle shows off Uriah as his model prisoner. Ten years later, as David and Agnes sit in front of the fire with their children, Mr. Peggotty arrives and tells them that he and his family have created successful lives for themselves in Australia, as has Mr. Micawber who has become a magistrate. The novel closes with David expressing his great love for Agnes.

Characters

Richard Babley
See Mr. Dick

Mr. Barkis
Mr. Barkis, whom David meets when he drives David to his boarding school, woos Peggotty and later marries her. He is a man of few words and is quite miserly. But Peggotty has a happy life with him, and he leaves her a large inheritance after he dies. He serves mainly as a plot device, providing some comic relief in his courtship of Peggotty.

Clara Copperfield
David's mother, Clara Copperfield, is loving but weak, definitely not strong enough to protect David from the cruelty of Murdstone and his sister. Clara appears quite "timid and sad" as she approaches David's birth after her husband dies, "very doubtful of ever coming alive out of the trial that was before her." She defers to everyone, including Peggotty, whom she often treats more like a mother than a servant.

Occasionally Clara shows some strength of character as when she defends her husband against Aunt Betsey's criticisms. Yet, her fear of losing Murdstone's love and protection weakens her to the point where she cannot protect her son. At one point, she tries to insist to Miss Murdstone that she is capable of running her own household, but she crumbles when Murdstone chastises her and thus relinquishes all control to him and his sister. She tries to make life easier for David by imploring him to love his new father and to obey him, and she tries to help David surreptitiously by whispering answers to his lessons. Yet she is not strong enough to intervene when Murdstone beats David or sends him off to school. Murdstone breaks her down to the point where she can only cover her ears to David's screams as Murdstone beats him, and she is afraid to show any kindness toward David for fear of offending her husband and so getting a lecture afterwards. At the end of her life, "a hard word was like a blow to her," and she ultimately could not survive under her husband's domination.

David Copperfield
David, the narrator of the novel, chronicles his movement from innocence to experience as he traces his life from birth to middle age. As a youth, he is trusting, idealistic, and devoted to friends and family. He continually defends those he loves against others' attacks, even when it would be

expedient to do otherwise, as when Aunt Betsey criticizes Peggotty, when he needs to please his aunt so she will let him stay with her.

He is also a romantic, envisioning himself as a hero, much like those he has read about in his father's adventure novels; he falls in love with every pretty girl he meets, insisting that he will kill himself if his love is not requited. In his innocence, he often trusts others too much. His forgiving nature allows him to accept his mother's abandonment of him after her marriage to Murdstone. When he matures, he recognizes that he has been blind to the true character of others, such as Steerforth, and to the workings of his own heart with regard to his choice of Dora for a bride. After Dora's death, he realizes that Agnes is a more appropriate companion for him.

Mr. Creakle

The cruel proprietor of Salem House, Mr. Creakle, frightens David during his time there. When he is an adult, David discovers that Creakle has become a prison warden, who self-confidently extols the virtues of the prison system.

Rosa Dartle

Rosa Dartle is a distant relative of Steerforth. Her "thinness seemed to be the effect of some wasting fire within her, which found a vent in her gaunt eyes." Rosa lives with Mrs. Steerforth as her companion. Steerforth gave her the scar on her lip when he was young during a moment of rage when he threw a hammer at her. David soon discovers that "she never said anything she wanted to say, outright; but hinted it, and made a great deal more of it by this practice." She cleverly keeps saying how ignorant she is, which tends to disarm others to the point where they give her the information she wants, often against their will. Steerforth insists that she is "dangerous," most likely due to her desire for power and her ability to get information. She shows her bigotry when she calls the Peggottys "a depraved worthless set" and insists that Em'ly should be whipped for seducing Steerforth. Her love for him becomes evident in her tirades against Em'ly and Mrs. Steerforth at the end of the book.

Mr. Dick

Aunt Betsey claims that Mr. Dick, an eccentric man who lives with her, is a "distant connexion" or relative of hers. Mr. Dick's "vacant manner, his submission to [his] aunt, and his childish delight when she praised him" causes David to "suspect him of being a little mad." David also sees evidence of mental problems in the fact that as Mr. Dick works on his autobiography he has difficulty keeping King Charles I from creeping into it. Mr. Dick later admits to David that he considers himself to have a simple mind. Aunt Betsey explains that "he has been ill-used" due to others' having bad opinions of him.

Aunt Betsey claims that he is not mad as some people think and is "the most friendly and amenable creature in existence," who gives wonderful advice. He has maintained a childhood innocence that allows him to thoroughly enjoy other people. Mr. Dick reveals his compassion and cleverness when he acknowledges that "a simpleton, a weak-minded person" like himself "may do what wonderful people may not do" because he will not be blamed for his actions and thus is able to bring Dr. Strong and Annie together.

Little Em'ly

David falls in love with Little Em'ly, Peggotty's niece, when they play together as children. She is a shy child but develops a desire to move up in class and become a lady. She is aware of the class differences between her and David, even as a young girl. She is good natured and affectionate with her family, but her desire to move up in class, coupled with her feelings for Steerforth, cause her to abandon them and break her engagement to Ham. After moving to Australia with her uncle, she devotes her life to helping others.

Mrs. Gummidge

Taken in by Mr. Peggotty after her husband, his partner, dies, Mrs. Gummidge has "rather a fretful disposition," especially when she thinks of her drowned husband. She often feels sorry for herself, as evidenced by her insistence that "everythink goes contrairy with me." She acknowledges that she irritates others because she feels more emotions and shows them. Mrs. Gummidge takes charge of the household, showing her gratefulness and compassion.

Uriah Heep

Conniving and deferential, Uriah Heep is fifteen when David first meets him. His goal is to gain power in a world that has denied him any, due to his position in the lower class.

Jack Maldon

Annie Strong's cousin, shallow, handsome, and confident Jack Maldon, serves as a plot device to complicate the Strongs' marriage, which allows Uriah an opportunity to meddle in others' affairs. His relationship with Annie also emphasizes the theme of loyalty.

Mr. Mell

Mr. Mell, David's instructor at Salem House, shows his affection for his mother who lives in a poorhouse and his humanity when he tries to deflect Creakle's cruelty. Mell also appears in the novel to provide Steerforth with an opportunity to reveal his true nature.

Mrs. Micawber

Fiercely loyal and supportive of her husband, Mrs. Micawber encourages Mr. Micawber through all of his misfortunes by continually extolling his virtues. Readers come to know her by her often repeated assertion, "I will never desert Mr. Micawber," which illustrates this loyalty. She has a constant belief that her husband's difficulties are only temporary, blaming his creditors for not giving him time to come up with payments. Like her husband, she is loquacious as well as kindhearted, evidenced by her treatment of David when he lives with them while working in the warehouse.

Wilkins Micawber

Ambitions and proud, Mr. Micawber unfortunately has no knack for making money. Yet he never lets this fact trouble him for long. Although he is often forced to dress shabbily, he always acts above his class, displaying genteel manners, confident that he will indeed rise above his often destitute situation. His home is as shabby as he is, but as David notes, it "like himself, made all the show it could."

He is good natured and amiable, always ready to give advice to help improve others' conditions, which he is confident he can do. He is even more loquacious than his wife, often trying the patience of his friends as they wait for him to get to his point, to which he never takes a direct route. Like his wife, he is generous and elastic, taking his misfortunes in stride, assured that his success will appear with the next opportunity. His debts often fill him with the profoundest misery to the point where he contemplates suicide, but an hour later, he is in high spirits again. Under the influence of Uriah, he turns sullen and distant, but he is able to regain his focus and, due to his careful planning, to expose Uriah's fraudulent activities. Mr. Micawber finally enjoys success when he is made a magistrate in Australia.

Edward Murdstone

After cruel and tyrannical Edward Murdstone marries David's mother, he rules the household autocratically. He forces Clara to distance herself from her son, which eventually destroys her, and abuses David and then sends him away to fend for himself.

Jane Murdstone

Edward Murdstone's sister Jane is "a gloomy-looking lady" who comes to live with David and his mother soon after the wedding. She carries metal boxes with her, which become a symbol of her metallic personality. As rigid as her brother, she takes control of the household after she arrives, manipulating Clara while insisting that she is helping her. David finds her arrogant with a "devil's humour" like that of her brother. Her cruelty toward David and his mother has more of an Evangelical bent than her brother's, as she proves when she determines everyone in church to be "miserable sinners," including David.

Clara Peggotty

David's nanny, called Peggotty, is devoted to him and to Mrs. Copperfield and becomes a surrogate mother to both of them. She is stern but loving as she raises David, frowning at him if he does not pay attention to the Sunday sermon, but listening night after night to him read his book on crocodiles. Before Murdstone and his sister arrive, David admits that he and his mother were "both a little afraid" of her and so "submitted [themselves] in most things to her direction," yet as soon as she feels that she has been short with them, she showers them with hugs and kisses. She often speaks her mind, as when she tries to persuade Clara not to marry Murdstone, and continually tries to find a way to counteract or soften Murdstone's decrees and harsh treatment of David by slipping him food or taking him on trips to see her family. Her kindheartedness prompts her to try to ease his and his mother's suffering.

Her loyalty is evident when she refuses to leave Clara even in the face of the Murdstones' tyranny and condescension. After Clara dies, she swears her devotion to David and treats him like a son. During his most difficult times, Peggotty reassures David that he will always be welcome in her home and that she will always try to help him in any way she can.

Dan Peggotty

Peggotty's brother Dan is a kind, generous, good-natured sailor who is devoted to his family. He tells David when he first meets him, "you'll find us rough, sir, but you'll find us ready." He has shown his readiness to take on responsibility when, even though he was quite poor, he took in and adopted his nephew Ham and his niece Little Em'ly, both orphans, as well as Mrs. Gummidge, the wife of a sailor who drowned. Peggotty insists he is "as good as gold and as true as steel." He shows infinite patience with and tender consideration for Mrs. Gummidge; when she gets upset and complains about her lot in life, he tries to make her as comfortable as possible and explains, "she's been thinking of the old'un," referring to her drowned husband. He proves his loyalty to his family when he devotes himself to finding Em'ly and then leaves his native England to relocate to Australia with her so that she can start a new life.

Ham Peggotty

Peggotty's nephew, Ham, is kindhearted and selfless, with "a simpering boy's face and curly light hair that gave him quite a sheepish look." Ham is a skilled boat-builder who has devoted himself to Em'ly. He is devastated when she runs off with Steerforth but never condemns her for it. He begs David to tell her that he is fine in order to ease her mind and blames himself for talking her into marriage. His selflessness and courage are also evident when he drowns trying to save Steerforth.

Dora Spenlow

David's first wife, Dora Spenlow, is spoiled, petulant, and immature when he first meets her. When they are engaged, thinking about running a household gives her a headache. After they marry, David becomes annoyed when others treat her like a child; he refuses at first to admit that she has never grown up. Neither is a skilled housekeeper, and servants and shopkeepers continually take advantage of them. By the end of her life, all recognize Dora's goodheartness. She shows some maturity and insight before she dies, understanding that David would have grown to regret their marriage and noting that she was too young and foolish for him to marry her.

James Steerforth

Charming and charismatic James Steerforth is David's best friend until he runs off with Em'ly. Steerforth possesses "an inborn power of attraction" and "carried a spell with him to which it was a natural weakness to yield, and which not many persons could withstand." David learns too late about the shallow, selfish nature of his friend.

Mrs. Steerforth

Mrs. Steerforth considers her son James to be her entire life. She is a proud woman who is concerned only about the welfare of her son, but that welfare is defined along class lines. When Mr. Peggotty begs her to support his marriage to Em'ly, she claims, "Such a marriage would irretrievably blight my son's career and ruin his prospects." Miss Dartle blames her for turning her son into a shallow self-centered man.

Annie Strong

Annie Strong takes good care of her husband and shows great affection toward him. Even though her mother persuaded her to marry him, Annie develops a strong sense of respect and love for him, which prevents her from being disloyal.

Dr. Strong

Kindhearted, amiable Dr. Strong is blind to his wife's feelings for her cousin Maldon. David claims that he is "the kindest of men; with a simple faith in him that might have touched the stone hearts of the very urns upon the wall." He displays a fatherly attitude toward his wife and never doubts her fidelity.

Tommy Traddles

A good school friend of David, Traddles shows his resilience and loyalty, often taking beatings for refusing to tell on his schoolmates. For this reason, David calls him, "the merriest and most miserable of all the boys." He shows his sense of justice when he comes to Mr. Mell's defense after Steerforth tries to humiliate him. As an adult, Traddles becomes "a sober, steady-looking young man of retiring manners," shy, still good natured and generous, as he reveals when he lends money to Micawber. His success as a lawyer enables him to reclaim the money Uriah steals from Aunt Betsey and Mr. Wickfield.

Betsey Trotwood

David's great-aunt on his father's side, Betsey Trotwood, is tough but also kind and generous. David finds her to be a "formidable personage," who was "mortally affronted by [his father's] marriage on the ground that [[his] mother was 'a wax doll,'" even though she had never met Clara. She takes charge of every situation, as when she arrives the day David is born, determines that Clara will have a girl, and demands that the child be called Betsey Trotwood Copperfield. Her distrust of human nature, due in part to a failed marriage, prompts her to insist that she will make sure that the child is brought up correctly, "well guarded from reposing any foolish confidences where they are not deserved." This distrust also causes her to take in young women as servants, "expressly to educate in a renouncement of mankind."

When he meets her, David notes that "there was an inflexibility in her face, in her voice, in her gait and carriage . . . but her features were rather handsome . . . though unbending and austere." Yet she respects a show of strength as when David stands up to her, defending Peggotty after Aunt Betsey criticizes his nanny. Her compassion is apparent in the fact that she saved Mr. Dick from an asylum and David from a life of abuse with Mr. Murdstone, eventually becoming a surrogate mother to him. She devotes herself to those she thinks worthy, such as Mr. Dick and David, and does not suffer fools like Uriah.

Agnes Wickfield

Agnes Wickfield becomes David's most trusted confidant and later his wife. She is completely devoted to her father, willing to sacrifice her own happiness for her father's sake. She offers sound advice and comfort to David, even though it encourages him to marry another woman when she is in love with him. She also shows strength of character when she disagrees with him concerning his opinion of Steerforth.

Mr. Wickfield

Mr. Wickfield is Agnes's father and a friend and lawyer to Aunt Betsey. He is devastated when his wife dies and so lets his daughter take care of him. He is not strong enough to stand up to Uriah and thus allows the man to take control of his affairs, which almost destroys him.

Themes

Class Consciousness

Characters in the novel represent different classes and illustrate the wide gulf between the classes in Victorian England. The most damaging effect from an awareness of the separation between the lower and middle classes occurs when Em'ly runs off with Steerforth. Em'ly is quite aware of the difference between her class and David's when he first meets her. When David notes that both of them are orphans, she calls his attention to one important difference: she tells him, "your father was a gentleman and your mother is a lady; and my father was a fisherman and my mother was a fisherman's daughter." By this statement, Em'ly means

that her antecedents worked hard to maintain a minimal standard of living, while David's parents had some measure of inherited wealth. Even at such a young age, Em'ly understands how money can radically affect one's life. Later, when she hopes to become a lady by marrying Steerforth, she is forced to realize how entrenched economically based prejudices can be. Mrs. Steerforth blames her for the situation, insisting that any association with Em'ly would "ruin his prospects."

David is also aware of class divisions and is distressed when he faces the possibility that he will never regain entry into the middle class. When he goes to work in the warehouse with his new associates there, he reveals "the secret agony of [his] soul, claiming, "[M]y hopes of growing up to be a learned and distinguished man [were] crushed in my bosom," and he is left broken-hearted. He does not associate with the other boys at the warehouse, thinking them beneath him. When David's fortunes change, he enjoys his status as a gentleman and is desperate to keep people from knowing how poor he had once been.

David's attitudes toward the lower class, however, are much different from the Steerforths'. Peggotty becomes his surrogate mother and the other members of her family his good friends. He even falls in love for a time with Little Em'ly, never considering that a match with her would be unacceptable. Yet he does maintain and reinforce class divisions when he never corrects Peggotty and her family when they refer to him as "Master Davy." Dickens appears to have mixed feelings about class consciousness as he has David maintain some distance from the Peggottys, but he portrays this family with an honesty and goodness of nature that is lacking in many upper-class characters. His attitude illustrates the progressive yet cautious attitude that was emerging in the more liberal circles of Victorian England: an effort to narrow the gap between the classes, but not to close it entirely.

Criticism of Social Institutions

The novel attacks social institutions Dickens viewed as unjust and cruel. The first is the boarding school system that permitted sadistic men, like Creakle, to be in charge. No one checks his power or tries to stop his cruelty; as a result, the children under his care are tormented physically and emotionally. Dickens also highlights the abusive situation that can result in the home where the man holds all power over the household, and no law or agency can be exerted on behalf of a wife or child. No one rebukes Murdstone for his tyranny over David and

Topics For Further Study

- The introduction to this chapter notes the universality of the novel. Write a poem or short story in a modern setting about an element of the novel that you find universal.

- Read Dickens's *Great Expectations* and compare its coming-of-age theme to that of *David Copperfield*. Does Pip in the first novel face the same difficulties as David? What accounts for the differences? Make up a chart comparing and contrasting the two in regards to this theme.

- Write a report on the treatment of children during the Victorian age. In your research, consider the following questions: How were orphans treated? How realistic was David's description of his harsh treatment at school? Were there any laws protecting children who were part of the labor force? Choose one of these topics to focus on for your report.

- Read a biography of Dickens and find specific parallels to incidents and people in David's life. Prepare a PowerPoint presentation of your findings.

---

his savage beating of him. Even after David's mother dies, Murdstone has complete control over the boy until Aunt Betsey intervenes. There are also no child labor laws to make illegal the employment of a ten-year-old boy for long hours of work in a warehouse.

The prison system also comes under attack in the novel when David and Traddles accept an invitation from Mr. Creakle, who has become a magistrate, to see the successful results of "the only true system of prison discipline; the only unchallengeable way of making sincere and lasting converts and penitents . . . solitary confinement." David and Traddles find the system not so solitary, since they observe the prisoners communicating with each other. They also discover its ineffectiveness when they meet Creakle's "Model Prisoner," whom he calls "Number Twenty Seven," who turns out to be Uriah Heep. After going through the prison's system of discipline, Uriah remains still his "umble" self and swears that he has been rehabilitated and would not relapse if he were released. David sees through this façade, and so recognizes the failure of the system, when the conniving Uriah mentions David's striking him, which gains him sympathy from the prison officials. Though this scene may come across as humorous, the fact is that the penal system was subjective, biased, easily manipulated. It may be fair to say it operated much of the time on the assumption that poverty is proof of corruption.

Dickens exposes inequities but offers no solutions. The tranquil domestic scene at the end of the novel is not disturbed by the memory of what David has suffered from social injustices. Yet Dickens's realistic portrayal of them calls readers' attention to the real damage they caused in Victorian England.

Style

Chapter Design

David Copperfield was serialized in monthly, one-shilling installments from May 1849 to November 1850. Dickens knew that serialization affected his audience's reading experience. He carefully constructed these installments so that each part relates to other parts and constitutes a complete unit in itself. He was concerned not only with *David Copperfield*'s installment arrangement, but also with the design of each installment's chapters, the only narrative units over which he had full control.

Serial publication caused Victorian readers to pause between issues. Read aloud by fathers to their families, these installments provided home entertainment much like an ongoing television series does in the twenty-first century. Chapters in *David Copperfield* mark new beginnings or hindrances for David as they move the plot ahead, thus tantalizing readers. The beginning and ending of chapters become narrative stress points, crucial in emphasizing the novel's thematic messages as well as providing a cliff-hanging effect to motivate readers to buy the next installment. Dickens's use of chapter titles marks this natural stress point and presents readers with important details that foreshadow David's future experiences and suggest a way to understand them.

Often chapter titles mark important stages in David's life, such as in chapter 3, "I Have a Change," announcing his trip to Yarmouth where he meets the Peggottys who will have a crucial effect on his development. The end of chapter 2 nicely sets up this change as it shows David's apprehension over leaving his mother and going off with Peggotty to a new place. Others, such as chapter 4, not only note a new development in David's life, but also suggest the effect that it will have on him. The title announces, "I Fall Into Disgrace," announcing the upcoming change in his household as well as the change in his relationship with his mother and the end of his idyllic childhood. Dickens constructs the end of the previous chapter to anticipate this upcoming change when he ends it with David's being frightened by Murdstone's ferocious dog. Dickens's chapter construction was affected by artistic issues and finances; the author created a plot that could handle these divisions, and he knew he would make more money on affordable installments than on attempting to market the novel in one or more, much more costly volumes.

Bildungsroman

David Copperfield is a bildungsroman, a novel that tells the story of maturation, of growing up. This novel presents itself as an autobiography with the mature David Copperfield writing his life story beginning with what he has been told about his birth. He wonders in the first lines of the novel if he will prove to be the hero of his own tale, but in this novel form the central character moving through adolescence into adulthood is most certainly its hero, the protagonist. The structure of the bildungsroman involves a movement from naïve innocence and total inexperience through a series of mishaps and apprenticeships toward a more mature state of experienced knowledge about the world and self-confidence. Though David Copperfield's world is a mixture of sweetness and corruption, he is not corrupted, though he is temporarily misled, as in trusting Steerforth, for example. The mature narrator shares the adult reader's worldly view of the novel's characters, sorry for the ways in which the child David is mistreated and happy about how bad

people get what they deserve, as is the case with Uriah Heep, and about how good people come along to be all right in the end, as is the case with the Peggottys and the Micawbers in their new lives in Australia. At the same time, the narrator sympathetically portrays the world from the child's point of view, drawing in youthful readers by telling a story about a hero with whom they can identify.

Historical Context

The Beginnings of Social Change

British society was divided at the end of the eighteenth century roughly into three classes: the aristocracy, the gentry, and the yeoman class. Yet the revolutionary fervor at end of that century, exemplified by the American and French Revolutions, was seeping into the social fabric of England. In the following several decades, class distinctions began to relax and be redefined. As people in the lower middle classes became more prosperous, they began to emulate their social betters, as did the landed gentry of the upper middle class. During the nineteenth century, increasing numbers of people rose financially through commercial work and factory production. These middle-class individuals increasingly became absorbed with a cultivation of the proper manners, dress, and décor, practiced by the gentry and lesser members of the aristocracy. Examples of this rising middle class can be seen with the Murdstones and the Steerforths in *David Copperfield*. David's parents, his aunt, and the Wickfields are members of the middle class, but they do not try to adopt the pretensions of the aristocracy.

Nineteenth-Century London

The contrast between the wealthy and poorer classes, however, was evident in London during the nineteenth century. A small portion of the city was occupied by well-kept residences and shopping areas. Upper and middle-class residents stayed in these areas, predominantly in the West End, fearing to venture into the remaining three-fourths of the city, especially in the rough East End, which was teeming with poverty, dense population, and corruption. The gulf between the rich and poor widened each year. New villages continually emerged, especially near the docks, but even though Londoners found work in the city's busy port, wages were not high enough to adequately provide for workers. The extreme stratification of

Compare & Contrast

- **1850s:** The lower classes crowded into English urban centers and working without any labor restrictions on their behalf are pessimistic about ever rising out of poverty. No social services are available to help them.

  Today: England has social programs such as national health insurance and subsidized housing that help improve the lives of those in the lower class.

- **1850s:** Voices emerge in protest against conditions for the working class, after a huge Chartist demonstration in 1848 in London. Protestors presented a petition for working-class rights to Parliament containing over two million signatures.

  Today: Protests in England during the beginning of the twenty-first century center on the war in Iraq, including anti-war marches and a movement to oust Prime Minister Tony Blair

from the Labour Party for his alliance with and support of President Bush's handling of the war.

- **1850s:** This period is the height of Victorianism in England, characterized by a devotion to strict codes among the middle and upper classes even regarding vocabulary. For example, it is considered improper to use the word, leg, in mixed company. The word, limb, is the preferred term.

  Today: Various languages, including different dialects of English, are spoken in England, from "posh," which identifies the speaker as part of the upper classes, to regional dialects, to Punjabi, the predominant language of Pakistanis, who make up a large portion of England's immigrant population. Slang and profanity are an accepted part of the English language as it is used on the streets.

---

the English urban centers was studied by Karl Marx and Friedrich Engels. Together, they wrote the *Communist Manifesto* (1848), and Engels wrote *The Condition of the Working Class in England* (1844), in which he describes graphically the living conditions in the center of London and Manchester and how these contrast with the wealthy residences on the outskirts. Together, they outlined the causes, effects, and political solutions to the problem of poverty which became the inspiration for the communist revolutions of the twentieth century.

Benthamism

Benthamism, also known as utilitarianism, became an important ideology in Victorian society, especially among the middle class. The term was associated with a philosophy of Jeremy Bentham (1748–1832), explained in his *Introduction to the Principles of Morals and Legislation* (1789), which was widely accepted among the Victorian middle class, affecting their habits and beliefs. By the 1820s, the philosophy gained a number of

disciples who promoted Bentham's theories in debates. Supporters gained political power in the 1830s when approximately one hundred were elected to the first reform-focused Parliament in England.

At the core of this philosophy was the belief in "the greatest happiness for the greatest number," a phrase borrowed from Joseph Priestley, a late eighteenth-century Unitarian theologian, which appeared in Bentham's *Introduction to the Principles of Morals and Legislation*. In *Victorian People and Ideas*, Richard D. Altick explains:

> utilitarianism was . . . wholly hedonistic; it made no allowance for the promptings of conscience, or for . . . the forces of generosity, mercy, compassion, self-sacrifice, love. Benthamite ethics had nothing to do with Christian morality.

At the heart of this belief was the supposition that self-interest should be one's primary concern and that happiness could be attained by avoiding pain and seeking pleasure, qualities that emerge in James Steerforth's character.

Evangelicalism

Another important middle-class movement in the nineteenth century was evangelicalism, a form of Protestant pietism. Evangelicalism focused less on doctrine and more on the day-to-day lives and eventual salvation of its followers. It set rigid patterns of conduct for its practitioners to follow in order that they might find atonement for their sins. Altick notes that "the Evangelical's anxious eye was forever fixed upon the 'eternal microscope' which searched for every moral blemish and reported every motion of the soul." Edward Murdstone and his sister's treatment of David provides good examples of this type of rigid, moralistic code.

Both utilitarian and evangelical movements, however, are also noted for their involvement in humanitarian activities during the Victorian period and especially for their calls for social reforms. Benthamites supported universal suffrage and education while the evangelicals successfully fought for amelioration of brutal prison conditions.

A Victorian Woman's Place

During the eighteenth and nineteenth centuries, women (like men) were confined to the classes in which they were born, unless their fathers or husbands moved up or down in the social hierarchy. The strict rules for each social class defined women and determined their lives. Women in the upper classes had the leisure to become educated; however, like their counterparts in the lower classes, upper-class women were not expected to think for themselves and were not often listened to when they did. Urges for independence and self-determination were suppressed in women from all classes. The strict social morality of the period demanded that middle-class women and those in classes above exhibit the standards of polite femininity, culminating in the ideals of marriage and motherhood. *David Copperfield* both reenforces (David's mother, Dora) and challenges (Betsey Trotwood) the period's attitudes toward women. Most female characters, however, operate within the confines of the middle class. Miss Trotwood's quick mind and independent spirit is tolerated because she is considered eccentric and is a widow.

Realism

Realism as a movement first appeared in Paris in the early 1800s as an effort to insure that art would not merely imitate life but would instead be an exact representation of it. In this sense, realistic works could be considered the literature of truth. Realism became a popular form of painting, for example in works by Gustave Courbet, and some literature in the mid-nineteenth century, for example in the novels of Gustave Flaubert. Novelists in this movement turned away from what they considered the artificiality of romanticism to a focus on the commonplace in the context of everyday contemporary life. They rejected idealism and the celebration of the imagination typical of romantic novels and instead took a serious look at believable characters and their often problematic social interactions.

In order to accomplish this goal, realist novels focus on the commonplace and eliminate the unlikely coincidences and excessive emotionalism characteristic of romanticism. Novelists such as Thomas Hardy discarded traditional sentimental elements as they chronicled the strengths and weaknesses of ordinary people confronting difficult personal and social problems. Writers who embraced realism use setting and plot details that reflect their characters' daily lives and realistic dialogue that replicates as far as possible the natural speech patterns of individuals in various classes.

One realistic part of *David Copperfield* is Dickens's portrait of the harsh conditions in London among the lower classes. Dickens was one of the first to chronicle in his fiction the monotonous, harsh, and sordid life of this group of people. Some scholars, however, determine that the endings of his novels, including the ending of *David Copperfield*, follow the romantic tradition.

Critical Overview

Charles Dickens is considered one of the great Victorian novelists, a reputation that was established soon after his novels began to be published. His first book, *The Posthumous Papers of the Pickwick Club* (1837), written when he was in his early twenties, became an immediate success in Britain and the United States. Soon after his death, scholars downplayed his literary significance, a pattern that continued for the next few decades. Yet in the 1950s, his reputation regained its status to the point that by the end of the twentieth century and the beginning of the twenty-first, no other English author except Shakespeare had merited as much critical attention.

In his *Irish Essays*, Matthew Arnold, a contemporary of Dickens, comments on the experience of writing the review of the novel: "what a pleasure to have the opportunity of praising a work so sound, a work so rich in merit, as *David Copperfield*."

Sally Field and Hugh Dancy in lamplit room in the 2000 film version of David Copperfield

Hallmark/The Kobal Collection/Nigel Parry

He finds "treasures of gaiety, invention, life" and "alertness and resource," in this "charming and instructive book." Arnold insists that "a soul of good nature and kindness govern[s] the whole!"

In his 1948 article, "The Art of 'The Crowded Novel,'" E. K. Brown praises "the beauty of [the novel's] structure," finding "the device of contrast . . . admirably used in the plot." Brown explores "the subtlety with which Dickens renders the settings," giving as an example Dickens's reference to Aladdin's palace as a metaphor for Mr. Peggotty's boat: "Dickens renders perfectly not

only the intimacy of the family with the sea . . . but what is more important to the idea of the novel, . . . the fairy-tale security and happiness of the family's life." In a discussion of the novel's complexity, he finds it "admirable" that such a "densely crowded" novel is "never confused" and points out how all the narrative elements come together to form the book's main ideas. Citing its universality, Brown claims, "the imagined group of characters . . . and the conflicts among them, after the lapse of almost a century, still seem so much a part of the streaming course of human life." Monroe Engel in his 1959 book *The Maturity of Dickens* agrees; he states that "*David Copperfield* has captured the imagination of readers for a century."

Bert G. Hornback in his 1968 essay on the novel echoes this sentiment in his conclusion: this is "Dickens's most ambitious undertaking; it is also his most complete, most satisfying, and most fully satisfactory achievement. To borrow a phrase from the text, if Agnes could do without it, we certainly could not."

Criticism

Wendy Perkins

Perkins is a professor of American and English literature and film. In this essay, she focuses on the darker characters in the novel and their effect on David Copperfield.

Several of the characters in *David Copperfield*, like Mr. Macawber and Peggotty, are so memorable because they are lovable and warm-hearted, offering support and comfort as they help David in his journey to adulthood. They also are valuable to him as they help counter the effects of the darker characters in the novel. Dickens provides a rather pessimistic view of human nature in his depiction of Mr. Murdstone, Mr. Creakle, James Steerforth, and Uriah Heep, who impede David's journey to selfhood and expose him to a world of cruelty and corruption. In his portrayal of these four men, Dickens explores how character can be negatively shaped through experience, especially when restrictive social mores and unregulated social institutions are part of that experience.

David's idyllic childhood ends when his mother marries Mr. Murdstone, which introduces David to the very worst in human nature. Dickens never provides any background information about Murdstone or about Creakle that might provide clues to the formation of their characters as he does with Steerforth and Heep. Thus, he suggests, the first two men are inherently evil through some defect in their character. This defect has a devastating effect on David.

Murdstone is a controlling, brutal man who David notes, "ordered me like a dog, and I obeyed like a dog." Murdstone initially tries to hide his true self when he insists to David that he wants to be "best friends in the world" in order to persuade Clara to think that he will be a good father. But

even though David has never come into contact with such evil before, he is an observant child and so is suspicious of this man who has "an eye that has no depth in it to be looked into." David understands that a kind word would have made him respect Murdstone, but his stepfather only offers platitudes before he marries Clara and gains control of the household.

Besides causing him to live in constant fear of being verbally and physically abused, Murdstone, along with his sister, denies David his childhood, first by not allowing him any free time to play at his home and then by forcing him into servitude in the London warehouse. David becomes "sullen, dull, and dogged" under Murdstone's tyranny. He escapes only through the adventure books his father left him that, he claims, "kept alive my fancy, and my hope of something beyond that place and time."

Murdstone unleashes his cruelty on David's mother as well, taking advantage of Clara's pliant nature in order to control David and the household. He admits that his goal is to form Clara's character, along with David's. When she does not conform to his demands, he threatens to stop loving her, knowing that she could not bear this. He is unconcerned that pushing her to separate herself from her son breaks her heart along with her spirit, which leads to an early death.

Murdstone forces David to encounter another person who is as evil as he is when he sends him to boarding school. Mr. Creakle, who runs Salem House, enjoys the power he has over the boys as Murdstone enjoyed the power he had over Clara and David. Creakle gloats to David, "when I say I'll do a thing, I do it, . . . and when I say I will have a thing done, I will have it done." His nature is as cruel as Murdstone's. David notes that "he had a delight in cutting at the boys, which was like the satisfaction of a craving appetite." Creakle compounds David's misery until he is able to establish a sense of community with the other boys at school.

The most popular boy in that community is James Steerforth, who decides that he will accept David as a friend. Steerforth, along with Uriah Heep, are more complex characters than Murdstone and Creakle, representing Dickens's belief that environment also has a profound effect on character and that a dark nature can emerge regardless of which class has nurtured it.

Steerforth is the most charming boy at school, a quality that he retains throughout his life. David notices Steerforth because of his attractiveness and bearing, but his loyalty to his new friend is forged when Steerforth is sympathetic to David's having to wear the "I bite" sign around school. He appears just as charming when David introduces him to the Peggottys and easily makes Em'ly fall in love with him.

Steerforth's true character, however, emerges soon after he and David become friends. David is thrilled to be so privileged as to be chosen to bunk next to Steerforth, not complaining when the older boy selfishly insists that he tell adventure stories long into the night, preventing him from getting much sleep. Steerforth's cruel streak appears during an altercation with Mr. Mell, one of the teachers at Salem House. Refusing to follow Mr. Mell's direction, the arrogant Steerforth reveals his class bigotry as well as his lack of compassion when he refuses to recognize Mr. Mell as a gentleman and calls attention to the impoverished condition of his mother, which eventually gets Mr. Mell dismissed from his position at the school. David is too blinded by his devotion to Steerforth to recognize the boy's cruel treatment of Mr. Mell, but Traddles notices it and declares, "Shame, J. Steerforth! Too bad!"

Steerforth's bigotry emerges in his response to the Peggottys, even after he spends many evenings with them, enjoying their company. He later refers to them disparagingly as "that sort of people" and claims, "there's a pretty wide separation between them and us. . . . They have not very fine natures." David's lack of maturity and continued innocence cause him to assume that Steerford's words were spoken merely in jest. David's lack of a clear sense of self prompts him to overlook Steerforth's condescension toward him as well. The older boy never treats David as his equal and takes to calling him "Daisy" in London because of his obvious innocence. Agnes clearly sees that David "has made a dangerous friend," but her dear friend is still too blinded by his trusting nature to accept her warning.

As his relationship with Em'ly develops, Steerforth does show signs of guilt but quickly blames his behavior on not having been raised by a father. He fails to note that David did not have a father either, except a very cruel one. But Dickens does suggest that Steerforth's environment shapes his character when he introduces his mother who cruelly dismisses Mr. Peggotty and his obvious distress over Em'ly's situation. She shows no concern for Em'ly, only for herself and her son, who she is sure will be ruined if he marries Em'ly.

Miss Dartle presents the most compelling evidence of Mrs. Steerforth's influence on her son's character when she attacks the elderly woman after Steerforth's death. She insists that Steerforth

> **In Uriah, Dickens has created a true grotesque, whose appearance and mannerisms become an outward expression of the evil within."**

was ruined by his mother's "pampering of his pride and passion," declaring, "from his cradle [you] reared him to be what he was, and stunted what he should have been" by encouraging his arrogance and selfishness.

When Em'ly runs off with Steerforth, David is forced to recognize his friend's damaged nature. He understands that there is something wrong with Uriah, however, as soon as he meets him. In Uriah, Dickens has created a true grotesque, whose appearance and mannerisms become an outward expression of the evil within. Initially, David tries not to judge him by his "cadaverous face" or the "snaky twistings of his throat and body," which occur "when he wanted to express enthusiasm, which was very ugly." Yet Dickens turns Uriah's evil into a supernatural force that cannot be overlooked: When David first meets Uriah, he sees the boy blowing into a horse's nostrils, "as if he were putting some spell upon him."

Uriah has learned to hide his true self through a veneer of "umbleness," which, he insists, defines him and his mother. He is able to manipulate others, especially Mr. Wickfield, through careful study of their weaknesses and by pretending that he would never assume to try to move above his class, maneuvers designed to gain their trust. His subtle watchfulness even works on David, who distrusts him immediately but does not initially realize that Uriah is taking advantage of David's "juvenile frankness."

When his true character emerges after Traddles exposes his criminal activities, Uriah reveals that, as was the case with Steerforth, his experiences have shaped him. In Uriah's case, the social system that created rigid rules making it almost impossible to move above one's class taught him how to gain power over people and so take the revenge that the system fostered within his heart. Uriah explains that he and his family were taught "a deal

What Do I Read Next?

- Dickens's *Great Expectations* (1860–1861) focuses on the coming of age of Pip, an orphan who must face the harsh realities of life in Victorian England. The novel is available from Random House (2006).

- A remarkable form of social protest is Jonathan Swift's "A Modest Proposal" (1729), which suggests an outrageous solution to the famine in Ireland: babies should be eaten. This essay, along with other short works by Swift, is available in *A Modest Proposal and Other Prose*, from Barnes and Noble (2004).

- Daniel Pool's *What Jane Austen Ate and Charles Dickens Knew: From Fox Hunting to Whist, the Facts of Daily Life in Nineteenth-Century England* (1993) examines the public and private world of the Victorians, including their customs, rituals, occupations, and living conditions.

- Sally Mitchell's *Daily Life in Victorian England* (1996) focuses on a variety of lifestyles during this period from country gentry to urban slum dwellers.

---

of umbleness" and were forced "to be umble to this person, and umble to that . . . and always to know our place and abase ourselves before our betters." His father reinforced this behavior, thinking that it was the best way for his son to "get on." Uriah admits that this training enabled him to gain a measure of power: "I got to know what umbleness did and I took to it. I ate umble pie with an appetite." After this admission, David acknowledges, "I had never doubted his meanness, his craft and malice; but I fully comprehended now . . . what a base, unrelenting and revengeful spirit, must have been engendered by this early, and this long, suppression."

Dickens's pessimistic view of human nature, as evidenced by the cruel actions of these four characters who have such a profound effect on David's life, is tempered by the goodness and compassion of his friends and family, who are often able to repair the damage that these four have accomplished. The novel also provides a forum for Dickens's views of the inherent nature of evil as well as a critique of a society that enables and shapes this darker side of humanity.

Source: Wendy Perkins, Critical Essay on *David Copperfield*, in *Novels for Students*, Thomson Gale, 2007.

Mark Spilka

In the following essay, Spilka explores and compares psychological projection in David Copperfield *and Franz Kafka's work.*

When we speak of psychological fiction, we generally mean the use of probing methods, like introspection or analysis; or we mean enveloping techniques, like point of view and stream of consciousness, which simulate the flow of inner conflict. But there is another kind of fiction, the projective novel, in which surface life reflects the inner self. *David Copperfield* belongs to that tradition. As the hero views the world, his feelings fuse with outward action, and his selection of events advances inward meaning. Franz Kafka saw this when he called *Amerika* his 'Dickens novel' in method and detail. By 'method' he apparently meant the dream-effects in *Copperfield:* the infantile perspective on a world controlled by elders, and the hero's progress through that world toward ultimate redemption. As Kafka knew, the childlike view connects unconscious tensions with the conscious scene. Because the child lacks self-awareness, and because he fails to understand his elders, his bafflement aligns two realms of feeling; and in a world of harsh repression, his need for inner growth becomes directive and informing. In his early fiction, Kafka borrowed about six stages of that growth from *Copperfield*, plus two regressions. These 'imitations' alone suggest a formal sequence for the novel; but keeping them in reserve, consider simply the method which he so admired, especially as it strengthens early chapters.

In Kafka, inner states are projected through fantastic situations, then treated in precise detail; in Dickens, outer scences are real, but are made to seem fantastic through projected feelings: in either case, the effect is of a surface charged with baffling implications. For Dickens, the creation of that surface came naturally, as part of his attempt to master childhood pain. In *Copperfield* he had summoned up the most anguished memories of youth: his wretched job in a blacking warehouse, his rejection by Maria Beadnell, and his earlier defeat within the home. With an artist's instinct, he had given form and texture to those episodes; and with genial and expansive humour, he had eased their pain and enlarged their meaning. Thus David's birth is to a world informed by sexual conflict— as heralded by his strident aunt, Miss Trotwood. Since her marriage to a younger man has ended badly, she has renounced the male sex and has even trained her maids to follow suit. Now she wants to train the approaching child, whose sex must be feminine and whose name must be her own: "There must be no mistakes in life and with *this* Betsey Trotwood. There must be no trifling with *her* affections". But the babe's name is David, a mistake which makes her vanish "like one of those supernatural beings" whom the boy is privileged to see by virtue of his birth on Friday midnight. From this renouncing spirit, he does see that marriage seldom works, and that the trouble seems to begin with sex in children; but her ghosthood is his own invention, and its comic form, his reaction to impending pain.

In Chapter 2 the pain begins. His first memories are of his mother and nurse Peggotty, as loving protectors. A fierce cock makes him shiver, and he dreams at night of geese with stretching necks, as a man might dream of threatening lions. There are two parlours in the house: in one he sits with Peggotty and his mother, in complete security; in the other he feels doleful, for Peggotty has told him of his father's funeral there. When his mother reads to them, in the second parlour, "how Lazarus was raised up from the dead", the boy becomes frightened; they are forced to quiet him, that night, by showing him the churchyard from his window, "with the dead all lying in their graves at rest, below the solemn moon". His father lies in one of those graves, and David fears his resurrection. Another night he suddenly asks about marriage: "if you marry a person, and the person dies, why then you may marry another person, mayn't you, Peggotty?" He is worried about the man who walks his mother home from church. When she

" **But as Kafka shows, David is another kind of modern hero—an Eduard Raban or Karl Rossmann, a younger Gregor Samsa; and Dickens' novel is one of our first and best examples of projective fiction.** "

returns that night, the man is with her, and the boy is jealous of his touch. His name is Murdstone, which David's aunt compares with Murderer, to fit his surface rôle; but Murdstone also means the *murd*ered man beneath his grave*stone*, who has risen now to assert his rights—and Dickens makes the tie with conscious skill. One day the boy agrees to a ride with Murdstone. Seated before him on his horse, he looks up at his face and thinks him handsome, especially in his mother's eyes. Then they come to the hotel where Murdstone's friends are waiting:

> They both rolled on to their feet, in an untidy sort of manner, when we came in, and said, "Halloa, Murdstone! We thought you were dead!"
>
> "Not yet," siad Mr. Murdstone.
>
> "And who's this shaver?" said one of the gentlemen, taking hold of me.
>
> "That's Davy", returned Mr. Murdstone. . . .
>
> "What! Bewitching Mrs. Copperfield's incumbrance?" cried the gentleman. "The pretty little widow?"
>
> "Quinion", said Mr. Murdstone, "take care, if you please. Somebody's sharp".
>
> "Who is?" asked the gentleman, laughing. . . .
>
> "Only Brooks of Sheffield", said Mr. Murdstone.
>
> I was quite relieved to find that it was only Brooks of Sheffield, for, at first, I really thought it was I. . . .
>
> "And what is the opinion of Brooks of Sheffield, in reference to the projected business?"
>
> "Why, I don't know that Brooks understands much about it at present", replied Mr. Murdstone; "but he is not generally favourable, I believe."
>
> There was more laughter at this, and Mr. Quinion said he would ring the bell for some sherry in which to drink to Brooks. This he did; and when the wine came, he made me have a little, with a biscuit, and,

before I drank it, stand up and say, "Confusion to Brooks of Sheffield!" The toast was received with great applause, and such hearty laughter that it made me laugh too; at which they laughed the more. In short, we quite enjoyed ourselves.

David is indeed confused by Murdstone's friends. That night he tells his mother of their talk, which pleases her immensely. Later, kneeling playfully by his bed, she makes him repeat their words, "Bewitching Mrs. Copperfield" and "pretty little widow". Again she responds with pleasure, and though she kisses him repeatedly, the scene conveys his bafflement at powers which keep her out of range, in areas where Murdstone is decidedly 'not dead'.

The next memory is of a trip to Yarmouth, arranged with special mystery. He meets Peggotty's family there, and the comedy turns on Mrs. Gummidge, the "lone lorn creetur" who exploits her husband's death for sympathy. With the orphan, little Em'ly, David soon achieves the security of childhood love, with no "provision for growing older", and with greater purity and disinterestedness "than can enter into the best love of a later time of life." His ideal, then, is sexless love with Em'ly or his mother; he even indicates that Em'ly should have toppled into the sea one day, and joined her father beneath the waves, to avoid her sinful future. Thus Yarmouth scenes advance the major conflict: beneath the peaceful surface and light comedy, pain and loss continue, and on the return trip home, they erupt with sudden force. His nurse becomes so ill at ease, on nearing home, that David calls in fear for his mother. He believes she too is dead, but Peggotty cries No! and tries to explain her agitation:

> "Master Davy", said Peggotty, untying her bonnet with a shaking hand, and speaking in a breathless sort of way. "What do you think? You have got a Pa!"
>
> I trembled, and turned white. Something—I don't know what or how—connected with the grave in the churchyard, and the raising of the dead, seemed to strike me like an unwholesome wind.
>
> "A new one", said Peggotty.
>
> "A new one?" I repeated.
>
> Peggotty gave a gasp, as if she were swallowing something that was very hard, and putting out her hand, said:
>
> "Come and see him".
>
> "I don't want to see him".

The shock jars loose his graveyard fears. He now shakes hands with Lazarus and greets his mother, but he cannot face them. The house seems altered. Later, when he roams into the yard, his feelings suffer full projection: "I very soon started back from there, for the empty dog-kennel was filled up with a great dog—deep-mounthed and black-browed like Him—and he was very angry at the sight of me, and sprang out to get me".

This is brilliant psychological fiction. Murdstone has become the risen and revengeful father; his powers involve the mysteries of sex, and somehow pull the mother out of range. In the meantime, the boy's hostility and fear suffuse the outward scene. The projective artistry is unmatched, and most of it seems conscious; in Chapter IV, moreover, it comes to full dramatic focus in a scene which Kafka found intriguing. Kept uninformed by nurse and mother, David has suffered deeply from the news of marriage. The shock might have been lessened, if Murdstone had responded with encouragement. Instead he offers 'firmness' and distrust. Idyllic spelling lessons, once directed by the mother, become drudgery under Murdstone and his sister. David stumbles in their presence, and when Murdstone brings cane to help his memory, the boy goes blank. In the struggle which follows, he bites the hand which touched his mother; he is beaten then with a vengeance and locked inside his room, where he rages helplessly upon the floor. Outside the wild household commotion is stilled. In the unnatural quiet, David crawls to the mirror and sees his face in the glass, "so swollen, red, and ugly that it almost frightened me. My stripes were sore and stiff, and made me cry afresh, when I moved; but they were nothing to the guilt I felt. It lay heavier on my breast than if I had been the most atrocious criminal".

This spectacle of a son locked in his room, shut off from his mother, and guilty of a crime against the father, appealed to Kafka; he used it in *The Metamorphosis* for his central situation, reshaping it to suit his needs—as the events themselves attest. Thus David lies by the window now, his head upon the sill, when Miss Murdstone brings in "bread and meat and milk". She glares at him with exemplary firmness, then locks him in again. His imprisonment lasts five days, which "occupy the place of years" in his remembrance. He listens to the household sounds of day, confuses time at night, and feels weighed down on awakening "by the stale and dismal oppression of remembrance". He is ashamed to show himself at the window, lest the boys outside should see him. During evening prayers he is allowed to stand alone, near the parlour doors, and look out on the averted faces of the family. On the last night of his restraint, he hears his name repeated in a whisper. The voice is Peggotty's; it reaches him through the keyhole, to which he puts his own lips in response, so that a mouth-to-ear communication begins on David's future (at one point, mouth-to-mouth). Then both fall to kissing and patting the keyhole, and David feels within him an indefinable love for Peggotty. She has reached him, he asserts, with "as much feeling and earnestness as a keyhole has ever been the medium of communicating". Kafka seems to challenge his assumption with key-manipulations by his giant insect, whose shape derives from Dostoevsky, but whose crime and punishment begin with Dickens. The strange ordeal of Gregor Samsa, an older and certainly a more regressive outcast, repeats the intensities of guilt, exclusion and frustration which Daivd undergoes; and the comparison affirms the unexpected depth of Dickens' 'method'.

After shock, whipping and exclusion, some kind of psychic damage seems inevitable, and the next ten chapters show its form. At Salem House, an older student, Steerforth, becomes the boy's protector. David loves and admires him, and serves him by reciting stories, "like the Sultana Scheherezade". Steerforth seems to like this girlish adoration. "If you had a sister", he tells him, "I should think she would have been a pretty, timid, little, bright-eyed sort of girl. I should have liked to know her". David's only 'sister', at this stage, is Em'ly; he will later bring these two together, and speak of his 'unconscious part' in their elopement. At the moment her budding womanhood disturbs him, and he is afraid to mention her. Steerforth's manhood is another matter; he admires him for his poise and charm, for powers which conquer elders. When Steerforth badgers Mr. Mell, the master (Creakle) promptly fires his helper—and David cheers his hero. In Kafka's novel, *Amerika,* Steerforth's counterpart is Mr. Mack, a sophisticated, patronizing figure who attracts and baffles young Karl Rossmann. Karl's attraction is an adolescent crush, like David's, but the sexual note has been enhanced by "sharper lights . . . from the times", which show Mack in collusion with his elders. Still, the lights in *Copperfield* seem sharp enough: Steerforth later joins the fathers, as sadist and destroyer, and is now an adolescent sultan.

From Steerforth David seeks vicarious confidence, knowledge and seductive power; in the future, he will even blind himself to get them. But the projective paths to mother-love are varied. On his return from school, for instance, his route is more direct. Hearing his mother sing in the parlour, he remembers how she sang to him in infancy. When he finds her there with Murdstone's baby, she puts his head upon her bosom, "near the little creature that was nestling there", and David longs for blissful death. He identifies himself with Murdstone's child, and with nurse and mother beside him, it seems "as if the old days were come back". Then the Murdstones return and break the spell. When he leaves for school again, his mother stands at the gate alone, holding the babe before her; and afterwards, in his sleep at Salem House, he sees her near his bed, "looking at [him] with the same intent face—holding up her baby in her arms". Her gesture seems to affirm his infant love, to fix it permanently in his mind. Thus, when mother and baby die, he remembers only "the young mother of my earliest impressions, who had been used to wind her bright curls round and round her finger, and to dance with me at twilight in the parlour. . . . The mother who lay in the grave, was the mother of my infancy; the little creature in her arms, was myself, as I had once been, hushed for ever on her bosom". In harsher terms, David has just appeased his guilt.

His projections take a comic turn with Barkis, the laconic carrier, who wants to marry Peggotty. When the boy first goes to school, Barkis waits in silence as the nurse embraces David and loads him down with pastry. Her buttons pop with every squeeze, and she leaves "without a solitary button on her gown"; but Barkis, like a grownup child, is more concerned with cakes than sex. They have roused his marital appetite, and with David as protective agent, he can risk the cryptic message: "Barkis is willing". So too is David willing. In a later chapter, he waits outside with Em'ly, in vicarious embrace, while Barkis and the nurse are married. He dreams that night about dragons, and wakens, in the morning, with Peggotty calling from below, as if Barkis were a dream "from first to last". Such proxy dealings might have appealed to Kafka. In "Wedding Preparations in the Country", young Eduard Raban wants to send his body ahead to meet his country sweetheart; in the meantime, he will rest in bed, as he had always done in childhood "in matters that were dangerous". Barkis too avoids the risks of courtship, like a frightened child; he also clings to boxes with the insecurity of Raban and Karl Rossmann, who seem to seek emotional support from baggage. Of course, he acts from slighter motives; but in marrying David's nurse, and in clinging to internal burdens, he reveals the boy's vicarious urges. In this sense, his death resembles that of Murdstone's child: it fixes David's attitude toward his nurse, just as Steerforth's death will fix his love for Em'ly. In each case, these characters die in their own right; but some of David's guilt dies with them, since they have allowed him to 'possess' his mother, nurse and 'sister'—all objects of the sexless love of childhood, with its hidden sexual base. Thus, as Barkis dies, he rests mutely on his box, which gives his form its only meaning; but at the last his mind begins to wander, as if under "the mysterious influence" of David's presence: he talks of driving him to school, and then speaks his comic phrase, "Barkis is willin'", which carries hidden weight.

During the early phase, emotional growth is blocked by further punishment. At Salem House, David is forced to wear the placard, "Take care of him. He bites", and the master whips him freshly for his crime. Mr. Creakle is another Murdstone: he turns his son out for protesting cruelty in the school and "usage of his mother". He prides himself on firmness, tweaks ears to make his point, and bursts from his chair like Murdstone's dog. With the zest of a "craving appetite", he delights in beating chubby boys like David. In London, David later works for Quinion, the manager of Murdstone's warehouse, who still refers to him as 'Brooks' and jokes about his sharpness. Through Creakle and Quinion, then, the father's power extends to realms beyond the home. This principle must have excited Kafka. In *Amerika* he joins David's 'menial labour' with his life at school, to create "The Hotel Occidental". Here Rossmann works for harsh parental figures, and sleeps in a dorm with other liftboys. His ultimate dismissal resembles Mr. Mell's: for, in line with Dickens, the social scene repeats the indignities of childhood; the world belongs to fathers, and each phase of youth is an attempt to get beyond them.

This section of the novel ends with David's flight to Dover, a flight which seems to summarize his past. His trunk is stolen by a youth who calls him a "pollis case" and threatens to expose him; he sleeps behind his school and dreams of Steerforth; an old-clothes dealer seizes him, with wild "goroos", like Creakle gone berserk; and a tinker steals his kerchief, then beats a kindly wife, as if the world were full of Murdstones. Throughout the journey, he keeps before him an image of his mother "in her youth and beauty"; but when he reaches Dover, where he hopes to find security with his aunt, the image disappears. In *Amerika* Karl Rossmann has troubles with his box, and with two unruly mechanics, on the road to Rameses. According to one critic, "Karl's inner world determines the character of his experiences", while David's world is "full of things and persons . . . essentially separate from his inward self, only temporarily and accidentally related to it". Kafka's 'imitation' tells us otherwise: to

integrate this journey, he drew from Dickens "the story of the trunk" (involving David's fear of further confinement), the clothes-exchange (involving bestial treatment), a schoolroom scene (suggesting Creakle and Steerforth), the stolen kerchief (involving Murdstone and Clara), and the image of the mother (involving infancy), which disappears with an older woman's kindness (suggesting inner peace). In other words, he followed Dickens' scheme of psychic integration, which is neither accidental nor temporary, but part of the sustained method from which these fourteen chapters draw direction, power, depth and meaning: the method, in short, which yields a truly brilliant stretch of psychological fiction.

Admittedly, the stretch abruptly ends with David's "new beginning"—and for the next five chapters, the novel seems to flounder. In his diaries, Kafka writes of "passages of awful insipidity" in which Dickens wearily repeats achieved effects; he speaks of "heartlessness" behind his sentimental style, and of rude characterizations which obstruct the story. The indictment is severe, but such chapters seem to confirm it. Thin characters like Mr. Dick and Dr. Strong, whose childlike traits are overpraised, suggest a form of fake emotion; and the repetitious effects are surely there. It seems more pertinent, however, that Dickens loses power when the projective method stops: for in these five chapters David reaches psychic rest; his inner troubles cease, and his connections with the outward scene are casual; at best, they extend the *breadth* of the novel, as he puzzles over the marriage of an old man and a young woman, a father's too-intense devotion to his daughter, a scapegrace husband, and a badly treated sister. These problems are thematic, but they leave him unengaged, and the novel seems impeded by their weight. Still, the expansive quality of David's style, his use of double perspective to forgive as parent while he errs as child, allows for excess baggage. Light comedy is in order: there is room for the Micawbers' economic dance, and for gargoyles like Uriah Heep. The trouble is, the comedy thrives upon the original psychic thrust, and Dickens' readers often miss the force behind it. One critic says the story happens around the hero, not within him. But the projective method shows otherwise: it provides the novel with its basic strength, and sustains even the excess baggage—apt, crude, fresh, insipid—if only by extended force.

Plainly the major plots relate to David's inner life. With Steerforth, for instance, he is again obsessed with self-distrust. Before their reunion, he is forced to yield his coach-seat to an older gentleman;

W. C. Fields as Wilkins Micawber and Freddie Bartholomew as a young David Copperfield in the 1935 film version of David Copperfield, *directed by George Kukor* MGM/The Kobal Collection

he passes by the lane where the 'goroo' man seized him; he passes Salem House, where Creakle "laid about him with a heavy hand". As on his first trip to school, a waiter treats him poorly. But with Steerforth's appearance, the waiter knows his place. The hero has returned in all his glory: hence David's shame at being beardless, his rechristening as 'Daisy', and his regressions with the servant Littimer, who makes him feel "about eight years old". At Steerforth's home, these hints are clarified through Rosa Dartle, whose scarred lip signals rage, and whose rage is based on sheer frustration. Brought up with Steerforth, and jealously in love

with him, she bears the hammermark of his rejection. Once she strikes him, "with the fury of a wildcat", when he coaxes her to play the harp, then taunts her with the hope of future love. Her scar pursues David to his bed, now, and even invades his dreams, though he tries to escape it. Kafka's wildcat in *Amerika* is the amorous Clara Pollunder, who pursues Karl Rossmann to his bedroom, throws him down on the sofa, and nearly chokes him. Karl even calls her a wildcat, in his rage and shame. Later he plays the piano, when suddenly Mr. Mack cajoles him from a nearby room, where he waits for Clara in his nightshirt. Like David,

Karl is immersed in sexual ambiguity and violence, which fascinate and repel him—and highlight his incompetence. For David too is sexually inadequate: repelled by violence, and blinded by vicarious desire, he can only follow Steerforth to the shoreline at Yarmouth, where he links his childhood love for Em'ly with the hero's death. His long pursuit may run to melodramatic claptrap; but projection lends it strength and point.

Indulgent humour marks the Dora plot. Through the double perspective, David's folly is accepted and forgiven. The doll-like Dora, the child-wife of the nineteenth century, is taken as a delightful hoax, a toy which breaks with possession, a sweet impossibility; and David's love is called "the first mistaken impulse of an undisciplined heart". But again the plot goes deeper. As critics often note, the girl resembles David's mother; her father, David's employer, is a businessman like Murdstone; and her paid companion is Miss Murdstone—as if Dickens had deliberately regrouped his early cast. In courting Dora, then, David reenacts the terms of childhood tension. When Miss Murdstone intercepts his letters, she shows them to the employer-father. As with the early spelling lessons, these figures disapprove of David's words and cut him off from his beloved. By David's own confession: "Miss Murdstone . . . looked so exactly as she used to look . . . in our parlour at Blunderstone, that I could have fancied I had been breaking down in my spelling lessons again, and that the dead weight on my mind was that horrible old spelling-book with oval woodcuts". Here Dora joins the mother, nurse and sister as objects of forbidden love. David's folly, his blindness to her incompetence, begins with spelling lessons at Blunderstone, and ends with a disastrous marriage and another death. Kafka seems to have caught these implications. In *Amerika* Rossmann travels with a businessman, Mr. Pollunder, to meet his daughter Clara. Clara herself resembles Rosa Dartle; but her sexual charade with Karl compares with David's country courtship. In each case, commercial bondage is expressed through sexual means; the fathers' powers have interfused, and the sons remain in double servitude.

In *Amerika* this theme extends to a later chapter, where Karl is trapped in an apartment drawn from Dickens' tenements. In the closing scene, however, he seems to find an escape from childhood. At the Nature Theatre of Oklahoma, he is accepted without question, just as David is received by Agnes Wickfield. Both endings seem unreal, and Kafka himself complains of Dickens' formal 'senselessness'. But his borrowed scenes belie him: they reveal projective loves and deaths which unify the novel and insure its progress. From his mother's death, through those of Barkis, Steerforth and Dora, David moves steadily away from childhood loves; and seems to reach maturity with Agnes. Dickens' authority here is weak, but so is Kafka's, in *Amerika*, when Rossmann seems to near adulthood. Significantly, both authors move toward darker novels. Pip, Richard Carstone and Arthur Clennam, Joseph K. and K., are older Karls and Davids whom the world imprisons. Here Dickens joins with other pioneer novelists, like Stendhal and Dostoevsky, for whom moral and spiritual maturity seem thwarted by the world's deficient fathers. One psychological critic undercuts this kinship; he holds that Copperfield "is never a hero of a modern novel, never a Raskolnikov, nor a . . . Julien Sorel". But as Kafka shows, David is another kind of modern hero—an Eduard Raban or Karl Rossmann, a younger Gregor Samsa; and Dickens' novel is one of our first and best examples of projective fiction. The wealth of comic action, the nostalgic tone, the author's great humour, have made the novel unpopular; but like David's progress, they all relate to childhood anguish and help to ease its pain.

Source: Mark Spilka, *"David Copperfield* as Psychological Fiction," in *"David Copperfield": A Norton Critical Edition*, edited by Jerome Hamilton Buckley, W. W. Norton, 1990, pp. 817–26.

Sources

Altick, Richard D., *Victorian People and Ideas*, Norton, 1973, pp. 117, 166.

Arnold, Matthew, "Mr. Creakle and the Irish," in *David Copperfield*, Norton Critical Edition, edited by Jerome H. Buckley, Norton, 1990, pp. 783, 784, 785; originally published in *Irish Essays*, Smith Elder, 1882.

Bloom, Harold, *Genius: A Mosaic of One Hundred Exemplary Creative Minds*, Warner Books, 2002, pp. 776, 777.

Brown, E. K., "The Art of 'The Crowded Novel,'" in *David Copperfield*, Norton Critical Edition, edited by Jerome H. Buckley, Norton, 1990, pp. 790, 791, 792, 793, 794; originally published in *Yale Review*, N.S. 37, 1948.

Dickens, Charles, *David Copperfield*, Norton Critical Edition, Norton, 1990.

Engel, Monroe, "The Theme of *David Copperfield*," in *David Copperfield*, Norton Critical Edition, edited by Jerome H. Buckley, Norton, 1990, p. 808; originally published in *The Maturity of Dickens*, Harvard University Press, 1959.

Hornback, Bert G., "David's Vocation as Novelist: Frustration and Resolution in *David Copperfield*," in *David Copperfield*,

Norton Critical Edition, edited by Jerome H. Buckley, Norton, 1990, p. 836; originally published in *Studies in English Literature, 1500–1900*, Vol. 8, 1968.

Further Reading

Kaplan, Fred, *Dickens: A Biography*, Johns Hopkins University Press, 1998.

This highly praised biography examines the relationships between Dickens's personal life and his art, especially the experiences of his youth. Kaplan also focuses on Dickens's view of himself and how he was seen by others as an artist and social reformer.

Myers, Margaret, "The Lost Self: Gender in *David Copperfield*," in *Gender Studies: New Directions in Feminist Criticism*, edited by Judith Spector, Bowling Green State University Popular Press, 1986, pp. 120–32.

In this essay, Myers claims that David is able to establish a firm sense of self only after allowing the feminine to integrate with the masculine in his personality.

Needham, Gwendolyn B., "The Undisciplined Heart of David Copperfield," in *Nineteenth-Century Fiction*, Vol. 9, No. 2, September 1954, pp. 81–107.

Needham explores the emotional development of David's character and its relationship to the novel's theme and structure.

Stone, Harry, "Fairy Tales and Ogres: Dickens' Imagination and *David Copperfield*," in *Criticism*, Vol. 6, 1954, pp. 324–30.

Stone examines Dickens's imaginative use of fairy tales in the novel, including the development of Betsey Trotwood's character in the clothes shop scene, highlighting the complexity of David's responses to his experiences.

The Deerslayer

James Fenimore Cooper

1841

The Deerslayer, or The First War-Path, by American novelist James Fenimore Cooper, was first published in 1841. It was the last of Cooper's series of five novels featuring the character of Nathaniel (Natty) Bumppo, also known as Deerslayer, Pathfinder, Hawkeye, Leatherstocking, and Trapper. Set in the wilderness area around Lake Otsego, New York, during one week in June between 1740 and 1745, *The Deerslayer* is an exciting story about the adventures of the woodsman known as Deerslayer and his Delaware Indian friend, Chingachgook. They meet at the lake to plot a rescue of Chingachgook's betrothed, a Delaware girl who has been abducted by the hostile Huron Indians. Deerslayer has never been on the warpath before, and this is a test of his manhood. Deerslayer's impetuous and lawless friend, Hurry March, the grizzled old trapper Thomas Hutter, and his two daughters—one beautiful and vain, the other pious and simple-minded—complete the main cast of characters. The novel presents the violence and unpredictability of life in a place where only a few white hunters and hunting parties of Indians have ever set foot. The interface between the wilderness and civilization, the pristine life of nature and the impact being made on it by human beings, makes this a fascinating story about a clash of values, a conflict which continued to shape the North American continent for the remainder of the century and beyond.

In the early 2000s, *The Deerslayer* may have far fewer readers than it did one hundred and fifty years before, but it has, together with the other four Leatherstocking Tales, become a classic of American nineteenth-century literature.

Author Biography

Known as the first great American novelist, James Cooper (the middle name Fenimore was added in 1826) was born on September 15, 1789, in Burlington, New Jersey, the twelfth of the thirteen children of William Cooper (a wealthy, landowning judge) and Elizabeth Fenimore Cooper. In 1790, the family moved to Cooperstown, in central New York, a settlement near Otsego Lake. The lake, known also as Glimmerglass, was later to be the setting for Cooper's novel, *The Deerslayer.*

Cooper entered Yale College in 1803, at the age of thirteen, but was expelled for misconduct two years later. He joined the Merchant Marines and was then a commissioned midshipman in the U.S. Navy. In 1811, after his father died and he inherited a fortune, Cooper married Susan Augusta DeLancey, who would bear him five daughters and two sons. The couple moved to Westchester in 1817.

The publication of his novel *Precaution* in 1820 marked the beginning of Cooper's literary career. Cooper followed with *The Spy* (1821), a tale of the American Revolution, which won him a wide readership. In 1823, he published *The Pioneers*, the first of the frontier novels on which his reputation came to rest. *The Pioneers* introduced the character Natty Bumppo (also to be known as Hawkeye, Leatherstocking, and Deerslayer), the rugged woodsman and hunter who is presented as a true American hero. The other novels to feature Bumppo are *The Last of the Mohicans* (1826), *The Prairie* (1827), *The Pathfinder* (1840), and *The Deerslayer* (1841). These five novels are known collectively as the Leatherstocking Tales.

From 1826 to 1833, Cooper and his family traveled in Europe. They lived in Paris from 1826 to 1828, and then visited London, Switzerland, Italy, and Germany, returning to Paris in 1830 and remaining there until 1832.

In 1833, Cooper returned to the United States, and the following year, he settled finally at Cooperstown, where he continued to write. He published *The Monikans* in 1835 and five volumes about his

James Fenimore Cooper   Getty Images

travels (1836–1838), beginning with *Sketches of Switzerland* (1836).

After his return from Europe, Cooper was frequently embroiled in controversy. In 1834, in *A Letter to His Countrymen*, he attacked American provincialism and the condition of American democracy. He entered into a legal dispute concerning a piece of land on Otsego Lake that the townspeople had become accustomed to using as a picnic area; Cooper claimed it was private property. He was also regularly attacked in the press as a man who had pretensions to being an aristocrat. This assertion led to a series of lawsuits in which Cooper's motivation was not so much to win damages but to curb what he saw as the irresponsibility of the press.

Cooper wrote over fifty books in all, including sociopolitical and sea novels, naval histories, and travelogues. By the time of his death, he had an international reputation and was probably more honored abroad than he was at home, where he was regarded as reactionary and too litigious, although the Leatherstocking novels were widely read and admired.

Cooper died on September 14, 1851, and was buried in the cemetery of Cooperstown.

Plot Summary

Chapter 1

The Deerslayer begins around noon on a sunny day in June, sometime between 1740 and 1745. It takes place around Lake Otsego, New York, then known as Glimmerglass. Two woods-men, twenty-six- or twenty-eight-year-old Henry March, often known as Hurry Harry, and his slightly younger companion, Nathaniel (Natty) Bumppo, known as Deerslayer, emerge from a small swamp and behold the lake. As they pause to eat their lunch and talk, they reveal differences in their characters. It soon emerges that Deerslayer has not yet killed a man in war or for any other reason; Hurry, who appears to be the more aggressive and ruthless of the two, says it is about time Deerslayer killed an Indian, since they are at war with them. Deerslayer has more respect for the Indians since he has lived among the Delawares and understands their culture. The two men then discuss three people they will soon be meeting, Tom Hutter, and his two daughters, Judith and Hetty. Tom, a widower, is a former pirate who for fifteen years has been living on the lake. Judith is beautiful but headstrong, and Hurry visits her often; Hetty is more humble, sweet-hearted, and dutiful, but does not possess great intelligence.

Chapter 2

Hurry and Deerslayer recover a canoe hidden in a hollow log. They paddle towards the first of Hutter's two homes, which is facetiously known as Muskrat Castle. It stands a quarter mile off-shore, a kind of fortress built on piles driven into a long, narrow shoal. It is relatively safe, since no one can attack it except by boat, and any attacker would be under merciless fire from Hutter's well-stocked armory. When they arrive at the castle, they find it empty. Deerslayer has a good look round, examining every aspect of the interior.

Chapter 3

The two men now paddle in search of Hutter's second home, which is a floating barge called the ark. At one point, Hurry goes ashore and shoots at and misses a deer. Deerslayer reproaches him for his lack of prudence, since the sound of the rifle may alert enemy Indians to their presence. They finally discover the ark concealed in bushes at the source of the Susquehanna River, at the southern end of the lake.

Chapter 4

Hurry leaps onto the ark and starts talking to Judith. Deerslayer climbs aboard more cautiously, and soon notes the presence of Hetty, who is sitting down doing needlework. Hutter realizes that his ark is in a vulnerable position and may be in imminent danger of attack by Indians. With the help of Hurry and Deerslayer, he pulls the ark upstream, using a rope attached to an anchor. As they reach the entrance to Glimmerglass, a band of six Indians in an overhanging tree prepares to leap onto the ark as it passes underneath them. More Indian warriors wait to follow them. But after the attackers make their leap, five fall into the water. Only the first manages to jump onto the ark, and he is immediately pushed overboard by Judith, who has rushed out of her cabin. The ark moves to safety on the open lake.

Chapter 5

Hutter outlines a plan to go on the offensive. He wants to scalp the Indian women and children that he knows are nearby in a hunting party so he can receive the bounty offered for scalps by the colony. Hurry agrees with the idea, but Deerslayer opposes it, saying it does not conform to his religion; Indians practice scalping, but white men do not. He offers to stay behind to protect the women. As Hetty talks to her father, it transpires that Judith does not like Hurry, in spite of his obvious interest in her. On the contrary, Judith shows by the attention she pays to Deerslayer that she is far more attracted to the younger man. She tells him that he is the first man she has met whom she did not regard as an enemy in disguise.

Chapter 6

Hutter, Hurry, and Deerslayer return to Muskrat Castle. Hutter suggests they will enhance their safety if they can collect two more canoes that are hidden in logs on the shore, thus depriving the Indians of the means to approach the castle. At midnight they go ashore in a canoe, locate the canoes and put them in the water so that they drift slowly up the lake, to be collected later. Then, as they paddle their canoe along the south shore of the lake, they locate an Indian encampment. They decide it is not a warriors' encampment and that there will be plenty of women and children there. Hurry and Hutter go ashore in search of scalps, while Deerslayer waits in the canoe to collect them when the expedition is over. But their plans go awry. Hutter and Hurry are captured by Indians, and as Deerslayer, alerted by the sound of a shriek, approaches in the canoe, Hutter tells him to return to the castle to guard the girls.

Chapter 7

After having slept all night in his canoe, Deerslayer collects one canoe and then goes to collect the other, which has drifted ashore. As he approaches the shore, an Indian shoots at him. Deerslayer is unhurt, makes it to the shore, and goes into the bushes. He sees his enemy reloading his rifle and has a chance to shoot him, but he feels this would be unchivalrous, since the man is at a disadvantage. He waits until he can confront the Indian directly on the shore. They talk to each other and appear to have reached an amicable solution, in which the Indian seems to accept that the canoes belong to white men not Indians. The Indian walks away, and Deerslayer is beginning to push the canoe when he sees the Indian preparing to fire at him from behind a bush. Deerslayer readies his rifle and they both fire simultaneously. The Indian is mortally wounded. Deerslayer refuses to scalp the dying man and treats him with respect. The Indian gives Deerslayer a new name, Hawkeye. As Deerslayer paddles out to the drifting canoe, he finds an unarmed Indian in it who is trying to take it to the shore. Deerslayer lets him escape unharmed.

Chapter 8

Back in the castle the following morning, Deerslayer informs Judith and Hetty of what happened. Judith is not too alarmed, as she expects the Indians to release their prisoners unharmed in exchange for a ransom of animal skins or gunpowder. She also continues to show her high regard for Deerslayer. Later that day, Deerslayer and the two girls leave the castle in the ark. Deerslayer has an appointment to meet an Indian friend of his at a large rock near the shore at sunset. The Indian is Chingachgook, a young Delaware chief, whose betrothed, Wah-ta!-Wah, has been abducted by another tribe of Indians, the Hurons. Deerslayer steers the ark in a zigzag fashion so as to confuse the Hurons (often referred to as Mingoes), who are tracking their journey from the shore.

Chapter 9

They arrive at the rock, and Deerslayer hopes he has deceived the Hurons as to his destination. Chingachgook is waiting for them, but as soon as he jumps aboard the ark, twenty hostile Indians leap from the trees and wade into the water, intending to board the ark. Deerslayer and Chingachgook pull hard and take the ark several hundred yards from the shore, leaving the Indians behind. Chingachgook informs them that Hutter and Hurry have not been harmed by their captors, although he also tells

Media Adaptations

- There have been several movie versions of *The Deerslayer.*

- *The Deerslayer and Chingachgook* (1920), starring Emil Mamelok and Herta Heden and directed by Arthur Wellin Ratin, was as of 2006 available on DVD from Alpha Video.

- *The Deerslayer* (1957), starring Lex Barker and Rita Moreno and directed by Kurt Neumann, was in 2006 unavailable.

- *The Deerslayer,* the 1978 low-budget made-for-television version, starring Steve Forrest as Deerslayer and Ned Romero as Chingachgook, was as of 2006 available on VHS from Anchor Bay Entertain.

Deerslayer that they will be scalped the next day. After Judith says she will offer her finest clothes as ransom, Chingachgook confirms that Wah-ta!-Wah is also being held in the same Indian camp. As the three talk together, Judith feels that she has known Deerslayer for a year rather than a day. She has a confidence in him that she has never felt for another man. All three are then surprised to see a canoe in the water. It is occupied by Hetty, who has set off on a mission of her own to rescue Hurry, with whom she is infatuated, and her father. Deerslayer and the others are deeply concerned, since they fear the canoe will fall into enemy hands and give them the means to attack the castle. They try but fail to stop Hetty.

Chapter 10

Hetty goes ashore and sets the canoe adrift. Deerslayer finds it and secures it to the ark. They locate Hetty on the shore. The simple-minded girl says she plans to go to the Indians and tell them that if they kill her father and Hurry, God will send them to everlasting punishment. She disappears into the forest where she spends the night. At dawn she sets off to find the Indian camp and meets Wah-ta!-Wah, who has been given the freedom to wander around the encampment. They take to each other immediately and tell their stories. Wah-ta!-Wah, whom Hetty calls Hist, is pleased to hear that Chingachgook is nearby. Hist leads Hetty to the camp, knowing that Indians treat the mentally deficient and the mad with a religious reverence that they do not show to others.

Chapter 11

In the camp, Hetty soon finds her father and Hurry, who are allowed to walk around unrestrained. She is pleased to learn that neither of them managed to scalp any Indians before they were captured. Then she is taken to the chiefs to whom she makes her request that her father and Hurry should be released. She gets out her Bible and speaks of the Christian God and the command to forgive enemies. But her words have no effect on the chiefs, who summon Hutter and Hurry and get them to admit that they went to the camp in order to collect scalps. The implication is that they deserve any punishment that may be dealt out to them.

Chapter 12

In the morning, back at the castle, Deerslayer and Judith decide that the best way to free Hutter and Hurry is to offer valuables as a ransom. In searching for something suitable, they open Hutter's old sea chest, which he has always kept locked. He has never spoken about its contents, except to Hetty. They find fine clothes, for both men and women. Judith changes out of her simple frock and into one of the dresses, and she looks so beautiful that Deerslayer remarks on it. But then he says that she looks even better without such finery, and she promptly changes out of it.

Chapter 13

Examining the chest further, they find two loaded pistols inlaid with silver. Chingachgook fires one of the pistols, the bullet going into the lake. Deerslayer fires the other, but it goes off before he was expecting it to, and fragments of the bullet fly in all directions. Judith trembles with fright but is uninjured. Next they find a surveyor's instrument and a set of exquisitely wrought ivory chess pieces in the chest. They decide to offer for ransom two rooks, castle-like shapes that are mounted on elephants. Shortly after this, an Indian boy arrives on a raft, bringing Hetty. Deerslayer allows him to examine two of the rooks, and he is captivated by them. Deerslayer sends him away with a message about the ransom offer. Meanwhile,

Hetty informs Chingachgook of the presence of Wah-ta!-Wah at the Indian camp. She tells him that Wah-ta!-Wah has said where she will be an hour after dark and has told him to come to her.

Chapter 14

Two Huron chiefs, one of whom is named Rivenoak, arrive on a raft. They are shown the rook and are entranced by the "beast with two tails," which they have never seen. After lengthy negotiations, which seem at one point to break down, a deal is struck: four rooks will buy the freedom of both Hutter and Hurry. The Hurons depart and return at sunset with the two white men. The Hurons leave on their raft and are about a hundred yards from the castle when Hurry tries to shoot at them. But the quick-moving Deerslayer prevents him.

Chapter 15

Deerslayer finds on the porch of the castle a bundle of sticks, several of which have been dipped in blood. This is a declaration of war. The sticks were delivered by an Indian boy, and Deerslayer and Chingachgook have to prevent Hurry from giving chase in a canoe and trying to scalp the messenger. A decision is then made to abandon the castle and take to the ark. Hutter hoists the sail and the ark is carried in a southerly direction, toward the eastern shore. Hutter, Hurry, and Chingachgook, who have decided to go on another scalping expedition against the Hurons, go ashore in a canoe. But they find the Indian camp deserted and return to the ark, where Deerslayer and Judith have been talking about many things, and Judith has again made plain her affection for him.

Chapter 16

While Hutter and Hurry sleep, Deerslayer and Chingachgook go ashore in a canoe to meet Wah-ta!-Wah at the place and time the Indian girl had disclosed to Hetty. But when they reach the spot, Wah-ta!-Wah is not there. Deerslayer eventually finds her at a new camp, where she is guarded by an old woman. Chingachgook makes a signal, imitating the sound of a squirrel, that alerts Wah-ta!-Wah to his presence. Deerslayer seizes the old woman by the throat and begins to throttle her, enabling Chingachgook to take Wah-ta!-Wah and run with her to the canoe. Deerslayer allows the woman moments in which to breathe, and during one of these moments, she lets out a shriek that alerts the warriors in the camp. Deerslayer drops her and goes back into the bushes.

Chapter 17

Deerslayer is captured by half a dozen Hurons and brought to their camp, where he engages in a dialog with Rivenoak. Rivenoak wants him to return to the ark and betray his friends, so that the Hurons can enter and kill them, but Deerslayer refuses. Deerslayer explains what brought him and Chingachgook to the camp. As Rivenoak consults his colleagues and Deerslayer talks with the Huron warrior who claims Wah-ta!-Wah as his wife, all of a sudden Hetty appears standing at the side of the fire. Judith has brought her to the camp in a canoe to try to secure his freedom with a ransom. Judith also wants to know what she should do in order to best serve him. Deerslayer replies that they should keep the ark moving and that he will never betray them, even though he knows he faces torture.

Chapter 18

At midnight, Hetty slips away from the camp. Judith collects her in a canoe. She quizzes Hetty about Deerslayer's precarious situation and makes it clear to her sister how she holds Deerslayer in much higher esteem than Hurry, for whom she has only contempt. She is determined to help Deerslayer in whatever way she can. Judith paddles the canoe but is unable to locate the ark. While they are discussing the matter they hear a rifle shot and observe that the shot has killed a Huron girl. Judith steers the canoe to the center of the lake for safety, after which she lets it drift. The two girls spend the night in the canoe.

Chapter 19

In the ark, Hutter and Hurry have no sympathy for Deerslayer, feeling that he brought his predicament upon himself. It transpires that it was a random shot from Hurry that killed the Indian girl, to the great distress of Wah-ta!-Wah. In the pre-dawn, the ark approaches the castle and makes contact with Judith and Hetty who are still in their canoe, with Wah-ta!-Wah. Chingachgook expresses a warning: he believes there are Huron warriors in the castle. Hutter and Hurry take no notice of this, however, and proceed unarmed to the castle. As he enters, Hurry calls out to Hutter that it is safe, but soon Chingachgook, who has remained behind, hears the sounds of a struggle. He steers the ark a hundred yards away from the castle. In the meantime, Hutter has been captured, while Hurry fights on.

Chapter 20

After a ferocious fight with several Hurons, Hurry is defeated and bound. At the suggestion of Wah-ta!-Wah, who is now referred to as Hist (the abbreviated form of the English version of her name), Hurry rolls off the platform of the castle, hoping to fall into the adjacent ark. But he misses the target and falls into the water. He is still bound hand and foot. Hist throws him a rope which he grasps with his teeth and his hands and is dragged to safety. Three Hurons then give chase in a canoe after Judith and Hetty. They are gaining on the girls when they break a paddle and abandon the chase. The Hurons then abandon the castle. When Judith and Hetty return to it they discover that their father, although still alive, has been scalped.

Chapter 21

It transpires that Hutter has also been stabbed, a mortal wound. He dies slowly, as Hetty and Judith tend to him. He confesses that he is not the girls' father, which pleases Judith, since there had never been much love between the two of them. After Hutter dies, his body is lowered into the lake, at the farthest end of the shoal on which the castle stands, near the place where he had buried his wife. After the burial, Hurry approaches Judith and makes her a marriage proposal, which she promptly refuses. Hurry tells her that the area of the lake no longer has any appeal to him, and she tells him to leave it and head for the nearest garrison, from which a party can be sent out to assist the girls. Judith also requests that the soldiers should not include a man named Captain Warley, although she gives no reason for this.

Chapter 22

In a canoe above Hutter's grave, Judith tells Hetty they are no longer safe living on the lake and must move to one of the settlements. Hetty does not want to leave, since she has lived all her life in nature and regards the settlements as places where wickedness flourishes. The women are then surprised to see Deerslayer approaching in a canoe. Deerslayer tells them he has been released on a furlough by the Hurons and has given his word that he will return by noon the following day.

Chapter 23

Deerslayer explains that he has been sent to convey some proposals from the Hurons, who now consider that the inhabitants of the castle lie at their mercy. They are prepared to offer Chingachgook safe passage back to his own tribe but insist that Hist must be returned to the Hurons. They want Judith to live with them and become the wife of a warrior who has recently lost his wife; they offer

Hetty safety, too; she will be honored and cared for. The Hurons also offer Hurry the chance to make an easy escape. Judith, Hist, and Chingachgook contemptuously turn down these proposals. Hetty also refuses but more gently. Hurry alone accepts the offer, and Deerslayer takes him ashore in a canoe. Deerslayer tells him to persuade the garrison to send out a force to pursue the Hurons and suggests that he lead it himself, since he knows the area so well.

Chapter 24

Deerslayer and Judith examine the remaining contents of Hutter's chest. Judith is eager to know whether it contains anything that will tell her more of her family history, since she now knows that Hutter was not her father. They find bundles of letters and other papers and piece together the story. Hutter was a pirate whose real name was Thomas Hovey. Judith's mother, who came from an educated family, was deserted by the man who fathered her two children, a European military officer, but who had never married her. Out of resentment and a desire to get back at the man who deserted her, Judith's mother married Hovey/Hutter, even though he was semi-illiterate and her inferior in every way. As Judith and Deerslayer talk, she makes it clear that she would like to be his wife. But Deerslayer cannot take this suggestion seriously, thinking that since he is an illiterate man of the woods he could never be a suitable husband for Judith.

Chapter 25

At dawn the next morning, Chingachgook and Hist agree that they will try to rescue Deerslayer from the Hurons. When Chingachgook makes his intentions clear to Deerslayer, the latter tells him his plan is madness, since he now has Hist to take care of. Deerslayer then talks to Judith, telling her that should he be killed by the Hurons, he would like Killdeer, the rifle formerly owned by Hutter and which Judith has given him, to be passed on to Chingachgook. Then Deerslayer and Chingachgook take turns shooting at ducks. Deerslayer has far greater skill than his Indian friend. Deerslayer then uses Killdeer to shoot and kill an eagle that was flying at a great height.

Chapter 26

Deerslayer regrets having killed the eagle for mere sport. Then he bids his companions lengthy farewells. He does not expect to see them again, since he presumes that the Hurons will torture and kill him. Hetty paddles the canoe that takes him ashore to return to the Hurons.

Chapter 27

At noon, Deerslayer returns to the Huron camp. Many of the warriors are surprised he honored his promise, but others are not. The senior warriors are seated on the trunk of a fallen log. The most important are Rivenoak and the Panther, the latter being known for his ferocity. After greeting Deerslayer, the chiefs confer for an hour, after which they tell him that he is to take as his wife Sumach, the widow of the warrior, Lynx, whom he killed. Deerslayer refuses, which so angers the Panther, who is Sumach's brother, that he hurls a tomahawk at Deerslayer's head. Deerslayer catches it with his hand and hurls it back, killing the Panther. In the confusion that follows, Deerslayer escapes. The Hurons pursue him; he jumps into a canoe, pushes it off from the shore with all his strength, and lies in the bottom to protect himself from rifle fire.

Chapter 28

Unfortunately for Deerslayer, the wind carries the canoe back to the shore, and he is recaptured. Rivenoak repeats his offer to marry Sumach and become an adopted Huron. Again, Deerslayer refuses. After a long conversation with Hetty, Deerslayer finds himself surrounded by a circle of Huron warriors. Preparations are under way for the commencement of his torture. He is bound and tied to a tree. After he turns down a personal appeal from Sumach, the signal is given for the torture to begin.

Chapter 29

The torture begins when Huron warriors throw tomahawks or knives at Deerslayer, the aim being that the weapon should hit the tree as near to his head as possible without actually striking him. Deerslayer faces his ordeal bravely, winning the respect of his captors. The Hurons are about to perform the same procedure with rifles when Hetty appears and reproaches them for their cruelty. The rifle shots disturb Deerslayer even less than the knives and tomahawks, and after he calmly endures the abuse of the Huron women, the Hurons decide it is time to begin the physical tortures.

Chapter 30

The proceedings are interrupted by the appearance of a beautiful, well-dressed woman who bears herself like a woman of rank. She demands of Rivenoak that Deerslayer be set free and offers more ransom. But then Hetty identifies the woman as Judith, her sister, and her ploy is thus doomed to failure. The torture by fire is about to start in earnest when there is another interruption, this time by the appearance of Hist, who manages to slip a knife to Judith, who passes it to Hetty, who starts to cut Deerslayer's bonds. She is swiftly stopped. Hist hurls abuse at Briarthorn, the Delaware who had abducted her and joined the Hurons. Next, Chingachgook suddenly appears and cuts Deerslayer's bonds and gives him his rifle, Killdeer. Briarthorn throws a knife at Chingachgook, but Hist turns it aside. Then Chingachgook throws a knife at Briarthorn, killing him. Sixty British troops then arrive and massacre the Hurons with their bayonets.

Chapter 31

After the battle, it is discovered that Hetty has been mortally wounded by a rifle shot. Only a few Hurons escaped the massacre. Rivenoak has been injured and taken prisoner. In the castle, Captain Thomas Warley, the leader of the British troops, talks with fellow officers about Judith. It appears that he had an affair with her some time in the past and is now, struck again by her beauty, considering renewing it. A few hours later, Hetty dies peacefully, her last act being to say goodbye to Hurry, of whom she was unusually fond. Judith is grief-stricken at the loss of her sister.

Chapter 32

Preparations are made for everyone to abandon the castle and the lake. Judith and Deerslayer take a canoe out on the lake, and Judith proposes marriage to Deerslayer. Deerslayer thanks her but refuses her offer, saying that they can never marry. Judith goes with the soldiers to the garrison, while Deerslayer rejoins Chingachgook and Hist. The following day, they return to the Delaware tribe, where they are greeted warmly. Fifteen years later, Deerslayer and Chingachgook, Hist, and their son Uncas return to Glimmerglass. The castle and the ark are in ruins, and it appears that no one has visited the lake since the final battle.

Characters

Briarthorn

Briarthorn is a Delaware who wanted Wah-ta!-Wah (called Hist) as his wife. He abducted her and went over to the Hurons. He tries to serve them well but is distrusted and only tolerated. When Chingachgook appears at the Huron camp in chapter 30, Briarthorn is angry and hurls his knife at the Delaware chief. The knife is deflected harmlessly by Hist, and Chingachgook throws a knife at Briarthorn, killing him instantly.

Natty Bumppo

See Deerslayer

Chingachgook

Chingachgook, whose name means Great Serpent, is a close friend of Deerslayer. He is by blood a Mohican, but he grew up among the Delawares. His father was Uncas, a great Mohican warrior. Chingachgook is named for his "wisdom and prudence, and cunning," even though he is still a young man and is on his first warpath. He is steady, dignified, and loyal; he always comes to Deerslayer's aid, as when he pledges to try to rescue him from the Hurons even though the odds against him seem insurmountable. Chingachgook is also courteous and a man of few words. He has traveled from Delaware country to meet with Deerslayer so that together they can rescue Wah-ta!-Wah (called Hist), Chingachgook's bride-to-be, who has been abducted and taken to the Hurons. As the plan is executed, Chingachgook distinguishes himself for his resourcefulness and courage. He also shows that he is deeply in love with Hist and is extremely respectful of her, which surprises Hetty who thinks that Indians always mistreat their women.

Deerslayer

Deerslayer, the hero of the tale, was raised by Moravian missionaries and lived for ten years among the Delawares. His real name is Natty Bumppo; he was given the nickname Deerslayer by the Delawares because of his prowess as a hunter. He respects their culture, and his great friend is the Delaware, Chingachgook. They have been hunting together for eight years.

Deerslayer is a few years younger than his friend Hurry March. He is about six feet tall, more slender than Hurry, but possessing great agility. Unlike Hurry, Deerslayer is not considered handsome, but his natural goodness is apparent in his appearance. His face gives the impression of "guileless truth, sustained by earnestness of purpose, and a sincerity of feeling, that rendered it remarkable." Deerslayer has a simple but unshakeable integrity, and everyone he meets quickly recognizes this.

Deerslayer has had little formal education and is illiterate. But he does not regret it. He is a man of "strong, native, poetical feeling," and he loves the woods in which he feels completely at home. He has a keen appreciation of the beauty of nature, and everywhere he looks he sees the handiwork of the Creator.

He often points out that he reads the book of nature rather than any printed book, and from nature he acquires all the wisdom and knowledge he needs.

Deerslayer has a highly developed moral sense. He seeks always to do the right thing and is clear in his mind about what that is. He is acutely aware of the requirements placed on him as a Christian man. Unlike Hutter and Hurry, for example, he refuses to take part in the practice of scalping, which he says may be lawful for an Indian but is not for a white man. He avoids killing whenever he can but will do so when he believes it is lawful and the situation demands it. For example, he kills Lynx only in self-defense. He has a reverence for life and kills deer only when food or skins for clothing are required. He does not believe in killing for sport, and he is bitterly repentant when just once he forgets his principles and shoots an eagle for the fun of it. "We should know *when* to use fire-arms, as well as *how* to use 'em," he says.

Having a straightforward nature, Deerslayer is true to his word, as is demonstrated by his honoring of the furlough given to him by the Hurons. He regards this as a moral duty, and duty "makes that which might otherwise be hard, easy, if not altogether to our liking."

Hist-oh!-Hist

See Wah-ta!-Wah

Thomas Hovey

See Thomas Hutter

Hetty Hutter

Hetty Hutter is Tom Hutter's simple-minded, naive stepdaughter. Innocent, vulnerable, and pious, she relies on her reading of the Bible for her moral compass. She has a love of truth and an intuitive grasp of what is right. She is distressed when her stepfather (whom she believes is her father) goes out with Hurry to take scalps. She abhors violence and has simple faith in the commandments not to kill and to forgive enemies. When the Hurons capture her father, Hetty goes to their camp to tell them about the Christian God who will punish them if they do not forgive their enemies. The Indians do not molest her because they regard such feeble-minded creatures with a kind of religious awe.

Without guile, trusting and meek, Hetty is infatuated with Hurry March and thinks the world has never seen anyone more handsome or stronger or braver. However, Hurry barely gives her a second glance. Hetty is rather dominated by her sister Judith, who has an easier command of words, but sometimes Hetty is able to check Judith's impetuosity by the clarity of her moral sense "that [was] so deeply engrafted in all her own thoughts and feelings; shining through both, with a mild and beautiful lustre, that threw a sort of holy halo around so much of what she both said and did." The fact that Hetty is accidentally killed in the final melee shows clearly that she is too pure to survive in the harsh world of reality.

Judith Hutter

Judith Hutter is Tom Hutter's stepdaughter. She speaks pleasingly and has had a good education, for which she is indebted to her deceased mother rather than her illiterate stepfather. Twenty years old, Judith is known for her great beauty and has been much sought after by any man passing through the lake area since she was fifteen years old. Hurry says she is "full of wit, and talk, and cunning." According to the Delawares, Judith is "fair to look on, and pleasant of speech; but over-given to admirers, and light-minded." In other words, she is accustomed to the adulation of men. She is superficial and susceptible to flattery; she admires dashing soldiers and fine uniforms. At some point in the past, she had an affair with Captain Warley and now refuses to speak of him.

Judith also loves fine clothes for herself and immediately puts on the gorgeous dress that is found in Hutter's chest. She is vain and knows how beautiful she looks in it, although as soon as Deerslayer says it does not suit her she changes out of it, since she wants him to think well of her. She has, in fact, taken a fancy to Deerslayer from the moment she first set eyes on him. She much prefers Deerslayer to Hurry March, and she ignores the latter's attempts to befriend her. Hurry is intoxicated by her beauty, but she regards him with disdain.

In the end, Judith is deeply hurt by Deerslayer's rejection of her bold proposal of marriage. She feels "Sorrow, deep, heart-felt sorrow," especially when she becomes aware that her reputation for being flighty has caused Deerslayer to be wary of her and unable to love her. It is with "a heart nearly broken by the consciousness of undue erring" that she says goodbye to him. Thus Judith becomes almost a tragic figure; the narrator describes her as "lovely but misguided."

Thomas Hutter

Thomas Hutter, whose original name was Thomas Hovey, is a former pirate who has lived in a virtual fortress facetiously known as Muskrat Castle on Lake Glimmerglass for fifteen years. He claims the entire lake for his own property and lives as a trapper. His wife has been dead for two years, and a son was killed some years earlier in a battle with the Indians, so all Hutter has left are his two daughters, Judith and Hetty. After Hutter's death, however, Deerslayer and the others find documents in an old chest owned by Hutter that reveal he is not the father of Hetty or Judith.

Hutter is direct in his speech and knows how to take decisive action. However, he is not exactly an admirable man. According to Hurry, he takes more after the ways of the muskrat than after any other creature. Hutter is ruthless, in part because of his long exposure to the harsh conditions of the wilderness. He lived in civilization before and appears to have had some education, the seeds of which "seemed to be constantly struggling upward, to be choked by the fruits of a life, in which his hard struggles for subsistence and security, had steeled his feelings and indurated his nature."

Although Hutter is not without goodness, which can be seen in the concern he shows over the welfare of his stepdaughters, he is also violent, greedy, and cruel; he thinks mostly of how he can gain from any given situation. For example, he goes on scalping expeditions, looking to scalp Indian women and children so that he can receive the bounty offered by the colony for Indian scalps.

Hutter eventually meets a violent death at the hands of the Hurons, who scalp him and stab him, leaving him to die slowly. He is mourned by Hetty but not by Judith.

Lynx

Lynx is the Huron warrior killed by Deerslayer, who was acting in self-defense. Lynx was married to Sumach. It is Lynx, as he is dying, who bestows on Deerslayer the name Hawkeye.

Harry March

Harry March is a woodsman and friend of Tom Hutter and Deerslayer. His nickname is Hurry, acquired because of his quick, bold nature. Sometimes he is called Hurry Skurry, because of his "dashing, reckless, off-hand manner." He is constantly on the move. Hurry is somewhere between twenty-six and twenty-eight years old and stands six feet four inches. He is immensely strong and also very handsome, and he is confident and bold in his manner. He holds his opinions fiercely even though they are usually not well thought out or considered.

Hurry is a deeply flawed character. Deerslayer comments that he cares for no one but himself. Like Hutter, Hurry is greedy and sees only what he can gain from any situation. He lacks chivalry and will not "hazard the safety of his own person, unless he could see a direct connection between the probable consequences and his own interest." He is also prejudiced in his views about race. He thinks Indians are no more than half human and regards white men as the superior race. He has committed much violence against the Indians, and he quiets his conscience by arguing that Indians have no human rights. He gets angry when his opinions are challenged.

Hurry is also reckless. In one incident, he fires a random shot in the darkness and kills a young Indian girl who had been acting as a sentinel. He affects an indifferent manner following this act of reckless destruction.

Hurry is attracted to Judith and tries to woo her. But she never shows the slightest interest in him, a rejection he feels keenly. By contrast, Hetty is fond of Hurry. Even though she finds him "rough and rude," she is still captivated by him. She does not really know him well, however, since he lavishes all his attention on her sister.

When Deerslayer conveys to Hurry the Huron offer of an easy escape, he is only too willing to take it, as the Hurons, knowing his character, fully expected him to. As he heads for the garrison, he does not seem to be ashamed of deserting the others. He goes resentfully, angered by Judith's rejection of him, and "as is usual with the vulgar and narrow-minded, he was more disposed to reproach others with his failures, than to censure himself." No one is sorry to see him go except Hetty.

Rivenoak

Rivenoak is the cunning old Huron chief. He is a skilled bargainer, as is seen when he negotiates with Deerslayer about the chess pieces. He is known for "eloquence in debate, wisdom in council, and prudence in measures." He admires Deerslayer's skill as a hunter and his fortitude under duress and does his best to persuade Deerslayer to become an adopted Huron, including trying various strategies to end Deerslayer's ordeal before it is too late. Eventually Rivenoak is captured by the British troops and taken to the ark.

Sumach

Sumach is the widow of Lynx, the Huron warrior killed by Deerslayer, and the sister of the Panther, who is also killed by Deerslayer. Sumach's name is derived from a berry that has an acid taste, which gives a clue to her personality. She is not greatly liked by the Hurons. When Deerslayer is captured, he is offered Sumach, who is much older than he is, as a wife. When he refuses the offer, Sumach is insulted and attacks him, pulling fiercely at his hair. Sumach is killed in the final battle by the British troops that come to the rescue.

Wah-ta!-Wah

Wah-ta!-Wah is a beautiful Delaware girl, also known by the English version of her name, Hist-oh!-Hist, which is abbreviated to Hist. Hist is the betrothed of Chingachgook. Slightly older than Hetty Hutter, she possesses a bright smile and melodious voice, delicate features, and even teeth. She speaks some English because her father had been employed as a warrior by the colony authorities. She has tact and ingenuity and knows how, within the confines of her place as a young woman, "to attract the attention she desired, without wounding the pride of those to whom it was her duty to defer, and respect." Hist has a narrow escape when Tom Hutter, on a scalping expedition, tries unsuccessfully to scalp her. After Hetty comes in search of her captured father, Hist befriends her. She also shows her bravery by playing an active role in the attempted rescue of Deerslayer. She slips a knife to Judith and then bravely admits to it when she is challenged. She can also be outspoken, and she roundly abuses Briarthorn, the man who abducted her from the Delawares. This surprises the onlookers, who had been more accustomed to her gentle ways. Hist also deflects the knife that is thrown by Briarthorn at Chingachgook.

Captain Warley

Captain Warley is a thirty-five-year-old British military officer. He is a confirmed bachelor but also something of a womanizer. In the past he has had an affair with Judith Hutter, and when he sees her again after the British troops carry out their rescue mission, he is again struck by her beauty and thinks about taking up with her once more.

Themes

Initiation and Testing

The main theme of the novel is the initiation of the young man Deerslayer, his rite of passage into true manhood. At the beginning he is untried and untested, but he develops into an authentic hero who successfully faces all the challenges presented to him.

Deerslayer has been given a civilized upbringing by the Moravian missionaries and the Delawares, and he has proved himself as a hunter, but he is not yet complete. He admits to Hurry March that there is no great valor in killing a deer. Now he must prove himself by going on his first warpath, with his friend Chingachgook, to rescue Hist, the Delaware's betrothed, from the Hurons. Unlike Hurry, his more experienced and ruthless companion, Deerslayer has never killed a man. His deadly encounter with Lynx is, therefore, of the greatest significance. During this incident, Deerslayer shows himself to be calm and self-possessed. He does not seek a quarrel with this Indian whom he encounters by chance, and he makes every effort to settle the matter peacefully. But when Lynx wrongly claims that one of the canoes belongs to the Indians, Deerslayer stands firm, insisting on the actual facts of the matter. He does not become angry, and he has no wish to kill, but he acts quickly when it becomes a matter of kill or be killed. Even then, he is courteous and considerate to the treacherous enemy Lynx, carrying the dying man to the lake, giving him water, taking his head in his lap and trying to comfort him in whatever way he can. He also refuses to scalp Lynx to gain a bounty from the colony, even though many would consider such an act to be legitimate. After the death of Lynx, Deerslayer refuses to exult or boast of his deed. He remains humble. Throughout this long incident he has behaved as a chivalrous warrior.

This key incident sets the tone for everything that follows. Immediately after the death of Lynx, Deerslayer behaves honorably toward the Indian he discovers in the canoe, allowing him to escape. He does not believe that the treachery of Lynx has somehow given him license to kill any Huron who crosses his path. But in the few days of adventure that follow, Deerslayer clearly demonstrates that he is a master of the art of legitimate warfare; he has the skill and the courage to excel. Yet he never sacrifices his principles. He refuses to go on a scalping expedition with Hurry and Hutter, because he does not regard scalping as a legitimate practice for a white man. In all things Deerslayer shows himself to be honest, patient, modest, pure-hearted, and loyal. He speaks the truth but does not speak hastily or without due consideration. He honors his word by returning from the furlough, even though on the surface this would appear not to be in his best interests. When he faces the ultimate test after being captured by the Hurons, he will not betray his friends to save his own life. Facing torture and imminent death, he remains stoic and self-possessed, never wavering for a moment, ready to endure whatever comes to him with courage and equanimity. Also, like the chivalrous hero of a medieval romance, Deerslayer proves his purity by resisting the

Topics For Further Study

- Research and make a class presentation on the history of the Lenape tribe (referred to in the novel as the Delawares). What happened to the Lenape during the eighteenth and nineteenth centuries? What were their relationships with the United States' government? Where do they live today?

- Working with a partner, investigate the issue of Native American-themed mascots in high school and college sports teams. Why do Native Americans object to these? Make a class presentation in which you explain both sides of the issue.

- As you read the novel, who did you find more sympathetic, Hetty or Judith? Why? Which character would make a better role model for young women today? Is Judith badly treated by Deerslayer? Is she superficial and vain, or is she a bold woman who knows her own mind? Write an essay in which you explore these topics.

- Write an essay in which you explore the following question: Is Deerslayer too good to be true? Cooper wrote that he had wanted to show some of Deerslayer's weaknesses so as to present "a reasonable picture of human nature, without offering a 'monster of goodness.'" Did he succeed? What weaknesses does Deerslayer exhibit, and how does he overcome them?

- Research on the Internet the history and beliefs of the Moravians. Who were the Moravians? Since Deerslayer was raised by Moravians, what would he have learned from them? Write an essay on the topic.

- Who is Leonard Peltier? What was the reason for the shoot-out on Pine Ridge Indian Reservation in 1975? Was it a modern version of the clashes between whites and Indians in the novel? Should Peltier be regarded as a political prisoner? Make a class presentation in which you discuss the case.

---

female seductress in the form of Judith. He does not allow himself to be bewitched by her beauty or to fall victim to her many ploys to win his love. He remains true to himself and his calling as a hunter, a man of the woods, an adventurer, a free and independent man, a man who certainly has obligations to his fellow creatures but whose destiny is not to become a domesticated husband leading a routine, limited life.

Clash of Values

There is a marked contrast in values between the characters, which fall broadly into two groups. In the first group are Deerslayer, Hetty Hutter, Chingachgook, and Hist. Deerslayer is a child of both civilization and wilderness who combines the best qualities of the two. He feels his being is in harmony with nature, but he is also aware of his obligations to God and his fellow man. Hetty Hutter, as an innocent who trusts in her Bible and her faith, who wishes no harm to come to anyone and who loves simply and well, is in some ways Deerslayer's

female counterpart, although being simple-minded she lacks Deerslayer's intelligence, practicality, and competence. Chingachgook is the highest example of what an Indian can aspire to. He is not bound by the same divine laws as the Christian white man— it is no sin for Chingachgook, being an Indian, to indulge in scalping, for example, but the young Delaware possesses dignity, sagacity, and loyalty. He is willing to risk his life for his friend Deerslayer. Chingachgook also exhibits a deep and respectful love for Hist, showing her "a manly kindness, equally removed from boyish weakness and haste." For her part, Hist is aware of her duties ("patient and submissive as became a woman of her people"), but also she reveals nobility and courage, telling Chingachgook that she would never be able to laugh again should Deerslayer be killed by the Hurons without her and Chingachgook's trying to save him. She says of herself, "She would rather go back, and start on her long path alone, than let such a dark cloud pass before her happiness."

Set against these characters, who embody all the most noble and desirable character traits, are those in the second group, consisting of Thomas Hutter, Hurry March, and Judith Hutter. Hurry is Deerslayer's opposite in every way. He is "loud, clamorous, dogmatical," in contrast to Deerslayer's even, prudent temperament. Hurry puts his trust in material rather than moral or spiritual values. He adheres to no higher principles that might impede his reckless pursuit of his own interests, and he has no regard for the rights of others, especially Indians, whom he views with absolute contempt. He desires only personal gain and financial profit, and he shares these unattractive qualities with Thomas Hutter. A key incident takes place when Hurry and Hutter—the latter a ruthless, violent man—set out on their scalping expedition to the Huron camp. The narrator explains that they go because of "a heartless longing for profit." Hurry has a "habitual love of gold, which he sought with the reckless avidity of a needy spendthrift." As for Hutter, he is expecting to find only women and children in the camp, who will be easy prey for what he has in mind. When the two men are disappointed to find the camp empty, they go prowling around "as if they expected to find some forgotten child"—a poor innocent whom they could murder. When they fail to find anyone, they fall to quarreling fiercely with each other. Appropriately enough, Hutter meets a violent end when he is himself scalped, and Hurry reveals his lack of moral values when he prefers to take the easy way out and head to the British garrison rather than help Chingachgook and Hist rescue Deerslayer.

As for Judith, she resembles Hurry in the sense that she values superficial qualities. Just as Hurry puts his trust in his own physical strength—and when that fails he has no strong will to sustain him—Judith identifies mostly with the physical level of life. She knows her own beauty, she loves fine clothes, and her head is easily turned by a shiny military uniform on a British soldier. She thinks that the mere presence of beauty confers some kind of merit on a person. She therefore stands in clear contrast to Deerslayer and Hetty, for whom inner qualities are more important than outer ones.

Style

Setting

The most prominent aspect of the setting is the lake, which has a symbolic as well as literal function in the novel. Together with the surrounding woods, Glimmerglass (Lake Otsego) represents the purity of nature, before the hand of man has touched it:

> On a level with the point lay a broad sheet of water, so placid and limpid, that it resembled a bed of the pure mountain atmosphere, compressed into a setting of hills and woods. . . . the most striking peculiarities of this scene, were its solemn solitude, and sweet repose. On all sides, wherever the eye turned, nothing met it, but the mirror-like setting of the lake, the placid void of heaven, and the dense setting of wood. . . . The hand of man had never yet defaced, or deformed any part of this native scene, which lay bathed in the sunlight, a glorious picture of affluent forest grandeur, softened by the balminess of June, and relieved by the beautiful variety afforded by the presence of so broad an expanse of water.

The above is the description given when Deerslayer sees Glimmerglass for the first time. He is transfixed with wonder by the scene, which is as fresh and untouched as the day it was first created by God. It therefore represents origins, the primal reality, the pure wilderness that was present before the arrival of human civilization. As a backdrop to the action and adventure described in the novel, it represents a kind of transcendence, a reality far removed from the savagery of war and the specter of human greed. Glimmerglass is, therefore, an aspect of eternity present in the temporal world. It represents what never changes, no matter what turbulence takes place among humans. This level of symbolism becomes clear in the description of the scene after the massacre of the Hurons by the British soldiers:

> When the sun rose the following morning, every sign of hostility and alarm had vanished from the basin of the Glimmerglass. The frightful event of the preceding evening had left no impression on the placid sheet, and the untiring hours pursued their course in the placid order prescribed by the powerful hand that set them in motion. The birds were again skimming the water, or were seen poised on the wing, high above the tops of the tallest pines of the mountains . . . In a word, nothing was changed.

Thus, Cooper suggests that human events are temporal, but there is something eternal and constant in nature, something that remains untouched and which refuses to record mortal strife.

Historical Romance

The novel belongs to the genre of romance. It has been variously described as an epic romance, a forest romance, an historical romance, and a pastoral romance. In romantic rather than realistic fiction, the characters and situations are more idealized and less true to real life. Medieval romance, for example, featured knights who went through a series of adventures—slaying monsters, for example—in which they proved their valor and their chivalry. In this respect Deerslayer, who has to prove himself on his first warpath, resembles a medieval knight.

Romances can often be allegorical, such as Edmund Spenser's verse romance, *The Fairie Queene*, in which virtues and vices are personified in the characters. *The Deerslayer* is allegorical in the sense that Hurry March and Hutter personify the qualities such as greed, violence, and selfishness, while Deerslayer personifies virtues such as courage, prudence, and integrity.

M. H. Abrams's description of prose romances in *A Glossary of Literary Terms* clearly puts *The Deerslayer* in that category. Such romances feature:

> Simplified characters, larger than life, who are sharply discriminated as heroes and villains, masters and victims; the protagonist is often solitary, and isolated from a social context; the plot emphasizes adventure, and is often cast in the form of a quest for an ideal, or the pursuit of an enemy.

The novels of Sir Walter Scott and Nathaniel Hawthorne are also examples of prose romance.

Historical Context

French and Indian Wars

The historical background of *The Deerslayer* is the periodic conflict between English and French forces for control of the North American colonies. The War of Austrian Succession (1740–1748), was fought mostly in Europe, but for England the chief interest lay in its overseas conflict with France and Spain over trading and colonial ambitions. In North America this period is known as King George's War (1744–1748), the most notable feature of which was the capture by the English colonists of the French fortress of Louisbourg on Cape Breton Island. However, Louisbourg was handed back to the French in the peace settlement of 1748. King George's War was the third of what became known as the French and Indian wars; the Indians became involved by forming alliances either with the French or the English. Such conflicts with France continued until the decisive Seven Years War (1756–1763) in which England overthrew French power in Canada and established itself as the controlling colonial power in North America.

Indians and Cooper

For information about Indians in colonial America a hundred years earlier, Cooper turned to the work of a historian, John Heckewelder, whose book, *Account of the History, Manners, and Customs of the Indian Nations, Who Once Inhabited Pennsylvania and the Neighboring States*, was published in 1819. Heckewelder was a Moravian missionary to the Delawares (also known as Lenape), and he developed great sympathy for and understanding of Delaware life and culture. Moravian missionaries from Germany had arrived in colonial Pennsylvania about 1740, working with the Delawares and traveling with them as they moved west. Many Delawares converted to Christianity. This historical fact helps to explain Deerslayer's background in the novel, since he was taught by Moravians and lived for ten years with the Delawares. It was Heckewelder who supplied Cooper with this background. Also, as Paul A. W. Wallace points out in "Cooper's Indians," it was Heckewelder who presented the model of Indians split into good and bad tribes that permeates not only *The Deerslayer* but also Cooper's *The Last of the Mohicans*. In the former group Heckewelder placed the Delawares and the Mohicans, presenting them in the tradition of the noble savage, a popular nineteenth-century idea about the innate nobility of indigenous people. Heckewelder heard and accepted the Delaware version of their history in which they were tricked by the Iroquois into disarming and becoming mediators and peacemakers with their Indian neighbors, following which the Iroquois induced other Indian tribes to attack the Delawares. This situation weakened the Delawares, greatly depleting their numbers, which explains the reference in *The Deerslayer* to the Delawares as "disparsed and diminished, that chieftainship among 'em has got to be little more than a name."

On the other side of the Indian divide, according to Heckewelder, were the Mingoes, or Iroquois (also known as the Five Nations and later the Six Nations), who were savage and treacherous. Following Heckewelder's lead, Cooper created Chingachgook as the chief representative of the noble, dispossessed Delawares, while Lynx, Rivenoak, and dozens of anonymous Indian warriors represent the treacherous Mingoes. Interestingly, although Cooper usually refers to the hostile Indians as Mingoes and Hurons, he once (at the beginning of Chapter 5), refers to them as Iroquois. This is an historical error, since the Iroquois were, in fact, allies of the English not the French during the French and Indian wars. Cooper was correct, however, in presenting the Hurons, who were allied with the French, as the enemy of the English and their allies. The Hurons were traditional enemies of the Iroquois.

Compare & Contrast

- **1740s:** Lake Otsego and its environs are visited only by a few hunters. Indians also visit the area, but no one Indian tribe lays claim to it. The first white pioneers of what will become Otsego County, New York, establish a settlement at Cherry Valley in 1739.

  1840s: Due to its many natural attractions of hills, valleys, streams, and lakes, the Otsego area gradually becomes established as a summer retreat. Great estates and houses are built there, and Cooper's Leatherstocking Tales make the area famous.

  Today: The town of Cooperstown, founded by James Fenimore Cooper's father in the 1780s and situated at the southern end of Lake Otsego, is a popular tourist destination. The Baseball Hall of Fame in Cooperstown attracts thirty thousand visitors each year.

- **1740s:** War between England and France includes skirmishes in the North American colonies. In 1745, the French attack and burn Saratoga, New York. Indian tribes maneuver for advantage by allying themselves to England or to France.

  1840s: Westward expansion of the United States results in battles between U.S. forces and various Indian tribes, as the government attempts to clear the way for further white expansion. These Indian wars continue into the 1880s.

  Today: According to the 2000 Census, 4.3 million people, or 1.5 percent of the total U.S. population, report that they are American Indian and Alaska Natives. The largest Indian tribes are Cherokee (302,569), Navajo (276,775), Sioux (113,713), and Chippewa (110,857). Twenty-six

percent of American Indians live in poverty, according to the 2000 Census. About 34 percent of the American Indian and Alaska Native population live on reservations, officially known as American Indian areas.

- **1740s:** The United States of America does not exist. The American colonists of New England (Connecticut, Rhode Island, Massachusetts, New Hampshire), the Middle Colonies (Delaware, New Jersey, New York, Pennsylvania) and the Southern Colonies (Georgia, North Carolina, South Carolina) are subjects of the king of England. However, during the 1740s, an influx of Scottish and Irish immigrants following the failed Jacobite uprisings in England fuel anti-English sentiment. The colonies gradually grow more unified amongst themselves and less loyal to the English government.

  1840s: The U.S. population in 1840 is 17,069,453. Population growth and territorial expansion continue rapidly. In 1845, Texas joins the Union as the twenty-eighth state. In 1846, war with Mexico begins, and the United States annexes New Mexico, formerly part of Mexico. The Mexican War ends in 1848 with the Treaty of Guadalupe Hidalgo, under which Mexico cedes five hundred thousand square miles of its territory in the western and southwestern United States.

  Today: The 2006 Census estimates U.S. population as 297,821,175, which is up 2,713,518 or 0.9 percent from the previous year. The population increases by one person every fourteen seconds. The United States is the preeminent military power in the world but faces stern challenges from international terrorism and the rapid growth of illegal immigration.

Critical Overview

On publication, *The Deerslayer* received mostly favorable reviews, some of which are quoted in George Dekker's and John P. McWilliams's *Fenimore*

Cooper: The Critical Heritage and others of which are cited in James Franklin Beard's "Historical Introduction" to the 1987 edition of the novel. Dekker and McWilliams quote an unsigned review in the *New-York Mirror* that presents an almost entirely

A scene from the French and Indian War, highlighting the alliance of certain Native Americans with the French against the British who are allied with other Native Americans, a feature of the conflict related in The Deerslayer © Kean Collection/Getty Images

positive view of the novel: "He [Cooper] is the most original thinker of any of our American novelists … unrivalled in descriptive powers, and unapproached in the heartiness of his patriotic feelings." The reviewer praises Cooper's "sketches of Indian character" and adds that "throughout the work there is more knowledge of human nature and more successful delineation of character than Mr. Cooper has generally had credit for." The only fault in the novel that the reviewer brings attention to is in the way the relationship between Deerslayer and Judith is presented. It seemed unlikely to the reviewer that such an admirable young woman would throw herself at such a rough character as Deerslayer and that he would not have become aware of her feelings much sooner than he does. This criticism aside, the reviewer concludes that Cooper "has shown a genuine American feeling which is unfortunately too seldom met with in American writers."

Beard cites reviews in other American magazines that largely echo these sentiments. For example, he quotes *The United States Magazine and Democratic Review* as asserting that

> by his admirable description and narrative talent, [Cooper] can keep the interest of his readers agreeably excited … recording the adventures and vicissitudes

of not more than four or five days spent on the waters, and about the shore, of a little inland lake in the heart of the howling wilderness.

Beard also quotes from the English publication *The Examiner*, which declares that "The book is full of fine description and vigorous character; no compromise is made with the wild and savage features of the time or of the scene." This reviewer also notes that "The heroine of the tale is, perhaps, somewhat harshly dealt with," a verdict on the fate of Judith that other contemporary reviewers echo and which has been repeated by modern critics of the novel.

Criticism

Bryan Aubrey

Aubrey holds a Ph.D. in English. In this essay, he analyzes The Deerslayer *in terms of the contrast between Deerslayer and Hurry Harry and what that signifies for the future of the American colonies, soon to become the United States of America.*

Visitors in the early 2000s to the crowded Lake Otsego area, one of New York's popular tourist

> " No modern reader with even a passing knowledge of Native American history since the coming of the white man can contemplate Hurry's sentiments, which are shared by Tom Hutter, without something of a shiver."

destinations, need an effort of the imagination to recreate for themselves Cooper's vision of the Glimmerglass, the pristine lake at the heart of the virgin wilderness where he set his final (although first in chronology) Leatherstocking Tale. As Cooper noted in his 1850 preface to *The Deerslayer*, it was not until 1760 that the first settlements appeared on the banks of Lake Otsego, so setting the story twenty years earlier than that gave him a sound basis for what in effect is a story about the origins of a nation, the choices it faces, the direction it is to take.

Many commentators remark on the symbolism of the Glimmerglass itself, the descriptions of which suggest a setting that is in some sense beyond time or change; it represents the eternity from which all temporal life emerges. The following description, which occurs as Deerslayer steers the ark, under the watchful, hostile eyes of the Hurons, to the rock where he is to meet Chingachgook, is typical:

> It was a glorious June afternoon, and never did that solitary sheet of water seem less like an arena of strife and bloodshed. The light air scarce descended as low as the bed of the lake, hovering over it, as if unwilling to disturb its deep tranquility, or to ruffle its mirror-like surface. Even the forests appeared to be slumbering in the sun, and a few piles of fleecy clouds had lain for hours along the northern horizon, like fixtures in the atmosphere.

Everything here, from the tranquil water to the slumbering forests and the stationary clouds, contributes to the feeling of time arrested or not yet born. Yet in the midst of this lake, which is serenity and beauty, is already the presence of something else, some intrusion on pristine nature: the Muskrat Castle of Thomas Hutter. Tom's castle is

a human dwelling rising up from the placid waters of the lake a full quarter of a mile from the nearest shore. So here are two aspects of life juxtaposed: nature untouched and nature already feeling the imprint of the human hand. Muskrat Castle is constructed as a fortress, much stronger and more formidable than the average log cabin of the era; it immediately suggests that now, the human world of opposing and competing values, of good and evil, with all its accompanying dangers, has arrived and taken up residence on the serene, undifferentiated surface of the lake. Indeed, the outer appearance of Muskrat Castle, because it is made up of logs of different sizes, is described as "rude and uneven"; it is as if the balance of nature has been upset.

When the reader gets to know Tom Hutter, it becomes clear how much disruption has been introduced into the natural order. Tom is an old rogue, a former buccaneer rumored to have associated with the notorious pirate Captain Kidd. He fled to the wilderness to escape the reach of the authorities and to cheat the hangman's noose. Lake Glimmerglass's first human guest is no Adam in a Garden of Eden. Although he treats his daughters well, Tom Hutter is a quarrelsome man whose previous dwellings were burned down on three occasions either by other hunters or Indians. Hutter reveals his character early in the story, with his bloodthirsty plan to scalp Indian women and children merely to collect the bounty offered by the colony. This is an example of humanity motivated by greed and material values to the exclusion of all decent feelings. As he puts it, "If there's women, there's children, and big and little have scalps; the Colony pays for all alike."

In this base desire to kill the innocent for monetary reward, Hutter is joined by Harry March, known for good reason as Hurry Harry. If there are two types of men who now wander in the formerly pristine wilderness, they are ably represented by Hurry, on the one hand, and Deerslayer, on the other. It is in the struggle between what these two represent that the soul of the emerging nation lies. The contrast between them is clearly and very deliberately laid out in the first three chapters. A clue lies in the first passage alluding to the two men, as they call out to each other in the woods: "The calls were in different tones, evidently proceeding from two men who had lost their way, and were searching in different directions for their path."

Different directions, indeed. As they talk with each other, Deerslayer declares it unlawful to take human life, except in warfare. Hurry, by contrast, takes the law into his own hands; he will kill anyone who robs him. (It saves the magistrates the trouble, he says.) Deerslayer has a religious sensibility that measures all things by how they conform to a moral law given by God. His thinking reflects his upbringing by the Moravian missionaries; he values truth above anything else. He even says that if Hurry were to kill any future husband of Judith (which Hurry says he would be prepared to do) he would inform on him to the colony, a comment which so angers Hurry that he seizes the younger man by the throat. Deerslayer remains calm and states his point again. They may be in the lawless woods, but that does not mean they are beyond the law of God: "there is a law, and a law maker, that rule across the whole continent. He that flies in the face of either, need not call me fri'nd." This religious attitude toward life shows itself again when Deerslayer, in stark contrast to Hurry, says he opposes the colony's practice of paying a bounty for the scalps of Indians. A law that runs counter to God's law should not be obeyed, he says. In contrast to Deerslayer's concern with God, law, and morality, Hurry thinks he has the right simply to do what he wants and take what he wants, regardless of obligations to others, whether human or divine. Unlike Deerslayer, he has little appreciation of the beauty of nature. When Deerslayer expresses his wonder at the loveliness of the lake, which soothes his mind, Hurry replies, "Lakes have a general character, as I say, being pretty much water, and land, and points, and bays." In other words, as far as Hurry is concerned, if you have seen one lake, you have seen them all. In contrast, Deerslayer's love of nature means that he is wary and even hostile to the spread of civilization, since he has seen some of the ill effects that such development brings. He tells Hurry that no one should be allowed to cut town timber without good reason, and he likes the fact that Glimmerglass has no name, "or at least no pale face name, for their christenings always foretel waste and destruction."

The differences between the two men are seen most tellingly in their attitude toward Indians. Hurry regards Indians as "half devil" and "half human." They are "murdering savages" who have "neither souls, nor reason." (When he utters the last remark he has apparently forgotten that only a couple of days earlier he had gone with Hutter to the Huron camp intending to murder women and children.) In contrast, Deerslayer, referring to the three races, white, black and Indian, replies, "God made all three, alike," although he allows each race its different "gifts," which means he is aware of cultural differences and does not judge the Indians adversely because their traditions and laws differ from those of the white man.

No modern reader with even a passing knowledge of Native American history since the coming of the white man can contemplate Hurry's sentiments, which are shared by Tom Hutter, without something of a shiver. Here are white settlers, proto-Americans still at this point under the British crown, declaring that Native Americans are less than human and regarding them as a "natural enemy," creatures that are "only a slight degree removed from the wild beasts that roam the woods." Bearing in mind the harsh policies and atrocities that would follow over the next century and a half, including massacres and even genocide of whole Indian tribes, it is hard not to be reminded, as twentieth-century European history has also reminded people, that defining another race as subhuman lays the groundwork for committing acts against them that would be unimaginable in any other circumstances.

The differences between Hurry and Deerslayer, laid out so clearly in the first three chapters, are apparent throughout the remainder of the novel. Whereas Deerslayer is "thoughtful," Hurry is "reckless." Deerslayer kills a man for the first time when he has no choice; he kills in self-defense. Hurry, by contrast, in an act of "unthinking cruelty," shoots a Huron girl who was acting as a sentinel. On several occasions, Deerslayer has to restrain Hurry from killing Indians when the situation does not warrant it. For example, in chapter 15, Hurry wants to kill the Indian boy who has delivered the declaration of war. Since he only understands motives relating to personal gain, Hurry cannot grasp the moral principle that compels Deerslayer to honor his furlough and return to the Hurons. Also, unlike Deerslayer, Hurry is not bound by feelings of loyalty and thinks nothing of deserting Hetty and Judith and returning to the garrison.

Here then, in the land that would within two generations become the United States of America, are two distinct types of men, with two radically different approaches to life. They are like the seeds that will determine how the young nation will develop and the principles that will govern its conduct. Although adventures in the wilderness of New York province in the 1740s may at first seem remote from the world of the twenty-first century, perhaps the thoughtful reader of *The Deerslayer* might consider the possibility that these representative types live on in the United States of the early

What Do I Read Next?

- *The Last of the Mohicans*, first published in 1826, is the most famous of Cooper's Leatherstocking Tales. Set in 1757, it describes the adventures of Deerslayer, now called Hawkeye, during the French and Indian wars. Hawkeye roams again in upper New York state with Chingachgook and also with Uncas, Chingachgook's son. The story contains the familiar mix of battle, pursuit, capture, and escape, and a dramatic massacre of an English garrison by Indians.

- Sir Walter Scott's historical romance, *Ivanhoe* (1819), is set in medieval England. Ivanhoe, the great chivalrous knight, returns from the Crusades in disguise and goes through many adventures that bring him into contact with the likes of Robin Hood and King Richard the Lion-Hearted before he ends up happily married to a noble lady.

- Nathaniel Hawthorne's psychological romance, *The Scarlet Letter* (1850), which is considered the masterpiece of this great American novelist, is set in Boston in the early days of the Massachusetts colony. It tells the story of a woman's adulterous relationship with a clergyman and explores issues of sin and spiritual redemption.

- *500 Nations: An Illustrated History of North American Indians* (new edition, 2002), by Alvin M. Josephy Jr., tells the stories of the diverse Indian nations of North and Central America, going back to the ancient Maya and Olmec civilizations of Mexico. Of particular relevance to readers of *The Deerslayer* are the sections that show how the lives of North American Indians were irreversibly changed by contact with white traders.

2000s: on the one hand, the determination to meet one's responsibilities to others, to the environment, and to God, and, on the other hand, the belief in the primacy of the individualistic for-profit motive, the valuing of self-interest above all. In the 1740s, this was the concern only of the American colonies; in the early 2000s, since the United States is the global superpower whose actions have effects far beyond its borders, it is the concern of all people around the world. What then is the essential soul of the United States: the humble, modest sincerity and truth of a Deerslayer, with his respect for nature and other cultures, or the recklessness of a Hurry Harry, who sees only what he wants and is aware of no moral law that might prevent him from seizing it?

Source: Bryan Aubrey, Critical Essay on *The Deerslayer*, in *Novels for Students*, Thomson Gale, 2007.

Donald Darnell

In the following essay, Darnell explores social hierarchy and the tragedy that can follow aspirations to rise above "one's place."

The Deerslayer: **Cooper's Tragedy of Manners**

Beginning with D. H. Lawrence's *Studies in Classic American Literature* in 1922, criticism of *The Deerslayer* for more than fifty years has ultimately examined it as a romance, emphasizing its mythic and pastoral qualities. While the persistence of this approach is not surprising considering the quest plot and Edenic setting of the work, what is remarkable is the absence of commentary on the strong textual evidence of a radically different dimension of the novel. This other dimension is most sharply focused in the ninth chapter when, following their rendezvous with Chingachgook and escape from the Hurons, Deerslayer explains to Judith Hutter an expected sound in the water:

"Sartainly something *did* move the water, oncommon like; it must have been a fish. Them creatur's prey upon each other like men, and animals on the land; osne has leaped into the air, and fallen hard, back into his own element. 'Tis of little use, Judith, for any to strive to get out of their elements, since it's natur' to stay in 'em, and natur' will have its way.'"

Readers familiar with previous *Leather-Stocking Tales* will be inclined to identify Deerslayer's speech as another of his characteristic sententious commonplaces. In point of fact, however, Cooper with conscious artistry has metaphorically identified a central conflict in *The Deerslayer* and developed the leitmotiv that structures and organizes one half the novel. Natty's remark is about knowing one's place, and *The Deerslayer*, its rich romantic, mythic, and pastoral elements notwithstanding, is, in a very substantial way, about social hierarchy and class, and the tragedy inherent in attempts to rise above one's social position. Cooper had ridiculed levelers and climbers earlier in *Homeward Bound* and *Home as Found* and would attack them with scathing sarcasm in the Littlepage trilogy and subsequent works. But in *The Deerslayer* he discovers that frustrated social aspiration can also be a source of tragedy and in the process creates his most memorable heroine in Judith Hutter.

The appearance of such a theme in a romance of the forest is incongruous, to say the least. Yet, the evidence is there in *The Deerslayer's* romantic world interpenetrated throughout by the assumptions, values, and mores appropriate to the novel of manners. Equally paradoxical is the fund of information about propriety, appropriateness of dress to social rank, and the dangers of attempting to rise above one's class—in short about manners, shared by persons with the most unlikely claims to such knowledge: Tom Hutter, Harry March, even Deerslayer. The result, then, is a striking and paradoxical fusion of romantic and novelistic worlds in which the values of the latter determine the fate of the heroine and give this last novel of the *Leather-Stocking Tales*, the most idyllic work Cooper wrote, its dark and somber cast. In an Edenic setting with a plot of violent forest warfare in which killing, scalping, and torture are the rule, the author finds his most tragic effects resulting from a young woman's frustrated social aspirations—the favorite subject of that most civilized of genres, the novel of manners.

The problem of manners is introduced early in chapter 1 in the dialogue between Deerslayer and Harry March concerning Judith Hutter's behavior when officers from the forts on the Mohawk visit the Glimmerglass. To March's declaration that Judith seems "beside herself," wearing finery and giving herself airs with "the gallants," Deerslayer observes that such conduct is "unseemly in a poor man's darter, . . . the officers are all gentry, and can only look on such as

> **"** In an Edenic setting with a plot of violent forest warfare in which killing, scalping, and torture are the rule, the author finds his most tragic effects resulting from a young woman's frustrated social aspirations—the favorite subject of that most civilized of genres, the novel of manners."

Judith with evil intentions." As precise knowledge of the ways of the social world is not typical information stored in the minds of Adamic heroes, one might well ask whence comes such wisdom to this child of nature. It is obvious that here and throughout the novel Cooper uses Deerslayer as the spokesman for his themes of the conflict between manners and morals, returning to a theme he had introduced twenty years earlier in *The Spy*, his first American novel.

In that work, the American Sarah Wharton, gentry herself, is bewitched by the savior-faire of the English officer Colonel Wellmere, who has a wife in England but is not deterred from marrying an attractive American girl of means. The wedding between Wellmere and Sarah is aborted, however, by the *deus ex machina* intervention of Harvey Birch. In *The Deerslayer* Cooper found the theme of betrayal across class lines still a powerful subject for literary examination, but in twenty years his perception of the theme had significantly deepened and his treatment had become more effective.

The dialogue between March and Deerslayer that introduces the theme of class differences also establishes "gallant" as synonymous with upper-class seducer of lower-class girls. "Gallant" and its synonyms "officer" and "gentry" appear throughout the novel in a highly specialized context to indicate members of a separate social class with a penchant for seduction and betrayal. With the exception of Hetty Hutter, every white character in the novel is aware of the connotation. The implications of the term established early, Cooper develops his theme of social aspiration and its consequences in the emphasis he gives to Judith's involvement with the gallants of the garrison. Having spent her winters in the neighborhood of the fort, Judith has "caught more than is for her good, from the settlers, and especially from the gallantifying officers," Harry tells Deerslayer. According to Hetty "Judith likes soldiers, and flaring coats, and fine feathers. . . . *She* says the officers are great, and gay, and of soft speech . . ." Tom Hutter admits his daughter has been "spoilt by the flattery of the officers who sometimes find their way up here . . ." What confirms beyond question the seriousness and significance of Judith's relationship with the officers, however, is Cooper's own assessment of her conduct, especially its implications in the social world: "She had many causes deeply to regret the acquaintance—if not to mourn over it, in secret sorrow—for it was impossible for one of her quick intellect not to perceive how hollow was the association between superior and inferior, and that she was regarded as the play thing of an idle hour, rather than as an equal and a friend, by even the best intentioned and least designing of her scarlet-clad admirers."

The passage is particularly important to the theme of the novel. It analyzes the caste system, continues the scarlet coat metaphor that permeates all discussions pertaining to rank and class, and sounds the motif of betrayal, the basis for the somber and tragic tone of the novel. It is significant that Cooper's assessment of Judith's plight precedes by only a page the quotation which introduced this study: "'Tis of little use, Judith, for any to strive to get out of their elements, since it's natur' to stay in 'em, and natur' will have its way."

Three chapters later nature has its way as Judith excitedly dons the beautiful brocaded gown from Hutter's chest, a gown that appears to have been made for her. While the ostensible reason for opening the locked chest is to secure articles to ransom Hutter and Harry March from the Hurons, Cooper uses the situation to discuss the validity of social separation. Consequently, chapter 12 becomes a key chapter in establishing the theme of caste and the important symbols and motifs which advance it. The reader learns that the large chest, which has never been opened in Judith's presence, had stood "a sort of tabooed relic before her eyes, from childhood to the present hour." When she attempts to open it she feels "resisted in an unhallowed attempt by some supernatural power." Having described the awe Judith feels regarding the chest, Cooper gives a detailed description of two articles

found there, a scarlet coat and a beautifully brocaded gown. The coat with buttonholes worked in gold thread is "not military, but . . . part of the attire of a civilian of condition, at a period when social rank was rigidly respected in dress." Urged by Judith to try on the coat, Deerslayer is incredulous that she wishes to see him in a "coat fit for a lord," and he refuses, declaring his gifts are his own, and he will live and die in them. More important to the social theme of the novel is the description of Judith's response to the gown and the dialogue it elicits: "Her rapture was almost childish, nor would she allow the enquiry to proceed, until she had attired her person in a robe so unsuited to her habits and her abode." Precisely why the gown is inappropriate is explained by Deerslayer. Judith should not keep the gown because "there's gifts in clothes, as well as in other things." His elaboration on this point comes by analogy from his own knowledge of Indian practice:

> "Now I do not think that a warrior on his first path, ought to lay on the same awful paints as a chief that has had his virtue tried, and knows from exper'ence he will not disgrace his pretentions. So it is with all of us, red or white. You are Thomas Hutter's darter, and that gownd was made for the child of some governor, or a lady of high station, and it was intended to be worn among fine furniture, and in rich company. In my eyes, Judith, a modest maiden never looks more becoming, than when becomingly clad, and nothing is suitable that is out of character."

Explicit as the dialogue and authorial commentary are, when examined in light of subsequent events in the novel, they raise important questions of interpretation: Specifically, where does Cooper stand on the issue of natural "gifts" vis-à-vis one's position in the social hierarchy, an issue that must be addressed in any final evaluation of the novel? The issue becomes further complicated when Cooper invests Judith Hutter's story of aspiration with tragedy and gives what might appear as an incidental plot embellishment a significant meaning in its own right. For if *The Deerslayer—The First War-Path*—is about Natty Bumppo's quest for a name in the heroic world, it is no less about Judith Hutter's search for identity in the social world. The reader will recall that the scalped and dying Tom Hutter tells Judith and Hetty he is not their real father and orders them to search his chest for information of their parentage. At this revelation Judith feels "an uncontrollable impulse of joy" and forbears to question Hutter further "lest something he should add, in the way of explanation, might disturb her pleasing belief that she was not Thomas Hutter's child." She grasps this notion and maintains it with passion to Harry March, who refers to her as Hutter's daughter: "I cannot tell you, Harry, who my father Was. . . . I hope he was an honest man, at least." With this expectation of finding an honest father, Judith again searches Hutter's chest in chapter 24, as crucial an initiation chapter for her as chapter 7 is for Deerslayer.

Within the chest, Judith and Deerslayer discover a small locked trunk. Forcing the lock, they find letters, fragments of manuscripts, and documents, all with the signatures carefully cut out and all names erased. Nor are there any addresses. In the account that follows, Cooper details his tragedy of class. Judith is gratified by the first group of letters, correspondence between her mother and her maternal grandmother indicating gentility and position. As she reads on, however, she discovers warnings and admonitions from the mother to the absent daughter in a letter coldly commenting on the "propriety of the daughter's indulging in as much intimacy, as had evidently been described in one of the daughter's own letters, with an officer 'who came from Europe, and who could hardly be supposed to wish to form an honorable connection in America'."

The next packet of letters, those by Judith's father to her mother, while "filled with the protestations of love [and] written with passion," exhibit "that deceit which men so often think it justifiable to use to the other sex." In them Judith discovers "a few points of strong resemblance between these letters and some it had been her own fate to receive." This "sad history of gratified passion, coldness, and finally of aversion" concludes after alluding to the births of Judith and Hetty and recording the mother's anguish at her lover's desertion. Thus Judith, the aspirant for a position and for recognition among the gallants of the garrison, discovers again the solid barriers of class. Her own mother, a genteel woman whose station in life was far higher than Judith's, was herself rejected by an English officer who would not marry a Colonial.

The letters between her parents are but the prologue to the sordid story of the relationship between her mother and Thomas Hutter explained in the next packet of letters Judith examines. In that correspondence, arranged "letter and answer, side by side," Judith learns that her mother made the first advances toward a marriage with Hutter, an ex-buccaneer with a price on his head. Hutter's letters, "coarse and illiterate," express a willingness to overlook her mother's "great error" for the "advantage of possessing one, every way so much his superior,

and, who, it also appeared was not altogether destitute of money." In what has amounted to a nightmare vision, a descent into the underworld analogous to Ike McCaslin's reading of the old McCaslin ledgers with their history of bondage, miscegenation, and incest in Faulkner's *The Bear*, Judith has pondered her mother's fate and her own destiny. She discovers class hierarchy, seduction, betrayal, and desertion with impunity by one's social betters—all of which actions have their basis in the social world, the source of Judith's tragedy.

Overwhelmed by this knowledge of her mother's past, yet unaware at this point that it foreshadows her own destiny, Judith, purged of social aspiration, turns to Deerslayer as one who will be faithful in a false world. Despite the fact that Deerslayer does not recognize her feeling for him nor understand that she has posed the possibility of marriage, Judith is not defeated. Rather she plans to win his love by rescuing him from the Hurons, to whom he must return at noon to honor his furlough. Joining "fertility of invention" and "decision and boldness" of character with reliance on her own and the Hurons' class sense, she dons the brocaded gown and demands Deerslayer's release by pretending to be an emissary from the English Queen. Except for Hetty's identification of Judith as her sister, the plan would have succeeded.

With the introduction of Captain Thomas Warley, Judith's former lover, who leads the rescue party from the fort, Cooper gives his final underlining to the theme of social hierarchy and social barriers. In a conversation with a junior officer, Warley, the arch-gallant of the garrison, resplendent in red coat, expounds the code of the wardroom, providing a dramatic illustration of Cooper's theme. He speaks for all "gentlemen," himself explicitly, for Judith's real father implicitly. "A hard featured, red faced, man, of about five and thirty; but of a military carriage, and with an air of fashion that might easily impose on the imagination of one as ignorant of the world, as Judith," Warley will make capital out of the expedition: "It shall not be my fault if she [Judith] is not seen and admired in the Parks!" To his ensign's question whether he contemplates matrimony, Warley answers, "I do suppose there *are* women in the colonies, that a captain of Light Infantry need not disdain; but they are not to be found up here, on a mountain lake; or even down on the Dutch river where we are posted." He "would not marry a princess, unless she were handsome," nor would he marry a handsome woman if she were a beggar. He concludes, "We are not a marrying corps."

The dialogue establishes the raison d'être of gallants. Against such a view and the overwhelming attraction of class, innocence and impressionable beauty are no match. A more accomplished woman would not have been seduced. None of Cooper's ladies, who know their own identities—an Eve Effingham or an Anneke Mourdaunt—would have been attracted. But when Judith seeks the identity of her real father, she discovers a gallant of the garrison who seduced and deserted her mother, and caused her out of desperation and a desire for vengeance to marry a man far beneath her. In the "wardroom scene" the reader discovers the reembodiment of Judith's father in Captain Warley.

But though Judith can now properly evaluate the Warleys of the world, her fate is to be linked with them. Sincerely preferring the honesty and moral worth of Deerslayer, she is nevertheless rejected by him because of her former intimacy with Warley and his own commitment to the heroic life. Alone in the forest world, she turns to her former lover, not out of attraction but out of a need to survive. At the novel's conclusion, fifteen years after her farewell to Deerslayer, we have our last word of Judith. An old sergeant at a garrison on the Mohawk who has recently returned from England informs Deerslayer, now Hawkeye, that "Sir Robert [Thomas] Warley lived on his paternal estates, and that there was a lady of rare beauty in the Lodge, who had great influence over him, though she did not bear his name." While the hero has lived up to his own *nom de guerre* and has an identity won on the shores of the Glimmerglass, Judith is still without a name.

Despite its finely rendered conclusion—the return of Deerslayer and Chingachgook fifteen years later to the scene of their first warpath, their discovery of the ruined castle and the stranded ark, and Deerslayer's inquiry after Judith—there is something troubling about the novel. Ideas introduced and dramatically rendered have not been worked out to their logical conclusions nor examined fully for their implications. If "'Tis of little use . . . for any to strive to get out of their elements, since it's natur' to stay in 'em, and natur' will have its way," has Judith Hutter not, in fact, followed nature? The point the novel makes again and again is that nature does have its way. Judith was clearly born for the drawing room and boudoir, not the solitude of the forest. She instinctively aspires to what is her natural realm—the social world. And while Cooper understands this, he cannot bring himself to forgive her presumption and provides constant reminders of her ill-advised departures from her place.

When the reader reexamines the account of Judith's discovery of the brocaded gown in light of subsequent events in the novel, he perceives the tension between Cooper's antipathy to social aspiration and his recognition of his heroine's legitimate claims to position in the social world. As Cooper speaking through Deerslayer explains: "There's gifts in clothes, as well as in other things. . . . You are Tom Hutter's darter, and that gownd was made for the child of some governor . . . and nothing is suitable that is out of character." Yet a few pages earlier Cooper in his own voice comments, "The dress happened to fit the fine, full, person of Judith, and certainly it had never adorned a being better qualified by natural *gifts*, to do credit to its really rich hues and fine texture" (italics added). The argument of gifts becomes complex when Judith wears the gown into the Huron camp while posing as an emissary of the English Queen. By the hero's own admission "'Twas a bold idee, and fit for a general's lady." The irony is compounded when the reader recalls Deerslayer's first sight of Judith in the gown at the Muskrat Castle: "I do'n't know a better way to treat with the Mingos, gal . . . than to send you ashore, as you be, and to tell 'em that a queen has arrived among 'em!" And it is precisely as a queen that Judith acts—adding courage and resolution to beauty. The awe with which Judith is regarded by the Indians (always unerring judges of character in Cooper's fiction) and Cooper's own commentary further complicate the issue: "Judith, in addition to her rare native beauty, had a singular grace of person, and her mother had imported enough of her own deportment, to prevent any striking or offensive vulgarity of manner; so that, sooth to say, the gorgeous dress might have been worse bestowed in nearly every particular. Had it been displayed in a capital, a thousand might have worn it, before one could have been found to do more credit to its gay colors, glossy satins, and rich laces, than the beautiful creature whose person it now aided to adorn."

Perhaps the proper gloss on this conflicting and confusing treatment of Judith Hutter is the commentary of another American also interested in the implications of rank and class, the letter of Thomas Jefferson to John Adams on the true aristocracy (October 28, 1813). In that letter Jefferson poses the qualities of genius and virtue to Adams's claims for birth, beauty, and wealth as the qualities necessary for aristocracy. Her lack of wealth and her sexual intimacy with Warley notwithstanding, Judith would seem to satisfy admirably the criteria of both men. Like Henry James, Cooper has endowed his heroine with natural beauty, grace, intelligence, boldness, courage, loyalty, and style (both natural and learned). Yet he has made it unmistakably clear that these qualities do not outweigh "low birth" and to think and act otherwise, to aspire to rise, is to know frustration and grief. In fact there is strong reason for believing that Judith is punished more for her social presumption than for her intimacy with Warley. So committed to pointing out the impropriety of transgressing class lines (no matter the quality of the aspirant), Cooper allows a double standard for sexual conduct. There is no explicit indictment of Warley by Cooper, nor does he risk complicating his presentation of the gallants of the garrison by making the kind of distinction between a Christian and a gentleman he makes in subsequent novels. The reader is left finally with the story of a young woman whose punishment exceeds her guilt. To his credit Cooper has made her fall comprehensible and forgivable, skillfully showing that the attraction the red coat held for both Judith and her mother was its symbolization of the *beau monde* they by their "gifts" and training were meant to inhabit. Their tragedy was that the Warleys were such inferior embodiments of their aspirations.

Perhaps Cooper's decision not to judge the Warleys himself stemmed from his instinct as a novelist which led him to recognize the dramatic effect to be achieved from Judith's rendering the judgment out of her feelings of frustration and anger. Whatever his motive, Cooper's decision results in the portrayal of a more fully developed heroine and a further underlining of his theme of class separation. For it is in those speeches denouncing the gallants of the garrison, in which scarlet coats and betrayal are always inextricably linked, that Judith emerges as Cooper's most passionate character: "if all men had as honest tongues [as Deerslayer], and no more promised what they did not mean to perform, there would be less wrong done in the world, and fine feathers and scarlet cloaks would not be thought excuses for baseness and deception!" More telling is the judgment she makes between the scalping mission of Hutter and March against the Hurons and the false promises of the officers: "Men will be men, and some even that flaunt in their gold and silver, and carry the king's commission in their pockets, are not guiltless of equal cruelty."

Desire for the richer life, the attraction of elegance and scarlet coats, seduction, class barriers, and betrayal—these are the themes that stir *The Deerslayer* no less than warpaths, courage, truth-telling,

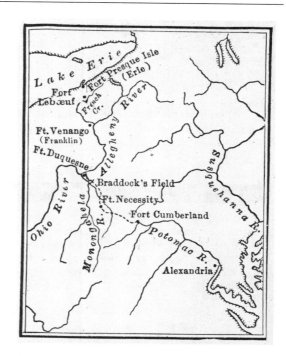

Map of the location of French forts in Pennsylvania during the French and Indian War and of a portion of Late Otsego, the location of the conflict in The Deerslayer © MPI/Getty Images

loyalty, and mythic quests. It is significant that in his last novel to treat his forest hero Cooper gave the conflict of manners and classes—a theme explored earlier in *Precaution*, *The Spy*, and *Home* novels—a tragic dimension in the portrayal of a lovely young woman destroyed by her society's assumptions about class. Though she speaks of her own feeblemindedness, Hetty Hutter provides the epigraph for Judith's story: "'Tis hard to live in a world where all look upon you as below them."

Source: Donald Darnell, "*Deerslayer*: Cooper's Tragedy of Manners," in *James Fenimore Cooper: Novelist of Manners*, Associated University Presses, 1993, pp. 58–67.

Sources

Abrams, M. H., *A Glossary of Literary Terms*, 4th ed., Holt, Rinehart, and Winston, 1981, p. 120.

Beard, James Franklin, "Historical Introduction," in *The Deerslayer or, The First War-Path*, State University of New York Press, 1987, pp. xlvi, xlviii.

Cooper, James Fenimore, *The Deerslayer or, The First War-Path*, "Historical Introduction" and Explanatory Notes by James Franklin Beard, State University of New York Press, 1987.

Dekker, George, and John P. Williams, eds., *Fenimore Cooper: The Critical Heritage*, Routledge & Kegan Paul, 1973, pp. 205–06.

Wallace, Paul A. W., "Cooper's Indians," in *James Fenimore Cooper: A Re-Appraisal*, edited by Mary Cunningham, New York State Historical Association, 1954, pp. 447–556.

Further Reading

Darnell, Donald, *James Fenimore Cooper: Novelist of Manners*, Associated University Presses, 1993, pp. 58–67.
    Darnell argues that in addition to its mythic and pastoral elements, *The Deerslayer* is about social hierarchy and class and the inability of a person to rise above his or her social position.

Long, Robert Emmet, *James Fenimore Cooper*, Continuum, 1990, pp. 120–31.
    Long analyzes *The Deerslayer* in terms of the failure of the characters to connect material and spiritual reality. He also shows how all the characters are tested and subjected to judgment.

Railton, Stephen, *Fenimore Cooper: A Study of His Life and Imagination*, Princeton University Press, 1978.
    In a study that encompasses all of Cooper's creative life, Railton argues specifically that this novel's themes are rite of passage and the right of possession. Deerslayer is constantly confronted with the question of which authority to obey and which to resist.

Ringe, Donald A., *James Fenimore Cooper*, updated edition, Twayne's United States Authors Series, No. 11, Twayne Publishers, 1988, pp. 64–69.
    Ringe regards *The Deerslayer* as the best of the Leatherstocking Tales for its complexity of meaning and its affirmation of the value of American life.

Empire Falls

Richard Russo
2001

Empire Falls (2001), by Richard Russo, is set in a small, working-class town that has fallen upon hard times. Unlike Russo's previous novels, which are set in upstate New York, this novel is set in Maine, where Russo lived for several years prior to its composition.

The themes explored in this novel are not peculiar to Maine, however. The story of long-suffering Miles Roby, trapped in Empire Falls by the mysterious motives of Francine Whiting, by economic necessity, and by his deep love for both his teenage daughter and his late mother, explores universal questions about how much is determined by free will and how much is determined by nature. The novel also examines whether the rich and powerful suffer consequences from their exploitation of those who are less fortunate, and it inquires if people ought to forfeit their own happiness in order to benefit others whom they love.

Distinguished by its rich characterization and Russo's trademark sense of humor, *Empire Falls* was awarded the Pulitzer Prize for Fiction in 2002.

Author Biography

Richard Russo was born James Richard Russo on July 15, 1949, in Johnstown, New York, but he grew up in Gloversville, an upstate New York town with many of the same difficulties as the fictional Empire Falls, Maine. The town's major industry—the

Richard Russo   Photograph By M. Spencer Green. AP Images.
Reproduced by permission

making of gloves—began to decline after World War II, when women ceased wearing gloves on an everyday basis. The author's father, James Russo, worked at a wide array of jobs, including glove cutting and construction work. After leaving Gloversville to attend college at the University of Arizona, Russo worked in construction with his father during the summers.

At the University of Arizona, Russo earned a Bachelor of Arts and Master of Arts in English and then began work on his Ph.D. in literature. As he neared the end of his dissertation, however, he began having second thoughts about his choice of study. Russo began writing fiction. Energized by this change in direction, he was able to complete his dissertation and earn his Ph.D. in 1980. He got an M.F.A. in creative writing the following year.

Russo supported himself by teaching at various universities while he penned his first three novels. The first of these, *Mohawk* (1986), is set in a fictional upstate New York tannery town (much like Gloversville) and populated by working-class characters. His second novel, *The Risk Pool* (1988), also set in the town of Mohawk, tells the story of Ned Hall and his complicated relationship with his father, a ne'er-do-well who abandons the family

early in Ned's childhood and later returns. Russo claims this to be the most personal of all his novels, as his own father was dying at the time he was writing it. This second novel was more widely acclaimed than his first. *The Risk Pool* won the annual award for fiction from the Society of Midland Authors.

Russo's third novel, *Nobody's Fool* (1993), is set in another fictional upstate berg, North Bath, New York. *Nobody's Fool* represents a turning point in Russo's career: it was the first of his novels to be made into a motion picture. The movie also introduced Russo and Paul Newman; Newman became a champion of Russo's work and later produced and starred in the 2005 HBO miniseries of *Empire Falls*. The success of the movie of *Nobody's Fool* brought Russo's work widespread attention, which ultimately allowed Russo to leave Colby College, where he was teaching, and become a full-time writer in the late 1990s. While he was still teaching at Colby, however, he wrote his fourth novel, *Straight Man* (1997), a satire of academia.

After retiring from teaching, Russo wrote *Empire Falls* (2001), considered by many critics to be his most ambitious work to that date, and Russo's ambition was rewarded in 2002 with a Pulitzer Prize in Fiction. The novel was also named by *Library Journal* as one of the Best Books of 2001.

In 2002, Russo published a well-received volume of short stories, entitled *The Whore's Child*. As of 2006, Russo was working on his next novel at home in Maine.

Plot Summary

Prologue

C. B. Whiting is the last in the line of Whiting males. The Whiting dynasty has ruled the town of Empire Falls for generations, owning the town's major employers, the shirt factory and the textile mill. Charles Beaumont Whiting grows up in privilege in the grandiose Whiting mansion. In his twenties, he moves to Mexico, where he dreams of being a poet and painter. However, his father summons him back to Maine to take over the management of the shirt factory. Ten years later, resigned to his life in Maine, Charles decides to build himself a hacienda across the river from Empire Falls. Before construction begins, however, he notices that great quantities of trash keep washing up on the banks of the river, on his future doorstep. Hired analysts explain that the "*design*" of the river, "*one of God's poorer efforts,*" is to blame for the problem. To improve the flow of the river, a channel is blasted through a strip of land Charles buys from a poor family named Robideaux.

The Whiting men have a common curse: they share their lives with women who make them miserable. C. B. Whiting chooses Francine Robideaux.

Part One: Chapters 1–8

In current day Empire Falls, the Empire Grill is a small diner run by protagonist Miles Roby, but owned (as much of Empire Falls is) by Francine Whiting. The shirt factory and the textile mill have been closed for over twenty years, but the town and the Empire Grill limp onward.

Miles and his daughter Tick are readjusting to Empire Falls after their annual trip to Martha's Vineyard, made possible by Miles's college friends who own a house there. Tick laments that she has no friends since she broke up with the volatile Zack Minty. Miles does his best to comfort her while coping with life at the Grill: the rundown dishwasher, a fry cook who has gone missing on his annual bender, and diner regulars such as Walt Comeau (also known as the Silver Fox), the loud boastful proprietor of the town's health club, who is sleeping with Miles's soon-to-be-ex wife.

Miles is a faithful parishioner of St. Catherine's, and in his spare time, he is painting the exterior of the church for free. He is good friends with Father Mark, the younger of the two priests at the parish; the elder, Father Tom, is senile. Miles and Father Mark chat over a cup of coffee when Father Tom enters and calls Miles a "peckerhead," and his mother—who has been dead for twenty years—a "whore." Miles attributes the outburst to Tom's dementia. Still, it causes him to think back on his mother and her untimely death of cancer.

Francine Whiting now controls what is left of the Whiting empire, since her husband took his own life over twenty years earlier. The same afternoon that Miles is accosted by Father Tom, Miles runs into Mrs. Whiting. She asks him about his recent trip and if he knows why he keeps going there every year. Miles replies that it is because his friends have a house there. Mrs. Whiting cryptically quotes from *The Great Gatsby* and then dismisses him with a wave of her hand.

Miles's wife, Janine, is now living in their house with Walt Comeau, while Miles is living in a tiny apartment over the Empire Grill. Janine's main attachment to Walt is sex. After twenty years

Media Adaptations

of marriage to Miles, Janine at forty had her first orgasm with Walt and is determined to make up for all the sex she has missed. Janine recently lost fifty pounds and is now an aerobics instructor at Walt's health club.

Tick, Janine and Miles's daughter, is in high school. Her favorite subject is art, and she has rearranged her schedule to accommodate it, by eating lunch alone in the cafeteria during sixth period. In art class, Tick sits at a table with her only friend, Candace, and John Voss, a silent boy who wears mismatched thrift-shop clothing. Candace carves her boyfriend's name on her chair with a stolen Exacto knife and accidentally slashes her thumb open. Tick faints at the sight. When she regains consciousness she spots the Exacto knife on the floor and slips it into her backpack before her teacher discovers it.

Miles's father, Max, is a seventy-year-old reprobate with a general disregard for niceties such as tact, personal hygiene, and integrity. Max badgers Miles to let him help paint St. Cat's, so he can make enough money to go to the Florida Keys for the winter. Miles points out that he is not getting paid. While arguing this point at the local donut shop one morning, they are joined by Jimmy Minty, an Empire Falls policeman Miles has disliked since childhood. Devious and spiteful, Jimmy always puts on an outward show of down-home friendliness. When Jimmy tells Miles to warn his brother David to be careful, because "Everybody knows he's growing marijuana," Miles loses his temper and tells him to shut up.

The idea that David could be growing marijuana, however, is not so far-fetched. David has had his problems with drugs and alcohol. Three years before, David, drunk, drove his car into a ravine. The accident ruined his arm but sobered him up. Now David's idea to serve ethnic dinners at the Empire Grill—one night Chinese, another Mexican—has boosted business and allowed the Grill to show a slight profit for the first time in years. After one particularly good evening, David suggests that they should petition Mrs. Whiting for a liquor license or go into business with Bea, Miles's mother-in-law, whose bar has an unused kitchen. Miles expresses his doubts. Angered by the negative response, David reminds Miles how heartbroken their mother would be to know that twenty years after her death, Miles was still running the Empire Grill.

Part One concludes with a flashback to a pivotal event in Miles's childhood, a trip that he and his mother took to Martha's Vineyard. They stay in a small cottage near the beach. Beautiful Grace is approached by numerous men on the island, but she rebuffs them. They eat every night at the cheapest restaurant they can find, where Miles eats steamer clams by the basket. One night, however, they have dinner in the main dining room, an expensive place, and Grace wears a new white dress. Miles complains loudly that steamer clams are not on the menu, and Charlie Mayne, who is eating alone at a neighboring table, suggests that he try the Clams Casino. To Miles's surprise, Grace invites him to join them for dinner.

After dinner Charlie takes them for a speedy ride in his yellow sports car, ending in a spot overlooking the beach, where the sun is just setting. Miles asks to go to the beach, and his mother agrees. When he returns, he spies his mother resting her head on Charlie Mayne's shoulder.

The next day, Miles is angry with his mother. He announces that he is going to tell Max about Charlie Mayne. His mother tells him he will have to wait for Max to get out of jail, because he has been arrested for being a public nuisance. Miles storms out, and while he is sitting on the beach, Charlie Mayne approaches and tries to talk to him, saying that everyone deserves a chance to be happy. When Miles asserts that his mother "*is happy*," Charlie replies, "*I was talking about me.*"

The next day they leave on the ferry. Grace is in tears, and Miles, seeing her distress, promises her he will not tell Max.

Part Two: Chapters 9–14

Miles is summoned to the Whiting hacienda. Mrs. Whiting claims she has a surprise for him. When he arrives, he sees that the surprise is Cindy Whiting, home from her latest stint in the state mental facility. In her early childhood, Cindy was hit by a car and crippled. Since then she has spent her life in and out of hospitals and institutions, as fragile mentally as she is physically. She has attempted suicide numerous times, twice citing her unrequited love for Miles as the reason.

Miles and Cindy were born on the same day, in the same hospital, and all his life, Miles's mother seemed to feel there was a connection between them and always instructed Miles to be kind to her. After Cindy's accident, Grace was especially insistent on this, telling Miles "they had a special duty" to help Cindy.

Cindy tells Miles that she still loves him, and his impending divorce gives her hope. Disentangling himself from her desperate embrace, Miles goes outside to meet with Mrs. Whiting.

In the gazebo by the Knox River, Mrs. Whiting tells Miles that the real reason he married Janine was his fear that if he did not, he would end up, at his mother's insistence, marrying pathetic Cindy Whiting. Miles is chilled by Mrs. Whiting's heartless attitude towards her daughter. Before he leaves the Whiting house, Miles asks Cindy to go with him to the homecoming game at Empire High. Afterwards, though, he is filled with dread at the prospect.

Meanwhile at Tick's school, principal Otto Meyer, Miles Roby's old friend, brings the outcast John Voss to the cafeteria where Tick is eating alone. Zack Minty and his friends are tormenting the boy so mercilessly at lunchtime that Meyer has decided he is better off here, eating later with Tick. He asks her to be a friend to the boy. Tick manages to draw John into conversation and learns that he lives with his grandmother because he was abandoned, first by his father, and then by his mother after she remarried. Their conversation is cut short, however, when Zack Minty enters and pleads his case to Tick, asking why she will not give him a second chance. He invites her to come with his friends to see him play in the homecoming game. Tick agrees to come if Zack will leave John alone.

At St. Cat's, Miles lets Max help him paint. In the time they have been working there, Max and old Father Tom have struck up an unlikely friendship. After working at the church one day, Miles and Max return to the Empire Grill, which is packed with customers for Mexican Night. Silent John Voss works there as a bus boy. Zack Minty and his crowd are at the Grill, and Zack asks Miles if Tick might get off work in time to go to a movie. Miles dislikes Zack.

After the night's excellent business, Miles, David, and Charlene—Miles's longtime crush and the Empire Grill's best waitress—go out to celebrate. When the subject of Mrs. Whiting comes up, however, David urges Miles to stop being so passive with her.

Part Two concludes with a flashback to Miles's teenage years, when he first learned to drive. Max Roby, after losing his license, sells the family car. Without a vehicle to practice on, Miles does poorly in his driver's education class. One day his mother informs him that Mrs. Whiting has volunteered to be his instructor.

On his first lesson in the high school parking lot, Mrs. Whiting instructs Miles to *"floor it."* When they are nearly out of the parking lot, Mrs. Whiting tells him to stop; he slams on the brake. Mrs. Whiting explains that now that he knows the extremes of what the vehicle can do, he should not be afraid. *"Power and control,"* she tells him.

Part Three: Chapters 15–22

At the homecoming football game, Miles helps Cindy Whiting as she makes her halting climb up the bleachers. Just moments after they are seated, Cindy loses her cane down through the bleachers. When Miles returns from getting it, he discovers that Cindy has been joined by Jimmy Minty, who is proudly pointing out his son Zack on the football field. While they watch, Zack makes a vicious late hit on the other team's quarterback, which has Jimmy on his feet cheering, even though the quarterback is clearly injured. Fed up with Jimmy, Miles makes a sarcastic remark, ridiculing Jimmy's grammar. Jimmy leaves with a warning to Miles: "You don't want Jimmy Minty for an enemy."

Janine is at the game but spends most of it in shock. She has just learned that Walt is not fifty, as he has claimed, but sixty years old.

Miles takes Cindy home, first stopping at the cemetery, at Cindy's request, to visit the graves of Miles's mother and C. B. Whiting, Cindy's father. The next morning at the Grill, Miles gazes at a newspaper photo of the office staff of the Empire Shirt Factory, circa 1966. His mother is in the

photo, and so is C. B. Whiting. When Miles looks more closely at the photo, he realizes that C. B. Whiting is none other than Charlie Mayne, the man they met on Martha's Vineyard.

Next, a flashback tells of Miles and Grace's return to Empire Falls after the Vineyard vacation. Rumors fly that the shirt factory and mills are closing. One day Honus Whiting calls a meeting of mill workers and announces that the mills are not closing; in fact, a new mill is being opened in Mexico. He explains that C. B. Whiting will go to Mexico to run this mill and that Honus himself will take over the management of the Empire Falls locations. When Miles comes home from baseball practice on the evening of this day, he finds his mother in the bedroom, sobbing.

Not long after, Grace takes Miles to church for confession. Miles waits for over half an hour while Grace confesses her sins to Father Tom. The next day Grace tells Miles that she has to go out for a while. Miles follows her. When she begins crossing the iron bridge over the river, Miles is sure she is going to jump. She continues across, however, and heads toward a gazebo, where a woman is waiting.

Back in present-day Empire Falls, Father Mark wakes up one morning to discover that Father Tom is missing. A search of Father Tom's room turns up a wastebasket full of now-empty offering envelopes from St. Cat's parishioners, and a brochure entitled, "Your New Life Awaits You in the Florida Keys." They discover the parish car is no longer in the garage.

Miles, fresh from his discovery that Charlie Mayne was actually C. B. Whiting, spends the afternoon at the church scraping old paint off its exterior, working hard while reviewing his entire life through the lens of this revelation. After working at the church—and learning about Max and Father Tom's escape—he goes to Bea's bar to propose that they go into business together.

Part Three ends with another flashback, this time to the year that the mill and shirt factory finally close, leaving Grace without a job. A lawyer calls Grace on behalf of a woman who has a broken hip and requires an assistant. The woman turns out to be Francine Whiting, who hires Grace. Grace also helps care for Cindy, whose refusal to work at physical therapy has rendered her most recent operation ineffectual. Grace asks Mrs. Whiting if they will ever speak of C. B. Whiting. Mrs. Whiting says no and makes Grace promise that if he ever contacts her, Grace will inform her immediately. Grace agrees.

Part Four: Chapters 23–32

Janine, despite her many misgivings, marries the Silver Fox, and Miles attends the wedding. After their discount honeymoon at a bed and breakfast, Walt returns to the Empire Grill as usual.

Miles and David spend most of their spare time at Bea's bar, trying to fix the place up enough to start their new business venture. David thinks Miles should tell Mrs. Whiting of their plans, but Miles is reluctant; he is sure Mrs. Whiting will find a way to ruin everything.

In a flashback to Miles's senior year of college, Mrs. Whiting summons Miles home to be with his dying mother. She tells him that if he comes home and helps run the Empire Grill for "a year or so," then she will take care of Grace's medical bills. Miles knows his mother will be furious at this arrangement. Her one dream for Miles is for him to get out of Empire Falls, away from Francine Whiting.

Max calls from Florida and tells Miles that he and Father Tom made it to the Keys as part of the crew of a schooner. Miles asks his father why Max never told him about his mother and C. B. Whiting. Max replies, "How come you never told *me*, son?"

At the high school, Zack Minty continues to persecute John Voss. One night, Zack uses his father's ring of master keys to let himself into John Voss's house, hoping to discover more about the boy, so he can torture him to even greater effect. Zack's friend Justin stays outside while Zack sneaks into the dark house. When Zack returns, all he has to say is, "This is SO F—— GREAT!"

At school, Tick notices that Zack's torment of John Voss has reached new heights. Zack lets himself into the cafeteria during sixth hour, when Tick and John are eating, to continue ridiculing him. Inexplicably, he inserts John's grandmother into conversation.

Principal Meyer receives anonymous notes asking the question, *"Where is John Voss's grandmother?"* When he goes to the cafeteria to ask John Voss about the notes, he discovers Zack Minty there. Meyer brings Zack to his office and asks him why he insists on persecuting John Voss. Then he asks Zack if he wrote the notes. Zack denies it, but the trace of a smile on his face as he does so convinces Meyer that Zack is the culprit.

Meyer drives to the Voss house to talk to John's grandmother. When he arrives the house is dark, and no one answers. Suddenly, he has a strong feeling that John's grandmother is not at home and

has not been for a long time. He breaks into the house and discovers he is correct. The house has no power or water. Meyer calls the police, who come to the house and start searching for her body, which they find in a nearby landfill. The police suspect that John's grandmother died of natural causes and that to avoid being sent to a foster home, John disposed of her body himself. Then a new search begins, this time for John Voss.

Meanwhile, a surprise health inspection at Bea's place results in the bar being shut down. Miles knows that Mrs. Whiting is behind it. As he leaves the restaurant to go confront her, Walt challenges him to an arm-wrestling match. For the first time, Miles accepts, and he slams Walt's arm on the bar so violently that he breaks his arm. With Walt in a heap on the floor, Miles leaves to find Mrs. Whiting.

Mrs. Whiting is at the old Empire Shirt Factory, showing the building to some out-of-town investors. Miles is confronted by Jimmy Minty, whom Mrs. Whiting has hired to stand guard. When Jimmy Minty refuses to let Miles enter, Miles punches him in the nose. A long fight ensues, until Mrs. Whiting finally emerges. Miles tells her he is giving her his notice; she will have to find a new manager for the Empire Grill. He also confronts her with the real reason she has kept him working for her all these years: "He preferred my mother, didn't he, Mrs. Whiting?" Mrs. Whiting gets in her Lincoln and drives away, and Miles and Jimmy Minty both end up in the hospital from their fight.

The day after this confrontation, Tick is painting in art class, when John Voss enters carrying a brown grocery bag. When Justin asks him what is in the bag, he reaches inside, pulls out a revolver and begins shooting. He shoots Justin, the teacher Mrs. Roderigue, and Candace, and then turns on Tick, who faints.

At the hospital, the police chief arrives and tells Miles to come with him. When they get to the high school, they find a gruesome scene. Justin Dibble and the teacher are both dead, and so is Otto Meyer. Miles learns that just as John was about to shoot Tick, Meyer stepped between them and saved her life. Miles finds Tick crouched behind the classroom door, clutching the Exacto knife Candace had stolen earlier. Miles carries her to his car and drives straight to Martha's Vineyard, intent only on getting Tick far away from Empire Falls.

On Martha's Vineyard, Miles and Tick stay in the friend's vacation house. Tick's progress is slow but steady: Miles enrolls her in the high school on the island. David calls and asks when they're coming home. According to David, new investment in Empire Falls has things looking up—developers are turning the old mill buildings into a brew pub and a mall, and Mrs. Whiting has put her house up for sale. Police discovered stolen merchandise in Jimmy Minty's house, and he has been forced to resign from the police force. Still, Miles is reluctant to return.

Out of nowhere, Max shows up on the island for a visit. Talking with Miles, Max admits that he was a disappointment for Grace as a husband and that if she had met C. B. Whiting first, she would have been happier. One day, Miles drives to the cottage where he and his mother stayed on their fateful visit to the island. He falls asleep there and dreams that he is a boy, confronting Charlie Mayne. Miles tells Charlie that Grace waited for him, and he never came. He says that Charlie killed Grace. Charlie tells Miles that he was the reason they could not run away together, and so it was really Miles who killed her. Miles awakens with the realization that it is time to return to Empire Falls.

When Miles returns to the cottage, Max tells him David just called and said that Francine Whiting has died, drowned in the Knox River during a flood. The next day, Miles, Tick, and Max head back to Empire Falls.

Epilogue

The epilogue of *Empire Falls* gives the details of C. B. Whiting's untimely end. He has been living in Mexico for many years now, since being banished from Maine as punishment for his affair with Grace. However, his father Honus Whiting has recently died, and for the second time in his life, Charles Beaumont Whiting has been summoned home from Mexico to take over the family business, this time by his wife, Francine, whom he despises. So on his way back to Empire Falls, he purchases a revolver, hoping to succeed where the other Whiting males have failed and kill his wife.

When he arrives at the house, however, and heads to the gazebo, where he imagines Francine will be, he sees that she is not alone. His daughter, Cindy, is watching through the patio door, and the true love of his life, Grace Roby, is beside his wife. When he sees his daughter, clutching the door handle for support, he recalls the day when, in a rage, he packed a suitcase, threw it in his car, and tore out of the garage without looking. It was C. B. Whiting who ran over Cindy, and Francine who shrewdly invented an anonymous hit-and-run driver in her

account to the police. C. B. never confessed his guilt until he fell in love with Grace Roby; Grace heard his confession and forgave him.

When Cindy sees her father, she calls, "Daddy!" and it is then that C. B. Whiting decides to use the revolver to end his own life, instead of Francine's.

C. B. Whiting does, indirectly, succeed in killing his wife. Because he altered the flow of the Knox River, he made it more prone to flooding, and it is one of these floods that sweeps Francine Whiting out of her gazebo and down the river.

Characters

Candace Burke

Candace Burke is Tick's new friend in art class. Candace is overweight, not particularly popular, and an unmotivated student, which is not surprising given that her mother's favorite endearment for her is "moron." Candace prefers discussing her love life to actually participating in class, and she begins most of her sentences with, "Oh-my-God-oh-my-God!"

Walt Comeau

Walt Comeau is a cocky, cheerful blowhard who challenges Miles to an arm-wrestling match every day. Walt wastes little time looking beyond the surface of any situation or person. To the Silver Fox, image is everything. Though he showers Janine with compliments on her appearance, these are the only compliments she gets.

To his credit, Walt has a positive outlook on life and seems genuinely fond of the regulars at the Grill. He remains optimistic about the town's prospects, just as he continues to believe he will someday beat Horace Weymouth at cards.

Charlene Gardiner

Charlene Gardiner is the Empire Grill's best waitress, a well-endowed, outspoken woman who feels it well within her rights to offer customers advice and enter into their conversations. Miles has pined for Charlene since high school, when he was fifteen and she was eighteen. She prefers bad men with fast cars, even after four failed marriages.

Bea Majeski

Bea Majeski is Janine Roby's mother and the proprieter of Callahan's, a local bar that is one of the few businesses in Empire Falls not owned by Francine Whiting. Bea is a no-nonsense, robust woman who speaks her mind and has little patience for her daughter's midlife crisis. She loves Miles and is mystified by Janine's attraction to Walt Comeau, whom she refers to as "that little banty rooster."

Father Mark

Father Mark is the younger of the two priests at St. Catherine's, Miles's church. Father Mark is gay, though he remains celibate, and also a pacifist who has taken part in anti-war demonstrations. Between his unpopular political stance and rumors about his sexual orientation, the diocese is not happy with Father Mark, which is why he was sent to Empire Falls in the first place. He and Miles have become good friends, perhaps because they are both sensitive, educated men—a bit of an anomaly in Empire Falls.

Otto Meyer Jr.

Otto Meyer is the principal of Empire High School, a job that has given him both his livelihood and bleeding ulcers. Otto, known to his high school classmates as "Oscar Meyer, the weiner," is an old friend of Miles; Otto came to his rescue in driver's education, preventing Miles from wrecking the driver's education car. Near the end of the novel, Otto saves Tick's life as well and sacrifices his own.

Jimmy Minty

Miles's next-door neighbor from childhood, Jimmy Minty, is now an Empire Falls policeman. Jimmy's father, William Minty, was a petty thief, wife-beater, and poacher, who made a little extra money now and then as an "enforcer" for the Whitings when mill workers threatened to unionize. Miles realizes that, in his own perverse way, Jimmy really does want to be his friend, but Jimmy is enough like his father that Miles has no desire to take him up on the offer.

Zack Minty

Zack Minty, who until recently was Tick's boyfriend, is cruel, coarse, and volatile. Zack keeps his friends (and girlfriends) not through common interests and shared opinions, but through intimidation and threats. His good looks and athletic ability have allowed him to get away with this behavior so far, but with his misconduct on the football field and his failing grades, it seems that Zack is riding for a fall.

Peter

Miles's college roommate Peter and his wife Dawn are now writers of TV sitcoms in Los Angeles.

Every summer they invite Miles to join them at their summer home on Martha's Vineyard.

Christina Roby

See Tick Roby

David Roby

David's brother Miles is Grace Roby's problem child. Practically abandoned by Grace as a boy when she became obsessed with the Whiting household, David responded by becoming a juvenile delinquent, a lifestyle he continued right into his thirties, until he ruined his arm in a drunk-driving accident. Now David appears to have cleaned up his act, but Miles still finds it difficult to believe he will not return to his delinquent ways.

Grace's last request from David was, "Look after your brother." David is frustrated with Miles's passive behavior and wants him to take control of his life.

Grace Roby

Miles's mother, Grace Roby, is a key figure not only in Miles's upbringing but in his present daily life; the lessons and love she gave him strengthen and hinder him at the same time. Grace, after many years as the unfortunate spouse of Max Roby, died at a relatively young age of cancer in Miles's last year of college.

Grace becomes a virtual deity in Miles's eyes, a symbol of all that is holy and good. When Miles imagines an all-loving God, "It pleased him to imagine God as someone like his mother, someone beleaguered by too many responsibilities, too dog-tired to monitor an energetic boy every minute of the day, but who, out of love and fear for his safety, checked in on him whenever she could." During their trip to the Vineyard, Grace's appearance is nothing short of angelic, in the white dress she bought to wear for Charlie Mayne. In the epilogue, C. B. Whiting's thoughts about Grace are steeped with religious imagery; as he considers telling her the truth about Cindy's accident, he thinks, "*If he were able to tell her, and if she were still able to love him, then wouldn't this be his salvation?*" Then, when he does tell her: "*As he'd always imagined, she heard his confession . . . and redeemed him.*" When he sees her years later, he realizes that "*The penance he'd once assumed for himself, he'd allowed her to perform in his stead.*" Like Jesus himself, Grace has taken on the weight of C. B. Whiting's sins.

Of course, Grace is merely human, as is demonstrated by her emotional abandonment of David as a child. In addition, on her deathbed, she is furious with Miles over leaving school and "clung to her anger as if that alone might keep her alive." The memory of her rage haunts Miles even now.

Janine Roby

Janine, Miles's soon-to-be-ex wife, is on a mission to make up for all the sex and all the orgasms that Miles "cheated" her out of in twenty years of marriage. After Walt gives her her first orgasm ever at the age of forty, Janine decides that Walt Comeau is what she wants, not Miles. Even as second thoughts turn to third, fourth, and tenth thoughts, Janine is too proud and stubborn to admit that marrying Walt is a mistake. Janine is defensive and quick to anger, the temperamental opposite of Miles.

Max Roby

Miles's father, Max, who is "sempty" years old, provides comic relief throughout the novel. Max's philosophy of life is embodied in the phrase, "So what?" Max looks out for Max and spends much of his time finding ways to get money while simultaneously avoiding work. When Miles was a boy, Max would disappear for months at a time, sometimes to work as a house painter, sometimes to simply do whatever he wanted. Miles's mother was left to support her family by working at the shirt factory.

There are signs, however, that contrary to Miles's opinion, Max is not "truly without conscience." For instance, one night at Bea's bar, Horace mentions C. B. Whiting's suicide, and Max blurts out, "Twenty-three years ago March," to the amazement of both Horace and Bea. Clearly Grace's affair with Whiting meant more to Max than he revealed. Later he admits to Miles, "It's a terrible thing to be a disappointment to a good woman."

Miles Roby

The protagonist of *Empire Falls* and the manager of the Empire Grill, Miles Roby is, as one of the characters in the novel describes him, "the nicest, saddest man in all of Empire Falls." He is also the most passive. Miles has learned to tolerate so much in the interest of not making trouble that he has lost touch with his own emotions and desires. He tells Father Mark that he was surprised to learn that his friends Peter and Dawn saw him as unhappy in his marriage. "I mean, if I was so unhappy, wouldn't I know?"

Miles steers a careful course in his life, always taking the middle road. While most people could relate to his desire to avoid the lows in life, Miles avoids the highs as well, as signified by his paralyzing fear of heights. This is not surprising, given that the most vivid example of great happiness in Miles's life was the joy his mother Grace experienced on Martha's Vineyard with Charlie Mayne. To Father Mark, Miles confesses "his lifelong worry that the intensity of his mother's brief joy had somehow been the root cause of the illness that killed her a decade later." No wonder Miles steers clear of ecstasy.

Another of Miles's key character traits is his inability to keep a secret; his facial expressions always give him away. Miles, through his own basic decency and Catholic upbringing, is not just morally incapable of lying, but physically as well. So thoroughly ingrained in Miles are the lessons of his Catholic education, that when he has a fleeting mental image of killing Father Tom (after Tom calls his mother a "whore"), he apologizes, reflecting the Catholic precept that evil thoughts, not just evil acts, are sinful.

The fact that in a single day, Miles has murderous thoughts about both Walt Comeau and Father Tom indicates that perhaps his capacity for tolerance is reaching its limit.

Tick Roby

Miles and Janine's daughter, Christina, called Tick, is Grace Roby all over again. She is like Grace in her sensitive, compassionate nature and her willingness to forgive: "[Tick is] the kind of person who forgives easily, who in fact cannot bear to think of a person wanting to be forgiven and having that forgiveness withheld."

What Tick lacks is Grace's strength. While she makes brave choices—such as breaking up with Zack Minty—she is then constantly fearful of the consequences. She is especially sensitive to the possibility of violence, as in the instance when she watches a movie about the D-Day invasion and her left arm goes numb. Her burdens, such as her fears, her parents' impending divorce, her mother's upcoming marriage to a man she despises, and her friendless status at school, are suggested by the enormous backpack she lugs to school, which is so heavy that Tick's spine shows early signs of scoliosis.

Doris Roderigue

Doris Roderigue is Tick's art teacher at Empire High. Mrs. Roderigue is an uptight, closed-minded woman who believes that clean-up is "the most important part of the whole artistic process." She dislikes Tick, mainly because Miles once embarrassed her in a public meeting.

Father Tom

While Father Mark is compassionate and understanding, Father Tom has always been stern and reprimanding, seeking to strike the fear of God into his parishioners. Now in his old age, he is senile and lashes out at others, using his favorite word, "peckerhead." He can no longer be trusted to keep confessions confidential; it was from Father Tom that Miles learned Janine was sleeping with Walt Comeau. Most importantly, it was Father Tom who, over thirty years before, heard Grace Roby's confession after her trip to Martha's Vineyard and instructed her to beg Francine Whiting's forgiveness.

John Voss

John Voss is the unnaturally quiet classmate of Tick. He comes to school with mismatched thrift shop clothing and unwashed, matted hair and rarely makes eye contact. John has been abandoned by both his parents and now lives with his grandmother. Late in the novel the reader learns that John's parents were drug dealers who, when John was a small boy, would stuff him into a laundry bag and hang him on the back of a closet door, so that he wouldn't interfere with business.

Tick does her best to be kind to John, even though she is afraid of him. As Zack Minty torments him, she notices that John "almost seems to feed on the abuse." To John, abuse is familiar and, perhaps, in a twisted way, comforting.

Horace Weymouth

Horace Weymouth is a reporter for the *Empire Gazette*, a good-natured cynic who comes into the Empire Grill every day to have a hamburger and beat Walt Comeau at cards. Horace has a large, purple fibroid cyst in the middle of his forehead; when Max suggests he should get it removed, Horace jokes, "I think it might be the source of my intelligence." Though he has decided, from his experience as a reporter, that most people are "selfish, greedy, unprincipled, venal, utterly irredeemable s—eaters," he treats everyone with kindness and respect, indicating that he still harbors a some optimism where human nature is concerned.

Charles Beaumont Whiting

C. B. Whiting is a dreamer born into a family of pragmatic achievers. When he is summoned home to Empire Falls from Mexico to take his place in the family business, he believes he is betraying his best self, the self that wants to paint and write poetry. However, C. B. Whiting is a weak man, not in the habit of standing up to others, and so he returns. Unfortunately for him, "*he'd never mastered the fine art of self-deception as most weak men do.*" His self-awareness contributes to his low opinion of himself.

Just like all the other Whiting males, C. B. Whiting chooses a wife who will make him miserable. His inability to stand up to her and to his father costs him the greatest love of his life, Grace Roby.

Cindy Whiting

Cindy Whiting, the daughter of Francine and C. B. Whiting, takes after her father: she is a dreamer who lacks the fortitude to make her dreams come true. She continues to believe that miracles are possible, that after each new operation she will be born anew. When these miracles do not occur, she is unwilling to work at physical therapy, convinced that the operation is a failure.

Cindy also clings to the notion that Miles may someday fall in love with her, though at some level, she is aware that this will never happen. For example, when Miles reassures her that he is pleased to see her, "She gave him a smile in which hope and knowledge were going at it, bare-knuckled, equally and eternally matched."

Francine Whiting

Perhaps the most mysterious character of the novel, Francine Whiting, who owns most of Empire Falls, is an incredibly shrewd woman. Her cold analyses of others' motives and desires, while tactless, are usually absolutely correct. It is as though, unencumbered by any emotions of her own, she is free to see others in a clear and objective light, though without a trace of empathy.

Francine Whiting fears losing control of her emotions. At no point in the novel does Mrs. Whiting have an outburst—she is never enraged, surprised, or even startled. Rather than laughing, she merely pronounces things "'hilarious,' despite a demeanor that suggested she didn't find them even remotely funny." Even her revenge is taken without passion, a slow, time-release sort of vengeance that is meted out over the course of thirty-odd years.

Near the end of the novel, Miles asks Mrs. Whiting, "When did you ever feel passion?" She replies, "Well, it's true I'm seldom swept away like those with more romantic temperaments." Ironic, then, that when she finally meets her demise, this is exactly what happens: she is swept away—not by romantic feelings but by the uncontrolled waters of the Knox River.

Themes

Human Nature versus Free Will

Early on, Russo poses the question of whether people's personalities and tendencies are fixed at birth, as their inherent nature, or whether they can change at will. In the prologue, C. B. Whiting feels that by leaving his painting and poetry behind in Mexico, he is *"violating his own best nature."* His father Honus is more of the opinion that, even if a man had a *"best nature,"* *"it was probably your duty either to deny it or whip it into shape, show it who was boss."* Francine Whiting believes differently. She tells Miles in her imperious way: "Lives are rivers. We imagine we can direct their paths, though in the end there's but one destination, and we end up being true to ourselves only because we have no choice." This remark is ironic coming from Mrs. Whiting, since she has spent years directing the paths of Miles and his mother, using their own natures against them to keep them where she wants them. Apparently Mrs. Whiting believes she herself is exempt from this inability to direct one's life because her mantra is "Power and control."

Later, Miles considers the question of nature versus free will in reference to his father: "It probably *was* admirable that his father never battled his own nature, never expected more of himself than experience had taught him was wise, thereby avoiding disappointment and self-recrimination." Disappointment and self-recrimination, of course, are all too familiar to Miles.

Empire Falls provides examples that show both that people are slaves to their inborn nature and that real change is possible. It does not seem likely, for instance, that Janine Roby is going to change. Though she claims, "People can change, and I'm changing," her mother observes, "You aren't changing, Janine . . . You're just losing weight." Janine just makes the same mistakes in new ways. She swings from one extreme to another: from Miles, a man with little passion, she jumps to Walt, a man whose passion is the only thing she enjoys.

David Roby, by contrast, seems to have achieved real change, though Miles continues to doubt him after three years of sobriety. He eventually realizes that he's been unfair to David: "He'd . . . meant to learn to trust him, but instead merely fell into the habit of waiting for him to f—— up again, even though he hadn't for a long time."

Miles finally changes his passive attitude, but as with David, it takes a traumatic event—the discovery of Charlie Mayne's true identity—to divert his well-worn path. The conclusion here is that without being shocked into self-awareness by a life-altering event, most people continue with their usual patterns.

Repression

Repression and its consequences is illustrated in several of the novel's key characters. For instance, Mrs. Whiting's description of Miles Roby as "a case study in repression" is fairly accurate. Miles allows the man who had an affair with his wife to eat regularly at his diner, live in his former house (while he resides in a tiny apartment over the Empire Grill), and even belittle his business tactics, all without a hostile word in return. In fact, he seems to go out of his way to give Walt the benefit of the doubt. Miles tells David, "I think he just comes in to let me know there's no hard feelings."

Similarly, Miles allows Mrs. Whiting to condescend to him on a regular basis. He does not object as she tactlessly espouses her theories on his personal motives and his marriage and speculates about his future actions as though his life were some sort of soap opera she enjoys switching on occasionally.

Miles is not really as saintly as he seems; he is simply repressing his anger. Russo demonstrates the consequence of all this repression through Miles's uncharacteristically violent outburst towards the end of the novel. When Mrs. Whiting attempts to block his new business venture with Bea, Miles snaps. First, he arm-wrestles Walt and actually breaks his arm. Miles is not described as a particularly athletic man; it is the sheer force of his pent-up rage that snaps Walt's arm. Then when Jimmy Minty tries to prevent him from seeing Mrs. Whiting, Miles attacks him.

There are parallels between Miles's repression and the more severe case of John Voss. John's repression is so complete that he hardly ever speaks at all, even though he has a lifetime of abuse to keep down. When the lid finally blows on John's anger—just one day after Miles's explosion—he doesn't just break someone's arm, he kills three people. Of course, the motives for repression in these two cases are different. Miles's repression is born, at least in part, from his Catholic upbringing and his need to keep his job at the Empire Grill. John's motives are probably more complex; most likely he had found that, in an abusive household, silence is the safest option. Both Miles and John, however, fear what will happen if they fully express their extreme emotions.

Topics For Further Study

- In his audio commentary on the DVD of the *Empire Falls* miniseries, Russo reveals that Timmy the Cat is actually Grace Roby reincarnated. How does this change your view of Timmy's actions? Reread the scenes of the novel featuring Timmy, and write a paragraph reinterpreting Timmy's actions in each scene.

- Like Empire Falls, many communities falter when major industries become obsolete or move to other regions. Think of at least three examples of cities that have declined due to such circumstances. Choose one of the three and find the following: population before and after, average income before and after, and median housing prices before and after. Make a chart showing the results.

- Though class distinctions are not as rigid in the United States as in some other countries, they still exist. List examples of class distinction from *Empire Falls*, both in the past (as in the flashbacks to Grace's life), in Miles's life, and in Tick's life at high school. Include on your list what the basis is for these distinctions: Is it money? Power? Intellect?

- Based on the descriptions in the novel, draw a map of Empire Falls, including the Knox River, the Whiting hacienda, the shirt factory, the Empire Grill, and the Whiting mansion. Include whatever other landmarks you remember from the book.

- Though the book has an omniscient narrator, the narrator takes the viewpoint of different characters in different chapters (for example, the high school chapters are written with Tick's point of view). However, Russo does not include segments written from Francine Whiting's or John Voss's point of view. Why do you think he chose not to do so? Choose a scene from the novel that involves Mrs. Whiting or John Voss and write it from this character's point of view.

It is possible that Francine Whiting harbors this same fear. Surely a woman so cool, measured, and calculating must be repressing more volatile emotions—rage, grief, remorse. If Mrs. Whiting does have a more emotional side to her, then, like Honus Whiting, she has "*beaten it into perfect submission.*" The consequence of her repression is an inability to experience any emotion at all.

In the end, Russo shows that there is no such thing as successful repression; the pent-up emotions will either explode to the surface or corrode a person from within.

Guilt

In the character of Miles Roby, Russo illustrates the crippling effect of excessive guilt. Miles's whole life has been directed by a combination of love, guilt, and fear. Because he loves his mother, he feels guilty when he does not come home to visit her while he is in college, even though his continued absence is exactly what his mother wants—she wants him as far away from Francine Whiting as he can get. Mrs. Whiting uses this guilt to manipulate Miles into coming home from school, even though he knows this will infuriate his mother. Then, of course, he feels guilty for disappointing her and not finishing his studies, guilty for increasing her suffering as her cancer consumes her.

In almost any situation, Miles is quick to blame himself. A large part of this guilt stems from Miles's Catholic upbringing. One cannot help but feel for young Miles, at age nine, as he prepares for confession after the fateful vacation on Martha's Vineyard:

> *Since returning from Martha's Vineyard he'd grown certain that he, not just his mother, had somehow sinned there, though he wasn't sure what sort of sin it was or how to explain it to the man on the other side of the lattice. He knew he'd betrayed his father by promising to keep his mother's secret, just as he was certain that if he broke that promise he would be betraying her. . . . He had come to confession armed with a list of sins he hadn't committed, sins he hoped were equal in magnitude to whatever he was concealing.*

Here, Miles is cornered by guilt: no matter what he chooses to do, he has betrayed someone. Grace, out of her guilt, follows Father Tom's directive to humiliate herself by begging Francine Whiting's forgiveness.

Max Roby and Mrs. Whiting are on the other end of the spectrum, feeling little or no guilt concerning their actions. Mrs. Whiting is cold and inhumane, and Max is compared to an ape more than once. The conclusion here seems to be that while some guilt is necessary and has a humanizing effect, too much is paralyzing, leaving a person unable to act.

Confusion of the Past and Future

In the first chapter of *Empire Falls*, Miles observes that when people look out the window of the Empire Grill, they look toward the abandoned textile mill and shirt factory, not in the other direction. "If the past were razed, the slate wiped clean, maybe fewer people would confuse it with the future." The citizens of Empire Falls continue to imagine that the mill and factory will be bought and revived, and Empire Falls will return to its past prosperity.

This confusion is further illustrated by the scale model of Empire Falls at the Planning and Development Commission office. One would expect that the Planning and Development Commission would be concerned mainly with the future, but the model depicts Empire Falls, circa 1959. As Mrs. Whiting points out, "Most Americans *want* it to be 1959, with the addition of cappuccino and cable TV." The only structure on the model that looks the same way it does in reality is the Whiting mansion, an indication, perhaps, that the past, present, and future of Empire Falls all belong to the Whitings.

Sexuality

In more than one instance, Russo likens sexual desire to a fever or illness. For instance, Father Mark, the younger priest at St. Catherine's, is battling his homosexuality in his struggle to remain celibate. He meets a young gay artist at a protest rally, who invites him to visit his studio and also to counsel him on a "spiritual matter." When he manages to resist temptation, Russo writes, "Father Mark's own crisis had passed, leaving him weak and relieved, as if a fever had broken."

In another scene, Miles's mother-in-law Bea muses that "Saying good-bye to sex was like waking up from a delirium, a tropical fever, into a world of cool, Canadian breezes." Later, Mrs. Walsh, the housekeeper at St. Cat's, is of a similar opinion. She no longer cares about sex and considers the fact that she ever did care "a kind of temporary lunacy," which, fortunately, "had been short-lived, not terribly virulent, and ultimately cured by marriage, as God intended."

The younger Janine Roby, of course, disagrees with Bea and Mrs. Walsh. Janine has just discovered the joys of sex after twenty years of passionless marriage to Miles. She credits Walt with awakening her sexuality and giving her her first orgasm. Her objective in marrying Walt is to "make up for all the sex she'd been cheated out of." This explains why she is so horrified to find that Walt is sixty, not fifty, as he claimed. "What if in a few short years all her well-hung man did *was* hang?" By the end of the novel, however, Janine's fever for Walt has cooled considerably. If marrying Walt could be considered insane—certainly Bea would characterize it as such—then Janine, too, could be said to be suffering from a temporary lunacy.

The only character in the novel that seems to derive any real joy from their sexuality is Grace Roby. During her brief affair with C. B. Whiting on Martha's Vineyard, Grace is happier and more radiant than Miles has ever seen her. Perhaps this is because Grace and C. B. Whiting are truly in love; most of the other couples in the novel are mismatched and miserable. Ironically, during her affair on the island, Grace also suffers from the consequences of sex with Max Roby—violent morning sickness.

In short, Russo's novel suggests that sexual desire in the wrong relationship (as in the case of Max and Grace) or experienced by a self-absorbed person who is not mature enough to truly love anyone (as in the case of Janine) is merely a physical condition, a hormonal imbalance.

Style

Setting

Empire Falls is a town mired in its own past. The once prosperous shirt factory and textile mill stand empty, a constant reminder of what the town has lost. Unable to imagine a new future, the town's citizens dream of returning to the past. At least once a year someone spots an expensive car parked at the old mill, and the same optimistic rumor begins circulating: someone is going to buy it and put the whole town back to work again.

This bleak setting is a key element of the novel because the local poverty narrows Miles's options. Here in Empire Falls he is trapped because by this town's standards managing the Empire Grill is a good job. With Tick just a few short years away from college, Miles feels he cannot afford to upset the status quo and defy Mrs. Whiting. He clings to her promise that she will leave him the Grill when she dies, though he has no proof of this, other than her word.

In a larger city, it would not be possible for one woman to have such a stranglehold on the economy. In Boston or New York, Mrs. Whiting would be just one more wealthy woman. In Empire Falls, she holds the purse strings for an entire community.

Finally, few of the citizens in this blue-collar town have an education beyond high school or an appreciation for the things that Miles enjoyed in his college years. As he discovered in his freshman year, *"This was where he belonged, among people who loved books and art and music, enthusiasms he was hard-pressed to explain to the guys lazing around the counter at the Empire Grill."* Having few neighbors who share these interests is a constant reminder to Miles that where he is now is not where he had once hoped to be.

Point of View

Empire Falls is told from an omniscient point of view. The reader is privy to the thoughts, emotions, and motives of all the major characters, with the exceptions of Francine Whiting and John Voss. Because of this arrangement, readers learn much more about the characters, even relatively minor ones, than in a story written from, for instance, a limited first-person viewpoint. For example, Otto Meyer Jr. could not be called a major character in the novel, but because of the omniscient narrator, readers learn that he feels he has failed as a parent, that he is taking mass quantities of antacids to calm his ulcers, that he does not favor capital punishment, that angry parents call and yell obscenities at him when he declares a snow day, and that his son Adam refers to him as "clueless." Knowing this about Meyer allows readers to appreciate even more his choice to protect a student at the risk of his own life. The point of view helps convey the breadth and depth of characters, giving the novel a full, rich quality and breathing life into the fictional community of Empire Falls.

Flashbacks

The mystery of the connection between Grace Roby, Francine Whiting, and C. B. Whiting is gradually revealed in chapter-long flashbacks to Miles's childhood and adolescence, printed in italics. By alternating these past scenes with present-day situations, Russo shows how Miles's relationship with his mother still affects him on an everyday basis. Also, through information revealed in the earlier flashbacks, Russo gives readers a chance to discover the true identity of Charlie Mayne before Miles does. Once Miles does make the discovery, the flashbacks illustrate how differently the past was experienced by Miles without that information and how he must now reinterpret his own childhood.

The combination of the omniscient narrator and the flashback also allows the reader to experience the story of C. B. Whiting, including the truth about Cindy Whiting's accident, Whiting's great love for Grace Roby, and the thought processes that led to his eventual suicide. C. B. Whiting's story is told in the prologue and epilogue, framing the rest of the novel. Without learning his story and his emotions, readers might view C. B. Whiting as a villain, a cad who promised Grace Roby happiness and then abandoned her without a second thought. By revealing his internal struggles, Russo portrays him as a sensitive, caring, but flawed man who lacks the fortitude to battle his formidable wife.

Foreshadowing

Russo drops clues that foreshadow future events and revelations. The true identity of Charlie Mayne, for instance, is hinted at early on, when Miles is in Mrs. Whiting's office of the Planning and Development Commission. A portrait of Elijah Whiting overlooks the scale model of Empire Falls, and this portrait and other Whiting portraits "all reminded Miles of someone, though he couldn't imagine who." In a flashback to his driving lessons with Mrs. Whiting, Mrs. Whiting claims that Cindy is "her father's daughter." A few moments later, when Miles sees part of Cindy's face in the rear view mirror, "Miles thought he saw someone else, someone vaguely familiar, someone he couldn't quite place."

The stolen Exacto knife that Tick retrieves and puts in her backpack foreshadows violence to come. Tick believes this violence will come from Zack Minty, who is angry with her for breaking up with him. Another harbinger of violence is the game that Zack calls "Polish Roulette," played by putting an unloaded gun to one's head and pulling the trigger. Zack is unnerved by John Voss's ability to play the game without flinching.

Humor

The story of a man whose mother died young of cancer, whose wife divorces him, and whose business barely makes a profit could be rather grim if it were not for the abundant humor in *Empire Falls*. A good deal of the humor is supplied by Max Roby, whose complete lack of tact makes for some hilarious moments. Upon seeing Jimmy Minty at the donut shop, Max greets him by saying, "Jimmy Minty . . . My *God*, what a stupid kid you were growing up." At Bea's bar, when Horace declines Max's offer to go to the Florida Keys, claiming he might get depressed and shoot himself like Hemingway, Max replies, "Try to miss that thing on your forehead . . . What a hell of a mess *that* would make."

Despite his troubles, Miles still has a sense of humor. Shortly after Janine and Walt get married, Miles receives an anonymous phone call:

> "Did you know your wife's on upper Empire Avenue screaming obscenities and kicking in the side of your Jeep?"

> "Here," Miles said, handing the phone to the Silver Fox. "It's for you."

The humor of *Empire Falls* serves to lighten the grim reality of the town's decline and Miles's disappointments. It also makes Miles, who in his extreme passivity could become frustrating for readers, a more likable and sympathetic character.

Metaphor

The unifying metaphor of *Empire Falls* is that of the river. It begins in the prologue, when C. B. Whiting attempts to alter the course of the Knox River so that garbage will no longer wash up on his doorstep. Ultimately, he fails; in a present-day scene, garbage is still washing up on the banks of the Knox River, by Mrs. Whiting's gazebo. There is a certain karmic justice to the garbage accumulating on the Whitings' lawn, since their factories polluted the river with dyes and chemicals for many years.

Though C. B. Whiting blasted away the Robideaux blight, he was later unable to blast away the true blight of his life, Francine Robideaux, even though he bought a revolver expressly for that purpose. It finally takes an act of nature to remove Francine, when the Knox River floods and sweeps her from her seat in the gazebo. If the river is life, then it is appropriate that Mrs. Whiting has constructed herself this comfortable perch from which to observe it. Throughout the story she is a keen observer of others, amusing herself by picking apart the motives and missteps of the citizens of Empire Falls.

Another recurrent metaphor is that of heights. As a boy, Miles loved to climb trees, but now "For all his early promise, Miles had scaled no heights." His paralyzing fear of heights is a metaphor for his fear of rising above his ordinary lifestyle and work, of taking a risk in order to gain something better. Miles is not the only character whose life is mired in mediocrity; when Janine is unable to get seats at the top of the stadium for the football game and instead spends it lower down with her mother brooding over her discovery of Walt's real age, Russo writes, "Janine understood about her mother's aching feet and why she hadn't wanted to climb all the way to the top . . . But damn, she'd hoped to get farther up than this." In these ways, Russo uses literal height or high places as a metaphor for development, for a character's ability to rise professionally or financially or in other ways.

Historical Context

Violence in Schools

In December 1997, a high school freshman in West Paducah, Kentucky, killed three students and injured five others when he fired about a dozen shots at the members of an informal prayer group. In a 2001 interview on www.randomhouse.com, Russo says it was this school shooting that first got him thinking about school violence and its causes. Just a few months later, in March 1998, two boys aged thirteen and eleven killed four students and one teacher and wounded ten others at a middle school in Jonesboro, Arkansas. Then in April 1999, at Columbine High School in Littleton, Colorado, Eric Harris and Dylan Klebold killed fifteen and wounded twenty-three in the worst school shooting to date in U.S. history. Parents across the country began demanding tighter security measures in schools, especially high schools. Russo's two daughters were in high school during this time.

Often, the students responsible for such shootings showed signs beforehand that something was wrong or even let others know of their intentions. According to a 2002 article in www.harvard magazine.com, "In many of the cases studied, fellow students knew about the shooter's plans and, in some cases, even knew the shooter had a gun with him before the attack began . . . But knowledge of the impending tragedy never made it to the adults in the community." This disconnect between adults and teenagers is mentioned several times in *Empire Falls*. For example, Russo writes:

> Most teachers, Tick has learned, feel no great compulsion to confront trouble. . . . The mystery of the Exacto knife stolen after the first art class . . . would be solved if Mrs. Roderigue ever visited [the] Blue [table], where Candace openly uses it on her "Bobby" carving.

The suggestion here is that the teacher is negligent in the case of the knife. Yet the more serious question of the school shooting is not so easily settled by blaming teachers. The principal goes out of his way to protect John Voss from another student, and yet John's psychological needs are not met and violence erupts.

Decline of the Textile Industry

Though the mill and shirt factory in Empire Falls closed over twenty years before the novel begins, a real crisis in the textile industry was taking place during the years that Russo was writing it. In 1997, the textile industry had a banner year, with near-record profits. However, sharp devaluations in Asian currencies, beginning in the latter half of 1997, caused U.S. prices to fall. Asian textile imports increased 80 percent between 1997 and 2001. Textile profits began dropping in 1998; in 2000, the U.S. textile industry posted a 350 million dollar loss—the first annual loss in its history. In a June 2001 statement to the U.S. Senate Committee on Commerce, Science and Technology, the American Textile Manufacturers Institute asserts, "In May 2001 alone, 9,000 U.S. textile workers lost their jobs. Over the past twelve months, ten percent of the textile workforce— 56,000 workers—lost their jobs." Between 1997 and September 2002, a total of two hundred and forty mills closed.

Critical Overview

The panoramic scope of *Empire Falls* prompted many critics to label it as Russo's most ambitious work to date. Is this ambition fully realized? Some critics answer with a resounding yes; Ron Charles of the *Christian Science Monitor* goes so far as to say, "The history of American literature may show that Richard Russo wrote the last great novel of the 20th century." Bruce Fretts of *Entertainment Weekly* says, "With this deeply ambitious book, Richard Russo has found new life as a writer."

Critics specifically praise Russo's compassion and empathy for his characters, even the less lovable ones: A. O. Scott of the *New York Times* cites his "humane sympathy for weakness and self-deception—a sympathy extended even to the manipulative Mrs. Whiting." Maria Russo of *Salon* notes that Russo writes "without sentimentality or nostalgia, just compassion for his characters' foibles and deep insight into the startling, sometimes disturbing varieties of human nature."

Russo's humor is also singled out for praise by many reviewers. "The deadpan wit of Russo's previous book, "Straight Man," runs all through this more weighty novel, particularly in his devastating (and devastatingly funny) descriptions of small-minded people," writes Charles. Fretts agrees, adding, "His one-liners can make you laugh out loud."

Some reviewers criticized the scope of the book. James Marcus of the *Atlantic Monthly* remarks that "at just over 500 pages the novel feels overstuffed," and Rita D. Jacobs of *World Literature Today* writes that the book "goes on for too long." Fretts disagrees; he calls the book "dense in the best sense of the word" and claims "hardly a word is wasted."

Another point disagreed on by reviewers is whether the school violence near the end of the novel is congruous with the rest of the book. Edward Hower, in a review in *World and I*, finds that this particular plotline "skirts uncomfortably close to melodrama at the story's end, adding a tinge of tragedy that seems incongruous." Jacobs writes, "when the surprises come at the end, they feel abrupt and forced." Scott, however, states, "the last section of the book explodes with surprises that also seem, in retrospect, like inevitabilities."

Paul Newman as Max Roby in the 2005 film version of Empire Falls   HBO/The Kobal Collection

On the whole, the book was warmly received, as evidenced by the Pulitzer Prize for Fiction awarded to Russo in 2002. As Tom Bissell in *Esquire* writes: "*There are bound to be other, flashier novels published this year, but very few will find such a deep, permanent place in one's heart.*"

Criticism

Laura Pryor

Pryor has a B.A. from University of Michigan and over twenty years experience in professional and creative writing with special interest in fiction. In this essay, she examines how the Knox River in Empire Falls *is a metaphor with more than one possible meaning.*

"Has it ever occurred to you that life is a river, dear boy?" Francine Whiting asks Miles Roby in *Empire Falls.* Apparently the idea of the river as metaphor has occurred to Richard Russo, because the Knox River comes to symbolize not just life in this novel, but God, death, and wealth.

Readers are first introduced to the waters of the Knox in the prologue, when C. B. Whiting

discovers the river's irritating tendency to deposit "*all manner of other people's s—*" on his lawn. Whiting comes to the conclusion that God is doing this to punish him for abandoning his true calling, the poetry and painting he left behind in Mexico. At one point he imagines that he hears the waters of the Knox calling to him, inviting him to commit himself to its depths (apparently the Knox knows who C. B. is destined to marry and is hoping to save him some grief). Rather than take the hint, C. B. Whiting decides to go to war with God and brings in experts who advise him to blast away a spit of land called the Robideaux blight.

Like God himself, the Knox giveth, and the Knox taketh away: Whiting achieves, at least temporarily, his goal of redirecting garbage from his doorstep, but in the bargain he gets Francine Robideaux, a far more formidable obstacle to his future happiness than any mere piece of land. Like the land she comes from—where little will grow and farming is next to impossible—Francine is a woman nearly barren of normal human emotion. When Francine gives birth to a daughter, motherhood does nothing to improve her drought of feeling; her newborn daughter is described as "*writhing and twisting at her mother's meager breast.*" Later, Cindy's struggles to elicit a few drops of affection from her mother are met with the same frustration.

> *Francine Whiting has much in common with Persephone, the Queen of Hades and mate of Hades himself, who ruled the underworld."*

If the river represents God and also love, then Francine's soul is in serious need of irrigation.

The name of the river presents other metaphoric possibilities. In building his hacienda, C. B. Whiting became the first Whiting to distance himself from the source of his wealth, namely, the people who worked in the mill and factory. By putting the river between himself and the rest of the town, he created a fortress—his own Fort Knox. This metaphor becomes even more appropriate with Francine Whiting in charge, given her tendency to hoard her wealth, meting it out to the town in small parcels with many strings attached. "When the woman was dead, it was hoped, the money would flow more freely," Russo writes, just like the Knox River after the Robideaux blight was blasted away.

Another interesting comparison suggested by the name, and also by Grace Roby's frequent use of the phrase *"crossing the river,"* is the similarity between the Knox and the River Styx. In Greek mythology, souls of the dead had to cross the River Styx to enter Hades, the underworld. A ferryman named Charon took the souls across the river, for which he required payment; the Greeks would bury their dead with a coin in their mouths to pay for their passage. Souls who came to the river without their fare at hand—or in this case, at mouth—had to wander the banks of the river for a hundred years before crossing. Once in Hades, souls were required to drink from the waters of the Lethe, another river, which made them forget completely their mortal lives.

The first time that Grace crosses the Knox River, she wears *"a dark dress that Miles hadn't seen her wear since the funeral of a neighbor,"* to visit Francine Whiting and beg her forgiveness. It is not until she begins working for her on a regular basis, though, that Grace Roby begins dying by

degrees. *"During the years that Grace worked for Mrs. Whiting, Miles saw her lose the last bloom of her womanhood,"* the narrator states, and then later, *"With each passing season, she grew more gaunt, more ghostlike."* As if she has drunk the waters of the Lethe, she becomes increasingly forgetful and distant with her family on the "living" side of the river, and more involved with the Whitings. *"On each dreaded vacation from St. Luke's [Miles had] witnessed his mother's increasing absence from their own home, even when she was present in the house."* Her effectiveness as a parent wanes as her *"vagueness about their own family"* increases; Miles is concerned that Grace is *"so forgetful about his brother."*

According to Greek myth, the waters of the Styx were so foul that to drink them was fatal. The waters of the Knox do not sound much tastier: *"Generations of Whitings had been flushing dyes and other chemicals, staining the riverbank all the way to Fairhaven."* The word "styx," translated from Greek, means "hateful"; the River Styx is then a river of hate. It seems appropriate that Francine Whiting should live next to such a river and even more so that its waters claim her life in the final pages.

Francine Whiting has much in common with Persephone, the Queen of Hades and mate of Hades himself, who rules the underworld. The god Hades is also called Pluto, which, in Greek, means "wealth." Hades, the man of the house, is less dreaded than his queen (whose name means "bringer of destruction.") Even though Persephone only lives in Hades a third of the year—much like Mrs. Whiting, who likes to winter in warmer locales—she is the more fearsome of the couple and, when in residence, takes a more active role in the workings of the underworld. Of course, Mrs. Whiting not only takes an active role, she eventually banishes her husband from Empire Falls entirely. It is unlikely that Persephone would be so bold.

The entrance to Hades is guarded by a three-headed dog named Cerberus; Mrs. Whiting's Hades is guarded by Timmy the Cat, who has just one head, though to Miles, who is bitten and scratched regularly by Timmy, it may seem like more. Timmy comes to the Whitings from the river itself and leaves by the river, ushering Mrs. Whiting into the hereafter: "astride the body, crouched at the shoulders of the dead woman, was a red-mouthed, howling cat." In the end, Mrs. Whiting is a mere mortal, though Miles's shock at her passing indicates that she never gave him that impression: "Miles shook his head, trying to imagine a world without Mrs. Whiting in it. Who would keep it spinning?"

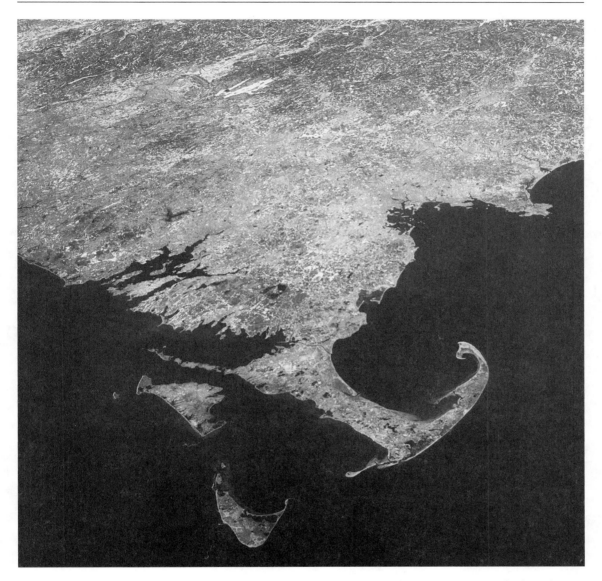

View from the space shuttle Atlantis, showing Nantucket, Boston, and Martha's Vineyard where key events in the novel take place © Corbis

So what the Knox River signifies depends on how the novel is interpreted. For those inclined to fatalism, there is Mrs. Whiting's theory: that life is a river, human destiny is predetermined, and the best people can do is to go with the flow. Certainly Max Roby would embrace this philosophy. Miles would be more inclined to think of the river as proof of God's power, as C. B Whiting ultimately does: "*When he . . . saw the swift water . . . he recalled his war with God over the moose and he realized for the first time that God had won, that as an arrogant sinner the only course left to him was penance.*" Maybe it is a combination, a life-giving entity created by God, then poisoned by the greed and arrogance of one family for generations. Then God, fed up with the Whitings, takes it back.

One thing is certain: the people of Empire Falls owe the Knox River a debt of gratitude. In sweeping Mrs. Whiting out of her gazebo, the river does more to brighten this town's future than any group of investors ever do.

Source: Laura Pryor, Critical Essay on *Empire Falls*, in *Novels for Students*, Thomson Gale, 2007.

HBO

In the following interview, Russo discusses the writing process, the protagonist in Empire Falls, *and the difficulties in translating the novel into a screenplay.*

[*Interviewer:*] *When did you start work on* Empire Falls, *the novel?*

[Richard Russo:] Actually, I've been working on *Empire Falls* coming up on a decade now. The idea would have gone back at least five years before that. What usually happens is that when I start getting close to the end of a novel, something registers in the back of my mind for the next novel, so that I usually don't write, or take notes. And I certainly don't begin. I just allow things to percolate for a while.

Most of my novels begin with a character in some sort of dramatic situation that I don't know how to solve. One of the first things that I had with *Empire Falls* was this notion of Miles Roby, a character that I was interested in. And I think from the start I thought of him as a man trapped not only by circumstance, but by love as much as by anything else. Mrs. Whiting has got Miles trapped. She's got him running that restaurant that he's promised to run until she dies, at which point she'll give him the restaurant. But she comes from a very long-lived family, so while he might want to do other things, as long as he's good to his word with her, she's got him trapped right where she wants him.

But the more important thing, the thing that always intrigued me about Miles was that he wasn't so much trapped by economic necessity, although that's the way he talks about it. He says, I can't move until the restaurant is mine, until I can sell it, I don't have the money. That's a theme that I'm sure is not new to me, but you don't see it all the time. And it interested me that a man in middle age could be trapped by a couple of different kinds of love. One of which resides in the past, and the other sort of in the future.

He's trapped by his affection for his dying mother, and what her dreams for him were, and not trying to betray those dreams. He gets into this situation coming home to Empire Falls and taking over that restaurant because of his love for her, and his refusal to abandon her when she gets ill. So he's trapped by the past, and by decisions that he's made in the past.

But the other great love of his life, of course, is his daughter. And it's her future that he's thinking of all the time. Even as he can think of things that he could do to make himself happier, they all seem to compromise his beloved daughter, Tick.

So the central characters in it are compromised by a past, and a future that are impinging upon the present all the time.

Do you usually have specific themes in mind that you want to explore?

No. It's usually the other way around. When I look back over my novels what I find is that when I think I'm finished with a theme, I'm generally not. And usually themes will recur from novel to novel in odd, new guises.

There's a way in which my early novels centered around fathers and sons, and male behavior, but the idea of family was kind of central to them. *Empire Falls* is, in a way, my first father daughter story. Which was, I suppose, inevitable given the fact that I have two daughters who were junior high school and high school age when I was writing this novel.

So it's not all that surprising that my interest in family, in the relationship of parents and children, which had manifested itself as fathers and sons in earlier work, and is now fathers and daughters in this novel.

It wasn't that I sat down in the beginning and said, oh, it's time I wrote a father daughter story. It's just I was interested in this character of Miles, and then suddenly his daughter was right there. And she began to take on the characteristics of my own daughters. And my devotion to my own girls began to play itself out in some sort of fictional form.

And lo and behold, I was writing again, coming from a slightly different direction on some things that I had been writing about in *Straight Man*, and in *Nobody's Fool*, and in *The Risk Pool*. Ultimately, your theme will find you. You don't have to go looking for it. [LAUGHS]

How do you approach structuring a story with so many complex interwoven characters?

That's a good question, because I'm struggling with it right now in a new novel where I'm doing exactly that. My belief, and sometimes beleaguered belief, is that even when I try to write a small, contained story, it's just the nature of my imagination for things to expand outward.

And so I've kind of learned over the years that usually my efforts to contain things don't work out very well. It's the reason I write so few short stories. And the reason my novels, even when I think that they're going to be short when I begin, ultimately turn out to be longer.

I see a character, and then I know suddenly who his father and mother were, and who his uncle was, and who his siblings were, and who his best friend was when he was growing up. And suddenly I've got what seemed like a very small painting now is a much larger canvas with a lot more people on it. And my belief has always been that if you follow these characters, they will tell you what their relationship is to each other, and to your story, and to their themes.

And so you just kind of have faith. You give them life, you set them loose in the world, and you have to trust as much as you can that they will come back to you with the answers that you don't possess. And will, ultimately, surrender themselves to a structure once that structure has been made known to you.

If that all sounds kind of mystical, it's because I really don't know how it works, but I trust that it does. I try to write the way I read, in order to find out what happens next. What these people are to each other, and what they are to the story. And structure is one of the things that I always hope will reveal itself to me. Because ultimately they do. They all have to work together eventually.

What was the process like, turning your novel into a screenplay? Did you have to kill a lot of your favorite children, as they say?

Well, no. I mean, the fact that we were doing it for HBO, and that we were going to have three and a half hours to spend made my job, um, I was going to say easier. In fact, what it actually did was made it doable. If it had been a two-hour movie, I would have had to turn it over to somebody else. I just couldn't see how it could be done.

The most difficult thing about writing the screenplay for *Empire Falls* was what I alluded to earlier. Was that the screenplay was based on a novel that had already cost me more than any other novel I'd written, emotionally.

When I finished with the novel I felt drained, in need of a blood transfusion. I decided to put together a collection of short stories just to avoid beginning another novel. I was so exhausted I just couldn't see my way clear to starting that.

I was working on another screenplay, and looking forward to somebody else, actually, doing

> " I see a character, and then I know suddenly who his father and mother were, and who his uncle was, and who his siblings were, and who his best friend was when he was growing up. And suddenly I've got what seemed like a very small painting now is a much larger canvas with a lot more people on it."

the screenplay for *Empire Falls*. Because I thought, at the time, what it needed more than anything else was a pair of fresh eyes. I was toast, I thought, at that point, and did not look forward to what I knew was not going to be an easy adaptation, even if we did have three and a half hours to accommodate the novel's complexities. It was still going to be difficult.

And I told Paul Newman when he was trying to convince me to do it that I just wasn't sure I was up to it. That I was tired, and I had given these characters everything I had. It was Paul, really, that talked me out of that, and said, of course you're tired now. But it really should be you. Nobody's going to know it as well as you do. And you're going to be surrounded with good people.

All of which I knew, but I needed some convincing on that point. I wrote a draft or two, which I shared with Paul. And then Marc Platt came on board, who was enormously helpful. I did several drafts with him, and with Scott Steindorff.

And just about the time that I was thinking once again that I was out of gas, we took it to the studio and got very good notes from HBO. I mean, HBO is really famous for hiring good people and staying out of their way until they ask for help, or need it. And that reputation is earned.

And then the final piece of the puzzle was (director) Fred Schepisi, who came in really at a time where everything seemed stale. Everything that I had done seemed a reworking of something that

What Do I Read Next?

- *The Great Gatsby* (1925), by F. Scott Fitzgerald, is one of Russo's favorite novels; Francine Whiting quotes the last line of it when she meets with Miles in the Planning and Development Office in chapter 2.

- Russo also counts Charles Dickens's *Great Expectations* (1860–1861) as one of his favorites and Dickens as one of his favorite authors. Russo's novels often have a large cast of quirky characters that more than one critic has described as Dickensian.

- Russo's second novel, *The Risk Pool* (1988), is probably the most autobiographical of Russo's books; the character of Sam in this novel was based, in part, on Russo's own father, who was dying at the time that Russo wrote the book.

- Russo was one of four authors to contribute essays about Maine to photographer Terrell S. Lester's book, *Maine: The Seasons* (2001). The other essayists are Ann Beattie, Richard Ford, and Elizabeth Strout.

- Another of Russo's favorite classics is *The Adventures of Huckleberry Finn* (1884–1885), by Mark Twain. Russo's use of humor is one of his trademarks; in an interview with bookseller Barnes & Noble in 2005, Russo said that Twain's classic "demonstrates that you can go to the very darkest places if you're armed with a sense of humor."

I had done before. I just couldn't see anything fresh anymore. And Fred came on board, and sat down with me over the script. And we'd actually done a couple of things that he thought were taking it in the wrong direction.

Fred got me to see things with those fresh eyes that I'd been looking for right from the start. And here was yet another new set of fresh eyes.

And so it was really, largely a matter of people keeping me as fresh as they could, and as enthusiastic, and as energized as was possible at the end of what was, for me, a very long road. I mean, there's always difficulty when you're adapting your own novel to the screen, which is why most writers don't adapt their own work.

What do you hope the audience will take away from the movie?

I guess I would retreat to what is both my glib and my truthful answer. I can be glib and truthful all at once here. [LAUGHTER] I remember when I was teaching at a state university in the Midwest. And the university would bring in one major figure to give a lecture. And the writer that we brought in to visit the university that year was Isaac Bashevis Singer. And he gave a wonderful reading that night. But during the day, all the honors students got together for an hour and a half just with Mr. Singer. And the students kept asking Mr. Singer, 'What is art?' And, 'What is the purpose of literature?' And he said, 'The purpose of literature is to entertain,' he held up one finger, 'to entertain and to instruct.'

Then he let his voice fall. And another student said, 'Well, yes, but shouldn't literature also . . .' And he interrupted him. He said, 'To entertain, and to instruct.' Three or four other students tried to get him to elaborate on these two principles, and even asked him, 'Which is more important?' And he said, 'I gave them to you in the order of importance' . . .

And here's this eighty-five-year-old man. And you just could not budge him. He had been asked a simple question, and he was giving a simple answer. And it was one he had been thinking about all his life: the purpose is to entertain and to instruct.

So, I would hope that people would first of all be entertained. Because I think it's very funny. And I think people will see that. They will marvel at these wonderful performances.

But I hope that if the purpose is to entertain and to instruct, that they will take something away from the movie that was at the center of the novel. I think when horrible things happen, people kind of look at each other and say, 'Why? Why did this have to happen? Help me understand this.' And the answers that they get are very often sociological. And often offered in a not a terribly helpful way.

You know, you say, 'Why did Columbine happen?' Well, people on the right say it's because of violence in movies and video games. People on the left say it's because of the availability of guns. And the argument goes on as if we have to choose between these explanations.

But really what people are asking is, 'What does it feel like when something like that happens? What does it feel like to be a parent? What does it feel like to be a child? And that's what stories do. They bring you there. They offer a dramatic explanation, which is always different from an expository explanation.

And I think that if people are instructed about anything, it should be about the nature of cruelty. And about why people behave so cruelly to each other. And what kind of satisfactions they derive from it. And why there is always a cost, and a price to be paid.

Source: HBO, "Interview with Richard Russo," in *HBO*, 2006.

failbetter.com

In the following interview, Russo shares how societal observations, his daughters' influence, and how being a parent has affected his work.

With his most recent novel, *Empire Falls*, Richard Russo returns to what should be familiar ground—hometown Americana—a place that won him such critical acclaim with his earlier novels of *Mohawk* and *Nobody's Fool*. But much has changed in America, and more specifically, in American small towns, within this past decade of economic development and over-reaching one time city-associated social troubles. Still as hilarious as ever, Russo's latest work, like the man himself, is easily accessible. He is a modern day master storyteller. Indeed, not only does such mastery result in an entertaining and effortless read, but a thought provoking one as well . . .

[*Interviewer:*] *Much is made of the common man / home town themes so prevalent in your novels, but perhaps a more common characteristic of your work has been the sense of humor that each book exudes.* Empire Falls *is no exception. In fact, at times it is quite hilarious. Often when an author*

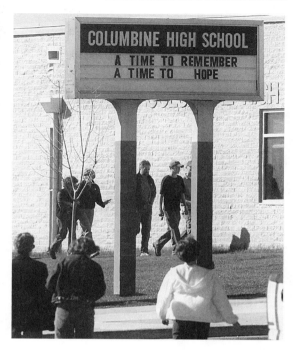

Students and faculty arrive at Columbine High School for a memorial service marking the one-year anniversary of the worst school shooting in U.S. history. A school shooting is one of the events portrayed in Richard Russo's Empire Falls © Reuters NewMedia Inc./Corbis

is asked to comment upon his or her work, it is the "serious" elements that are so easily expounded upon. But our first question is this: What difficulties do you encounter in writing humor? As a writer of literary fiction, do you ever wonder whether your sense of humor will undermine or prevent readers or critics from taking an otherwise epic novel like Empire Falls *seriously?*

[*Russo:*] At the risk of appearing disingenuous, I don't really think of myself as "writing humor." I'm simply reporting on the world I observe, which is frequently hilarious. Here's the thing. Most of what we witness in life is too complex to take in whole. Because of this we unconsciously edit what we see, select what to really record and what to ignore, which is why people who look at the same thing don't necessarily see the same thing. I've been in many an English department meeting where I was the only one strangling to keep from laughing. Yet when I reported on those same department meetings in my academic novel *Straight Man*, many of the same people who didn't find the

"At the risk of appearing disingenuous, I don't really think of myself as 'writing humor.' I'm simply reporting on the world I observe, which is frequently hilarious."

experience funny when they were living it, did laugh when they saw the same events through my eyes. Comic writers don't so much invent funny things as strip away the distractions, the impediments to laughter. "Try to see it my way," we urge. "Only time will tell if I am right or I am wrong."

I never worry about people not taking my work seriously as a result of the humor. In the end, the comic's best trick is the illusion that comedy is effortless. That people imagine what he's doing is easy is an occupational hazard. Cary Grant never won an Oscar, primarily, I suspect, because he made everything look so effortless. Why reward someone for having fun, for being charming? In "serious" fiction (as in "serious" film) you can feel the weight of the material. You expect to see the effort and the strain of all that heavy lifting, and we reward the effort as much as the success. Comedy is often just as serious, and to ignore that seriousness is misguided, of course, but most writers with comic world views have accustomed themselves to being sold at a discount. Most of us wouldn't have it any other way.

[Interviewer:] Though you have returned to a "small town story" (this time our story is set in Maine not Mohawk) the scope of Empire Falls *seems much larger in scale in comparison to your other books. There are timeline shifts and a larger number of significant characters and sub-plots. What difficulties or challenges did the new book present that you had not previous encountered as a writer?*

[Russo:] I don't think this book presented any "new" challenges as a result of its scope. Think of it, rather, as a juggling act. The number of objects that have to be kept in the air at one time, along with the variety of their shapes and weights, is what

determines the degree of difficulty. It's easier to juggle three same-size rubber balls, than it is five objects that vary in shape and weight. For many of my readers *Empire Falls* and *The Risk Pool* are their two favorite Russo novels. I don't know which is the better book, but *Empire* was much the more difficult to write. It's more complex, less autobiographical, and it's told from an omniscient point of view that's far more demanding than the relatively simple first person of the earlier novel. I'm not aware of anything all that "new" in *Empire*, just a greater complexity and variety of elements.

[Interviewer:] In your previous novels, whether it was The Risk Pool *or* Nobody's Fool, *the father-son relationship was one of the main focal points of the book. Amy Tan, an author who has successfully explored the mother-daughter relationship, has stated that she is quite relieved that she has not had a daughter of her own. Ironically, though married and with a loving family, you yourself have no sons. Is this, in some small way, a relief or a regret?*

[Russo:] I've never regretted not having sons. And perhaps there is even some relief, though I'd never thought of it in those terms until you posed the question. A father of sons is supposed to know what he's doing, whereas a father of daughters is entitled to be incompetent. That sort of thing. Raising children is a task that requires great imagination, but it seems to be expected (especially these days) that imagination will fail to transcend gender, which may mean that the fathers of daughters and the mothers of sons, will be judged less harshly for their failures of imagination.

[Interviewer:] Empire Falls *focuses upon the father-daughter relationship, that between Miles and Tick. Having two daughters of your own, how much personal research found it's way into the new book? And have your kids offered their critique of the book?*

[Russo:] Both my daughters were in high school when I began *Empire Falls*, a novel that centers, at least in significant part, on the experience of high school. I've thanked both girls on the acknowledgments page for their willingness to talk with me about their high school experience, especially as it related to cruelty, which drives so much of the novel's narrative. I used a fair amount what they told me, usually in altered form, but I think their greater gift was that their stories caused me to remember things that had happened when I was their age, the kind of terrible, thoughtless, psychic cruelty that was inflicted on some kids every day of their young lives.

Both my daughters have now read *Empire Falls*, though neither has been particularly talkative about it. My favorite small critique came from my younger daughter who remarked, regarding one of the more vividly cruel incidents in the novel, "I didn't remember telling you about that." She hadn't. It was something I'd remembered and embellished from my own adolescence, not hers.

[*Interviewer:*] *Besides the thin teenager Tick, there are several prominent and complex female characters in your new novel, whether it is weight watching Janine, the blunt conversationalist Charlene, levelheaded barkeep Bea, or best of all, the manipulating Mrs. Whiting. That said, however, Miles is clearly still the protagonist of the book. The logical next step would seem to dictate that you might have a central woman protagonist in your next novel. Is this a possibility? Have you grappled with this idea before—and/or—what problems would you expect to encounter in such an endeavor?*

[*Russo:*] You anticipate my every move. I want very much to place a woman in the center of at least one novel of mine, though the idea does make me nervous. I question, among other things, my motives. One of the reasons I'm glad to be full-time writer these days, and not a member of the Academy anymore, is the kind of lethal atmosphere that's taken root there, largely as a result of Critical Theory and all its attendant idiocy. Courses in The Literary Imagination have now been replaced by courses that suggest no such thing exists, or has ever existed. Old white males, it's now suggested, betray on every page their race, their gender, the nature of the times that informed their narrow, bigoted thinking. *Huckleberry Finn* is taught not as a great work of the imagination, but rather to reveal the author's prejudice, everything he was unable to transcend. I'd be the first to admit that the literary imagination, mine or anyone's, can't be expected to transcend all human limitations. There is evidence of anti-Semitism in *The Great Gatsby*, for instance. Authors are flawed, just like everybody else. But the fact that my imagination may be unequal to certain tasks doesn't mean that I shouldn't push it to its limits. Does anyone wish that Flaubert had written his novel about Mr. Bovary?

That said, wanting to place a woman at the center of one of my novels because I have every right to do so, may not be a good enough reason. A far better one might be that, as my recent fiction suggests, in middle age I'm simply getting more interested in women's lives. How could I not be? My wife and I have been married for almost thirty

years; I'm the father of two daughters. Also, in middle age, I'm less timid, less afraid of getting things wrong, or of being told I'm getting them wrong. What scares writers most, I suspect, in writing across gender, is sex. Dickens wrote wonderfully about young girls and old women; it was the sexual identity of women that seemed to flummox him, and I sympathize. Tick Roby in *Empire Falls* and Beryl Peoples in *Nobody's Fool* are two of my best characters, but their ages allow me to finesse that which is most troublesome and mysterious, that which I'd least like to fail at rendering believably. Then again, as other people have pointed out to me, my writing is reticent on sexual matters anyway, regardless of gender.

[*Interviewer:*] *For an author whose previous works seem to portray a timeless microcosm of either small town Americana or, as in* The Straight Man, *the mind-numbing neuroses of academia,* Empire Falls *is a timely work that has some clear connections with the problems of modern day society. I am referring to the implications of the troubled boy John Voss. Did you find yourself writing about the tortured school teen from the angle of an inquisitive author, or more from the view of a real life parent seeking a plausible explanation for such tragedies?*

[*Russo:*] I'd been thinking about school violence since the incident in Paduka, however long ago that was, and I was right in the middle of writing *Empire Falls* when the events at Columbine took place. I'm not sure I can separate the inquisitive author and terrified father functions, at least not now, after the fact. But after the Columbine shootings, when everyone was asking why, I remember thinking (in inquisitive-author-mode) that answering this kind of question is what fiction is best at. The sociological explanations for school violence—the easy availability of guns, too much violence in the media, too little parental supervision of today's youth—are not terribly satisfying. We suspect that if solutions to these very difficult problems could be engineered, the question of why would still remain. What we really want to know is more like, What did it feel like to aim the gun and pull the trigger? What sequence of events led to this moment? The only knowledge that will be even remotely satisfying is the kind that comes from living that horrible moment imaginatively and understanding what led up to it. That's what literature offers us—the visceral experience of the living moment. So, yes, I was interested in investigating that. But it was out of my role as a terrified parent that the book really grew, I suspect. Like Miles Roby, I've often thought that as parents we have to be vigilant, and the first chapter of the novel opens with Miles anxiously awaiting his daughter's return from school, hoping to catch sight of her, to make sure she's okay. What Miles also knows (and I fear) is that no matter how vigilant you are, the moment you're needed most, you'll likely be elsewhere, dealing with some other distraction. Such knowledge is the basis for parental night sweats, and I've come to think of this book in exactly those terms—one long, vivid, parental night sweat.

[*Interviewer:*] *Another, perhaps more universal societal observation/implication of the new book is the socio-economic implications of revitalization. The image of wealth and beauty of a place like Martha's Vineyard is in sharp contrast to the dreary existence of a dying Maine town. Nevertheless, the line between the two towns is not so permanent, just ask the year-round resident of a place like the Vineyard who can no longer afford to live there, or invite a few wealthy New Yorkers to flee the urban life to a simple town such as Empire Falls, possibly open up some quaint B&Bs and boutiques. Next thing you know, The Empire Grill becomes a successful Starbucks-like chain in every American town from Maine to Montana. In this viscous economic cycle, where does it all end? What's the answer? Most importantly, what words of wisdom would a character like Max Roby have to say?*

[*Russo:*] Earlier this spring, when I was on book tour with *Empire Falls* in Chicago, Bill Young (the world's greatest literary escort) took me slightly out of our way to show me something he assured me I'd love. It was Cabrini Green, the infamous housing project, now in a state of transition. Some of its horrid high rises have been razed; others await demolition, while the people who still reside in them await relocation somewhere less Dresden-like. But it wasn't the project itself that Bill wanted to show me, but rather the Starbuck's that had opened right across the street. Snap and develop that photo and many people will accuse you of doctoring it. I'm reminded of a line spoken by Peter Falk in an old movie: "This can only mean one thing, but I don't know what it is." Here's a prediction though: the people who'll be drinking designer coffee at three bucks a pop may not be in the picture yet, but they will be. And so it goes.

[*Interviewer:*] *Some readers may have had a hard time reading your work without imagining Paul Newman as one of the characters (for instance, I had him pegged for Max this time)—though*

I'm not sure that this is a bad thing. Much has been written and made of the success of Nobody's Fool—*the book, the movie, and your own subsequent screen-play writing. What, if any, negative consequences have come as a result of your success?*

[*Russo:*] I got a nice phone call from Paul a couple of months ago. He wanted to tell me how much he'd enjoyed *Empire Falls*. Before hanging up, he said, "If there's a movie I want to play Max. Nobody'd be better at it, either." Too true.

Thanks to technology, I don't think the movie business is as damaging to writers as it used to be, at least not to those of us who live on the opposite coast. Actually, I'm not sure it was ever the movie business that was so poisonous to writers like Fitzgerald and Faulkner, but rather "the life." L.A. (like Las Vegas) is more disorienting than anything else, thanks to its noise and glitter, the ever-present sun reflected off the shimmering water of countless swimming pools. Live there and you can't help but get caught up, and until recently if you wanted to be a screenwriter, you had to live there. Now I can deliver a script as an e-mail attachment and live in Maine, a fine, mostly quiet, unpretentious place where I can hear myself think. For more on this subject have a look at my recent story "Monhegan Light" in the August *Esquire*.

[*Interviewer:*] *We understand that you are currently working on a short story collection. Known primarily as a novelist, is this new territory for you? You once stated that that one of the wonderful things about being a writer is that once you have finished one book, the next day you can start another one and "begin another life." With the forthcoming collection, what kinds of lives can we look forward to reading about?*

[*Russo:*] It's taken me over a decade to come up with a slender volume of stories. Many of them derive from material that for various reasons I've removed from my novels and then recast. I'm absurdly proud of several of the stories for the simple reason that short fiction requires a tighter hold on the fictional reigns than I'm often capable of exerting. I love the shape and structure of good short stories, the fact that they can be experienced whole. What are the stories about? Well, there's an abused nun; an elderly, disoriented college professor on vacation; a gaffer with a grudge; a woman fleeing her husband; a painter who needs a hip replacement; a kid who suspects that inanimate objects may have inner lives; a writer who fears he may have been poisoned by the town where he grew up. The usual suspects.

Source: failbetter.com, "Interview with Richard Russo," in *failbetter.com*, Vol. 2, No. 3, Summer/Fall 2001.

Joseph Epstein

In the following excerpt, Epstein discusses how a small town's aura of bad luck, its struggle against resignation, and an unlikely hero are the subject of Russo's Empire Falls.

Jonathan Franzen, make no mistake, is a talented writer, with all the many moves of the contemporary novelist. He can do fancy fornication, anarchic humor, different cities (New York, Philadelphia, St. Louis), the police in a thousand voices. He has wide knowledge of how things work in the worlds of upscale restaurants and goofy leftist academic circles, and even knows a thing or two about investment banking. He includes in the novel a jaunt to Lithuania, where Chip helps operate an Internet scam for an entrepreneurial fraud named Gitanas and thereby enables his creator to get in a few shots at American capitalism.

In his *Harper's* essay, Franzen mentioned wanting to write about "the things closest to me, to lose myself in the characters and locales I love." Despite the improbably warm conclusion he supplies for his novel—Alfred having finally been put in a nursing home, the family, in a fashion, rallies 'round—his characters have long since lost their color by having been thoroughly rinsed in contempt. If the contemporaneity of their lives holds one's interest, one is nevertheless unlikely in the end to care very much for or about them. Missing from this novel is something vital, which literary talent alone cannot supply.

That something was intimated by Matthew Arnold in an 1887 review of Tolstoy's *Anna Karenina*, which Arnold had read in French translation and which blew him away. In this novel Matthew Arnold found what millions of readers have found after him: "great sensitiveness, subtlety, and finesse, addressing themselves with entire disinterestedness and simplicity to the representation of human life." In his essay, Arnold devotes a paragraph to comparing Tolstoy's treatment of the theme of romantic love and adultery in *Anna Karenina* with Flaubert's treatment of the same theme in *Madame Bovary*. By contrast with Tolstoy's novel, he judges Flaubert's to be a work of "petrified feeling," over which, as Arnold writes, there "hangs an atmosphere of bitterness, irony, impotence; not a personage in the book to rejoice or console us; the springs of freshness and feeling are not there to create such feelings."

> Understanding, in this novel, is in the nature of the human struggle, and, like that struggle itself, is never complete on this earth."

Jonathan Franzen is not Gustave Flaubert, except perhaps in his dreams, and I suspect Richard Russo will forgive me for saying that neither is he Leo Tolstoy. But there is indeed a freshness of feeling to Russo's *Empire Falls* that is entirely absent from *The Corrections* and that evokes, in contemporary terms, precisely what Arnold was getting at.

This is all the more impressive since the *mise-en-scène* of Russo's novel is itself almost unrelievedly bleak. A town in Maine that sits on a polluted river and has lost its industry and its hope, Empire Falls is not merely in danger of going down the crapper but, at one point late in the novel, is actually compared by Miles Roby, the book's central character, to the very thing down which it is headed: "This crapper, it occurred to Miles [inspecting broken plumbing], was his hometown in a nutshell. People who lived in Empire Falls were so used to misfortune that they'd become resigned to more of the same."

The dying town of Empire Falls is controlled by the widow of a dynastic family, the Whitings, whose men have displayed a knack for marrying women they soon learn to despise, to the point of longing to kill them. As for the other townspeople, some of them are still there because staying even after the jobs left "was easier and less scary than leaving," while some stayed out of pride, because their parents and grandparents had lived in Empire Falls and because they did not want to be driven away by the greed of outsiders. Among them all, the future is the least used tense. "Ambition," the father of a local cop liked to tell his son: "It'll kill you every time."

Miles Roby's own father is an itinerant and highly inept housepainter ("By the time they'd discover his shoddy work in Boothbay, he'd be painting someone else's windows shut in Bar Harbor"), a drinking man, and a sponge whose two-word philosophy of life is, "So what?" Miles himself, in his early forties when the novel begins, is about to be divorced and is the father of a talented but psychologically fragile adolescent daughter. He is out of shape, no great sexual athlete, a man who left college to tend to his dying mother and never subsequently escaped the trap of his hometown.

This mother was a saintly woman who believed that we are all put on earth to make things more fair. "We have a duty in this world, Miles. You see that, don't you?" she told him when he was still young. "We have a moral duty." Dying of cancer in her forties, she has left Miles with a strong case of terminal decency.

At the heart of the plot of *Empire Falls* is the mysterious connection between Miles and the wealthy widow Francine Whiting, for whom he runs a bar and grill. She both encourages and taunts him; he lives in simultaneous thrall and contempt of her. What the novel slowly reveals is that Miles's mother once had a love affair with Mrs. Whiting's long-dead husband—an act about which his mother feels forever remorseful while the quite remorseless Mrs. Whiting prefers, instead, revenge, served cold and parsimoniously and taken out, decades after the affair, on her husband's lover's son.

Empire Falls is an intricately plotted novel, with lots of back story to fill in the earlier lives of the main characters. The intricacy of the plot allows Russo to arrange things so that the unpredictable is made to seem entirely plausible, which is one of the things that good fiction accomplishes. But what gives *Empire Falls* gravity is its persuasive staging of the struggle of a decent man to do the right thing, which means to put those he loves before himself. "Her heroes may be insipid," Virginia Woolf once wrote of the novels of Jane Austen, "but think of her fools!" Fools aplenty there are in this novel, but in Miles Roby, Richard Russo has created a hero not in the least insipid. Because of this, *Empire Falls* possesses the element that is entirely missing from *The Corrections:* a moral center.

A fine equanimity pervades *Empire Falls.* This no doubt has much to do with its author's not having set out to mock his characters or to show the height of his superiority through the depth of his disdain. But it is far from a solemn book. A wry comedy animates plot and characters alike. "You're kind and patient and forgiving and generous," Miles is told by a waitress at his restaurant, "and you don't seem to understand that these qualities can be really annoying in a man, no matter what the ladies' magazines say." According to the same waitress, customers tend to tip in proportion to bra cup size. Miles himself remarks that his years in college, away from town, were like being in a witness protection program. But beyond the comedy, Russo is implicated in the lives of these characters in a way that implicates us, his readers: his major effort is to understand them— and to understand that this understanding, too, has its limits.

This is a novel in which God figures. Miles Roby, a former altar boy, still goes to Mass. His manner of tithing is to paint the decaying exterior of the town's Catholic church for nothing. He believes in God, though prefers to think of Him as all-loving rather than all-knowing. One gathers his position here is shared by Richard Russo. Understanding, in this novel, is in the nature of the human struggle, and, like that struggle itself, is never complete on this earth.

Want to make God smile, an old joke has it, tell him your plans. Life, or so this novel instructs, is immensely complicated for people who wish to live it other than selfishly: an obstacle course in which desire is every day set in an unending match against duty. The power of *Empire Falls* lies in its capacity to return us to this daily scene of moral conflict in a manner that is genuine, gripping—and entirely believable.

"If making things prettier than they are is a lie," says Miles Roby's sixteen-year-old daughter, Tick, "then making them seem uglier is another." She is speaking about painting, but the same goes for novelists. The point is to get those "things" as nearly right as possible, to get as close as one can to being *dans le vrai.* This is never easy, but one of the ways a novelist may know he is at least on the right track is when neither Oprah nor the committee of the National Book Awards singles him out for honors.

In a scene in *Empire Falls* set in one of the town's working-class bars, a moper at the end of the bar, forced to watch Oprah Winfrey on television, complains: "If we got to listen to a fat woman talk, can't she at least be a white one?" To which the barkeeper, a Polish woman in her sixties, replies: "Oprah's smarter than any five white men you can name, Otis." And more influential, she might have added, than any twenty literary critics you never heard of.

Source: Joseph Epstein, "Surfing the Novel," in *Commentary,* Vol. 113, No. 1, January 2002, pp. 32–37.

Sources

American Textile Manufacturers Institute, "The Current State of U.S. Manufacturing and the Impact of the Manufacturing Recession," in Statement to U.S. Senate Committee on Commerce, Science, and Technology, June 21, 2001, p. 1.

Bissell, Tom, Review of *Empire Falls*, in *Esquire*, June 2001, p. 42.

Charles, Ron, "Grease Spots on the American Dream," in *Christian Science Monitor*, May 10, 2001, Features Section, Books, p. 18.

"A Conversation with Richard Russo," in randomhouse.com, 2001, www.randomhouse.com/knopf/authors/russo/qna.html (accessed September 17, 2006).

Fretts, Bruce, "Maine Attraction: Richard Russo's *Empire Falls* Draws Readers into the Tangled Lives of Small-town New Englanders," in *Entertainment Weekly*, May 18, 2001, pp. 72–3.

Graff, Garrett, "Behind the Rampages," in *Harvard Magazine*, September-October 2002, http://www.harvardmagazine.com/on-line/0902128.html (accessed August 31, 2006).

Hower, Edward, "Small-Town Dreams: Disappointment Haunts the Characters in Richard Russo's Depiction of Life in a Hapless Maine Backwater Town," in *World and I*, No. 10, October 2001, p. 243.

Jacobs, Rita D., Review of *Empire Falls*, in *World Literature Today*, Vol. 76, Spring 2002, p. 153.

Marcus, James, Review of *Empire Falls*, in *Atlantic Monthly*, June 2001, p. 104.

"Meet the Writers—Richard Russo," in barnesandnoble.com, Spring 2005, http://www.barnesandnoble.com/writers/writer.asp?z=y&cid=968838 (accessed September 2, 2006).

Russo, Maria, Review of *Empire Falls*, in salon.com, May 21, 2001, http://archive.salon.com/books/review/2001/05/21/russo/index.html (accessed July 28, 2006).

Russo, Richard, *Empire Falls*, Vintage Contemporaries, 2002.

Scott, A. O., "Townies," in *New York Times Book Review*, June 24, 2001, p. 8.

Further Reading

Gutman, Richard J. S., *American Diner: Then and Now*, Johns Hopkins University Press, 2000.
   In this book, Gutman traces the history of the American diner from horse-drawn lunch carts to the classic streamlined stainless steel diners. Included are numerous photographs of the various types of diners, sample menus, and anecdotes about diners across the country.

Moran, William, *The Belles of New England*, Thomas Dunne Books, 2002.
   This book chronicles the history of New England's textile mills, the women who worked in them, and the dynastic families who profited from them.

Russo, Richard, *The Whore's Child and Other Stories*, Vintage Contemporaries, 2003.
   Many stories in this collection have a much darker tone than Russo employed in his novels. The title story is a subplot that was edited from his novel *Straight Man*.

Yates, Richard, *The Collected Stories of Richard Yates*, Henry Holt, 2001.
   Russo's moving introduction gives a fine appreciation of this collection of short stories by the late Richard Yates, whose writing influenced many other celebrated authors, including Raymond Carver, Andre Dubus, and Richard Ford.

The Good Earth

Pearl S. Buck

1931

Pearl Buck was one of the most widely read American novelists of the twentieth century. When she published her most popular and critically acclaimed novel, *The Good Earth*, in 1931, she was living in China as the wife of a Christian missionary. By that time, she had lived in China for about forty years and brought to her portrayal of Chinese rural life a knowledge that few if any Western writers have possessed.

The novel is about a poor farmer named Wang Lung who rises from humble origins to become a rich landowner with a large family. Although Wang Lung is a fundamentally decent man, as he becomes wealthy and acquires a large townhouse he becomes arrogant and loses his moral bearings, but he manages to right himself by returning to the land, which always nourishes his spirit.

The Good Earth contains a wealth of detail about daily life in rural China at the end of the nineteenth century and in the first quarter of the twentieth century; it shows what people ate, what clothes they wore, how they worked, what gods they worshiped, and what their marriage and family customs were. The novel is written in a simple but elevated, almost Biblical style, which lends dignity to the characters and events. It was widely praised for presenting American readers with an accurate picture of a country about which they knew very little in the 1930s. As of 2006, *The Good Earth* had never been out of print and had sold millions of copies in many different languages.

Author Biography

One of most popular American authors of the mid-twentieth century, Pearl Buck was born on June 26, 1892, in Hillsboro, West Virginia. Her parents, who were Christian missionaries, took her to China when she was three months old. Spending her childhood in Chinkiang, China, Buck was able to read Chinese as well as English literature when she was only seven years old. When she was eight, her family was endangered by the Boxer Uprising of 1900, which targeted Western missionaries for killing.

After attending a boarding school in Shanghai, Buck returned with her family to the United States, and in 1910, she enrolled at Randolph-Macon Woman's College, in Lynchburg, Virginia.

She graduated in 1914, and she soon returned to China, marrying John Lossing Buck, an American agricultural specialist. The couple lived in a village in North China. In 1924, Buck taught English literature at the University of Nanking. The following year, she returned to the United States and enrolled at Cornell University, from which she received an M.A. in 1926. After returning to China in 1927, Buck and her husband found themselves caught up in revolutionary violence in Nanking. A mob looted their house as they lay in hiding in a tiny room in a nearby house.

During the 1920s, Buck developed her writing craft, publishing stories and essays in magazines. Her first novel, *East Wind, West Wind* was published in 1930. It was followed by *The Good Earth* in 1931, which won the Pulitzer Prize in 1932 and the William Dean Howells Medal in 1935. The novel, which was a runaway bestseller, was made into a Broadway play and a film. Buck was now a prolific writer, and two novels soon followed: *Sons* (1932) and *A House Divided* (1935), which followed the saga of the family of Wang through later generations.

Buck returned permanently to the United States in 1934. She divorced her first husband and married Richard Walsh, the president of a publishing company. The couple lived in Pennsylvania and adopted six children.

In 1938, Buck became the third American and the first American woman to be awarded the Nobel Prize for Literature. The award was for Buck's outstanding publications, *The Good Earth*, *The Exile* (1936; a biography of her mother), and *Fighting Angel* (1936; a biography of her father).

Buck continued to publish for the remainder of her life, but her later books were not as highly

Pearl S. Buck International Portrait Gallery. Reproduced by permission

regarded by critics as her work of the 1930s. However, throughout her writing life, her books remained popular with readers, and at the time of her death, her books had been translated into more languages than those of any other American writer. In all, she published over seventy books, including novels, short stories, biographies, an autobiography, poetry, plays, and children's literature, as well as translations from the Chinese. She was also involved in humanitarian causes and was an outspoken advocate for civil right and women's rights. She sought to promote understanding between Eastern and Western cultures.

Buck died on March 6, 1973, at the age of eighty.

Plot Summary

Chapters 1–3

As *The Good Earth* begins, Wang Lung, a poor farmer in north central China, is preparing to get married. He is looking forward to having a woman to do the household chores since his mother died six years earlier. He lives with his father, an old man who complains a lot.

Media Adaptations

- *The Good Earth* was filmed by Metro Goldwyn Mayer in 1937, directed by Sidney Rainer. As of 2006, the film was available on video cassette. A play based on the novel was written by Owen Davis and Donald Davis and produced in the Theatre Guild in New York City on October 17, 1932.

Early in the morning, Wang Lung puts on his best clothes and walks into the town. He is on his way to the House of Hwang, the wealthiest family in town, where he has been promised a slave girl as a wife. The marriage has been arranged by his father, and he has never met the girl, although he knows she is not pretty.

Arriving in town, he visits the barber and then the butcher, where he buys meat for the evening wedding feast. Outside the House of Hwang, he is at first too frightened to go in, and he goes to a restaurant and buys noodles and tea. When he returns to the House of Hwang at noon, he is taken to the Old Mistress, who summons the female slave, named O-lan. The old mistress says O-lan is a virgin and a good worker, although somewhat slow and stupid. Wang Lung is pleased to have her, and on their way home, he takes her to a temple, where he burns incense to the gods. When they arrive home, O-lan prepares the food, and Wang Lung's neighbors and relatives arrive for the feast.

As the days go by, Wang Lung begins to enjoy married life. O-lan, although she is mostly silent, is a good cook and a competent housekeeper. By summer, she has started to work with him in the fields, too.

Soon O-lan becomes pregnant. Refusing help from anyone, she gives birth to a baby boy, to the delight of Wang Lung and his father.

Chapters 4–6

Following a local custom, Wang Lung buys fifty eggs and dyes them red in honor of the new baby. In a short time, O-lan resumes her work with her husband in the fields. That year, the harvest is a rich one, and the frugal Wang Lung manages his affairs well, in contrast to his lazy uncle and his wife. During the winter, he even manages to save some silver pieces.

For the New Year celebrations, O-lan makes rice cakes, and Wang Lung and she take their son to the House of Hwang. O-lan presents the boy to the Old Mistress and gives the cakes to the ladies in the house. O-lan learns from the cook that the Hwang family has fallen on hard times because of the spendthrift habits of the young men, and the family wishes to sell some land. Wang Lung decides to buy the land and is proud of his new acquisition.

In spring, he and O-lan labor on their new land. In the fall, O-lan gives birth to a second son, and Wang Lung is happy with his good fortune. His plentiful harvests continue, he saves money from the sale of his produce, and he earns a reputation in the village as a man of substance.

Chapters 7–9

Wang Lung is angered by the laziness of his uncle's family. His uncle has a wife and seven children, but none of them works, and the family is always in need. One day Wang Lung's uncle complains of his ill-fortune and asks Wang Lung for money. Reluctantly, Wang Lung gives him nine pieces of silver.

O-lan gives birth to a baby girl. Neither he nor O-lan is pleased by this, since girls are not valued as highly as boys.

There is a summer-long drought, and only one piece of Wang Lung's land bears harvest. But Wang Lung remains well off, and he buys more land from the House of Hwang as that family's fortunes continue to decline.

The drought continues into autumn. Food becomes scarce, and Wang Lung and O-lan are forced to kill and eat their ox in order to survive. Wang Lung gives his uncle some beans, but when the man returns for more, Wang Lung refuses. His uncle turns against him.

In the winter, hungry villagers, encouraged by Wang Lung's uncle, come to Wang Lung's house, intent on stealing food. But they find little food there. The famine gets so bad that people eat grass and the barks of trees, as well as dogs and horses.

O-lan gives birth to another girl, but the infant dies, either strangled or smothered by O-lan. With his family penniless and starving, Wang Lung decides they will travel south to escape the famine. He and O-lan sell their furniture but keep their land.

Chapters 10–13

Wang Lung and his family begin their walk south, then catch a train. When they arrive in the city of Kiangsu (based on Nanking), Wang Lung buys mats and builds a hut that rests against the wall of another house. They get rice from the public kitchens for the poor. The following day, the family begs on the streets, except for Wang Lung, who hires a rickshaw and conveys people around town. But for all his hard work, at the end of the day, he has made almost no profit. Fortunately, however, O-lan and their sons have collected enough money to pay for their rice the following morning.

As Wang Lung pulls the rickshaw each day, he gets to know the city, but he does not feel at home there. He hears young men speaking to crowds at street corners, saying that the Chinese must have a revolution and rise up against the foreigners. Wang Lung meets a foreigner for the first time when he gives a ride to an American woman in his rickshaw.

In the city, food is plentiful, but Wang Lung and his family cannot escape their poverty. When the younger son steals pork from a butcher, Wang Lung beats him. He decides he must get back to his land as soon as possible. But he has nothing to sell that would finance the move back, and he refuses to entertain his wife's idea that he should sell their daughter into slavery.

Chapters 14–16

When spring comes, Wang Lung still longs to return to his land. He does not understand city life. Sometimes men hand him papers with writing on them, but since he cannot read, he does not understand the message. One such paper has a picture of a man hanging on a cross; another shows a fat man stabbing a man who is already dead. A man tells Wang Lung that this depicts a rich capitalist killing the poor. Wang Lung is mystified; he does not understand this way of seeing the world.

One day Wang Lung sees several men seized by soldiers, and a shopkeeper informs him that there is war somewhere, and the soldiers need people to carry their supplies. Wang Lung narrowly escapes being seized himself. Frightened, he stops going out in the day and takes a night job pulling wagonloads of boxes through the streets.

The city is filled with fear, and there are rumors that the enemy is approaching. Wang Lung loses his job and runs out of money. He is desperate. Then comes the news that the enemy has

arrived in the city. In the violence that follows, a mob breaks into the rich house that adjoins Wang Lung's hut. Wang Lung is swept up into the action but, unlike the others, does not steal anything. But then he finds himself alone in an inner room with a man who has been in hiding. The frightened man thinks Wang Lung will kill him and offers him money. Wang Lung takes the man's silver.

The next day Wang Lung and his family return to their land, where he buys seeds, grain, and an ox. He is visited by his neighbor Ching, who fared badly during the famine. Wang Lung gives him seeds and offers to plough his land. Wang Lung is pleased to hear that his uncle has left the village, and no one knows where he is.

Back on his land, Wang Lung is happy again. One night he discovers that O-lan had stolen some jewels from the rich person's house. He insists that he must have all but two pearls so he can buy more land from the House of Hwang.

On visiting the formerly great house, he learns that bandits have stolen all the remaining wealth and that only two people still live there, the Old Lord and a former female slave named Cuckoo. Cuckoo tells him there is land available for sale, and Wang Lung purchases it with the jewels he took from O-lan.

Chapters 17–19

Wang builds additional rooms to his house and buys Ching's land. Ching comes to live with him and helps on the land. Wang Lung hires laborers and builds another room for the house. O-lan gives birth to twins, a boy and a girl, and Wang Lung is happy. The only sad thing in his life is that his first daughter is mentally retarded and never learns to speak.

There are many years of good harvests. Wang Lung hires more laborers and builds another house. He no longer works in the fields but spends his time supervising his workers and marketing his produce. He sends his eldest son to school so the boy can learn to read and write and help him at the grain markets. Wang Lung also sends his younger son to school, and he is proud of them both.

One year there is a flood, and two-fifths of Wang Lung's land is under water. He is not worried, however, because his storerooms are filled. But he is restless. Now he has money, but he is not as happy as he was before. He is aware that he now occupies a higher social status, and he starts to patronize a more sophisticated tea house in town than the one he has been going to for years. In the evening, he hears women's voices coming from the upper floor of the tea house. One night, with the help of Cuckoo, whom he encounters by chance in the tea house, he is shown to the room of one of the women, whose name is Lotus. Captivated by the slender Lotus, Wang Lung visits her every night and does not return home until dawn. He is infatuated with Lotus all summer and buys her expensive gifts. He even takes O-lan's pearls and gives them to Lotus.

Chapters 20–22

Wang Lung's uncle returns. He knows how wealthy his nephew is, so he decides that he and his wife and son will move in with him. Wang Lung is appalled, but tradition demands that he cannot reject his uncle. His uncle's wife soon discovers that Wang Lung has a mistress and informs O-lan. Wang Lung decides to move Lotus into his house, and he builds a new court with three rooms to accommodate her. Lotus agrees to come in exchange for many expensive gifts.

After Lotus arrives, Wang Lung spends his time with Lotus rather than O-lan. While O-lan accepts the presence of Lotus, she does not accept the presence of Cuckoo, because when they were both slaves in the House of Hwang, Cuckoo did not treat her well. Wang Lung builds a new kitchen so the two women can stay apart. But there is little peace for Wang Lung. He tires of Lotus's petulance and the fact that she does not like his children. After Lotus becomes angry with them one day, Wang Lung's love for her cools. In the fall, he turns again to the earth, which has always nourished his life. As he works in the fields, he no longer feels so attached to Lotus.

Wang Lung's eldest son has learned to read and write and helps his father at the grain market. Wang Lung decides he must find a wife for his son, but he has difficulty finding a suitable match. His son becomes moody and plays truant from school, for which Wang Lung beats him with a stick.

Chapters 23–25

Lotus and Cuckoo tell Wang Lung that a wealthy grain dealer named Liu has a young daughter who would make a suitable wife for his son. Wang Lung hesitates to agree to this idea, but after he finds that his son has been visiting a prostitute in town, he tells Cuckoo to negotiate the match.

Wang Lung confronts his uncle, who has been constantly abusing Wang Lung's hospitality. He tells him that he must leave the house. But his uncle

shows him the lining of his coat, in which there is a false beard of red hair and a length of red cloth. Wang Lung then realizes that his uncle is one of the Redbeards, a gang of robbers that has been marauding in the area. He realizes that he cannot throw his uncle out of the house for fear of reprisals.

Wang Lung is upset because Liu refuses to allow his fourteen-year-old daughter to marry for another three years.

Wang Lung's son, now nearly eighteen, says he wants to study in one of the great schools in the south. Wang Lung angrily refuses permission. But after O-lan tells him that his son has been visiting Lotus, Wang Lung goes unexpectedly one night to Lotus's court. Finding the two of them together, he beats his son severely. Lotus claims that she and the young man only talk; he has never been in her bed. But the next day, Wang tells his son to leave for the south. Then he turns his attention to his second and third sons. He apprentices the former in the grain market and decides that the latter will become a farmer. He then thinks of O-lan and notices she is sick. He summons a doctor who says that O-lan will die.

Chapters 26–28

For many months, O-lan lies in bed, slowly dying, and her future daughter-in-law comes to the house to look after her. O-lan says she will not die until she sees her eldest son married. The son returns, and the night of the wedding feast, O-lan finally dies.

After her death, Wang Lung moves into the court where Lotus lives. Within a few days, Wang Lung's father dies, and he and O-lan are buried at the same time.

In the summer, there is a catastrophic flood. Wang Lung's land is under water, but his house, which is on higher ground, survives. There is a severe famine in the village because there are no harvests, and people starve. There is no harvest the following year either, and Wang Lung has to conserve his dwindling resources. To add to his troubles, his uncle and his family are always complaining, demanding money, and reminding Wang Lung that were it not for their protection, his house would long ago have been attacked by the Redbeards. Not only this, his uncle's son lusts after the wife of Wang Lung's son. Wang Lung decides to ply his uncle and his wife with opium that will dull their minds and make them less troublesome.

After the flood recedes and the villagers return to their homes, Wang Lung lends them money to restore their property. The trouble between Wang Lung's eldest son and his cousin continues, and at his son's suggestion, Wang Lung decides to move his family into the empty inner courts of the House of Hwang.

Chapters 29–31

While the rest of the family moves, for a while Wang Lung remains on his land with his mentally retarded daughter and his youngest son. Wang Lung's uncle's son leaves to join in a war in the north, to Wang Lung's relief. He starts to spend more time at the house in town and is proud when his daughter-in-law gives birth to a son.

Wang Lung's faithful steward, Ching dies, and Wang Lung buries him near the family plot. Lonely without Ching and tired of all his labor, Wang Lung takes his son and daughter and lives permanently in the house in town. Persuaded by his eldest son, Wang Lung buys the outer courts of the house as well. The son ensures that the rents are raised, forcing the tenants out. Wang Lung then spends lavishly, restoring the house to its former splendor. Some time after this, he employs a tutor for his youngest son and puts his second son in charge of managing his land.

Over the next five years, Wang Lung has four grandsons and three grand-daughters. Also, his uncle dies.

One day a horde of soldiers, one of whom is the son of Wang Lung's uncle, descends on the town. They are rough and violent, and some of them take up residence in Wang Lung's courts. The son of Wang Lung's uncle behaves especially badly and comes into conflict once again with Wang Lung's eldest son. Anxious to placate him, Wang Lung gives him a female slave named Pear Blossom.

Chapters 32–34

Wang Lung is nearly sixty-five years old, but he can find no peace. The wife of his eldest son and the wife of his second son quarrel; the eldest and the second son dislike each other; the youngest son says he want to become a soldier, which displeases Wang Lung, and Lotus is angry with Wang Lung when he takes Pear Blossom as a mistress. His passion for Pear Blossom does not last long, however, although he still spends time with her.

Wang Lung now has eleven grandsons and eight granddaughters. He thinks of his life as nearly over, and he decides to return to his land, with Pear Blossom and his daughter, to live out the remainder of his days.

In the fall, he overhears his first two sons discussing a plan to sell the land after his death. He is angry, and they try to reassure him that the land will not be sold, but unseen by him they exchange a knowing smile, indicating they have no intention of keeping this promise.

Characters

Ching

Ching is a farmer and neighbor of Wang Lung. He is a small and quiet man with a face "like an ape's." Honest and decent, Ching is ashamed of the fact that during the famine he joined with the mob that went to Wang Lung's house to steal. He took a handful of Wang Lung's beans, but only because his child was starving. A short while later, Ching gives Wang Lung some dried red beans to atone for his actions. During the famine, Ching's wife dies, and he is forced to sell his daughter to a soldier to save her life. When Wang Lung returns from the city, he helps Ching. He later buys Ching's land and employs Ching to help him manage all his land. Ching becomes a loyal employee, and there is mutual respect between the two men. When Ching dies, Wang Lung grieves for him even more than he did for his father.

Cuckoo

Cuckoo is a sharp-voiced, shrewd woman who for much of her life is a slave at the House of Hwang. But after the old mistress dies and the house is sacked by bandits, she becomes the mistress of the Old Master and manages his affairs. She also acts as intermediary for Wang Lung to meet Lotus. When Lotus moves to Wang Lung's house, Cuckoo attends her as a servant. This arrangement causes friction in the house because O-lan dislikes Cuckoo and will not speak to her. As the years go by, Cuckoo and Lotus develop a more equal relationship and become friends. Cuckoo is very skilled at looking after Lotus's interests.

Old Master Hwang

Old Master Hwang, the patriarch of the Hwang family, allows his family to decline into poverty and ruin. He insists on taking in new concubines every year, even when he cannot afford to do so, and he seems to exert little control over his sons.

Old Mistress Hwang

Old Mistress Hwang is the matriarch of the Hwang family. When Wang Lung goes to her house to fetch his bride, Old Mistress is rather stern and haughty. She is addicted to opium. When the family fortunes go into decline, Old Mistress sells much of the family land. She dies of shock when bandits raid the house and tie her to a chair and gag her.

Liu

Liu is a wealthy, good-hearted grain dealer with whom Wang Lung does business. The two men also arrange for their families to be linked through marriage. Liu's daughter marries Wang Lung's eldest son, and Wang Lung's second daughter is promised to Liu's second son. Also, Wang Lung's second son is apprenticed to Liu.

Lotus

Lotus is a courtesan who entertains men on the upper floor of the tea shop that Wang Lung frequents. She is slender and alluring, with tiny hands and feet. When he first meets Lotus, Wang Lung is captivated by her charm and falls under her spell. He does whatever she asks of him, and he also brings her expensive gifts. Eventually, Wang Lung moves Lotus into his own house, so that he does not have to share her with others, and he builds new rooms for her. Wang Lung's uncle's wife comments that Lotus "reeks of perfume and paint" and is not as young as she looks, but Wang Lung does not seem to care. An idle woman, Lotus lies around on her bed all day, nibbling at food and being bathed and oiled by Cuckoo. In the evenings, she decks herself out in her fine clothes. For Wang Lung, "there was nothing so wonderful for beauty in the world as her pointed little feet and her curling helpless hands." Lotus can also be bad-tempered, especially with Wang Lung's children, and eventually Wang Lung's love for her cools.

O-lan

O-lan is Wang Lung's wife. Before she is given to him in marriage, she spent ten years as a slave at the House of Hwang. O-lan is a plain, taciturn woman who accepts her lot in life without complaint. She makes a good wife for Wang Lung, since she is a competent housekeeper, an excellent cook, and a hard worker in the fields. She also has a lot of common sense. When Wang Lung complains about having his uncle's family living with them, she says it cannot be helped, so they must make the best of it. But Wang Lung does not love his wife. He treats her cruelly when he insists on taking the jewels she cherishes and using them to buy land. When Wang Lung becomes wealthy, he becomes dissatisfied with O-lan's appearance. He

thinks of her as "a dull and common creature, who plodded in silence without thought of how she appeared to others." He starts to criticize her, and she bears his reproaches silently. She knows he does not love her. After Wang Lung acquires Lotus as a mistress, he no longer sleeps with O-lan. O-lan dies after a long illness, the night of her eldest son's wedding feast.

Pear Blossom

Pear Blossom is a young slave. Wang Lung bought her during a famine, when she was half-starved. She is small and delicate and helps Cuckoo and Lotus. Later, even though Wang Lung is old enough to be her grandfather, he takes Pear Blossom as his mistress.

Son of Wang Lung's uncle

The son of Wang Lung's uncle is a worthless young man who is nothing but trouble from the beginning. He is the only son of his father but contributes nothing to the family's welfare. He is a bad influence on Wang Lung's eldest son, who is younger than he, and he takes him into town to visit prostitutes. The two young men later quarrel, and the son of Wang Lung's uncle reveals another of his faults: he is a womanizer who has designs on the wife of Wang Lung's son. Later, he leaves to become a soldier, although he has no intention of ever taking part in a battle. Some years later, he is one of the horde of soldiers that descend on Wang Lung's town and stay in the inner courts of the former House of Hwang. He is hated and feared, and Wang Lung gives him the slave Pear Blossom to satisfy his lusts so that he will not harm the other women.

Wang Lung

When the story begins, Wang Lung is a young farmer eking out a precarious living from his small amount of land. He is a hardworking, dutiful man who looks after his old father. Because Wang Lung is poor, he can only acquire a former slave as a wife. When he goes to the great House of Hwang to claim his bride, he is terrified. A humble man from the fields, he knows nothing of city life. He is accustomed to frugal habits and is shocked at how much everything costs.

After he acquires a wife, Wang Lung begins to prosper. He fathers two sons, his harvests are good, he saves money and buys more land. The only adversity he suffers is from things over which he has no control. When drought leads to famine, he takes his family to a big city in the south, just so they can survive. But Wang Lung is still a man from the country, and he never adjusts to city life. He misses his land. Working on the land gives him peace and contentment, and whenever he is away from it, he suffers.

Wang Lung is an honest man, but he falls prey to temptation when he takes silver from a frightened man as a mob runs through the rich house in the city. The money enables him to return to his land, and once more, he prospers, winning the respect of others in the village; he has become a man of substance. But as he gets more wealthy, he forgets some of the values that enabled him to succeed. He no longer works on the land and is sometimes idle, and he thinks his humble wife is not good enough for a wealthy man such as he. His former humility is replaced by a certain amount of pride at the fact that when he goes into the tea shop, people whisper about him, pointing him out as a rich landowner. He starts to patronize another tea shop which he had formerly despised because there was gambling there as well as "evil women." But soon he gets smitten by one of those very "evil women," the courtesan Lotus, and for a while he loses his moorings altogether, lavishing gifts on her and becoming vain about his own appearance. He eventually frees himself from this obsession by going back to work on the land. His life is not entirely peaceful, however, since he spends much of his time worrying about his sons and other family matters. When he is very old, he leaves his house in the town and returns to live in the old earthen house on his land.

Wang Lung's father

Wang Lung's father is an old man who lives with his son. Wang Lung looks after him and makes sure he has enough food, even during the famine. He seems to remain cheerful and says he has seen worse days. The old man travels south with the family but refuses to beg on the streets with O-lan and the boys. He just trusts that he will somehow receive enough food.

Wang Lung's first daughter

Wang Lung's first daughter is mentally retarded, perhaps because during her first year of life there was little food for her to eat. She never learns to speak but sits around with a sweet, empty smile on her face. Wang Lung takes good care of her, calling her "my poor little fool."

Wang Lung's first son

Wang Lung's first son is sent to school at age twelve so he will be able to help his father, who cannot read or write, in his dealings at the grain market. He proves himself to be an able scholar, and later, when he is nearly eighteen, he continues his education at a prestigious school in the south. He returns when his mother dies, and he marries a girl from a wealthy family. As a young man, he is quite different from the way his father was at the same age. He is accustomed not to poverty but to wealth, and he does not have his father's love of the land. He spends money lavishly to renovate the former House of Hwang because he thinks that his family should live in a style commensurate with their wealth.

Wang Lung's second daughter

Wang Lung's second daughter, the twin of his third son, is a pretty child. Wang Lung and O-lan decide to bind her feet so it will be easier for her to find a husband. The girl is later betrothed to the son of Liu. When she is thirteen, to escape the undesirable attentions of the son of Wang Lung's uncle, she is sent to live with Liu.

Wang Lung's second son

Wang Lung's second son is apprenticed to Liu, the grain dealer. Unlike his elder brother, this middle son is a competent, careful businessman, and Wang Lung trusts him with the financial management of his land. But the son turns out to be too parsimonious. He provides the slaves and servants with the least he can give them, causing Cuckoo to sneer at him in protest; he complains to Wang Lung that so much money is being spent on restoring the former House of Hwang that it will eat up his inheritance, and he even complains that his own wedding costs too much.

Wang Lung's third son

Wang Lung's third son is a quiet boy, and Wang Lung does not know much about what interests him. Wang Lung's plan is for the boy to become a farmer, but the boy says he wants to learn to read. Wang Lung thinks this is unnecessary for a future farmer, but he accedes to his son's request and employs a tutor. After the band of unruly soldiers come to the village, the boy listens to their stories and says he wants to be a soldier. The boy is fond of Pear Blossom and disappears from home after his father takes Pear Blossom for himself.

Wang Lung's uncle

Wang Lung's uncle is a lazy good-for-nothing who fails to cultivate his lands and look after his family. Instead, he persuades Wang Lung to give him money. Eventually, when Wang Lung has become wealthy, his uncle insists on moving into his nephew's house, along with his wife and son. Once there, they all make nuisances of themselves and contribute nothing to the household. The uncle takes advantage of Wang Lung's unwillingness to behave harshly to a relative and cements his position at the house by revealing that he is a member of the Redbeards, a gang of robbers, and claiming that it is only his presence in the house that prevents the Redbeards from robbing it. Wang Lung solves the problem presented by his uncle by getting him addicted to opium, after which the old man lies around smoking all day and no longer creates trouble.

Wife of Wang Lung's first son

The wife of Wang Lung's first son is the daughter of Liu. She tends to O-lan in her final illness and then marries the son when she is sixteen. O-lan and Wang Lung think highly of her. However, she is not so popular with Wang Lung's second son and his wife. The two women hate each other, and the second son tells Wang Lung that the wife of the eldest son talks all the time about all the luxury in her father's house and encourages her husband to spend too much money on unnecessary things.

Wife of Wang Lung's second son

The wife of Wang Lung's second son comes from a good family in a nearby village. She quarrels constantly with the wife of Wang Lung's eldest son, who regards her as ill-bred.

Wife of Wang Lung's uncle

The wife of Wang Lung's uncle is a self-pitying, lazy woman who never bothers to clean her house. She has seven children, six of whom are girls. When Wang Lung becomes wealthy, she moves into his house, with her husband and son. She abuses Wang Lung's hospitality, eating the expensive foods that Cuckoo brings for Lotus and complaining a lot. Like her husband, she eventually becomes addicted to opium, which makes her passive and manageable.

Themes

Love of the Land

Throughout the novel, the land is the "good earth"; it nourishes Wang Lung, physically, emotionally, and spiritually. When he toils in the fields, he is happy; as a farmer, he knows his true place to be on the land, as it has been for many generations of his family before him. When he is forced by famine to go south to the city, he is out of his element, cut off from what sustains his life, and this contrast between country and city occurs repeatedly throughout the novel. When Wang Lung hears that the young lords of the House of Hwang no longer have any direct contact with the land, he immediately decides that he will start his two young sons working in the fields, "where they would early take into their bones and their blood the feel of the soil under their feet, and the feel of the hoe hard in their hands." Working on the land restores Wang Lung's spirits at crucial moments in his life. Whenever he is troubled, physical labor on the land restores him. It liberates him from his unhealthy infatuation with Lotus and has the same effect after the plague of locusts has gone: "For seven days he thought of nothing but his land, and he was healed of his troubles and his fears." While all else in life may fluctuate, the land alone remains. Even when Wang Lung is old and rich and living in a town house, his link with the land cannot be broken—"his roots were in the land"—and every spring he feels the call to return to it, even though he no longer has the strength to hold a plow. To lose connection to the land is to lose connection to life. This is why he says to his sons, when he hears that they are planning to sell the land, "If you sell the land, it is the end."

The Corrupting Influence of Wealth

The theme that wealth corrupts occurs repeatedly and is connected to the theme of losing connection to the land. At the beginning of the novel, the House of Hwang is a symbol of great wealth and luxury. When Wang Lung arrives with the meat he has bought for the wedding feast that night, the gateman tells him that in this house, they feed such meat to the dogs. Arriving in the main hall, Wang Lung is so overawed by its size and splendor that he almost falls over. The wealth of the House of Hwang has been built up over the generations simply because of their ownership of land. But over time, they have forgotten the source of their wealth. The young lords of the House go abroad and spend money wastefully; they never go to the land and see it for themselves. Instead, they rely on agents to handle affairs for them, and they simply collect the money. Eventually, the House of Hwang falls. As Cuckoo tells Wang Lung, "And in these generations the strength of the land has gone from them and bit by bit the land has begun to go also."

Although Wang Lung takes this observation to heart, he also goes through a phase in which wealth

Topics For Further Study

- Closely examine the brief incident described in chapter 14, in which Wang Lung encounters a Christian missionary. What image does it present of Christianity? Does the passage suggest that Christian missionary work in China is positive or negative? What reasons might Buck have had for presenting Christian missionary work in this light? Write an essay in which you present your analysis.

- Obtain a copy of the 1937 movie version of *The Good Earth* and make a class presentation, with video clips if possible, of the main differences between the book and the movie. Take especial note of how O-lan is portrayed. Also consider why all the leading parts were taken by white rather than Chinese actors.

- Consider some of the stereotypical ways in which Chinese and other Asian people were viewed by Americans during the twentieth century. Consider films and television programs. Why did the West cultivate such negative views of non-Western cultures? Make a class presentation in which you discuss such stereotypes and show how portrayals of Asians and Asian-Americans in the media today are more positive than in former times.

- Team up with another student and make a class presentation in which you compare John Steinbeck's *The Grapes of Wrath* (1939) to *The Good Earth*. What themes do the two books have in common? Does Steinbeck's book suggest a reason why *The Good Earth* was received so enthusiastically by American readers during the 1930s?

---

makes him forget the principles of thrift and hard work on which his life is based. He also forgets his origins and becomes quite a snob. The old tea shop he has frequented for years is no longer good enough for him, and neither is his wife, or so he decides. When he meets Lotus, she makes him ashamed of smelling like a country fellow, and he starts to have his clothes specially made in a fashionable cut by a tailor in town. He also wears velvet shoes such as those worn by the Old Master Hwang. In a telling moment, O-lan says that he reminds her of the young lords in the House of Hwang. Wang Lung mistakenly takes this as a compliment. It appears that he is in danger of going down the same path trodden by the young lords. Even after he recovers from his infatuation with Lotus, he still thinks of himself as a cut above the common man. When he goes into one of the poorer areas of town and sees the common people, he despises them as "filthy" and walks past them "with his nose up and breathing lightly because of the stink they made." He forgets that not too long ago he was a common man himself and rarely washed until he met Lotus, thinking "the clean sweat of his labor washing enough for ordinary times."

The third example of the corruption of wealth is Wang Lung's eldest son. He has never lived as close to the land as his father and has been raised in a wealthy house. He is contemptuous of the common people, and they laugh at him for his snobbish attitude, saying that he has forgotten the smell of manure on his father's farm. He is always spending money lavishly and does not seem aware that all the wealth comes from the land. O-lan remarks, just as she had done to Wang Lung, that the behavior of her eldest son reminds her of the young lords in the House of Hwang. The desire of both the eldest and the second son to sell the land after Wang Lung's death suggests that they may indeed be following in the path of those who so catastrophically mismanaged the House of Hwang.

Inferior Status of Women

In the society depicted in the novel, women occupy an inferior position. O-lan is a slave before she marries and is accustomed to working from dawn until midnight. As a wife to Wang Lung, she becomes almost a domestic slave. She is expected to do all the cooking and housekeeping and to work alongside her husband in the fields as well.

She knows her place and accepts the conditions of her life without complaint, even though Wang Lung has little respect for her. Once, early in the marriage, Wang Lung finds himself wondering about her former life as a slave. But then he is ashamed of his own curiosity; "She was, after all, only a woman."

A revealing moment comes when O-lan gives birth to her first daughter. It is a disappointment to both her and her husband. "It is only a slave this time—not worth mentioning," she says, and Wang Lung, preoccupied with dealing with his uncle, does not even look at the newborn. He thinks of the birth almost as a curse ("the birth of daughters had begun for him"). A female child is not even considered part of the family into which she is born, for as soon as she is of child-bearing age she will marry and become part of another family.

The undervaluing of women can also be seen in the fact that during harsh times, the daughters of the poor are often sold into slavery, so that the other members of the family can survive. When O-lan smothers her second daughter, who is born during the famine, she is merely acting on a culture-wide devaluation of female life. It is more than unlikely that her actions would have been the same had the child been a boy.

Style

Imagery and Symbolism

The novel is a realistic one but also on occasions employs imagery and symbolism. The traditional Chinese practice of foot-binding, for example, is used as a symbol of Wang Lung's desire to improve the social status of his family. The binding of girls' feet over a period of years resulted in a deformed foot that sometimes was no longer than three inches. Foot-binding was a painful process, but a small foot was considered desirable. Wang Lung finds Lotus alluring because she has tiny feet. Also, if a girl had bound feet it was easier for the family to find her a husband. The practice was not common amongst the poor, however, because poor women had to work; they could not afford to be merely decorative objects. Since O-lan is a kitchen slave, her feet were not bound. However, when Wang Lung acquires wealth and determines that his wife is not good enough for him, what repels him most are her "big feet," and he looks at them angrily. To appease him, she offers to bind the feet of their younger daughter. O-lan does this

successfully, and the result is that the girl "moved about with small graceful steps."

Wang Lung's braided hair is also used as a symbol. It represents the traditional way of life. When as a young man Wang Lung visits a barber on his way to collect his bride, the barber wants to cut off the braid to make him look more fashionable, but Wang Lung will not hear of it. He says he would need his father's permission to have it cut—another indication of his adherence to traditional customs. However, when Wang Lung meets Lotus, he forgets all about the values that have sustained his life, and when she mocks him for having what she calls a "monkey's tail," he has it cut off straightaway, so he can look fashionable. But when he gets home, O-lan is horrified by what he has done. "You have cut off your life!" she says, thus establishing a symbolic link between the way a man's hair is worn and the traditional ways of life.

Historical Context

Revolutionary Change in China

During the period covered by the novel, China went through dramatic political change. Although *The Good Earth* focuses mostly on rural existence, which was resistant to change, on two occasions Wang Lung comes into contact with wider social forces. The first occurs when he is in the city of Kiangsu (Nanking), and he hears all the revolutionary talk and sees soldiers in the city, recruiting for a war. Then a revolutionary army arrives, and mob violence breaks out. The atmosphere and events described in these sections of the novel are based on the growing social unrest in China during the first decade of the twentieth century. For decades, the political institutions of Chinese imperial rulers had become increasingly corrupt and incompetent, failing for example to defend China from foreign invasions. The social discontent thus generated culminated in the Revolution of 1911, in which the Ch'ing dynasty collapsed. The trigger for the revolution was an uprising that broke out in October of 1911, between nationalist revolutionaries and the military in the city of Wuhan. For four months, many provinces rose up against imperial rule. There was heavy fighting in Nanking. Buck's parents, the Christian missionaries Absalom and Carie Sydenstricker, were in Nanking at the time and were advised to evacuate, but they refused to do so.

Compare & Contrast

- **1930s:** In the Chinese city of Nanking, invading Japanese troops kill an estimated 369,366 Chinese civilians and prisoners of war between December 1937 and March 1938. About 80,000 women and girls are raped; many are then mutilated and murdered.

  Today: For decades Japan refused to apologize to China for atrocities committed during World War II. In 2005, Japanese prime minister Junichiro Koizumi apologizes for the fact that Japan caused grief and pain to many people in Asian nations during the war. But he does not mention Nanking by name.

- **1930s:** China is under the rule of the Nationalist Party, led by Chiang Kai-shek. The Chinese Communist Party opposes the nationalists but in the 1930s is on the defensive. In 1934, the communists begin their famous 6,000-mile Long March from Hunan to northwest China, where they establish a base.

  Today: China is ruled by the Communist Party, but economic reforms over the past twenty years have introduced many capitalistic practices. The private sector of the economy is growing fast as China develops into a major world power.

- **1930s:** In Shanghai, a Chinese city subject to many international influences, educated, sophisticated women forge new roles for themselves that leave old ideas about appropriate gender roles behind. They regard themselves as free and liberated, but traditionalists see in them the dangers of modernity and foreign influences. The lives of Chinese women in rural areas and less modern cities, however, remain hard, with few recognized rights.

  Today: The Chinese government makes great strides in protecting women's rights and advancing women's political and social status. Gains have been made in education, health care and employment, although discrimination still exists in the workplace, and women from poor areas frequently have their rights violated, especially in matters of family and marriage.

On February 12, 1912, a Chinese Republic was established with revolutionary leader Sun Yat-sen as its first president. He proclaimed the goals of the republic as nationalism, democracy, and socialism. But he soon came under pressure and resigned in favor of Yuan Shi-k'ai, a revolutionary general. Yuan Shi-k'ai declared himself emperor in 1915, but he died the following year before he could advance his imperial ambitions. His death severely weakened the republican government and led to the period known as the Warlord Era (1916–1927), in which provincial armies vied for power, often producing devastating results for local populations. It is this period that is referred to in chapter 31 of *The Good Earth*, when the horde of soldiers descend on Wang Lung's town and tyrannize the local people. This action signifies the widespread chaos in China during this period, which was not finally resolved until the triumph of the communists in 1949.

Foot-binding and the Role of Women in China

In traditional, pre-twentieth century Chinese society, women were assigned a position inferior to that of men. The qualities that were valued in women were obedience and loyalty. As is apparent from *The Good Earth*, the birth of a girl was not greeted by the family with as much pleasure as that of a boy. As Xiongya Gao explains in *Pearl S. Buck's Chinese Women Characters*, if a couple's first child was a girl, this was considered a disappointment; if the second was a girl also, it was cause for grief; and a third girl was considered a tragedy. The wife would be blamed for her failure to produce a son. It was not unusual for an infant girl in a poor family to be smothered or sold into slavery (as *The Good Earth* demonstrates).

Young girls in traditional Chinese families faced other hazards growing up, including having their feet bound. The practice of binding the feet began among the aristocracy in the tenth century and spread throughout China. Foot-binding was started when a girl was between the age of four and six and would continue for over a decade. The feet would be bound tightly with bandages so that the toes were bent under the sole of the foot and the arch pushed upward. The procedure, which resulted in broken and misshapen bones, was extremely painful and resulted in deformed feet. Such feet were subject to infection and disease; after some years of binding, the foot would be virtually dead and would smell. But the tiny, crippled foot was looked on by Chinese men as a most desirable thing. As Gao puts it, "Such a product of cruelty, of women's tears and suffering, had come to be greatly admired, played with, and worshiped by men. It [the foot] became the most erotic organ of the female body." In other words, women were deliberately crippled in the name of beauty and eroticism.

For the cruelty of the practice, one need look no further than the description in *The Good Earth*, when the daughter of Wang Lung tells her father that she weeps "because my mother binds a cloth about my feet more tightly every day and I cannot sleep at night" The bandages on the foot were usually changed every two days, and rebound more tightly, causing greater pain.

If a girl did not submit to foot-binding the chances of her finding a husband were slim. She was told that she had to have her feet bound in order to be pleasing to men. Part of the attraction for men was that a woman with bound feet was physically weak and could more easily be controlled. Such women were kept secluded in the home. They could not walk far or sometimes at all without leaning on a man. Having a girl with bound feet was a sign of the family's social status. It meant they could afford to have an unproductive female in the house. Big, unbound feet (like O-lan's in the novel) were a sign of poverty and low status.

At the beginning of the twentieth century, however, voices were raised in China against the inferior status of women and the practice of foot-binding. Jonathan Spence, in *The Gate of Heavenly Peace*, quotes from an essay published in 1904 by a young woman named Qiu Jin, who protested about the oppression of women in Chinese culture. Her description of the prevailing attitude toward the birth of a daughter recalls a number of passages in *The Good Earth*. The father will

immediately start spewing out phrases like "Oh what an ill-omened day, here's another useless one...."

He keeps repeating, "She will be in someone else's family later on," and looks at us with cold or disdainful eyes.

Qui Jin also protested against foot-binding:

They take out a pair of snow-white bands and bind them around our feet, tightening them with strips of white cotton; even when we go to bed at night we are not allowed to loosen them the least bit, with the result that the flesh peels away and the bones buckle under.

Foot-binding was banned by the Chinese government in 1911. During this period, also, as Spence reports, Chinese society was starting to address the issue of the status of women. The number of girls' schools increased, and magazines and newspapers were published that focussed on women's issues. Christian missionaries and Chinese reformists were also influential. In 1919, the first girls were admitted to Peking National University.

Critical Overview

On publication in 1931, *The Good Earth* was a huge critical and popular success. It was chosen for the Book of the Month Club, which in the 1930s was a guaranteed way to generate high sales for a book. In fact, *The Good Earth* was the bestselling book in the United States in 1931 and 1932. It was reviewed in all the major newspapers and magazines and received near universal acclaim. It was awarded the Pulitzer Prize in 1932. Over the years it was translated into thirty languages.

What reviewers most liked about the novel was that it was the first book to give Western readers insight into what Chinese society was really like. It was not a fanciful portrait of China as seen through the distant gaze of a Westerner, and it did not present the Chinese in terms of the unflattering stereotypes that were common in the West at that time. For example, a reviewer for the *New York Times* comments that the country portrayed in the book is "a China in which, happily, there is no hint of mystery or exoticism. There is very little in [Buck's] book of the quality we are accustomed to label, 'Oriental'" (quoted in Peter Conn, *Pearl S. Buck: A Cultural Biography*). In *The Nation*, Eda Lou Walton comments that Buck's "complete familiarity with her material allows her to present her characters as very human and very real, as people who engage our sympathies." H. C. Harwood, in *Saturday Review*, remarks: "The opening chapters of *The Good Earth* are so lovely that one forgets the Far East, one forgets everything but humanity." Harwood also commented on how

Luise Rainer as O-Lan and Paul Muni, in the motion picture The Good Earth, *1937* © The Kobal Collection.
Reproduced by permission

[W]ithout effort or anger an alien civilization is quietly presented. It is so easy to be funny about China, and so easy to be funny about the collisions of alien cultures. Mrs. Buck turns away from all that and explains Wang Lung.

The novel was also well reviewed in a number of Chinese journals, although some Chinese intellectuals professed to dislike it. Buck's defenders felt this was because she had revealed a side of Chinese life (poverty, inequality) that the Chinese educated class would sooner not have exposed.

In the early 2000s, there was a revival of interest in *The Good Earth* among contemporary readers because the book was selected for Oprah Winfrey's Book Club.

Criticism

Bryan Aubrey

Aubrey holds a Ph.D. in English and has published many articles on twentieth century literature. In this essay, he discusses the religious beliefs of the society depicted in the novel and how Wang Lung's attitude toward religion gradually changes.

> In his old age, then, Wang Lung shows that he has not quite renounced the religious beliefs and customs that are observed as a matter of course in his society. But the years have changed him."

In *The Good Earth*, Buck's saga of rural Chinese life over several generations, the three great religions of China—Confucianism, Taoism, and Buddhism—make almost no appearance. In Chinese history, there has generally been a distinction between the religious beliefs and practices of the educated classes and those of the peasantry. Over the centuries, the common people have known little of the intellectual or devotional practices of these great faiths. Instead, as Ninian Smart explains in *The Religious Experience of Mankind*, "religion, interwoven with magic, had an immediate practical significance in the struggle for worldly benefits and in the common round of agricultural and family festivals." It is these early religious beliefs and superstitions, which seem to have remained unchanged for many hundreds and perhaps thousands of years, that are presented in *The Good Earth*, against the background of Wang Lung's changing attitude towards them.

The first insight into the religious beliefs and practices that govern life in the small village in which Wang Lung lives comes when, as a young man, he returns from the House of Hwang with his bride, O-lan. The first thing he does is take her to the western field on his property, where a tiny earthen "temple" stands. It was built by Wang Lung's grandfather, and Wang Lung's father tends to it with great care. It is part of their family tradition. Inside stand two earthen figures depicting a male and a female god. They are covered in robes of red and gilt paper which Wang Lung's father makes for them every New Year. Wang Lung burns incense to these gods of the fields, in whom all the townspeople believe, so that they will bless his marriage and make it fruitful. Although at this stage Wang Lung appears to believe in these gods and their power, the author gives a hint that they may not be as all-powerful as he believes.

The gods look spruced up in their new robes, but this will not last, because "each year rain and snow beat in and the sun of summer shone in and spoiled their robes." These are gods who are damaged by the very things they supposedly control.

In addition to believing in the power of the gods, Wang Lung also believes in omens and evil spirits. He is relieved to find that the sticks of incense he has brought with him to the temple are not broken, for that would be an evil omen. Then later, when he comes home with O-lan and his baby son from the House of Hwang, he shows his superstitious nature. He boasts about how beautiful the baby is, but then he is fearful because he is walking under an open sky with his baby and any evil spirit could see the child, and, presumably, cause him harm. So Wang Lung covers the child's head and speaks out loud to confuse any lurking evil spirit, saying it is a pity the child is a female and has smallpox and that he and O-lan should pray that it may die. It appears that this is a world in which malicious spirits practice trickery and must be outwitted by human ingenuity.

Such are the basic religious beliefs of this late-nineteenth and early-twentieth century Chinese peasant society. But as the novel continues, it becomes apparent that Wang Lung is not a slave to ancient beliefs about the gods. He is at heart a practical, down-to-earth man who learns to look for comfort, solace, and peace not to the capricious gods but to the earth, the land, the bringer of sustenance and the giver of life. He is quite willing to reject the gods, but he never rejects the land.

It is during the famine that Wang Lung's attitude to the gods starts to undergo a radical change. Like Job in the Bible, when suffering comes Wang Lung expresses his frustration with God. But he goes further even than Job, directly accusing the "Old Man in Heaven" of being wicked, although he does feel a twinge of fear at doing so. When he goes to the temple, instead of burning incense, he spits on the face of the god. But the god and his consort "sat there unmoved by anything and Wang Lung gnashed his teeth at them." Wang Lung repeats these sentiments when the famine is over and he has returned from the city. Peering into the temple, he sees that the statues of the gods have fallen into ruin. No one has been paying them any attention; their faces have been washed away by the rain and their paper clothes are in tatters. These are impotent gods, indeed, and Wang Lung seems to relish the feeling of revenge that the sight of them produces in him: "Thus it is with gods who do evil to men!" he says.

What
Do I Read
Next?

- Buck's novel *Sons* (1932) is the second volume in the trilogy that begins with *The Good Earth*. Beginning where the previous volume ends, *Sons* is about the lives of Wang Lung's three sons, the eldest (the landlord), the second (the merchant), and especially the youngest son, who becomes a warlord. None of the sons respects the father's legacy. As literature, *Sons* is not considered the equal of *The Good Earth*; nonetheless, it is a tale well told.

- *Splendid Slippers: A Thousand Years of an Erotic Tradition* (1998), by Beverley Jackson, is an account of the Chinese practice of foot-binding. Jackson describes the history of foot-binding, what the procedure involved, and the erotic fascination associated with bound feet. She also compares foot-binding to other exotic practices supposedly aimed at enhancing female beauty, such as the custom of the women of Burma who appear to stretch their necks by wearing a series of heavy necklaces. (Actually,

the collar bone collapses toward the rib cage as x rays have proven.)

- John Henry Gray's *China: A History of the Laws, Manners, and Customs of the People*, published by Dover Books on Literature and Drama in 2003, is a reprint of the original book that was published in 1878. Gray was the archdeacon of Hong Kong, and this readable history covers the period when Wang Lung, in *The Good Earth*, was a young man. It covers topics such government, prisons, religion, Confucian philosophy, marriage, servants and slaves, sports, funerals, and commercial activities such as agriculture and tea and silk production. It includes 140 illustrations of scenes from daily life.

- *The Cambridge Illustrated History of China* (1999), by Patricia Buckley Ebrey, is a much praised, scholarly work that covers with pictures and text some four millennia of Chinese history and culture.

Wang Lung's religious skepticism sees him through into middle age and beyond. When he is getting on in years and Ching warns him of an approaching flood, he repeats his earlier sentiments with even greater vehemence: "I have never had any good from that old man in heaven yet. Incense or no incense, he is the same in evil." He even tells Ching that he thinks God enjoys looking down and seeing men drowning and starving. Not surprisingly, the humble Ching is shocked and asks that his employer not talk in such a way. But Wang Lung just walks off, muttering to himself. It appears that a prosperous, successful man has no need for religion.

But often in crises or moments of emotional intensity, people suddenly return to the beliefs they think they have outgrown. So it is with Wang Lung—although with a twist. Some years after the flood, he is awaiting the birth of his grandson. When he hears from Cuckoo that it will be a long and difficult birth, he gets frightened and feels the need for spiritual support. He buys incense and

goes to the temple in the town, "where the goddess of mercy dwells in her gilded alcove." He summons a priest to make the offering. But then a thought strikes him: what if the grandchild is a girl not a boy? To offset this possibility, he strikes a more assertive note in his newly recovered piety: "If it is a grandson I will pay for a new red robe for the goddess, but nothing will I do if it is a girl!" Then he goes to the small temple on his own land, burns incense as an offering and says much the same thing to the two gods there "who watched over fields and land." In his old age, then, Wang Lung shows that he has not quite renounced the religious beliefs and customs that are observed as a matter of course in his society. But the years have changed him. As a young man he respected the gods and was submissive to them; as a mature man, he railed against the malevolence and injustice of the gods; now, as an old man, he is willing to take them into partnership, to deal with these vexing gods as an equal, as if they were bargaining partners and he were negotiating the price of purchasing new land or selling his goods. They may be gods, but he is Wang Lung, man of substance and not to be trifled with. Over the years, he has learned his lessons; that life is hard and unpredictable; that the gods may have little care for human happiness, that he must make his own way and cleave to the land, which he venerates with the kind of fervor that others reserve for those inscrutable gods.

Source: Bryan Aubrey, Critical Essay on *The Good Earth*, in *Novels for Students*, Thomson Gale, 2007.

Xiongya Gao

In the following excerpt, Gao considers Buck's depiction of the sympathetic character O-Lan, a "representative of the Chinese peasant women," and expounds on how the author "humanizes the Chinese people."

The Good Earth, upon its publication, caught the reader's attention immediately. About its realism, Florence Ayscough wrote (1931):

> I have lived for many years in such a country and among such people as Mrs. Buck describes, and as I read her pages I smell once more the sweet scent of bean flowers opening in the spring . . . ; all as it was and is there in the Yangtze Valley.

Similarly, Paul Hutchinson (1931) pointed out that there had never been a novel that "looked more deeply and understandingly into actual Chinese life." The novel's greatest effect, however, is that it humanizes the Chinese people for the American public. The readers feel a kinship toward Buck's characters, who engage their sympathies and with whom they could easily identify. Thus Carl Van Doren, in *The American Novel* (1940), commented that "*The Good Earth* for the first time made the Chinese seem as familiar as neighbors." The writer of a review in *New Statesman and Nation* (1931) said:

> I can recall no novel that frees the ordinary, flesh and blood, everyday Chineseman so satisfyingly from those screens and veils and mirrors of artistic and poetic convention which nearly always make him, to the Western reader's eye, a flat and unsubstantial figure of a pale-colored ballet.

Although Wang Lung is the main character, around whom the events in the novel revolve, O-lan seems able to gain more sympathy from the readers. A plain-looking, inarticulate, submissive, and enduring woman, O-lan plays a critical role in the ups and downs of Wang Lung and his family. Like the humble and wordless good earth, O-lan is rich in resources and silently produces and keeps

life going. More than the good earth, O-lan is an intelligent, courageous, and capable woman, who makes the right decision at the right time for the family and keeps it going in health toward happiness.

In what follows, it will be shown that O-lan is a very individualized character while at the same time representative of the Chinese peasant women of her times. Like all other women, she is made aware of where her place is both in society and at home. She has also learned the principles of the Three Obediences and Four Virtues that society requires from a woman. However, it is important to see that, under such unfavorable situations, she is able to use her limited power to steer the fate of the family towards prosperity.

The first thing we notice of O-lan is her plain looks. Before we meet her for the first time, we already know from Wang Lung's father that she is not supposed to be a pretty woman, whom a poor house like theirs does not need. At first glance, she appears to be "a square, rather tall figure," with "neat and smooth" hair, and "clothed in clean blue cotton coat and trousers." And "He [Wang Lung] saw with an instant's disappointment that her feet were not bound." Looking more closely, Wang Lung finds out that:

> She had a square, honest face, a short, broad nose with large black nostrils, and her mouth was wide as a gash in her face. Her eyes were small and of a dull black in color, and were filled with some sadness that was not clearly expressed. It was a face that seemed habitually silent and unspeaking, as though it could not speak if it would . . . there was not beauty of any kind in her face—a brown, common, patient face.

The only thing Wang Lung can comfort himself with is that she has no pockmarks on her dark skin and her lips are not split.

As for O-lan's personality, Buck let us view her first through the eyes of the Old Mistress of the House of Hwang. According to the Old Mistress, O-lan is a "good slave, although somewhat slow and stupid," "does well what she is told to do and she has a good temper." Next, Buck has Wang Lung, who is naturally eager and curious to find out what his bride is really like, watch her closely for the next few months after their marriage.

To Wang Lung, O-lan seems to be dull and slow. For instance, when Wang Lung wants to know if there is a side gate on their way out of the House of Hwang, "she nodded after a little thought, as though she did not understand too quickly what he said." All the way out of the house, where she has been a slave for ten years, her face is expressionless, and her eyes "dumb" when she looks at him. Above all, the reader is constantly struck by O-lan's silence. "She never talked . . . except for the brief necessities of life." She does everything in her submissive ways, a virtue she has been forced to adopt. When Wang Lung shows her the box and the basket to take home, she places the heavy box on her shoulder without a word. When Wang Lung changes his mind and commands her to take the basket instead, she simply obeys, "still speechless." Once a wife, she does her daily chores without a word; she works with Wang Lung in the fields quietly. Even in childbirth, she is silent. She appears so inarticulate that one wonders if she is capable of thinking. Wang Lung could make nothing of her. So he contents himself with the thought that she is, after all, only a woman.

However, this seemingly ordinary peasant wife surprises the reader more and more as the story goes on. As we observe more of her, especially after she is out of the House of Hwang, we find that the Old Mistress is not altogether right about her. Even Wang Lung has quite a few surprises from O-lan's intelligence and ability. He admits to himself that "she was a woman such as not commonly found."

We find, as the story reveals little by little, that O-lan is not only hardworking, dutiful, enduring, but also intelligent, competent, and has a practical mind to get things done toward good. Silent or inarticulate though she may be, she carries with her a quiet dignity that catches the reader's heart.

Evidence of O-lan's good qualities is bountiful throughout the novel. Her image as a hardworking, dutiful, and enduring woman who always serves as a provider is set from the very first day of the wedding. According to Chinese custom, even a girl from a poor family gets to wear red, has the day off from daily chores, and is waited upon on her wedding day. O-lan, however, never gets to enjoy what a wife is normally entitled to. She has no wedding clothes and no formal wedding ceremony. Out of the House of Hwang, on their way toward the small earthen house of his ancestors, they stop to burn incense before the gods in the wayside temple to the earth, which is supposedly the moment of their marriage. She has to start working hard to fulfill her duty as a wife as soon as she steps into Wang Lung's house. The only celebration they have is the wedding "feast," but O-lan is the one who prepares it and stays in the kitchen, working the entire time until all the guests are gone. Through

> " We find, as the story reveals little by little, that O-lan is not only hardworking, dutiful, enduring, but also intelligent, competent, and has a practical mind to get things done toward good. Silent or inarticulate though she may be, she carries with her a quiet dignity that catches the reader's heart."

the wedding feast, O-lan not only proves her own capability but also brings Wang Lung the pride he has never had among his folks, for with what little meat she has, she has "skillfully brought forth all the force of the meat itself, so that Wang Lung himself had never tasted such dishes upon the tables of his friends."

As the wedding feast symbolizes, O-lan, in the days to come, takes what little life has to offer her and makes the best of it. Rather than just doing well what she is told to do, as the Old Mistress says about her, she does the daily chores "without a word and without being commanded to do them." Every day, she is the first one to arise at dawn to light the stove and the last one to go to bed at midnight after making sure every household matter has been well taken care of. Furthermore, she goes to work with Wang Lung in the fields. Thus, she actually works much harder than Wang Lung, for she has the extra housework to do, meals to prepare, and the ox to be fed after a whole tiresome day's work in the fields. She never stops working, even when she is heavy with child. Except for the firstborn. O-lan will stop working in the fields only when she had to go back to deliver. Right afterward, she would come back to work at Wang Lung's side as if she had done nothing extraordinary. Even for the first childbirth, she surprises Wang Lung by stopping in her labor to prepare food for him and his father. When her family becomes rich, she refuses to use a slave and insists on doing everything by herself until too sick to work anymore.

It is interesting to note that O-lan's diligence is both typical of Chinese peasant women and unique to herself. The Chinese people are noted for their willingness to work hard, and Chinese women are even more capable of doing so simply because they have more responsibilities than men. However, O-lan's diligence seems to exceed that of peasant women in general. For example, we can safely say that very few women are able to prepare food for their family during childbirth labor. This interdependence of typicality and individualization well illustrates Buck's skill in characterization: individualization, although seemingly the opposite to typicality, grows out of typicality rather than running counter to it.

O-lan never complains, seldom asks anything for herself for all the work she has done, and endures quietly any hardship that comes her way, both physically and emotionally. For her endurance, the reader can hardly forget the vivid scenes of her child delivering. Once critic, Barbara LeBar (1988), rightly points out that O-lan makes mockery of modern "natural" child-birth. O-lan "simply has a child. And she bears it along—without a doctor, without a midwife, without even her husband", and, I would like to add, without scream. Furthermore, she goes back to work beside her husband without a word right after she gives birth to their second son, thinking not about herself but that the rice has to be gathered into sheaves before the rain.

During the year of famine, the entire family starves, but O-lan is the one who suffers most. Here is what Wang Lung sees after O-lan kills the infant girl to avoid another mouth to feed:

> Her eyes were closed and the color of her flesh was the color of ashes and her bones stuck under the skin—a poor silent face that lay there, having endured to the utmost, and there was nothing he [Wang Lung] could say. After all, during these months he had only his own body to drag about. But this woman had endured what agony of starvation with the starved creature gnawing at her from within, desperate for its own life!

Apart from physical hardships, O-lan endures much emotional pain. When Wang Lung gets tired of O-lan and becomes infatuated with Lotus, he reproaches her for not dressing properly and having feet too big to be fit for a landowner's wife. O-lan takes the reproach humbly and hides her feet under the bench. At Wang lung's anger, she only says in a whisper: "My mother did not bind them, since I was sold so young. But the little girl's feet I will bind."

The most unbearable thing that O-lan confronts is the time when Wang Lung forces her to give up the two pearls, which she wants to keep not for her own sake, but as a future wedding gift for her younger daughter. When Wang Lung laughs at the sight of the pearls O-lan puts in the hands,

> O-lan returned to the beating of his clothes and when tears dropped slowly and heavily from her eyes she did not put up her hand to wipe them away; only she beat the more steadily with her wooden stick upon the clothes spread over the stones.

When Wang Lung takes Lotus into the house, O-lan goes to work in the fields and comes back silently, saying nothing to anyone, and goes into the kitchen to do her duty as she always does. At night, she sleeps alone by herself, burying her sorrow all in her heart.

One wonders how O-lan could endure so much in silence. Is she really dull and not capable of thinking? Wang Lung cannot make anything of her, thus giving up his attempt to understand her. However, the discerning reader would find that O-lan is anything but dull.

O-lan's silent endurance of hardship and pain has its roots in the mistreatment women of her times received from society. As indicated in chapter 2, Chinese society offered women so little that they had learned to expect little from life. Even to gain that little, they had to make much effort and to endure the kind of suffering that their male counterparts did not. This is especially true for a woman like O-lan, who comes from the bottom of society as a slave girl. Having been freed from slavery and becoming a landowner's wife is already more than she could expect; any hardship in this capacity would seem nothing compared with what she has had to endure as a slave.

O-lan's silence can also be explained by her miserable past experiences. Having been sold at the age of ten to the House of Hwang in times for famine, O-lan has been severely oppressed and mistreated for ten years. From her habitual slavegirl gesture of raising her arms as if to defend herself from a blow, and her brief unconscious words in her last hours, we gather that she has been forced to accept the fact that she is ugly and therefore not to be loved. Even among the slaves, she is at the bottom, not even allowed to appear before the great lord of the house. She has been beaten for the smallest mistake she makes and anyone can scold her for no fault of her own. There is no place for her to speak. Besides, women were viewed as inferior and supposed to be submissive to men. So, once married to Wang Lung, she tries to do all in her silent obedience. Her silence is therefore one of her trademarks, indicating her personality, her background, and her effort to make her behavior acceptable.

Despite the oppression, O-lan, like other women, "has her joys and sorrows and experiences a full range of human emotions" (Li 1989, 99). In her silence we see her pride, desire, stubbornness, and temper. She is proud of the fact that she is doing well as Wang Lung's wife, for there is "not one slave with a new coat like mine" in the House of Hwang; she is proud of her first son because "there was not even a child among the concubines of the Old Master himself to compare to him in beauty and in dress." She is also proud of having been a mother, who has produced so many sons for the family. Such pride, as Doyle (1980) comments, "is particularly touching because O-lan wants and expects so little from life."

O-lan has a love for beauty. When she hands all the jewels to Wang Lung, she asks to keep two smooth white pearls for herself. At this,

> Wang Lung, without comprehending it, looked for an instant for an instant into the heart of this dull and faithful creature, who had labored all her life at some task at which she won no reward and who in the great house had seen others wearing jewels which she never even felt in her had once.

To his puzzled eyes, O-lan only says: "I could hold them in my hand sometimes." Later, when Wang Lung cruelly takes them from her to give to Lotus, O-lan said nothing, but her tears, which have been seldom shed, suggest that she is heartbroken.

The quiet O-lan also possesses self-dignity. For instance, while she tolerates Lotus for Wang Lung's sake, she refuses to serve or speak to Cuckoo, who, when a superior in the House of Hwang, was cruel and picky. She protest to Wang Lung, which she seldom does, against the presence of Cuckoo in her house and shows her disdain by ignoring Cuckoo's existence. She says, "with a sullenness deeper than ever upon her face, 'I am not slave of slaves in this house at least.'"

O-lan is in fact very intelligent, thoughtful, and much more practical than Wang Lung—qualities that seem to have been lost in her silence. She is like a pond of still water that runs deep. Buck only occasionally offers her reader the opportunity to glance at her depth. For instance, before she and her husband return to visit the House of Hwang with their firstborn, O-lan astonishes Wang Lung with her careful planning. He has not expected her, with the way she has gone about her work, to have thought about their unborn child and what she will do when she returns to the house where she used to be a slave. But he finds the child fully clothed and the mother in a new coat also. It turns out that, although she says nothing a while working by his side in the fields, she has been making plans for the event by herself all along.

O-lan's intelligence is shown in many cases—not only in terms of the way she sees things, but also in terms of how she expresses her own opinion and gets things done while still seeming to remain obedient and submissive. When Wang Lung first thinks of buying land from Hwang, she responds with much shrewdness. Though, at first, she does not think that buying land from Huang is a good idea, she does not immediately state her opinion against Wang Lung. Instead, she makes it clear that she supports his idea of buying land, for she thinks it better than putting money into a mud wall. Meanwhile, she shows more consideration for the practicality of buying land from Hwang, pointing out that the land is too far away and they would have to walk the whole morning to reach it. Seeing that Wang Lung's mind is set on buying it, however, she submits to his decision, again thinking about it in more practical terms: "rice land is good, and it is near the moat and we can get water every year."

During the famine, she helps Wang Lung to resist his uncle and two city slickers who have been pressing him to sell their land. She sees farsightedly that if they sold the land then, they would have nothing to feed themselves when they return from the south. She will sell the furniture since they have to move, but she will not sell the hoes and plows, which they will need to work on the land. In the city, it is O-lan who is shrewd enough to know what kind of mats are the best buy and clever enough to shape them into a comparatively comfortable hut, with a rounded roof and a matted floor, as a family shelter.

O-lan is also more practical than Wang Lung in many other ways. Wang Lung cannot bear to kill the ox and eat the meat, while O-lan sees an ox as an ox, which should be sacrificed to save human lives. Similarly, when their second son brings home some meat, Wang Lung throws it away because it is stolen. O-lan simply picks up the meat, washes the dirt off and puts it back into the boiling pot, for "Meat is meat," as she says quietly, and it is the time of famine.

However, in doing all this, O-lan never lets herself appear more intelligent than Wang Lung, never complains or criticizes Wang Lung for his improper behavior, and almost never openly speaks a word against him. When Wang Lung is incapable of carrying out a certain task, she takes things over in her own hands only as if simply to complete what Wang Lung has left unfinished. She knows that she ought to appear subordinate to her husband.

Though O-lan does not speak, she sees everything clearly. It is she who senses the incestuous relationship between their eldest son and Lotus and suggests sending him away to the south to avoid a family scandal. She also discerns that Wang Lung is more and more like the lords in the great house and that what has happened in the House of Hwang would happen in their family. However, she is now helpless, as Wang Lung has forsaken her. She knows that Wang Lung does not love her, a fact that Wang Lung later learns from his daughter. Wang Lung feels sad "because with all her dimness O-lan had seen the truth in him."

When O-lan chooses to speak, she does it logically and forcefully. Here is what she says to the villagers who come to loot their house:

> It is not yet time to take our table and the benches and the bed from our house. You have all our food. But out of your own houses you have not sold yet your table and your benches. Leave us ours. We are even. We have not a bean or a grain of corn more than you—no, you have more than we, now, for you have all of ours. Heaven will strike you if you take more. Now, we will go out together and hunt for grass to eat and bark from the trees, you for your children, and we for our three children, and for this fourth who is to be born in such times.

When she marries Wang Lung, O-lan knows what is expected of her and, compared to being a slave, her social status is instantly elevated. Therefore, she does not mind the hard work as a wife and takes a submissive position to her husband. Besides, she cares very much for Wang Lung, to whom she gives all her devotion and for whose happiness she will do anything. The reason for her silence is not that she does not know how to speak, but because she has deliberately chosen not to speak and has long formed such a habit. Though we know that she is often more shrewd than Wang Lung, she never shows it off and is always supportive and submissive to Wang Lung's will. Only when compelled by crises, when Wang Lung is too weak-minded to deal with the situation, does she come forward. When this happens, she is still supportive to her husband, never making him feel embarrassed. She does what has to be done or says what has to be said when needed.

Putting all these good qualities—endurance, silence, intelligence, resourcefulness, and practicality—together, we see in O-lan a very individualized character. Her individuality, it should be noted, is believable as well, because it embodies the typical characteristics of the Chinese peasant women in her times and reflects the actual social conditions under which she lives.

O-lan manages not only to achieve some measure of happiness and autonomy for herself, but also brings love, warmth, and comfort into Wang Lung's house and steers Wang Lung's life toward success, wealth, and happiness. Before O-lan's coming to the house, Wang Lung has to take care of the house and his old father besides working daily in the fields. Life is miserable for him. With O-lan's coming, his life turns dramatically from the first day of his wedding, when O-lan takes all the household chores over to herself. Wang Lung begins to enjoy "this luxury of living" he has never had before. Now, he can afford to lie "in his bed warm and satisfied," "tasting and savoring in his mind and flesh his luxury of idleness" "while in the kitchen the woman fed the fire and boiled the water." Even hard work in the fields becomes a luxury, because when it is done he can go back to his house, which O-lan has made clean and comfortable, and where food is always ready and delicious for his appetite.

With O-lan's diligence, thriftiness, and skillful management, the family's livelihood is much improved. Before marrying O-lan, no matter how hard Wang Lung worked, they were poor. Now they are able to save money on fuel and fertilizer, for O-lan gathers them herself. With O-lan working with him in the fields, he is even able to have some extra money at the harvest time to buy a piece of land. More importantly, O-lan has produced children, especially sons, one after another, rendering the house full of life.

Apart from the physical changes O-lan has brought to Wang Lung's life, she gives Wang Lung pride, happiness, and confidence. Just look how proud Wang Lung is at the wedding feast, how delighted when their first son is born, and how happy when he gives the red eggs to his friends and the villagers to celebrate the "big happiness." "Wang Lung felt his heart fit to burst with pride. There was no other woman in the village able to do what his had done, to make cakes such as only the rich ate at the feast." When they go to House of Hwang, with his whole family dressed in new clothes O-lan has made and the cakes O-lan has prepared, Wang Lung, for the first time in his life, holds his head high with self-esteem.

These are enough to illustrate O-lan's importance in Wang Lung's life. But O-lan does more. If any ordinary wife can accomplish what O-lan has done to make the life of the family better, O-lan is quite extraordinary for her crucial actions at critical times to steer her husband's and the family's fate.

The first extraordinary act of O-lan is the killing of the ox in the time of famine. It is not that O-lan has a harder heart, but that she knows that, with nothing else to eat, the ox must be killed for the family to survive. Besides, as she sees it: "Eat, for there will be another one day and far better than this one." The meat of the ox saves the family from starving to death.

Another critical moment is when the villagers, driven by hunger and desperation, come to loot Wang Lung's house. It is O-lan who, with her pregnant belly, brings them back to their senses. Later, by selling these bits of furniture O-lan has saved, they are able to make the trip to the south.

When Wang Lung, in a moment of weakness, is about to agree to sell their land for a little money to feed the family, O-lan comes forward to prevent it. When she is talking, "There was some calmness in her voice which carried more strength than Wang Lung's anger." Afterward, O-lan helps Wang Lung to make up his mind to go south.

The most shocking thing O-lan does, especially to the Western eye, may be the killing of her second infant girl at its birth. However, her "reasons for so acting," as Ms. LeBar says (1988), "are as compelling as any in fact or fiction." Firstly, they could not afford to feed another mouth when the whole family is already starved. Secondly, in her condition, she herself cannot possibly feed the new baby, who, therefore, cannot survive for long anyway. Thirdly, O-lan does it so that they can have less worry and difficulty to make the trip to the south, which, as it later turns out, will save the life of the whole family. Weighing the pros and cons, knowing Wang Lung does not want this girl at such a time, O-lan makes the decision to do the unimaginable and takes the guilt all to herself. LeBar thinks that O-lan "terminated an unwanted pregnancy in a way not too much different from the way it is done in modern times at local abortion clinics." To explain this seemingly cruel action, Pearl Buck says, in *My Several Worlds* (1954):

It was inevitable that the very reality of their lives made them sometimes cruel. A farm woman could strangle her own newborn girl baby if she were desperate enough at the thought of another mouth added to the family, but she wept while she did it and the weeping was raw sorrow, not simply at what she did, but far deeper, over the necessity she felt to do it.

Wang Lung's rise to wealth owes much to O-lan, particularly to the jewelry O-lan discovers in a rich man's house during a looting. Taking the jewelry may suggest dishonesty on O-lan's part, but the situation O-lan is placed in seems to justify her act. First, this is something O-lan would not normally do if she were not swept into the mass looting. Second, having been a slave in a rich man's house before, she knows how extravagantly the rich live. When her family faces starvation, it is only human for her to take whatever comes her way. Besides, as Li Bo noted (1989),

It was not an uncommon thing in China during the 1920s and 1930s for the poor people to break into rich people's houses and seize their properties because they regarded the rich as their oppressors and exploiters. O-lan never felt guilty about her robbery because it was not considered a bad thing in her time.

The jewels O-lan gets enables Wang Lung to buy more and more land and finally takes Wang Lung to the position he has never dreamed of reaching. Wang Lung himself knows in his heart that all the riches he has gotten would have been impossible if O-lan had not found the jewels and had not given them to him when he commanded her.

What is more important, O-lan is the central good force of the family, serving as a cohesive tie to hold the family together. With O-lan as the wife and mother, there is plenty of love, warmth, comfort, and a healthy atmosphere in the house, which, as Doan (1965) points out, "are essential for family happiness." The old father becomes healthy and contented; the children are well cared for, among whom the retarded daughter receives special attention; Wang Lung himself is satisfied and happy, at least for the first several years.

From this, we see that it is O-lan who sees the family through all the crises; it is O-lan who gets done what has to be done; it is O-lan who holds the family together; and it is O-lan on whom Wang Lung's wealth and fate rest. No wonder that, to Buck, O-lan, with her almost inexhaustible resource of life, symbolizes the good earth which has borne and sustained the life of the Chinese peasants for more than two thousand years:

The woman [O-lan] and the child were as brown as the soil and they sat there like figures made of earth. . . . But out of the woman's great brown breast the milk gushed forth for the child . . . if flowed like a fountain . . . life enough for many children, and she let it flow out carelessly, conscious of her abundance.

The crucial role O-lan plays in the family is significant in many ways. First, it adds much individuality to O-lan as a complex, dynamic character, making her unique and memorable. Second, it reflects Buck's feminist point of view. *The Good Earth* is considered an epic, telling the ups and downs of Wang Lung, but it is O-lan who is the driving force for his rise to prosperity and higher social status.

As if the events discussed thus far are not enough to suggest O-lan's importance, Buck sets up a contrast in Wang Lung's family between the time when he works with O-lan and the time when he turns away from her. During the former time, Wang Lung's family survives crisis one after another and gradually obtains prosperity. However, as soon as Wang Lung turns away from O-lan, love, warmth, and peace vanish from the house and lust, quarrelling, and sickness set in. Wang Lung's morality deteriorates greatly once he turns from O-lan to Lotus. He thinks himself entitled to frequenting the teahouse in town and having concubines, giving no consideration to O-lan's feelings. He becomes a brute, pouring all his anger upon O-lan because she is too common, too ugly to suit his new status.

Yet Lotus, whom Wang Lung feels he needs now as a rich man and later takes home to be his second wife, is nothing more than a sexual object for Wang Lung, a toy for him to play with. Once Wang Lung becomes infatuated with Lotus, he neglects O-lan entirely. He never notices that O-lan's health has greatly deteriorated and "he had not thought why she had been willing at last to stay in the house and why she moved slowly and more slowly about." O-lan finally dies of a stomach illness, due to much hardship, fatigue, and a long time of neglect of her disease.

Without O-lan, the house falls apart: "for the first time Wang Lung and his children knew what she had been in the house, and how she made comfort for them all and they had not known it." No one seems to know how to light the stove and how to cook and no one bothers to clean the house. The retarded girl is once left outside in the cold the whole night and almost dies from the illness she gets as a result. The old father is neglected and dies soon after O-lan's death. There are plenty of women in the house, but Wang Lung knows in his heart that there will never be the kind of love and care O-lan once gave him and his children. The house is divided and declining.

As a representative of the old-fashioned Chinese country women, a Confucian model of a caring mother and a faithful wife, O-lan's qualities are more appreciated when compared to other, minor characters in the novel: Wang Laung's concubines Lotus and Pear Blossom, and Cuckoo, Lotus's slave.

Lotus is everything O-lan is not. She entices Wang Lung because she loves his money. It is there no surprise that she contributes nothing to the family but jealousy and turmoil. While O-lan is the central force that unites the family, Lotus is a bad disease, infecting and weakening it. Every time Wang Lung is with Lotus, he comes home ill-tempered toward everyone. With her, Wang Lung does not only part from O-lan, but is also shunned by his children. To make it worse, Lotus develops an incestuous relationship with Wang Lung's eldest son, bringing shame and pain to the family.

Pear Blossom, a young girl whom Wang Lung takes as a third wife in his old age, shares some similarity with O-lan. She remains faithful to Wang Lung and takes care of the retarded daughter for O-lan until the end of her days. However, she lacks the kind of courage and ability we have seen in O-lan.

Cuckoo, a slave, cannot compare to O-lan, a former slave herself. She is a snob, bullying fellow slave girls below her position but fawning on her superiors and the rich, from whom she thinks she can benefit. When her master is rich, she tries to entice him. Once his family's wealth collapses, she betrays him. She uses the money she has taken from the old master to run a teahouse, but when she sees less work and more comfort and security to be gained in going into Wang Lung's house with Lotus, she chooses to be a slave again. Her behavior is even despised by O-lan who, as we have seen, seldom thinks ill of others: "You may have lived in the courts of the Old Lord, and you were accounted beautiful, but I have been a man's wife and I have borne him sons, and you are still a slave."

It is also interesting to compare O-lan with Madame Wu, in *Pavilion of Women*. At first sight, we see primarily differences. O-lan is quiet and inarticulate; Madame Wu is eloquent. O-lan does not come forward unless in some crisis that Wang Lung cannot handle; Madame Wu is always in the forefront of every family affair. O-lan does not have much control over the family decisions; Madame Wu is the maker of all decisions in the House of Wu. They even differ in appearance: While O-lan is plain-looking, Madame Wu is beautiful.

All these differences are, however, only superficial. They have many commonalities between

A scene from the MGM production The Good Earth, *starring Paul Muni and Walter Connolly, and directed by Sidney Franklin, 1937* © General Photographic Agency/Stringer/Hulton Archive/Getty Images

them. They are both intelligent, courageous, hard-working, capable, and dignified; they both play crucial roles in the fate of their respective families.

How can we explain these differences on the one hand and similarities on the other, then? Such an explanation, in fact, is not hard to obtain. It can be sought in the origins of the two characters and the socioeconomic conditions they find themselves in. In terms of origin, O-lan's is humble whereas Madame Wu's is not. Having been a slave makes O-lan short of words and submissive. Being born and bred in a family of wealth provides Madame Wu the opportunity to be educated, thus becoming eloquent and dominant. In terms of socioeconomic conditions, O-lan is married into a poor peasant family, which means that her life will be characterized by hardship and submissiveness to her husband, whereas Madame Wu is wedded to a wealthy husband with a big family, which means that she will have the responsibility to oversee all affairs of the house, providing her with a stage to display all her intelligence and ability.

However, these differences do not necessarily prevent them from sharing positive qualities, qualities that can only be found in their very being. In other words, Buck may have offered the two characters different stages to perform and allowed them to act in different ways toward similar events in their respective lives, but she has bestowed on them the same nobility and admirability, hence the same credibility as literary characters.

O-lan possesses better qualities than her husband. O-lan, like many of Buck's Chinese women characters, is shown to have "more integrity, more steadfastness, more endurance in the crises and affairs of life", while Wang Lung displays weakness in such situations. As he changes from a poor peasant to a wealthy landlord, he completely loses his integrity. He no longer works hard, and instead forsakes the land, takes concubines, betrays his wife, and lives and idle and corrupted life. In times of difficulty, he is happy and grateful to have O-lan as his wife. When he rises to prosperity, he deplores her ugliness and thinks that O-lan no longer fits his position.

Portraying Wang Lung as such does not only reveal Buck's conviction that Chinese women are better than men, but also that men's corruption has been caused, in part at least, by society. Buck tells us, through the narration, that Wang Lung is only doing what other men of wealth and leisure are supposed to do. Therefore, O-lan is, as Charles W. Hayford

(1992) points out, "betrayed (but not broken) as much by her husband's weak character as by social attitudes."

Through O-lan, Buck seems to suggest that, although oppressed, Chinese women, even the peasant women, have the same fine qualities as women elsewhere in the world. They have strength, courage, and insight as well as a practical mind to steer the fate and future of a family and to struggle for dignity and happiness.

Source: Xiongya Gao, "Peasant Women: *The Good Earth*," in *Pearl S. Buck's Chinese Women Characters*, Associated University Presses, 2000, pp. 91–106.

Pradyumna S. Chauhan

In the following essay, Chauhan illuminates the epic qualities in Buck's novels.

It was certainly the power of Pearl S. Buck's fiction that brought her to the tables of presidents and into the counsels of ambassadors. It was the enchantment of her stories that captivated millions around the globe and won her the Nobel Prize, making her the first woman recipient of both the Pulitzer and the Nobel awards for literature. And yet the keepers of academic gates have hardly shown much zeal for her work. When they have praised her, as did Henry Seidel Canby in his 1938 review of *The Good Earth*, or Carl Van Doren in his 1940 study *The American Novel, 1789–1939*, the compliment has been as stinted as it has been patronizing. Confronted by such critical climate, one scans the academic skies, but, like Wang Lung in the years of drought, sees not a sign of a fertilizing cloud, not a mention of Pearl S. Buck in academic journals or critical debates in the country, not even when popular fiction receives rising scholarly attention and when multiculturalism happens to be the rallying cry on quite a few campuses.

In view of such general timidity, I find a special reason to commend the faculty and the administration of Randolph-Macon Woman's College for their having opted to stir up some critical and academic dialogue about Buck's stature as a writer while they could as well have had a party to celebrate the glorious career of their distinguished alumna.

The neglect of Pearl S. Buck's fiction, even if benign, is, to an observer, a matter of cultural bafflement. Today, while women writers of smaller talents are avidly read, little notice is taken of the substantial work that Pearl S. Buck produced, and the best of it excellent by many critical standards. Whether it is some critical orthodoxy, or a popular prejudice against her chosen subject, or an aspect

of her life that keeps Buck's work from being assimilated as part of our intellectual heritage is an issue that belongs, I think, to another topic. I shall, therefore, forbear from speculating about the causes of her exclusion from the academy.

I shall only indicate why she read, rather than explain why she is not being read, especially at universities and colleges where her work has the potential of doing much social good.

Unlike Thomas Lask, who regards her books as "facile" and "slick," or Paul A. Doyle, who finds her stories improbable and simplistic, I find in Buck's tales the compelling power, and in her style the touches of sublimity, which, as in the case of all great literature, release the readers from the numbing round of their daily life and transport them to new regions of thought and feelings. To read her trilogy *House of Earth* is to confront in all its fullness the part of humanity that had, by and large, gone unrepresented in Western literature. Not only does Buck install at the world's banquet table a guest frequently heard of but seldom seen there; she also confers human decency and literary dignity upon peasants and slaves, upon the disinherited of the earth who seldom had their portrait taken. The peasants who had been granted only entrances and exits—except in Hardy's, Hauptmann's, or Brecht's fiction—are now allowed the whole stage to themselves. Pearl S. Buck enfranchises the mute and the inarticulate half of humanity simply by creating a literary space where they can enact the sheer truths of their impoverished existence. Nowhere is a better proof of this daughter of America's commitment to democracy to be found than in her trilogy. And if her work is infinitely gentler than Soviet writing, where a worker falls in love with his tractor and lives happily thereafter, it is because the human spirit is dearer than any ideology.

To take Pearl S. Buck's true measure, it may be necessary to recall that an average English novel tends to fasten itself on a particular scene, attend to a set of characters, and see them through a course of action by the time the curtain is ready to come down. When we are done with the novel, if we remember it at all, what we turn over in our mind is some traits of a character, the nature of a locality, or the social and psychological issue from which the story evolved. Not so with the *The Good Earth*, however. What we are left with is a feeling of immensity, the sensation of having watched from space the life of earthlings, embroiled in a struggle for existence—ploughing, fighting, mating, dying—while the earth keeps turning and turning, sometimes parched by the sun, sometimes swept by floods, at times invaded by locusts and pestilence. Like Tennyson's gods looking down upon the Lotos land, then we watch from high

> Blight and famine, plague and earthquake, roaring deeps and fiery sands
> Clanging fights, and flaming towns, and sinking ships, and praying hands.

The reader reviews from the author's grandstand, again in Tennyson's words,

> . . . an ill-used race of men that cleave the soil,
> Sow the seed, and reap the harvest with enduring toil.

Now such a capacity in the writer to wrest from the obscuring flux of life sharp patterns of human existence and to a project their ceaseless cavalcade through tumbling seasons of the earth is a rare gift indeed. And it is the gift, generally, of an epic writer, of one endowed with a macroscopic vision, of a writer who sees life and sees it whole. That hers was such a vision is borne out by passage after passage in *The Good Earth*. We are told what Wang Lung and O-lan encountered working in their field: "Sometimes they turned up a bit of brick, a splinter of wood. It was nothing. Some time, in some age, bodies of men and women had been buried there, houses has stood there, had fallen, and gone back into the earth. So would also their house, some time, return into the earth, their bodies also. Each had his turn at this earth." After reading this, the earth appears no strange place, nor death a terror. This couple but rehearses what generations of human ancestors have perpetually gone through.

Ezra Pound, summing up Henry James's achievement, remarked upon the latter's epic talent, which, according to him, consisted in James's capacity to "show race against race; immutable; the essential Americanness, or Englishness, or Frenchness." Buck's powerful narrative conveys to the reader not only the Chineseness of her characters, but also a feel of what it must have been like to be living in the era between the old dynasty and the modern state.

It conveys something else, too: the recurring scheme of life on the planet, caught amid the cycles of seasons and the alternating pattern of plenty and scarcity. Equipped, like an epic writer, with a prophet's vision that can not only see, but also reveal to others, the patterns that are embedded in human lives and Nature's kingdom, Buck brings all this to her readers, and without leaving them with any sense of despondence either. When we are told that "the woman and the child were as brown as the soil and they sat there like figures made of earth

> **"Equipped, like an epic writer, with a prophet's vision that can not only see, but also reveal to others, the patterns that are embedded in human lives and Nature's kingdom, Buck brings all this to her readers, and without leaving them with any sense of despondence either."**

[and] there was dust of the fields upon the woman's hair and upon the child's soft black head", we find there is nothing for tears in their plight. Eternal like the earth, they are possessed of its strength. There is such vitality in their motion that nothing, it seems, can stop this fountain of life. If we begin Buck's novel with some curiosity, we end it with wisdom.

Now such an effect is rarely achieved by a realistic novel, which specializes in compiling a record of each fact like a police diary. Its chronicle can, at best, show us the root and branches of some trees, but never the shape of the entire wood. The latter effect is achieved by works like Homer's *Odyssey*, or a novel like Tolstoy's *War and Peace*, where the entire social fabric is rendered for our contemplation. The only two American novels that come close to this stature are Melville's *Moby Dick* (1851) and Steinbeck's *The Grapes of Wrath* (1939). What makes Buck's achievement all the more remarkable is the fact that her novel arrived nine years before Steinback's and might well have served as a model for his work.

Let us briefly examine precisely how she goes about her work: she makes up a captivating tale, captivating not so much because its subject is exotic as because its appeal is universal. The story that opens with a young man's preparation for his marriage takes us through his contented years with his wife, his struggles against grinding poverty, and the virtual starvation of his family. Then, when the heavens relent, Wang Lung attains prosperity, reaches mid-life crisis, goes through certain flings, and is smitten by anxiety for his children, who embark on searches of their own. Things approach a closure with his wife's, then his father's death. Soon after his children have reached adulthood, we find him preparing to meet his death, after which, we know, his children will abandon the lands into which he had poured his sweat and blood and of which he had become a part. Thus, within the covers of a book, we see two generations pass away and the third ready to spring out on its own.

The reason her story is gripping and credible is that Buck, like a true epic writer, transplants details that are realistic to a plot that is both fantastic and mythic. Wang Lung, like all culture heroes—like a Theseus, a Moses, a Rama—leads his people on a frightening journey from "the Northern province of Anhwei" to the southern city of Nanjing. What they encounter in the urban ghetto is chronic deprivation, moral anarchy, and political lawlessness. Wang Lung, an Eastern Job, suffers physically and psychologically, yet never gives up either his courage or his dream.

On the contrary, he brings his people through, brings them not only home, but to a peak of prosperity, founding, in the bargain, a family which shall have to be reckoned with for a least another three generations. At its base, the plot is but a variation of the Cinderella story, of a rags-to-riches romance, all the more engaging because first we witness here human life stripped of all pretensions, in its bare essentials: in its hunger and cupidity, in its sexuality and self-centeredness. But we stay to witness, too, daring and noble self-sacrifices. For, of characters, there is God's plenty here. If we come across social leeches, like Cuckoo, we find here mothers, too, like O-lan, who is at once patient and courageous, pragmatic yet noble. If we are confronted by the bullying gateman at the ancient house of the north, the one who keeps twisting the three hairs of his mole, we meet, in the south, the crusty hot-water seller, the one who hides Wang Lung behind his cauldron when the soldiers come looking for the able-bodied in the shantytown. A garrulous old lord is balanced on Buck's canvas by a seductive young slave. A revolutionary finds, as a counterpoint, a missionary, who goes about distributing pictures of Christ on the cross to uncomprehending heathens. Faithful neighbors like Ching serve as a counterbalance to robbers like the rapacious uncle. The mob of a city and the laborers of the fields, all find their place in this gigantic portrait of humankind.

Similarly, all the enterprises of life, from courting through wedding to copulation, birth, and burial, are covered here. The pages of the novel, as a consequence, seem bristling with motion and vitality. What ennobles the narrative is the stature of Wang Lung, who, though a contemporary of Prufrock, is more like a Prometheus. O-lan, too, compels by her determination a comparison with the heroines of Greek Tragedies. By discovering for us innate nobility and willful tenacity among the poor peasants of China, Pearl S. Buck makes us realize the worth of the people written off as of no consequence unless they are acting as a mob.

The crowded canvas of the epic novel is accompanied by a comprehensive range. For what makes an epic different from any other genre is that it casts its net wide and captures the entire communal life of a people: their manners, their rituals, their customs; their food and dress and medicines; their forms of government and their ways of worship. *The Good Earth* shows us all: the rituals of the community, the social gestures, the superstitions, the New Year's feast, the wedding gifts, and the burial ceremonies. The earth gods, we realize, must be remembered at all crucial occasions—upon the marriage and the birth, at mournings and festivals—and they must be remembered even when they curse and afflict the people who adore them. The whole range of behaviors confronts us, thus, not only with the social picture of a people, but also with their "unconscious metaphysics," the ethos which defines them as a memorable entity.

What lends epic qualities to the novel, though, is not merely the mythos and the human crowd. At work here is, to use Longinus' words, in addition to "the faculty of grasping great conceptions," besides "dignified and spirited composition," a grand style, one forged under the mighty influence of the Bible.

If we look at the text closely, we notice the repetitive phrase and the recursive image of time so typical of Old Testament narrative. We may be running full tilt and, suddenly, we ram into expressions like "his heart pained him with longing for that which was passed." "Was passed," not the ordinary "had passed." We are reined in by phrases like "he was so amazed at what had come about", reminiscent of the suggestive grandeur of the simple, almost austere, phrasing of the King James version of the Bible. The mythical resonance of the plot, which speaks to our unconscious, is, in this novel, enhanced by a style whose dignified echoes have become part of our collective auditory imagination.

The larger picture of the novel is framed by a fearful symmetry: it opens with the coughing shadow of Wang Lung's father waiting for his boiled water, and closes with Wang Lung's occupying the spot where his father used to lean against the wall; it begins with the grandfather waiting for the warm bodies of his grandchildren, and ends with the father who is mocked by the cold stares of his sons plotting to sell the land he had acquired with heroic efforts. The land acquired, acre by acre, with blood and sweat, and preserved for posterity by an iron will, is sold off by the progeny for creature comforts. The grand human tale, subverted by a terrible irony, reveals life to be but *vanitas vanitatum* leading us to deep contemplation.

It is a mischief to equate Pearl S. Buck's fiction with popular romance. Even if we were to ignore the generosity and the decency of the novelist's conscience, her sensitivity to women's cruel situation, her quiet anger at social injustice, the aesthetics of the novel would have enough, besides its ethics, to keep the readers embroiled in a debate. Therefore when critics complain that Pearl S. Buck "lacks a Camus-like intellect" and that she suffers from a Victorian reserve in handling sexual material, one knows that they are asking for a pint of gin at a health shop. But the history of reading is filled with such misreadings. What is amusing in our situation is our inability to abandon old positions even after we have witnessed several critical revolutions. Some readers would slight *The Good Earth* because, they argue, historically it is inaccurate. But she was not writing a book of history; she was writing an epic, a story not merely of three generations but of entire China, of the human life itself. History, Aristotle warns us, "relates what has happened," and poetry/epic "what may happen." Buck's novel carries a greater truth than the chronicle of one-shot events. Its tale has a larger validity, for it can as well be read as an extended allegory of the fates of all families, Japanese, Indian, or American.

When we correct one angle of a square, all the angles of the square, we know, correct themselves. If we can but bring ourselves to read Buck's works as we read other received texts—exploring their verbal and thematic complexities—we may discover that the best of her work is what appears but once in the greatest of literary traditions—a powerful and abiding tale told by an untutored imagination.

One thing is very clear: if there is no one to fight for the turf, the turf will not be protected. And here rests a challenge for all those who believe that their lives and minds have been enriched by their contacts with Pearl S. Buck's work.

Source: Pradyumna S. Chauhan, "Pearl S. Buck's *The Good Earth*: The Novel As Epic," in *The Several Worlds of Pearl S. Buck: Essays Presented at a Centennial Symposium, Randolph-Macon Woman's College, March 26–28, 1992,* edited by Elizabeth J. Lipscomb, Frances E. Webb, and Peter Conn, Greenwood Press, 1994, pp. 119–24.

Sources

Buck, Pearl, *The Good Earth*, John Day, 1965.

Conn, Peter, *Pearl S. Buck: A Cultural Biography*, Cambridge University Press, 1996, p. 126.

Gao, Xiongya, *Pearl S. Buck's Chinese Women's Characters*, Susquehanna University Press, 2000, p. 36.

Harwood, H. C., Review of *The Good Earth*, in *Saturday Review*, Vol. 151, No. 3942, May 16, 1931, p. 722.

Smart, Ninian, *The Religious Experience of Mankind*, Fontana, 1970, p. 218.

Spence, Jonathan D., *The Gate of Heavenly Peace: The Chinese and Their Revolution, 1895–1980*, Viking Press, 1981, p. 51.

Walton, Eda Lou, "Another Epic of the Soil," in *Nation*, Vol. 132, No. 3, May 13, 1931, p. 534.

Further Reading

Doyle, Paul A., *Pearl S. Buck*, revised edition, United States Authors Series, No. 85, Twayne, 1980.
    This is a concise and readable introduction to the entire range of Buck's work.

Harris, Theodore F., in consultation with Pearl S. Buck, *Pearl S. Buck: A Biography*, John Day, 1969–1971.
    Written by her close friend and collaborator, this two-volume work is, as of 2006, the most comprehensive biography of Buck.

Leong, Karen J., *The China Mystique: Pearl S. Buck, Anna May Wong, Mayling Soong, and the Transformation of American Orientalism*, University of California Press, 2005.
    Leong explores American orientalism during the 1930s and 1940s, focusing on three women who were associated with China: Buck, Anna May Wong, and Mayling Soong. Leong shows how these women negotiated the cross-cultural experience of being American, Chinese American, and Chinese against the backdrop of the emergence of the United States as an international power and the growing participation of women in civic and consumer culture.

Liao, Kang, *Pearl S. Buck: A Cultural Bridge across the Pacific*, Greenwood Press, 1997.
    Liao analyzes the reasons for the success of Buck's early novels and the critical neglect of her later work. He argues that the social, historical, and cultural values of Buck's work exceed their aesthetic value.

In Babylon

Marcel Möring

1997

Paul Binding, in his review of *In Babylon* for the *Times Literary Supplement*, calls Marcel Möring "one of the most important Dutch writers of his generation." After the publication of *In Babylon* and its eventual translation into seven languages, readers all over the world were able to confirm Binding's assessment.

In Babylon focuses on sixty-year-old Nathan Hollander during the four days he spends with his niece in the family's old hunting lodge in a forest outside Rotterdam, Holland, cut off from the world by a raging blizzard. As the two struggle to stay warm, Nathan tells Nina the story of their family, tracing it back four hundred years to his great-great-grand-uncle Chaim Levi and up through the recent death of their uncle Herman, who collapsed after having sex with a prostitute. Nathan's story is occasionally interrupted by strange voices, booby trapped doors, and ghostly visits from family ancestors.

The two come to believe that the house may be haunted by the ghost of Nathan's brother Zeno, who is also Nina's father. By the end of the four days, Nathan and Nina question their connection to their family as well as their knowledge of themselves. As Möring expertly interweaves ghost stories, fairy tales, myths, and family history, he explores the tensions between past and present, fantasy and reality, and the compelling need to discover a clear sense of self and place.

over ten countries and won the AKO Prize, the Dutch equivalent of the Booker Prize. *In Babylon* (1997), his third novel, won two Golden Owl awards the year after it appeared in print. Due to the great success of his novels, Möring is considered to be one of the most important twentieth-century Dutch writers.

Marcel Möring © Ulf Andersen/Getty Images

Author Biography

Marcel Möring was born in 1957 in Enschede, Holland, near the Dutch-German border to a Dutch Reformed father and a Jewish mother. A decade later, the family moved north to Assen, Holland. While still a child, Marcel received a Bible from his father and thus began the author's lifelong interest in religion. Möring decided against going to college, having concluded early on that he only wanted to be a writer. He noted in an interview with HarperCollins, "I decided to become a writer when I was thirteen. . . . I had written a poem . . . and whilst reading it the next day, thought: I like this, I want to do this the rest of my life."

In the 1980s, Möring worked as a correspondent for local newspapers, and in the 1990s, he had several reviews and essays published by Dutch, German, and American journals and magazines, including *Esquire*. Möring also wrote several plays that were produced in Holland. His novels, however, brought him to the attention of the literary world. In 1990, his first novel, *Mendels Erfenis*, was published in Holland and became a critical and popular success. His second novel, *Het Grote Verlangen* (The Great Longing) appeared in 1993 and was eventually published in

Plot Summary

Part One

Nathan Hollander, the first-person narrator of *In Babylon*, begins his story with his memory of finding his uncle Herman dead in a hotel in Rotterdam, Holland, after the uncle had sex with a young prostitute. Nathan observes that Herman would most likely "have enjoyed dying that way." This incident prompted Nathan to think about his past and his future, acknowledging that he feels "old and worn," and to see himself as "an eyewitness, a stowaway in time."

The scene shifts to the present, Herman's hunting lodge in Holland in 1995 outside Rotterdam, where sixty-year-old Nathan and Nina, his niece, are snowed in. Nina has been successfully working as Nathan's European agent for the fairy tales Nathan has written. She had given him a ride to the lodge, but the car got stuck in the snow, and she could not leave. To pass the time, Nina reads the biography Nathan has written about Herman, enhanced by additional stories that Nathan tells her about their family, whom Nina considers "a bunch of loonies." They discover the cellar is fully stocked with food and wonder who put it all there, along with the barricade formed at the top of the stairs out of the house's furniture, including a piano, hanging precariously above them. Nina half seriously declares the house to be haunted. To keep warm, they chop and burn pieces of the barricade.

Nathan admits that his uncle gave him the lodge under the condition that Nathan would write Herman's biography. During the drive there, Nathan thinks he sees the ghosts of his relatives: Uncle Chaim, Magnus, Herman, Manny, and Zeno. He remembers a happy time five years earlier when the family was together at the lodge, the day that Herman announced that he was giving it up, and they all celebrated Zoe's engagement.

Back in the present, Nina is getting spooked by the house and so leaves without telling Nathan. When he goes out to look for her, he sees a little man running in the snow. Freezing and unable to find her, he returns to the lodge where he chops up pieces of the barricade and throws them on the fire. A few hours later, he hears Nina banging on the front door. After she stumbles in, half frozen, Nathan takes off her wet clothes in an effort to warm her, but the act becomes charged with sexual tension. Nina explains that she drove the car into a snow bank and had to walk back to the lodge.

Later, they hear a faint rustling noise, and then a lantern crashes down the stairs. They hear "a voice from the depths of something dark and far away." They soon realize that what they are hearing is a tape recording. Nina is convinced that it is Zeno's voice on the tape. In an effort to distract her fears, Nina asks Nathan about the biography.

Nathan tells the story in pieces. It begins in the seventeenth century with his great-great-granduncle Chaim Levi, who lived from 1603 to 1648 on the border of Poland and Lithuania. He and his nephew Magnus, both clockmakers, are Nathan's most distant ancestors. After Chaim died, Magnus roamed over Europe for twenty-one years until he settled in Holland. Generations later, Nathan's father Manny and his uncle Herman moved Nathan, his mother, two sisters, and a brother to the United States.

Nathan insists that he has been visited frequently over the years by the ghosts of Chaim and Magnus who help fill in the history of the family. The first time they appeared was when he was ten and living with his family in New Mexico where he witnessed the first test explosion of the atom bomb.

Nathan continues the story with more specific details of Chaim's and Magnus's lives. Chaim invented the pendulum clock and was devastated when a group of marauding Cossacks during the Chmielnitzki Massacres of 1648 killed his wife. The Cossacks murdered over one hundred thousand Jews during this period. The same year, after Chaim died and the Cossacks burned down his house, Magnus began his European wanderings. He decided to stay in Holland, known as the Lowlands, because he found a contented community that welcomed him, including a young woman with whom he fell in love and soon married. Magnus and his bride moved to Rotterdam on the west coast of Holland where he changed his name from Levi to Hollander in honor of his new home. Eight generations of Hollanders were born there. The next two generations left before the outbreak of World War II.

Nathan's parents met in a Rotterdam park in 1929. Manny instantly fell in love with Sophie, but Uncle Herman "felt the earth move under his feet" when he met her. His arrogance, however, clashed with her sense of independence, and she married Manny because she respected his passion for creation. A year later, Nathan's sister Zoe was born followed in quick succession by Zelda and Nathan, and nine years later by Zeno.

In the early years of their marriage, Manny worked as a mechanical engineer for a crane factory and had little time for inventing things, and Sophie was worn out with domestic duties. In 1938, their lives were complicated by the growing tension in Europe over German aggression. After Germany invaded Czechoslovakia in 1939, Uncle Herman determined that they were not safe in Holland and should immigrate to the United States. When Nathan's grandparents refused to go, Herman tried to convince Manny that as Jews, they were not safe anywhere in Europe. A visit from German refugees convinced them to go, and the clan continued its journey west.

On the trip to the United States, five-year-old Nathan fell in love with Reisele Minsky, a girl on the same ship. While they were crossing the ocean, Germany invaded Poland, which changed the relaxed atmosphere on board. Soon after they arrived in the United States, Manny ran into Enrico Fermi, a famous physicist and a close friend of Nathan's grandparents, at Columbia University. Fermi set Manny up with a job as an instrument maker.

One night in 1943, Manny came home and announced to his family that they were moving to Los Alamos, New Mexico, to work on secret government business. This business turned out to be the Manhattan Project, which involved the development of the atomic bomb. Back in the present, Zeno's ghost appears to Nathan, but he does not welcome it as he does Chaim and Magnus. Nathan insists that Zeno is merely a dream.

Part Two

On the second day at the lodge, Nathan and Nina are frightened by what they think is an apparition peering out from a cupboard, but it turns out to be a portrait that someone had hung there apparently to frighten them.

Later, Nathan's story continues with the separation of his parents in 1948. The family had returned to New York from Los Alamos the year before. Over the years, Manny and the children had adapted to and embraced American culture, but Sophie hated it, "the bigness, the muchness, the filled to burstingness . . . the absence of discretion." She had also been frustrated by the never-ending tasks of motherhood, leaving her no time to paint, which had become her obsession. Nathan notes that Manny had already left the marriage in spirit, not knowing what to do to make Sophie happy.

Seeing no way out of her predicament, Sophie convinced Manny to return to Holland. A year later, he came back to New York alone where he made a fortune with his mattress invention. The couple's separation and subsequent divorce started Nathan on his writing career. He wrote long, detailed letters to his father, whom he would see only once a year, in an effort to tell him "everything . . . he needed to know" so that he would come back to them. Nathan claims that the correspondence turned him into "the family's emotional switchboard" as everyone wanted to know what was in the letters. Unfortunately, Manny's only responses to his son's letters were postcards with a terse "*Regards, Papa,*" written on them. Nathan could not understand his father's apparent lack of interest in the family.

A year later, Nathan received a long letter from Uncle Herman, who was living with Manny in New York. The letter began a correspondence that would last until Herman's death, and it motivated Nathan to continue to write. That first letter also inspired five-year-old Zeno to speak for the first time. Looking over Nathan's shoulder, Zeno began to read the letter. No one knew he could talk, much less read.

Zeno's childhood was relatively ordinary, although he was reticent. When he was ten, he had some sort of spell and spent the next year in bed. He later explained the cause of his spell as his acknowledgement of his own mortality. For the first few weeks he slept for most of the time, but after that, he began to read everything he could get his hands on. His personality changed after that year from being a quiet child to being an annoying know-it-all who devoured books and newspapers and never seemed to forget what he read.

Initially, Nathan was his teacher, but Zeno soon surpassed him intellectually. Zeno developed an extensive library bought by money he earned washing cars and finding and selling rare books. He soon began to supplement his income by working as a magician's assistant. His penchant for theatrics caused him to steal the show one night when he made his brother and sister disappear.

Foreshadowing Zeno's future as a cult leader, Nathan noted after the performance, "Zeno would make a good prophet of doom."

Years later in 1965, Zeno became the "silent prophet" of a group of fifty young people that eventually grew to several hundred. He soon became famous; newspaper articles and scholarly articles were written about him, and he gave speeches on religion and contemporary youth. Zelda became his champion and protector, while Nathan blamed her for encouraging what he considered to be Zeno's "madness."

As his status grew, he became the leader of a cult of those searching for truth. The political left embraced him while the right condemned him, and his relationship with his family, except Zelda, grew more strained and distant. Zeno disappeared in 1968 and was never heard from again.

Back in the present, Nathan explains how much he loves the lodge because in the past he spent happy times there with his family. This visit was his first in five years. He notes that he spent his life traveling and that the lodge has been his only real home. He wants to die there.

He thinks about an argument that he had with Herman when the two went on a trip to Israel, focusing on Nathan's refusal to consider the country his homeland as Herman did. As the two discussed the remaining family members, Herman noted that no one was sure Zeno was Nina's father and therefore that she was a Hollander. After she was born, Sophie grew tired of the speculation and decided that they should all accept her as part of the family regardless of whether they had any proof. During a conversation on the day that he died, Herman warned Nathan about the loneliness he would experience if he continued to refuse to allow anyone to get close to him.

Nina tells Nathan that in the past, she did not want to be a part of the family, but now she does because she wants to understand her history. Nathan explains that he has a photographic memory for events and so is qualified to record the family's history. Later, she asks him to read one of his fairy tales called "The Tower" about the Tower of Babel, a biblical story about a group of proud people who build a tower to reach heaven, but their efforts are confounded by divine interference, which causes them to speak in different, mutually unintelligible languages. The moral of the tale is that "when men have no common goal and no longer speak the same language, the foundations will crumble."

Nathan insists that it is time for Nina to "make peace" with Zeno, but she resists, arguing, "How . . . can I make peace with someone . . . who would have nothing to do with me?" Nathan insists that since he has told her details about the family and about himself, she must tell him about herself, "quid pro quo," but Nina does not respond.

When they go upstairs to try to gain access to Nathan's bedroom, they find that the door is locked and that a cabinet has been nailed to it. Nathan wrenches the cabinet free enough for them to slip into the room where they see what they initially believe is a man nailed to the wall. When they calm down, they realize that it is a dummy dressed in Nathan's clothes with a face that resembles his. They both assume that Zeno put it there, which makes Nina furious and determined to leave and makes Nathan cry. She tells Nathan, "I hope he burns in Hell." But he insists: "Don't hate him. Don't fall into his trap." He silently determines not to let Zeno's tricks get to him and vows to protect Nina. He does acknowledge, though, that the experience has changed him from a man who could never settle down to one who longs for a home, marriage, and peace.

Later, Nathan tells Nina about his first wife, Molly, an American who sang in the chorus in London musicals. He left her less than a year after they were married when he became afraid that he was losing himself in the relationship. As Nina sleeps, Nathan thinks of a trip he took to Frankfurt, Germany, with Herman. There he learned that Herman had been to Bergen-Belsen, a World War II Nazi concentration camp, after the war as a researcher and had seen there evidence of the Holocaust. He came back later to Germany to help the Germans face their guilt.

He then thinks about his second wife, Eve, an English travel agent, admitting, "with Eve, I came very close to finding the peace that I had been searching for all my life." Yet, he had soon grown cold and withdrawn.

Part Three and Part Four

The next morning, Nina seduces Nathan. Afterwards, she asks Nathan to tell her another fairy tale. This one, which is unnamed, is about a boy named Berg whose father, a forester, had disappeared. Block, the new forester, was cruel to Berg and his mother until Berg stood up to him. The next morning Berg's father reappeared. After he finishes the story, Nina tells him that she is going to marry him over his protestations that he is too old for her.

Later that day, they decide to search another bedroom, but the door is blocked from within. As Nathan kicks it open, a sandbag slams into him knocking him out. While he is unconscious, he envisions that Magnus comes to him and tells him a parable of a man who was searching for order and learned how to accept chaos. At the end of the story, the man becomes Nathan. When Nathan awakens, Nina rails against Zeno whom she blames for all of the booby traps in the house. Nathan admits to himself that he loves her and would spend his life with her "if it weren't so wrong."

The narrative shifts to the night Herman died. Nathan took the prostitute, Rolinda, home and stayed with her for a while to help calm her. He agreed to meet her the next night when they went to the stable where she kept her horse. As they talked, Rolinda noted similarities between Nathan and Herman, providing the first clue that the two may be father and son. After a frustrating night trying to capture Rolinda's horse, Nathan left before she got a chance to tell him something. Nina was waiting for him when he got back to the hotel. She asked him questions about the family's medical history that caused Nathan to think about the similarities between him and Herman and to conclude that Herman is his father.

While Nathan daydreams about his past, Nina disappears. After Chaim and Magnus appear, the latter tells about how he became a follower of Shabbetai Zevi, who declared himself the messiah approximately twenty years after the Chmielnitzki Massacres and engaged in sexual adventures with the woman who would become his bride. As Magnus finishes his story, Chaim begins to fade until he disappears, insisting that he has told everything.

Nathan admits to Magnus that he feels like the American legendary Rip Van Winkle who woke up after a twenty-year nap and found the world a changed place. Then he suddenly determines that the person who set all of the traps must be up in the attic.

Part Five

The last chapter mixes fragments of the future, when Nathan lies dying in an Israeli hospital, with the present, when he has a final confrontation with Nina, and the past stories about the family. In the hospital, he confuses the nurse with Reisel, the girl he fell in love with on the ship to the United States. In the present, Nathan appears to find Nina half frozen in the attic. However, this may be a dream, since when he continues the story, it is he who almost freezes in the attic.

Nina nurses him back to health in the present at her house in Amsterdam. Nathan accuses her of setting the traps in the lodge, insisting that it could not have been Zeno because even if he were alive, he did not hate Nathan. When she denies it, he wonders if he imagined seeing her in the attic.

Nathan asks her if she thinks that he drove Zeno away and insists that he is dead, which makes Nina fly into a rage and attack him. When he pushes her away, she hits her head and is knocked unconscious. The novel ends as he leaves Amsterdam, noting that he does not have any answers to the questions that he has raised about his family.

Characters

Eve Hollander

Eve Hollander, Nathan's second wife, was an English travel agent. She had more influence on Nathan than Molly did. Her positive nature eventually prompted Nathan to alter his pessimistic attitude, at least for a while. He admits, "with Eve, I came very close to finding the peace that I had been searching for all my life." Her patience and determination eventually caused him to see through her eyes and discover that "the world was worth seeing." Ultimately, though, this marriage fell apart as Eve recognized that Nathan did not "want to be known."

Herman Hollander

Nathan's uncle, Herman Hollander, became a famous sociologist after the family immigrated to the United States. His death after having sex with a prostitute, which is the first incident of the novel, conjures an image to Nathan of "a warrior fallen in battle and laid in state . . . on this disheveled altar." He was a short man yet sometimes "gave the impression of being twice his size." Nathan insists that he was a demagogue, always giving a lecture, and had "a severe case of megalomania," as, Nathan claims, all socialists do since Herman assumed "he [knew] what's best for the world."

His arrogance and inability to listen to another's point of view, coupled with his pessimistic view of mankind, made him clash with Sophie, the woman he never stopped loving. As a result, Sophie married Manny instead of Herman. Yet, in his later years when he became "an ageing Casanova," he softened his views on the world and so could be "finally at peace in the company of the woman [Sophie] with whom he would spend his last years." His pessimistic view of human nature did have a positive effect on the family when he recognized the Nazi threat early enough to convince them to leave Holland for the United States.

He retained his need for control to the end of his life as evident in his declaration that he would give the lodge to Nathan only under the condition that the latter write a biography about him. Although he was one of the first in the family to take Nathan's profession seriously, he hoped that the biography would steer his nephew in another direction.

Herman did not appreciate Nathan's fairy tales because he "didn't like obscurity. He had worked all his life towards the clarification of things that were uncommonly vague and in the wake of that pursuit he regarded every form of art . . . as an ideal way of gaining insight." Herman wanted to deal only with facts, dissecting and analyzing information until he understood it completely.

Magnus Hollander

Magnus Hollander, Chaim's nephew, visits Nathan along with Chaim to tell Nathan about the past as well as occasionally offer his advice for the present. Like his uncle, he becomes a figurehead in the sense that he was a wanderer, the Hollander family's second dominant trait. Nathan sees him as an iconic "Wandering Jew," traveling for twenty-one years before reaching the Lowlands in Holland. Nathan projects his own restlessness onto Magnus when he describes him as always "roaming, searching," displaying a "continual uncertainty about where he was and when."

Manny Hollander

Manny, born Emmanuel, is Nathan's father. Manny "didn't have much of a knack for social intercourse," especially since he was often lost in his own "musings about new, smaller, better machines," which eventually made him quite successful. What attracted Sophie to him was his "passion of creation." She respected his ability to "start out with nothing and to make something out of it." Yet this passion pulled him away from his family. He had chosen Sophie because she was independent and so "thought she would leave him in peace, just as he would her." He became estranged from his children after Sophie took them back to

Holland, which was exacerbated by his inability to communicate with them.

Molly Hollander

Molly Hollander, Nathan's first wife, was born in Brooklyn. She was twenty-three when he met and soon after married her. She serves, like his second wife, Eve, to highlight aspects of Nathan's character, especially his inability to allow someone to get close to him. He leaves her abruptly one day, which devastates her.

Nathan Hollander

Nathan Hollander, referred to as "Nuncle" by Nina and "N" by the rest of the family, considers himself to be a respectable man who follows the rules. He admits to Nina that he never indulged in the hedonistic behaviors of the 1960s and so is shocked when she seduces him. Herman refers to him as a "Calvinistic bastard" because of his strong work ethic. Nathan reveals his sentimental nature in his ambition to freeze his good memories of the family at the lodge by detailing them in the family history.

Nathan is a loner who has never established a sense of place for himself. As a result, he has become a wanderer, moving from place to place, living in hotels. At this point in his life, he regrets this status and longs for a home and for a sense of connection to his family. Nina explains his solitary life when she insists, "you've lived the life of a fugitive. When the going gets tough, you run away." His second wife, Eve, clarified the motive for this tendency when, after he insisted that he loved her, she replied, "for love you need submission, and that's something you know nothing about." His inability to love someone completely and to constantly be in control of his emotions has ruined his two marriages and left him alone. By the end of the novel, he still has not found a clear understanding of himself or his place in his family, but he accepts the little knowledge that he has gained.

Nina Hollander

Nina Hollander, Nathan's niece, is an attractive, intelligent young woman who is stranded with her uncle for four days in the lodge. Nathan thinks that he has a clear understanding of her, but his judgment gets clouded by her actions at the end of the novel. Initially, she appears to be self-sufficient and confident, which becomes evident when she seduces him, although she is spooked by the strange occurrences in the lodge. Nathan finds her "rebellious and sharp, a combination of Zeno's agile mind, Zoe's sense of beauty, and Zelda's seriousness." She also appears to be bitter about her father, which has caused her to be estranged from the family.

Nathan is unable to explain her behavior at the end of their stay in the lodge when she suddenly, with no warning, disappears. Her feelings toward Zeno become hazy after she attacks Nathan during a conversation about who might have booby trapped the lodge. Her incomplete characterization reflects Nathan's lack of knowledge about the motives of any of the women that he knows.

Sophie Hollander

Sophie Hollander, Nathan's mother, was a woman with a strong independent streak "who had life figured out long before life understood her." She was certain of her convictions, declaring herself a socialist from a young age. Sophie soon "learned to dispense with bourgeois formalities" and had such "a directness that made most people blush." She chose Manny because he "could appreciate her independence and willfulness."

Sophie was committed to socialism "because she couldn't see how the God of Abraham, Jacob, and Isaac was making the world any better," and so it became her religion. As set in her convictions as Herman was in his, she became critical of traditional Judaism, claiming that God was "not doing his job." She was as passionate about socialism as Zelda was about Zeno's prophesies. Like her daughter, Sophie was also idealistic in the sense that she hoped the practice of socialism would make the world a better place.

Zelda Hollander

Zelda Hollander, Nathan's sister, gave her fervent support to Zeno and his prophetic visions. She never married, devoting herself solely to her brother and his mission. Nathan notes her monomaniacal devotion to her brother when he claims, "Zelda's great tragedy was that she had been born a nun in a Jewish family."

Zeno Hollander

Zeno Hollander, Nathan's brother and New Age prophet, disappeared thirty years earlier. In the HarperCollins interview, Möring claims, "I was fascinated by Zeno's darkness, the way he allowed himself to submerge in his own myth, his barely hidden self-hate." Until the age of five, he seemed to be an ordinary child, but at ten he begins to change to the extent that Nathan claims, "he was living in a totally different world than the rest of us." Zeno showed his extreme sensitivity at this age when he recognized his own mortality and believed that happiness was unobtainable.

Zeno appears calculating as he engineers his emergence as a cult leader, testing out ideas on Nathan to "find out how far and how fast he could go." He used his sister "as his mouth and eyes and ears," letting her think that she was guiding him. It is not clear whether he turns vindictive toward Nathan, since the latter never discovers who booby trapped the lodge.

Chaim Levi

Chaim Levi, Nathan's great-great-grand-uncle, is the first ancestor to be chronicled in the family history. Born in 1603 in the area that in the early 2000s borders Poland and Lithuania, Chaim "died of woe" forty-five years after his wife was brutally killed by invading Cossacks. He, along with his nephew Magnus, has been visiting Nathan for fifty years, relating his memories of the past, in which he continues to live. Nathan provides few other details about his personality, employing Chaim more as a figurehead, the initial clockmaker who began the family's interest in time.

Rolinda

Rolinda, a young prostitute, inadvertently causes Herman's death during sexual intercourse with him. Her inexperience and youth are revealed in her response to his death as she talks Nathan into coming home with her. She is persuasive with him, perhaps because she is quite attractive and also because she insists that she wants to tell him something, most likely that Herman is his real father.

Themes

Time and Regret

The Hollanders have been associated with time since Chaim Levi began making clocks and passed on his skills to his descendants. Nathan continues that association when he tries to condense time in a history of the family. Möring, in his interview for HarperCollins online, explains the connection between time and regret, noting, "sometimes I have the feeling that life is all about time and us trying to get a hold on it. And we always fail. In the end time defeats us." Nathan expresses the same sentiment when he tells Nina, "just before your time runs out you realize that you should have been better prepared, that you could have made more out of it if only you'd started sooner and now it's too late." The regret that Nathan feels at his age prompts him to try and find a stronger connection between himself and his family, including Nina, with whom he hopes, at one point, to establish a sense of home.

Zeno had recognized the destructive consequences of regret, insisting that one feels it only "when it's too late." To him, regret "is mourning for the irreversibility of things," like the damage that has been done to his relationship with his family. Nathan notes the sense of regret and of irreversibility for all in his family. He recalls Herman claiming, "If I hadn't been such an arrogant know-it-all, who had to blurt out everything that popped into his mind, I'd have won" Sophie. Zelda insists that if only she had taken care of Zeno better, he would not have disappeared. The point seems to be that after time passes one begins to reflect and evaluate ones earlier choices, an assessment which is necessarily after the fact and ineffectual because what has been done is done.

Religion and the Search for Meaning

Religion had an impact on Nathan on board the ship that took him and his family to the United States as they were escaping the Nazi occupation in Europe. As he listened to a playmate's father telling tales from the Talmud and Midrash, holy Jewish books, he claimed "a whole new world opened up for me." As a result, he notes, "a stowaway began growing inside me and he looked like a hunched Talmud and Torah Jew." While he remembered the stories he discovered in these books, they gave him little comfort in his search for his place in the world. As an adult, he determined that there was no God. He also rejected Israel as his homeland, in the face of great protest by Herman, feeling no connection to the nation until the end of his life, when, finding solace no where else, he decided to live out his last days among people he could regard as family.

Other members of the family created their own religions. Sophie's socialism became hers as she determined that only this system could save the world. Zeno reinvented himself as a New Age prophet, insisting that he gave his followers insight into themselves and the world. Nathan, however, found his claim to be a lie and argues that Zeno "merely guided their uncertainty and discontent towards the path of discipledom." He considers his brother's prophecies to be a "dangerous combination of sixties optimism, a passion for mysticism and blind faith in one's own morality." Nathan's

Topics For Further Study

- Write a poem or a short story that focuses on the subject of being an outsider of a family, a social group, or a culture.

- Read *Anne Frank: The Diary of a Young Girl* and prepare a PowerPoint presentation noting the historical details of Frank's story as well as her response to her harrowing life in hiding.

- Research and write a report on the treatment of Jewish refugees in the United States prior to and at the start of World War II.

- Zeno's cult following is a reflection of the movement in the 1960s toward alternative forms of spirituality. Research those forms along with the various cults that appeared in the 1970s and 1980s. Be prepared to lead a discussion on how leaders of these cults came to power and were able to have such a great influence on their followers.

claims appear to be justified when, soon after Zeno's disappearance, three people commit suicide. A note found on one of the bodies read, "We have found eternal silence," which was the ultimate goal of Zeno's followers. Zeno's devotion to his role as cult leader causes a split between him and Nathan that is never healed. All of the characters fail to find fulfillment in their pursuit of religion; in fact, it often causes them to be isolated from others, especially family members. Möring suggests that no matter how complex and often painful family connections can be, they can provide more sense of belonging and peace, if only for brief moments.

Style

Setting

Möring handles setting details symbolically in an effort to create a supernatural atmosphere in this ghost story. As Nathan and Nina approach, the "house looked like the head of a giant," sitting "on top of a densely wooded hill in the middle of the countryside, a hill straight out of some dark fairy tale." While Nathan tells her the story of their family, weaving in fairy tales and ghost stories, he claims, "Around us the darkness bowed over the glow of the flames and it was as if we were sitting in a cave: the storyteller and the last member of his tribe, waiting until the fire, and finally they, too, turned to ashes." In this way, Nathan links the ghost stories of the past to the one they are living in the present.

The sense of danger the two feel in the house is heightened by Möring's use of personification as the blizzard rages: "the horizonless white world was forming outside," as "the blizzard snarled and shrieked." Nathan notes the extreme threat they face, insisting, "this isn't just another snowstorm, this is a national disaster. Entire villages are cut off from the civilized world."

The danger does not abate inside the lodge: "the wind grabbed hold of the shutters and ran its hands along the house looking for chinks, holes, some way to get in. It wailed and moaned like a restless spirit." Their fears, caused by the relentless cold gripping the house, are heightened by the booby traps they find. When they discover the barricade someone has formed with pieces of furniture, Nathan insists, "it looked as if that huge stockpile was there in preparation for something that was yet to happen." In the library, he imagines whispers that declare, "You're all ours now. It's you and us and the house. We'll never let you go." Möring's use of personification, exaggeration, and imaginative visions also illustrates the tension between reality and fantasy that Nathan will struggle with as he tries to define his place within his family.

Significance of the Title

The word, Babylon, is most often used to suggest an atmosphere of vice and luxury. When the ancient city was destroyed in 689 B.C., many saw it as a sign of divine vengeance. The use of the word in the title of the novel most likely applies to Nathan's relationship with his niece, which develops throughout. Nathan is troubled by his sexual relationship with her, considering it to be a form of incest, but not enough to resist it. Yet there is no divine vengeance that destroys the relationship, for Nathan does not believe in God. The relationship ends because of the confused nature of Nathan's and Nina's parentage and their family conflicts. Perhaps Möring is using the term, along with Nathan's and Nina's sexual relationship, as a symbol of the betrayals that have generated those conflicts and which eventually destroy the bonds they have established with each other.

The title could also be a reference to the Biblical story of the Tower of Babel, constructed in a city that is now thought to be Babylon. Nathan tells a version of this story to Nina, focusing on the process of building the tower and the problems that arise when the builders who speak different languages cannot communicate with each other, and as a result cause the foundation to collapse. This reference suggests the miscommunication that existed in Nathan's family, and his attempts to shore up its foundation by writing a family history.

Historical Context

The Onset of World War II

The world experienced a decade of aggression in the 1930s that culminated in World War II. This second world war resulted from the rise of totalitarian regimes in Germany, Italy, and Japan. These militaristic regimes gained control, partly as a result of the Great Depression experienced by most of the world in the early 1930s and from the conditions created by the peace settlements following World War I. The dictatorships established in each of these three countries encouraged expansion into neighboring countries.

In Germany, Adolf Hitler strengthened the army during the 1930s. In 1936, Benito Mussolini's Italian troops took Ethiopia. From 1936 to 1939, Spain was engaged in civil war involving Francisco Franco's fascist army, aided by Germany and Italy. In March 1938, Germany annexed Austria, and in March 1939, it occupied Czechoslovakia. Italy took Albania in April 1939.

One week after Nazi Germany and the U.S.S.R. signed the Treaty of Nonaggression, on September 1, 1939, Germany invaded Poland and World War II began. On September 3, 1939, Britain and France declared war on Germany after a German U-boat sank the British ship *Athenia* off the coast of Ireland. Another British ship, *Courageous*, was sunk on September 19. All the members of the British Commonwealth, except Ireland, soon joined Britain and France in their declaration of war.

The Holocaust

The Holocaust is the name given to the Nazi persecution and extermination of European Jews. By the end of World War II, six million Jews had died, along with millions of other so-called objectionable people, such as handicapped persons, Gypsies, intellectuals, and homosexuals. The impetus for this persecution came before the war, in the early 1930s when Adolf Hitler came into power in Germany. Hitler gained support for his persecution of the Jews by blaming them for Germany's economic and social problems and claiming that the country lost World War I because of a Jewish conspiracy. Wealthy Jews who recognized the impending danger fled Nazi Germany, but others who could not afford to relocate or who hesitated too long were destined to die.

In 1933, Germans classified the Jews as *Untermenschen*, meaning subhuman. A year later, more discrimination was legislated. The yellow Star of David was marked on the windows of Jewish shops, which were forbidden to Christian Germans. Jews were relegated to special areas on buses, trains, and park benches and were openly ridiculed and bullied. The Nuremberg Laws, passed in 1935, took away German citizenship from any person who had one Jewish grandparent, denying these people the right to marry non-Jews. It became increasingly difficult for Jews to find shops that would sell them food and medicine.

Violence against the Jews became an accepted practice beginning on November 10, 1938, after Krystalnacht, the Night of the Broken Glass. This was the first night of a week-long terror campaign, ordered by Hitler after a Jew killed a Nazi in Paris. Ten thousand Jewish shops in Germany and the occupied territories of Austria and Sudetenland were destroyed and looted while Jewish homes and synagogues were burned. Ninety-six Jews lost their lives while over one thousand were injured. Thirty thousand were arrested and sent to concentration camps. This night marked a crucial turning point in Germany's treatment of the Jews, the commencement of Hitler's Final Solution, the extermination of European Jewry in every occupied country.

Approximately 140,000 Jews lived in the Netherlands in 1939, including 25,000 German-Jewish refugees who had fled during the prewar years. The majority lived in Amsterdam. By the end of the war, 75 percent had died. While many citizens collaborated with the Nazis, the Dutch underground helped hide and eventually saved thousands. Because of the survival of her diary, Anne Frank is a well-known Dutch Jew who hid during the war years but was eventually discovered. She and her family were sent to Bergen-Belsen, where all of them but her father died.

The Development of the Atomic Bomb

In 1939, several prominent scientists, including Albert Einstein, informed President Franklin D. Roosevelt of German efforts to build an atomic bomb. Soon after, Roosevelt authorized the Manhattan Project, which began work on creating the bomb, in the hopes that it would be completed before the Germans developed theirs.

During the next six years, more than two billion dollars were spent on the Manhattan Project, which was supervised from start to finish by J. Robert Oppenheimer. The first bomb was tested near Los Alamos, New Mexico, on the morning of July 16, 1945. The incredible explosion that could be seen over one hundred miles away heralded the start of the Atomic Age. After the blast, most who worked on the bomb were shocked by its power and capacity for destruction. Several of them subsequently signed a petition against its use, which was ignored by the government.

The atomic bomb has been used twice: first, the United States detonated it over Hiroshima, and second, the United States dropped it over Nagasaki, both cities in Japan. The explosion in Hiroshima, which vaporized or burnt everything in an area of three miles, immediately killed an estimated 66,000 people and injured another 69,000. Nagasaki lost 39,000 in the initial blast and over 25,000 people were injured. Both cities were practically completely destroyed.

Critical Overview

In Babylon received enthusiastic reviews, especially in Holland where it became a bestseller. Paul

Binding, writing for the *Times Literary Supplement*, praises the novel's themes, writing that it "evokes a deep sense of loss and impermanence, together with a courageous facing up to restlessness." Binding declares it to be "a moving and convincing testimony to the continuing tension between the desire for assimilation and the awareness of separateness."

Noting the novel's interplay between past and present, Binding argues that the novel has "all the penetration we expect." He finds its theme carried out until the end of the novel, which, he claims "is both moving and disturbing." He asserts, "Confrontation with the past isn't quite enough, its thoughtful pages seem to be suggesting; there will always remain the intractable world."

Binding, however, finds fault with some of the novel's techniques. He claims that "its concern with the weight of history has led the author away from territory he knows personally . . . to what he knows only from research." This shift "has led Möring to make use of the techniques of magic realism," which, Binding insists, is too conventional. He also finds fault with Möring's use of historical figures, writing that "In order to give the Hollanders paradigmatic stature, many noteworthy worldly attainments and friendships with the great are accorded them." He concludes that this is an unsatisfactory substitution "for the more difficult business of making ideas and theories palpable" since it "encourages a sort of vicarious snobbery in the reader, putting an easy relationship with the famous in place of a reappraisal of ordinary human beings."

Marc A. Kloszewski, in his review for the *Library Journal*, offers a mixed assessment of the technique of this "imperfect but amiable enough novel," writing that it "wears its 'epic' garments lightly, with many appealing personalities and much humorous dialog nicely captured through Knecht's translation." However, he finds "too much territory to be covered" and fears that "the reader will be left wondering how exactly all of this ties together."

A review in *Publishers Weekly* gives mostly praises in its assessment of this "grand, engrossing novel." The reviewer insists that "only occasionally does the narrative linger too long in the past or a philosophical discussion . . . [and so] impede the flow of the text." Yet overall, its "prose is fluid and erudite, and the transitions between the many eras masterfully achieved." The review concludes that "as historically instructive as it is suspenseful, this is an impressive, accomplished tale."

The setting for In Babylon *is a snowbound lodge, similar to the scene depicted here* © Per Eriksson/
Iconica/Getty Images

Brian Kenney in a review for *Booklist* declares the novel's setting to be "absolutely beguiling." He finds more careful construction in the novel, claiming that "as much fun as the magical and mythical can be, Möring wisely keeps returning us to the tense reality of uncle and niece and the questions their situation poses." Noting a smooth link between the thematic and structural elements of the novel, Kenney argues that "miraculously, as the past and the present begin to converge, Möring largely succeeds in keeping this unwieldy fictional package tied together." Kenney concludes, "it's worth it to be reminded that fiction can be both emotionally moving and artistically inventive."

Criticism

Wendy Perkins

Perkins is a professor of American and English literature and film. In this essay, she examines the novel's intricate narrative structure and its relationship to Nathan's search for self.

Prior to the twentieth century, authors traditionally structured their novels to reflect their belief in the stability of character and the intelligibility of

experience. By the end of Jane Austen's *Pride and Prejudice* (1813), for example, Elizabeth Bennet has discovered and acknowledged her true self while proving the novel's ultimate affirmation that young people get the marital partners they deserve. Novelists in the twentieth century, however, have challenged these assumptions about stability and intelligibility as they expanded the genre's traditional form to accommodate their characters' questions about the nature of truth. Modernists of the first several decades and postmodernists later in the century structured their narratives to trace their characters' internal quest for an authentic self and to illuminate the problems that can arise in such a search. Their innovative constructions frustrate readers' expectations about closure and thus force readers to recognize that the process of gaining knowledge of oneself and one's world can be problematic. Marcel Möring, a postmodernist, structured the narrative of his novel *In Babylon* (1997) to reflect this late-twentieth century sensibility.

Modernists such as Virginia Woolf in *Mrs. Dalloway* (1925) and William Faulkner in *The Sound and the Fury* (1929) experimented with shifts in narrative voice and subjective, internal dialogue to suggest the difficulty in discovering concrete truths regarding the complexity of human

"Nathan, though, has a difficult time getting a firm grasp on his family's history, including his own."

experience. Postmodern authors such as Donald Barthelme in *Snow White* (1967) and John Fowles in *The French Lieutenant's Woman* (1969) deconstructed traditional narratives by providing alternate endings and mixed genres in order to reflect the same sense of complexity. Marcel Möring's *In Babylon* also illustrates the intricacies of postmodern experimentation in its juxtaposition of various genres, including ghost stories, fairy tales, and historical and personal narratives. As Möring constructs his story of sixty-year-old Nathan Hollander and his attempts to come to a clear understanding of his family and his position in it, the author incorporates all of these genres, revealing the difficulties inherent in the search for self.

Nathan's biography of his uncle Herman, which he was commissioned to write in exchange for ownership of Herman's lodge, has become a family chronicle. Nathan feels compelled to "tell everything" from the life of his great-great-granduncle Chaim Levi down to the present because he feels "the weight of their stories" on him. Herman's extensive library has become his "ship to the other world" of his family's history.

Nathan introduces the first genre shift into his biography when he admits: "our family is obsessed by the origin of things. Everything has to be told in the form of a creation myth." He, too, feels compelled to tell the story of the creation of his family in an effort to clarify his own story, but his recognition of the mythic quality of the chronicle suggests that he will have a difficult time separating truth from fiction.

Nathan's history juxtaposes his and his ancestors' memories of their lives with historical details, an arrangement that accentuates the novel's mythic elements as his family claims that they have been involved with important events and people. He was told that his father worked with physicist Enrico Fermi, who had been a close friend of Nathan's grandparents and later participated in the Manhattan Project, while his mother danced in the chorus of the Ziegfeld Follies, a famous review on Broadway in the 1930s and 1940s, and became friends with famous dancer/actor, Gene Kelly. Nathan's task is enlivened yet complicated by this mix of fact and probable myth.

Yet he claims, "we Hollanders regarded ourselves . . . as a family of guides," and so he counts on them to help him in his journey of self discovery. Möring explains in an interview in Harper-Collins online, that "family . . . is the only concept of belonging that makes any sense." He concludes that "what counts is that your identity is formed by your siblings and your own personal history; your memory, that is. That is who you are and what you are. It is what will guide you through life." Nathan, though, has a difficult time getting a firm grasp on his family's history, including his own. He is not sure who his or Nina's father is or whether his brother Zeno hated him enough to try to torment or even kill him by setting up booby traps in the lodge. By the end of the novel, he is also not sure of Nina's involvement in the events of the past four days.

Nathan notes his feelings of separation from his family, which started during his adolescence in New York when his father worked all day, his mother was wrapped up in her painting, and his sisters were preoccupied with their approaching womanhood. He admits to Nina, "so I kept silent and I listened and as I listened I lost the distinction between then and now, here and there, reality and fantasy." As he discusses this sense of separateness, he claims, "I don't really play a part in the story of my family. I was there, that's all. That's my second talent: I'm always there."

His first talent, which sprang from his ability to blur the line between reality and fantasy, is storytelling, specifically writing fairy tales. He started to write them down after Chaim and Magnus began their nightly visits when he was fifteen. "Hand-in-hand," he explains, "we traveled through the forest of stories," for "the only way to understand the world . . . is by telling a story."

Nathan tries to understand and explain his world by incorporating fairy tales into his family narrative. One such story focuses on two rivals who find a way to resolve their differences after the daughter of one and the son of the other fall in love. The spiritual leader of the community tells them "not to smell, not to hear, and not to see, and then, when all roads to the mind are closed, to open the heart and make the world anew, to see it anew, hear

What Do I Read Next?

- *Anne Frank: The Diary of a Young Girl*, published in 1947, chronicles the courageous life of its author, a gifted Jewish teenager after she and her family go into hiding in Nazi-occupied Amsterdam. Anne was eventually arrested and later died, along with most of her family, in a Nazi concentration camp.

- Marcel Möring's second novel, *Het Grote Verlangen* (The Great Longing, 1993), won the AKO Prize, the Dutch equivalent of the Booker Prize. Its narrator, thirty-year-old Sam van Dijk, attempts to remember his past and reestablish ties with his siblings. He lost his memory and was separated from his brother and sister after his parents were killed in an auto accident when he was twelve.

- Jeffrey Eugenides's Pulitzer Prize-winning novel, *Middlesex* (2002), focuses on the life of a hermaphrodite and the story of her multi-generational Greek-American family as well as her struggle to establish a clear sense of self. She sets her epic story, which moves from 1922 to 2001, against a changing historical backdrop, including the Turkish invasion of Greece, Prohibition, the Great Depression, World War II, the civil rights movement, and the Vietnam War.

- *Night* (1958) is Elie Wiesel's autobiographical story of Wiesel's internment in a Nazi concentration camp and his overwhelming feelings of guilt for having survived when so many others, including his father, did not.

---

it anew, smell it anew." This tale becomes symbolic of Nathan's struggle to see his family and his place in it in new ways in an effort to define himself.

He realizes, however, the difficulties in employing the fairy tale genre in his search. The beginning and ending of fairy tales are marked by "'Once upon a time . . . and 'They lived happily ever after.'" Between this "obscure beginning" and "obscure end" falls "our story, and our limitation," for "we are always aware that what we have read, or seen, is that which was already visible or readable, the representation of something obscure."

Nathan's incorporation of a ghost story into his narrative both illuminates and clouds his knowledge of his family. His and Nina's time in the lodge becomes a classic ghost story with mysterious voices drifting through the rooms, a cellar stocked with food, and booby traps in the bedrooms. Their initial explanation of these phenomena is that Zeno has come back to the house to haunt or possibly harm them, especially Nathan, with whom he had a troubled relationship. Yet after examining the house more closely, Nathan finds it hard to imagine that Zeno had the skill to orchestrate all of the ghostly details.

Elements of the ghost story also exist in the visitations by dead family members who can be seen only by Nathan and who help him clarify details about the family life. Yet, these visitations could be only the product of Nathan's admitted blurring of the real and the fantastic in an effort to justify his own version of those details.

Möring comments on the connection between memory and the past in the HarperCollins interview, noting his fascination with "the way time shapes us, the way we shape time and how memory . . . never fails to determine our lives and actions." He explains:

> we allow our pasts to exist in the now and we project the now into the future. When we speak, in the past tense, about a powerful experience, we relieve that experience, so in a way the past has become present again.

In this sense, Nathan allows his and his ancestors' memories of the past to shape his present vision of them and of himself. He admits, "the past was always very much alive in our family." His memory of his interactions with Zeno affects his present in his belief that Zeno has booby-trapped the house, which becomes symbolic of the complex relationship he had with his brother.

Paul Binding, in a review of the novel for the *Times Literary Supplement*, notes that "confrontation with the past isn't quite enough, its thoughtful pages seem to be suggesting; there will always remain the intractable world." Nathan, he claims, will always be "a wanderer . . . never finding a house or a community to call home," as Nathan himself admits when he declares, "This century, this life, the history of my family, it has all passed me by and left me . . . in total bewilderment."

Explaining his intermingling of genres in his history of his family, Nathan notes, "the world is made up of unfinished stories" that we try to "extrapolate. . . . We try to give them a beginning and an end. We try, on the basis of those fragmented stories, to understand the world." What we ultimately come to, Nathan suggests at the end of the novel, is only a partial knowledge of ourselves and the world and hopefully a reluctant acceptance of the little that we can understand.

This acceptance is illustrated during Nathan's last day in the lodge when he is visited by Magnus who tells him a story about a man's struggle to find himself. As the man journeys over a plain with an overwhelming feeling of emptiness, he realizes that he cannot find a place where he belongs. After intense contemplation of his predicament, he eventually is able to acknowledge and accept "the chaos, the self-generating chaos" of his world and his inability to find his place in it. At the end of the story, Nathan becomes the man as he gives up his quest for ultimate knowledge. Möring echoes this sentiment in the HarperCollins interview when he insists that the novel's task is "to raise questions, to make the reader doubt his own convictions."

By the end of the novel, Nathan is no longer searching for his place in the world. He has chosen to live out his last days in Israel, "a Jewish sanctuary," he claims, where he can find some connection, albeit an incomplete one, to the past. He insists that Israel is "the only place I can be. Only place in the world where a person without family can still feel at home. Land full of Sophies and Mannys and Hermans and Zoes and Zeldas," where he can find some peace with his ghosts, his memories, and a fragmented knowledge of himself.

Source: Wendy Perkins, Critical Essay on *In Babylon*, in *Novels for Students*, Thomson Gale, 2007.

Publishers Weekly

In the following review, Möring is praised for his "fluid and erudite" prose, seamless transitions between eras, and the "instructive" history he traces.

The arc of this grand, engrossing novel spans four centuries and two continents. Trapped by "the winter to end all winters" in an isolated house in the country, Nathan Hollander, a 60-year-old Dutch fairy-tale writer, and his niece, Nina, the last of the Hollanders, delve deep into their family history. In order to claim the house, left to him by his uncle Herman, a famed sociologist who died in the arms of a prostitute, Nathan was required to compose a biography of the dedeased; now that the project is nearly complete, Nathan has "allowed" himself to revisit the home where he spent much of his youth. After arriving in a ferocious snowstorm, Nathan and Nina must combat not only the fierce cold but also the mysterious work of some hostile force. To relieve the grimness of their plight, Nathan shares Herman's biography—which he describes as "more of a family chronicle"—with Nina, so she can learn the history of the clan from which she was long estranged. As the two uncover the house's mysteries, Nina learns of Chaim and Magnus, ancestral ghosts who have visited Nathan for 50 years; of the family profession: clock making; of their migration from Poland to Holland in the 17th century, where they took on their adopted country's name; of their flight to America during WWII and their return to Holland; of Nathan's brother and Nina's father, Zeno, a "20th-century prophet" who disappeared 30 years earlier. Möring's prose is fluid and erudite, and the transitions between the many eras masterfully achieved; only occasionally does the narrative linger too long in the past or a philosophical discussion (sometimes related via a fairy tale) impede the flow of the text. As historically instructive as it is suspenseful, this is an impressive, accomplished tale of a perennially uprooted family and its last remaining members seeking their home in an inhospitable world.

Source: Publishers Weekly, Review of *In Babylon*, in *Publishers Weekly*, January 31, 2000, p. 77.

Paul Binding

In the following review, Binding compares In Babylon *and* The Great Longing *and notes that* In Babylon *incorporates magic realism and traces a larger Jewish history.*

With *The Great Longing*, his second novel, Marcel Möring established himself as one of the most important Dutch writers of his generation (he was born in 1957). The book was a great commercial and critical success, and it has since transcended its status as *the* Dutch novel of 1993, and acquired the lustrous compelling glow of an icon to the decade now ending. Picaresque yet also subtly and intricately constructed, it contains a tender portrait of the three young siblings at its centre, but its examination of contemporary culture is unflinching. It is a sustained poem about urban life, detritus and all. *The Great Longing* was evidence of an original and empathic mind; now, British readers can assess Möring's third novel, which has been translated, like the earlier book, into fluent and versatile English by Stacey Knecht. *In Babylon*, which was first published in Dutch in 1997 is, however, a very different work.

The main part of the novel traces the mental development of sixty-year-old Nathan Hollander, a celebrated writer of fairy tales, over the four days he spends with his niece, Nina, holed up in an old forest hunting lodge, cut off by a severe snowstorm. The lodge, large and romantic, is a house he has known for many years, for it belonged to his Uncle Herman, a famous sociologist. Now, after his uncle's unexpected and rather squalid death (*in flagrante delicto*, underneath an amateur tart in a seedy Rotterdam hotel), the place is his—provided he satisfies the terms of the will by writing Herman Hollander's biography. During the days of cold and discomfort, Nina (who is also Nathan's agent) reads through what he has written and asks searching questions. Nathan's narrative provokes enquiries into areas of the family's past over which a silence has hitherto prevailed. It seems that Nathan may be Herman Hollander's son, not his nephew, and that Nina, who was believed to be the daughter of Nathan's strange brother, Zeno, a charismatic cult-leader who has vanished without trace, may be no relation at all. Certainly, her provocative behaviour does not appear to be that of a niece.

Behind these mysteries lies the whole hazy history of the gifted Hollanders. The adopted name was a grateful tribute to the country in which they found themselves, having left behind the shtetls and forests of Lithuania. Family stories, the progenitors of the fictions Nathan has gone on to write, have preserved the spirit-animated world of the Hasidim, rather than the traditions of the more stolid Dutch culture in which so many Hollanders, past and present, have distinguished themselves. Nathan confronts his inheritance with unease.

In Babylon is preoccupied with a larger history than in *The Great Longing*, dwarfing the personalities of the present day. It is a Jewish history, and it evokes a deep sense of loss and impermanence, together with a courageous facing up to restlessness.

The novel is a moving and convincing testimony to the continuing tension between the desire for assimilation and the awareness of separateness. And it must surely encourage readers to look at *The Great Longing* in a new, Jewish light.

Yet, for all its ample riches, *In Babylon* is not in the end as successful as the second novel; its concern with the weight of history has led the author away from territory he knows personally (which gave his earlier work its freshness and originality) to what he knows only from research. And this has led Möring to make use of the techniques of magic realism—now as hoary and conventional as the missing heirs and destroyed wills of nineteenth-century fiction. These include characters who every now and again pop up from a past century to converse with those in the present; eccentric, galvanic family-members and their attendant legends; and transformations of place (the hunting lodge, once so well-known to Nathan, becomes a realm of terror, mysteriously full of booby-traps put there by some unknown agency). In order to give the Hollanders paradigmatic stature, many noteworthy worldly attainments and friendships with the great are accorded them. Thus, the eminent physicists Albert Einstein and Enrico Fermi were family friends, and they have walk-on parts here. This substitution of resonant names for the more difficult business of making ideas and theories palpable, in the rendering of personal life, encourages a sort of vicarious snobbery in the reader, putting an easy relationship with the famous in place of a reappraisal of ordinary human beings. How much more satisfying was Möring's picture of Raff and Sam and their associates in *The Great Longing*, as they moved on from one rough unsatisfactory enterprise to another.

It would be unfair to Marcel Möring—beyond doubt one of the most imaginative and perceptive novelists writing today—to end with adverse criticism. The treatment of the way past scenes and present comprehensions work on Nathan Hollander's tired mind, as it gropes towards a personal and suprapersonal future, has all the penetration we expect. And the last section, "The Stranger", set after Nathan's decision to take himself to Israel, is both moving and disturbing. Confrontation with the past isn't quite enough, its thoughtful pages seem to be suggesting; there will always remain the intractable world, and a Dutch-Jewish fairy-tale writer, once a refugee from Nazi Europe in America, then a returned exile in Holland, but always a wanderer—in and out of women's lives, never finding a house or a community to call home—is obliged to choose the desert-land of remote fore-bears as the place in which to die.

Source: Paul Binding, "Finding a Place to Die," in *Times Literary Supplement*, translated by Stacey Knecht, July 2, 1999, p. 23.

Sources

Binding, Paul, "Finding a Place to Die," in *Times Literary Supplement*, July 2, 1999, p. 23.

"*In Babylon*—An Interview with Marcel Möring," in *Harper-Collins Publishers Australia*, http://www.harpercollins.com.au/global_scripts/product_catalog/author_xml.asp?author id=AUS_0002540&tc=ai (accessed July 25, 2006).

Kenney, Brian, Review of *In Babylon*, in *Booklist*, Vol. 96, No. 13, March 1, 2000, p. 1195.

Kloszewski, Marc A., Review of *In Babylon*, in *Library Journal*, Vol. 125, No. 6, April 1, 2000, p. 131.

Möring, Marcel, *In Babylon*, translated by Stacey Knecht, 1999, Perennial, 2001.

Review of *In Babylon*, in *Publishers Weekly*, Vol. 247, No. 5, January 31, 2000, p. 77.

Further Reading

Groueff, Stephane, *Manhattan Project: The Untold Story of the Making of the Atomic Bomb*, Backinprint.com, 2000.
  Groueff explains the process by which this massive project was managed, which necessitated practical as well as creative solutions to the problems faced in the development of the bomb.

House, Wayne, *Charts of Cults, Sects, and Religious Movements*, Zondervan, 2000.
  House examines several religious movements in the twentieth century and compares them with Christianity.

Laqueur, Walter, *Generation Exodus: The Fate of Young Jewish Refugees from Nazi Germany*, University Press of New England, 2001.
  Laqueur focuses on a generation of Jews who were able to get out of Germany and Austria before and during the war and traces the difficulties this group of refugees faced during the resettlement process.

Martin, Walter Ralston, *The Kingdom of the Cults*, Bethany House Publishers, 2003.
  This work examines the teachings and effects on followers of New Age cults and of major world religions, including Buddhism, Islam, Jehovah's Witnesses, and Mormonism.

Independence Day

Richard Ford
1995

Independence Day, by Richard Ford, is set in the fictional New Jersey town of Haddam (reportedly based on Princeton) and also roams over Connecticut and upstate New York. The plot is not complex. Frank Bascombe, a divorced realtor in his mid-forties, goes on a road trip over the Fourth of July weekend in 1988. After trying to sell a house to a couple who do nothing but complain and find fault, he visits his girlfriend at her house on the Jersey shore. Then he heads for Connecticut to pick up his troubled fifteen-year-old son Paul, who lives with Bascombe's former wife and her second husband, whom both Bascombe and Paul dislike. Bascombe plans to use the trip to establish a deeper relationship with his son. They visit the Basketball Hall of Fame and then the Baseball Hall of Fame in Cooperstown, New York, where a distressing and unexpected incident disrupts Bascombe's plans and forces him to end their trip early.

Bascombe's constant ruminations on life in general and in the United States in the 1980s give *Independence Day* much of its depth and character. The novel can be seen as an inquiry into the nature of independence, a quality that Bascombe seeks to cultivate and tries to pass on to his son. But Bascombe also realizes that independence is a complex notion that may carry its dangers, too, in terms of social isolation and lack of community. During the course of the weekend, he discovers a new sense of optimism about his future and his willingness to connect with others in a meaningful way.

Richard Ford © Jerry Bauer. Reproduced by permission

Author Biography

Richard Ford was born on February 16, 1944, in Jackson, Mississippi, the only child of Parker Carrol Ford, a traveling salesman, and Edna Akin Ford. When Richard Ford was eight years old, his father had a heart attack after which the boy spent much time with his grandparents in Little Rock, Arkansas. His father died from a second heart attack in 1960.

Ford left home when he was seventeen, working for the Missouri Pacific Railroad and living in various towns in Arkansas and Missouri. He then enrolled at Michigan State University, where his dyslexia ensured that he read slowly. He later observed that this slow reading was excellent preparation for a writer who crafts each sentence so carefully. Ford received a Bachelor of Arts degree in English in 1966. Two years later he married Kristina Hensley, whom he had met at Michigan State, and the couple moved to New York, where he worked as an assistant science editor. After spending a semester in a law school, Ford decided that he wanted to be a writer, and he enrolled in the Master of Fine Arts in creative writing program at the University of California, Irvine. He graduated from there with his M.F.A. in 1970.

Ford's early attempts to have his short stories accepted for publication brought only frustration. He decided instead to try his hand at writing a novel, and in 1976, *A Piece of My Heart* was published by Harper and Row. The novel tells the story of a drifter and a law student who encounter each other on an island in the Mississippi delta. A second novel, *The Ultimate Good Luck*, about a Vietnam veteran who travels to Mexico to free a man from prison, followed in 1981. However, sales were not high, and Ford decided to take a break from fiction writing. He became a sportswriter for the magazine *Inside Sports*, but the publication folded soon after, and Ford decided to return to writing fiction. The result was *The Sportswriter* (1986), which sold more than sixty thousand copies and made Ford's reputation. This novel was named by *Time* magazine as one of the five best books of the year. The protagonist of *The Sportswriter* is Frank Bascombe, a novelist turned sportswriter who is plunged into a crisis by the death of his young son.

The following year, Ford published *Rock Springs*, his first collection of short stories, and was immediately acclaimed as one of the modern masters of the short story. His next novel, *Wildlife* (1990), was not as successful, either in terms of reviews or sales, but the publication of *Independence Day* in 1995 confirmed his reputation as a leading contemporary American novelist. *Independence Day* is a sequel to *The Sportswriter* and continues the story of Frank Bascombe. The novel was awarded the PEN/Faulkner Award and the Pulitzer Prize. It was the first novel to win both awards.

After that, Ford published two short story collections, *Women with Men* (1997) and *A Multitude of Sins* (2002), and a third novel featuring the character, Frank Bascombe, entitled *The Lay of the Land* (2006).

In addition to his writing, Ford has taught writing and literature at the University of Michigan, Princeton University, Harvard University, Williams College, and Northwestern University in Evanston, Illinois. As of 2006, Ford lived in Louisiana.

Plot Summary

Chapter 1

Independence Day begins early on a Friday morning on the Fourth of July weekend in 1988, in Haddam, New Jersey. The narrator is Frank Bascombe, a forty-four-year-old divorced realtor, the father of a son and a daughter who live with Ann, his ex-wife, in Connecticut. Bascombe is about to set off for a weekend trip with his fifteen-year-old son, Paul, but before he collects Paul, he plans to visit his girlfriend Sally Caldwell, who lives in South Mantoloking on the Jersey shore. He feels their relationship may have reached a crisis point and that they may not be seeing each other much longer. But his main concern is with Paul, who has recently been arrested for shoplifting condoms and for assaulting a female security guard who apprehended him. He is due to appear in court on the Tuesday, July 5th. Since that incident, and Paul's psychological evaluation, Bascombe has tried to keep more in touch with Paul, taking him out and also talking to him in early morning telephone conversations. Now he will be picking Paul up in Connecticut and going on a road trip in which they will visit the basketball and baseball halls of fame. He hopes this will be an opportunity for him to connect with his wayward, highly intelligent but emotionally immature son and steer him back on the right course.

Chapter 2

Bascombe's day starts with a visit to one of the two rental houses he owns to collect the rent. The houses are adjacent to each other in a quiet black neighborhood. The house he visits now is rented by a mixed-race couple, the McLeods, and Larry McLeod tends to act aggressively when Bascombe stops by for the rent. On this occasion, however, no one answers the doorbell, even though Bascombe is certain that someone is at home.

After a quick visit to his office, he drives to a motel where he picks up Joe and Phyllis Markham. They want to move into the area from Vermont, and Bascombe hopes to sell them a house by noon. The problem is that the Markhams cannot really afford to buy the kind of house they want in this area, which means that up to now they have been disappointed with all the forty-five houses that Bascombe has shown them. When Bascombe arrives, he finds that the Markhams have just quarreled and that Joe is in a sour mood. Bascombe tells him he wants to show them a house in nearby Penns Neck, and Joe reluctantly agrees.

Chapter 3

Bascombe shows them the house, a remodeled farmhouse owned by Ted Houlihan, a recently widowed engineer. Bascombe knows the house is not exactly what they want, but he also knows they can afford it, and he thinks they may be dispirited enough to buy it. When he arrives, he realizes it is

the nicest house on the street. Joe immediately inspects the house carefully but appears to be unimpressed, while Phyllis is delighted by what she finds. However, her enthusiasm is soon curbed when she finds out from Houlihan that the property adjoins a minimum security state prison. Houlihan insists that it is more like a country club than a prison and presents no problem to the residents of the house. But Phyllis is not convinced, thinking it might be a problem for Sonja, their twelve-year-old daughter and also indicating that she herself does not want to live next door to a prison. Meanwhile, Joe has changed his mind and says he likes the house. Bascombe tries to encourage them that the house is a good value, and they would be happy there. He takes them back to their motel so they can consider their options.

Chapter 4

Bascombe recalls the events that led up to his becoming a realtor. Before that he had been a short-story writer and a sports journalist. His son Ralph had died of Reye's syndrome, and this loss had negative effects on his marriage, eventually leading to a divorce. Bascombe quit his job, moved to Florida and then to France, where he had a brief affair with a much younger woman, and then returned to Haddam and looked around for a fresh challenge. In 1984, he was thinking of reconciliating with Ann, but Ann announced she was getting married to Charley O'Dell, an architect about fifteen years older than she, and they were moving to Connecticut. Bascombe was deeply disturbed by this news, since he had never expected her to remarry, and they had remained close friends after the divorce. When she moved, he sold his house and bought hers. He then took some training and became a realtor at the Lauren-Schwindell firm in Haddam. He liked the work and felt happy with his life, which, broadly speaking, he still does.

Bascombe makes a second call on the McLeods to collect the rent. As he stands on the porch, a neighbor, Myrlene Beavers, thinks he is trying to break into the house and calls the police. Bascombe talks to Betty McLeod, who tells him that Larry is not at home. Bascombe knows this is not true. A policeman arrives, and Bascombe has to explain that he not breaking in; he is just trying to collect the rent.

Chapter 5

Bascombe goes to check on a hot-dog stand he co-owns in a semi-rural location near Haddam. His business partner is an older man named Karl

Bemish, a widower. Bascombe discovered the place by accident and went into partnership with Karl to help the business out of a financial mess. He soon sorted it out, changing the name from Bemish's Birch Beer Depot to Franks and decided he would sell only root beer and Polish wurst-dog. Karl tells him he is worried that two Mexicans who have been driving by slowly, are planning to rob him.

Bascombe leaves Karl, and as he drives on the Interstate to visit his girlfriend, he recalls the sad fate of Clair Devane, a young black former girlfriend of his, who also worked as a realtor in the same office. Clair was murdered at a condo that she was showing to a client. Her murder remains unsolved.

He arrives at Sally's beach house in South Mantoloking. Sally is out, and he takes a nap. When he wakes it is twilight, and Sally has returned. He feels their relationship may be at a turning point, but neither of them says anything explicit to that effect. They have dinner, and at ten-thirty Sally says it is time for him to go.

Chapter 6

At a rest area off the turnpike, Bascombe calls his ex-wife Ann, who tells him that their son Paul got into an argument with Charley, Ann's husband, and hit him in the jaw with an oarlock, knocking him down. After this disconcerting conversation, Bascombe returns a call from Joe Markham, who has been leaving him angry messages. Markham says that he and his wife have now found another realtor in a different town. Bascombe then calls Sally, wanting to return to her house for the night, but she is not at home, so he starts off on the next leg of his journey to Connecticut. He pulls into a motel parking lot, where a number of police cars and an ambulance are assembled. After he pays for his room, he chats to Mr. Tanks, a guest at the motel, who tells him that two teenage boys broke into a room, robbed a couple, and killed the man. After chatting to Mr. Tanks about real estate, Bascombe goes to his room. He half-dreams, half-muses about Clair Devane, the murdered realtor, and the three-month romance he had with her one winter after she joined the realty office. As he lies in bed, he feels that the night's events have left him in a kind of limbo, unable to move. Death seems very close.

Chapter 7

In the morning, Bascombe sets off again. He calls Ted Houlihan to tell him that the Markhams are still thinking about whether to buy his house. Ted replies that he has some other people looking

at it, which annoys Bascombe because Ted has signed a contract giving Bascombe's firm an exclusive right to sell the house. By mid-morning, Bascombe arrives in Deep River, Connecticut, where Ann and the children live. Under the mailbox outside their house he finds a dead grackle on the ground, and he wonders whether his son is responsible for it. He picks up the dead bird and throws it into the bushes. At that moment a policeman drives up and quizzes him about what he is doing. Having satisfied the suspicious policeman, he parks outside the house and greets his daughter Clarissa. He tries to talk to her about Paul, but all she will say is that his problems are all stress-related. She thinks he would be happier if his father would come to live in Deep River, or nearby. Later, Ann informs him about the seriousness of Paul's condition; he has been driving his mother's car recklessly (without permission and without a license) and seems out of control. She reports on the comments of Dr. Stopler, Paul's psychiatrist, and suggests that Frank also see Stopler, as a co-parent. They talk about their past relationship, which in Bascombe's mind is not satisfactorily resolved. He retains a vague hope that they might remarry, but they finally agree that it is too late now to fix anything that might have been wrong in their relationship. Paul arrives, smirking, and he and his father go to the car to begin their trip.

Chapter 8

On the journey, Bascombe tries hard to be a good father and selects topics of conversation he thinks will help him get through to his son, such as a discussion about the Framers of the Constitution. Paul, however, is not interested, although they are able to joke with each other. They arrive at the Basketball Hall of Fame in Springfield, Massachusetts, and look at the exhibits. While Paul wanders off, Bascombe calls Sally and tries to persuade her to fly up to Albany, New York, and join them on their trip to the Baseball Hall of Fame. But she declines.

After forty-five minutes at the Basketball Hall of Fame, Bascombe and Paul resume their journey, with Bascombe still struggling to find ways to talk to his son. They drive on across the Hudson River and past Albany. As they approach Cooperstown in the evening, Paul begins turning the pages of a book of essays by Ralph Waldo Emerson, which his father really wants him to read, but he mocks Emerson's words and then tears a page out of the book, to Bascombe's annoyance. They pass the Baseball Hall of Fame and drive up to the Deerslayer Inn, where they will be staying.

Chapter 9

Bascombe goes to his room to rest while Paul wanders off on his own to explore. A little later, Bascombe receives a telephone message from Phyllis Markham, saying that they have changed their minds and would like to buy the Houlihan house. Bascombe tries to reach Houlihan to inform him that an offer will be forthcoming, but he cannot reach him. He calls Sally, and they have another inconclusive conversation about their feelings for each other. She agrees to meet him in New York the following day, after Bascombe has dropped Paul off at the train station.

Bascombe is hungry, but he is too late to get dinner at the hotel. He asks Char, the young female chef, if she can recommend anywhere for him to go, and she suggests a place called the Tunnicliff. She says he can walk her over there since it is on her way home. While he waits for her to change clothes, he is surprised to discover on the bookshelves in the parlor a book of short stories he published in the late 1960s. At first he plans to give it to Char, but then, exasperated by a greeting that has been written in it, which brings his troubled relationship with Ann to the surface of his mind, he hurls the book across the room. He then picks it up and puts it back where he found it. Char arrives in a sexy outfit, but Bascombe has lost interest in walking with her to the Tunnicliff, and she goes off alone. At that moment Bascombe hears Paul make a facetious remark; his son is sitting close by in a rocking chair and has heard the entire conversation between Char and his father. They start to talk about an incident that happened when Paul was a child, and for the first time they seem to be able to have a serious conversation.

Chapter 10

In the morning, Bascombe calls Ted Houlihan to let him know that the Markhams are about to make an offer for his house. But Houlihan says he has already sold the house to a Korean family. Bascombe threatens to sue him for breach of contract, although he knows he will not do it.

Bascombe and Paul go out to breakfast, where they have their best talk so far, and then on the Baseball Hall of Fame. There are some protesters outside. The nature of their grievance is unknown to Bascombe, so he and Paul take a walk. Bascombe is still eager to spend some quality time with his son. He takes him to a batting cage at Doubleday Field and tries his skill at one with the title "Dyno-Express," which has a machine that pitches the ball to the batter at seventy-five miles per hour. The machine pitches the ball to him five times, and

he manages to hit the ball on two occasions. But then Bascombe and his son quarrel and start to scuffle. When they break away from each other, Bascombe tries to make light of it, but Paul is still angry as he goes off to try his luck with the bat. The first ball he faces hits him full in the face and knocks him flat on his back. He appears to be badly injured, and someone calls an ambulance. In the confusion, Bascombe's stepbrother, Irv Ornstein, who just happens to be there, tries to reassure him. Bascombe has not seen Irv for twenty-five years.

It transpires that Paul has been hit in the eye. He is transported by helicopter to the hospital at Oneonta. Irv offers to drive Frank to the hospital, since he is not permitted to accompany Paul in the helicopter.

Chapter 11

At the hospital, Bascombe waits nervously while Paul is examined. Then a young female doctor, Dr. Tisaris, tells him that Paul has a dilated retina, which is a serious eye injury, and they would like to get him into surgery before the day is out. Bascombe calls his ex-wife, who says she will get another medical opinion and fly up by helicopter to the hospital. In the meantime, Bascombe sees his son, whose is quite calm and not in any pain. To pass the time until Ann arrives, Bascombe goes for a walk with Irv, who explains to him his philosophy of life and his views on marriage.

Chapter 12

Ann arrives at the hospital, bringing Henry Burris, a specialist from Yale, with her. Ann persuades Bascombe to agree to allow Paul to be transported to New Haven, where Burris will perform the surgery. Bascombe talks to Burris and has complete faith in his abilities. He says goodbye to Paul, who says he will come and stay with him for a while when he gets out of the hospital. Bascombe is delighted to hear this, since this is what he has wanted all along. Paul is placed in an air ambulance, and Bascombe says a poignant farewell to Ann.

Independence Day

Bascombe is back at his house in Haddam, New Jersey, on the morning of the Fourth of July. He has informed the Markhams by telephone that they have lost their chance to buy the Houlihan house, and they are now willing to consider renting one of the two houses Bascombe owns in Haddam. He has also heard from Ann that Paul came through his surgery in satisfactory condition, although he would be at risk for developing glaucoma by the age of fifty and would need glasses long before that. The Markhams arrive, inspect the house, and agree to rent it. Bascombe then drives into town, observing all the preparations for the Fourth of July parade. He recalls two telephone conversations he had the previous night, one with Karl Bemish, which ended with a quarrel, the other with Sally. Because of what happened to Paul, he and Sally were unable to meet in New York City as they had planned, but she was very sympathetic when she heard about Paul's accident. After they talked, Bascombe felt optimistic about life and his relationship with Sally.

Back in the present, Bascombe watches some parachutists come down on the Haddam green and feels happy to be in Haddam on the holiday. He continues his drive and stops outside his old house, which is now an ecumenical center. His friend Carter Knott comes up to him, and they chat for a few minutes, after which Bascombe drives off to watch the parade. He feels optimistic that Paul will come and live with him in the near future and that he may even marry again some time.

Characters

Clarissa Bascombe

Clarissa Bascombe, the twelve-year-old daughter of Frank Bascombe and Ann Dykstra, is more emotionally mature than her brother Paul, even though she is several years younger than he, and she and her father have a good, playful relationship. She already has definite political views, declaring herself, like her father, to be a Democrat.

Frank Bascombe

Frank Bascombe, the narrator of the novel, is the father of Paul and Clarissa and the ex-husband of Ann Dykstra. In his mid-forties, he is a realtor in Haddam, New Jersey, an occupation he enjoys and performs well. Formerly he was a sportswriter for a magazine, and before that he wrote fiction and published a volume of short stories. A staunch Democrat living in a city that is heavily Republican, Bascombe hopes for a Democratic victory in the upcoming presidential election.

Bascombe has been divorced for seven years. After he recovered from that very turbulent event in his life, he entered a period of relative contentment and stability that he calls his "Existence Period." He is reasonably happy with this stage of his life, a life which he regards as "more or less normal-under-the-microscope." Bascombe sees himself as

a reasonable man who looks at life honestly and tries to live as best he can. He believes he has found "maturity's balance," a kind of balance of opposites in which "interest can mingle successfully with uninterest . . . intimacy with transience, caring with the obdurate uncaring." As a divorced man who lives on his own, he has gained some independence, which he values greatly, but this has come at the price of forming close attachments to others. Part of this desire to stand a little aloof from other people is due to the fact he does not have much faith or trust in his own powers of judgment, so he tends to avoid making big decisions.

Two of the significant people in Bascombe's life express judgments about him that tend to undermine his own rather complacent view of himself. His ex-wife Ann feels some hostility toward him and is determined to keep her distance, even though Bascombe still entertains vague thoughts that one day they might reconcile and remarry. At one point Ann says to him, "You just want everything to seem perfect and everybody to seem pleased. And you're willing to let *seem* equal *be*. It makes pleasing anybody be an act of cowardice." Bascombe's current girlfriend, Sally Caldwell, also has an assessment of him that might be somewhat jarring to his self-image. He reports that Sally told him he was living in a state of "mechanical isolation that couldn't go on forever," and she does not wholly trust him. At one point she tells him he is "smooth and . . . cautious and . . . noncommittal," qualities that make it difficult for her to accept him fully.

Paul Bascombe

Paul Bascombe, the fifteen-year-old son of Frank Bascombe and his former wife, Ann, is a highly intelligent but wayward youth who has run foul of the law. He stole three boxes of condoms from a store and assaulted a female security guard who apprehended him. He now faces criminal charges of assault and battery. Paul has been evaluated by a psychiatrist who found no major psychological disturbance, and an evaluation made of him by counselors at a camp to which his mother sent him declared him to be intellectually advanced for his years but emotionally immature. One of Paul's problems seems to be obsessive thinking about the past. He is still troubled, for example, by the death of the family's dog, Mr. Toby, that was killed by a car when Paul was six.

Paul tells his father that he is frequently thinking about the fact that he is thinking, "by which he tries to maintain continuous monitorship of all his thoughts as a way of 'understanding' himself and being under control and therefore making life better." Paul is also given to making strange barking noises. He has a quirky sense of humor and is always making remarks that show his ability to play with words. He rarely gives a serious, heartfelt answer to his father's numerous attempts to get through to him, although Frank Bascombe seems to understand the boy's sense of humor.

Paul's appearance is not attractive. He dresses poorly and appears to pay no attention to personal hygiene. His father says of his own son that he is someone "you'd be sorry to encounter on a city street." When Bascombe picks him up for their road trip together, Paul strikes him as being suddenly taller and heavier, and his "gait is a new big-shoe, pigeon-toed, heel-scrape, shoulder-slump sidle by which he seems to give human shape to the abstract concept of condescending disapproval for everything in sight."

Myrlene Beavers

Myrlene Beavers is an elderly and rather deranged African American woman who lives across the street from Bascombe's two rental properties in Haddam. She keeps an eagle eye on happenings in the neighborhood, and when Bascombe visits the McLeods' for the rent, she thinks that he is breaking in to the house and calls the police.

Karl Bemish

Karl Bemish is the sixty-five-year-old owner-operator of a hot-dog stand called Franks in a semi-rural location not far from Haddam, New Jersey. He is "a big, sausage-handed, small-eared guy who looked more like he might've loaded bricks for a living." A widower, Bemish worked in the ergonomics field for thirty years but then decided to try something different. He bought a birch beer stand (calling it Bemish's Birch Beer Depot) on a whim, without knowing anything about the retail trade or the food service industry. He was successful at first but soon ran into trouble, lacking knowledge about how to put his innovative ideas into practice. Bascombe met him by chance and went into partnership with him, taking a controlling interest. He soon erased the debt and Franks became a profitable business.

Henry Burris

Henry Burris is a sixty-year-old southerner who is a highly renowned eye surgeon. He runs the Yale-Bunker Eye Clinic in New Haven, Connecticut, and Ann arranges for him to perform the surgery on Paul.

Sally Caldwell

Sally Caldwell, Bascombe's forty-two-year-old girlfriend, is an attractive blond woman. Her husband, Wally, disappeared in Chicago two weeks after returning from Vietnam, leaving Sally to raise their two children alone. In 1983, she bought a beach house facing the sea in South Mantoloking, New Jersey. She owns an agency that finds tickets to Broadway shows for people who are terminally ill. Bascombe has been seeing her for nearly a year. He describes her as "angularly pretty, frosted-blond, blue-eyed, tall in the extreme, with long, flashing model's legs." They appear to enjoy their relationship, but there is no commitment on either side to making it permanent.

Char

Char is a single mother of about thirty who works as the chef at the Deerslayer Inn. She is outspoken and rather vulgar. Bascombe describes her appearance: "Frizzy blond hair, pallid indoor skin, blotchy where I can't now see, thick little wrists and neck, and wandering breasts not well captained inside her chef's get up." Bascombe arranges to walk with her to a bar but later thinks better of it and is glad he has avoided any involvement with her.

Clair Devane

Clair Devane was a bright and enterprising young black woman who worked as a realtor in Bascombe's office. Originally from Talladega, Alabama, she was a divorced mother of two children. After she joined the realtor office, she had a brief affair with Bascombe. Two years later, Clair was raped and murdered while showing a condo to a client. Her murder was unsolved.

Ann Dykstra

Ann Dykstra is Bascombe's former wife. She is now married to Charley O'Dell and lives in Deep River, Connecticut, with her two children from her former marriage. Ann initiated the divorce from Bascombe, against his wishes, when he could not get over the death of their son, Ralph, and left home for a while and saw other women. Bascombe is still in love with Ann and would like to remarry her, but she is decidedly cool toward him. She tells him bluntly that Charley is a better man than he, that she trusts Charley because he tells her the truth, whereas she did not trust Bascombe and believes he never told her the whole truth about anything. However, Ann's marriage to Charley is not working out well. She does not admit this to Bascombe, but both children tell him there have recently been fierce quarrels between their mother and her husband.

Erik

Erik is the young policeman who drives up just as Bascombe is tossing a dead bird into the bushes outside Ann's house. He is suspicious of what Bascombe is doing there and interrogates him.

Catherine Flaherty

Catherine Flaherty is a young woman with whom Bascombe had a love affair two years after his divorce. She was a medical student at the time.

Ted Houlihan

Ted Houlihan is a recently widowed, retired engineer who is selling his house in Penns Neck, New Jersey. It is the house that the Markhams are shown around. According to Bascombe, Houlihan "is a sharp-eyed little white-haired seventy-plus-year-old . . . and looks like the happiest man in Penns Neck." Houlihan has been diagnosed with testicular cancer and plans to go to Tucson, Arizona, where his son, who is a surgeon, will operate on him. Ted upsets Bascombe by selling his house to a Korean family through another realty company, even though he had signed an exclusive contract with Bascombe's firm.

Carter Knott

Carter Knott is a friend of Bascombe in Haddam, New Jersey, although they do not see each other often. A Vietnam War veteran, Knott was a successful entrepreneur and businessman. Now on his second marriage, he is wealthy and has retired from work to supervise his investments.

Vonda Lusk

Vonda Lusk is the receptionist at the Lauren-Schwindell realty firm where Bascombe works. She was best friends with Clair Devane.

Joe Markham

Joe Markham and his wife, Phyllis, are disillusioned with the public schools in Vermont and want to move to Haddam, New Jersey, where the schools are reputedly better, so that their daughter, Sonja, will have a better chance in life. Joe, who has a son by a previous marriage, is a former schoolteacher who has just found a job in the production department of a textbook publisher near Haddam. He also makes pots and sand-cast sculptures and has been quite successful at selling them.

However, Joe is a morose, verbally aggressive man who is unhappy about the fact that he cannot find a house he likes in Haddam that is also within his budget. He is rude on a number of occasions to Bascombe, but Bascombe ignores his provocations because he wants to sell him a house.

Phyllis Markham

Phyllis Markham is Joe Markham's wife. In her forties, she has a son by a previous marriage and a twelve-year-old daughter, Sonja, with Joe. She occupies her time helping her husband's business by designing slick sales pamphlets for his work, but she has health problems and is feeling a lot of pressure as she and Joe try to make the move from Vermont to Haddam. According to Bascombe, "she carries herself as if there were a new burden of true woe on the earth and only she knows about it." He thinks she has a "malleable and sweet putty face." Phyllis shows much patience in coping with her difficult husband, and eventually, after a frustrating search for real estate, she is content to rent the house Bascombe owns.

Betty McLeod

Betty McLeod is the white wife of Larry McLeod. Bascombe describes her as "a sallow, pointy-faced little Grinnell grad, off the farm near Minnetonka." She is not a friendly woman and spends most of her time inside the house with her children. Bascombe thinks she always looks disappointed, as if she regrets the choices she has made.

Larry McLeod

Larry McLeod is a middle-aged black man who works in the mobile-home construction industry in a town near Haddam. He rents one of the houses that Bascombe owns. A former Green Beret, McLeod is an aggressive man and is difficult to deal with. He does not pay the rent promptly. When Bascombe calls on him to try to collect the rent, the realtor notices a large automatic pistol lying on a table, which makes him wary of his tenant.

Charley O'Dell

Charley O'Dell is the husband of Ann, Bascombe's former wife. He is a wealthy, sixty-one-year-old architect. Bascombe, who dislikes Charley and refers to him contemptuously as "the bricklayer," first met him four years earlier. He describes him then as "tall, prematurely white-haired, rich, big-boned, big-schnozzed, big-jawed, literal-as-a-dictionary architect." Charley does not get on well with Bascombe's son, Paul, and it also appears that his marriage to Ann is in difficulties.

Irv Ornstein

Irv Ornstein is Bascombe's half-brother, the son of Bascombe's mother's second husband. Bascombe has not seen Irv for twenty-five years, and then he bumps into him immediately after Paul is injured. Irv just happens to be in the same place at the same time. He reassures Bascombe, drives him down to the hospital, and tells him about his life. Irv works as a flight simulator; he has been divorced twice and spent some time on a kibbutz in Israel. He does not have a clear sense of where his life is going, but he seeks continuity.

Dr. Stopler

Dr. Stopler is the psychiatrist in New Haven, Connecticut, who evaluates Paul. Bascombe calls him a "fancy shrink."

Mr. Tanks

Mr. Tanks is a large African American man in his forties who wears a green Mayflower moving van uniform. He is a long-haul trucker. Bascombe meets him at the motel where a murder has just been committed. Mr. Tanks is divorced and says he virtually lives in his rig. He owns a house in Alhambra, California, but is thinking of moving to the East Coast. Bascombe offers him some advice about real estate.

Dr. Tisaris

Dr. Tisaris is the young female doctor who examines Paul at the hospital in Oneonta after he injures his eye.

Themes

Independence

Against a background of Independence Day, the novel sets out to explore the nature of human independence. What is independence? How is it achieved? Is there a price to be paid for it? How does independence relate to community and commitment and service to others? The novel's main character, Frank Bascombe, has attained a certain kind of independence. He has recovered from the turbulence that accompanied the death of his son Ralph and his divorce seven years earlier.

He lives on his own, away from his two surviving children. This period of his life he characterizes as the "Existence Period . . . the part that comes *after* the big struggle which led to the big blow-up." It is a time of relative stability that involves a lot of solitude, but which is "self-directed and happy." He explains that "The Existence Period helps create or at least partly stimulates the condition of honest independence." However, this condition of independence is a rather cautious, limited one. Bascombe says he does not always trust his own judgment about matters and knows, based on past experience, that there are good reasons for not doing so. He admits that he ignores things he does not like or which worry him rather than dealing with them. In the Existence Period, he tends to keep others at a distance. A telling detail is the fact that he sees Carter Knott, whom he regards as his best friend in Haddam, only about once every six months, and even then they chat for less than two minutes and are careful to avoid any serious conversation. Bascombe is also reluctant to become deeply involved with his girlfriend, Sally Caldwell. He admits that he likes the thrill "of early romance yet lack[s] the urge to do more than ignore it when that sweet sorority threatens to develop into something else." Bascombe is wary of making any commitment to Sally that would involve the loss of his independence.

Bascombe also tries to teach his son about the need for independence. Trying to lead into the subject by talking about Independence Day, he plans to tell Paul that the day is "an observance of human possibility, which applies a canny pressure on each of us to contemplate what we're dependent on . . . and what ways we're independent or might be." Bascombe's goal is to help his son heal the wounds of the past so that he can become "free and independent rather than staying disconnected and distracted." He wants him to jettison the past, not to remember everything (like the unfortunate death of the family dog when Paul was six) and not to try so hard to keep everything under control. He wants him to develop self-determination, and this involves one's own sense of judgment. "A lot of things we think are true aren't . . . You have to make your own assessments," he says to Paul.

Towards the end of the novel, Bascombe seems to acknowledge that his Existence Period may not be as satisfactory as he has formerly thought. He acknowledges that independence is a "complex dilemma," and he is far more willing to

Topics For Further Study

- What does Independence Day mean for you? How does the July 4th holiday differ from other American holidays, such as Thanksgiving or Memorial Day? How do you spend your time, and what do you reflect on, during these times? Write a personal essay on the subject.

- Read Emerson's essay "Self-Reliance" and make a class presentation about it. Identify the major points and explain why Bascombe wants Paul to read this essay. Is it a good choice of reading for Paul? Why do you think Paul reacts as he does to it?

- Get together with a group of three other classmates and discuss what independence means to you. How are you dependent on or independent of your parents and other family members? Is independence a goal of yours? Are there any drawbacks to being independent? What is the relationship between independence and community? Do you take your values from your family, your group of friends, or develop them yourself?

- Write an essay in which you analyze the character of Paul. What has gone wrong in his life? What are the underlying reasons for his being in trouble with the law? Does Frank approach him in the right way? Explore other ways in which to approach the character of Paul, including the possibility that there is really not much wrong with him at all. Does he remind you of anyone you know?

---

engage more deeply with others, especially Sally, who comments on the "mechanical isolation" of his Existence Period. He still seeks independence, which he refers to as "God-required but not God-assured," but he also feels that he may marry again, and he certainly looks forward to his son coming to stay with him. The last two sentences of the novel, as he mingles with the Fourth of July crowds, suggest this new awareness of his necessary involvement with other humans: "My heartbeat quickens. I feel the push, pull, the weave and sway of others."

Continuity and Community

Since independence in human life can never be total, another theme of the novel is the search for community and the feelings of continuity and permanence that come with it. As a realtor, Bascombe meets many people who are in a transition phase in their lives, wanting to buy a house and establish themselves in a new community. The Markhams, for example, are leaving Vermont where they have lived for many years and want to put down roots in Haddam. But they find this easier said than done. Frustrated in their search, they stay in motels—symbols of transience and the random gathering of strangers—and end up renting a house rather than buying one. But once they have decided on this, Bascombe remarks that the illusion of permanence takes over, and they act as if they are long-time residents.

On his road trip, Bascombe also encounters people who are in transit and searching for a sense of community. Mr. Tanks, for example, who makes a living by moving other people, is estranged from his ex-wife, and virtually lives in his removals truck, is thinking of selling his home in California and expresses the wish to Bascombe to live in a "neighborhood," although he does not have much idea of where that might be. Bascombe's instincts as a realtor take over, and he advises Mr. Tanks about the current housing market. Bascombe instinctively seeks to help others, by means of his professional knowledge, in their search for community. One of the reasons he bought the two houses in Haddam that he now rents out was to establish "a greater sense of connectedness."

He acknowledges that he lacks this in his own life, but he understands "the sense of belonging and permanence" towards which the residents of the area aspire.

Style

Metaphors

The guiding metaphor throughout the novel is of real estate as the reality of life itself. A house is a temporary structure, but people take refuge in it as a safe place on their life journey. A house gives security with which to weather the storms of life and seems to give significance and permanence to a person's existence. But Bascombe concludes that the power of place, of a home to confer meaning on human life, is more a product of hope than reality. When he visits the home where he once lived with his wife and children, and which has now been transformed into an ecumenical center, he asks:

> Is there any cause to think a place—any place—within its plaster and joists, its trees and plantings, in its putative essence *ever* shelters some spirit ghost of us as proof of its significance and ours?

He answers his own question in the negative, adding that people should "quit asking places for what they can't provide." This is the same sentiment he expresses earlier in the novel, when he visits Sally's beach house. The house is familiar to him in the sense that it has some significance in his life history and his memory, and yet it is also unfamiliar, refusing to confer the full measure of significance that he half-hopes such a place should. He concludes that people should "cease sanctifying places" that once held significance for them, because the truth is that in spite of what may have once taken place there, "Places never cooperate by revering you back when you need it. . . . Place means nothing." It is because of this belief that Bascombe values independence so highly. No one can depend on a house; one can only depend on oneself.

Historical Context

The Presidential Campaign of 1988

Independence Day takes place against a backdrop of a developing presidential race in which Bascombe and some of the other characters take a keen interest. In early July 1988, preparations were underway for the conventions of the two major parties in which each would nominate a candidate for the presidential election in November. Bascombe is a Democrat and hopes that Michael Dukakis, the governor of Massachusetts, who is already assured of winning the Democratic nomination, will become the next president of the United States. Dukakis was generally considered, as Bascombe puts it, an "uninspirational" candidate, but he won the Democratic nomination because he took credit for what was known as the Massachusetts Miracle, the economic revival of the state during his tenure as governor. Dukakis based his campaign on his perceived managerial competence and ability to improve the economy by creating new jobs. Republicans fought back by trying to typecast him as an ultra-liberal, tax-and-spend Democrat. In the novel, for example, Karl Bemish, who plans to vote Republican, refers to Dukakis's home state of Massachusetts as "Taxachusetts."

Bemish is an example of those voters who were known at the time as Reagan Democrats. The term was used to describe traditionally Democratic, mostly white, working-class voters who switched to the Republicans in the 1980s, when Republican Ronald Reagan was president (1981–1989). Reagan Democrats tended to perceive the Democratic Party as no longer working for their economic interests but being controlled by special interest groups and catering to minorities and other disadvantaged groups. These voters also tended to be more conservative on national security issues, an area in which Reagan was perceived as strong. They also supported Reagan's policy of cutting taxes. In the novel, Bascombe regards the Reagan Democrats as "turncoats."

The Democratic primary campaign in 1988 was notable for the success of the Rev. Jesse Jackson Jr., who won eleven primaries, receiving a total of 6.9 million votes. After he won the Michigan primary, he was briefly regarded as the leading contender for the Democratic nomination, but he failed to hold on to his advantage, allowing Dukakis to capture the nomination. In the novel, Bascombe considered himself a Jackson supporter during some of the primaries but "finally decided he couldn't win and would ruin the country if he did." Bascombe may have had in mind Jackson's position as the most liberal of the Democratic candidates. Jackson aimed to build what he called a Rainbow Coalition made up of minorities, the working poor, women, and gay people. He favored reversing Reagan's tax cuts, spending more money on social welfare programs, and cutting the defense budget by up to 15 percent over four years.

Unlike Bascombe, most of the characters who express a political opinion in the novel are Republicans. Charley O'Dell, for example, is a staunch supporter of what Bascombe's daughter Clarissa calls "the party of money, tradition and influence." (Clarissa is no doubt repeating her father's opinion.) Irv Ornstein is also a Republican, who expects to vote for the Republican candidate, Vice President George Bush, but feels uneasy about what he describes as Bush's "indecisiveness." This was a common view of Bush at the time. Although Bush had been Reagan's vice president for eight years, he did not generate much enthusiasm amongst Republican voters. Bascombe, who lives in the solidly Republican city of Haddam, New Jersey (a fictional creation), comments that Haddam voters "love Reagan like Catholics love the Pope, yet also feel dumbfounded and double-crossed by the clownish spectacle of Vice President Bush as their new leader." Conservative voters were especially wary of Bush because they felt, in addition to the fact that Bush was not generally regarded as a strong leader, that he did not share their core principles on key social issues, such as abortion. When Bush first ran for president in 1980, he was perceived as a moderate rather than a conservative. Indeed, Bush had then been a supporter of abortion rights, but he had changed his position when the pro-life Reagan selected him as his vice-presidential running mate.

During the election campaign in the fall of 1988, Bush managed to step out of Reagan's shadow and assert his own leadership qualities. In a generally negative campaign, the Republicans managed to create an impression in the public mind that Dukakis was soft on crime. The Bush campaign also exploited Dukakis's veto of a bill in Massachusetts that would have required school-children to recite the Pledge of Allegiance, implying that Dukakis was unpatriotic.

Although according to opinion polls, Dukakis held a lead of up to 18 percent over Bush in the summer of 1988, he lost the lead following the Republican convention in late summer. Bush went on to win the election comfortably, winning forty states to Dukakis's ten, with a 54 percent share of the total vote to Dukakis's 46 percent.

Critical Overview

Reviewers in general regarded *Independence Day* as a worthy successor to Ford's earlier novel featuring Frank Bascombe, *The Sportswriter*. According to the reviewer for *Publishers Weekly*, *Independence Day* "is an often poetic, sometimes searing, sometimes hilarious account" of Bascombe's life around the Fourth of July: "Frank struggles through the long weekend with a mixture of courage, self-knowledge and utter foolishness that makes him a kind of 1980s Everyman." In *Newsweek*, Jeff Giles shares this enthusiasm for Frank Bascombe, describing him as "a great mythic American character" in what is "a long, exhausting but finally exhilarating sequel to *The Sportswriter*." In Giles's view, the novel picks up steam when Bascombe arrives at his ex-wife's house and starts out on the trip with his son: "The halls-of-fame sequence is a genuinely heartbreaking study of a screwed-up father trying to reach his screwed-up kid."

In *Time*, Paul Gray also focuses on the character of Bascombe, describing him as an "entertaining storyteller . . . [whose] conviction that it is possible to behave honorably—even while selling real estate—and to be useful to his fellow citizens commands respect." However, Gray comments that Bascombe "has a way of attracting misery to those around him" and does not seem especially aware of this fact, making him "a bigger mystery to the reader than he is to himself."

Some reviewers had reservations about the plot, commenting that there were too few actual events to sustain interest in the narrative. For example, Charles Johnson, in the *New York Times Book Review*, writes:

> [T]here is only the thinnest of story lines in the 451 pages of *Independence Day*. The novel often bogs down in repetitive descriptions of place and setting. Some events—Frank's effort to collect his rent from the McLeods, his arrival at a motel in Connecticut just after a killing has occurred and the mystery of the realtor's murder—lead nowhere.

Johnson does, however, acknowledge the "brilliant character sketches" in the book and concludes:

> Bascombe has earned himself a place beside Willy Loman and Harry Angstrom in our literary landscape, but he has done so with a wry wit and a *fin de siècle* wisdom that is very much his own.

View of Fourth of July parade down Main Street from the top of city hall. Bristol, Vermont.
© James P. Blair/Corbis

Criticism

Bryan Aubrey

Aubrey holds a Ph.D. in English and has published many articles on twentieth century literature. In this essay, he discusses how during the course of the novel Frank Bascombe progresses from a too rigidly held independence to a more open attitude toward other people.

Frank Bascombe's journey through 1980s America is a secular one. In all his meetings and conversations with people, not one of them (with the possible exception of Karl Bemish) expresses a belief in God. The characters do not have a religious faith or suggest even for a moment that they look to God for support in difficult times. Bascombe himself tells Karl quite explicitly that he is an atheist. These are people who must make their way through the minefield of human experience without the traditional props and succor that religion has offered to troubled souls.

Given the absence of religion to help people deal with the inescapable vulnerability that is the human condition, it might seem odd—as it indeed seems to Bascombe—that his girlfriend Sally

Caldwell remarks, while they are discussing how they perceive themselves, that she sees him "in an odd priestly mode." Bascombe responds that being seen as some kind of priest is the worst thing imaginable, "since priests are the least self-aware, most unenlightened, irresolute, isolated and frustrated people on the earth." Bascombe gives no clue as to why he has arrived at such a negative appraisal of priests, but Sally's observation has more in it than he might care to acknowledge. In a world that has no religious faith, Bascombe acts as a kind of secular shepherd of souls, helping people find and settle into their temporary resting places—their homes—where they can find shelter from life's storms.

Bascombe's dealings with Joe and Phyllis Markham are a case in point. In the course of showing them over forty houses in and around Haddam, Bascombe gets to know, like a priest hearing a confession, many of their secrets and a lot about their hopes, desires, and frustrations, not to mention the stresses in their marriage. At one point, after the couple arrives having argued on the way down, Phyllis even asks Bascombe to mediate between them ("I wonder if you'd mind just talking to him"). Bascombe is used to this kind of thing and is not bothered by "steely silences, bitter cryptic asides, eyes

> These images of falling are a metaphor for letting go rather than holding on for dear life to all the props and supports with which the average person surrounds himself. It is a kind of independence, a flowing in the moment without care of past or future."

rolled to heaven and dagger stares passed between prospective home buyers." Mostly, in addition to offering whatever helpful comments about real estate that he can muster, he acts as a nonjudgmental listener, a person who can be a receptacle for his clients' anger and frustration without reacting in a personal way. When, for example, Joe Markham treats Bascombe with thinly disguised contempt and later leaves messages on his answering service, calling him all kinds of unpleasant and obscene names, Bascombe does not let it affect the evenness of his manner. Like a priest, he has a broad understanding of people's sins and follies, and he also has a certain sense of mission about his work. "I do like to help the poor and displaced," he later says to Karl, and when he finally manages to get the Markhams installed in a house they can at least tolerate, he takes his leave having "done the best I can by everyone" and asking rhetorically, "What more can you do for wayward strangers than to shelter them?"

But if Bascombe can be seen as a kind of Good Samaritan and secular priest, he is a priest without a theology to guide him. Not only this, he has little belief or trust in the strengths and virtues of the traditional family unit. It is hard to blame him. There is barely a single intact, harmonious family in the novel. Bascombe is unhappily divorced, with a fifteen-year-old son whose life is in crisis (a common result of so-called broken homes); his ex-wife is now unhappily (so it would appear) remarried; Bascombe's stepbrother Irv Ornstein is divorced twice and his second wife wants no contact with him. The unstable Markhams are on their second marriages, with Joe's son from his first marriage possessing a conviction for armed robbery; Sally Caldwell's husband, Wally, disappeared twenty years earlier and

has not been heard of since. Marriage is thus presented as a risky undertaking, with the chances of success small and the possibility of lasting pain large. Irv Ornstein resists making any commitment to his current girlfriend, fearing that if he does he will lose his own identity and regret it for the rest of his life. When Irv shows Bascombe an old black and white family snapshot that he has carried around with him for years, it strikes the reader (and Bascombe, who calls it "[Irv's] precious artifact") as a relic from a bygone age. The family unit may once have been the foundation unit of society, but it can no longer lay claim to such a position.

With neither faith in God nor family to sustain him, Bascombe has cobbled together a kind of private, secular faith in the value of independence, which he has carefully cultivated during what he calls his Existence Period, the time of stability that followed the turbulence caused by the death of his first son and his subsequent divorce. But he has paid a price for his independence in separateness from others. Although he is helpful and considerate to people, he has guarded himself too carefully and lacks any really intimate relationships that might nourish his heart. He does not believe that he could ever marry again and refers to himself as a "suspicious bachelor." He has convinced himself that he is "more or less self-directed and happy," but the reader guesses that his assessments of himself are not always accurate. His ex-wife Ann, for example, says that he "may be the most cynical man in the world."

However, toward the end of the novel, after Paul's accident, a new quality enters Bascombe's life that has not been seen before. It is hope. Just as Paul is about to be airlifted to the hospital, Bascombe observes Ann shaking hands with Irv Ornstein. He cannot hear over the sound of the turning rotors of the helicopter, but he sees Ann's lips moving and Irv seeming to mouth back what she is saying: "Hope, hope, hope, hope, hope." They are of course referring to Paul's injury, hoping that it is not quite as serious as they fear it may be. (Their hope is rewarded.) But the hope seems to extend beyond this narrow meaning to Bascombe's life as a whole. When he talks to Sally about Paul's accident, he tells her of "some odd feeling of peculiar and not easily explainable hope" that extends to optimism about the future of his relationship with Sally and the possibility that they might actually make a commitment to each other. It is as if the shock of the injury to Paul has blasted away from Bascombe his carefully cultivated stance of detachment and forced him to become more real, open, and honest.

He repeats his new-found sentiment the next day, as he looks back on the call he made to Sally from a dark gas station in the village of Long Eddy, New York:

> I could sense like a faint, sweet perfume in the night the *possibility* of better yet to come, only I had no list of particulars to feel better about, and not much light on my horizon except for a keyhole hope to try to *make* it brighter.

The next day, Independence Day, Bascombe has yet another realization, this time about his relationship with his son, that "yesterday may have cleaned our air and accounts and opened, along with wounds, an unexpected window for hope to go free."

Bascombe, of course, still has much to learn, and in the later stages of the novel, a new approach to living makes its appearance at the periphery of his life. It is an approach that does not involve trying to control the way things work out. This is relevant for Bascombe since when Paul sustained his injury, his carefully laid plans for the weekend went badly awry. This was not the outcome he was planning for. There is a foreshadowing of this sense that life is not within one's control, however hard one tries, at the beginning of Chapter 10, when Bascombe is awakened early in the morning in his room at the Deerslayer Inn by the sound of a loud radio coming from outside. There is a talk show in progress, and a caller named Bob says the following:

> You know, Jerry, the truth is I just began to realize I didn't care what happened to me, you know? Worry and worry about making your life come out right, you know? Regret everything you say or do, everything seems to sabotage you, then you try to quit sabotaging yourself. But then *that's* a mistake. Finally you have to figure a lot's out of your control, right?

Bascombe merely reports this without commenting on it, but another key moment comes almost at the end of the novel, when he watches four parachutists land as part of the Fourth of July celebrations. He watches them "careening to earth within five seconds, landing semi-gracefully with a hop-skip-jump close by the Dutch dance floor." He marvels at how they are able to jump from "the old safety, the ordinary and predictable, which makes a swan dive into invisible empty air seem perfect, lovely, the one thing that'll do." These images of falling are a metaphor for letting go rather than holding on for dear life to all the props and supports with which the average person surrounds himself. It is a kind of independence, a flowing in the moment without care of past or future. Bascombe comments on the parachutists, and the implied metaphor of letting go, that he would never consider doing this himself: "I ... would always find a reason not to risk it ... I'm no hero." But the reader may at this point once more find that Bascombe is what literary critics call an unreliable narrator; what he says about himself is not always the way things really are. After all, letting go is part of what he has been urging Paul to do, since Paul is irrationally clinging to the memory of things that happened in the long-ago past and is also busying himself watching himself thinking. The truth is that by the end of the novel, Bascombe has become much more open to real communication with people, which involves letting go of fixed concepts and being willing to change.

On the very last page of the novel there is yet another key moment. Late at night Bascombe is awakened by his telephone ringing. The person at the end of the line does not identify himself and just mumbles a few unintelligible sounds. But Bascombe responds by saying he is glad the person has called, and then says, "Let me hear your thinking. I'll try to add a part to the puzzle. It can be simpler than you think." This suggests his openness to communication not just with the people he knows but with anonymous voices and minds everywhere, as if he is more ready to absorb and respond to the stream of life as it occurs moment to moment, forming ever-new patterns that are held for a time and then pass on to something new. Bascombe may or may not be a hero, but it will surely seem to most readers that he is learning how to live in a new way, a way that will lead him to new destinations and places that perhaps he has never even imagined for himself. The parachutist jumps because he has trust and can leave the old and the familiar behind; Bascombe, although he may tell readers otherwise, is in fact in the process of suiting up, ready to take the plunge into the unknown, letting the winds of time and change uphold him and place him where he needs to be.

Source: Bryan Aubrey, Critical Essay on *Independence Day*, in *Novels for Students*, Thomson Gale, 2007.

Huey Guagliardo

In the following essay, Guagliardo discusses the "dislocatedness" and self-imposed isolation the protaganist experiences in a mobile society. In an attempt to connect with his son, the protagonist takes him on a journey to find their "place" in the world, and along the way discovers a greater understanding of the meaning of independence.

The psychological and spiritual journey of Ford's suburban Everyman, Frank Bascombe, progresses further in *Independence Day*, the author's most richly developed novel. Five years have passed, and Frank is now forty-four, and his son, Paul, briefly introduced in *The Sportswriter* as a tenderhearted ten-year-old who tries to contact his dead brother by carrier pigeon, is now a troubled teen who has been arrested for shoplifting. Paul is also prone to emit "unexpected barking noises," and he spends a great deal of his time "thinking he's thinking," that is, monitoring his thoughts in an attempt to gain understanding and control of his life. Like *The Sportswriter*, this novel also takes place over a holiday weekend. Its events begin on a Friday and end on Monday, the 4th of July, 1988. This time it is the nation's birthday that marks an important passage in the life of a Ford character. As Frank says, it is "a weekend when my own life seems at a turning or at least a curving point." The 4th of July/election year setting also provides Ford with ample opportunity to render the state of American culture in the latter half of the twentieth century; and *Independence Day* is clearly the novelist's most insightful commentary to date on contemporary life, with particular emphasis upon the dissolution of those important human connections long sustained by families and communities. A major portion of the plot involves an automobile trip that Frank and Paul take to the basketball and baseball halls of fame as part of the absent father's attempt to bond with the son he feels is rapidly slipping away from him. That Frank chooses this quintessentially American pilgrimage—the 4th of July, the possibilities of the open road, the halls of fame—as his means of bonding with Paul demonstrates the extent to which Ford's protagonist embraces suburban America's ideals even as his own experiences reveal the culture's many failures and breakdowns.

Frank's own life has changed considerably over the five-year period. His ex-wife, Ann (he now uses her first name), remarried and moved with Frank's two children from Haddam, New Jersey, to Connecticut, after which Frank moved into the house formerly owned by Ann and quit his job as a sportswriter to become a "Residential Specialist" for a real estate firm. As a result of these events, Frank has entered a phase of his life that is even more passive than his life as a sportswriter. He refers to this phase as "the Existence Period," which implies, among other things, a midlife willingness "to let matters go as they go and see what happens."

In *Independence Day*, Frank's "relocation"—new home and new point of view—as well as his new job in an industry that supposedly stresses the notion that "location is everything" are extremely significant in expressing Ford's concern with the question of what it really means to locate oneself and gain one's independence in a complex and often dangerous world.

As the novel begins, we see that life in still-quite-prosperous Haddam has been somewhat devalued, along with its real estate. Crime and violence have spread even to this once-quiet suburb. The modern world is a dangerous place, and there seems to be no escape from life's randomness. Frank himself has been mugged, his neighbors burglarized, and a colleague/ex-girlfriend raped and murdered. Haddam, in short, has failed to protect its residents from the violence and uncertainty of the world. It is a community on the edge; or, as Frank expresses it: "there's a new sense of a wild world being just beyond our perimeter, an untallied apprehension among our residents, one I believe they'll never get used to, one they'll die before accommodating." As in Ford's other novels, there is once again a strong sense of the marginality of human existence, a marginality that Frank, once a writer, understands more keenly than most of his neighbors. The Existence Period is Frank's newest way of coping with life's unpredictability and with his own feeling of being "*waaaay* out there at the edge."

According to Frank, selling real estate is the "ideal occupation" for someone gliding along in the Existence Period. Frank regards the real estate profession, like sportswriting, as a peripheral occupation, as "being on the periphery of the business community." Frank explains that "the one gnostic truth of real estate" is "that people never find or buy the house they say they want." Instead, "The premise is that you're presented with what you might've thought you didn't want, but what's available, whereupon you give in and start finding ways to feel good about it and yourself." To Frank, this scheme makes perfect sense: "Why should you only get what you think you want, or be limited by what you can simply plan on? Life's never like that, and if you're smart you'll decide it's better the way it is." Being a realtor also provides Frank with the perfect position from which to observe the "dislocatedness" so prevalent in modern suburban life. As a realtor he must constantly deal with people who, like himself, are trying to find their place, to locate themselves; but he soon discovers that no one is really at home, that in a sense we are all homeless nomads searching desperately for what he refers to as that "homey connectedness." Always an astute observer of contemporary American society, Ford finds the realty profession to be the ideal vehicle for commenting on the rootlessness and sense of longing that are characteristic of an increasingly mobile population.

Frank's view of reality and of realty, his Existence Period philosophy that we seldom get what we plan on and might as well learn to accept the fact, is dramatized in a comical episode involving a couple from Vermont, Joe and Phyllis Markham, who are searching for a dream house that does not exist in the Haddam market. The episode also points to the disintegration of families and communities in American culture, as well as to a general pattern of rootlessness. The Markhams' lives have followed an all-too-familiar pattern in a society in which families and communities are dissolving. They were each married to another, but "spouses wandered off with other people's spouses; their kids got busily into drugs, got pregnant, got married, then disappeared to California or Canada or Tibet or Wiesbaden." The middle-aged Joe and Phyllis reinvented themselves, found each other, married, and built comfortable lives in Vermont; but, like so many restless Americans, they eventually decided to pull up stakes in search of a dream. Now they find themselves living in a motel and running out of money. Their "predicament of homelessness" is emphatically suggested by their beat-up, borrowed Nova with the "muddy bumper sticker that says ANESTHETISTS ARE NOMADS." On a "rainy summer morning" with "the seeds of gloomy alienation sown in," Frank prepares to show his clients a house "in the Haddam area," a suburb of a suburb, so to speak. Joe Markham, however, makes clear just how important location is to him: "I don't want to live in an area. . . . Nobody ever said the Vermont area, or the Aliquippa area. . . . They just said the places." Frank views Joe as a man "who's come to the sudden precipice of what's left of life a little quicker than he knows how to cope with." Frustrated after showing the Markhams forty-five houses, Frank tries to convince them to see things from his point of view and to settle for a house which, while below their expectations in a number of ways, realistically represents the best that they can expect for their money. However, the house is not actually in Haddam, the most desired location, and, to make matters worse, it has a minimum security

> **As in Ford's other novels, there is once again a strong sense of the marginality of human existence, a marginality that Frank, once a writer, understands more keenly than most of his neighbors.**

prison in its backyard. Selling "the positive aspects of close-by prison living" requires the realtor's best attempts at "pseudo-communication." Although the prison behind the fence is an all-too-real reminder of the dangers lurking just beyond the perimeters of suburban life, Frank tries to minimize its importance with the less-than-comforting reminder that "No one knows his neighbors in the suburbs anyway. It's not like Vermont." In spite of himself, the cantankerous Joe Markham seems ready to surrender to the influence of Frank's Existence Period philosophy. Even before being shown the house, he ironically announces: "I've completely quit becoming. . . . I'm not out on the margins where new discoveries take place anymore." His poor wife, Phyllis, perhaps realizing that they have, in fact, reached the edge of their possibilities, unenthusiastically resigns herself to the thought that "maybe no one gets the house they want."

Although Frank's passive, stoical life in the Existence Period may help him to cope with disappointment and uncertainty, and in so doing provide him with a false sense of independence from life's travails, such a view of the world definitely has its drawbacks. Most notably, as he is well aware, the view can result in "physical isolation and emotional disengagement ... which cause trouble equal to or greater than the problems" which it solves. As he explains, "[I]t is one of the themes of the Existence Period that interest can mingle successfully with uninterest ... intimacy with transience, caring with the obdurate uncaring." Later, he confesses that "intimacy had begun to matter less to me." A certain disinterest or uncaring is often evident in Frank's dealings with others, particularly the homeless Markhams. Even more significantly, however, his emotional detachment

What Do I Read Next?

- *The Sportswriter* (1986) is the first of Ford's novels to feature Frank Bascombe, who at this time is a sportswriter, struggling to come to terms with the death of his older son, Ralph, from Reye's syndrome, and his recent divorce. The novel takes place over an Easter weekend, during which Bascombe shows he is able to survive but is unable to make deep contact with others.

- *Rabbit at Rest* (1990), by John Updike, is the fourth and final volume in Updike's saga about the life and times of Harry "Rabbit" Angstrom. Set in Pennsylvania in 1989, Rabbit is now fifty-five years old, a sick man who has premonitions of death. Like *Independence Day*, Updike's novel presents the protagonist's observations, memories, and reflections in the United States in the late 1980s, a time of large government budget deficits, terrorism, AIDS, drug abuse, junk food, and environmental decay, to name only a few of the negative trends of the decade.

- *Nobody's Fool* (1993), by Richard Russo, is set in a small town in upstate New York and features the problem-strewn life of Sully, a sixty-year-old man who is still haunted by the memory of an abusive father. In addition, Sully has troubles with his landlady, who wants to evict him; his estranged son; his ex-wife; and his longtime girlfriend. In addition to the characterization, the novel is notable for the author's wit and his knowledge of the small-town setting.

- *Reckoning with Reagan: America and Its President in the 1980s* (1994), by Michael Schaller, is an even-handed account of the Reagan presidency that gives full measure to Reagan's achievements in restoring confidence to the United States but which also sheds light on the less attractive sides of the Reagan legacy, including the growth of income inequality despite economic recovery and growth.

---

is shown by his willingness to allow a satisfying romantic relationship with his lady friend, Sally Caldwell, to end without the least bit of resistance on his part. In fact, he admits to Sally that at times he feels "beyond affection's grasp." Most important, Frank may even sense and fear that, in addition to physical distance, an emotional distance is gradually separating him from his son, Paul. His ex-wife, Ann, views him as a "half-hearted parent" and suggests that he should think of his children "as a form of self-discovery." By the end of the novel, Ann's advice proves prophetic.

Frank plans the 4th of July/halls of fame weekend trip in order to connect with Paul and help the boy to find his way in the world, but the trip ends up being more a journey of discovery for the father than it is for the son. Frank has brought along two "key 'texts' for communicating" with Paul on this "voyage meant to instruct," Emerson's "Self-Reliance" and Carl Becker's *The Declaration of Independence*. Frank explains: "The impulse to read

Self-Reliance is significant here, as is the holiday itself—my favorite secular one for being public and for its implicit goal of leaving us only as it found us: free." Believing that "independence is . . . what [Paul] lacks—independence from whatever holds him captive: memory, history, bad events he struggles with, can't control, but feels he should," Frank hopes to initiate his son into some of the more useful tenets of his own Existence Period philosophy. But perhaps it is Frank's own gradual emergence from the Existence Period, his growing realization that "laissez-faire is not precisely the same as independence," that "independence and isolation [are] not the same," which allows him to embark on this journey that will take both Paul and himself "From Fragmentation to Unity and Independence."

Frank's pairing of the words "unity" and "independence" is an important one, for it is evidence of his intuitive understanding that true freedom requires strengthening, not severing, ties with others.

In fact, Frank tries to drive this point home to Paul by explaining that the founding fathers "wanted to be free to make new mistakes, not just keep making the same old ones over and over as separate colonies. . . . [Thus] they decided to band together and be independent and were willing to sacrifice some controls they'd always had in hopes of getting something better—in their case, better trade with the outside world." The importance of strengthening ties, of "establishing a greater sense of connectedness," is further emphasized in the novel in a variety of subtle ways: by the pair of tiny ribbon bows which Clarissa, Frank's daughter, gives to her father and brother before they embark on their journey; by the bow tie pasta which Sally Caldwell prepares especially for Frank; and by a seemingly offhand reference which Frank makes to "the poignant line" in Thornton Wilder's nostalgic *Our Town*. Wilder's decidedly American play, of course, is also about making connections—to a family, to a community, and to a nation—and the importance of such connections is expressed by that play's leitmotif, "Blessed Be the Tie That Binds." While *Our Town* depicts a simpler life in the past, Ford's equally American novel depicts "the perilous character of life" in the present time when the ties are becoming frayed, that is, when the most important human connections are in a state of dissolution.

If true independence requires solidarity with others, it also requires surrendering the desire for control and accepting one's connection to the past as a useful guide to living in the present. In his own life, Frank has had his difficulties in all three areas. He maintains a posture of detachment from others; he vacillates between a desire to control life and a desire to surrender to it, and he would like to jettison much of his past. As Frank puts it, "[W]hen you're young your opponent is the future; but when you're not young, your opponent's the past and everything you've done in it and the problem of getting away from it. (My son Paul may be an exception.)" In *The Sportswriter*, Frank had observed that "You can get detached from your beginnings . . . just by life itself, fate, the tug of the everpresent." There is a scene at the Deerslayer Inn in Cooperstown in which Frank discovers a link to the past of which he, as much as Paul, is a captive. The bad memories of a failed marriage and of other events which he regrets and would like to forget all return when he finds an old copy of a book of short stories that he once published. He looks at the photograph on the dust jacket depicting an image of himself as a young writer, an image which may remind the reader of Harry Quinn, a man who chose to reject the past and to live in the moment, and which also serves as a reminder of Ford's view of the writer's "marginality in our culture": "I take a look at the . . . author photo . . . a young man, though this time with a completely unwarranted confidence etched in his skinny mouth, ludicrously holding a beer and smoking a cigarette (!), an empty sun-lit (possibly Mexican) barroom and tables behind, staring fixedly at the camera as though he meant to say: 'Yep, you just about have to live out here in the wild margins to get this puppy done the way God intended. And *you* probably couldn't hack it, if you want to know the gospel.' And I, of course, *couldn't* hack it; chose, in fact, a much easier puppy on a much less wild margin."

Although Frank's peripheral, Existence Period life in the suburbs of New Jersey is considerably "less wild" than either Harry's Mexico or the young Frank's marginalized life as a writer, it is, in its own way, fraught with perils; and Frank is only deceiving himself when he refuses to acknowledge the fact that he is as much a captive of events beyond his control as is his son.

For much of the novel father and son cannot seem to connect. Frank frets about "[n]ot owning the right language" to communicate with a boy who has erected his own protective barriers—his periodic barking noises and his habit of wearing headphones—against human contact. Indeed, in *Independence Day*, there is a great deal of emphasis upon the role that language plays in helping one to achieve or avoid connections with others. As Frank looks over the copy of his old collection of short stories, he takes some satisfaction in the knowledge that the book is "still striving to the purposes I meant it to: staging raids on the inarticulate, being an ax for the frozen sea within us, providing the satisfactions of belief in the general mess of imprecision." As he tries to connect with Paul the next morning, Frank expresses his faith in the affirmative power of language: "My trust has always been that words can make most things better and there's nothing that can't be improved on. But words *are* required." Of course, Frank is also experienced in using language to distance himself from others. The pride that Frank takes in his skillful use of "a form of strategizing pseudo-communication" as a realtor comes to mind, along with his attempts at "pseudo-intimacy" with Sally Caldwell. With Paul, however, Frank's failure to find the right language is quite painful, leaving him as "lonely as a shipwreck." At times even their "oldest-timiest, most reliable, jokey way of conducting father-son business" fails, and their "words get carried off in the breeze, with no one to care if [they] speak the intricate language of love or don't."

After a visit to the Basketball Hall of Fame and a night spent at the Deerslayer, father and son finally begin to make some progress toward meaningful communication; but just as the two seem on the verge of connecting, the trip ends abruptly when Paul is injured in a batting cage accident. The boy steps face-first into a fastball from a pitching machine, a device that represents the many things in life over which we have little or no control. Frank has tried to teach Paul to "let some things go" and surrender to life's uncertainties: "you're trying to keep too much under control, son, and it's holding you back." Ironically, though, Frank himself must relearn that very lesson, and it is the injured Paul who sends his father the message: "Tell my dad he tries to control too much. He worries too much too." Indeed, although Frank has been willing to give in to uncertainty in many areas of his life, he has been as unwilling as Robard Hewes or Harry Quinn to surrender to the affection of another.

As Frank ministers to his injured son, a connection from the past steps from a crowd of onlookers to minister to Frank. It is Irv Ornstein, a step-brother whom he has not seen in twenty-five years. Interestingly, in *The Sportswriter* it was Irv Ornstein who, in a roundabout way, was responsible for helping Frank to connect with his relatives in Florida. Irv offers to drive Frank to the hospital as Paul is taken away in an ambulance, and Frank surrenders to Irv's "full authority." At the hospital where Paul's injuries are treated, Irv and Frank become reacquainted. Irv, it seems, is "going through an 'odd passage' in life" which, in many ways, mirrors Frank's own experience. A designer of flight simulators, Irv feels as if he is living a simulated existence. Like Frank, he is unable to commit to a relationship. As Frank puts it, "[Irv] complains of feeling detached from his own personal history, which has eventuated in a fear . . . that he is diminishing; and if not in an actual physical sense, then definitely in a spiritual one." Once again we have the idea, also expressed by Harry Quinn, that the person who tries to protect himself from life's uncertainties ends up with nothing and, in fact, runs the risk of being absorbed into nothingness. Frank, who himself has occasionally experienced a "'fear of disappearance,'" can easily relate to such feelings; and he concludes that "Irv is entering his own Existence Period, complete with all the good and not-so-good trimmings, just as it seems I'm exiting it in a pitch-and-tumble mode." It is, of course, possible that Frank is merely experiencing an illusion, what he himself refers to as "one of the Existence Period's bedrock paradoxes . . . that just when you think you're emerging, you may actually be wading further in." Nevertheless, Paul's accident and the chance meeting with "Irv-the-solicitous" seem to provide the impetus needed for Frank finally to exit from and advance beyond the Existence Period. As Irv says, "Incidents we can't control make us what we are." Or, as Frank himself says, "[T]here's nothing like tragedy or at least a grave injury or major inconvenience to cut through red tape and bullshit and reveal anyone's best nature." Frank's encounter with Irv might be compared to the reader's encounter with Ford's novel, for just as the feeling of solidarity with the sympathetic Irv seems to release Frank from his isolation, so the reader may be freed from his or her own isolation by the same feeling of solidarity with the author and his characters.

The novel ends on Independence Day, with Frank's having gained independence from his self-imposed isolation and from his fear of emotional engagement. He makes progress toward improving his strained relationship with his ex-wife, Ann, and he proposes that Paul change locations and come to live with him. He even manages to find a suitable location (one of his own rental houses) for the wandering Markhams. "What more can you do for wayward strangers than to shelter them?" he says. More important, Frank reconciles with Sally Caldwell, after a long and intimate telephone conversation during which they discuss "possibilities for commitment." He looks with hope toward the future, to a possible marriage with Sally, and to the "Permanent Period" of his life, which will surely be marked by that "greater sense of connectedness" for which he has been searching.

Frank's reference to the "Permanent Period" echoes a passage from one of Ford's own essays, entitled "Accommodations," in which the author reminisces about spending a large part of his childhood in his grandfather's hotel. "In the hotel," writes Ford, "there was no center to things, nor was I one. . . . I simply stood alongside. . . . And what I thought about it was this: this is the actual life now, not a stopover, a diversion, or an oddment in time, but the permanent life, the one which will provide history, memory, the one I'll be responsible for in the long run." According to Ford, this type of marginalized life, a life without a

Visitors inspect plaques in the Baseball Hall of Fame, where Frank Bascombe takes his son Paul
© Bob Rowan/Progressive Image/Corbis

center, taught him that "Home is finally a variable concept." Such a life, he says, "promotes a cool two-mindedness: one is both steady and in a sea that passes with tides. Accommodation is what's wanted, a replenished idea of permanence and transience . . ." Like Ford himself, Frank Bascombe seems to have developed a certain ambivalence, or "two-mindedness," with respect to his feelings of marginalization. The "Residential Specialist," whose job it is to find accommodations for others, seems to have accommodated himself to the notion that being truly at home may not be possible in a world where human beings so often feel like homeless nomads or castaways. Perhaps a clean, newly renovated "rental" is the best accommodation one could hope for in either a fluctuating realty market or a chaotic world. Indeed, the house that Frank offers to the Markhams, with its "new white metal siding and new three-way windows with plastic screens glistening dully in the sunlight," might be compared to Hemingway's little café, that symbol of light and order in "A Clean, Well-Lighted Place." While Frank may seem as resigned to his fate as any Hemingway hero, at the same time he discovers that a "homey connectedness" with others might be available even on the wildest margins, and that whatever

permanence is possible in this impermanent world derives more from that sense of connectedness than from any sense of place. Frank asks: "[Is] there any cause to think a place—any place—within its plaster and joists, its trees and plantings, in its putative essence *ever* shelters some spirit ghost of us as proof of its significance and ours?" His answer: "No! Not one bit! Only other humans do that . . ."

The final scene of *Independence Day* suggests that the best way to deal with life's marginality is to reach out to the other marginal people in the darkness. The novel's closing calls to mind a scene toward the conclusion of Walker Percy's *The Moviegoer*, in which Binx Boiling, when asked what he plans to do with his life, replies: "There is only one thing I can do: listen to people, see how they stick themselves into the world, hand them along a ways in their dark journey and be handed along, and for good and selfish reasons." In what is perhaps the most moving passage in Ford's fiction, and the author's own testament to the "efficacy of telling" ("The Three Kings"), Frank is awakened from a sound sleep in the middle of the night by a ringing telephone. Most likely it is Paul on the line, but the caller is less important than the fact that Frank responds with healing words and with what he once referred to as "the real stuff," the *"silent intimacies . . .* of the fervently understood and sympathized with." The passage clearly shows how far Frank's journey has taken him. And for the Ford reader who may also take consolation from the healing words of a gifted writer at the height of his power, it represents a fitting culmination to everything that the author has written thus far:

> And when I said hello from the darkness, there was a moment I took to be dead silence on the line, though gradually I heard a breath, then the sound of a receiver touching what must've been a face. There was a sigh, and the sound of someone going, "Ssss, tsss. Uh-huh, uh-huh," followed by an even deeper and less certain "Ummm."

> And I suddenly said, because someone was there I felt I knew, "I'm glad you called." I pressed the receiver to my ear and opened my eyes in the dark. "I just got here," I said. "Now's not a bad time at all. This is a full-time job. Let me hear your thinking. I'll try to add a part to the puzzle. It can be simpler than you think."

> Whoever was there—and of course I don't know who, really—breathed again two times, three. Then the breath grew thin and brief. I heard another sound, "Uh-huh." Then our connection was gone, and even before I'd put down the phone I'd returned to the deepest sleep imaginable.

> And I am in the crowd just as the drums are passing— always the last in line—their *boom-boom-boom*ing in my ears and all around. I see the sun above the street, breathe in the day's rich, warm smell. Someone calls out, "Clear a path, make room, make room, please!" The trumpets go again. My heartbeat quickens. I feel the push, pull, the weave and sway of others.

In his dream, Frank is no longer alone on the periphery of life. Instead, he is a bystander among bystanders, a castaway among castaways, immersed in the great current of human experience and excited by the infinite possibilities that it offers. The dream is another sign that the Existence Period of his life has ended, and the Permanent Period has begun.

Source: Huey Guagliardo, "Marginal People in Ford's Novels," in *Perspectives on Richard Ford*, edited by Huey Guagliardo, University Press of Mississippi, 2000, pp. 21–32.

Sources

Ford, Richard, *Independence Day*, Alfred A. Knopf, 1995.

Giles, Jeff, "Seems like Old Times," in *Newsweek*, June 12, 1995, p. 64.

Gray, Paul, "Return of the Sportswriter," in *Time*, June 19, 1995, p. 60.

Johnson, Charles, "Stuck in the Here and Now," in *New York Times Book Review*, Vol. 100, June 18, 1995, p. 28.

Review of *Independence Day*, in *Publishers Weekly*, Vol. 242, No. 17, April 24, 1995, p. 59.

Further Reading

Chernecky, William G., "'Nostalgia Isn't What It Used to Be': Isolation and Alienation in the Frank Bascombe Novels," in *Perspectives on Richard Ford*, edited by Huey Guagliardo, University Press of Mississippi, 2000, pp. 157–76.
  Chernecky offers an analysis of *The Sportswriter* and *Independence Day*. In the former, Frank Bascombe has a solipsistic worldview that alienates him from the world around him and deprives him of seeing any meaning in life. In the latter, he has mellowed and is less judgmental and solipsistic. He is able to create bridges in order to reach other people.

Hobson, Fred, "Richard Ford and Josephine Humphreys: Walker Percy in New Jersey and Charleston," in *The Southern Writer in the Postmodern World*, University of Georgia Press, 1991, pp. 41–72.
  Hobson sees in Ford's narrator, Frank Bascombe, a continuation of the tradition of the cerebral southern narrator found in the novels of William Faulkner, Robert Penn Warren, and others. Hobson argues that Bascombe is fascinated by the past, by family, and by place, even though he tries to persuade the reader that he is not.

Lee, Don, "About Richard Ford," in *Ploughshares*, Vol. 22, No. 2–3, Fall 1996, pp. 226–35.
  This article presents an overview of Ford's life and work, up to and including *Independence Day*.

Walker, Elinor Ann, *Richard Ford*, Twayne's United States Authors Series, No. 718, Twayne, 2000, pp. 133–76.
  This lengthy analysis of *Independence Day* includes an examination of how Ford explores the nature of language. Characters use both the power and the imprecision of words to connect or to distance themselves from each other.

No-No Boy

John Okada
1957

No-No Boy, by John Okada, was first published in 1957. Set in Seattle after the end of World War II, it tells the story of Ichiro Yamada, a young Japanese American who refused to serve in the U.S. armed forces during the war and was consequently imprisoned for two years. Now, following his release, Ichiro regrets the decision he made and fears that as a "no-no" boy he has no future in the United States, in spite of the fact that he was born and educated there. During the two weeks in his life described in the novel, he gradually learns to put aside his self-hatred and rediscover a sense of hope and belonging.

No-No Boy made little impact on first publication, but interest in the novel grew in the 1970s, and in the early 2000s, it was established as one of the classic, pioneering Asian American novels. It opens a window on the Japanese American experience in the immediate postwar period, particularly on the generational conflict between the Issei (the first generation of Japanese immigrants, who were born in Japan) and the Nisei (the second generation, born in the United States), and the struggles of the Nisei to come to terms with their dual heritage. As such, the novel has relevance for the experience of many immigrant communities in the United States.

Author Biography

John Okada was born in Seattle, Washington, in September 1923, of Japanese American parents.

John Okada University of Washington Press, 2001. Reproduced by permission

He attended Broadway High School, but his college education at the University of Washington was interrupted by World War II, during which Okada's family was interned in Idaho because they were Japanese American. Okada volunteered for service in the U.S. Air Force. He served in army intelligence, translating Japanese radio transmissions and dropping propaganda leaflets over Japanese-held islands in the South Pacific. He was discharged in 1946 with the rank of sergeant.

Okada completed his education after the war, graduating with a Bachelor of Arts from the University of Washington and a Master of Arts degree in sociology from Columbia University in 1949. After this he returned to Washington and earned a Bachelor of Arts degree in library science. He worked in the business reference department of the Seattle Public Library and then moved to Detroit to take up a better paid position in the Detroit Public Library. He also worked as a technical writer for Chrysler Missile Operations in Michigan. During this time, Okada worked on writing fiction, resulting in the publication of his novel, *No-No Boy*, in 1957. The novel had no immediate impact. Okada then began work on a second novel, which focused on the experiences of the Issei, the first generation of Japanese to immigrate to the United

States. He was never able to complete it. In the late 1960s, Okada served briefly as head of the circulation department at the University of California, Los Angeles.

Okada died of a heart attack on February 20, 1971, at the age of forty-seven. He was survived by his wife, Dorothy, whom he met at Columbia University in the late 1940s, as well as a son and a daughter. After his death, his wife offered all his papers to the Japanese American Research Project at the University of California, Los Angeles. But the project refused to take an interest, and Okada's wife then burned the papers, which included the almost complete first draft of Okada's second novel.

It was only after his death that Okada's work began to be recognized. As of 2006, he was acknowledged as a powerful early voice in the recording and interpreting of Asian American experience.

Plot Summary

Preface

No-No Boy begins with a preface which explains that after the Japanese attack on Pearl Harbor on December 7, 1941, Japanese in the United States became the objects of hostility and suspicion. They were rounded up and sent to internment camps.

Chapter 1

In Seattle just after the end of World War II, Ichiro Yamada, a twenty-five-year-old Japanese American, steps off a bus. He has just returned home from two years in an internment camp for Japanese Americans and two years in prison for refusing to join the U.S. armed forces. As he walks down the street, he does not feel at home. An old Japanese American friend named Eto greets him. Eto served in the U.S. Army, and he turns hostile when he learns that Ichiro is a "no-no" boy. He said no to serving in the U.S. armed forces and also refused to swear allegiance to the United States. Ichiro turns away and continues walking along the street until he reaches home, a cramped space behind a grocery store, where his mother, father, and younger brother Taro live. His father greets him warmly, and then his mother returns from the bakery.

Ichiro is bitter about his experience. He feels he made the wrong choice and should have fought for the United States, the land of his birth, and he blames his mother for his wrong choice. He is at odds with both his parents, who have lived in the United States for thirty-five years but speak only Japanese. He is especially resentful of his mother. She insists on believing that Japan won the war and that a ship will soon be sent to take them back to Japan. Ichiro thinks his mother is crazy. He feels he is neither Japanese nor American, and this distresses him. He blames himself as well as his mother. Taro resents him; he plans to go into the army instead of college. The two brothers are like strangers to each other.

That evening Ichiro and his mother visit another Japanese family, the Ashidas. Like Ichiro's mother, Mrs. Ashida believes that Japan won the war and a Japanese ship will take them back to Japan. Ichiro loathes her, and he persuades his mother that they should leave since it is getting late. They visit another Japanese family, the Kumasakas, who have purchased a home and seem reconciled to living in the United States. Ichiro inquires about their son Bob. He does not know that Bob was killed in the war, fighting in the U.S. Army. An army buddy of Bob's named Jun explains how Bob was killed in action.

As they leave, Ichiro again reviews his reasons for not joining the army. He decides he was weak and unable to do what he should have done. Returning home at midnight, he finds his father, who has been drinking, still up. He says he has been celebrating Ichiro's return. Ichiro finds out that unlike his mother, his father does not believe that Japan won the war. He has letters from relatives in Japan begging for help, asking for money, clothing, and food.

Chapter 2

At breakfast the next morning, Mrs. Yamada tells Ichiro that in reality it is Bob's mother who is dead since she did not conduct herself like a Japanese, and since she is no longer Japanese, she is the equivalent of being dead. She insists that she and her husband remain Japanese and that Ichiro is Japanese, too. Angry, Ichiro calls her crazy, grips her wrists and starts to drag her across the room. When his father intervenes, Ichiro strikes him, knocking him against the wall. He immediately apologizes, and his father understands why Ichiro is so angry. He gives Ichiro money so he can visit his friend, Freddie. Freddie, who has been out of prison for five weeks and has developed a defiant attitude, is pleased to see him.

Chapter 3

Ichiro leaves Freddie and walks down the street, trying to determine his place in the United States, where he was born and educated. He hopes that over time there will be a place for him; he will buy a home and have a family. Remembering when he studied engineering at the university, he takes the bus to the campus, where he visits Baxter Brown, his former teacher. The professor encourages him to return to his studies, but Ichiro is disappointed with their superficial conversation. He stops to buy a hamburger and encounters his friend Kenji, who has lost a leg in the war. Ichiro tells him he does not plan to enroll at the university. They walk to Kenji's new Oldsmobile, which has been specially redesigned so he can drive it. It was given to him by the federal government, in addition to education and pension benefits, because of the injury he received in combat. However, Kenji's leg has gangrene and may still kill him. Nonetheless, Ichiro would willingly change places with him because at least Kenji has become fully American. Ichiro returns home where his father is trying to persuade Taro, whose eighteenth birthday it is, to finish high school before he joins the army. Taro and Ichiro exchange angry words, and Taro storms out of the house.

Chapter 4

That evening, Kenji and Ichiro go to a casino in the Chinatown area of the city and then to a drinking club. Kenji tells him not to keep blaming himself. As the club fills up, a Japanese man, Bull, greets Kenji warmly but insults Ichiro, since he knows Ichiro is a no-no boy. Other young Japanese laugh at him, and Ichiro notices Taro in the club, too. Angry, Ichiro drinks some more and then follows Taro outside, since Taro says he wants to talk to him. He walks into a trap. In an alley, two youths accost him and insult him for being Japanese. One of the youths kicks him, and he stumbles. Ichiro fights back but is thrown to the ground. Kenji intervenes and drives the two youths away. He and Ichiro drive off in Kenji's car. They stop at a small farmhouse just outside the city, where Kenji's Japanese friend Emi lives. She has been virtually deserted by her husband, Ralph, who is determined to remain with the U.S. Army in Germany. By his physical appearance, Ichiro reminds her of her husband, and that night they sleep together. The next morning she tries to encourage him to put all his bitterness behind him, identify with being an American, and take action to create a better future for himself.

Chapter 5

When Ichiro returns home, he has another harsh exchange with his mother who does not want him to see Kenji again. His father then reads her a letter from her sister in Japan, who writes of the hardship they are enduring and asks them to send food for the children. Mrs. Yamada does not believe the letter is from her sister, and she goes and sits silently in the bedroom. Ichiro thinks she may no longer be sure that Japan won the war. At lunch time she refuses to eat, and her husband worries about her.

Chapter 6

Kenji returns home, where he greets his father. Father and son, who respect and love each other, share a drink, but the father feels the pain of knowing his son may soon die. While Kenji naps, his father goes out and buys a chicken for roasting. Kenji's sister Hanako and his brother Tom arrives. It is a happy family, but they are all worried about Kenji. After dinner, Kenji's married sisters, Hisa and Toyo, arrive with their husbands and children. The family gathering is lively, but Kenji slips out at about ten, planning to drive overnight with Ichiro to the hospital in Portland, Oregon. As they drive to Portland, they are stopped for speeding, but Kenji throws the ticket away. He believes that he does not have long to live.

Chapter 7

After saying goodbye to Kenji, Ichiro takes a hotel room and searches for a job. He is interviewed for a position as draftsman in a small engineering office. The pleasant owner of the company, Mr. Carrick, has a favorable view of the Japanese, and he offers Ichiro the job on the spot. The pay is good, but Ichiro cannot bring himself to accept it straightaway. He explains that he was in jail for refusing the draft. Mr. Carrick reacts sympathetically, but Ichiro has already decided that the job should go to someone who is fully American. He returns to the hotel to sleep but wakes in the middle of the night and goes to a café, where he rebuffs the attempts of the waiter, a Japanese American who is a U.S. Army veteran, to befriend him. In the morning, he drives to the hospital to visit Kenji, who tells him that he is dying. Kenji tells Ichiro to go back to Seattle and stay there until people learn to leave him alone. Ichiro returns to Seattle immediately and visits Emi, who tells him that her Japanese neighbor would offer him work, but Ichiro is not interested. There is an attraction between Emi and Ichiro, but Ichiro will not act on it because he believes Emi's husband will soon return from Germany.

Chapter 8

Ichiro's mother has not eaten for two days and is behaving strangely. Her husband is worried about her but can do nothing to help. She goes to the bathroom and runs the water for a bath, while Mr. Yamada drinks whisky and recalls the happy early days of their courtship. At nine o'clock in the evening, Ichiro drives to Kenji's home, where Kenji's father informs him that Kenji died at three o'clock that afternoon. After they grieve together for a while, Ichiro returns home to find his mother has drowned in the tub. He rouses his father, who has fallen into a drunken sleep, and informs him of his mother's suicide.

Chapter 9

The Buddhist funeral is held several days later. Friends and relatives gather, and Mr. Yamada even seems to be enjoying the situation. Ichiro feels awkward; the ceremony means little to him, and he is embarrassed by the speeches made in praise of his mother. Leaving before the funeral is over, he meets up with Freddie, who is living recklessly so that he never has to think much about his own unhappiness. Freddie tells him that he would be able to get a job at the Christian Reclamation Center, a charitable community. Ichiro goes home and receives a visit from Emi, who has heard about the deaths of Kenji and Ichiro's mother. She says she is divorcing her husband at his request. They go out dancing together, and a man they do not know buys them a drink. When Ichiro returns home early in the morning, he finds his father preparing a parcel to send to Japan. He seems relieved that his wife is no longer alive to dictate to him what he should do.

Chapter 10

Ichiro goes to the Christian Reclamation Center, where the man in charge, Mr. Morrison, offers him a job even though Ichiro confesses that he evaded the draft. Ichiro says he will think about it and talks to Gary, a friend of his who works there and who also refused the draft. Gary enjoys his work and feels that his life is on the right track. After Ichiro says he is going to turn the job down, Gary tells him about the prejudice he faced in his previous job at a foundry. Ichiro takes the bus home, thinking about his situation and seeing a ray of hope because of the goodness he has encountered in some people.

Chapter 11

Freddie and Ichiro go to the shoe shine parlor and then to a pool hall, where Freddie causes trouble and they have to leave. After this, Ichiro suggests they go back to his house, but Freddie wants to go to the Club Oriental, even though he knows there are people there who are out to get him. At the club, Bull picks a fight with Freddie and drags him outside. Ichiro intervenes and bloodies Bull's nose. Freddie digs his heel into Bull's stomach. Freddie then runs to his car and drives away recklessly. He hits another car, goes into the wall of a building, and is killed. Ichiro apologizes to Bull, who is howling and crying. Ichiro walks away feeling hopeful about the future.

Characters

Freddie Akimoto

Freddie Akimoto is a Japanese American friend of Ichiro. Like Ichiro, Freddie has just returned to Seattle, although whether he was in an internment camp or a prison is not stated. Freddie now has a defiant attitude. He lives recklessly, filling his time with activities such as drinking, fighting, womanizing, playing poker, and going to the movies. He lives this way to distract himself from his own unhappiness. Ichiro thinks Freddie is just running away from reality, but Freddie thinks Ichiro is stuck in a rut. Freddie is killed after he gets involved in a fight at the Club Oriental and drives off recklessly.

Mrs. Ashida

Mrs. Ashida and her husband come from the same village in Japan as the Yamadas. The two families are friends. Agreeing with Mrs. Yamada's sympathies, Mrs. Ashida's loyalties are to Japan. Mrs. Ashida believes that Japan won the war.

Birdie

Birdie is a black man who defends Gary at the foundry when the other workers are hostile to him.

Professor Baxter Brown

Baxter Brown is a professor of engineering at the university and Ichiro's former teacher. He encourages Ichiro to resume his studies.

Bull

Bull is a loud and rough Japanese American who is friendly to Kenji but not to Ichiro or Freddie.

He and Freddie twice get into a fight at the Club Oriental.

Mr. Carrick

Mr. Carrick is the owner of the small engineering business to which Ichiro applies for a job. He is a decent man who likes Japanese people. He tells Ichiro that the internment of Japanese during the war was a big mistake and a black mark in the annals of U.S. history. When Ichiro confesses that he refused the draft, Mr. Carrick is sympathetic and tells Ichiro not to blame himself. Mr. Carrick's kindness and generosity help to give Ichiro hope that he may have a future in the United States.

Emi

Emi is an attractive, twenty-seven-year-old Japanese American whose husband, Ralph, is stationed with the U.S. Army in Germany and shows no signs of wanting to return. Ichiro is introduced to Emi by Kenji. He and Emi sleep together, and Emi gives Ichiro sound and encouraging advice about how he can move forward in his life. When she hears that her husband wants a divorce, she again seeks out Ichiro's company, and they go dancing together. She is a positive influence on Ichiro.

Gary

Gary is a Japanese American friend of Ichiro. He works as a sign painter at the Christian Reclamation Center. He enjoys his work and wants to become an artist. Like Ichiro, he has served time in prison, but unlike his friend he regards it as the best thing that happened to him because it enabled him to sort out his goals. He realizes that he has wasted a lot of time but now he believes he is moving in a positive direction.

Hanako Kanno

Hanako Kanno, Kenji's sister, works as a bookkeeper in an office in Seattle.

Kenji Kanno

Kenji Kanno is a young Japanese American who volunteered to fight in World War II. He was wounded and lost most of his leg and was awarded the Silver Star. The U.S. government has rewarded his sacrifice by giving him a new car, specially designed so he can drive it, as well as education and pension benefits. However, Kenji's wound is gangrenous, and he knows he may die soon. But he faces his fate with courage. What most upsets him is not his own condition but the bigotry, meanness, and racial prejudice he observes in others, attitudes that are foreign to his own nature. Kenji is a friendly, well-adjusted man, generous and level-headed, who is liked and respected by everyone. He comes from a close-knit, affectionate family, and he tries to help others, including his friends Emi and Ichiro, who is in every way his opposite. Kenji dies in the hospital in Portland.

Mr. Kanno

Mr. Kanno is Kenji's father, a good-hearted man who is close to his son and allowed him to volunteer for service in the U.S. armed forces. Mr. Kanno originally came to the United States to get rich and then return to Japan, but he eventually got used to and appreciated the fact that he could create a life for himself and his family there. After his wife died, he was left to raise six small children, which he did with much struggle. Now the children are grown, and he is comfortably off, although he grieves about the wound his son suffered in the war.

Tom Kanno

Tom Kanno, Kenji's brother, works as a drafter at an aircraft plant and is a baseball fan.

Mr. Kumasaka

Mr. Kumasaka and his wife are friends of the Yamada family. Unlike the Ashidas, Mr. and Mrs. Kumasaka have bought a house and are reconciled to staying in the United States. Their son Bob was killed fighting for the United States in the war, and they are still grief-stricken.

Eto Minato

Eto Minato is an old acquaintance of Ichiro. When the two meet after the war, Eto, who has been in the U.S. Army, is friendly to Ichiro until he finds out that Ichiro did not serve. Then he insults him and spits on him. Freddie later says that Eto was only in the army six months and then wangled himself a medical discharge.

Mr. Morrison

Mr. Morrison is the good-natured employer at the Christian Reclamation Center. He enjoys working in a job that allows him to help people, and he offers Ichiro a job without hesitation.

Rabbit

Rabbit is a black man who works at the shoe shine parlor.

Ichiro Yamada

Ichiro Yamada is the twenty-five-year-old Japanese American "no-no" boy of the title. He was born in the United States to first-generation Japanese immigrants and had begun his education in engineering at the university in Seattle when the war interrupted his plans. He was interned by the U.S. government, and partly out of loyalty to his Japanese mother and partly because he lacked the courage to do what he felt was the right thing, he refused to serve in the U.S. Army. As a result, he served two years in prison.

When he returns to Seattle after the war, he is confused, not knowing his place in the United States. Facing hostility from Japanese Americans such as Eto and Bull, Ichiro is filled with self-hatred and blames himself for his predicament. He is at odds with his own family, especially his mother, whom he thinks is crazy, and he regards his father as a weak man for whom he has no respect. He does not mourn his mother's death. Ichiro is also at loggerheads with his younger brother, Taro.

Ichiro feels more American than Japanese, but he also feels that he does not belong to either country. His feelings of guilt and his apparent need to go on suffering for his mistake prevent him from accepting an excellent job offer in Portland, since he convinces himself that the job should go to someone who is fully American in a way he can never be.

For two weeks, Ichiro stumbles along, experiencing deep introspective moods in which he ponders how he got into this mess and whether he will ever have a decent life in the United States. He is fortunate in that he encounters a number of people who are kind to him and give him helpful advice, such as Kenji and Emi, both of whom tell him not to blame himself. He also meets helpful, pro-Japanese employers who offer him a chance to get his life moving forward again. Finally, he begins to feel a glimmer of hope that he can one day become fully a part of the diverse community that populates the United States.

Mr. Yamada

Mr. Yamada, Ichiro's father, is a weak man, dominated by his strong-willed wife. Unlike her, he does not believe that Japan won the war, but he exerts little effort to tell her the truth. He regards her as a sick woman and worries about her, feeling that perhaps he is in some way partly responsible for her sickness. Mr. Yamada is a well-meaning man who tries to befriend his son, but Ichiro's opinion of him is scathing: "Pa's okay, but he's a nobody. He's a [g— d——], fat, grinning, spineless nobody." Mr. Yamada's main weakness is alcohol. On the night his wife commits suicide, he slowly drinks himself into a stupor. After her death and at the funeral, he seems more relieved than in mourning.

Mrs. Yamada

Mrs. Yamada, Ichiro's fanatical mother, rigidly maintains her allegiance to Japan and insists on believing that Japan won the war. She despises the United States even though she has lived there for thirty-five years. She refuses to learn or speak English and refers to Japanese Americans who serve in the U.S. armed forces and Japanese people who do not conduct themselves as Japanese as already dead. Mrs. Yamada entirely dominates her husband, who is too weak to stand up to her, and her relationship with Ichiro is full of tension. He rejects her completely, regarding her as insane. Eventually, when she receives a letter from her sister in Japan, it becomes impossible for her to believe any longer that Japan won the war. But she will not admit that openly. Instead, she retreats to her bedroom, refuses to eat, and exhibits signs of extreme psychological disturbance, such as lining cans up on the shelves and then hurling them to the floor, repacking them in boxes and then going through the whole procedure again. Eventually she commits suicide by drowning herself in the bathtub.

Taro Yamada

Taro Yamada, Ichiro's younger brother, is just eighteen. He is restless and refuses to study. He is determined to defy his parents' wishes and join the U.S. Army rather than go to college. He dislikes his brother because of Ichiro's refusal to serve in the armed forces, and he even leads Ichiro into a trap outside the Club Oriental, where two thugs try to beat him up.

Themes

Generational Conflict

The novel presents a type of generational conflict that is peculiar to immigrant families. The older, first generation parents identify with their country of origin, whereas the younger generation born in the new country identifies with it rather than the ancestral home. So it is with Ichiro Yamada, but in this case the generational conflict is sharpened by the facts of war.

When Ichiro is asked the two questions in the internment camp, he does not have the courage, maturity, or self-knowledge to answer what he truly feels in his heart. His real allegiance lies with the United States, but he holds back from stating it because he cannot free himself from the powerful influence of his mother, who will not allow him to develop an identity separate from hers. Her love is conditional. She says she is proud to call him her son, but he knows this is only because of his refusal to serve in the U.S. armed forces. Had he made a different decision, she would have rejected him. For her, there can be no compromise. She is incapable of seeing a situation from any point of view other than her own. She may think that she loves her son, but she is in effect smothering him, trying to make him deny who he really is. In return, all Ichiro can offer her is hostility, bitterness, and rage. His mother now is as much of a stranger to him as Japan, her country of origin that he has never seen. They literally speak different languages. The conflict can only be resolved by his mother's death, and Ichiro feels no grief at her passing.

Ichiro has no respect for his father either and regards him as weak. But his father is not as fanatical as his mother and is prepared to allow Ichiro, and also Ichiro's younger brother Taro, to go their own ways. His reasonableness in this respect allows him to maintain at least a semblance of a relationship with his son, and after the death of his wife, there is a hint that Ichiro and his father may develop a more genuine bond of sympathy.

The familial conflicts which afflict Ichiro are sharply contrasted with the bonds of love and affection that bind Kenji and his family together. Kenji's father accepted Kenji's decision to join the army, although it was not what he would have wished. But his flexibility and wisdom allow their family to remain united, without rancor, in contrast to the bitter divisions that tear the Yamada family apart.

Assimilation and Overcoming Self-blame

Despite his Japanese heritage, Ichiro knows in his heart that he is American. He knows also that when he answered no to the two questions in the internment camp he was not being true to who he

Topics For Further Study

- Conduct some interviews with some first- and second-generation immigrants from any country, either from your school or the local community, and make a class presentation on the different attitudes each generation has to its country of origin and to the United States. How do the second-generation immigrants, born as U.S. citizens, regard the United States? Do they make efforts to learn about the culture of their parents?

- Asian immigrants are sometimes known as the model minority. Research this expression. What does it mean and why are Asians thought to embody it? Is the term accurate? Do Asian immigrants succeed more consistently than, say, Hispanic immigrants? If so, why should this be? Write an essay in which you describe your research and present some conclusions.

- Write an essay in which you examine how the Kanno family is presented in chapter 6 of the novel. How does Mr. Kanno's life embody the American dream? How does his family reflect the ideal of Japanese immigrant assimilation of mainstream American culture?

- Write a letter to the editor of a newspaper, warning readers of the dangers, in the current U.S. war on terror, of treating Arab Americans or Muslim Americans any differently from any other group of American citizens. As a main part of your letter, use the example of the unjustified internment of Japanese Americans in the 1940s. Include pertinent facts and relate them to the present situation in the United States.

---

really is. He makes his feelings plain early in the novel, when he first returns home:

> [O]ne is not born in America and raised in America and taught in America and one does not speak and swear and drink and smoke and play and fight and see and hear in America among Americans in American streets and houses without becoming American and loving it.

His task now is to integrate American mainstream life. But he faces a double barrier. Not only does he have to convince white Americans that he is a true American, he also faces hostility from other Japanese Americans who despise him for being a "no-no" boy. During the two weeks in which the novel takes place, Ichiro embarks on an inner journey in which he must convince himself that a life in the United States, as an American, is possible for him. Having once turned his back on himself and the country that he knows is his, he must learn to face them both again. He must overcome his tendency to blame himself for his predicament and also his own feeling that he, having once rejected the United States, is now forever unacceptable to it. Time and again, he encounters

people, especially the employers Mr. Carrick and Mr. Morrison, as well as Kenji and Emi, who show him that the United States is in fact a land of generosity, compassion, and inclusiveness. These people are far less concerned about the choice Ichiro made in the internment camp than he is himself. His actions then do not matter to them, and they show him only kindness and affection. By the end of the novel, Ichiro has made progress toward the realization that his troubles are of his own making. He is ready to make a free choice to accept his rightful place, knowing that the United States is a vast community in which injustice and hatred certainly exist, but which also offers the possibility of forgiveness and a new start for those who have lost their way.

Style

Setting

The novel gives a realistic picture of the Japanese immigrant area of Seattle, which includes

Jackson Street, where Ichiro and his family live, and extends from Fifth to Twelfth Avenue. Known as "Japanese town," it is adjacent to another immigrant area known as Chinatown. Both areas are known for the prevalence of gambling, prostitution, and drinking. They are also impoverished and have gotten worse in the four years Ichiro has been away: "Everything looked older and dirtier and shabbier." In Chinatown, the brick buildings are "more black than red with age and neglect." The young people in these areas spend their time aimlessly in the pool halls, the cafés, and the taverns, although they seem not to lack ready cash to enjoy themselves in the evenings.

The home of Ichiro's parents, behind the grocery store they own, is "a hole in the wall with groceries crammed in orderly confusion on not enough shelving, into not enough space." The cramped, inadequate quarters reflect the difficult lives of first-generation immigrants who have had to struggle and make do with little as they tried to establish themselves in a new country. The Ashidas, friends of the Yamadas, also live in less than ideal circumstances. They have only four rooms, on the second floor of a three-story house, in which two adults and three children live together. In a telling detail, the living room is described as "sparsely furnished." The Kumasakas, by contrast, live in more prosperous circumstances, in a "freshly painted frame house" with a "neatly kept lawn." The details are significant because this family has shown more willingness to assimilate American culture. They have decided to stay in the country permanently, and their son fought and died for the United States in the war. As a result of this assimilation, their home "is like millions of other homes in America."

Historical Context

Internment of Japanese Americans

After the surprise Japanese attack on Pearl Harbor on December 7, 1941, the U.S. government considered that Japanese Americans were a threat to national security because they might support Japan rather than the United States. Much of this suspicion was fueled by racism, the belief that Japanese immigrants were somehow different and could never be fully American. The American fear of Japanese immigrants was evident historically in a law passed in 1924 that prohibited intermarriage between Japanese men and white women. There was also a prohibition on Japanese immigrants sponsoring wives from Japan.

Convinced by his advisors that Japanese Americans were being recruited as spies, President Franklin D. Roosevelt issued Executive Order 9066 on February 19, 1942. The order revoked the civil rights of Japanese Americans, despite the fact that two-thirds of them were U.S. citizens. About 112,000 Japanese Americans from all over the Pacific coast were rounded up and sent to internment camps in nine states. Most of the camps were built on Native American reservations.

The internment was a devastating experience for the Japanese, since they were forced to quickly abandon their homes and businesses. It also damaged their culture. The Japanese are a self-reliant people, but in the camps they were forced to depend on the U.S. government to meet their basic needs. The internment was especially hard on the Issei, the first generation immigrants, many of whom, like the Yamada family in *No-No Boy*, had been living in the United States for thirty or forty years. They lost everything they had worked for.

In January 1943, the U.S. government decided to recruit second-generation Japanese immigrants into an all-Japanese combat unit. All males in the internment camps were required to answer a series of questions, which included whether they were willing to serve in the U.S. armed forces and whether they would swear allegiance to the United States, defend the country against any attack, and renounce obedience to the Japanese emperor. Most of the internees answered yes to these questions, giving the lie to the idea that all Japanese immigrants were threats to national security. However, several hundred, including Ichiro in *No-No Boy*, did not, and they were sent to prison for disloyalty.

In 1944, the Supreme Court upheld the Executive Order 9066, but the U.S. government finally rescinded it on January 2, 1945. All Japanese American prisoners were released from the internment camps. In 1988, the U.S. Congress passed a law that provided for payment of twenty thousand dollars each to the surviving Japanese-American victims of internment.

Japanese American Literature in the 1950s

In the 1950s, the United States was generally unwilling to face up to what had happened to

Compare
&
Contrast

- **1940s:** In 1945, the Japanese American 442nd Regimental Combat team is awarded 18,143 Medals of Valor and 9,486 Purple Hearts, making it the highest decorated military unit in U.S. history.

  Today: Americans of Japanese descent make their mark in many fields of activity. In 1999, General Eric Shinseki becomes the thirty-fourth chief of staff, United States Army, and serves in that position until his retirement in 2003.

- **1940s:** In 1945, defeated Japan is forced to accept U.S. occupation. Those Japanese considered war criminals are tried and hanged. Japan is given a constitution and the work of reconstruction begins. Japan no longer possesses a Pacific empire.

  Today: Japan is a staunch U.S. ally and a major economic power in Asia and globally.

- **1940s:** After release from internment, many Japanese Americans move to parts of the country other than the West and Northwest Coast in order to restart their lives.

  Today: The number of Japanese Americans in the United States is approximately 1,148,000. The largest communities remain in California and Washington, but there are also sizable Japanese American communities in New York, Texas, Illinois, Oregon, Colorado, Pennsylvania, New Jersey, and Florida. Each year, about seven thousand Japanese immigrants enter the United States.

Japanese Americans during World War II. It was considered more important to present a picture of the United States in which nonwhite immigrants were able to integrate into the mainstream culture. This was during the cold war between the West and the Soviet Union, and the cultivation of an optimistic image of the United States was considered necessary in countering Soviet charges of U.S. economic and racial inequalities. The U.S. postwar alliance with Japan was also a factor. Given this political and cultural environment, the type of Japanese American literature favored by mainstream publishers was mostly innocuous autobiographical accounts of immigrants who told of their struggle as newcomers to establish themselves in U.S. society and the success and assimilation of their children. Monica Sone's autobiographical *Nisei Daughter* (1953), which was a commercial success, told of her experience during internment, but she was careful to present an image of Japanese Americans that she believed would be acceptable to white Americans. She made it clear, for example, that she regarded the United States rather than Japan as her home and that Japanese immigrants were fully capable of assimilating American life. More challenging accounts of race relations in the United States were left to African American authors, with the publication, for example, of Ralph Ellison's *Invisible Man* (1952). It was for these reasons that it took two decades before *No-No Boy*, a more controversial, hard-hitting account of the Japanese American experience than *Nisei Daughter*, won a wide readership.

Critical Overview

When *No-No Boy* was published by mainstream publisher Charles E. Tuttle in 1957, it was largely ignored by both the literary establishment and the Japanese American community. The latter had yet to come to grips with the Japanese American experience of internment during World War II and the controversial issues of racial and national identity that are at the core of the novel. At the time of Okada's death, fourteen years later, some of the fifteen hundred copies printed remained unsold.

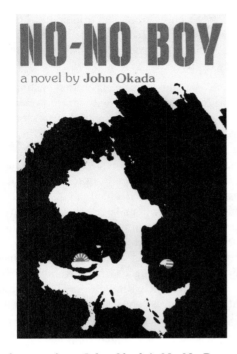

Book cover from John Okada's No-No Boy

University Of Washington Press, 2001. Copyright © 1976 By Dorothy Okada. Reproduced by permission

However, in the 1970s, the novel was rediscovered by a group of Asian American writers, including Jeffrey Paul Chan, Frank Chin, David Ishii, and Lawson Fusao Inada. They realized that *No-No Boy* was an important milestone in Asian American literature, as well as a powerful novel in its own right. Thanks to the work of the Combined Asian American Research Project, *No-No Boy* was reprinted in 1976 and quickly acquired wide readership and critical acclaim. Inada, writing in 1976, calls *No-No Boy* "a great and lasting work of art. It is a *living* force among us. And it is just one of the many beautiful and courageous stories of the continuing story of what we know as Asian-America." Over the following thirty years, the novel continued to attract the attention of scholars. In "To Belong or Not to Belong: The Liminality of John Okada's *No-No Boy*," William Yeh comments on the "enduring relevance of Okada's work, an honest and uncompromising, occasionally didactic and melodramatic, examination of the aftereffects of the World War II draft resistance by *Nisei* (second-generation Japanese Americans)." Yeh analyzes both the novel itself and the reception it received in terms of "liminality, or 'betweenness,'" in the sense of standing not fully in either American or Japanese culture. The relationship between Ichiro and his mother has attracted interest from psychoanalytic critics. Bryn Gribben, in "The Mother That Won't Reflect Back: Situating Psychoanalysis and the Japanese Mother in *No-No Boy*," points out that many of the elements in *No-No Boy* can be explained in terms of psychoanalysis:

> the controlling mother, her refusal to look into a mirror with her son and face their separateness, and her death by water all signify, in traditional Western psychoanalysis, a psychosexually rooted crisis in masculine identity formation, based on separation and differentiation from the mother.

Okada's work is well received at long last though regrettably years after his death.

Criticism

Bryan Aubrey

Aubrey holds a Ph.D. in English and has published many articles on twentieth century literature. In this essay, he discusses Ichiro Yamada's search for psychic wholeness and his lost sense of belonging.

At the beginning of *No-No Boy*, Ichiro Yamada is in the midst of an identity crisis as he tries to put his life back together following his release from two years in prison. The unity of his family has been shattered irreparably, and he does not know where he belongs, feeling that he was "born not soon enough or not late enough" and is therefore "neither Japanese nor American." Using a structural rhythm that alternates between Ichiro's encounters with various Japanese Americans and white Americans and his intense reflections about his own situation, the novel tells the story of his search for psychic wholeness and his lost sense of belonging.

There are lessons for Ichiro everywhere he goes and from everyone he meets. Not all of these experiences are helpful to him, however, especially at the beginning of the novel, when everything that happens seems to fuel his self-doubt and his fear that he has forever lost his chance to be fully accepted as an American. It is easy to understand his predicament. Along with thousands of other Japanese Americans, the U.S. government put him in a camp, as he tells Mr. Carrick, "to prove to us that we weren't American enough to be trusted" and then imprisoned him for refusing to swear allegiance to the nation of his birth, so he has every

> In Kenji, Ichiro finds true friendship. A Nisei who fought and was wounded in the war, Kenji declines to reproach Ichiro for his refusal to serve. He does not feel even a twinge of anger or resentment about the matter."

reason to fear white America will never accept him, whatever he does to redeem himself. "Being American is a terribly incomplete thing if one's face is not white and one's parents are Japanese of the country Japan which attacked America," he says. He is unfortunate in that so soon after his return to Seattle he encounters second-generation Japanese Americans such as Eto and Bull, who identify strongly with being American and have no time for a man who in their eyes chose to ally himself with the enemy.

But it is interesting to note that these men are, like Ichiro, Japanese Americans. The hostility Ichiro anticipates from white Americans simply never materializes. There is a large discrepancy between what he expects to find, given his own fear and self-hatred, and what he does find, although it is a long time before he is able to fully recognize this. In his heart he knows all along that his future has not been destroyed and that the United States, even for him, is still a land of opportunity. This can be seen by his thoughts when he walks down the street after his first meeting with Freddie Akimoto, another "no-no" boy, who acts as a foil for Ichiro. Ichiro tells himself that there surely must be the hope of redemption. He remains a U.S. citizen; he is permitted to vote, and he is free to travel and study and marry. Over time, he says, there will be forgiveness in the country that is known for its "vastness and goodness and fairness and plentitude," and he will buy a home, start a family, and be as American as everyone else. But as soon as he conceives this vision, he denies it. "Swallowed up by the darkness of his soul," he cannot overcome his negative frame of mind. Even then,

however, he knows that "the trouble [is] inside of him"; the enemy he faces is more internal than external. It is he, no one else, who finds himself "guilty of treason."

These points are clearly demonstrated in Ichiro's three encounters with white Americans. The first is with Baxter Brown, his former engineering professor at the university. Brown makes it clear from the outset that he is sympathetic to Japanese Americans and is aware of the injustice of the internment: "Families uprooted, businesses smashed, educations disrupted. You've got a right to be sore." Brown makes the assumption that Ichiro had been helping the U.S. war effort in some capacity, and Ichiro is too unsure of himself to reveal the truth, but Ichiro hardly has cause to complain about being excluded from his former place of study, since Brown urges him to return. White America is prepared to open its doors to him.

The same point is made when Ichiro goes for a job interview at Carrick and Sons in Portland. Mr. Carrick could not be more welcoming. He greets Ichiro with a phrase in Japanese and says he has had some good Japanese friends. Like Brown, he expresses regret about the internment and even goes so far as to apologize for it as "a big black mark in the annals of American history." He also offers Ichiro the job on the spot. When Ichiro confesses he refused the draft, Mr. Carrick shows great sympathy and understanding. He does not judge Ichiro. Later, Ichiro realizes that Mr. Carrick, and others like him, "offered a way back into the great compassionate stream of life that is America," and this marks an important milestone in Ichiro's journey toward recovering his sense of belonging.

The third white American Ichiro meets is Mr. Morrison, who speaks to him in exactly the same, kind, tolerant, open-minded, and generous way that Mr. Carrick does. Like Mr. Carrick, he greets Ichiro with a few words of Japanese and says he admires the Japanese people. He understands Ichiro's problem as a "no-no" boy immediately, even without Ichiro telling him, since his employee Gary has exactly the same problem. Like Mr. Carrick, Mr. Morrison offers Ichiro a job immediately.

The reader may feel that the close similarities between these two characters and how they interact with Ichiro, coming so close together in the narrative, detract from the literary merits of the novel. It seems that Okada the author may have

What Do I Read Next?

- Joy Kogawa's *Obasan* (1981), which has won many awards, examines the effects of internment and forced relocation on Japanese Canadians. The focus is on the Nakane family, and the story is told from the perspective of Naomi, an unmarried schoolteacher. The book is relevant for American readers since the policy of the Canadian government on its Japanese citizens was similar to that of the United States.

- Louis Chu's *Eat a Bowl of Tea* (1961) is set in New York's Chinatown after World War II. One of the first Chinese American novels, it has won praise for its language, which expresses idiomatic Cantonese in English. The themes of the novel include generational conflict and the disillusionment of Chinese immigrants with the American dream.

- *Seventeen Syllables and Other Stories* (revised edition with four new stories, 2001), by Hisaye Yamamoto, a second-generation Japanese American immigrant, covers the whole range of Japanese American experience, including the internment camps and the tensions between first-generation and second-generation immigrants. Yamamoto's stories also place particular emphasis on the lives of women.

- *Prisoners Without Trial: Japanese Americans in World War II* (1993), by Roger Daniels, is a concise introduction by one of the foremost historians of Japanese American history to the incarceration of nearly 120,000 Japanese Americans during World War II. Topics discussed include the historical prejudice against Asian Americans, the upholding by the Supreme Court of the evacuation, life in the relocation centers, and the difficulty of resettling people after the war was over.

---

been, at least in this instance, more concerned with making a didactic point than in creating realistic characters. His treatment of Mr. Carrick and Mr. Morrison seems to reflect the predominant belief in the 1950s, that white America was now successfully extending the hand of friendship to the Japanese Americans whom it had once regarded as a subversive influence.

Certainly, Ichiro's external problems, as opposed to his internal doubts, lie not with white America but with the Japanese American community, which is divided not only between the Issei (first-generation immigrants, born in Japan) and the Nisei (second-generation, American born), but also between the Nisei themselves. Those who fought in the war, the novel implies, have something to prove—that they are fully American—and tend to become aggressive super-patriots, intolerant of those who cling to their Japanese heritage. Ichiro, for example, fears that his brother, Taro, who is about to enter the army, will end up like these arrogant Nisei, "walk[ing] the streets of America as if you owned them always and forever."

But Ichiro is fortunate in that not all the Nisei are like Eto, or Bull, or those who tormented Gary, the third "no-no" boy in the novel, when he worked at the foundry. Ichiro also has Kenji and Emi to show him a better path, as well as Freddie to show him the way not to live.

In Kenji, Ichiro finds true friendship. A Nisei who fought and was wounded in the war, Kenji declines to reproach Ichiro for his refusal to serve. He does not feel even a twinge of anger or resentment about the matter. He also manages to give Ichiro some good advice. As he lies dying in his hospital bed, he warns about how the Japanese in Seattle are putting up psychological fences around themselves, cutting themselves off in their own little enclave: "They [b——] and hollered when the government put them in camps and put real fences around them, but now they're doing the same damn thing to themselves." He feels strongly that ethnic differences should be transcended; he sees people as people, not as members of a particular group that differentiates them from another group. He tells Ichiro to return to Seattle where things will work out well for him in the long run. "The kind of trouble you've got, you can't run from it," he tells his friend.

Running from his troubles is the mistake made by Ichiro's other friend, Freddie, who cultivates a defiant, me-against-the-world attitude that merely compounds the problem. Ichiro realizes that Freddie has "blindly sought relief in total, hateful rejection of self and family and society," and Ichiro eventually comes to the understanding that such a path leads nowhere. Unlike Freddie, Ichiro is able to reflect honestly on his experiences and face his fears. At the end of the novel, Freddie's sudden and violent death symbolizes the fact that his way was untenable in the long term. Instead, it is Ichiro who finds the ray of hope he so desperately needs.

In this rediscovery of hope he has much to thank Emi for. She is a sweet, practical, down-to-earth woman who does not let her own sorrows—the desertion by her husband, Ralph—make her bitter. She reminds Ichiro of the greatness of the country of which he is a citizen ("This is a big country with a big heart. There's room for all kinds of people") and also helps him to get beyond his constant negative self-talk. A key incident occurs in chapter 9, when Ichiro takes Emi to a dance, where a man they do not know insists on buying them both a drink. Ichiro is suspicious. He offers Emi a variety of explanations involving ulterior motives on the part of the man, who appears not to be Japanese, until Emi coaxes out of him the comment, "I want to think . . . that he saw a young couple and liked their looks and felt he wanted to buy them a drink and did." Emi confirms for him, "You keep on thinking that. That's how it was." Emi is quietly encouraging Ichiro not to read into situations things that are not there but to have a simple, more accepting attitude. Up to this point, Ichiro has made up a story for himself about his own life and his place (or lack of it) in the United States, but the story is neither helpful to him nor true. In silencing the negative, fear-based workings of his mind, which only impose a veil over what is really happening, he gives himself a better chance of finding that "elusive insinuation of promise" that will enable him to make his way once more in the land of his birth.

Source: Bryan Aubrey, Critical Essay on *No-No Boy*, in *Novels for Students*, Thomson Gale, 2007.

Elaine H. Kim

In the following excerpt, Kim recounts Okada's depiction of the splintering effects of internment on Japanese American families and communities.

Unquestionably, internment propelled to crisis dimensions the conflicts and tensions already existing in the Japanese American family and community. But no Japanese American literary work depicts the fragmenting effects of internment on the family and community more vividly or poignantly than John Okada's *No-No Boy* (1957). The novel is set in Seattle just after the end of the war, when the disfiguring effects of the internment and the racial hysteria that made it possible were discernible in Japanese American communities all along the West Coast. Like *All I Asking for Is My Body*, *No-No Boy* is about the *nisei*'s rebellion against the *issei* generation, about the *nisei*'s desire for an identity separate from his parents'. Clearly, the *nisei*'s rejection of his parents is linked to his desperate desire for acceptance in American society, which the *nisei* believes is made impossible by his Japanese heritage. The *nisei*'s unfulfilled longing to participate in American society causes the fragmentation and disfiguration of both his family and his community.

No-No Boy is replete with contradictions and unanswered questions: whether the self-deluded *issei* who are still waiting for a final Japanese victory are fanatical fools or the hopeless victims of a racist society in search of temporary comfort; whether the *nisei* veterans who fought in the American army are brave and heroic, or self-hating martyrs; whether the Japanese American community is a comforting haven or destructive to the individual Japanese American. The question that underlies all the others is whether America is in fact the desirable land of democracy and freedom or a racist, predatory society.

The *nisei* of John Okada's novel are driven almost to self-destruction by their desperate desire to belong in America. In the *nisei* world, there is hardly a sacrifice too great for the prize of acceptance. War veteran Kenji loses his leg and eventually his life, while the people of the community think of him as an enviable hero. Ichiro's "mistake," the mistake of refusing the draft, is serious enough for him to be totally ostracized by the community. Another "no-no boy," Freddie, is killed by someone whose hatred of him makes him feel important among his peers. Brothers betray brothers, children turn against their parents, who become alcoholic or commit suicide; husbands desert wives, and wives commit adultery. The community is torn apart by the almost hysterical desire of its members to be accepted as genuine Americans, no matter what the cost.

Like the world of *Eat a Bowl of Tea* and *All I Asking for Is My Body*, Okada's community has been sustained by self-deception that must now come to an end. Like Ben Loy and Mei Oi, like Tosh and Kiyo, Ichiro has been deceived. His mother's fanatical loyalty to Japan has led him to imprisonment for refusing the draft and then to the hatred of his fellow *nisei*, who are themselves desperate to prove their loyalty through their collective reputation. Ichiro's mother's fanaticism culminates, after her stubborn refusal to admit Japan's defeat, in her insanity and eventual suicide.

Ichiro's mother, "dried and toughened" through the many years of hardship in America, is unable to "accept a country which repeatedly refused to accept her or her sons" and turns all her hopes toward Japan. She walks twenty-six blocks to save 35 cents on ten loaves of day-old bread from a bread factory, saving her pennies for what she dreams will be her eventual triumphant return to Japan. Ashida-san works the night shift at a hotel, "grinning and bowing for dimes and quarters from rich Americans who he detested, and couldn't afford to take his family on a bus," but always comforted by the thought of ships on their way to conquer America. Although Ichiro understands that these *issei* are the victims, not the originators, of the hatred that destroys their rationality, he cannot forgive them, because they have allowed their stubbornness and weakness to make them irrational and resistant to truth or change. He blames them for refusing to face the fact that they were never going to return to Japan, that their real future was in America. Even though "growing families and growing bills and misfortunes and illness and low wages and just plain hard luck were constant obstacles to the realization of their dreams," they should have tried to learn English, to integrate themselves into white society, to buy homes and make long-term commitments to an American future. They should have "exchanged hope for reality" and reconciled themselves, instead of clinging to illusions and rationalizations. But what makes Ichiro bitterest is that the *issei*'s inability to face reality is passed on to their children.

When his mother dies, Ichiro feels no regret. He has suspected her of an "incurable strain of insanity," which he hints might be a "Japanese" insanity that might spread through the family to him. The affliction is "Japanese" to the extent that it revolves around loyalty to Japan and reminds Ichiro of Japanese fascism and militarism. Just as many

> " The Japanese Americans in *No-No Boy* are not the patient, law-abiding hard-working, docile model minority: they are tormented, uncertain, and incapacitated by self-hatred."

issei are susceptible to false hopes and illusions, many *nisei* are also weak and vulnerable. Ichiro asks himself:

> Was it she [Ichiro's mother] who was wrong and crazy not to have found in herself the capacity to accept a country which repeatedly refused to accept her or her sons . . . or was it the others who were being deluded, the ones . . . who believed and fought and even gave their lives to protect this country where they could still not rate as first-class citizens because of the unseen walls?

While some *issei* are subject to unrealistic hopes of being saved by Japanese ships from humiliation and drudgery, many *nisei* are afflicted by stifling, narrow-minded thoughtlessness caused by their feelings of inferiority and insecurity. Ichiro's mother is a "rock of hatred," whose "curse" has sent him into prison and shame, but his former friend, a *nisei,* spits on him for being a "no-no boy" and the other *nisei* assume the roles of moral judges on his deviant actions. Their desperation to prove themselves as Americans drives them to idolize and accept those who wear war wounds as proof of their loyalty and despise those who refused the draft. Ichiro feels forced to escape from the diner and the tortured young *nisei* working there who "had to wear a discharge button on his shirt to prove to everyone who came in that he was a top-flight American."

Because of their desperation to be "Americans," hatred of "no-no boys" is prevalent among the *nisei*. Bull threatens Ichiro and Freddie at a night club just to win approval from the crowd. Emi's husband re-enlists in the army because his brother had refused the draft and he feels he must prove his own loyalty again and again. Even Ichiro's younger brother, Taro, betrays Ichiro by leading him into an ambush so that Taro can win acceptance from his peers.

The fragmented and warped Japanese American community in *No-No Boy* almost disintegrates during the course of the novel. Ichiro himself is characterized as incomplete and fragmented. He and his brother Taro are two halves of the same person, joined by a common weakness. Ichiro thinks he refused to join the army because he was too cowardly or too unimaginative to go against his mother's wishes. Taro joins the army and betrays his brother because he too is cowardly. Taro rejects Ichiro because he hates "that thing in his elder brother which had prevented him from thinking for himself," and yet Taro is also unable to think for himself. According to Ichiro, what differentiates the two brothers is only time and circumstance:

> Taro, my brother who is not my brother, you are no better than I. You are only more fortunate that the war years found you too young to carry a gun. . . . And you are fortunate because the weakness which was mine made the same weakness in you the strength to turn your back on Ma and Pa and makes it so frighteningly urgent for you to get into uniform to prove that you are not a part of me.

Just as Ichiro fears that his mother's insanity has contaminated him, he finds his father's weakness in himself and in his brother. The old man is described as a "fat, grinning, spineless nobody" who is afraid to challenge his wife's delusions even in crisis. In fact, none of the characters in *No-No Boy* can be healthy and complete. Ichiro and Kenji, a returned *nisei* veteran, are also two parts of an incomplete whole. But while Ichiro is despised and outcast from the *nisei* community because he has refused the opportunity to prove his loyalty in battle, Kenji is the veteran whose gangrenous amputated leg serves as an immediate and indisputable sign of his "manliness." The fusion of the two men takes place when Kenji "procures" Emi for Ichiro:

> "She needs you," said Kenji, "No, I should say she needs someone. Just like you need someone. Just like I need someone sometimes. I won't apologize for her because then I'd have to apologize for myself. . . . I'm only half a man, Ichiro, and when my leg starts aching, even that half is no good."
>
> The hot color rose to his face as he lashed out at Kenji angrily. "So you're sending in a substitute, is that it?"

The interchangeability or the complementary nature of the two men is brought out clearly when they ask each other if they would ever change places: Ichiro, the detested, and Kenji, the dying. In the topsy-turvy world where Japanese American men are required and require each other to risk their lives and their manhood, to sacrifice their families and their wives, to prove their loyalty to America, Ichiro would change places with his dying friend if he could:

> I'll change with you, Kenji, he thought. Give me the stump which gives you the right to hold your head high. Give me the eleven inches which are beginning to hurt again and bring ever closer the fear of approaching death, and give me with it the fullness of yourself which is also yours because you were man enough to wish the thing which destroyed your leg and, perhaps, you with it but, at the same time, made it so that you can put your one good foot in the dirt of America and know that the wet coolness of it is yours beyond a single doubt.

But Kenji, mutilated and slowly dying, would not change places with Ichiro. The measure of manliness and loyalty becomes all the more ironic and bizarre when it begins to be considered in terms of inches of amputation. As pieces of Kenji's leg are chopped away, as the stump comes closer to his body and his "manhood," the two men wonder how many inches of leg is worth the sacrifice and whose problem is worse:

> "We've both got problems, bigger than most people. That ought to mean something."
>
> . . . "I was thinking all the time we were silent that I decided that, were it possible, I might very well trade with you."
>
> "For eleven inches, or for the seven or eight that'll be left after the next time?"
>
> "Even for two inches. . . ."
>
> "Mine is bigger than yours in a way, and then again, yours is bigger than mine."

In Ichiro's world, nothing can be complete. Kenji is losing inches of his body little by little. Ichiro describes himself as "half a man" and his mother as a withered, stunted adolescent. The individuals in the Japanese American community described in *No-No Boy* are stunted and incomplete because their options are limited. Faced with a choice between the army and the concentration camp, between America and Japan, between his country and his parents, Ichiro chose prison, saying no to both impossible options, and is outcast for his choice. Kenji is forced to choose between his wife and his country. Taro chooses between his brother and his country. Virtually all the *nisei* in the novel are subjected to a choice between Japan, which represents their race and their parentage as much as it does militarism or fascism, and America, which represents the realities of racial bigotry as well as the dream of democracy. Faced with such choices, individuals felt cut in half, as Ichiro does:

> There was a time when I was your son. . . . Then there came a time when I was only half Japanese because one is not born in America and raised in America and taught in America without becoming partly American. . . . But it is not enough to be American only in the eyes of the law and it is not enough to be only half an American and know that it is an empty half. I am not your son and I am not Japanese and I am not American. I can go someplace and tell people that I've got an inverted stomach and that I am an American, true and blue and Hail Columbia, but the army wouldn't have me because of the stomach. . . . I wish with all my heart that I were Japanese or that I were American. . . . I do not understand you who were the half of me that is no more and . . . I do not understand what it was about that half that made me destroy the half of me which was American and the half which might have become the whole of me if I had said yes I will go and fight in your army because that is what I believe and want and cherish and love.

Ichiro describes the torment of being torn between desire to belong and knowledge of rejection: "[I]t is not an easy thing to discover that being American is a terribly incomplete thing if one's face is not white and one's parents are Japanese of the country Japan which attacked America. It is like being pulled asunder by a whirling tornado."

Like the characters and community, the America in *No-No Boy* is not yet whole and complete. Kenji notices Japanese discriminating against blacks and concludes that race hatred is eroding the Japanese American community and the world beyond it:

> The Negro who was always being mistaken for a white man becomes a white man and he becomes hated by the Negroes with whom he once hated on the same side. And the young Japanese hates the not-so-young Japanese who is more Japanese than himself, and the not-so-young, in turn, hates the old Japanese who is Japanese and, therefore, even more Japanese than he. . . .
>
> And Kenji thought about these things and tried to organize them in his mind so that the pattern could be seen and studied. . . . And there was no answer because there was no pattern and all he could feel was that the world was full of hatred.

What Ichiro detests in his mother is her irrational absolutism, which allows her to equate good and evil with nationality. She gloats over the death of her friend's son, who has joined the American army. To Ichiro, tragedy makes "no distinction as to what was wrong and what was right and who was Japanese and who was not."

Ichiro detests no less the race prejudice that allows the internment of the Japanese Americans because of their nationality alone. He longs to be accepted for "what he is," not as a Japanese or an American or a Japanese American: "If Smith would do the same for Eng and Sato would do the same for Wotynski and Faverghetti would do likewise for whoever happened by. Eng for Eng, Jap for Jap, Pole for Pole, and like for like meant classes and distinctions and hatred and prejudice and wars and misery." Kenji hates the ghetto, hoping that there will be no "Jackson Street wherever I'm going to." He concludes that racism can be ended only when communities are broken up and scattered and distinct national and racial groups can no longer be identified. He advises Ichiro to leave the Japanese American community and try to find anonymity somewhere far away: "Marry a white girl or a Negro or an Italian or even a Chinese. Anything but a Japanese. After a few generations, you've got the thing beat." But Ichiro wants to belong to the *nisei* community and to be a part of America at the same time. Before the war, poverty and segregation had been tolerable to him because at least his peers faced similar problems. What obsesses him now is that he might have forfeited his chance to move with other *nisei,* his chance to attain the American dream that had become possible for the *nisei* who had volunteered to fight in the U.S. Army. Ichiro is acutely aware of the furniture, rugs, and phonographic equipment in Kenji's family's house, which to him symbolize belonging in America:

> Ichiro looked out at the houses, the big, roomy houses of brick and glass which belonged in magazines and were of that world which was no longer his to dream about. Kenji could still hope. A leg more or less wasn't important when compared with himself, Ichiro who was strong and perfect but only an empty shell. He would have given both legs to change places with Kenji.

Ichiro's desire for material comfort is part of his desire to be acceptable, an average all-American. Ichiro hopes that someday there will be a place for him in America's "vastness and goodness and fairness and plenitude" and that in time he too will "buy a home and love my family and . . . [be] walking down the street holding my son's hand and people will stop and talk with us about the weather and the ball games and the elections," just like in the movies and magazines.

Throughout the novel, Ichiro has hovered between hope and despair, between bitter anger and almost pathetic gratitude for a kind word from a white man. What he finally comes to understand is that the contradictions within himself and within his community also prevail in America. The same America that is abundant, beautiful, and desirable is also an America where racial hatred and injustice flourish. Ichiro realizes that he is not alone after all, not even when he is on the outside looking in, but that almost everyone else is probably on the outside too. Perhaps, he concludes, there is no "in" after all. What had seemed to be individual alienation might be common to all, and it might be causing people to commit acts of hatred towards each other:

> [W]hat about the young kid on Burnside who was in the army and found out it wasn't enough so that he has to keep proving to everyone who comes in for a cup of coffee that he was fighting for his country like the button on his shirt says he did because the army didn't do anything about his face to make him look more American? And what about the poor niggers on Jackson Street who can't find anything better to do than spit on the sidewalk and show me the way to Tokyo? They're on the outside looking in, just like that kid and just like me and just like everybody else I've ever seen or known. . . . Maybe the answer is that there is no in. Maybe the whole damned country is pushing and shoving and screaming to get into someplace that doesn't exist, because they don't know that the outside could be the inside if only they would stop all this pushing and shoving and screaming, and they haven't got enough sense to realize that. . . . And then he thought about Kenji in the hospital and of Emi in bed with a stranger who reminded her of her husband and of his mother waiting for the ship from Japan and there was no answer.

Ichiro's final affirmation comes when he understands the connections between himself and other human beings. He has felt totally alone and ostracized as a "no-no boy," misunderstood and hated by everyone. His search has been a search for wholeness, for completion and connections. The connection emerges as compassionate love that has the potential to combat the damage done to America's potential, to the *issei,* to the diseased *nisei* community. This love is a "good sharp knife" that cuts out the tumors. Ichiro's painful compassion for and understanding of the fellow *nisei* who hate him because they are also on the outside looking in even helps him understand the *issei* he once hated and resented.

In a transparent bid for attention and approval from his peers, Bull causes a "no-no boy" to die in an accident. Ichiro is overcome by compassion for his friend's killer when he looks into his "frightened, lonely eyes" peering through a film of tears and begging for solace. Ichiro and his friend's killer are together in sorrow and struggle, victimized by racism and the feelings of inferiority that drive them to make terrible and self-destructive mistakes. He decides that he should

not "disappear," should not leave his community, his roots, and his past:

> A man does not start totally anew because he is already old by virtue of having lived and laughed and cried for twenty or thirty or fifty years and there is no way to destroy them without destroying life itself. That he understood. He also understood that the past had been shared with a mother and father and, whatever they were, he too was a part of them and they a part of him and one did not say this is as far as we go together, I am stepping out of your lives, without rendering himself only part of a man. If he was to find his way back to that point of wholeness and belonging, he must do so in the place where he had begun to lose it.

No-No Boy ends with the hope that the America in Ichiro's heart will one day become a reality: "He walked along, thinking, searching, thinking and probing and, in the darkness of the alley of the community that was a tiny bit of America, he chased that faint and elusive insinuation of promise as it continued to take shape in mind and in heart."

No-No Boy was not welcomed by the American public, much less by the Japanese American community, at the time it was first published. According to Charles Tuttle, the Japan-based publishers: "At the time we published it, the very people whom we thought would be enthusiastic about it, mainly the Japanese-American community in the U.S., were not only disinterested but actually rejected the book." No doubt the Japanese American community was protecting itself from being revealed in such an unflattering light, even a decade after internment. The Japanese Americans in *No-No Boy* are not the patient, law-abiding hard-working, docile model minority: they are tormented, uncertain, and incapacitated by self-hatred. The community described in the novel has been violently distorted by racism. Nor is American society portrayed in a very favorable light. What is desirable does not yet exist.

Most of Okada's characters are not fully developed. The fragmentation and disintegrating influence of American racism on the Japanese American community and its members are depicted through the incompleteness of each individual character: Ichiro is filled out by Kenji, Taro, Freddie, and Bull. *No-No Boy* explores creatively the effects of racism on the Japanese American community and on the individual Japanese American psyche. It is an important book not only because it is a pioneer effort but also because it is a moving and contemporaneous expression told by an insider of an experience heretofore largely ignored in American culture.

Source: Elaine H. Kim, "Japanese American Portraits," in *Asian American Literature: An Introduction to the Writings and Their Social Context*, Temple University Press, 1982, pp. 148–56.

Sources

Gribben, Bryn, "The Mother That Won't Reflect Back: Situating Psychoanalysis and the Japanese Mother in *No-No Boy*," in *MELUS*, Vol. 28, No. 2, Summer 2003, p. 31.

Inada, Lawson Fusao, "Introduction," in John Okada, *No-No Boy*, University of Washington Press, 1979, p. vi.

Okada, John, *No-No Boy*, University of Washington Press, 1979.

Yeh, William, "To Belong or Not to Belong: The Liminality of John Okada's *No-No Boy*," in *Amerasia Journal*, Vol. 19, No. 1, 1993, p. 121.

Further Reading

Chu, Patricia, *Assimilating Asians, Gendered Strategies of Authorship in Asian America*, Duke University Press, 2000, pp. 55–61.

Chu discusses the novel in terms of Ichiro's rejection of Japanese authenticity in the form of his mother in order to construct himself as an Asian American subject.

Ling, Jingi, "*No-No Boy*," in *A Resource Guide to Asian American Literature*, edited by Cynthia Sau-ling Wong and Stephen H. Sumida, Modern Languages Association of America, 2001, pp. 140–50.

Ling discusses the reception of the novel, the biographical background of the author, the historical context, critical and pedagogical issues, and supplies a list of other Asian American works that cover similar themes.

———, "Race, Power, and Cultural Politics in John Okada's *No-No Boy*," in *American Literature*, Vol. 67, No. 2, June 1995, pp. 359–81.

Ling argues that Ichiro's attempt in postwar Seattle to articulate Japanese American dissent in terms of ethnic pride reflects the limited options available to Okada given the social and aesthetic milieu in which he wrote. Ling also argues that the novel transcends Ichiro's ideological fatalism.

Sato, Gayle K. Fujita, "Momotaro's Exile: John Okada's *No-No Boy*," in *Reading the Literatures of Asian America*, edited by Shirley Geok-lin Lim and Amy Ling, Temple University Press, 1992, pp. 239–58.

Sato analyzes the novel's binary opposition of Japan and the United States through examination of two of the novel's subtexts, the loyalty oath and the Japanese folk tale known as Momotaro.

Stones from the River

Ursula Hegi
1994

Stones from the River, by Ursula Hegi, is the story of a dwarf who lives in the fictional small town of Burgdorf, Germany, through the first half of the twentieth century. The novel is an intimate look at what it was like for ordinary people to live through the rise of Adolf Hitler and the devastation wrought by the Third Reich. The novel conveys the horrors of Nazism and the Holocaust as these become apparent in the small town. The advent of Nazism provides the context for an in-depth analysis of certain universal psychological tendencies, chief among which are the search for identity through group membership, the desire for social acceptance, and the fear of ostracism.

The novel demonstrates the nature of difference and how policies of exclusion divide a community. It also exposes the ways in which the Catholic Church and the fascist state engendered fear and promoted discrimination. Townspeople are persuaded by beliefs about community solidarity and outsider status, and the plot enumerates the diverse human impulses and choices at work when various people live in close proximity over decades, weathering global conflict twice in their lives.

In her acknowledgments, Hegi thanks her godmother, Käte Capelle, who "broke the silence by documenting her memories of the war years." The novel exposes the little-known reality as it was experienced by the small-town German population. It addresses the common question about how decent Germans could have allowed the Holocaust to happen. *Stones from the River* was well received in

1994 when it first appeared, but it became a best-seller in 1997 when it was chosen for Oprah's Book Club list.

Author Biography

Ursula Hegi, author of *Stones from the River* and at least nine other books, was born in Düsseldorf, Germany, on May 23, 1946. When she was eighteen, she moved permanently to the United States, settling in New Hampshire, where she married and raised two sons. Though her academic degrees are variously reported, several sources indicate she received both her B.A. and M.A. from the University of New Hampshire in the late 1970s and that, after graduating, she remained at the university in a teaching position. Apparently in the 1990s, she lived in Spokane, Washington, and taught at Eastern Washington University. Thereafter, she lived in New York State and wrote full time. She has served as a conference participant or visiting professor at a number of academic institutions, including University of California at Irvine, University of North Dakota, University of New Hampshire, and Barnard College.

Though she began writing as a child, Hegi waited until she was in her forties to pursue a career in writing. As a German American, she was aware that Americans knew more about Germany's World War II history than many Germans did, who had reached their adulthood in a culture sworn to secrecy about the Holocaust. Some of Hegi's works draw upon a cluster of characters that were born before or during the world wars and lived part or all of their lives in the fictional town of Burgdorf, near Düsseldorf, Germany. Two of these works are *Floating in My Mother's Palm* (1981), a collection of interrelated stories, and the novel, *Stones from the River* (1994). Two Burgdorf residents who immigrated to the United States and their descendents are the focus of her novel *The Vision of Emma Blau* (2000), which tells the German-American, multi-generational story of a family-operated grand apartment house in New Hampshire. A cultural change of pace is Hegi's *Sacred Time* (2003), a work with three narrators, which tells the story of an extended Italian family living in the Bronx in the 1950s.

Hegi also wrote *Tearing the Silence: On Being German in America* (1997), a compilation of fifteen interviews with German-born immigrants in the United States, which explores problems of identity for Germans who must cope with the legacy of

Ursula Hegi   Photograph by Gordon Gagliano. Reproduced by permission

Germany's Nazi past. In addition to this work and those mentioned above, Hegi has published two collections of short stories: *Unearned Pleasures and Other Stories* (1994) and *Hotel of the Saints: Stories* (2001). She is also the author of many reviews and other kinds of articles published in a variety of journals.

Hegi has received a number of grants and awards, including five PEN Syndicated Fiction Awards. She was nominated for a PEN Faulkner Award for *Stones from the River*, which in 1997 became a bestseller after it was chosen for inclusion by Oprah's Book Club.

Plot Summary

One: 1915–1918

The novel opens with a reflection on the time when the protagonist, Trudi Montag, as a child assumed that everyone had her gift for knowing "what went on inside others," a time predating her understanding of "the agony of being different." The narrator jumps ahead to Trudi's pubescent molestation by four boys. That event showed Trudi that praying does not change things. For the first three months after Trudi's birth, the unstable Gertrude Montag refuses to touch her baby, and the child is cared for by neighbor women.

Trudi's father, Leo Montag, returns from World War I in October 1914. He impregnates his wife immediately and resumes his work, running the pay-library. Gertrude gives birth July 23, 1915, to a dwarf daughter, who is called Trudi. Gertrude persists in abnormal, even scandalous behavior, and Leo takes to locking her into the third-floor sewing room. Soldiers return home, disheartened and humiliated. They take over the daily responsibilities that have been handled by the women.

Two: 1918–1919

Late in the fall 1918, Gertrude tells Trudi the story of her ride on Emil Hesping's motorcycle, how they fell and Gertrude got gravel under the skin of her left knee. On the day of this accident, or about that time, Gertrude had a brief sexual relationship with Emil. Gertrude believes now that her infidelity and the damage to her knee, which is its outward sign, caused Leo to be injured in his left knee on the same day while fighting on the Russian Front.

Leo takes Gertrude to Grafenburg, where she remains in an asylum for seven weeks. She comes home about Christmas time and suggests a sibling for Trudi, who rejects the idea. Gertrude tells Trudi that storks can be persuaded to deliver a baby if people leave sugar cubes on the windowsills over night. Because Trudi does not want a baby to come, she secretly eats the sugar. Born prematurely, the baby boy, Horst, dies. Trudi feels responsible for his death.

Gertrude returns to the asylum where she contracts pneumonia and dies. At the funeral reception, Trudi catches Herr Buttgereit kissing the baker's wife and senses intuitively the power of knowing what others do not want her to know. Talk at the party touches upon refugees moving into the area, and the locals are "united against newcomers." The unknown benefactor leaves a phonograph and some records in the pay-library, and the music comforts Trudi. She turns four and misses her mother "with a bottomless panic." Leo takes Trudi to see fireworks for her birthday. Secretly, Trudi visits Doktor Rosen, asking for a pill to make her grow.

Three: 1919–1920

Trudi hangs from doorframes in hopes of growing. Leo's sister, Helene Montag Blau, visits from the United States with her son, Robert. During the visit, Trudi and Robert become friends. Together, they discover a bee entangled in a spider web, and Robert cuts it gently free without tearing the web. After he leaves, Trudi becomes friends with Georg Weiler, who lives next door. His mother, Hedwig Weiler, dresses him like a little girl, refuses to cut his hair, and will not allow him to play with boys. The two children, outwardly so different looking, are ostracized by their peers.

During the flood of 1920, Franz Weiler drowns when he goes to the Rhein with some drinking buddies and entertains them by doing handstands on the dike. Frau Weiler insists Franz was en route to mass; however, the townspeople know otherwise. The point is made that the age-old local habit was to uphold the façade, to maintain family respectability. The narrator writes: "a complicity of silence . . . had served the town for centuries." A week later, the unknown benefactor gives Georg lederhosen (leather pants with leather suspenders), though his mother does not permit him to wear them.

Four: 1920–1921

When she was a little girl, Hedwig Weiler was sexually abused by her alcoholic stepfather, and she developed a belief that men's souls are contaminated. Her generalized distrust of Georg causes him to learn to lie. At Georg's urging, Trudi cuts his hair, though she anticipates that as he becomes more like other boys, she will lose him as a friend. Leo lovingly assures Hedwig that "it was time."

Trudi does the shopping: Anton Immers's butcher shop, Buttgereits's farm for white asparagus, and Braunmeiers's farm for eggs and milk. Trudi takes to swimming alone in the river. At Catholic school, the nuns find Trudi pushy and intrusive. Though she is bright and enthusiastic, she must learn to wait to be called on and not volunteer to answer questions. The children exclude her whenever they can from games, and the nuns do not help the situation. They teach the children religious precepts that encourage feelings of German superiority and prejudice toward non-Christians.

At the end of summer, the Eberhardts's pear tree is heavy with fruit, and the children eat pears, but their sweetness gags Trudi, who chokes whenever she tastes sugar and is reminded that she caused her brother's death. Renate Eberhardt has a baby, whom she names Helmut. He is beautiful, with golden hair and blue eyes, but Trudi intuits that Helmut could destroy his mother. Because Trudi has no friends, Leo buys her a little dog, that she names Seehund. Owning the dog makes Trudi appealing to Eva Rosen, and their friendship develops privately, though Eva ignores Trudi at school. Trudi asks the priest for the name of the patron saint of dwarfs; all he can suggest is St. Giles, patron saint of cripples.

Five: 1921–1923

In a confidential moment, Eva reveals that she is different, too. She has a red birthmark that spirals across her chest and around her nipples. Eva anticipates that when she has babies, she will lactate "red milk." Trudi does well in school but likes history best; she compares playground bullies to Napoleon. Leo tells her that Germans have a history of sacrificing everything for one leader, and this is because Germans fear chaos. Hans-Jürgen lures Eva and Trudi into the barn to see some kittens. He takes one up, swings it around, and throws it against the wall, killing it. When Hans burns a cat's paw, his father breaks his arm for having a match in the barn. When Eva shuns Trudi, Trudi tells Helga Stamm about the birthmark.

Six: 1923–1929

At age thirteen, Trudi attends a carnival and sees another dwarf, the circus entertainer, Pia, who has a trailer in which the furniture is scaled down to fit her body. Leo adjusts the furniture in the pay-library to fit Trudi's body. Trudi goes swimming alone and happens to see four boys swimming naked. When they spy her, the boys drag her into Hans-Jürgen's barn and molest her. One of the boys is Georg Weiler, her childhood friend. Alexander Sturm arrives and calls out to Frau Braunmeier, causing the boys to flee. Wrapped in a cow blanket, Trudi gets back to the river and collects her clothes. She throws stones in the river, calling them by the boys' names.

Seven: 1929–1933

In the aftermath of this attack, Trudi refuses food, cannot sleep, and stays indoors wrapped in loose clothes and a blanket. She cannot bear to have Seehund with her, since the dog witnessed her degradation. She remains indoors all winter and into the spring. In April, the floods arrive, "loosen[ing] her rage." Trudi takes revenge on her assailants by spreading false stories about them. Her stories cause Fritz Hansen's bakery to lose business and Paul Weinhart to miss out on an apprenticeship. She tells Hans no woman will ever love him, but she holds off doing something to Georg Weiler. Helmut Eberhardt joins a youth group (soon to be the Hitler-Jugend [HJ]) and attempts to hurt Rainer Bilder, a morbidly obese boy.

Media Adaptations

A boycott of Jewish stores occurs and an anti-Semitic torch parade takes place, in which Helmut marches with a beatific look on his face, as though he is receiving communion. Hitler becomes chancellor, and Trudi sees him when she visits Düsseldorf. The priest's sermon against sins of the flesh causes people to borrow more romance novels from the pay-library. Trudi wonders why the priest never attacks novels about soldiers being killed in battle. Prayers for the fatherland become more common during mass. In the spring 1933, two hundred authors are labeled indecent, and their books are burned around the country; Leo and Trudi hide books by these authors in the pay-library. Ingrid Baum's religious fanaticism shows the extreme effect Catholicism can have on a conscientious person who believes she has sinned.

Eight: 1933

Klaus Malter, the eligible young dentist, begins socializing with Ingrid Baum and Trudi. Both young women are attracted to him, but Ingrid pulls back in strict piety, and Klaus rejects the idea of being involved with the dwarf Trudi. The Nazis come to power, and people take a wait-and-see attitude. Jews are identified as a political problem. Ilse and Michel Abramowitz lose their passports. Rainer Bilder disappears.

Nine: 1934

Dressed neatly in his Hitler-Jugend uniform, ten-year-old Bruno Stosick hangs himself. His father, Günter Stosick, so objected to the group that he forced his son, a champion chess player, to withdraw. Trudi and Ingrid go to Düsseldorf to a movie and see an anti-Hitler flyer on the bus. The movie and the news bulletins are examples of Nazi propaganda. Back in Burgdorf, Fienchen Blomberg, a girl of nine, is stoned by Hitler-Jugend members.

Frau Weiler beats off the boys with a broom, warning she will tell their parents. Leo holds the girl while Doktor Rosen attends to her wounds. Next day, Frau Weiler is arrested for attacking children. Leo goes with her to the police station, swearing the boys were eighteen and the victim just a little child. Frau Weiler spends a week in jail, which enrages her. Leo tells her to be quiet and keep the vigil; they can help Jews more effectively if they act covertly. Günter Stosick is forced to resign from the chess club, and he and his wife are shunned during mass. Ingrid continues her blind faith in the absolute word of the Catholic Church, repeating the rosary and asserting that she is not the one to decide what is right and wrong. Though her father abused her, she believes it is she who is the unredeemable sinner.

Ten: 1934–1938

More children join the political clubs: the boys join Hitler-Jugend; the girls join the Bund Deutscher Mädchen (Alliance of German Girls [BDM]). They are indoctrinated to be true to the Führer and not to trust their own judgment. One benefit of membership is these teens move more easily from school into apprenticeships and jobs.

Eva Rosen and Alexander Sturm marry one month before passage in September 1935 of the Nürnberg laws, which prohibit the intermarriage of Jews and Christians and deny Jews their German citizenship. Eva and Alexander have a costume party, in defiance of the laws that are shrinking the world of the Jews, and Eva wears a nun's habit. Seehund dies of old age. Trudi and Leo celebrate his fifty-first birthday. In the face of Jewish persecution, onlookers practice silence "nurtured by fear and complicity." When Anton Immers's son marries, the father entertains wedding guests with stories of his World War I service, and the guests begin telling their own stories of seeing him in battle.

In March 1938, German troops enter Austria, and feeling his age, Leo turns most of the library work over to Trudi. Pastor Beier hears confessions of Burgdorf women who love Leo, and the priest would like to hear more about "Leo Montag's successes," yet celibate Leo confesses only three times a year and never mentions a love interest. By contrast, Emil Hesping plays the field, but Lotte Simon always takes him back.

Eleven: 1938

The 1938 spring of Anschluss (Germans in Austria), the Rhein floods again. Gifts from the unknown benefactor appear in many houses. Lotte

Simon is arrested in front of her store, and its contents are confiscated. The storefront becomes the Hitler-Jugend headquarters. Trudi and Leo quickly take valuables from the milliner's apartment and hide them in the pay-library for safekeeping. When she returns four months later, Simon lives in a room elsewhere in town, a broken woman.

In November 1938, during Kristlnacht (Crystal Night), mobs vandalize Jewish stores and synagogues, wasting property and making a terrible mess for which the Jews are later taxed. Twelve hours before his wedding, Helmut Eberhardt and two other HJ members break into the Abramowitz house, destroying personal property and hauling off Michel Abramowitz to be beaten. Through the night Leo stands beside Ilse Abramowitz, waiting by the window. Finally, they see Michel crawling along in the street. At Helmut's wedding the next day, Trudi whispers to Renate what her son has done. Ruth Abramowitz comes to comfort her parents; she foolishly believes that being married to a Christian physician will protect her from the Nazis. The local synagogue is destroyed by fire; townspeople watch the fire, having learned "to take the horrible for granted."

Twelve: 1939–1941

Helmut and his wife move into the upstairs rooms of his mother's house, but he relentlessly badgers Renate to sign over the house to him. He wants to occupy the larger ground floor rooms and have her live upstairs. She refuses to buckle under his pressure. Resolute in her compassion and generosity for suffering people, Renate continues to befriend Jews, even though Helmut warns her that doing so is unpatriotic. In June 1939, Helmut warns her that she could be arrested. On September 1, 1939, Hitler invades Poland. Helmut turns in his mother, and she is arrested. By December, Jews must wear a yellow six-pointed star on their outer clothes. The following year, Hilde gives birth to a little boy, and Helmut is killed in action. Hilde lives upstairs with her son, keeping the downstairs clean and ready for the return of her mother-in-law. But Renate never comes home again.

Ingrid goes off to teach a large class of children, and Klaus Malter ends a six-year courtship in order to suddenly marry Jutta Sturm. Jews in many cities are forced into crowded housing.

Thirteen: 1941–1942

At the age of twenty-six, Trudi answers a newspaper romance ad and meets Max Rudnick in Düsseldorf. Klaus Malter's mother, a professor and

Christian, is arrested. Herr Blau turns away a young Jewish man who comes in the night seeking a hiding place. Afterward, Blau deeply regrets his refusal to help the man and seeks ways to make amends for it. Lotte Simon is relocated and later writes to Ilse Abramowitz about the labor camp conditions. Max pursues Trudi; he says her being a dwarf bothers her, not him.

Fourteen through Sixteen: 1942

Trudi discovers Erna Neimann and her son Konrad hiding under the pay-library and takes them in. Seeing an urgent need, Leo and Trudi develop the means to hide people, making house rules and excuses to discourage those who want to visit. With the help of Emil Hesping and Herr Blau, they dig an escape tunnel between the pay-library and the Blaus's house. Working together on the tunnel gives Trudi a new sense of community. Ilse Abramowitz says she would "rather be subjected to injustice . . . than to be the one who inflicts it on others." She predicts that the Germans "might survive, but they'll never recover."

Eva is questioned about her parents' escape by car to Switzerland. She has chosen to stay behind because of Alexander and is convinced if she were arrested Alexander would voluntarily go with her. Eva goes into hiding at the pay-library. Erna Neimann and Konrad must be moved to another hiding place, and for a special farewell dinner, Leo burns banned books and cooks a roast with vegetables. Eva decides to return for one night to her husband, but she is informed on by the butcher and arrested. Alexander cowers before the Gestapo, "paralyzed with fear," as his wife is taken away.

Matthias Berger gives a recital at Fräulein Birnsteig's estate in October 1942. Trudi makes a comment about the Nazi flags and is immediately arrested. After three weeks confined in the Theresienheim, the local convent hospital taken over by the Nazis, she is interrogated by the officer who arrested Lotte Simon. She sees right through this man, realizing at once that he does not believe in what he is doing and will be a suicide within the year. She tells him a story about a man born with his heart outside his body. The officer releases Trudi with a warning.

Trudi tells Max Rudnick that while she looks different on the outside, she is really like everyone else on the inside. Max says this is not so: "Each one of us is different." Every person is unique; even people who look and act alike are different from one another on the inside. Max and Trudi have a

romantic and sexual relationship. Max is a watercolorist, and his room is decorated with paintings of buildings transformed into red and yellow flowers. These images signify sexual orgasm to Max, but they also foreshadow the destruction of Dresden in which he is killed.

Seventeen: 1943

In February 1943, Trudi learns that Max is married but has been separated from his wife for a long time. Ingrid returns to Burgdorf, pregnant. Her father persuades the father of her child, Ulrich Hebel, to come to Burgdorf and marry Ingrid, who gives birth to a daughter, Rita, one week after the wedding. Ingrid is convinced the baby is the outward sign of her depravity. Ingrid becomes pregnant again and then her husband is killed in action, and this second child, Karin, is born after Ingrid is widowed. Ingrid sees the facts surrounding her daughters' births as signs of her sinfulness.

Alexander Sturm joins the army. His guilt about abandoning Eva is so great that he hopes to be killed in battle. Hans-Jürgen is missing in action in Russia; Fritz Hanson returns to Burgdorf without his jaw. The identity of the unknown benefactor is revealed. Emil Hesping attempts to steal the small statue of Hitler and is shot in the act. The police realize he is the benefactor when they find a ledger in his apartment going back years, noting needs and clothing and shoe sizes of townspeople, and dates on which gifts were delivered. His brother, the bishop, visits Leo. They discuss Emil's courage and love. The bishop reveals that Emil embezzled money from the gym in order to pay for the gifts.

Eighteen: 1943–1945

A postcard comes from Zurich; Erna and Konrad Neimann have made it safely into Switzerland. In June 1944, Michel Abramowitz dies in his sleep, and his wife is arrested after she takes her cane to the HJ headquarters, breaks up the interior and hurts the young men in there who were responsible for beating up her husband. After Ilse is deported, Leo acts like a widower again. He wants to get the Abramowitzs's valuables to Ruth in Dresden. He and Trudi drive there and search in vain for her. Alexander Sturm deserts, having had no success in getting himself killed in action. He returns to the attic where Eva was arrested and jumps from the window to his death.

Max gets a week off from the factory, and in February 1945, just before his thirty-eighth birthday, he agrees to take the Abramowitzs's valuables to Dresden and search for Ruth. He apparently is killed in the firebombing of Dresden in which thousands die. American tanks arrive in Burgdorf in March 1945.

Nineteen: 1945–1946

People resolve not to discuss the war. Eva's parents are alive in Sweden. German POWs from Russia arrive, starving and in rags; German POWs from England arrive well-fed and in clean clothes. When Americans question local people about having supported the Nazis, these individuals disavow any such loyalty and seek supportive statements from Leo and Trudi. Babies are born; even the widowed midwife, Hilde Eberhardt, has or adopts a baby and names it Renate in memory of her mother-in-law. The town makes itself pretty again; the site of the synagogue is paved over, making a parking lot.

Twenty: 1946–1949

Trudi sees the "crippled state of her community." Jutta and Klaus have a baby, Hanna, and Jutta paints a picture that reminds Trudi of Alexander and Eva. Matthias Berger visits from the seminary and tells Trudi how he was sexually abused by other seminarians. He abhors his homosexuality and resolves to return to the seminary because being there, he believes, is good for his soul. In April 1947, Ingrid attempts to save her children from lives of sin by throwing them off a bridge. She believes this will expedite their innocent flight to heaven. Rita drowns, but witnesses save the baby, Karin. Ingrid slips further into a psychotic state and dies. Karin is raised by Ingrid's brother, Holger, and his wife, who together hide the fact of Ingrid's existence; Karin grows up believing that her uncle and aunt are her biological parents. In November 1948, Hans-Jürgen murders his girlfriend and her male companion; he is tried and people testify to his history as a psychopath, but Trudi does not tell what she knows about him. Rainer Bilder reappears, so thin people barely recognize him. Now a journalist, he interviews Hans-Jürgen in jail and writes an article that describes Hans-Jürgen as "lonely and troubled," seeming to blame the town more than Hans-Jürgen himself. The murderer is sent to the asylum at Grafenberg. Ironically, ten years later, the released Hans-Jürgen murders Rainer Bilder's brother.

Twenty-one: 1949–1952

After the war, anti-Semitism continues. Trudi spends time with little Hanna and notices as she continues to work in the library that she views her own stories differently, seeking their meaning rather than using them against her neighbors. Trudi makes a nice dinner for Leo's sixty-seventh birthday, and he dies the following afternoon. Hundreds attend his funeral, including Matthias who returns by train. At the reception held in Frau Blau's house, Trudi remarks that her father had predicted that war could come again, so long as Germany "has a need for violence to settle conflict." In the weeks following the funeral, Trudi finds many gifts left on the doorstep of the pay-library. The house feels large, but her grief is larger. In the final scene, Trudi broods about the nature of story, thinks about a dream in which she meets Georg and he asks her what will become of him. She feels enormous compassion for the people who have loved and lived in her stories, and she knows her story-making will continue.

Characters

Ilse Abramowitz

Frau Ilse Abramowitz is like a mother to Trudi Montag, to whom she is more affectionate than her own children. She secretly loves the widowed Leo Montag, channeling her erotic attachment to him into maternal love for his dwarf daughter. Frau Abramowitz has what her husband, Michel, sees as a dangerous ability to adapt to the growing anti-Semitism, and when the Nazis come for the Abramowitzs's passports, she surrenders them without telling her husband, believing cooperation and obedience are safer than resistance. Generous and conciliatory, Frau Abramowitz insists that preserving one's dignity is essential; she also maintains it is better to be the persecuted than the persecutor. Yet after her husband dies, she takes her cane and literally breaks up the Hitler-Jugend office, whipping the young men there who previously broke into her home and brutally beat up her husband. Despite her lifelong philosophy of nonviolence, Ilse Abramowitz goes down fighting. She is arrested and dies in a concentration camp.

Michel Abramowitz

Both a lawyer and photographer, prosperous Michel Abramowitz is wounded in World War I yet returns to Burgdorf to live an upper middle-class life with his wife, Ilse, and their children, Ruth and Albert. Soon the household has a telephone, and the family enjoys outings in the countryside in their recently purchased 1908 Mercedes. In the years between the wars, Michel and Ilse Abramowitz travel widely, collecting photos of such remote places as China. When the Nazis gain power, Albert, now living in Argentina, tries repeatedly to get his parents out of Germany. By this time, Ruth is married to a Christian doctor who is so successful she believes she is not at risk. Herr Abramowitz is realistically pessimistic about the family's destiny within the Nazi state, and when he and his wife lose their home, he entrusts the family valuables to Leo Montag. Though he fears the worst, Michel Abramowitz has the luxury of dying at home in his sleep in 1944.

Sister Adelheid

Sister Adelheid is caught celebrating mass and is locked up as insane. She aspires to being a priest, and for challenging the church hierarchy in this way, she is put under lock and key. To Trudi, Sister Adelheid confides that life in the convent is "Picky and petty and always the same." Sister Adelheid voices part of this novel's criticism of the Catholic Church, particularly its hierarchy, authoritarianism, and guilt-engendering control tactics.

Ingrid Baum

Ingrid Baum and her family move to Burgdorf after World War I. Her father, who owns a bicycle shop, sexually abuses her as a child, a crime that goes unexposed. Rather than blaming her father, Ingrid attributes the cause of his abuse to her own depravity. As an adult, Ingrid prays several hours a day, subordinating herself totally to the will of the Catholic Church. Her abusive father continues to taunt her, and Ingrid is swallowed up by a fatal self-hatred. That she becomes pregnant out of wedlock and then gives birth to a second child after her husband's death proves conclusively to Ingrid that her nature is corrupt. In a psychotic attempt to rescue her daughters from sin, she decides to cast them off a bridge, drowning them in order to expedite their flight to heaven. She succeeds with her firstborn, Rita, but the infant Karin is rescued by passers-by. After Ingrid dies, Karin is raised by Ingrid's brother, Holger, and his wife, and she grows up believing them to be her biological parents. Karin is impregnated at age thirteen by her maternal grandfather.

Matthias Berger

Child prodigy Matthias Berger is the chosen pupil of Fräulein Birnsteig, the famous concert pianist who lives in an estate just outside Burgdorf.

Matthias is tormented by his homosexual orientation; attempting to control those impulses, he enters the seminary where he is physically abused by other seminarians. When he confides in Trudi, she reminds him of what her father has said, that "much of what the church calls sin is simply being human." Not convinced by that unorthodox view, Matthias abandons his music and suppresses his sexual orientation by remaining in the seminary, a choice he believes is unsafe for his body but good for his soul.

Fräulein Birnsteig

The famous pianist and Jew, Fräulein Birnsteig owns an expensive estate in the countryside beyond Burgdorf. Annually, she gives a free concert for local children and their schoolteachers. Philanthropic in other ways, Fräulein Birnsteig selects one piano student each year to tutor free of charge. Nazis take over her estate during the war but allow her to continue to live there. She commits suicide in January 1945 after hearing that her adopted son has died in a concentration camp.

Flora Blau

Elderly Flora Blau and her husband, Martin, live next door to the pay-library. Of Dutch descent, Flora Blau excels at cleaning, and the house always smells of fresh floor wax. She polishes her keys and rubs her windowsills so often that the child Trudi believes Frau Blau's one arthritic finger is bent from dusting too much. Having "powdered cheeks and a broken heart," Frau Blau longs for their son, Stefan, who in 1894 ran away to the United States.

Helene Montag Blau

Sister of Leo Montag and third wife of Stefan Blau, Helene Montag returns from the United States with her son, Robert, for a visit after her sister-in-law, Gertrude, dies. Robert is a good friend to Trudi during the five-week visit. Loyal always to the local people and town of her birth, Helene mails gifts, provisions, and money to help Leo and Trudi and others during the early years of World War II.

Martin Blau

A retired tailor, elderly Herr Blau regrets that he once turned away a Jewish man who came to the house in the night seeking shelter. When Blau discovers that the Montags are hiding Jews, he offers to help, eager to exonerate himself. He sews clothes for the Jews and helps dig the escape tunnel that joins his house with the pay-library.

Hans-Jürgen Braunmeier

The sadistic Hans-Jürgen Braunmeier is a contemporary of Trudi Montag. He is physically abused by his father, but when Hans comes to school with bruises and a broken arm, no one steps in to help. Hans is also punished repeatedly in school for his antisocial conduct. The nuns exclude him from the annual piano concert and make sure St. Nicholas brings him no treats. In adulthood, Hans-Jürgen becomes a murderer.

Helmut Eberhardt

Born in 1920 shortly after the death of his father, Helmut Eberhardt is the beautiful, blond, blue-eyed baby of the widowed Renate Eberhardt. However, as soon as Trudi touches baby Helmut, she knows he has "the power to destroy his mother." Helmut marries the midwife Hilde Sommer in 1938, and in 1940 she bears him a son, Adolf. Also in 1940, Helmut is killed in battle. Townspeople gather for his burial, sympathetic toward Hilde and yet glad Helmut is dead because they know he had his own loving mother arrested and taken away to a concentration camp where she died.

Hilde Sommer Eberhardt

The midwife Hilde Sommer Eberhardt is older and weighs more than her husband, Helmut. At first, she acquiesces to his domination, moving with him into the second floor of his mother's home and observing how he works on his mother to sign over the house to him. When Renate Eberhardt refuses to buckle under her son's pressure, Helmut has her arrested for being kind to Jews. During the war years and thereafter, Hilde lives with her son in the upstairs rooms, cleaning and maintaining the ground floor rooms in readiness for the return of her mother-in-law. Many years after the war, Hilde gives birth to or adopts a daughter, whom she names Renate. As a midwife, she is generous and dutiful, and the townspeople respect her for her loyalty to her mother-in-law's memory.

Renate Eberhardt

Generous, resolute Renate Eberhardt is beloved by her neighbors. She has a lush flower garden, with a lovely pear tree in the center. The garden conveys her love of life and nature as well as her lack of the typically Germanic need for order. She loves her son, Helmut, with a love that freezes after he becomes a ruthless, self-seeking autocrat. Very much living according to her own values, Frau Eberhardt continues to help Jews even after the Nazi laws forbid it, and she stands up to her son, refusing to sign over her house to him or retire out of his way to the second floor. Because he wants the house, Helmut turns in his mother for befriending Jews: she is arrested and taken to a concentration camp. As a soldier, Helmut is haunted by his mother's love for him. After Renate's disappearance, her pear tree bears only tainted fruit.

Emil Hesping

Though his brother is a bishop, Emil Hesping does not attend church. He avoids military service during World War I, remaining in Burgdorf and managing several gymnasiums. He is generally criticized for being a womanizer but tolerated as a charming, good-hearted person. He is a devoted friend of Leo Montag and feels an erotic attachment to Leo's wife, Gertrude, with whom he once had a sexual encounter. Hesping is discovered to be the town's unknown benefactor. The truth comes out that he has embezzled money from the gyms in order to purchase gifts and secretly deliver these to townspeople in need. During World War II, he assists Leo and Trudi in digging the escape tunnel, and he risks his life repeatedly by driving Jews from the Montag home to their next hiding place. Emil Hesping is murdered by the Nazis when he is caught trying to remove a statue of Hitler. Afterward, the bishop describes his brother as courageous, and Leo calls him the town's only hero.

Anton Immers Sr.

The butcher, Anton Immers, trades sausage for Kurt Heidenreich's World War I officer's uniform and has Michel Abramowitz take his portrait wearing it. This photograph hangs in the butcher shop, masking the fact that Immers was rejected for military service because of a curved spine, the result of a 1912 accident. Years later, Immers begins to "believe that fabrication," and eventually the townspeople do, too. During World War II, both he and his son are Nazi sympathizers and express strong anti-Semitic views.

Klaus Malter

Red-bearded Klaus Malter, a young dentist, opens a practice in Burgdorf and attracts the attention of several unmarried women. Both Ingrid Baum and Trudi Montag become attached to him; however, Ingrid refuses his attention, and he rejects the prospect of a relationship with the dwarf Trudi. For several years, he dates the prim Brigitte Raudschuss, but then suddenly he falls in love with Jutta Sturm, an eccentric artist, whom he marries.

The couple has one child, Hanna, whom Trudi loves as she would her own daughter.

Gertrude Montag

Born in 1885, Gertrude Montag "absorbed the joys and pains of others," a sensitivity that either drives her crazy or manifests as a psychotic symptom. Three days after she gives birth to the dwarf daughter named after her, Gertrude runs away from home for the first of many times. In order to contain her and keep her safe, her husband, Leo, locks her in the third-floor sewing room, where Gertrude spends her days playing with cut-out paper dolls. Gertrude has an aversion to Emil Hesping, with whom she had a brief sexual encounter. Erratic, impulsive, and willful, Gertrude is committed to a neighboring mental institution on two occasions. Between these two stays, Gertrude gives birth prematurely to a son, Horst, who dies immediately. In 1919, during her second time in the institution, she contracts pneumonia and dies.

Leo Montag

Self-described as a "reluctant" soldier, Leo Montag is the first casualty to return from World War I, a plate disk now lodged in his left knee. A reader and thinker, Leo is the third-generation owner of the pay-library. He has a gaze that makes others feel both "respected and sheltered." A good listener, he draws women to him but remains sexually neutral. Leo does not reveal himself to others or seek to be understood by them. Yet he receives without judgment and keeps the confidences of others. A reserved person generally, Leo is nonetheless an open critic of the Catholic Church and the Nazi Party. He treats others humanely and bravely defends those who are rejected or abused.

Trudi Montag

The dwarf Trudi Montag, only daughter of Gertrude and Leo Montag, is the protagonist of *Stones from the River*. She is blue-eyed and has lovely blond hair, two Aryan traits valued by the Nazis, yet her abnormal body type associates her with those other so-called undesirables whom the Nazis slated for medical experimentation and extermination. A storyteller by nature and a librarian by profession, Trudi buys and trades books, markets gossip, and twists news to suit her purposes. Seeking to be like others, to be loved for who she is, Trudi constantly experiences "the agony of being different." Capable of revenge, Trudi nonetheless finds love and a sense of self-worth as she comes to understand that difference is what makes individuals unique and acceptance and membership in a community are universal human desires.

Erna Neimann

The Jewish biologist, Erna Neimann, and her son, Konrad, take shelter under the pay-library where they are discovered by Trudi, who takes them in and protects them. Neimann brings word to the Montags about how in other cities Jews are being herded into certain houses and then shipped away in boxcars. By a mere accident of timing, she and her son escape similar deportation. Their presence in the pay-library instigates the creation of an escape tunnel between the pay-library and the Blaus's home next door. Of all the people hidden by the Montags, the Neimanns are the only ones who later write, revealing that they indeed reached safety in Zurich.

Pia

Pia is the first dwarf Trudi sees, a talented circus performer, whose trailer has scaled-down furniture and who speaks to Trudi about the fact that there are other dwarfs in the world. Pia has been married, and she has a normal-size adult son. Self-accepting, Pia speaks in defense of difference and on behalf of self-love and tolerance of others. Though she never sees Pia again, Trudi remembers her advice about how to love oneself.

Doktor Rosen

The Jewish doctor in town is a woman with an invalid husband and one daughter, Eva. Doktor Rosen tells Trudi there is no pill that will make her grow, that her condition is genetic. Successful before the Third Reich comes to power, Doktor Rosen's practice suffers in the years leading up to World War II. She and her husband manage to find a car and drive out of Germany to safety in Switzerland. Making a fatal mistake, their daughter elects to remain behind with her Christian husband, Alexander Sturm.

Max Rudnick

A schoolteacher who has the bad luck to be overheard making a joke about Hitler, dim-sighted Max Rudnick loses his job and is obliged to move to Düsseldorf where he works first as a tutor and later in a factory. With a look in his eyes "too deep to be concerned about surfaces," Max falls in love with Trudi Montag, and they have a close, fulfilling relationship for more than a year. Max speaks for the importance of individuality and points out how Trudi uses her body type as a defense to keep people away.

Lotte Simon

Lotte Simon, a successful milliner and Jewish spinster, owns her own apartment and shop. While local women and those from nearby towns come to her for her stylish hats and completely trust her judgment in matters of fashion, Fräulein Simon remains an outsider. Over the years, she has an on-again off-again sexual relationship with Emil Hesping. Lotte Simon is arrested by the Nazis; her hats are confiscated; and the shop becomes the local headquarters for the Hitler-Jugend. She returns diminished after four months in captivity. Later she is deported to a labor camp. She writes to Ilse Abramowitz about conditions there and then is heard of no more.

Alexander Sturm

Alexander Sturm inherits a toy factory and constructs an apartment building in Burgdorf. A Christian, he is nonetheless mesmerized by the beautiful Eva Rosen, whom he marries one month before the 1935 Nürnberg laws prohibiting such unions. To his great consternation and guilt, Alexander cowers when the Nazis arrest Eva. Later he enlists in the army, hoping to die in battle. When he emerges without even a wound from repeated military action, he deserts, returns to Burgdorf, and commits suicide by jumping from the window of the apartment building attic where Eva was arrested.

Eva Rosen Sturm

Eva Rosen, tall and beautiful, becomes a childhood friend of Trudi Montag. Eva has the looks Trudi envies, yet Eva has a large red birthmark across her chest, which makes her feel inferior to others. Eva experiences ostracism at the Catholic school because she is a Jew. Defiant and proud, she marries the Christian Alexander Sturm. Though she successfully hides in the pay-library, she is discovered in the Sturm apartment house and arrested. She dies in a concentration camp.

Unknown Benefactor

See Emil Hesping

Hedwig Weiler

Abused by her stepfather and then married to Franz Weiler, an abusive alcoholic, Hedwig Weiler runs the grocery store next door to the pay-library and after she is widowed raises her son Georg alone. Frau Weiler dresses her son in smocks like a girl and leaves his hair in long curls, wishing to keep him separate from the evil she believes lurks in most men's hearts. Georg and Trudi are childhood friends, but when she cuts his hair at his urging, she recognizes

that his becoming like other boys separates him from her. Later with three friends, Georg participates in the molestation of Trudi Montag. He marries Helga Stamm, daughter of an unwed mother.

Themes

Difference

The story of the dwarf Trudi Montag directs attention to the experience of being different, both its discomforts and its power. The novel explores definitions of human deviation and what causes people to hide their own abnormalities and conform outwardly to communities based on apparent sameness. Trudi; her exhibitionistic manic mother, Gertrude; Georg Weiler next door whose mother dresses him like a girl; Rainer Bilder, the morbidly obese schoolboy; Eva Rosen with the birthmark across her nipples; drooling Gerda, and many others, all diverge in various ways from normal body type and/or a range of normal function, and they are treated in ways that convey their inferior status: they are ignored, rejected, ridiculed, shunned, or abused. They suffer low self-esteem, ostracism, loneliness.

These German townspeople value order, comeliness, obedience, and conformity. Aberrant individuals, even if they are tolerated, get aligned with what is to be avoided, with what is believed to be bad. The townspeople are united in their resistance to German refugees who move in after World War I. Newcomers, such as the Baums, who are very like long-time Burgdorf residents, are still viewed as outsiders, as is Fräulein Simon, the Jewish milliner. Women depend on her fashion sense and good taste but exclude her socially. Moreover, some abnormalities are more suggested than apparent; for example, some parents' sexual and physical abuse of their own children may go undetected, the parents treated as upstanding members of the community while the deviance is hidden (as in Ingrid's being sexually abused) or ignored (as in Hans-Jürgen's broken arm and bruises that no one inquires about).

Across the community, people seek group identity and conform to certain social modes of behavior. By so doing, they align themselves with the acceptable and detach themselves from what is believed to be unacceptable. One example of this tendency is shown in Anton Immers, the butcher, and the portrait he displays of himself in a World War I officer's uniform. The pretense of military service

Topics For Further Study

- Investigate online the Auschwitz Memorial and Museum and read Elie Wiesel's *Night*. Give a presentation to your class, showing pictures of the museum and describing what happened at Auschwitz and other concentration camps during World War II, relying on Wiesel's eyewitness report in his book.

- A few Burgdorf women help Renate Eberhardt pack for her arrest and anticipated deportation. Do some research on what Jews were allowed to take in their suitcases and what happened to their possessions. Then choose a small suitcase or backpack and put in it the valuables you would choose to take with you if you were being deported. Unpack the bag in front of your class, explaining your choices and telling about what happened to the things the Jews packed.

- The medical term for Trudi Montag's genetic condition is achondroplastic dwarfism. Write a paper in which you explain the symptoms of her condition and its effects on Trudi as shown in the novel.

- Read Hegi's collection of short stories, *Floating in My Mother's Palm*, and write a paper on what you learn about Burgdorf and its residents that adds to your understanding of *Stones from the River*.

- Do some library research on Nazi propaganda films, and then write a paper on the subject, using the description Hegi gives of a film Ingrid Baum and Trudi Montag see in Düsseldorf as a starting point. How does the film they see communicate beliefs and values that convey anti-Semitism and support Nazi treatment of Jews? You might like to include in your discussion a Hollywood film that also incorporates propagandistic messages and explain those messages, too.

- Write a short story from the point of view of Eva Rosen Sturm, Renate Eberhardt, or Ilse Abramowitz, telling about the person's arrest and what happened to her after she was removed from Burgdorf.

---

mitigates his shame in being found unfit to serve, and in time the pretense eclipses the fact that he did not serve. A different example is given in the story of the chess champion, Bruno Stosick, the boy who yearns to be like other seemingly ordinary children. Bruno secretly joins the Hitler-Jugend, seeking peer approval and club membership, but his anti-Nazi parents force him to withdraw from it. Without this group validation, the child plunges into depression and hangs himself. When the Nazis come to power, Bruno's father is forced out of the chess club, and no one sits near him and his wife during Catholic mass. By this time, explicit disapproval of the Nazis is dangerous, and others want to pass for having party loyalty or indeed are loyal to it. Former friends and neighbors shun Bruno's parents as if they are to blame for his suicide. In the butcher's case, the difference is a physical handicap; in the boy's case, the difference is an exceptional talent. In both cases, the person seeks group identity, the appearance of sameness in order to mask individual difference and gain group validation.

Anti-Semitism and the Catholic Church

In a well-crafted novel, themes are closely interrelated: one idea builds on another. Anti-Semitism as it is dramatized in this novel is closely connected to the theme of difference. Hegi's novel implicates those in the Catholic Church who complied with the Third Reich, Christians whose beliefs about Jews seemed to justify their being cast out of the community. The novel faults the Church for conditioning its members into blind obedience, for persuading people to follow authoritarian dictates rather than to think for themselves. The parish priest sermonizes against the romance novels on loan at the pay-library but never denounces novels that celebrate war. Then, too, the church service changes, with prayers for the fatherland taking an increasingly prominent part.

At the same time that this visible compliance by the Catholic Church is criticized by Trudi and her father, reports surface about what happens when clergy resist the totalitarian state. The fugitive priest named Adolf who hides for a while in the pay-library reports being arrested while celebrating mass and escaping into a forest right before deportation to the concentration camp at Buchenwald. Hiding in a cemetery, the priest experiences an all-consuming hunger that eclipses his faith in God. He looks around at the grave markers, which have been left standing for the Christian dead but which have been broken up if marking the graves of Jews. He says: "I thought I'd go insane. I could not understand how some people's graves could be marked while others were obliterated without evidence. It felt more horrible than any other injustice I'd ever known." After Emil Hesping is killed and he is revealed to have been the unknown benefactor, his brother the bishop talks with Leo about Emil's courage. The bishop admits that many bishops who openly resisted have been "pulled out of high positions." He notes only the bishop of Münster spoke out without being harmed. Emil's brother has been covertly instrumental in helping Jews move on from the pay-library, yet he resents having to work secretly, in what he calls "furious silence." Darkly, he and Leo agree that the extermination of Jews was the plan of the Third Reich from the very beginning.

The apparently compliant position of the Catholic Church regarding anti-Semitic policies is taken as justification by some Catholics for their feelings of resentment regarding Jewish prosperity after World War I. Jews in Burgdorf are prosperous and envied by others who struggle economically. Michel Abramowitz is able to buy a used Mercedes; Fräulein Simon owns her own thriving hat shop, Doktor Rosen has a successful medical practice. Outside town, the Jewish pianist, Fräulein Birnsteig lives in a sumptuous estate. Hegi's novel helps readers understand how it came to be that ordinary, church-going small-town people were swept along with a nationalistic political machine set on mobilizing the latent hatred of Jews in order to eradicate them.

Hegi does not idealize Jews. Some are commendable, some not so; each one is a complex human being, like those who persecute or protect them. The generosity and loyalty of the Abramowitzs is dramatized side-by-side with the failure of Erna Neimann, in hiding at the pay-library, to acknowledge the risk the Montags take on her behalf and the theft of silverware by another Jew in hiding there.

Regarding those who either participated in the abuses of Jews or did nothing to stop them, the fact is that as the Third Reich gained power, the survival instinct of ordinary people took over. Persecuted or not, people found themselves fearing for their lives. It is perhaps easy to condemn people who cannot be kind to one another in civil times, but when each fears for his own life, kindness is for many the first social grace to go.

In sum, the novel invites readers to reflect on the role of the Catholic Church with regard to anti-Semitic policy and to acknowledge the importance of independent thinking and moral behavior, even when it contradicts the homily from the pulpit. Leo Montag makes it clear: kindness matters most. It is a precept that can be very hard to follow in life-threatening conditions.

Style

Setting

The geographical location, landscape, buildings, along with the time in history and the seasons of the year, can be important parts of any novel's setting. In addition, the general environment, consisting of the social, economic, religious, and political world in which the characters live, creates a backdrop against which the novel's action is understood. The fictional town of Burgdorf, within walking distance of the Rhein River, easy driving distance of Düsseldorf, and a couple hours by car from Dresden, is the geographical setting. The novel includes details about the two Catholic churches; the Theresienheim convent hospital, which is later appropriated by the Gestapo; and the more remote Grafenburg asylum with its stone walls topped with jagged glass.

The pay-library is both home and business for Leo Montag and his daughter. Their bedrooms and the sewing room where Gertrude is confined are upstairs. Behind the library on the ground floor are the kitchen and living room. There is a cellar, and during the war a dirt tunnel from the cellar to the Blaus's cellar next door serves as an escape route for Jews in the event the house is searched by Gestapo. Under the house in the back is a dark place where Gertrude and Trudi crouch together and where Trudi discovers Erna and Konrad Neimann hiding. This building is Trudi's home, but it also serves as the center of the town. Stories are borrowed and exchanged here, both literally as patrons pay to borrow books and socially as Trudi gathers and exchanges gossip, altering news and reports of others when it suits her purposes.

This story cannot exist outside the national political and economic environment which frames it. The German defeat in World War I and the economic depression following, the blind obedience demanded by the Catholic Church, the rise of Adolf Hitler and his anti-Semitic platform, along with the Nazi organizations, such as the youth groups, intended to build a proud national identity, all combine to create the environment for and determine the nature of both plot and character.

Metaphoric Language

Vividness and immediacy are achieved in descriptions which use words in unexpected, fresh ways. In metaphoric writing, comparisons between dissimilar things often convey exactly the picture the author has in mind. For example, the fireworks on Trudi's fourth birthday are described in terms of water: they "drenched the sky" with "showers of stars that shot up and spilled high," emphasizing the streaming movement of what is actually explosion and fire. But when describing heavy rains and people smoking as they watch the river approach flood stage, Hegi makes a surprising comparison to sewing and cloth: "Threads of cold rain stitched the earth to the gray sky," and townspeople at dawn stared at the rising water, "shrouded by the smoke from their cigarettes." The people work to reinforce the dykes in a constant rain, until "the sun finally untangled itself from the clouds." By contrast, Hegi compares the process of falling asleep to jumping in a lake: Erna Neimann finally falls asleep in the pay-library, "as though flinging herself into a bottomless lake." The beauty and strength of Hegi's prose is, in part, felt in the author's poetic use of metaphor to help readers imagine something all the more clearly because it is compared to something else.

The River as Symbol

A symbol is a figure of speech (meaning a word used in other than a literal sense) that both refers to something that exists objectively and suggests other levels of meaning at the same time. Quite different from metaphor or simile, the symbol retains this objective referent while it may have layers of additional meaning ascribed to it in a given text. According to *A Handbook to Literature*, some literary symbols are used so frequently that they embody "universal suggestions of meaning, as flowing water suggests time and eternity." Literally the Rhein River flows near Burgdorf; there is

a dyke to protect the farmland and village from its repeated floods; and accidents occur along the river (as when Franz Weiler does handstands on the dyke, loses his balance, and drowns). On this level, the river is part of the novel's setting, an objective referent. In addition, the river symbolizes the action of storytelling, the ways in which narratives flow out, generated by certain people or events. Just as a river transports boats or objects along with its current, stories transport ideas and beliefs and allow people to be carried away imaginatively from their immediate lives into the world created by the narrative. In addition, the action of the river is compared to Trudi's ways of obtaining stories from her neighbors. Hegi writes:

> As the river, she washed through the houses of people without being seen, got into their beds, their souls, as she flushed out their stories and fed on their worries about what she knew. . . . Whenever she became the river, the people matched her power only as a group.

Trudi takes Konrad imaginatively to the river by telling him stories about it: "she painted the Rhein for him with words that let him see." Throughout the decades of her life, Trudi would be able to envision the river as she did her stories: "It was like that with stories: she could see beneath their surface, know the undercurrents, the whirlpools that could take you down, the hidden clusters of rocks. Stories could blind you." In this novel, the river is both literally the water that marks the seasons of ebb and flood, and symbolically the nature of narrative, the flow of plot and the imaginative transport possible via stories and the storyteller who tells them.

Historical Context

Adolf Hitler's Rise to Power

In her acknowledgments, Hegi thanks Ilse-Margret Vogel and Rod Stackelberg for checking the novel for its historical accuracy. The novel presents a fictional story occurring within an accurately portrayed period in German history, making reference to specific historical events. Hegi's novel begins with Leo Montag being the first local soldier to return from World War I; he appears in town in October 1914, two months after the battle of Tannenburg on the Eastern Front in which the Germans defeated the Russians. But while the novel does not dwell on World War I, it does include the effects of the German defeat: shortages of goods and a struggling economy robbed of its civilian labor

Compare & Contrast

- **1940s:** IG Farben produces xyklon-B (hydrogen cyanide [HCN]), a delousing chemical created by German Jew Fritz Haber for use in World War I, and supplies it to the SS (the Schutzstaffel, the military organization of the Nazi Party) to be used in gas chambers at Buchenwald and elsewhere.

  Today: After the break up of IG Farben, several of its major companies remain in business. Two of these are Bayer and BASF.

- **1940s:** Crystal Night, in which mobs vandalize and destroy synagogues and Jewish-owned shops across Germany, initiates hate crimes against Jews that continue throughout the early 1940s.

  Today: In 1993, residents in Billings, Montana, squelch attacks by white supremacists against local Jews. Over ten thousand homes and businesses display a picture of a menorah in their windows in a show of solidarity with Jewish residents, and Christians crowd local synagogues for services rather than attending their own churches. The white supremacists are embarrassed and leave town. This kind of solidarity with Jews and other minorities who suffer prejudice continues into the new millennium.

- **1940s:** The forced labor and extermination camp complex known as Auschwitz-Birkenau, located in Oswiecism, Poland, is run by Commandant Rudolf Höss. About 1.6 million people die here during the Holocaust, approximately 1.3 million Jews, along with an estimated 300,000 Soviet POWs, Polish Catholics, Gypsies, and other groups. In 1947, Höss is hanged at Auschwitz for war crimes.

  Today: Auschwitz-Birkenau Memorial and Museum, in Oswiecism, Poland, has been visited by over twenty-five million people. From the 1990s on, an average of a half million visitors come annually to the museum. The museum has a website which shows pictures of the existing buildings and evidence gathered by the Allies of what the Nazis did here. Children under the age of fourteen are discouraged from visiting the museum.

---

force. Hegi emphasizes how in the absence of their men, village women took over the business of ordinary life, becoming both self-reliant and cooperative. After the war, when German soldiers returned disillusioned by defeat, the women were relegated to their traditionally secondary status in family life, their concerns reduced to the lines for food and the challenge involved in getting dinner for their families.

Between the wars, in the years when Trudi grows into young adulthood, German society struggled financially, strapped with enormous war debt assigned to the nation by the Treaty of Versailles. The treaty, which brought an end to World War I, demilitarized a thirty-mile strip along the right bank of the Rhein and restricted German development of arms. The humiliations imposed on Germany by the treaty became a rallying cry for Adolf Hitler (1889–1945) in his rise to power. Facing frequent bankruptcies, demoralized, and struggling, small-town people became all the more competitive and angry, suspicious of outsiders, ready to assign blame. It was in this general discontent and economic depression that the Weimar Republic was established. Weimar was a democracy that would eventually permit Hitler to ascend to power. The novel traces, always from the small-town perspective looking out toward the national situation, the ominous and insidious social and political shifts, which were misconstrued as positive for quite some time.

Shortly after World War I, Hitler joined a military intelligence unit (the Press and Propaganda Department of Group Command IV of the Reichswehr), a right-wing group whose platform became extremely anti-Semitic. Hitler drew people and money into this group with his forceful speeches on the unfairness of the treaty. He advocated revoking civil rights for Jews and expelling Jews who came into Germany after World War I began. He blamed Jews for the prevailing economic instability, including high inflation, which gave the Christian German population some group on which to project its own shame in losing the war. He argued for nationalism, connecting Jews to internationalism. Hitler's group now called itself the National Socialist German Workers Party and adopted the red flag bearing the swastika as its symbol (the swastika was a symbol Hitler first saw on Catholic Church walls where he attended school as a child). By 1921, Hitler was chairman of the Nazi Party. By 1923, he advocated the overthrow of the Weimar Republic as too liberal and urged cleansing the Berlin government of all communists and Jews. He incited a revolution against the government, was tried for treason, and sent to prison, where he wrote his partly autobiographical political tract, *Mein Kampf: My Struggle*, which explains a lot about his development, his totalitarian philosophy, and the devastating effects it was to have in the Holocaust. In his book, Hitler claims that Jews bastardize the German race and corrupt the German national character and culture. He urges Germans not to marry Jews or Slavs. Released after five months, Hitler sought power through the electoral process. The conservative upper class thought Hitler was an uneducated demagogue, but he was popular among the working class.

In a complex series of maneuvers, Hitler won elective office and then dismantled the government that allowed that election, centralizing power in his office. By 1933, all political parties other than the Nazi Party were illegal, and all books considered disloyal to Nazism were ordered to be destroyed. By 1934, he had completed a purge of the Nazi Party to eliminate dissent. Heinrich Himmler supervised those political executions and took charge of the Gestapo, the secret police. A campaign against Jews (who numbered about 600,000 in Germany) began. The 1935 Nürnberg Laws defined a person as a Jew who had one Jewish grandparent, thus about 2.5 million Germans, in addition to the 600,000 who considered themselves Jews, were now targeted. These laws denied Jews citizenship and barred them from marrying non-Jews. (Interestingly, some historians speculate that Hitler's maternal grandfather, who was illegitimate, may have been half Jewish.)

Kristlenacht (Crystal Night) in 1938 was a campaign of mob violence in which synagogues and Jewish-owned businesses were attacked, the name coming from the broken glass that filled the city streets. By 1939, Jews were required to wear a yellow six-pointed star on their outer clothing. The failure of Christian churches, both Protestant and Catholic, to act openly in resistance to Nazi treatment of Jews is noted in Hegi's novel, in which many Christian clergy and congregations stood by in fear and did nothing, while others worked both openly and covertly against anti-Semitic actions. Increasingly, as the populace saw the cost of open resistance in human life and liberty, covert actions took over. Emil Hesping's brother, a Catholic bishop, remarks that only the bishop of Münster was able to openly criticize the Nazis without bringing immediate harm to himself. Father Adolf, the priest in hiding at the pay-library, reports being arrested for his anti-Nazi stance while celebrating mass. Hitler, who was himself a Roman Catholic, signed an agreement with the Vatican, assuring the continuance of Catholic services in Germany, yet these services were violated when anti-Nazi sentiments were expressed from the pulpit. Repeatedly critical of the Catholic Church, Leo Montag warns against the German love of a strong ruler, and the arbitrary rules of Catholicism that discourage independent thinking and promote political cooperation instead of solidarity with non-Christians against a totalitarian state.

Hitler was given credit for transforming unruly young people who joined the youth groups, for putting the unemployed back to work in civic programs, and for improving the economy. As conditions worsened for Jews, the Christian population saw improvements for themselves. Weekly news programs and movies promoted Nazi ideology.

World War II began when German troops invaded Poland in September 1939 and Great Britain and France declared war on Germany. The United States entered the war in December 1941. By 1944, the Allied forces occupied much of Europe, and German cities were being destroyed by air attacks. As extermination of Jews and many other so-called undesirables accelerated in concentration camps, Hitler recognized he had lost the war and committed suicide in Berlin in 1945.

Critical Overview

Since its appearance in 1994 and continuing into the early 2000s, Hegi's *Stones from the River* has received wide-ranging and positive reviews, enhanced by the novel's 1997 selection for Oprah's

Portrait of Anita, a female dwarf, standing beside a man of more average stature to demonstrate her size © Topical Press Agency/Getty Images

Book Club. Kitty Harmon, in a long *Publishers Weekly* review article, states that this novel is:

> Hegi's attempt to understand the conspiracy of silence in towns like Burgdorf throughout Germany—a conspiracy that countenanced persecution of Jews during the war and enabled a community to quiet its conscience once the truths of the Holocaust were revealed.

Hegi is quoted in this review as remarking that once she came to the United States, she realized "Americans of [her] generation knew more about the Holocaust than [she] did." Discussion of the Nazi devastation was "absolutely taboo," she is quoted as saying. In *Stones from the River*, Hegi challenges that taboo by dramatizing how ordinary Germans coped, adapted, resisted, and conformed during the Third Reich. A 1994 review in *Booklist* notes: "Though Hegi's canvas is broad here, the focus is always on individual lives, not on the horrific events that swirl around them." A 1994 *Publishers Weekly* review notes that in this "powerful novel," protagonist Trudi Montag "exploits her gift" for drawing out people's secrets. The review also states that the book describes the "vast amnesia that grips formerly ardent Nazis" after World War II.

Commenting on Oprah's "reading revolution," a 1997 review by Lisa Schwarzbaum in *Entertainment Weekly*, notes that because of the novel's selection, Scribner was advised to print "an extra billion copies," and Oprah Winfrey is quoted as saying that readers who finish the "big" novel will find rewards in it "just as big." Hegi's accomplishment is summed up in a 2002 review by Judith Robinson in *Library Journal*: Hegi depicts "the emergence of Nazi Germany on an intimate canvas of a small town and its humanly flawed population." Robinson notes that the novel helps readers start to understand how political shifts occur and gain sway and how an unsuspecting populace concerned with its own day-to-day obligations may be swept into something they never envisioned or invited. Another review in *Booklist*, this time of Hegi's *Tearing the Silence: On Being German in America* asserts that Hegi's work recognizes "the German—and human—capacity for evil."

Criticism

Melodie Monahan

Monahan has a Ph.D. in English and operates an editing service, The Inkwell Works. In the following essay, Monahan explores how storytelling conveys characterization and affects plot in Stones from the River.

Ursula Hegi's *Stones from the River* is about storytelling. It is about fairy tales and old wives' tales, about memories based on fiction, church-spawned morality tales, political agenda and film propaganda, and ultimately the writing of history. Storytelling is one way of selecting from and compressing complex, multifaceted human experience into the arbitrary linearity of chronology. In providing ways to understand self and world, stories perpetuate or mask the truth and shape individuals' beliefs about themselves and others. Storytelling can even shape events, putting a certain interpretation on past occurrences, influencing the outcome of present events, and giving direction to future choices and policy. The novel shows how stories provide formulas for denial, how fantasy augments reality for certain sexual or psychological purposes, and how old tales or mythologies assert their world-views and cause some individuals to see the world in their terms. Ultimately, the novel is about the power of story.

The immediate setting, a small-town pay-library where the protagonist works as a librarian, is central to the novel's focus on storytelling. The dwarf Trudi Montag is both an insider and an outsider, a person who lives at the hub of the community and yet is somehow ignored when people speak privately to one another in her presence. She is literally a purveyor of stories, since she buys, organizes, and checks out novels to patrons. These people gather in the pay-library to visit; to confide in Trudi's father, Leo Montag; and to exchange news. As she matures, Trudi capitalizes on what she hears or knows about others, markets and trades gossip, and in revenge for being scorned and violated learns to punish offenders by making up false stories against them. Able to keep her own secrets, Trudi exposes the secrets of others as a kind of social currency.

Trudi's story is directly linked to the novel's central composite symbol, the river and the stones that come from it. A universal symbol for time, according to the definition given in *A Handbook to Literature*, the river seems to signify in this text the flow yet constancy of time as it moves across or through events. Within its banks, the river signals chronology, since events are commonly plotted in linear arrangement, as the chapter headings suggest by designating specific years. The stones mentioned in the title may then be the people who enact the events; at least that seems to be the message in the passage following Trudi's violation by four boys. Trudi throws stones into the river, assigning the boys' names to the stones, throwing several with the name of Georg Weiler, her next-door neighbor and early childhood friend. Add to this scene the description of Trudi, born of "two long and angular people" and yet shaped "like a pebble—round and solid" and one gets the correlation Hegi is drawing. Furthermore, an early story Gertrude tells Trudi, about the motorcycle fall with Emil Hesping in which gravel gets embedded in Gertrude's skin, connects the stony particles to the larger story of Gertrude and Hesping. Gertrude presses the child's fingers against her left knee to feel the stony bits, and the intuitive child takes "in the story beneath the anguish" and feels "the secret shaping itself into images." Even as a preschooler, little Trudi understands her mother's sense of guilt and the causal link Gertrude sees between her marital infidelity and Leo's injury on the same day and similarly in the left knee.

Since her home is a library, Trudi grows up surrounded literally with hundreds of stories. The wider culture of her hometown, Burgdorf, is also

> " The stories that matter are the ones that help people cherish their uniqueness and empower them to create community by acting kindly toward one another."

full of stories. Many of these project their own versions of the facts or actually hide the truth. One of these stories is asserted by the portrait of the butcher, Anton Immers, posing in a World War I officer's uniform. Deformed by an accident and bent to one side, Immers actually did not qualify for service. Yet the portrait tells another story, showing him dressed in a uniform and standing as erect as he can. When Immers looks at the portrait, he imagines having "fought in the war" and being "highly decorated." As time passes, he comes to believe the "fabrication," and the following generation is "fed that illusion as history." The story Hedwig Weiler tells about her husband's death is also a rewriting of events. She tells people Franz was en route to mass when he fell into the river and drowned. Eyewitnesses know that the inebriated Franz fell because he was entertaining his drinking buddies by doing handstands on the dyke. Yet "no one contradicted Frau Weiler." Rather, townspeople perpetuated "the façade." This "complicity of silence . . . had served the town for centuries." Hegi writes that only a few individuals "would preserve the texture of the truth" and not let "its fibers slip beneath the web of silence and collusion." It is this nexus of story-making and truth-withholding that is part of the novel's focus.

One old wives' tale or fairytale is used as a metaphor for human reproduction. To prepare Trudi for the advent of a sibling, Gertrude tells her daughter that storks are persuaded to deliver babies if sugar cubes are left for them on windowsills. Fearful that a normal baby would garner more parental love than she receives, Trudi secretly eats the sugar. Then when baby Horst is born prematurely and dies, Trudi believes she caused his death. Her mother had told her on another occasion that "people die if you don't love them enough"; Trudi did not "love" enough: she ate the sugar, and thus

What Do I Read Next?

- An early work by Hegi is the collection of interrelated stories entitled *Floating in My Mother's Palm* (1990), which introduces many characters, including Trudi Montag, who appear in subsequent novels. These evocative, poetic stories take place in Burgdorf, Germany, the setting Hegi uses for *Stones from the River*.

- Readers of *Stones from the River* who would like to know more about the life Stefan Blau has after he immigrates to the United States may enjoy Hegi's *The Vision of Emma Blau*, which was published by Simon and Schuster in 2000. This novel tells the story of Stefan Blau's three wives—the third of whom is Leo Montag's sister, Helene—and the bicultural family's life in Blau's large apartment building in New Hampshire. The novel spans nearly a century and ends with the story of Blau's granddaughter, who is the woman named in its title.

- Hegi has written several other excellent novels. One of these is *Sacred Time*, first published by Simon and Schuster in 2003, which tells the story of three generations of an Italian family living in the Bronx. This novel employs three first-person narrators.

- Eva Hoffman's autobiography, *Lost in Translation: A Life in a New Language*, available in a Penguin edition (2003), tells the story of Jewish immigrants to Canada who grow up in a world in which one culture predominates in the home and another in the world outside it. Hoffman's parents survived the Holocaust by hiding and running; Hoffman herself was born immediately after World War II, but her parents' experience colored her childhood.

- Ian McEwan's popular novel *Atonement*, which was published by Doubleday in 2002, is set in England, on one day in 1935 and a subsequent day during the British retreat from Dunkirk, early in World War II. Written in prose similar to that of Henry James, this novel is about an accusation that ruins two lives and a subsequent question about whether the accusation was true. The novel explores the way in which past events can be reexamined and reinterpreted years later.

- Corrie ten Boom's autobiography, *The Hiding Place*, available from Chosen Books (2006), tells the true-life story of a Christian family in the Netherlands who hid many Jews during World War II and whose members were finally arrested and taken to concentration camps. Ten Boom alone survived the camps.

---

she killed her brother. Years afterward, and even when Trudi fully understands the stork story as myth, sugar continues to gag her with guilt. When Gertrude dies shortly after Horst and four-year-old Trudi is not permitted to feel for the gravel in her dead mother's knee (to prove the corpse's identity), Trudi fantasizes that the body in the coffin is not her mother's, that Gertrude is hiding and will come back as soon as Trudi grows taller. In these and other instances, a story is invented to work out a more acceptable vision of past or future events.

An important illustration of how story connects with self-concept and can affect outcomes occurs when as a young adult Trudi is arrested and then interrogated by a Nazi officer. To manipulate the situation to her advantage, Trudi uses her intuitive understanding of people's beliefs and destinies. She senses that this officer does not believe in what he is doing and that he is destined to be a suicide within the year. When he asks her what it is like to be a "*Zwerg*" (dwarf), she knows it is a game and that she must play the dwarf and draw him into a story about being different. Trudi tells the officer a story of a man born with his heart on the outside of his chest cavity. She tells how the man had his suits designed to hide this abnormality, yet the heart pushed out visibly against the jacket. She tells the officer that in the man's dreams, "his chest was smooth, his heart safely anchored within his body." Trudi feels empowered, knowing that this story may save her life. She says she understands how the man felt because in her dreams she is tall. She tells the officer how as a child she hung from doorframes hoping to lengthen her body to conform to normal height, just like the man longed to be like other children when he was a little boy.

Using her intuition that the Nazi officer is hiding something about himself that makes him different from his fellow soldiers, Trudi draws him out by sympathetically telling a story about how difference makes one vulnerable to rejection and degradation. The story strikes such an immediate chord of sympathy with the officer that he begins feeding details into the story himself. Trudi has made a connection with him, linking her outward difference to his inner difference via the story. He knows the story she tells because it is as much his story as it is hers. During the Third Reich, a dwarf, even a blue-eyed, blond one, was destined to become "a medical experiment" and eventually be exterminated. By telling this particular story to this particular listener, Trudi penetrates the officer's outer conformity to a military identity in order to connect to his inner sense of his own separateness. He connects with the dwarf storyteller because he identifies with the man in her story. This connection causes him to release her. In this scene, as in many others, Hegi explores how storytelling can shape events and transform people's beliefs about themselves and about their culture and past.

Many other stories in the novel shape people's perception of the world. These include Eva Rosen's story about the cat in her father's bedroom window, Erna Neimann's story about the rich girl who takes Konrad's cat, Trudi's story about Hans-Jürgen's not being loved by any woman, Hanna's portrait of the swirling couple, and even Max Rudnick's watercolors of buildings transformed into red and yellow flowers. On the national scale, the propaganda machinery of the Third Reich produces films and newsreels, like those Ingrid Baum and Trudi see in Düsseldorf, that use stories to fuel a general atmosphere of hate, which in turn serves the anti-Semitic policies designed to achieve Hitler's Final Solution.

In *Stones from the River*, Hegi demonstrates how stories serve different purposes, how they come out of guilt and engender it (Gertrude's story of the bike accident), how they come out of rage

and effect revenge (Trudi's stories about her assailants), how they satisfy certain kinds of longing (Trudi's sexual fantasies), how they seek to obscure physical inferiority within the costume of conformity (Immers' military portrait). Stories arise from fear or from a sense of the unknown, and they create connection or prove wrongdoing (the old women's explanation of why the pear tree's fruit is spoiled after Renate is betrayed by her son and sent to the death camps).

Pia's story of a glorious island initially gives thirteen-year-old Trudi the hope that dwarfs can live altogether in a place. She asks Pia, "'Why can't we all be in one place?'" Pia responds, "'We are. It's called earth.'" Pia understands what many people have yet to learn: that all humans live together in one place, here on the Earth, and being different is what each and every one of them has in common with all the rest. Pia tells Trudi to know that she is never alone and when she feels alone to give herself a big hug, to literally embrace her uniqueness. Out of this self-acceptance can come the courage to create community despite differences.

Some stories in the novel are designed to hide the truth or to revise historical record. The danger of historical revision is that it may allow evil to grow undercover. This danger is dramatized in the story of the hidden sexual abuse of Ingrid Baum by her father; Ingrid's existence is denied by her family, and her daughter, Karin, is at thirteen impregnated by her grandfather. Had the family faced the original abuse, Ingrid's life would have been different and that difference would have created a better life for Karin and Ingrid's other daughter, Rita. In this case and in other ways, the novel seems to suggest that, ultimately, the stones thrown in the river must be pulled to the surface and examined. Against a tide of interpretations and the perpetuation of chosen stories, one must seek the truth. Trudi recalls her father's insistence that "being kind is the most important thing." *Stones from the River*, which tells the stories that defined a small town in Germany, conveys this message: seek truth, act kindly. Doing so is possible in so far as one strives for and achieves some level of self-acceptance. The stories that matter are the ones that help people cherish their uniqueness and empower them to create community by acting kindly toward one another. Ultimately, Trudi realizes that for her the ongoing engagement with story-making seeks discernment about "what to enhance . . . what to relinquish. And what to embrace."

Source: Melodie Monahan, Critical Essay on *Stones from the River*, in *Novels for Students*, Thomson Gale, 2007.

Victoria J. Barnett

In the following review, Barnett discusses the outsider protagonist in Stones from the River, *whose storytelling breaks the destructive silence, liberating those who have maintained, through the silence, "the illusion of a heile Welt (an intact world)" during the oppressive time of Nazism.*

At the end of Margarethe von Trotta's film "The Leaden Time" (1981), the young son of a murdered terrorist turns to his aunt. "Tell me about my mother," he says. For the viewer, the mother's story seems to have ended; but for the boy the story is the beginning. As viewers leave the theater, they wonder: what version of the past will his aunt give him? Whether she tells the truth or lies, he will have to struggle to weave what he learns of the past into the meaning of his own existence.

Most of us want to understand the links between our own identities and those of our families, communities and countries. In Germany, this process is burdened by the legacy of Nazism. Asking questions about the past imposes moral responsibilities upon both the narrator and the listener.

Germans' deeply emotional debates about the past are not so much about facts as about meaning, about moral interpretation. In the "historians' debate" during the 1980s, for example, revisionist Ernst Nolte did not deny that millions of Jews were murdered. Nolte's argument was that mass murders came about almost accidentally: they were a lamentable step that the Nazi regime, under wartime pressures and dangerously threatened by the Soviet Union, found "necessary." In revisionist history, the death camps were just one more tragic cost of a war that included the bombings of European cities, the deaths of millions of soldiers, and the forced flight of millions of ethnic Germans from eastern Europe at the end of the war.

U.S. historian Charles Maier has called this "Bitburg history"—an attempt to put all the "victims of fascism" under the same historical label, thereby avoiding the problematic issue of who was morally responsible for this bloodshed. The historians' debate is really about identity, not history. Like the boy in von Trotta's film, Germans were asking who they are, where they came from, and whether the past offers them a foundation upon which to live.

The resulting tension—between the young and old, between those who seek to remember and those who would rather forget—has been a theme in German films, television programs and novels since the 1950s. It is the subject, for example, of the film "The Nasty Girl" (1990), based upon the true story of Anna Rosmus, a student in Passau. When she combed town archives to write a paper on Passau during the Nazi era, Rosmus uncovered disagreeable truths about some of the town's leading citizens. In the film the "nasty girl," originally the darling of her school and town, is ostracized and threatened by the townspeople once it becomes clear that she is after the truth, not pleasant fictions.

Her persistence makes her an outsider. In Germany after Nazism, outsiders refuse to keep silent. They collect secrets, they tell stories. Their lives no longer fit the patterns of a society that would rather forget. Postwar German fiction is populated with such characters. Often some physical or psychological attribute distinguishes them visibly from those around them. This raises echoes of the outsider status that the Nazis forced upon all those who did not fit "Aryan" ideals.

A recent addition to this group is Trudi Montag, the central character in Ursula Hegi's new novel. Trudi is a dwarf—which, of course, immediately brings to mind the other dwarf in postwar German literature, Oskar Matzerath in Gunter Grass's *The Tin Drum*. Although the two books are very different, each chronicles the life of an outsider who comes of age during the Nazi era.

Trudi is born an outsider. As opposed to Oskar (who decides to stop growing), Trudi desperately wants to grow, even hanging upside down in a futile attempt to stretch her short torso. But despite her longing for acceptance and friendship, Trudi recognizes early the morally stifling consequences of belonging. When she starts school, the nuns scold her for "pushiness," pointing out that other girls "kept silent even if they knew the answers." Throughout her life, Trudi's difference liberates her from expectations about women, and she evades the rules that constrain those who belong. Adults ignore her and say "things they would never say around other children. If she didn't remind people that she was there, she got to listen to all kinds of secrets." Stealthily, she begins to gather the stories people would rather conceal.

After Trudi is nearly raped by four village boys, she furiously throws stones for each boy into the river. Later, more methodically, she begins to gather stones and stories for all the people in her life. She piles by the river one stone for each story she knows: stories of anger, revenge, longing and love. Her stories are her power, for Trudi knows secrets about the villagers that they themselves do not know. Beneath the surface of normal life in Nazi Germany, Trudi sees madness and moral emptiness.

Because of their physical stature, Oskar and Trudi are treated as children, as powerless and irrelevant. Actually, both rapidly leave childlike innocence behind. Oskar's recognition of the world's absurdity and Trudi's vision of its secrets give each character a form of power.

With the beginning of the Third Reich, Trudi is no longer the only outsider in her village. In a selection process that begins long before the death camps, people either scuttle to become part of the Nazi mainstream or—because they think differently or are Jewish—they become outsiders. Those who become part of Nazi society lose their sense of who they and their neighbors are. Only those who remain outside retain the ability to see what is really happening. One of the most shocking incidents in Hegi's book comes long after Trudi's size has ceased to be in the forefront of her or the reader's mind. Arrested and interrogated by a Gestapo officer, she realizes that he sees her not as an opponent of the regime (she has been hiding Jews) but as a potential victim—as a dwarf who could easily fall under the euthanasia guidelines.

For both authors, the Third Reich is part of a continuum (for Hegi, of silence; for Grass, of moral chaos) that begins long before 1933 and is not broken after 1945. Further, they contend that the failure to deal honestly with the past ensures the continuance of moral corruption. This belief marked much of the literature that emerged from Gruppe 47, a collection of postwar writers that included Ingeborg Bachmann, Uwe Johnson, Heinrich Boll and Gunter Grass. Much of their work concerns not only the past but lingering moral questions: What consequences does this confrontation with the Nazi past have for our own identity as moral beings? Was Nazism a moral aberration, or did it prove how easily moral values are weakened and corrupted?

For people of faith, of course, these are religious and spiritual questions as well. Yet the alienation of many of these writers and their fictional protagonists from the church is striking. Part of the reason is the poor record of the Protestant and Catholic churches under Nazism. In *Stones from the River*, the Catholic parish is a picture of conformity and hypocrisy. Though one of the priests and the bishop help the village's resistance group, they are alienated from "the Church," and their resistance takes place outside it. Everyone—from simple old

> But despite her longing for acceptance and friendship, Trudi recognizes early the morally stifling consequences of belonging."

farmers to Nazi informers—goes through the old rituals of the mass as though nothing were amiss. Through silence the villagers maintain the illusion of a *heile Welt* ("an intact world"); in its silence the church is part of that illusory world. "The silence of the war was in direct contradiction to [Trudi's] storytelling. It was much closer to the silence of the church—fostering belief instead of knowledge, smothering mystery, muffling truth."

Many writers were disillusioned by the churches' behavior both under Nazism and after the war, when organized religion accommodated to the new circumstances in East and West. Beneath this disillusionment, however, is the more fundamental problem of defining morality and asking what kind of ethical society might have been possible after the Nazi experience. This attitude is expressed by Trudi's father, Leo, who "never felt the division within the town as acutely as he did in the chapel. Once, the parish had felt like something whole, one body of people connected in one belief and many shared values . . . but now that belief had become tainted by those who used it to proclaim their superiority."

Nazism's corruption of people's values is so powerful that it shakes the very heart of Leo Montag's faith. The moral and religious values that before 1933 had seemed so strongly woven into all levels of society had unraveled so quickly under Nazism that it became difficult for many to believe in them at all. The surreal, chaotic world of Grass's *Tin Drum* and the stony hypocrisy of the Catholic Church in Heinrich Boll's *The Clown* (1963) are defiant postwar assertions that Germany can never return to "normal." When morality within religious or political institutions no longer seems possible, the only beings who can act as the voice of conscience are outsiders, symbolized in these novels by a dwarf and a clown.

What happens to these outsiders? Here, Grass and Hegi's novels have different outcomes. Against his will, Oskar Matzerath begins to grow after the war, and becomes symbolically entrapped by the guilt of the postwar world. In contrast, Trudi Montag finds ways to liberate others. She had initially gathered her stories and stones to gain power and revenge against those who had hurt her. But her purpose changes: "In the telling, she found, you reached a point where you could not go back, where—as the story changed—it transformed you, too. What mattered was to let each story flow through you."

Trudi comes to understand that her gift is not to make these stories happen, but to understand life itself. Through her stories, she has gained compassion. She uses her prophetic powers in a new way, to help herself and her listeners learn "what to enhance and what to relinquish. And what to embrace." This hopeful ending may be the product of the author's own distance from her native land. Born in Germany in 1946, Hegi has lived in the U.S. since 1965. But it may also be a product of the passage of time and of the process of Vergangenheitsbewaltigung, or mastering the past, which has gone on now for 50 years.

This process has been more successful in the arts than in politics or history. Perhaps this is because fiction can better reveal the intersection between explicable human history and the deeper, irrational psychological currents that move individuals. How else can we explain Hitler's charisma, and the bizarre mixture of mythology and racism that suddenly became the governing principle of an entire society? How else can one explain the behavior of people raised in a highly developed, religious culture who, in the name of the "Aryan ideal," murdered millions of people in unspeakably barbaric ways?

The task of Vergangenheitsbewaltigung is to use its insights to alter human circumstances, just as the river in Hegi's book eventually shows Trudi the purpose of her stories: ". . . it would always be the nature of the river to remember the dead who lay buried beneath its surface. What the river was showing her now was that she could flow beyond the brokenness, redeem herself, and fuse once more."

The stories of the dead and the living in Trudi's river join the myriad stories—of dwarfs, terrorists' sons, "nasty girls" and others—that have been told since 1945 to fill a void. Had Germans, confronted by their children's questions during the 1950s and 1960s, responded with tears, anguish and remorse—with anything but explanations, self-justification and silence—they would have laid an entirely different foundation from which to look at the past and the future. If there is a single message that recurs in the work of postwar German writers and filmmakers, it is the destruction wrought, both during and after the Third Reich, by silence.

Source: Victoria J. Barnett, "*Stones from the River*," in the *Christian Century*, Vol. 111, No. 23, August 10, 1994, pp. 755–57.

Kitty Harmon

In the following interview, Hegi talks about wrestling with her country's past and the "conspiracy of silence" in Stones from the River.

In the years after Ursula Hegi's arrival in the U.S. at the age of 18, she intentionally turned her back on Germany, the country of her birth. She married an American, became an American citizen and chose America as the setting for her first two books. Now in her late 40s, Hegi finds that it's not possible to reject one's origins, especially in the ease of 20th-eentury Germany. "The older I get," she says, "the more I realize that I am inescapably encumbered by the heritage of my country's history."

Hegi began revisiting that heritage in *Floating in My Mother's Palm*, a highly praised novel published by Poseidon in 1990. In it Hegi introduces various inhabitants of a fictional German town called Burgdorf. Like Hanna, the narrator of *Floating*, Hegi grew up in a small town near Dusseldorf in the 1950s, observing the foibles and flashes of generosity of people within a tight, small community. Now, with Poseidon's publication of *Stones from the River* (Fiction Forecasts, Jan. 17), Hegi extends her portrayal of Burgdorf's characters and the exploration of her own heritage to include the several decades preceding her birth: the years leading up to World War II, the war itself and its immediate aftermath. The stories in the two books are interwoven with such seamless ease that readers will find it difficult to believe that the new book was not written first.

Stones from the River is Hegi's attempt to understand the conspiracy of silence in towns like Burgdorf throughout Germany—a conspiracy that countenanced persecution of Jews during the war and enabled a community to quiet its conscience once the truths of the Holocaust were revealed. "When I came to this country," Hegi says, "I found that Americans of my generation knew more about the Holocaust than I did. When I was growing up you could not ask about it; it was absolutely taboo. We grew up with the silence. It was normal and familiar; these are terrible words considering the circumstances." Like the narrator in *Floating*, Hegi wryly recounts how history lessons in school started with the classic Greeks and Romans, ended with World War I and began all over again with ancient Greece and Rome. "We knew a lot about those old Greeks and Romans," she says.

Hegi weighs her words carefully and often asks if there isn't a better term to describe this or that emotion, as if entreating her interviewer to respect her words and not give them nuances she doesn't mean them to have. She speaks English flawlessly but with a pronounced accent, and her long blonde hair and rosy complexion reveal her Teutonic ancestry. Hegi says that sometimes she dreads it when people ask her where she's from. "I wish I could say some other country, not Germany. As a German, I feel implicated by what happened."

Still, Hegi had no intention of digging up the unspeakable parts of her country's past in her third novel. In fact, she recalls emphatically denying, in an interview with National Public Radio's Bob Edwards, that she would be revisiting the inhabitants of Burgdorf in her next book. But, she recalls, as soon as she left the studio, the voice of Trudi, a character in *Floating*, began speaking inside her head, demanding her "own book." This almost mystical connection with Trudi continued: not long afterward, Hegi and her companion, Gordon Gagllano, were driving from Portland to home near Spokane, Washington, listening to Beethoven's Ninth Symphony, when she got the urge to jot down some notes. Soon she had filled half a legal pad, often with complete passages that appear unchanged in *Stones*. "Trudi was in that car with us—even Gordon felt her presence," she says.

Trudi is a Zwerg, a dwarf whose handicap sets her apart from the community. This "otherness" mirrors her refusal to take part in the complicity of silence and enables her neighbors to confide in her. She collects their stories and uses them to barter for information, divulging or withholding or changing details as needed and thus developing her own power in the community. Hegi says that Trudi did not become the protagonist of *Stones* because of her physical deformity, but because she was already a fully developed character in *Floating* whose voice cried out to be heard.

When asked about the inevitable comparisons with *The Tin Drum*, Hegi shrugs. "Yes, I know, 'another novel about a dwarf in Germany during the war.' It worried me in the beginning—well, it stopped me for about five minutes. But the character was so strong in her insistence to be heard that to stop writing wasn't possible."

> **Hegi says she is drawn to write about things that she doesn't dare look at but needs desperately to figure out—'the things that won't leave me alone.'**

A faculty research grant in 1986 enabled Hegi to return to Germany for the first time in 15 years to research background material for *Floating*. This was immeasurably helpful, she says. "It added a whole layer of sensuousness—the sounds, the smells, the tastes—that you can only get from being there." When she visited her hometown, she looked around for the Zwerg she remembered from her childhood, a woman whom she had barely known but who, she says, "obviously must have made a big impression on me." Having failed to find her, Hegi was sitting in a cafe when the object of her search appeared at her table, having heard that Hegi was looking for her. Instead of replying to Hegi's tentative questions about some of her relatives, the woman shot back, "I hear you've been divorced." Only after Hegi had shared the details of her marital breakup would the gossipy Zwerg tell her about her grandparents. It was this bartering for information that contributed to the development of Trudi's character.

Although Trudi's voice presented itself to Hegi "whole and complete, like a gift," the process of fleshing out the narrative was much more difficult. Hegi took a second trip to Germany before finishing *Stones*, visiting the concentration camp at Buchenwald and other similar sites. This time, research was not the purpose. Hegi was compelled to make what she feels was a pilgrimage. "I was afraid to go [to the camp]," she says, "but as a German-born woman I felt I had to. Writing the book was what gave me the courage."

To provide details of the period, Hegi immersed herself in historical material on the Holocaust, reading dozens of books and collections of journals written by concentration camp inmates. "There were many, many times when I wished I could leave the research alone, but I couldn't.

It was an important part of my own journey, of integrating the past within myself."

Serendipity had a hand in furnishing some of the most helpful details. A German-American writer named IlseMargret Vogel, who called Hegi to congratulate her after the publication of *Floating*, was able to provide much material about the Resistance movement during the war; she was the first person who talked openly to Hegi about that time. Their conversations gave Hegi the courage to write to her godmother and ask for information, despite the fact that the older woman had previously refused to talk about the war years. Her godmother complied by recording her memories on tape. To Hegi, this constituted a gift of major proportions. "One sentence would become an entire story," she says.

She continues to be pessimistic about the interest of the German people in their tarnished past. Although she'd like *Stones* to be published in Germany "more than anywhere else in the world," she expects that it would make her the target of criticism there. "I would be tearing open the silence," she says, "something that even now many people aren't ready to face. I've come a long way in the past five or six years. Three years ago, even, we couldn't have had this conversation." In fact, it is an approach-avoidance dynamic that fuels much of her writing. Hegi says she is drawn to write about things that she doesn't dare look at but needs desperately to figure out—"the things that won't leave me alone."

Hegi's development as a writer came in fits and starts. While growing up in Germany, she wanted to write but lacked craft and encouragement. She wrote a novel after arriving in the States but collected enough rejection letters from publishers to convince herself to destroy the manuscript and stop writing altogether for three years. At the age of 28, with two sons, aged five and one, Hegi enrolled at the University of New Hampshire for a B.A. and then an M.A. and she stayed on to lecture in the English department until her divorce in 1984. On arriving at UNH she found herself within a community of writers and impulsively wrote "writer" as her occupation on a passport application. Soon thereafter, agent Gail Hochman sold her first novel, *Intrusions*, for publication by Viking in 1981. The University of Idaho Press issued a decade's collection of her stories in 1988. Hegi favored a university press because she surmised they would keep a short-story collection in print much longer, "and they did—it's still available in hardcover after six years."

Kathy Anderson at Poseidon was the first editor to make an offer for *Floating* and ironically lost her job the week the novel received a glowing review in the New York Times Book Review. Poseidon editor Ann Patty subsequently signed Hegi to a two-book contract and edited *Stones*. Hegi was uneasy about the transition, but when Patty called after reading the manuscript and said, "Trudi is the dwarf in all of us," she knew they would work well together. Now that Patty, too, has left Poseidon and the imprint is closing, Hegi has been assigned to Mark Gompertz at Simon & Schuster, at Gail Hochman's request. Hegi is approaching her 15-year anniversary with Hochman and says that the consistent connection with her agent has been invaluable while dealing with a procession of editors.

Hegi lives in Nine Mile Falls in eastern Washington with Gagliano, an architect, and a black mutt they named Moses ("as in, found by the river"). When weather permits, she kayaks on or swims across the Spokane River in front of their home. She is tenured at Eastern Washington University, where she teaches courses in fiction writing and literature in the M.F.A. program; she also serves on the board of the National Book Critics Circle.

For someone who feels so strongly about human rights, Hegi became politically aware relatively recently. Citing one incident that spurred her activism, she recalls a demonstration against a neo-Nazi group across the border in Hayden Lake, Idaho. She had decided not to participate in the event, believing it was a mistake to attract more media attention to white supremacist agendas, and was in her car driving elsewhere when a sudden insight flooded her mind. She realized that this was "exactly what happened in Germany—the silence. In the beginning everyone considered the Nazis a bunch of thugs; no one took them seriously." She phoned Gordon to meet her, and they joined the thousand people who had gathered in protest. "It was important that each and every one of us was there," she says.

Hegi has finished her next novel, called *Salt Dancers*, which is set in the Pacific Northwest. She is currently working on two new projects, waiting to see which will take over. *The Passion of Emma Blau* is the third novel with origins in Burgdorf, beginning with the immigration of Helene, a character who appears in *Stones*, to the U.S., and tracing the stories of successive generations of German-Americans. She is also developing a nonfiction work on the experience of being German in America.

When asked if she considers herself a German-American, Hegi hesitates, and it is the German side of the designation that gives her pause. "I don't really know," she says. "It doesn't have to do with choice. America is my country of choice, and I feel a connection to it even though it's not perfect. I have very little connection to my country of origin."

And yet Hegi says that in writing *Stones* her relationship with her native land altered more than she expected, and it will probably continue to change. "In the early years here, I went out of my way to avoid meeting other Germans," she says. "Now I seek them out in order to understand."

Source: Kitty Harmon, "Ursula Hegi: The German-Born Novelist Continues to Confront Her Native Country's Past," in *Publishers Weekly*, Vol. 241, No. 11, March 14, 1994, pp. 52–53.

Sources

Harmon, Kitty, "Ursula Hegi: The German-born Novelist Continues to Confront Her Native Country's Past," in *Publishers Weekly*, Vol. 241, No. 11, March 14, 1994, pp. 52–54.

Hegi, Ursula, *Stones from the River*, Scribner, 1994.

Holman, C. Hugh, and William Harmon, *A Handbook to Literature*, Macmillan, 1986, p. 494.

Ott, Bill, Review of *Stones from the River*, in *Booklist*, Vol. 90, No. 14, March 15, 1994, p. 1327.

Review of *Stones from the River*, in *Publishers Weekly*, Vol. 241, No. 3, January 17, 1994, p. 400.

Review of *Tearing the Silence: On Being German in America*, in *Booklist*, Vol. 93, No. 21, July 1997, p. 1793.

Robinson, Judith, Review of *Stones from the River*, in *Library Journal*, Vol. 127, No. 6, April 1, 2002, p. 159.

Schwarzbaum, Lisa, Review of *Stones from the River*, in *Entertainment Weekly*, No. 371, March 21, 1997, pp. 65–67.

Further Reading

Adelson, Betty M., *Dwarfism: Medical and Psychological Aspects of Profound Short Stature*, Johns Hopkins University Press, 2005.

Adelson, a psychologist and the mother of an adult dwarf daughter, summarizes how dwarfism was understood and treated during the twentieth century. She examines social factors that affect the dwarf community and describes the day-to-day challenges that dwarf individuals face.

Goldhagen, Daniel Jonah, *Hitler's Willing Executioners: Ordinary Germans and the Holocaust*, Knopf, 1997.

Thoroughly researched and documented, Goldhagen's book disproves myths that suggest that ordinary Germans did not know what was happening during the reign of the Third Reich. Indeed, Goldhagen documents how tens of thousands of ordinary Germans engaged in hunting down and exterminating Jews.

Kautz, Fred, *The German Historians: "Hitler's Willing Executioners" and Daniel Goldhagen*, Black Rose Books, 2002.

Kautz summarizes Goldhagen's book and then examines the rejection of it by three important German historians: Eberhard Jackel, Hans-Ulrich Wehler, and Hans Mommsen. Kautz looks at the way these scholars evaluated Goldhagen's work and makes some cautionary remarks about the writing of history.

Mamet, David, *The Wicked Son: Anti-Semitism, Self-Hatred, and the Jews*, Knopf, 2006.

A provocative writer, Mamet explores modern anti-Semitism and connects it to the way some Jews internalize that hatred. The title uses the metaphor of the Wicked Son, the child at the Passover Seder who asks about the story's meaning. Mamet analyzes how some Jews seek meaning anywhere but in Judaism and how in the eyes of the non-Jewish world, Judaism remains the religion of the Wicked Son.

O'Brien, Mary Elizabeth, *Nazi Cinema as Enchantment: The Politics of Entertainment in the Third Reich*, Camden House, 2006.

O'Brien's book analyzes the propaganda films produced during Hitler's regime and how they seduced German audiences, offering anti-Semitism couched in traditional values, community identity, and the hope for a better standard of living. In her analysis of thirteen films, O'Brien shows how Germans were enchanted by happy depictions of Aryan family life and messages that justified the Nazi regime.

Ulrich, Herbert, *Hitler's Foreign Workers: Enforced Foreign Labor in Germany under the Third Reich*, Cambridge University Press, 2006.

Ulrich analyzes how the Nazis used millions of foreigners as forced labor in Germany during World War II. Ulrich explores the workers from the point of view of the Nazi leadership and also from the point of view of the workers themselves.

Waiting

Ha Jin
1999

Waiting (1999) is a novel written in English by Ha Jin, a Chinese author who as of 2006 was teaching creative writing at Boston University in Boston, Massachusetts. The book is based on a true story that Jin heard from his wife when they were visiting her family at an army hospital in China. At the hospital was an army doctor who had waited eighteen years to get a divorce so he could marry his long-time friend, a nurse. But now his second marriage was not working. Jin thought that this situation would make a good plot for a novel, and he began working on *Waiting* in 1994.

The plot revolves around the fortunes of three people: Lin Kong, the army doctor; his wife Shuyu, whom he has never loved; and his girlfriend at the hospital where he works, the nurse Manna Wu. Beginning in 1963 and stretching over a twenty-year period, *Waiting* is set against the background of a changing Chinese society. It contrasts city and country life and shows the restrictions on individual freedoms that are a routine part of life under communism. But *Waiting* is primarily a novel of character. It presents an in-depth portrait of a decent but deeply flawed man, Lin Kong, whose life is spoiled by his inability to experience strong emotions and to love wholeheartedly.

Author Biography

Ha Jin was born on February 21, 1956, in a small rural town in Liaoning province, China, the son of

Danlin and Yuanfen Jin. His father was an army officer. In 1969, when Jin was fourteen, he volunteered to serve in the Chinese Army, stationed at the northeastern border between China and the Soviet Union. The minimum age for enlistment was sixteen, but Jin lied about his age because he wanted to leave home. This was during the time of upheaval in China known as the Cultural Revolution; the schools were closed so there was nothing for Jin to do in his hometown. He found army life quite exciting at first, since tensions between China and the Soviet Union were high and there were rumors of an impending Russian attack.

Jin remained in the army until 1975. After leaving the army, he wanted to go to college, but they were still closed. So he worked for three years as a telegrapher at a railroad company in Jiamusi, in northeast China. During this time, he began to learn English, listening to an English study program on the radio.

In 1977, when colleges reopened, Jin passed the entrance exam and enrolled at Heilongjiang University in Harbin. He received a Bachelor of Arts degree in English in 1981 and then studied American literature at Shandong University, where he received a Master of Arts degree in 1984. In 1985, Jin came to the United States to begin a Ph.D. program in the English Department at Brandeis University.

After 1986, when his scholarship ran out, Jin supported himself by working odd jobs, including night watchman, housecleaner, and busboy. During this time he first began to write in English. His poems impressed the poet Frank Bidart, who was teaching at Brandeis, and this recognition led to a series of events that together resulted in the publication of a volume of Jin's poetry, *Between Silences: A Voice from China*, by the University of Chicago Press in 1990.

When he first came to the United States, Jin had every intention of returning to China on completion of his studies. But when he saw on television what happened in China's Tiananmen Square in 1989, he decided to remain away. At Tiananmen, the Chinese government ordered the army to attack pro-democracy demonstrators, and hundreds of people were estimated to have been killed.

Jin received his Ph.D. from Brandeis in 1993 and became assistant professor of creative writing at Emory University in Atlanta, Georgia. In 1996, his first collection of short stories, *Ocean of Words: Army Stories*, was published, quickly followed by a second collection of stories, *Under the Red Flag*,

Ha Jin   © Marc Brasz/Corbis

in 1997. These stories are set in a rural town in China during the Cultural Revolution. Jin's first novel, *In the Pond*, was published in 1998. Like all Jin's works, it is set in China. It tells the story of an artist who has to spend his time working at a fertilizer plant to support his family.

Jin's second novel, *Waiting*, was published in 1999. It won the National Book Award and the PEN/Faulkner Award for Fiction. After that, Jin continued to publish poetry, short stories, and novels regularly, including the novels *The Crazed* (2002) and *War Trash* (2004). As of 2006, he remained in the position of professor of creative writing at Boston University, Boston, a role he assumed in 2002.

Plot Summary

Prologue

Waiting begins in Goose Village in China in 1983. Lin Kong, an officer and doctor in the Chinese army, has returned from the army hospital in Muji City, where he works, with the intention of divorcing Shuyu, his wife of twenty years. He has been doing this every summer for many years. The

Media Adaptations

- In 2004, *Waiting* was adapted by Brilliance as an audio book. As of 2006, it was available from Amazon.com.

court always turns down his request because at the last minute Shuyu changes her mind and refuses to agree to it. Lin's marriage was arranged by his parents, and although he does not dislike his wife, he has never loved her either, and they have not had sexual relations for seventeen years.

In the courtroom, Shuyu's brother Bensheng protests that Lin is acting unfairly to his wife, and the judge declines Lin's request. Lin returns home and tells his girlfriend Manna Wu that he will seek a divorce the following year, because according to the law an officer could divorce his wife after an eighteen-year separation, with or without her consent.

Part 1

Chapter 1

In 1964, Manna is a nursing student at the military hospital in Muji, where she falls in love with a lieutenant named Mai Dong. An immediate marriage is not possible, but Manna promises Mai Dong she will marry him sooner or later. Mai Dong is transferred to a new regiment eighty miles away, and after several months, he tells her he is going to Shanghai, where he will marry his cousin. Manna is heartbroken. At the age of twenty-six, she despairs of ever getting married.

Chapter 2

From her earliest days at nursing school, Manna had been friends with Lin Kong, one of her teachers. He seems to her to be a scholarly man, and she borrows books from him. She is also impressed by the fact that he can read Russian. He invites her to his dormitory to help him make dust jackets for his books. She finds him easy going and good natured.

Chapter 3

In the winter of 1966, hospital staff go through a training exercise in which they march four

hundred miles through the countryside, practicing treating the wounded and rescuing people from a battlefield. Lin is the head of a medical team, and Manna also takes part in the training. During a forced march, Manna can barely walk because of blisters on her feet. Lin helps her. At the farmhouse where the nurses are billeted, Lin drains Manna's blisters and then helps her for several days until her feet are healed.

Chapter 4

Manna grows curious about Lin and wonders what his wife is like. She thinks she should distance herself from him, but her interest continues to grow. One evening, she sees Lin in the company of Pingping Ma, the hospital librarian, and she grows agitated, wondering whether they have a romantic relationship. She decides she must do something to stop Pingping Ma from taking Lin away.

Chapter 5

Manna leaves an envelope on Lin's desk. Inside is a ticket for an opera which is to be performed that evening in the hospital theater. He decides to go and is surprised when he finds Manna sitting in the seat next to him. During the opera, which is about a battle between Chinese and Japanese forces, Manna places her hand on top of his. That night, Lin wonders whether this is the beginning of an affair. When he encounters her the next day and she suggests they go for a walk on Sunday, he is willing to begin an affair.

Chapter 6

During their walk they talk about the social and political upheaval in China. Within a month they are meeting several times a week in the evening. By August they see each other frequently during the day, and people begin to gossip about them, saying they are having an affair. Ran Su, vice-director of the hospital's political department, tells Lin he is heading for trouble, and Lin promises that he and Manna will not have sexual relations. Worried, he regrets having started a relationship with her. The next day, Lin tells Manna that although he loves her, they cannot be together.

Chapter 7

In 1968, Manna sees a photograph of Lin's wife. She teases him that Shuyu looks like his mother rather than his wife. The picture confirms her belief that Lin cannot be attached to his wife and will eventually leave her. Manna's friend Haiyan suggests she should sleep with Lin and gives Manna the key to her sister's house, saying that her sister will be away over the weekend. Manna is thrilled, but when she tells Lin about the idea, he says it is too risky. He insists that she return the key to Haiyan before the weekend. Manna reluctantly agrees but worries that Lin does not love her enough to take a risk.

Chapter 8

That night, Lin reviews his decision. He convinces himself that he loves Manna but that the bond between them need not be sexual. He dreams that he makes love to an unknown woman in a field, and he ejaculates in his sleep. In the morning his roommates find out about his "wet dream" and tell him he should not be ashamed of it. But Lin is confused by the dream because in real life he could never imagine doing such a thing.

Chapter 9

Lin wants to divorce his wife, although he feels guilty about deserting her. Manna has become tired of waiting and says that if he does nothing, it is over between them. For a while they stop seeing each other, but Lin is in turmoil over the situation.

Chapter 10

Lin sees Manna at a formal banquet. When he stops at her table and advises her not to drink too much, she responds with a hostile remark. After the banquet, she embraces him and apologizes, but she is drunk and says she wants him to make love to her. After he takes her home, Lin thinks seriously about getting a divorce.

Chapter 11

Lin visits his wife and daughter and finds it relaxing to be with his family again. In the evening, Bensheng, his brother-in-law, asks Lin to lend him some money. Lin does so with the agreement that Bensheng will help them thatch their roof in the fall. Lin is amazed at how well Shuyu manages the money he sends her each month, but during his ten-day leave, he cannot bring himself to ask for a divorce. One night Shuyu says that she wants to sleep with him so she can give him a son, but he says he has no need of one.

Chapter 12

A week after his return, he confesses to Manna that he failed to ask for a divorce. When he suggests they break up, she storms out of the room. A week later, Lin apologizes and says he will seek a divorce in the future. The following summer, when Lin returns home again, Manna has high hopes. But when Lin returns he tells her that Bensheng threatened to

retaliate if Lin divorced his sister, so Lin had not pursued it. He promises to figure out some way of getting a divorce.

Part 2

Chapter 1

By 1972, Lin is pessimistic about being able to obtain a divorce, having failed the previous year. He offers Manna the chance to meet his cousin Liang Meng, who lives about eighty miles away and wants a girlfriend. Manna is unenthusiastic about the idea but agrees to meet him in June.

Chapter 2

When Liang Meng arrives, Lin introduces him to Manna, and the three of them talk for a while at the hospital. The next morning, Liang Meng and Manna meet at Victory Park in the city and take a walk. When they sit on a bench, he shows her some of his drawings, which do not interest her. When she returns home she tells Lin that she is not attracted to Liang Meng and does not want to see him again.

Chapter 3

The next summer, Lin and Shuyu again go to the divorce court. But after Lin refuses to reveal the name of the woman he plans to marry, the judge refuses to consider the case. Outside the court a hostile crowd has assembled, stirred up by Bensheng, but Lin leaves without being harmed. The next afternoon, Ren Kung, Lin's elder brother, visits and tries to persuade Lin not to leave Shuyu, since a divorce would affect everyone in the family.

Chapter 4

A week later, Ran Su informs Lin that Commissar Wei has asked the hospital to recommend a woman for him to marry. The Party Committee has been considering recommending Manna. Lin raises no objections, saying he is a married man and should not hold her back. Manna agrees to meet the commissar. Secretly, Lin is upset at the prospect of losing her and angry at the commissar. At the same time, he has a feeling of relief, since if he loses Manna he will not have to continue to ask for a divorce.

Chapter 5

Commissar Wei meets Manna at the army's hotel in Muji. He is courteous and a good listener. He asks her what books she has read recently. Taking a copy of Walt Whitman's *Leaves of Grass* from his briefcase, he says he has read it four times. He then lends her the book for a month. When she has read it, she is to tell him what she thinks of it. In the evening, Manna and the commissar go to a movie together. At the theater she is introduced to a stern-faced officer named Geng Yang.

Chapter 6

Manna does not understand *Leaves of Grass* and asks Lin to help her. He writes a report on the poems, which Manna copies out in her own hand in a six-page letter and sends to Commissar Wei. In anticipation of moving to Harbin and marrying the commissar, she gets Lin to teach her how to ride a bicycle. After a few weeks, however, Manna is informed that the commissar will not pursue the relationship because he was not satisfied with her handwriting. He needed someone with good handwriting to help him with secretarial work. Manna feels humiliated and returns to Lin, her passion for him rekindled.

Chapter 7

Lin is taken ill with tuberculosis and is quarantined in the hospital's tuberculosis building. His roommate is Geng Yang, who has almost recovered from the illness. Lin takes Manna to visit him. Later, Geng Yang urges Lin to take decisive action regarding his divorce.

Chapter 8

After Lin recovers, he is sent to Shenyang City on an army program. Before he leaves, he and Manna take Geng Yang out to dinner in a restaurant. Geng Yang again urges Lin to seek a divorce and suggests that he use money to accomplish his goal. That evening Lin devises a plan to pay his brother-in-law two thousand yuan to ensure that he does not oppose the divorce. But he does not have enough money, and Manna refuses to contribute.

Chapter 9

While Lin is away, Manna visits Geng Yang, who is about to leave the hospital, in order to pick up some books that Geng Yang borrowed from Lin. In his hospital room, Geng Yang rapes Manna. She runs back to her dormitory and weeps. She fears that if she reports the crime, she will not be believed, since she went to his room voluntarily.

Chapter 10

The next morning, she learns from the hospital that Geng Yang has checked out of his room. She knows he has already left Muji. Not knowing what to do, she consults Haiyan, who tells her she should keep quiet about what happened and not even tell Lin until some time in the future. Over

the following days, Manna is depressed, but she is relieved when she discovers she is not pregnant.

Chapter 11

Lin returns six weeks later, and within two weeks, Manna tells him about the rape. He is angry at Geng Yang but also angry with himself, thinking that had he been more decisive he would have married Manna by now, and Geng Yang would not have been able to get at her. He also fears that Haiyan will not keep Manna's secret.

Chapter 12

Word gets out about Manna's rape, and Mrs. Su insults her. Manna blames Haiyan, but Haiyan tells Lin it was her husband's fault: he let the secret slip out when he was drunk. The years go by, and each year, Lin fails to obtain a divorce. Finally, in 1983, he decides to bring Shuyu to the People's Court in Muji. After eighteen years' separation, he is going to divorce her, whether she agrees to it or not.

Part 3

Chapter 1

Shuyu arrives at the army hospital and receives medical treatment. The nurses are intrigued by her bound feet. She also has a haircut that makes her look ten years younger. The hairdresser tells her to sneak into Lin's bed at night, then he will not be able to divorce her. But she says she would not do that.

Chapter 2

Lin tells Shuyu that in the divorce court she must tell the judge that she wants Lin to find a good job for Hua in the city. At the court, the divorce is approved within half an hour. After the divorce, Shuyu remains in Muji, living on her own in the dormitory house. Lin writes a letter to Hua, begging her to come to Muji, where a job awaits her. She replies that she does not want to live in the city, so Lin decides to return to his village to try to persuade her.

Chapter 3

In the village, Bensheng informs him that a man named Second Donkey wants to buy his house. But Second Donkey has offered only three thousand yuan, whereas Lin thinks the house is worth four thousand. He also finds out that Hua has a boyfriend in the navy who is encouraging her to move to the city. That night, he and Second Donkey agree to a price of thirty-two hundred yuan for the house and furniture. Lin gets close to his daughter, which pleases him, and also quarrels with Bensheng.

Chapter 4

Hua returns with Lin to Muji and starts a new job. Her mother goes to live with her. In November, Lin and Manna marry at a ceremony attended by half of the hospital staff and their families. Manna becomes emotional and has to go home early during the festivities. Lin finds the wedding boring.

Chapter 5

Lin finds Manna to be passionate in bed, and he has to work hard to satisfy her. He feels he owes this to her, since she waited so long for him. His colleagues tease him because he is losing weight. He tells Manna that they should slow down and save some energy for work, and they agree to have sex less often.

Chapter 6

In February, Manna finds she is pregnant at the age of forty-four. Lin worries about her health and suggests an abortion, but she insists on having the baby. Her pregnancy is hard. She vomits a lot and her face becomes bloated. Lin finds their married life tedious and chaotic.

Chapter 7

Manna resents the fact that Lin goes out twice a week in the evenings to teach chemistry to a group of orderlies. She begins to feel wretched and lonely. One night she follows him and observes him through an open window as he teaches the class of young women. He seems to be enjoying himself, and she thinks he is flirting with them. The next day she rebukes Lin for taking the teaching position without consulting her. They quarrel but are later reconciled. However, Manna still feels lonely on the evenings when Lin goes out.

Chapter 8

As her pregnancy advances, Manna grows irritable. She goes into labor prematurely, and she and Lin walk to the hospital. Haiyan, who is an obstetrician, arrives to help. After an excruciatingly painful labor, during which Manna seems almost to lose her mind and curses her husband, she gives birth to twin boys.

Chapter 9

In the weeks following the birth, Manna gets weaker and weaker. A cardiogram indicates that she has a heart condition. Many visitors arrive with food and congratulations on the birth of the twins, who are christened River and Lake. Manna's health continues to deteriorate, and also after a couple of months, both babies develop dysentery. A number of remedies fail until a folk remedy cures them.

Chapter 10

Lin and Manna watch a television program about people who have responded to an instruction by the party and acquired wealth through entrepreneurship. Formerly this way of making money was illegal. Manna and Lin are shocked to see Geng Yang on the screen. He has made big money by reorganizing a construction company. Manna weeps and Lin comforts her. From then on, they sleep in the same bed again, which they have not done since Manna became pregnant.

Chapter 11

Manna's heart grows weaker, and a doctor tells Lin that she does not have many years to live. Manna's temper grows worse, and Lin struggles to get the housework done. He is grateful that Hua comes on the weekends to help. Manna eventually returns to work part-time. When Manna yells at Lin over a pot of burned rice, he storms out and asks himself whether marrying her was a wise decision.

Chapter 12

Lin bicycles to visit Shuyu and Hua two days before the Spring Festival. They greet him warmly, and he has a feeling of being at home. But he finds their kindness hard to bear and feels he has made a mess of his life. For the first time, he expresses some affection toward Shuyu and confesses to her his sadness. He returns to Manna the next day, and together they prepare for the Spring Festival. Hua arrives and tells her father that Shuyu says she will wait for him. He says he is not a man who is worth waiting for.

Characters

Mai Dong

Mai Dong, a young lieutenant, is in charge of a radio station at the headquarters of the Muji Sub-Command. In 1964, he meets and falls in love with Manna Wu. He wants to marry her immediately, but she persuades him that they should wait. Manna regards him as a gentle but weak man, and she wishes he were stronger. Mai Dong's radio station is transferred to a newly formed regiment nearly eighty miles away, but he is not happy there. He gets a discharge and breaks Manna's heart when he tells her he is returning to his hometown of Shanghai to marry his cousin.

Fengjin

Fengjin is Hua's boyfriend. He and Hua are former classmates, and he is now in the navy.

Hua Kong

Hua Kong, the daughter of Lin and Shuyu, grows up working in the fields in Goose Village. Later she works in Bensheng's grocery store. Lin wants her to get a job in Muji City, but initially she is reluctant to do so. Eventually she agrees to make the move, and she works for the Splendor Match Plant. She lives in an apartment with her mother and proves to be a dutiful daughter. Lin is pleased that he is able to establish a warm relationship with her, despite the many years in which he barely saw her.

Lin Kong

Lin Kong is an army officer and doctor at the army hospital in Muji City, where he has been since 1963. He is also a teacher, and one of only four medical school graduates on the hospital staff in the 1960s. Lin is a tall, quiet, good-natured man who is on good terms with everyone. For the first few years of his tenure at the hospital, he is elected model officer every year. His fondness for books earns him the nickname Scholar or Bookworm. However, Lin has not found happiness in his family life. Although Shuyu is a good wife to him, he does not love her, partly because he does not find her physically attractive. He fathers a daughter by Shuyu, but after that he ceases to have sexual relations with her and lives alone in Muji, visiting his wife in Goose Village only on annual leaves.

Lin's life changes in 1966 when he begins a romantic relationship with Manna, who is four years his junior and was formerly his student. For seventeen years Manna is his girlfriend. He keeps promising that he will divorce Shuyu and marry Manna, but he allows something to thwart him, either Shuyu's last minute change of mind or the opposition of Bensheng, his brother-in-law. Since Lin is not ruthless in pursuing his goals, his situation tends to stagnate. His indecisiveness also seems to hold him back in his career. He is too passive, unable to shape his life in a positive way. Only once does he seem to acquire a leadership position, and that is in 1966 when he is in charge of twenty-eight people on an arduous training march. But his prestige dips when his nonsexual affair with Manna is noted by his colleagues at the hospital, who no longer elect him model officer. He holds much the same job in 1983 as he did twenty years earlier, whereas other characters in the story ascend the career ladder.

Lin is aware that he lacks passion and that he does not often feel intense emotion. He will not take any risks in his relationship with Manna, which is why their love affair remains unconsummated for seventeen years. He feels little resentment when Commissar Wei shows an interest in Manna, despite the fact that he may lose her. Lin's flaw is that he is unable to develop emotionally, so he never learns how to love his wife Shuyu, even though she is devoted to him. Nor is Lin able to make a success of his second marriage, and this weighs upon his mind. He knows he should have been more decisive and married Manna sooner. He also regrets that never in his life has he loved a woman wholeheartedly. He is always ambivalent, his mind going one way then another, trying to analyze things rationally from every possible point of view. In the end he refers to himself as "a useless man," a man who has not known himself well enough to strive for his own happiness or be aware of his desires or needs.

Ren Kong

Ren Kong is Lin's elder brother. Unlike Lin, Ren did not receive an education, since his parents expected him to work in the fields. He and Lin are therefore not close, since they did not grow up together. Ren Kong is a good-hearted man who never complains about being deprived of an education. However, he appears to have had a hard life and looks fifteen years older than his age. He is married with three sons.

Shuyu Kong

Shuyu Kong is Lin Kong's wife. She married Lin in 1962, but Lin has never been happy with her. It was a marriage arranged by his parents, and as soon as he saw Shuyu he was disappointed. Even as a young woman of twenty-six, she looked like she was in her forties, with leathery hands and a wrinkled face. She also has tiny, bound feet, which are no longer fashionable. By the time Shuyu is in her late forties, she is a small, withered woman who still looks much older than her age. However, Shuyu is devoted to Lin and performs all her duties as wife without complaint. She also nurses Lin's parents in their final illnesses. She is a simple, rather naïve, illiterate woman and is quite content with her life in the village. She is a good housekeeper and frugal with her limited resources. She even manages to save some money, and instead of keeping it for herself, she tries to give it to Lin, since she thinks he must need it. When the divorce finally goes through, Shuyu accepts it, but she still thinks of Lin as a member of her family. She is pleased, for example, when she hears that Manna is pregnant because that will mean their family will become larger. Lin arranges for Shuyu to move away from Goose Village into the city, where she shares an apartment with her daughter, Hua. Shuyu adjusts well to the change in her circumstances and is content with her lot. She never reproaches Lin for deserting her. On the contrary, she continues to treat him with great warmth and kindness.

Bensheng Liu

Bensheng Liu, an accountant of the production brigade, is Shuyu's younger brother. He opposes Lin's desire to seek a divorce from Shuyu and on several occasions actively intervenes to prevent it. Lin is aware of Bensheng's hostility but maintains cordial relations with him because sometimes he needs Bensheng's assistance. Even so, he does not regard Bensheng as a trustworthy man. However, in Lin's absence, Bensheng and his wife, who are childless, develop a strong bond with Hua and treat her as their own daughter. Hua is fond of her uncle Bensheng, but she also knows how greedy he is. He thinks of nothing but money, and eventually he owns a prosperous grocery store. When he hears that Lin has fathered twin sons, he is extremely jealous.

Pingping Ma

Pingping Ma is a young librarian at the hospital where Lin and Manna work. Manna thinks she is ugly, but when she sees Pingping Ma out on a walk with Lin one evening in the mid-1960s, she fears they may be involved in a romantic relationship.

Liang Meng

Liang Meng is one of Lin's cousins. An educated man who is a middle school teacher, he is also a widower with three children. In 1972, when he tells Lin that he is seeking a girlfriend, Lin introduces him to Manna, but after Liang Meng and Manna walk together in the park, Manna tells Lin she is not interested in developing a relationship with Liang Meng.

Haiyan Niu

Haiyan Niu is Manna's friend when they are both in nursing school. Manna admires the streak of wildness in Haiyan's nature and sometimes turns to her for advice, although she does not trust her friend to keep secrets. Haiyan later takes one and a half years of training to become an obstetrician, and it is she who delivers Manna's twin sons. Haiyan marries Honggan and they have a son.

Honggan Niu

Honggan Niu is married to Haiyan. He is an officer in charge of recreational activities in the Propaganda Section and later becomes vice-chairman of a lumberyard in Muji.

Second Donkey

Second Donkey gets his nickname from his donkey-like face. He lives in Goose Village and is a friend of Bensheng. Second Donkey buys Lin's house.

Snow Goose

Snow Goose is a nursing student who has a reputation as a flirt. She was an actress with an opera troupe but was transferred to the army hospital in Muji after she had an affair with an officer. Snow Goose, who gets her nickname from her long white neck, is one of the young women who receive instruction in chemistry from Lin after he marries Manna. Manna is jealous of her when she sees her smiling at Lin.

Mrs. Su

Mrs. Su is the wife of Ran Su. After her son drowns in a river, she becomes deranged and unreliable. She takes to insulting Manna after she hears that Manna was raped.

Ran Su

Ran Su is the vice-director of the hospital's political department, who eventually becomes vice-commissar and then commissar of the hospital. He is a decent, fair-minded man who wins a lot of respect at the hospital when he declines to send his wife, who suffers from dementia, to a mental asylum. Ran Su is also a friend of Lin's, since they share an interest in books.

Commissar Guohong Wei

Commissar Guohong Wei is a well educated man in his fifties with good manners. He looks more like a professor than an officer. Wei has divorced his wife and is seeking to remarry. He makes an arrangement to meet with Manna but later decides not to pursue an interest in her. In 1981, Wei dies in prison, where he had been incarcerated for his connections with the Gang of Four, a group of out-of-favor politicians.

Manna Wu

Manna Wu is the girlfriend and then wife of Lin Kong. Manna is an orphan whose parents were killed in a traffic accident in Tibet when she was three. Raised in an orphanage in Tsingtao City, she worked for three years as a telephone operator before enrolling in 1964 at the nursing school in Muji. When she graduates she remains at the hospital as a nurse. Eventually she becomes head nurse.

Manna is tall and quite athletic, playing table tennis and volleyball, and although she is not beautiful, she has a pleasant voice. When she is a student, she dates a lieutenant named Mai Dong, and they plan to marry. But Mai Dong returns to Shanghai and marries his cousin. Manna then has difficulty finding a husband since after graduation she is twenty-six years old and considered almost an old maid. All the other nurses are much younger and it is they who receive all the attention from the male officers. It is under these circumstances—without family or a home to go to when on leave, and without good marriage prospects—that Manna begins her long friendship with Lin Kong. She is the one who initiates the romantic development of what begins as a simple friendship between teacher and student. She knows that Lin is married but convinces herself that he will leave his wife and eventually marry her.

As the years go by, Manna presses Lin to get a divorce, but she has no power to compel him. Other suitors are presented to her, such as Lin's cousin, Liang Meng, and Commissar Wei, but she remains attached to Lin. However, the love affair with Lin is never consummated during seventeen years of courtship because the strict rules of the hospital prevent them from meeting outside the hospital compound, and they are unwilling to take any risks. She loses her virginity not to Lin, but in a brutal rape by Geng Yang.

When she and Lin finally do marry, Manna releases all her pent-up sexual passion, but she also becomes irritable, moody, and irrationally jealous. She gives birth to twins at the age of forty-four, and in the midst of her agonizing pain during labor, she reveals her bitter resentment that Lin had forced her to wait so long before being able to marry and have children.

After Manna becomes a mother, her health begins to fail. She has a heart ailment and a doctor says that she has only a short while to live.

Geng Yang

Geng Yang is a heavily built, powerful, decisive man who is an officer in the army with the Third Border Division. He is introduced to Manna when she goes to the movie with Commissar Wei. She sees him again when he is recovering from tuberculosis and is Lin's roommate. Lin likes Geng Yang because he is straightforward and carefree. He speaks his mind and expresses himself in vulgar language. Manna likes him as well, but then when she calls on him in his hospital room when Lin is out of town, Geng Yang turns vicious and rapes her. Later, in the new political atmosphere that encourages capitalism, Geng Yang becomes wealthy by reorganizing a construction company.

Themes

Duty versus Desire

Lin Kong finds himself torn between what he really desires and the demands that duty places on him. To a lesser extent, the same is true for Manna Wu. For Lin, submission to perceived duty and the will of others is a pattern established early in his life. His marriage to Shuyu was arranged for him by his parents, who wanted Lin to marry so that his bride could look after his sick mother. Lin agreed "out of filial duty." When he met Shuyu in person and was not attracted to her, he protested but still yielded to his parents' desires. So Lin carries out his duty but finds himself trapped in a shell of a marriage.

When he begins his relationship with Manna and wants to marry her, he is constrained by his duty as an army officer not to break the strict rules the hospital imposes on relations between men and women who are not married to each other. Although at the hospital everyone knows they are a couple, they cannot live together. All they can do is eat at the same mess table and take walks within the compound. They must not be together outside. In this way the society depicted attempts to frustrate individual desires and prevent liaisons between men and women which threaten to disrupt the smooth functioning of the group. The same goal, to preserve a stable social structure even if it involves the thwarting of individual desire, is apparent in the obstacles that are placed in the way of anyone seeking a divorce. The rule that an officer must wait eighteen years before he can divorce his wife without her consent is one of these restrictions. It was invented by a high-placed army bureaucrat in 1958, but no one has had the nerve to challenge it. Also, when Lin tries to obtain a divorce, he first has to obtain a letter of recommendation from his army bosses. Even then, the authorities seek to discourage him by playing on his sense of duty. In 1983, the divorce court judge, for example, sternly reminds him of his social position:

> [Y]ou are a revolutionary officer and should be a model for us civilians. . . . This is immoral and dishonorable, absolutely intolerable. . . . Do you deserve your green uniform and the red star on your cap?"

The approach taken to dissuading Lin has not changed much over the years. In the late 1960s, according to the village newspaper's report of the proceedings at the divorce court, the judge tried to make him feel guilty by spouting party propaganda: "*You have forgotten your class origin and tried to imitate the lifestyle of the exploiting class.*"

Lin is susceptible to such appeals not because he is such a fervent revolutionary officer (he does not question party doctrine but he is no zealot either) but

Topics
For Further
Study

- What role do dreams play in the novel? What is the significance of Lin's dreams in Part 1, chapters 4 and 8, and Manna's dream in part 3, chapter 10? Write an essay in which you present your interpretation.

- Discuss the dilemma faced by Manna after she is raped. Why does she not report the crime? Research the occurrence of acquaintance rape in the United States. Then imagine that a friend of yours has been raped by an acquaintance, and write a letter to her advising her what she should do and why in response to the crime.

- Compare attitudes and policies toward divorce in China, as depicted in the novel, with divorce in the United States. Research statistics of divorce rates in China and compare them to U.S. divorce statistics. What are the differences between the two countries, and what are the causes of the differences? Make a class presentation about your findings.

- Describe some of the ways that the government or army authorities intrude on people's personal lives in the China as depicted in the novel. How do these intrusions delineate a difference between Chinese and U.S. culture, society, and politics? Write an essay in which you discuss your findings.

because he is a man easily swayed by what others expect of him. It is in this sense that duty holds him back from ruthlessly pursuing what he really wants in life. He is not willing to challenge the rigid system in which he lives, that allows little deviation from the personal and career path approved by the authorities. For example, Lin is worried that if Bensheng, his brother-in-law who opposes his desire to divorce Shuyu, follows through on his threat to report him to the army authorities, he will not get a promotion that would otherwise be almost guaranteed. When Ran Su, director of the political department, calls him in to his office, Lin is fearful that the divorce court may have reported him. He does not seethe with the injustice of it and resolve to pursue his desire with more determination; he simply fears for the consequences of what he has already done. Desire is thus quashed by an array of political and psychological customs and restraints that place duty and the perceived needs of the society above desire and the need of the individual to pursue happiness.

City versus Country

Throughout the novel, there is a contrast between the countryside and the city, the old feudalism and the new communism. As a young man, Lin believes he is living in the "New China," which is modernizing and outgrowing the old ways, but he

is presented with a bride from the country who has bound feet, an unmistakable sign of China's backward past. Lin thinks that people in the city would laugh at her feet, and indeed, when Shuyu does visit Muji City many years later, her small feet are an object of great curiosity to the nurses at hospital, who also laugh at the simplicity of her approach to life. For her part, Shuyu is amazed at the creature comforts that she finds in the city, and she thinks the nurses have a wonderful life, working indoors instead of toiling in the fields and wearing smart uniforms. The simple Shuyu, who does not know how to dress properly or present herself in the best light, is contrasted with Manna, the educated career woman in the city. Manna (like Lin) reads books; Shuyu is illiterate. Shuyu has no sex drive, but Manna's, when unleashed, almost proves too much for Lin. In that regard, Manna is a liberated city woman (whatever the constraints on her behavior in other areas). While Shuyu is happy to maintain a simple, sexless devotion to her husband, Manna is demanding and chronically dissatisfied with Lin.

Values and customs are different in the rural areas. Lin realizes that it "would make no sense to anybody in the countryside" for him to divorce a wife because he does not love her. Since Shuyu does everything that is expected of a wife in the village, she would be considered beyond reproach. Practicality rather than romantic love is the determining factor. Also, in the country, the extended family living in close proximity is a more significant factor than it is in the city. Lin's brother Ran King counsels him against divorce because it would affect everybody in the family; the boys in the village have already started calling Lin's nephews names over the matter. Lin, however, accustomed to army life in the city under the direction of the ruling Communist Party, is shocked by this news. "How ridiculous people are," he thinks. "What does my marriage have to do with my nephews' lives?" Lin's alienation from these more traditional notions of family is also noticeable when Shuyu suggests that she and Lin produce a son to carry on the family line. Lin regards this as a "feudal" idea; he does not care about such things, possibly because he has been taught by the communists that the continuance of the revolutionary spirit of the party is more important than old-fashioned notions about the maintenance of a family line. Thus in the contrast between country and city is seen the contrast between the traditional China and the changes wrought by communism and emerging modernity.

Style

Setting

Waiting tells its story of thwarted and ultimately disappointing love against what to the American reader is an exotic backdrop of Chinese society in all its variety, in which the old and the new coexist. The contrast between old and new is often apparent. For example, when Lin goes home to the village, he visits the graves of his parents, taking with him some food Shuyu has cooked, which he offers to his deceased parents. He also places some paper money around the graves, but he does not burn it as the villagers do, which is the traditional way of sending money to the nether world. How different is the scene at the wedding of Lin and Manna, in which at the beginning of the ceremony bride and groom are invited to pay tribute to the Communist Party and Chairman Mao. The couple bows three times before the portrait of the late chairman of the party and a banner displaying the communist emblem of a crossed sickle and hammer. Only after the bows are completed can the actual wedding take place. Traditional customs are thus contrasted with the new customs and rituals of China under the communists.

Folk Medicine Motif

The old China is also seen in a number of motifs (recurring elements in a literary work). One of these is Chinese folk medicine. Various remedies for ailments are mentioned. Sesame oil and walnuts are used in a recipe for curing kidney stones; Lin wonders if to satisfy Manna's sexual desire he should resort to an aphrodisiac made up of ginseng, angelica roots or seahorses, and steep them in a bottle of wheat liquor; and, most prominently, the twins' serious case of dysentery, which seems to resist all medicines, is finally cured by a concoction made up of mashed taro mixed with white sugar and egg yolk.

Foot-binding Motif

Another recurring motif is foot-binding. This centuries-old, widespread practice in China only died out during the twentieth century. Small feet were considered extremely attractive and increased a girl's marriage prospects. Foot-binding was begun when the girl was as young as five. The toes were folded under the foot and tightly bandaged. The procedure was painful and resulted in a deformed and stunted foot that sometimes measured no more than three inches. In the novel, Shuyu's bound feet are four inches long, and she is in effect semi-disabled, unable to fetch water from the communal well. Lin has to have a well sunk in their yard to overcome the difficulty. For his part, Lin does not like his wife's bound feet, viewing the practice as a throwback to an earlier era. Not surprisingly, when Shuyu has treatment at the army hospital in Muji, her feet are an object of great interest to the nurses, who watch her tottering about across the square. They are surprised that a woman under the age of seventy should have bound feet.

Historical Context

China's Cultural Revolution

In the early 1960s, when *Waiting* begins, China had been under communist rule for a decade and a half, since the establishment of the People's Republic of China in 1949. Under the leadership of Mao Zedong, the nation made great strides during the 1950s in modernizing its backward economy, although this was not without setbacks. The failure of the Great Leap Forward, an economic plan in the late 1950s, contributed to the famine that devastated China in 1960 and 1961.

In 1966, the period known as the Cultural Revolution began. It was set in motion by Mao and was initially directed against senior Chinese leaders such as Liu Shaoqi and Deng Xiaoping who Mao believed were taking the country on a backward road to capitalism. He claimed that the communist bureaucracy was in danger of becoming no better than the exploiting class they had supposedly replaced. Mao encouraged large groups of radical young people, known as Red Guards, to tear down all the old

Compare & Contrast

- **1960s:** The Cultural Revolution produces chaos in China as revolutionary Red Guards rampage the country, attacking old institutions and condemning thousands to death for being counter-revolutionaries.

  1980s: In the late 1980s, China undergoes a period of political liberalization. In 1989, large peaceful crowds gather in Beijing's Tiananmen Square to demand democratic political reform. The Chinese government declares martial law and on June 4 orders the army to attack the demonstrators. Hundreds of people are killed.

  Today: China is ruled by the Communist Party. There are eight registered small parties controlled by the Communist Party but no significant political opposition groups. The Chinese government identifies the Falungong spiritual movement and the China Democracy Party as subversive groups.

- **1960s:** China suffers from famine and its population is rapidly growing. However, the government declines to introduce a population policy.

  1980s: China adopts a one-child policy in order to curb population growth. Abortion is available on demand. Propaganda, education, incentives, and coercion are all used to promote the one-child policy. The goal is zero population growth by 2000.

  Today: As a result of the one-child policy, China is one of the most rapidly aging countries in the world. The one-child policy is no longer applied so rigidly.

- **1960s:** Tensions between China and Russia are high. In 1969, Chinese and Russian forces clash at the Ussuri River on the northern Chinese frontier.

  1980s: Relations between Russia and China remain poor. Both countries fear that war could break out between them. Russia's invasion of Afghanistan in 1979, and the war in that country that continued into the 1980s, is a reminder to China of the threat posed by Soviet expansionism.

  Today: In 2005, Russia and China announce a strategic partnership on a range of issues in order to counteract Western military and fiscal influence. Russia provides a significant amount of China's energy needs, and China provides financial guarantees and loans to Russia.

---

structures of society, including old customs, old ideas, and old culture. Red Guards rampaged in mobs, targeting intellectuals. Students turned on their teachers and beat and humiliated them. Then the Red Guards turned their ire on Liu, Deng, and their followers. For several years China suffered into near anarchy and chaos. Factories and schools were closed; tens of thousands of people were arbitrarily accused of being counter-revolutionaries and were executed or imprisoned. In *Waiting*, Manna and Lin discuss the Cultural Revolution in 1967 (part 1, chapter 6). At the army hospital in Muji, the staff had divided into two factions and would argue, each accusing the other of deviating from Mao's teachings. Manna and Lin also talk about the fighting in large cities. At one point in 1968, virtual civil war broke out as Red Guards attempted to seize government and party headquarters around the nation.

The period of violence and instability came to a gradual end during the early 1970s. The Red Guards were disbanded and sent to work in agriculture in the countryside. China remained, however, a repressive, totalitarian society. As Alan Hunter and John Sexton state in *Contemporary China*, China under communism was

> one of the world's most regimented states. The population was organized into structures that facilitated social and political control. The mass media served as propaganda instruments, cultural life was stultifying and dissent virtually impossible."

This is clear from at least one incident in *Waiting*, when the hospital's political department orders all the staff to turn in any books they have that contain "bourgeois ideology and sentiments, particularly those by foreign authors."

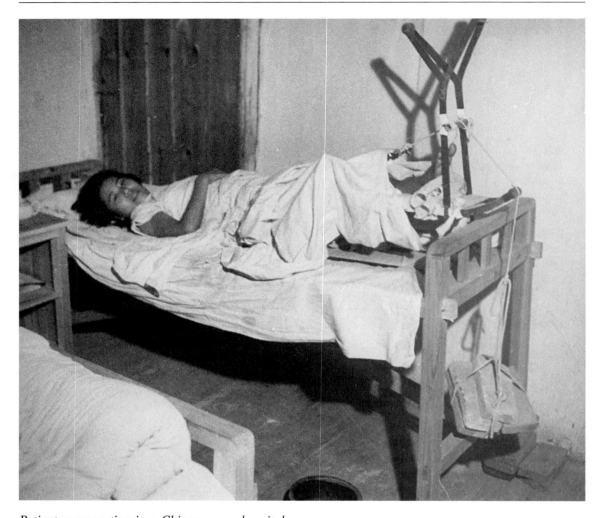

Patient recuperating in a Chinese army hospital © Jack Wilkes/Time & Life Pictures/Getty Images

China in the 1980s

In 1978, Deng Xiaoping, who had been under attack during the Cultural Revolution, returned to power. His goal was to modernize Chinese agriculture, industry, science, and technology and to encourage foreign investment. These policies bore fruit in the 1980s, during which China's annual economic growth rate was about 9.5 percent. Deng also allowed the introduction of capitalistic practices into the Chinese economy. Trade and prices were influenced by market forces rather than being determined by centrally planned government production mandates. These new policies were applied at first in what were known as Special Enterprise Zones (SEZs) in south China, which received foreign investment. When the SEZs were successful, the methods they practiced were extended to other industries and other parts of the country. A new breed of Chinese entrepreneurs

emerged, and the accumulation of private wealth was no longer officially disparaged. This is the context in which the incident in *Waiting* in which Manna watches a television show entitled *To Get Rich Is Glorious* should be understood. The show features people who have become rich through innovative business practices. The narrator comments:

> Every one of these entrepreneurs became a legendary figure. A few years ago their ways of making money were illegal, but now the nouveaux riches were held up as examples for the masses to follow.

Critical Overview

Waiting was received respectfully by American reviewers. "[Q]uiet but absorbing," writes the reviewer for *Publishers Weekly*, who notes that the novel explores the "dilemma of an ordinary man who misses the best opportunities in his life simply by trying to do his duty—as defined first by his traditional Chinese parents and later by the Communist Party." For this reviewer, the strongest section of the novel is part 3, when Lin and Manna are married: "the final chapters are moving and deeply ironic."

Entertainment Weekly praises the author's "unnerving insight" and "elegant irony." A reviewer in the *New Yorker* writes admiringly of "This suspenseful and bracingly tough-minded love story" and notes that "No one questions the state's right to control its citizens' hearts—and loins—and Jin's characters are as free of Freudian insights as they are of the traditions of romantic love." In *Time*, Paul Gray notes that Jin "casts a wise, rather than a cold, eye on his characters' struggles, both with an inflexible social system and their own weaknesses." Gray also expresses the view that *Waiting* is a "deliciously comic novel," pointing out Jin's "impeccably deadpan manner."

Francine Prose wrote a long review of Jin's novel in the *New York Times Book Review*. Like Gray, Prose comments on the humor in the novel, especially in the section in which Lin writes an essay on Walt Whitman's poetry in order to help Manna. Prose is also full of praise for Jin's "deceptively simple fiction [that] resonate[s] on many levels: the personal, the historical, the political," and gives much insight in a small space to Chinese society from the 1960s to the 1980s. Noting that "Throughout the book, tender private dramas are enacted against the coarse backdrop of party ideology," Prose argues that the tension in the novel is generated by "the force with which [Manna and Lin] are constantly pulled in several directions."

Criticism

Bryan Aubrey

Aubrey holds a Ph.D. in English and has published many articles on twentieth century literature. In this essay, he analyzes Waiting *as a novel of character, focusing on the protagonist, Lin Kong, and the foil with whom he is contrasted, Geng Yang.*

Waiting is primarily a novel of character, and the character in question is Lin Kong. Like that

> **What happens in the case of Lin is that the psychic and sexual energy— to use Jin's terms—that should be directed outward gets turned inward and results in feelings of guilt, self-reproach, and self-doubt. Lin knows that he has failed those who are close to him."**

other great literary procrastinator, Shakespeare's Hamlet, Lin is more suited to thinking than to acting. His chronic indecisiveness in pursuing his relationship with Manna condemns him, and her, to a life of "waiting." Too passive to initiate action, he allows his life to be shaped by others. Moreover, just as Hamlet has a foil in the character of Laertes, who does not hesitate to take decisive action, so Lin Kong has a foil in the character Geng Yang. (A foil is a character that sets off another character by contrast.)

Geng Yang is everything Lin Kong is not. When Manna first meets him, she finds him interesting because he is so unlike anyone else she has known, so "manly," which is not a word that could be used to describe the quiet, bespectacled, scholarly Lin. Lin is a rather refined man, whereas Geng Yang is coarse and vulgar in his speech. When he and Lin are both recovering from tuberculosis and share a room in the hospital, Geng Yang makes suggestive comments about the nurses and questions Lin about whether Manna is really a virgin. However, Lin does not allow this direct approach to offend him; on the contrary, he likes Geng Yang, seeing him as "a man full of certainty and capable of decisive action, a real go-getter." Since it is common for people to admire in others what they lack in themselves, it is perhaps not surprising that Lin is drawn to this no-nonsense military man who knows how to get what he wants and does not allow obstacles, whether internal or external, to stop him. Indeed, it is Geng Yang who comes up with the idea of bribing someone in the village so that Lin will be able to get the divorce he so badly wants.

Geng Yang is also shrewd in his assessment of others. He quickly takes stock of Lin, and his observation is absolutely accurate. This is what he tells Lin when they are both in the hospital:

> I know your type. You're always afraid that people will call you a bad man. You strive to have a good heart. But what is a heart? Just a chunk of flesh that a dog can eat. Your problem originates in your own character, and you must first change yourself. Who said "Character is fate?"

When Lin replies, "Beethoven," Geng Yang's response is, "Yes. You know so much, but you can't act decisively." Geng Yang's point is that what happens to people in their lives is a product of their own character, not the result of external causes or some unalterable fate. He then goes on to produce a saying of Chairman Mao that says much the same thing. Geng Yang well knows how to get through to Lin, the obedient party member who has been known to lecture at the hospital on the work of Chairman Mao.

Of course, Geng Yang later demonstrates by his brutal rape of Manna that a comparison between him and Lin does not in the end come out in his favor. Lin is a moral man who would never force himself on a woman. But certainly his basic goodness is compromised by his inability to act decisively, with courage and determination. After many years of their long-drawn-out attachment, Manna is well aware of this aspect of his personality: "She knew the workings of his mind: he would always choose an easy way out." At one point she berates him for his attempt to think through their situation. "All you can do is think, think, think," she says with exasperation and rushes out through the door.

Lin's indecisiveness stems in part from the fact that he does not know how to love fully. He is incapable of loving his first wife, Shuyu, despite her many years of loyalty and devotion to him. He simply does not, until the very end of the novel, see her as a person in her own right, with desires and emotions of her own. Since he lacks empathy, he is stuck on the surface of things, influenced by relatively trivial matters such as Shuyu's unprepossessing appearance. During his long courtship with Manna, he thinks he loves her, but he loves her in a detached kind of way, without passion. It is as if all the passion has been bled out of him. For seventeen years, Lin is content not to have sex with either Shuyu or Manna (or anyone else), and in one of the book's richly comic episodes, he is barely able to satisfy Manna when her desire is finally unleashed after their marriage. Lin also realizes after

finally entering into the marriage that he sought for so long that he cannot give his heart fully to Manna, or to anyone.

There may be a reason for Lin's personality flaws located in the society and the times in which he lives. In an interview published in *Asia Week* in 1999, the author himself, Ha Jin, commented that Lin's inability to love may

> allegorically . . . sum up a sort of internal psychological damage to the Chinese [after the Cultural Revolution]. I think one of the major tasks of the Revolution was to disable people so they can't love others—disable emotions, so that psychological energy, sexual energy or creative energy could be focused on the revolutionary cause.

This is an interesting explanation, coming from a man who lived through the Cultural Revolution as a child. Certainly, much of Lin Kong's energy is channeled into his work. At one point, he deliberately wears himself out working, so that he will go straight to sleep at night rather than thinking endlessly about his situation with Manna. Although he does not come across as a man fanatically devoted to the revolutionary cause, he is quietly supportive of it. He does not question the wisdom of Chairman Mao or the right of the authorities to dictate to him what he should do. He is submissive to authority and scared of taking risks. He internalizes all the rules imposed on him and genuinely thinks they are for the best.

What happens in the case of Lin is that the psychic and sexual energy—to use Jin's terms—that should be directed outward gets turned inward and results in feelings of guilt, self-reproach, and self-doubt. Lin knows that he has failed those who are close to him. After Manna tells him about the rape, he blames himself for his indecisiveness, thinking that had he married Manna, Geng Yang would not have been able to commit his crime. "Such a wimp!" he curses himself. His laments gather force in part 3 of the novel, after his second marriage, when the consequences of his actions over many years become most painfully apparent to him. When he reads the passionate love letters Manna received from Mai Dong, he realizes that "Never had he experienced that kind of intense emotion for a woman; never had he written a sentence charged with that kind of love." He tries to figure out why that should be, concluding that perhaps it was because he had read too much or was better educated or that he was a scientist by training: "Knowledge chills your blood." By the penultimate chapter of the novel, when it is clear that his marriage is not destined to be a happy one, his introspection reaches

What Do I Read Next?

- Da Chen comes from the same Chinese generation as Ha Jin. Like Jin, he writes in English and lives in the United States. His *The Colors of the Mountains* (2001) is an autobiographical coming-of-age tale that gives vivid insight into the devastating effects on a family of China's Cultural Revolution and tells of Chen's own triumph over adversity.

- *Ocean of Words: Stories* (1996) is Ha Jin's first collection of short stories. They are set on China's northern border in the 1970s, when tensions between Russia and China were high and many feared that war was imminent. Ha Jin draws on his own experience of army life at the border during this period to create stories about the lives of the Chinese soldiers who live in close proximity to one another and share emotions such as fear, curiosity, and embarrassment. Although the situations may be remote from the experience of American readers, Ha Jin writes with such insight and humanity that the reader cares about the characters.

- *Spring Moon* (reprint edition, 1990), by Bette Bao Lord, is a portrait of five generations of a Chinese family, from the late nineteenth to the twentieth century. It also gives vivid insight into the huge political and social upheavals that took place during this period. The main character is Spring Moon, a daughter of the wealthy house of Chang.

- *The Three-Inch Golden Lotus* (1985), by Chi-Tsai Feng, is a novel that focuses on the traditional but long-discontinued Chinese practice of foot-binding. Set in the late nineteenth and early twentieth century, the novel follows the story of a girl called Fragrant Lotus, whose elegantly bound feet attract the attentions of the wealthy Tong Ren-an. Tong chooses his daughters-in-law based on what he regards as the beauty of their bound feet. After Tong's death, Fragrant Lotus, whose entire success in life has been based on her bound feet, has to deal with the rise of the Natural Foot Society, which calls for an end to foot-binding.

- *Snake's Pillow, and Other Stories* (1998), by Zhu Lin, consists of six stories set in contemporary China. Set in the rural area of Jiangnan in east-central China, most of the stories focus on the lives of women and how, in a changing society, they are exploited by men.

---

its most profound level as he engages in a dialogue with himself about his feelings for Manna. A voice inside tells him that he has never really loved Manna and that he knows very little about love. He has never known his own mind or his own heart. This inner voice rises to a crescendo filled with regret and self-loathing: "Fool ... Eighteen years, the prime of your life, gone, wasted, and they led you to this damned marriage. You're a model fool!"

Against this background of Lin's remorse, the final scene of the novel, in which Lin visits Shuyu and Hua in their urban apartment, becomes deeply poignant. It is also replete with irony. As Lin and Manna sink into unhappiness, Shuyu flourishes, looking healthy and younger in her new environment. Lin is deeply touched by the peaceful life created by mother and daughter and feels he is at home, even though he is not at home—he is merely visiting the woman he deserted for another. When he drinks too much and calls Shuyu his sweetheart, it is the first time he has ever said an endearment to her. In an ironic reversal, he begs Shuyu to wait for him, since Manna has only a short time to live. Thus the wheel turns full circle, and the "waiting" which characterizes the life of this "superfluous man" (as he disparagingly refers to himself) goes on. This is a man who did not appreciate what he had until he threw it away. The final impression left on the reader is that the most appealing character in the novel is not the procrastinating, inadequate Lin but his ex-wife Shuyu, who in her quiet dignity and devotion, her simplicity, her optimism and her refusal to complain about her lot deserves far more than her emotionally crippled ex-husband ever gave her.

Source: Bryan Aubrey, Critical Essay on *Waiting*, in *Novels for Students*, Thomson Gale, 2007.

Dwight Garner

In the following essay, Garner comments on Ha Jin's mastery of written English, his struggles with spoken English, and on how he is someone who seems to not have fully immersed himself in American culture.

On a bright fall morning in 1985, Xuefei Jin walked out of Logan airport in Boston and took his first real gulp of American air. It almost sent him to his knees. "There is a unique American smell that hits you when you arrive here," he says. "It is very sweet, like chemicals or a kind of perfume. It makes you sick for a while." Jin had flown from Beijing, a student visa stuffed into his pocket, to study American literature at Brandeis University. "I know people who came here from Asia and vomited for days. They couldn't even brush their teeth because the water smelled so different."

Xuefei (pronounced shu-FAY) Jin, who writes under the pen name Ha Jin, is a courtly and soft-spoken man who punctuates stories like this one with a quick, apologetic laugh—a laugh that says, "How silly this must all sound." He employs it often when talking about his early years in America, while recalling, for example, the menial jobs he took to pay the rent—busing tables at a Friendly's restaurant, cleaning houses, working as a night watchman at a chemical factory—or remembering why he initially thought all Americans must be rich. ("There were so many squirrels, and no one was trying to eat them.") It's a laugh that pops up everywhere, vanishing only when he talks about his decision, in the days following the Tiananmen Square massacre, in 1989, not to return to his native country. Or when he recalls the difficult months he spent trying to get permission from the Chinese government so that his wife, Lisha Bian, and later his young son, Wen, could join him in America.

Jin's laugh is abundantly in evidence on the windy December afternoon he takes me on an impromptu driving tour of Emory University in Atlanta, where he has taught since 1993. It's a bumpy ride in his small Chevrolet; every so often, Jin brakes suddenly, as if he has gotten lost in his own backyard. His driving skills are almost as shaky as his command of spoken English —his Mandarin accent, with its hard "r" sound, remains strong. "It is very easy to lose your way in Atlanta," he says. "So many street names begin with the word 'peach.'" He rolls down the window to look around, and he sucks down another deep lungful of American, air. "I am very grateful for fall and winter," he says. "The rest of the year, Atlanta is pollen central."

Jin has more or less adjusted to America's complicated oxygen supply. But watching him grapple with the intricacies of its spoken language—he often drops his articles, and an excruciatingly exact rendering of the quotation above would be, "Rest of year, Atlanta pollen central"—is an experience that will startle anyone who first encountered his voice through his fiction. On the page, Jin has the kind of effortless command that most writers can only dream about. His first novel, *Waiting,* the story of a Chinese doctor who wants to end his arranged marriage so he can marry a more modern woman, recently won a National Book Award, a mere 11 years after Jin began writing seriously in English. In the 50-year history of the awards, only two other writers who weren't native English speakers have taken home the fiction prize: Isaac Bashevis Singer and Jerzy Kosinski.

Waiting begins with the kind of economical but perfectly turned sentence that abounds in Jin's work—"Every summer Lin Kong returned to Goose Village to divorce his wife, Shuyu"—and it casts a spell that doesn't break once over the course of the book's 308 pages. Set in northern China in the 1980's and based on a true story, the novel is a delicate portrait of a decent but oddly passionless man. It is also about a love triangle in which there's little genuine love to be found.

Like all of Jin's work, *Waiting* has the stripped-down simplicity of a fable. The novel's protagonist, Lin Kong, is an urban doctor who left behind in the countryside the woman his family chose for him to marry—a loyal wife whose Old World servility and bound feet embarrass him. Because he can't work up the nerve to force her to grant him a divorce, and because adultery is punished severely by the Communist Party, he is forced to wait 18 embittering years before he can be with the clever, educated nurse he thinks he loves. During those years he lives "like a sleepwalker, pulled and pushed by others' opinions." Worse, he comes to realize he may have been waiting for the wrong woman.

Waiting is set just after the end of the Cultural Revolution, and Jin forcefully evokes a world in which both petty rules and local gossips could ruin a life in an instant. It's a world he remembers all too well. "In China there was no privacy," the 43-year-old writer says. "Your banker would tell your neighbors how much money you had in your bank account! It was something you didn't even question."

These kinds of memories remain vivid for Jin, which helps explain why none of his fiction is set in America, even though all of it has been written since his arrival here in 1985. (In addition to *Waiting,* he has published a novella, two short-story collections and two volumes of poetry.) Unlike almost every other Asian-American novelist who has attracted notice in the United States—Gish Jen, Amy Tan and Chang-rae Lee, to name but a few—Jin steers clear of the bumpy politics of assimilation.

The exoticism of his northern Chinese locales separates him from these writers, but so does the almost classical rigor of his storytelling. If the lucidity and focus of *Waiting* puts you in mind of Russian masters like Gogol and Chekhov, that's no accident. Jin reads and rereads these writers, he says, to remind him of what fiction is supposed to be. "You read so many novels these days by young writers and they feel so ephemeral," he says. "They are full of references to TV shows and movies. What's important is to get human feeling onto paper. That's what is timeless, and that's what you get from Tolstoy and from Gogol and from Chekhov."

In a funny way, says the Chinese-American novelist Gish Jen, the timeless quality of Jin's writing may be among the few really new things happening in American fiction right now. "The whole idea of looking to masters instead of overturning something is very Chinese," she says. "On some level, Ha Jin has chosen mastery over genius. It's as if he said, 'I am going to make something like *that.*' This never happens with American writers. We are too beset with the anxiety of influence. What he's doing is very challenging, and I am interested to see how the American literati pick it up and deal with it."

The glamorous world of the literati is something Jin himself knows little about. He is a small, somewhat awkward man who can appear to be here but not here in America, and that's not just because he gets lost easily or still struggles with spoken English. Jin has almost zero affinity for American popular culture—he can't remember the last movie he saw, and his TV knowledge is limited to unhip shows like "Walker, Texas Ranger." In many ways, he resembles the brilliant but slightly bumbling

> **"** On the page, Jin has the kind of effortless command that most writers can only dream about."

foreign academic in one of his own favorite novels, Vladimir Nabokov's *Pnin.*

Jin's monkishness becomes apparent the moment you step into his house, a small brick ranch in a drab suburb northeast of Atlanta. The faux-wood-paneled living room is decorated in a style that might best be described as Grad School Provisional. Besides books in English and Chinese, there are a couple of inexpensive vinyl-covered couches, and, most notably, there is a Ping-Pong table that takes up half the room. ("My wife always beats me," Jin says.) Yet he plays only rarely, he confesses. Often he works so late that he ends up sleeping in his office—in a small bed placed near his computer.

As Xuefei Jin picks at the platters of food that have been spread across the livingroom coffee table—there are oranges, cookies and plastic jugs of Gatorade and apple juice —he tells me he's not sure what surprises him more: that he has become a writer, or that he has made a life for his family in America. "It wasn't supposed to work out this way," he says. "This is not where I thought I would be."

When Jin arrived at Brandeis in 1985, he not only didn't plan on becoming a writer, he also didn't plan on staying in the United States. "I just wanted to get my Ph.D. so I could get a good teaching job when I went back," he says. To ensure that Jin would indeed return, the Chinese government made him leave his wife and young son behind. "My first years here were very exciting but very lonely," he says. "My wife and I wrote many, many letters."

Jin's scholarship ran out after a year, and he began working odd jobs to cover his living expenses. It was while at one of these jobs, as a night watchman at a chemical factory, that he began doing his first writing in English—a language that he studied for several years in China, but one that he had not yet come close to mastering. "I was just dabbling," he says of these early experiments. But as he wrote, he sensed a freedom in English that he had never felt in his native language. "I had written a few poems in Chinese, but I wasn't happy with them. The Chinese language is very literary and highbrow and detached from the spoken word. It doesn't have the flexibility that English has. So I slowly began to squeeze the Chinese literary mentality out of my mind."

At the prompting of a professor, Jin took some of his work to the poet Frank Bidart, who was teaching at Brandeis. "It was extraordinary to find something this shaped from someone whose first language was not English," Bidart recalls. "He had this remarkable idiom." One of Jin's poems, "The Dead Soldier's Talk," was so good that Bidart read it over the telephone to Jonathan Galassi, who was then poetry editor of *The Paris Review* (and now editor in chief of Farrar, Straus & Giroux). Galassi immediately accepted the poem; a few years later, Jin's first book of poetry, *Between Silences,* was published by the University of Chicago Press.

Around this time, Jin began experiencing severe stomach problems. The Chinese government grudgingly allowed his wife to come to the States to care for him; the pains soon went away, and in 1989 he prepared to return to China with his wife. But something happened, Jin says, "that changed everything for me." Student protesters had gathered in Tiananmen Square, and Jin and Bian spent several days glued to the television screen in their small Boston apartment. "I was not mentally prepared for what happened," he says of the government's crackdown. "I had always thought that the Chinese Army was there to serve and protect the people." Disillusioned, Jin decided not to return to China and began working to get his son, Wen, out of the country as well. To his astonishment, Chinese authorities allowed Wen to board a flight to the United States a few months later.

Wanting to write fiction as well as poetry, Jin enrolled in a master's program at Boston University, where his work was embraced by teachers like Leslie Epstein. But his accent, which was still terribly thick, made workshop discussions difficult. What's more, Jin's subject matter turned off some classmates. One of his classmates was Jhumpa Lahiri, whose first collection of stories, *Interpreter of Maladies,* appeared last year. "He is such a gentle man, but his stories really pushed people's buttons," she says. "There were a lot of brutal rape scenes in them. One was about a man who castrates himself. I remember people being shocked and outraged by some of it."

Epstein remembers those heated discussions well. "Ha Jin is one of the great poets of rape," he says. "One of his best stories, 'Man to Be', has this terrible, terrific rape scene in which a man recovers his humanity when he looks into the eyes of the woman he is about to rape." One of the most powerful moments in *Waiting,* too, is a rape scene. While Lin Kong dithers about divorcing his wife, his girlfriend is brutally raped, and Lin Kong is convinced, perhaps with some justification, that it is his fault. "Indecisiveness," he thinks, "had opened the door to the wolf."

Jin laughs uncomfortably when I tell him that he has been described as a "great poet of rape." "My stories are not gentle stories," he says. "The question for me has always been, How do you write about terrible things without resorting to vulgarity? I think I might push things farther than people expect. But that's how you test yourself as a writer."

Jin has remained in academe, having taught writing at Boston University for a few years before moving to Emory. Settled in Atlanta, Jin began publishing his work. His first story collection, *Ocean of Words*, appeared in 1996 and won a PEN/Hemingway prize; a 1997 collection, *Under the Red Flag*, won the Flannery O'Connor Award for Short Fiction. As the awards for his work began piling up, Jin says, he began to be asked the same question over and over at readings and book signings: how can someone write English so fluidly, yet speak it so haltingly? "I always give the same response," he says. "On the page, I can spend all the time I need. I can be patient. I can work and work until I think I've almost got it right."

Jin was born in 1956 in the Northern Chinese City of Jinzhou, where his father, a military officer, was stationed. At age 7, he was shipped off to boarding school, where he studied for two years, until Mao Zedong ordered all of China's schools closed at the start of the Cultural Revolution.

He returned home to chaos. "Because my grandfather had been a landowner, my mother was criticized very severely," he recalls. "People did terrible things to her. She was once thrown into a trash can." Soldiers burned books owned by Jin's father in a bonfire on the city's streets.

With no school to attend and little else to do, Jin joined the Little Red Guard, where he spent a few years "wearing red armbands, waving flags and singing revolutionary songs" before lying about his age and signing up, at 14, with the People's Liberation Army. At the time, there were rumors that Russia was planning an attack on China, and Jin did not want to die at home in a bomb shelter. "Like everyone else, I wanted to be a hero, a martyr," he says. Jin spent a year shivering on the Russian border, a year that provided the raw material for his first collection, *Ocean of Words*, a cycle of stories about Chinese soldiers who await the outbreak of war and struggle, sometimes comically, to cleanse themselves of "bourgeois sentiment."

The Russian attack never came, but something else happened: Jin came upon a worn Chinese translation of *War and Peace*. "I was almost illiterate and could barely read it," he says. "But I remember thinking to myself: What a revelation this is. I'm here fighting the Russians, and Tolstoy showed me that the Russians were just like me."

Jin was discharged when he was 19. Because the schools were still closed, he took a job as a telegraph operator in a remote northern city. For once he had ample time to read. Even better, a local radio station began broadcasting an English-language program from 5 to 5:30 a.m. six days a week. He listened avidly and set himself a goal: to read Friedrich Engels's *Condition of the Working Class in England* in its original English. "It was a stupid goal," he says. "I didn't come close."

When China's colleges finally reopened in 1977, Jin was admitted to Heilongjiang University in the northeastern city of Harbin as an English major. He spent four years there, listening to tapes and reciting English phrases until his mouth felt as if it would fall off into his hands. "I hated it," he says. "I simply couldn't say the words. They twisted your tongue, your muscles, too much. We all went to the clinic regularly to get painkillers."

In the early 80's, just as China was beginning to liberalize, Jin enrolled at Shandong University in eastern China, where he got a master's degree in what was becoming a fashionable intellectual topic: American literature. "Like everyone else, I became obsessed with Faulkner, with Roethke, with Bellow," he says. "It was finally O.K. to read these writers."

At Shandong University, Jin met visiting U.S. scholars who encouraged him to study in America. Around this time, Jin also met his future wife, who was teaching mathematics at Shandong. What's more, he stumbled upon the story that would ultimately emerge in *Waiting*. While visiting Bian's parents, who were army doctors, he heard the story of another doctor at their hospital who had waited 18 years to get a divorce. "Intuitively, I knew this would make a great story," he says, "but I never thought I would write it. You needed skill to write a story like that. I didn't have it."

When Jin finally did sit down to begin *Waiting,* in the early 90's, he still wasn't sure he could bring the story off. "I was terrified because I didn't know if it was any good," he recalls. Fortunately, LuAnn Walther, an editor at Pantheon, found the novel very good indeed. After years of advances and royalties that were rarely more than a few thousand dollars, Pantheon bought *Waiting* at auction for $50,000, and the foreign rights later sold for another $50,000. "I finally felt like I could breathe," Jin says.

It has grown dark outside, and the oranges and cookies are almost gone, when Jin suggests heading out in search of some real food. We pile into his car along with Bian and Wen and drive to a Malaysian restaurant in Chamblee, another suburb. With the recent influx of Asian immigrants, the area has been nicknamed "Chambodia." Along the way we pass strip malls with Korean hair salons and Vietnamese noodle shops, and Jin points out several excellent Chinese bookstores. As much as he appreciates the bookstores, he says, they are a constant reminder that his own books are not available in mainland China. None of his work has been published there. "The American media sometimes portrays me as a dissident, as an exile, although I'm not sure I really am one," he says. News that a Taiwanese publisher will translate *Waiting* has inspired some hope. "I'd like my parents and my brothers and sisters to be able to read my work."

At the restaurant, Jin digs into a whole sauce-covered snapper and discusses his future projects. He is currently polishing a collection of short stories that are set in the same city where *Waiting* takes place and developing a novel that he describes as being about insanity. "It's about a professor in China who has had a stroke but who remains quite articulate," Jin says. "He talks a lot of nonsense but also a lot of truth." Once these books are finished, Jin says, he plans to put China behind him and write his first novel set in the United States. "I have been gathering some ideas," he says.

The idea of writing about America clearly intimidates him, so I'm almost entirely kidding when I ask him if he'll try a frenetic, jumbo-size Atlanta novel along the lines of *A Man in Full*. Jin takes the question seriously, however. He has read Tom Wolfe's book, and he praises its abundance of "great detail" while making it clear that it's not his kind of thing.

"I may not understand America very deeply in that way," he says, "but perhaps I can make sense of it from a different angle, from an immigrant's perspective." Jin smiles. "This book will be a great hurdle for me. I will have to write it *very slowly*."

Source: Dwight Garner, "Ha Jin's Cultural Revolution: The Émigré Novelist, a Former Soldier under Mau, Still Has Trouble Speaking English. So How Can He Write like Henry James?" in *New York Times Magazine*, February 6, 2000, pp. 38–41.

Linda Simon

In the following essay, Simon discusses how Ha Jin's characters struggle with the waiting imposed on them because of love, a repressive political structure, and social customs.

When Ha Jin came to America in 1985 to become a graduate student at Brandeis University, he and his wife left their two-year-old son in their native China. Four years later, the massacre at Tiananmen Square awakened Jin to the realities of Chinese politics and convinced him to change his plans to return home after completing his degree. Instead, with the help of the U.S. Embassy, he managed to extricate his young child from, as he put it, "the middle of the chaos." He would never return, he decided, as much for his son as for himself. "The government [is] so cruel," Jin told an interviewer later. "People died for no other reason, just for a bunch of old hooligans who want to keep in power. I was really very embittered. I wanted him to be American. That was very clear. That was one of the reasons I decided to stay."

Jin's feelings of embitterment and disillusion have informed his fiction: *Under the Red Flag*, which earned him the Flannery O'Connor Award for Short Fiction in 1996; *Ocean of Words*, which won the PEN/Hemingway Award in 1997; and now *Waiting*, the winner of the 1999 National Book Award for Fiction.

In all these works, Jin explores the lives of ordinary men and women as they confront tensions between traditional values and new political imperatives. They struggle for status, power, and wealth in the baffling and threatening new social order generated by the Cultural Revolution.

Waiting focuses on the plight of star-crossed lovers whose public obligations conflict with their personal desires. More than a tale of thwarted love, the novel is an indictment of the repressive political structure and social customs, corruption, and deeply embedded psychological constraints that shape contemporary Chinese culture.

In simple, precise prose (Jin has been writing in English, his adopted language, since 1988), the novel tells the story of Lin Kong, a Chinese army doctor working in the small city of Muji, and his eighteen-year-long, unconsummated affair with Manna Wu, a nurse at the hospital, from the time they meet in 1966. The two cannot marry until Lin divorces his wife, which requires her consent, or until the couple has lived apart for eighteen years—an arbitrary number invented by a powerful bureaucrat. Each summer, Lin returns home to the hamlet of Goose Village to persuade his wife, Shuyu, to grant him a divorce. Each summer she agrees; but as soon as she faces the judge, she recants and refuses. Lin can do nothing, he thinks, but return to Manna and repeat the process the next year.

As Jin chronicles Lin's frustrated efforts to liberate himself from his marriage, we become intimately acquainted with village life and Shuyu's place within her culture. Unlike most modern women, Shuyu had her feet bound as a child, a process that she recalls as excruciatingly painful. But her mother was convinced that small feet—"called Golden Lotus, like a treasure," Shuyu explains—would make her a prize in marriage. "Mother said it's my second chance to marry good, 'cause my face ugly. You know, men are crazy about lotus feet in those days. The smaller your feet are, the better looking you are to them." But bound feet, far from attracting Lin, repulsed him.

He and Shuyu had been brought together by a matchmaker at the request of his parents, while Lin was a medical student. His mother was ill, and his father urged Lin to find a wife so there would be someone to help with housekeeping. Lin agreed, but when he finally met the woman chosen for him, he was deeply disappointed: Shuyu looked older than her years, she was illiterate, and her bound feet, he decided, made her a laughingstock. But when he tried to break the engagement, his parents reminded him that the village would censure him. They convinced him that Shuyu's kindness outweighed her lack of beauty.

After they were married, Lin never allowed Shuyu to visit him at the army hospital—her appearance embarrassed him—and although he returned to her every summer and had a child with her, they essentially lived apart. While he was away, she cared for her in-laws through their last illnesses, brought up her daughter, Hua, and remained devoted to Lin. Her refusal to divorce came not from anger or spite but out of an abiding love for her husband. Jin presents Shuyu as a woman whose life is bound by hardship and, despite Lin's financial support, relative poverty, yet she shows

no resentment toward her husband, only hopeful-
ness that one day he will return and love her.

Self-criticism

Shuyu emerges as the most sympathetic character in this novel, capable of deep love and devotion, aware of her own feelings, yet necessarily
resigned to powerlessness in her marriage and her
culture. Her only power lies in her refusal to grant
Lin a divorce, and here she does manage to exert
her will and thwart her husband's plans. Lin, on
the other hand, is overwhelmed by the constraints
imposed upon him politically, socially, and cul-
turally. As a man and an army officer, he would
seem to have a position of power, but the reality
is far different. He feels always subjected to the
judgment of others: his fellow officers, his superiors, his roommates, and even Manna. Coveting
yearly election as a model officer, he usually gains
this prize. After his relationship with Manna becomes hospital gossip, he fails the election for the
first time.

Lin is shaken when he learns the reasons:

> Some people complained about his lifestyle. One of-
> ficer reported that Lin once had not stood at atten-
> tion like others when the national anthem was
> broadcast, even though they had been in the bath-
> house, all naked in the pool. A section chief re-
> marked that Lin shouldn't keep his hair so long and
> parted right down the middle. The hairstyle made
> him look like a petty intellectual, like those in the
> movies.

Immediately, Lin asks one of his roommates
to give him a crew cut. Yet he knows that his appearance is only part of the reason others voted
against him. He guesses that a much more serious
offense is his reluctance, at political studies meetings, to disclose "his inmost thoughts, as though he
were supposed to make a self-criticism."

Lin has little ability for self-reflection—even
the self-criticism demanded by the political system.
He never fully understands his feelings toward
Shuyu, Manna, or his daughter. His plea for divorce
becomes a rote activity, enacted largely to please
Manna, who herself seems motivated as much by
the public perception of her relationship with Lin
as by her own feelings. In Manna, we see Shuyu's
counterpart in a so-called modern woman, mod-
estly educated and living independently. Still,
Manna knows that her future lies in marriage—and
not just to anyone but to a man of some stature in
the community. Her marketability as a wife, however, depends heavily on her reputation: She must
be a woman whose behavior and appearance are

> " More than a tale of
> thwarted love, the novel is an
> indictment of the repressive political
> structure and social customs, corruption,
> and deeply embedded psychological
> constraints that shape contemporary
> Chinese culture."

without blemish. And she must wait for a man to
choose her.

During her protracted relationship with Lin, at
one point she is singled out as a possible mate for
Commissar Wei, a high-ranking official in his
fifties who divorced his first wife and has asked his
subordinates to recommend a replacement. Under
the circumstances, Lin cannot object to the match,
and Manna agrees that "this was an opportunity she
shouldn't miss. The man was a top officer in the
province—if her relationship with him developed
successfully," she thinks, "he could arrange for her
to be transferred. Possibly the commissar could
place her in a crash program for training doctors or
in a college to earn a diploma."

Wei meets Manna, they attend a showing of a
sentimental Korean movie at the Workers' Cultural
Palace, and he presents Manna with a copy of Walt
Whitman's *Leaves of Grass*, with instructions that
she write a response about it and send it to him.
Manna is worried by this gesture, as is Lin: They
both see the assignment as a test. "You must take
the report seriously," Lin tells her and agrees to
help her write it. Lin, one of the few men in his
community who reads anything besides political
tracts and the work of Chairman Mao, is gravely
disturbed by the book:

> To him, this was a bizarre, wild book of poetry that
> had so many bold lines about sexuality that it could
> be interpreted either as obscenity or as praise of hu-
> man vitality. Moreover, the celebration of the poet's
> self seemed to verge on a kind of megalomania that
> ought to be condemned. But . . . on the whole this
> must be a good, healthy book; otherwise the com-
> missar wouldn't have let Manna read it.

Lin decides to focus his attention on Whitman's celebration of the working class, but he is

stumped when he tries to elaborate on the symbolic meaning of grass. Finally, he manages to assert that "the grass gathered the essence of heaven and earth, yin and yang, and the material and the spiritual, and that it unified the body and the soul, the living and the dead, celebrating the infinity and abundance of life. In brief, it was a very progressive symbol, charged with the proletarian spirit." As confident as they can be that Lin's report is satisfactory and politically correct, Manna copies it over and sends it to Commissar Wei. Then, as she has done in so many other circumstances, she waits.

Weeks later, Manna learns from a hospital aide that the commissar has decided not to pursue his relationship with her. Although her report impressed him, her handwriting did not. Wei, in the process of preparing a book manuscript, "needed someone whose handwriting was handsome to help him with secretarial work." Manna was not in love with or even attracted to Wei, but his reaction was humiliating, subjecting her to public ridicule. "What," she asks herself, "was more fearful than being surrounded by gossiping tongues?" In her world, nothing could be worse.

The next page

When Lin finally is granted his divorce, he feels that "a new page of his life" surely will open. But this new page contains some surprising revelations. First, the divorce inspires him to establish a relationship with Hua, whom he had neglected throughout her childhood and youth. Shuyu's only demand in agreeing to the divorce is that Lin find a job for Hua in the city, liberating her from the demeaning poverty of Goose Village. Hua, though, is not convinced that city life would be a benefit; she wants to stay in the country, she tells her father, and become "a socialist peasant of the new type." Lin is angered that his daughter has thoughtlessly swallowed such propaganda, and he goes to Goose Village to persuade her to start a new life for herself in Muji. Western readers are unlikely to believe that affixing labels to matchboxes at the Splendor Match Plant could offer a desirable future, but in fact, Hua discovers that the job, which comes with dormitory housing and a decent salary, offers her a new level of self-respect—certainly it is better than life in Goose Village.

Throughout the novel, Jin offers readers a vivid and indelible portrait of rural and provincial landscapes, realized in a few deft strokes. Here, for example, is what Lin sees when he returns to Goose Village to persuade Hua to come to the city:

> On the ground, near the wattle gate of the vegetable garden, was spread a bloody donkey's hide. It was

almost covered up by dead greenheads. Judging by the sweetish odor still emanating from the skin, a lot of dichlorvos had been sprayed on it to prevent maggots. The air also smelled meaty and spicy, with a touch of cumin, prickly ash, and magnolia-vine. Hua, a violet towel covering her hair, was stirring something in a cauldron set on a makeshift fireplace built of rocks.

What she is stirring is five-flavored donkey meat, the flesh of her uncle's prized possession, the animal on which he depended to transport groceries and supplies. No one can allow a dead animal simply to rot away, so, thinking he would get more money from cooked meat than raw, Hua's uncle enlisted her help in cooking a vat of stew to sell to villagers. From this scene, Lin is convinced, more than ever, that he must rescue his daughter; and he experiences, unexpectedly, a passionate and heartfelt impulse.

Besides becoming closer to Hua, Lin, once divorced, also discovers a new relationship with Shuyu, who leaves Goose Village to live with Hua in the city. For the first time in her life, Shuyu has her hair cut professionally, and as her appearance changes, so do her spirits and her outlook on life. Lin realizes that she is a woman with whom he could have a real friendship; he realizes, in the end, how much he loves her. But of course, it is too late.

Although Jin admits that he intended the novel to be a universal story of a man's inability to love and appreciate what he has when he has it, Lin is an unlikely candidate for Everyman. His passivity seems both anachronistic and connected to his unique historical and cultural context. With his limited perspective, circumscribed experiences, and lack of connection to literature, philosophy, art, and psychology—sources that might give him insight into his own feelings and behavior—Lin is unable to act on his own behalf or even to understand what he truly wants.

At the end of the novel, Lin engages in conversation with an inner voice that forces him to examine his feelings about Manna and his own responsibility for his fate. As Jin presents it, this is the first such reflection that Lin has ever had about his life, but it leaves him only "weary," feeling "too old to take any action," and wistful about the life he might have had. A visit to Shuyu and Hua intensifies his feeling of regret and impotence. But what can be done? He has married Manna, they are parents of infant twin sons, and he is caught, once again, in a web of circumstances. His only way out, he thinks, will come through external change:

Manna has a bad heart; she cannot last much longer; and Shuyu lives just minutes away.

The story, then, ends as it began: Manna is waiting, only now, she awaits death; Shuyu is waiting, hopefully as ever, for her husband to return; and Lin is waiting: for love, liberation, or perhaps an inner revolution that, Ha Jin implies, is the only real basis for cultural enlightenment.

Source: Linda Simon, "Love among the Revolutionaries—Chinese Expatriate Ha Jin Writes of Love, Freedom, and Repression in His Native Land," in *World and I*, Vol. 15, No. 5, May 2000, p. 247.

Sources

Chun, Kim, "Author Ha Jin on the Rewards of *Waiting*; Emory University Professor Talks About His Novel," in *AsianWeek.Com*, Vol. 21, No. 17, December 16, 1999, http://www.asianweek.com/1999_12_16/ae_hajinwaiting .html (accessed September 5, 2006).

Gray, Paul, "Divorce, Chinese-Style: A Fine First Novel, *Waiting*, Revels in One Man's Comically Thwarted Quest for Personal Happiness," in *Time*, Vol. 154, No. 19, November 8, 1999, p. 144.

Hunter, Alan, and John Sexton, *Contemporary China*, Macmillan, 1999, p. 27.

Jin, Ha, *Waiting: A Novel*, Pantheon Books, 1999.

Prose, Francine, "The 18-Year-Itch: In Ha Jin's Novel, a Doctor and the Woman He Loves Must Wait Nearly Two Decades to Consummate Their Relationship," in *New York Times Book Review*, Vol. 104, No. 43, October 24, 1999, p. 9.

Review of *Waiting*, in *Entertainment Weekly*, October 29, 1999, p. 107.

Review of *Waiting*, in *New Yorker*, November 1, 1999, p. 114.

Review of *Waiting*, in *Publishers Weekly*, Vol. 246, No. 34, August 23, 1999, p. 42.

Further Reading

Bonavia, David, *The Chinese*, Penguin, 1989.
Bonavia is a journalist who has lived and worked in China, and his book presents a realistic picture of life in China in the 1980s. Bonavia describes every aspect of Chinese life from city to country, covering such topics as education, crime, birth control policy, marriage, sex, and consumerism, as well as Chinese language and literature, economic and foreign policy, and the Cultural Revolution and its aftermath.

Davis, Marcia, "Work of Heart: Honored for His Fiction, Ha Jin Considers the Facts of His Life," in *Washington Post*, May 14, 2005, p. C01.
This is an interview with Jin after he was awarded the PEN/Faulkner Award for the second time, for his 2004 novel, *War Trash*. Jin speaks about his life, his literary achievements, and his plans for future works.

Geyh, Paula E., "An Interview with Ha Jin," in *Boulevard*, Vol. 17, No. 3, Spring 2003, pp. 127–40.
In this interview, Ha Jin discusses his life and work.

Sturr, Robert D., "The Presence of Walt Whitman in Ha Jin's *Waiting*," in *Walt Whitman Quarterly Review*, Vol. 20, No. 1, Summer 2002, pp. 1–18.
Sturr discusses the influence of Whitman on Jin, the prominence given to Whitman's *Leaves of Grass* in *Waiting*, and what purpose it serves. Sturr also discusses the Cultural Revolution in China and how it affected attitudes toward American poets and writers such as Whitman.

Glossary of Literary Terms

A

Abstract: As an adjective applied to writing or literary works, abstract refers to words or phrases that name things not knowable through the five senses.

Aestheticism: A literary and artistic movement of the nineteenth century. Followers of the movement believed that art should not be mixed with social, political, or moral teaching. The statement "art for art's sake" is a good summary of aestheticism. The movement had its roots in France, but it gained widespread importance in England in the last half of the nineteenth century, where it helped change the Victorian practice of including moral lessons in literature.

Allegory: A narrative technique in which characters representing things or abstract ideas are used to convey a message or teach a lesson. Allegory is typically used to teach moral, ethical, or religious lessons but is sometimes used for satiric or political purposes.

Allusion: A reference to a familiar literary or historical person or event, used to make an idea more easily understood.

Analogy: A comparison of two things made to explain something unfamiliar through its similarities to something familiar, or to prove one point based on the acceptedness of another. Similes and metaphors are types of analogies.

Antagonist: The major character in a narrative or drama who works against the hero or protagonist.

Anthropomorphism: The presentation of animals or objects in human shape or with human characteristics. The term is derived from the Greek word for "human form."

Antihero: A central character in a work of literature who lacks traditional heroic qualities such as courage, physical prowess, and fortitude. Antiheroes typically distrust conventional values and are unable to commit themselves to any ideals. They generally feel helpless in a world over which they have no control. Antiheroes usually accept, and often celebrate, their positions as social outcasts.

Apprenticeship Novel: See *Bildungsroman*

Archetype: The word archetype is commonly used to describe an original pattern or model from which all other things of the same kind are made. This term was introduced to literary criticism from the psychology of Carl Jung. It expresses Jung's theory that behind every person's "unconscious," or repressed memories of the past, lies the "collective unconscious" of the human race: memories of the countless typical experiences of our ancestors. These memories are said to prompt illogical associations that trigger powerful emotions in the reader. Often, the emotional process is primitive, even primordial. Archetypes are the literary images that grow out of the "collective unconscious." They appear in literature as incidents and plots that repeat basic patterns of life. They may also appear as stereotyped characters.

***Avant-garde*:** French term meaning "vanguard." It is used in literary criticism to describe new writing that rejects traditional approaches to literature in favor of innovations in style or content.

B

Beat Movement: A period featuring a group of American poets and novelists of the 1950s and 1960s—including Jack Kerouac, Allen Ginsberg, Gregory Corso, William S. Burroughs, and Lawrence Ferlinghetti—who rejected established social and literary values. Using such techniques as stream of consciousness writing and jazz-influenced free verse and focusing on unusual or abnormal states of mind—generated by religious ecstasy or the use of drugs—the Beat writers aimed to create works that were unconventional in both form and subject matter.

***Bildungsroman*:** A German word meaning "novel of development." The *bildungsroman* is a study of the maturation of a youthful character, typically brought about through a series of social or sexual encounters that lead to self-awareness. *Bildungsroman* is used interchangeably with *erziehungsroman,* a novel of initiation and education. When a *bildungsroman* is concerned with the development of an artist (as in James Joyce's *A Portrait of the Artist as a Young Man*), it is often termed a *kunstlerroman.* Also known as Apprenticeship Novel, Coming of Age Novel, *Erziehungsroman,* or *Kunstlerroman.*

Black Aesthetic Movement: A period of artistic and literary development among African Americans in the 1960s and early 1970s. This was the first major African-American artistic movement since the Harlem Renaissance and was closely paralleled by the civil rights and black power movements. The black aesthetic writers attempted to produce works of art that would be meaningful to the black masses. Key figures in black aesthetics included one of its founders, poet and playwright Amiri Baraka, formerly known as LeRoi Jones; poet and essayist Haki R. Madhubuti, formerly Don L. Lee; poet and playwright Sonia Sanchez; and dramatist Ed Bullins. Also known as Black Arts Movement.

Black Humor: Writing that places grotesque elements side by side with humorous ones in an attempt to shock the reader, forcing him or her to laugh at the horrifying reality of a disordered world. Also known as Black Comedy.

Burlesque: Any literary work that uses exaggeration to make its subject appear ridiculous, either by treating a trivial subject with profound seriousness or by treating a dignified subject frivolously. The word "burlesque" may also be used as an adjective, as in "burlesque show," to mean "striptease act."

C

Character: Broadly speaking, a person in a literary work. The actions of characters are what constitute the plot of a story, novel, or poem. There are numerous types of characters, ranging from simple, stereotypical figures to intricate, multifaceted ones. In the techniques of anthropomorphism and personification, animals—and even places or things—can assume aspects of character. "Characterization" is the process by which an author creates vivid, believable characters in a work of art. This may be done in a variety of ways, including (1) direct description of the character by the narrator; (2) the direct presentation of the speech, thoughts, or actions of the character; and (3) the responses of other characters to the character. The term "character" also refers to a form originated by the ancient Greek writer Theophrastus that later became popular in the seventeenth and eighteenth centuries. It is a short essay or sketch of a person who prominently displays a specific attribute or quality, such as miserliness or ambition.

Climax: The turning point in a narrative, the moment when the conflict is at its most intense. Typically, the structure of stories, novels, and plays is one of rising action, in which tension builds to the climax, followed by falling action, in which tension lessens as the story moves to its conclusion.

Colloquialism: A word, phrase, or form of pronunciation that is acceptable in casual conversation but not in formal, written communication. It is considered more acceptable than slang.

Coming of Age Novel: See *Bildungsroman*

Concrete: Concrete is the opposite of abstract, and refers to a thing that actually exists or a description that allows the reader to experience an object or concept with the senses.

Connotation: The impression that a word gives beyond its defined meaning. Connotations may be universally understood or may be significant only to a certain group.

Convention: Any widely accepted literary device, style, or form.

D

Denotation: The definition of a word, apart from the impressions or feelings it creates (connotations) in the reader.

Denouement: A French word meaning "the unknotting." In literary criticism, it denotes the resolution of conflict in fiction or drama. The *denouement* follows the climax and provides an outcome to the primary plot situation as well as an explanation of secondary plot complications. The *denouement* often involves a character's recognition of his or her state of mind or moral condition. Also known as Falling Action.

Description: Descriptive writing is intended to allow a reader to picture the scene or setting in which the action of a story takes place. The form this description takes often evokes an intended emotional response—a dark, spooky graveyard will evoke fear, and a peaceful, sunny meadow will evoke calmness.

Dialogue: In its widest sense, dialogue is simply conversation between people in a literary work; in its most restricted sense, it refers specifically to the speech of characters in a drama. As a specific literary genre, a "dialogue" is a composition in which characters debate an issue or idea.

Diction: The selection and arrangement of words in a literary work. Either or both may vary depending on the desired effect. There are four general types of diction: "formal," used in scholarly or lofty writing; "informal," used in relaxed but educated conversation; "colloquial," used in everyday speech; and "slang," containing newly coined words and other terms not accepted in formal usage.

Didactic: A term used to describe works of literature that aim to teach some moral, religious, political, or practical lesson. Although didactic elements are often found in artistically pleasing works, the term "didactic" usually refers to literature in which the message is more important than the form. The term may also be used to criticize a work that the critic finds "overly didactic," that is, heavy-handed in its delivery of a lesson.

Doppelganger: A literary technique by which a character is duplicated (usually in the form of an alter ego, though sometimes as a ghostly counterpart) or divided into two distinct, usually opposite personalities. The use of this character device is widespread in nineteenth- and twentieth-century literature, and indicates a growing awareness among authors that the "self" is really a composite of many "selves." Also known as The Double.

Double Entendre: A corruption of a French phrase meaning "double meaning." The term is used to indicate a word or phrase that is deliberately ambiguous, especially when one of the meanings is risqué or improper.

Dramatic Irony: Occurs when the audience of a play or the reader of a work of literature knows something that a character in the work itself does not know. The irony is in the contrast between the intended meaning of the statements or actions of a character and the additional information understood by the audience.

Dystopia: An imaginary place in a work of fiction where the characters lead dehumanized, fearful lives.

E

Edwardian: Describes cultural conventions identified with the period of the reign of Edward VII of England (1901–1910). Writers of the Edwardian Age typically displayed a strong reaction against the propriety and conservatism of the Victorian Age. Their work often exhibits distrust of authority in religion, politics, and art and expresses strong doubts about the soundness of conventional values.

Empathy: A sense of shared experience, including emotional and physical feelings, with someone or something other than oneself. Empathy is often used to describe the response of a reader to a literary character.

Enlightenment, The: An eighteenth-century philosophical movement. It began in France but had a wide impact throughout Europe and America. Thinkers of the Enlightenment valued reason and believed that both the individual and society could achieve a state of perfection. Corresponding to this essentially humanist vision was a resistance to religious authority.

Epigram: A saying that makes the speaker's point quickly and concisely. Often used to preface a novel.

Epilogue: A concluding statement or section of a literary work. In dramas, particularly those of the seventeenth and eighteenth centuries, the epilogue is a closing speech, often in verse, delivered by an actor at the end of a play and spoken directly to the audience.

Epiphany: A sudden revelation of truth inspired by a seemingly trivial incident.

Episode: An incident that forms part of a story and is significantly related to it. Episodes may be either self-contained narratives or events that depend on a larger context for their sense and importance.

Epistolary Novel: A novel in the form of letters. The form was particularly popular in the eighteenth century.

Epithet: A word or phrase, often disparaging or abusive, that expresses a character trait of someone or something.

Existentialism: A predominantly twentieth-century philosophy concerned with the nature and perception of human existence. There are two major strains of existentialist thought: atheistic and Christian. Followers of atheistic existentialism believe that the individual is alone in a godless universe and that the basic human condition is one of suffering and loneliness. Nevertheless, because there are no fixed values, individuals can create their own characters—indeed, they can shape themselves—through the exercise of free will. The atheistic strain culminates in and is popularly associated with the works of Jean-Paul Sartre. The Christian existentialists, on the other hand, believe that only in God may people find freedom from life's anguish. The two strains hold certain beliefs in common: that existence cannot be fully understood or described through empirical effort; that anguish is a universal element of life; that individuals must bear responsibility for their actions; and that there is no common standard of behavior or perception for religious and ethical matters.

Expatriates: See *Expatriatism*

Expatriatism: The practice of leaving one's country to live for an extended period in another country.

Exposition: Writing intended to explain the nature of an idea, thing, or theme. Expository writing is often combined with description, narration, or argument. In dramatic writing, the exposition is the introductory material which presents the characters, setting, and tone of the play.

Expressionism: An indistinct literary term, originally used to describe an early twentieth-century school of German painting. The term applies to almost any mode of unconventional, highly subjective writing that distorts reality in some way.

F

Fable: A prose or verse narrative intended to convey a moral. Animals or inanimate objects with human characteristics often serve as characters in fables.

Falling Action: See *Denouement*

Fantasy: A literary form related to mythology and folklore. Fantasy literature is typically set in non-existent realms and features supernatural beings.

Farce: A type of comedy characterized by broad humor, outlandish incidents, and often vulgar subject matter.

Femme fatale: A French phrase with the literal translation "fatal woman." A *femme fatale* is a sensuous, alluring woman who often leads men into danger or trouble.

Fiction: Any story that is the product of imagination rather than a documentation of fact. Characters and events in such narratives may be based in real life but their ultimate form and configuration is a creation of the author.

Figurative Language: A technique in writing in which the author temporarily interrupts the order, construction, or meaning of the writing for a particular effect. This interruption takes the form of one or more figures of speech such as hyperbole, irony, or simile. Figurative language is the opposite of literal language, in which every word is truthful, accurate, and free of exaggeration or embellishment.

Figures of Speech: Writing that differs from customary conventions for construction, meaning, order, or significance for the purpose of a special meaning or effect. There are two major types of figures of speech: rhetorical figures, which do not make changes in the meaning of the words, and tropes, which do.

Fin de siecle: A French term meaning "end of the century." The term is used to denote the last decade of the nineteenth century, a transition period when writers and other artists abandoned old conventions and looked for new techniques and objectives.

First Person: See *Point of View*

Flashback: A device used in literature to present action that occurred before the beginning of the story. Flashbacks are often introduced as the dreams or recollections of one or more characters.

Foil: A character in a work of literature whose physical or psychological qualities contrast strongly with, and therefore highlight, the corresponding qualities of another character.

Folklore: Traditions and myths preserved in a culture or group of people. Typically, these are passed on by word of mouth in various forms—such as legends, songs, and proverbs—or preserved in customs and ceremonies. This term was first used by W. J. Thoms in 1846.

Folktale: A story originating in oral tradition. Folktales fall into a variety of categories, including legends, ghost stories, fairy tales, fables, and anecdotes based on historical figures and events.

Foreshadowing: A device used in literature to create expectation or to set up an explanation of later developments.

Form: The pattern or construction of a work which identifies its genre and distinguishes it from other genres.

G

Genre: A category of literary work. In critical theory, genre may refer to both the content of a given work—tragedy, comedy, pastoral—and to its form, such as poetry, novel, or drama.

Gilded Age: A period in American history during the 1870s characterized by political corruption and materialism. A number of important novels of social and political criticism were written during this time.

Gothicism: In literary criticism, works characterized by a taste for the medieval or morbidly attractive. A gothic novel prominently features elements of horror, the supernatural, gloom, and violence: clanking chains, terror, charnel houses, ghosts, medieval castles, and mysteriously slamming doors. The term "gothic novel" is also applied to novels that lack elements of the traditional Gothic setting but that create a similar atmosphere of terror or dread.

Grotesque: In literary criticism, the subject matter of a work or a style of expression characterized by exaggeration, deformity, freakishness, and disorder. The grotesque often includes an element of comic absurdity.

H

Harlem Renaissance: The Harlem Renaissance of the 1920s is generally considered the first significant movement of black writers and artists in the United States. During this period, new and established black writers published more fiction and poetry than ever before, the first influential black literary journals were established, and black authors and artists received their first widespread recognition and serious critical appraisal. Among the major writers associated with this period are Claude McKay, Jean Toomer, Countee Cullen, Langston Hughes, Arna Bontemps, Nella Larsen, and Zora Neale Hurston. Also known as Negro Renaissance and New Negro Movement.

Hero/Heroine: The principal sympathetic character (male or female) in a literary work. Heroes and heroines typically exhibit admirable traits: idealism, courage, and integrity, for example.

Holocaust Literature: Literature influenced by or written about the Holocaust of World War II. Such literature includes true stories of survival in concentration camps, escape, and life after the war, as well as fictional works and poetry.

Humanism: A philosophy that places faith in the dignity of humankind and rejects the medieval perception of the individual as a weak, fallen creature. "Humanists" typically believe in the perfectibility of human nature and view reason and education as the means to that end.

Hyperbole: In literary criticism, deliberate exaggeration used to achieve an effect.

I

Idiom: A word construction or verbal expression closely associated with a given language.

Image: A concrete representation of an object or sensory experience. Typically, such a representation helps evoke the feelings associated with the object or experience itself. Images are either "literal" or "figurative." Literal images are especially concrete and involve little or no extension of the obvious meaning of the words used to express them. Figurative images do not follow the literal meaning of the words exactly. Images in literature are usually visual, but the term "image" can also refer to the representation of any sensory experience.

Imagery: The array of images in a literary work. Also, figurative language.

In medias res: A Latin term meaning "in the middle of things." It refers to the technique of beginning a story at its midpoint and then using various flashback devices to reveal previous action.

Interior Monologue: A narrative technique in which characters' thoughts are revealed in a way that appears to be uncontrolled by the author. The interior monologue typically aims to reveal the inner self of a character. It portrays emotional experiences as they occur at both a conscious and unconscious level. Images are often used to represent sensations or emotions.

Irony: In literary criticism, the effect of language in which the intended meaning is the opposite of what is stated.

J

Jargon: Language that is used or understood only by a select group of people. Jargon may refer to terminology used in a certain profession, such as computer jargon, or it may refer to any non-sensical language that is not understood by most people.

L

Leitmotiv: See *Motif*

Literal Language: An author uses literal language when he or she writes without exaggerating or embellishing the subject matter and without any tools of figurative language.

Lost Generation: A term first used by Gertrude Stein to describe the post-World War I generation of American writers: men and women haunted by a sense of betrayal and emptiness brought about by the destructiveness of the war.

M

Mannerism: Exaggerated, artificial adherence to a literary manner or style. Also, a popular style of the visual arts of late sixteenth-century Europe that was marked by elongation of the human form and by intentional spatial distortion. Literary works that are self-consciously high-toned and artistic are often said to be "mannered."

Metaphor: A figure of speech that expresses an idea through the image of another object. Metaphors suggest the essence of the first object by identifying it with certain qualities of the second object.

Modernism: Modern literary practices. Also, the principles of a literary school that lasted from roughly the beginning of the twentieth century until the end of World War II. Modernism is defined by its rejection of the literary conventions of the nineteenth century and by its opposition to conventional morality, taste, traditions, and economic values.

Mood: The prevailing emotions of a work or of the author in his or her creation of the work. The mood of a work is not always what might be expected based on its subject matter.

Motif: A theme, character type, image, metaphor, or other verbal element that recurs throughout a single work of literature or occurs in a number of different works over a period of time. Also known as *Motiv* or *Leitmotiv.*

Myth: An anonymous tale emerging from the traditional beliefs of a culture or social unit. Myths use supernatural explanations for natural phenomena. They may also explain cosmic issues like creation and death. Collections of myths, known as mythologies, are common to all cultures and nations, but the best-known myths belong to the Norse, Roman, and Greek mythologies.

N

Narration: The telling of a series of events, real or invented. A narration may be either a simple narrative, in which the events are recounted chronologically, or a narrative with a plot, in which the account is given in a style reflecting the author's artistic concept of the story. Narration is sometimes used as a synonym for "storyline."

Narrative: A verse or prose accounting of an event or sequence of events, real or invented. The term is also used as an adjective in the sense "method of narration." For example, in literary criticism, the expression "narrative technique" usually refers to the way the author structures and presents his or her story.

Narrator: The teller of a story. The narrator may be the author or a character in the story through whom the author speaks.

Naturalism: A literary movement of the late nineteenth and early twentieth centuries. The movement's major theorist, French novelist Emile Zola, envisioned a type of fiction that would examine human life with the objectivity of scientific inquiry. The Naturalists typically viewed human beings as either the products of "biological determinism," ruled by hereditary instincts and engaged in an endless struggle for survival, or as the products of "socioeconomic determinism," ruled by social and economic forces beyond their control. In their works, the Naturalists generally ignored the highest levels of society and focused on degradation: poverty, alcoholism, prostitution, insanity, and disease.

Noble Savage: The idea that primitive man is noble and good but becomes evil and corrupted as he becomes civilized. The concept of the noble savage originated in the Renaissance period but is more closely identified with such later writers as

Jean-Jacques Rousseau and Aphra Behn. See also Primitivism.

Novel of Ideas: A novel in which the examination of intellectual issues and concepts takes precedence over characterization or a traditional storyline.

Novel of Manners: A novel that examines the customs and mores of a cultural group.

Novel: A long fictional narrative written in prose, which developed from the novella and other early forms of narrative. A novel is usually organized under a plot or theme with a focus on character development and action.

Novella: An Italian term meaning "story." This term has been especially used to describe fourteenth-century Italian tales, but it also refers to modern short novels.

O

Objective Correlative: An outward set of objects, a situation, or a chain of events corresponding to an inward experience and evoking this experience in the reader. The term frequently appears in modern criticism in discussions of authors' intended effects on the emotional responses of readers.

Objectivity: A quality in writing characterized by the absence of the author's opinion or feeling about the subject matter. Objectivity is an important factor in criticism.

Oedipus Complex: A son's amorous obsession with his mother. The phrase is derived from the story of the ancient Theban hero Oedipus, who unknowingly killed his father and married his mother.

Omniscience: See *Point of View*

Onomatopoeia: The use of words whose sounds express or suggest their meaning. In its simplest sense, onomatopoeia may be represented by words that mimic the sounds they denote such as "hiss" or "meow." At a more subtle level, the pattern and rhythm of sounds and rhymes of a line or poem may be onomatopoeic.

Oxymoron: A phrase combining two contradictory terms. Oxymorons may be intentional or unintentional.

P

Parable: A story intended to teach a moral lesson or answer an ethical question.

Paradox: A statement that appears illogical or contradictory at first, but may actually point to an underlying truth.

Parallelism: A method of comparison of two ideas in which each is developed in the same grammatical structure.

Parody: In literary criticism, this term refers to an imitation of a serious literary work or the signature style of a particular author in a ridiculous manner. A typical parody adopts the style of the original and applies it to an inappropriate subject for humorous effect. Parody is a form of satire and could be considered the literary equivalent of a caricature or cartoon.

Pastoral: A term derived from the Latin word "pastor," meaning shepherd. A pastoral is a literary composition on a rural theme. The conventions of the pastoral were originated by the third-century Greek poet Theocritus, who wrote about the experiences, love affairs, and pastimes of Sicilian shepherds. In a pastoral, characters and language of a courtly nature are often placed in a simple setting. The term pastoral is also used to classify dramas, elegies, and lyrics that exhibit the use of country settings and shepherd characters.

Pen Name: See *Pseudonym*

Persona: A Latin term meaning "mask." *Personae* are the characters in a fictional work of literature. The *persona* generally functions as a mask through which the author tells a story in a voice other than his or her own. A *persona* is usually either a character in a story who acts as a narrator or an "implied author," a voice created by the author to act as the narrator for himself or herself.

Personification: A figure of speech that gives human qualities to abstract ideas, animals, and inanimate objects. Also known as *Prosopopoeia*.

Picaresque Novel: Episodic fiction depicting the adventures of a roguish central character ("picaro" is Spanish for "rogue"). The picaresque hero is commonly a low-born but clever individual who wanders into and out of various affairs of love, danger, and farcical intrigue. These involvements may take place at all social levels and typically present a humorous and wide-ranging satire of a given society.

Plagiarism: Claiming another person's written material as one's own. Plagiarism can take the form of direct, word-for-word copying or the theft of the substance or idea of the work.

Plot: In literary criticism, this term refers to the pattern of events in a narrative or drama. In its simplest sense, the plot guides the author in composing the work and helps the reader follow the work. Typically, plots exhibit causality and unity and have a beginning, a middle, and an end. Sometimes, however, a plot may consist of a series of disconnected events, in which case it is known as an "episodic plot."

Poetic Justice: An outcome in a literary work, not necessarily a poem, in which the good are rewarded and the evil are punished, especially in ways that particularly fit their virtues or crimes.

Poetic License: Distortions of fact and literary convention made by a writer—not always a poet—for the sake of the effect gained. Poetic license is closely related to the concept of "artistic freedom."

Poetics: This term has two closely related meanings. It denotes (1) an aesthetic theory in literary criticism about the essence of poetry or (2) rules prescribing the proper methods, content, style, or diction of poetry. The term poetics may also refer to theories about literature in general, not just poetry.

Point of View: The narrative perspective from which a literary work is presented to the reader. There are four traditional points of view. The "third person omniscient" gives the reader a "godlike" perspective, unrestricted by time or place, from which to see actions and look into the minds of characters. This allows the author to comment openly on characters and events in the work. The "third person" point of view presents the events of the story from outside of any single character's perception, much like the omniscient point of view, but the reader must understand the action as it takes place and without any special insight into characters' minds or motivations. The "first person" or "personal" point of view relates events as they are perceived by a single character. The main character "tells" the story and may offer opinions about the action and characters which differ from those of the author. Much less common than omniscient, third person, and first person is the "second person" point of view, wherein the author tells the story as if it is happening to the reader.

Polemic: A work in which the author takes a stand on a controversial subject, such as abortion or religion. Such works are often extremely argumentative or provocative.

Pornography: Writing intended to provoke feelings of lust in the reader. Such works are often condemned by critics and teachers, but those which can be shown to have literary value are viewed less harshly.

Post-Aesthetic Movement: An artistic response made by African Americans to the black aesthetic movement of the 1960s and early '70s. Writers since that time have adopted a somewhat different tone in their work, with less emphasis placed on the disparity between black and white in the United States. In the words of post-aesthetic authors such as Toni Morrison, John Edgar Wideman, and Kristin Hunter, African Americans are portrayed as looking inward for answers to their own questions, rather than always looking to the outside world.

Postmodernism: Writing from the 1960s forward characterized by experimentation and continuing to apply some of the fundamentals of modernism, which included existentialism and alienation. Postmodernists have gone a step further in the rejection of tradition begun with the modernists by also rejecting traditional forms, preferring the anti-novel over the novel and the antihero over the hero.

Primitivism: The belief that primitive peoples were nobler and less flawed than civilized peoples because they had not been subjected to the tainting influence of society. See also Noble Savage.

Prologue: An introductory section of a literary work. It often contains information establishing the situation of the characters or presents information about the setting, time period, or action. In drama, the prologue is spoken by a chorus or by one of the principal characters.

Prose: A literary medium that attempts to mirror the language of everyday speech. It is distinguished from poetry by its use of unmetered, unrhymed language consisting of logically related sentences. Prose is usually grouped into paragraphs that form a cohesive whole such as an essay or a novel.

Prosopopoeia: See *Personification*

Protagonist: The central character of a story who serves as a focus for its themes and incidents and as the principal rationale for its development. The protagonist is sometimes referred to in discussions of modern literature as the hero or antihero.

Protest Fiction: Protest fiction has as its primary purpose the protesting of some social injustice, such as racism or discrimination.

Proverb: A brief, sage saying that expresses a truth about life in a striking manner.

Pseudonym: A name assumed by a writer, most often intended to prevent his or her identification as the author of a work. Two or more authors may work together under one pseudonym, or an author may use a different name for each genre he or she publishes in. Some publishing companies maintain "house pseudonyms," under which any number of authors may write installations in a series. Some authors also choose a pseudonym over their real names the way an actor may use a stage name.

Pun: A play on words that have similar sounds but different meanings.

R

Realism: A nineteenth-century European literary movement that sought to portray familiar characters, situations, and settings in a realistic manner. This was done primarily by using an objective narrative point of view and through the buildup of accurate detail. The standard for success of any realistic work depends on how faithfully it transfers common experience into fictional forms. The realistic method may be altered or extended, as in stream of consciousness writing, to record highly subjective experience.

Repartee: Conversation featuring snappy retorts and witticisms.

Resolution: The portion of a story following the climax, in which the conflict is resolved. See also *Denouement.*

Rhetoric: In literary criticism, this term denotes the art of ethical persuasion. In its strictest sense, rhetoric adheres to various principles developed since classical times for arranging facts and ideas in a clear, persuasive, appealing manner. The term is also used to refer to effective prose in general and theories of or methods for composing effective prose.

Rhetorical Question: A question intended to provoke thought, but not an expressed answer, in the reader. It is most commonly used in oratory and other persuasive genres.

Rising Action: The part of a drama where the plot becomes increasingly complicated. Rising action leads up to the climax, or turning point, of a drama.

Roman a clef: A French phrase meaning "novel with a key." It refers to a narrative in which real persons are portrayed under fictitious names.

Romance: A broad term, usually denoting a narrative with exotic, exaggerated, often idealized characters, scenes, and themes.

Romanticism: This term has two widely accepted meanings. In historical criticism, it refers to a European intellectual and artistic movement of the late eighteenth and early nineteenth centuries that sought greater freedom of personal expression than that allowed by the strict rules of literary form and logic of the eighteenth-century neoclassicists. The Romantics preferred emotional and imaginative expression to rational analysis. They considered the individual to be at the center of all experience and so placed him or her at the center of their art. The Romantics believed that the creative imagination reveals nobler truths—unique feelings and attitudes—than those that could be discovered by logic or by scientific examination. Both the natural world and the state of childhood were important sources for revelations of "eternal truths." "Romanticism" is also used as a general term to refer to a type of sensibility found in all periods of literary history and usually considered to be in opposition to the principles of classicism. In this sense, Romanticism signifies any work or philosophy in which the exotic or dreamlike figure strongly, or that is devoted to individualistic expression, self-analysis, or a pursuit of a higher realm of knowledge than can be discovered by human reason.

Romantics: See *Romanticism*

S

Satire: A work that uses ridicule, humor, and wit to criticize and provoke change in human nature and institutions. There are two major types of satire: "formal" or "direct" satire speaks directly to the reader or to a character in the work; "indirect" satire relies upon the ridiculous behavior of its characters to make its point. Formal satire is further divided into two manners: the "Horatian," which ridicules gently, and the "Juvenalian," which derides its subjects harshly and bitterly.

Science Fiction: A type of narrative about or based upon real or imagined scientific theories and technology. Science fiction is often peopled with alien creatures and set on other planets or in different dimensions.

Second Person: See *Point of View*

Setting: The time, place, and culture in which the action of a narrative takes place. The elements of setting may include geographic location, characters' physical and mental environments, prevailing cultural attitudes, or the historical time in which the action takes place.

Simile: A comparison, usually using "like" or "as," of two essentially dissimilar things, as in "coffee as cold as ice" or "He sounded like a broken record."

Slang: A type of informal verbal communication that is generally unacceptable for formal writing. Slang words and phrases are often colorful exaggerations used to emphasize the speaker's point; they may also be shortened versions of an often-used word or phrase.

Slave Narrative: Autobiographical accounts of American slave life as told by escaped slaves. These works first appeared during the abolition movement of the 1830s through the 1850s.

Socialist Realism: The Socialist Realism school of literary theory was proposed by Maxim Gorky and established as a dogma by the first Soviet Congress of Writers. It demanded adherence to a communist worldview in works of literature. Its doctrines required an objective viewpoint comprehensible to the working classes and themes of social struggle featuring strong proletarian heroes. Also known as Social Realism.

Stereotype: A stereotype was originally the name for a duplication made during the printing process; this led to its modern definition as a person or thing that is (or is assumed to be) the same as all others of its type.

Stream of Consciousness: A narrative technique for rendering the inward experience of a character. This technique is designed to give the impression of an ever-changing series of thoughts, emotions, images, and memories in the spontaneous and seemingly illogical order that they occur in life.

Structure: The form taken by a piece of literature. The structure may be made obvious for ease of understanding, as in nonfiction works, or may obscured for artistic purposes, as in some poetry or seemingly "unstructured" prose.

Sturm und Drang: A German term meaning "storm and stress." It refers to a German literary movement of the 1770s and 1780s that reacted against the order and rationalism of the enlightenment, focusing instead on the intense experience of extraordinary individuals.

Style: A writer's distinctive manner of arranging words to suit his or her ideas and purpose in writing. The unique imprint of the author's personality upon his or her writing, style is the product of an author's way of arranging ideas and his or her use of diction, different sentence structures, rhythm, figures of speech, rhetorical principles, and other elements of composition.

Subjectivity: Writing that expresses the author's personal feelings about his subject, and which may or may not include factual information about the subject.

Subplot: A secondary story in a narrative. A subplot may serve as a motivating or complicating force for the main plot of the work, or it may provide emphasis for, or relief from, the main plot.

Surrealism: A term introduced to criticism by Guillaume Apollinaire and later adopted by Andre Breton. It refers to a French literary and artistic movement founded in the 1920s. The Surrealists sought to express unconscious thoughts and feelings in their works. The best-known technique used for achieving this aim was automatic writing—transcriptions of spontaneous outpourings from the unconscious. The Surrealists proposed to unify the contrary levels of conscious and unconscious, dream and reality, objectivity and subjectivity into a new level of "super-realism."

Suspense: A literary device in which the author maintains the audience's attention through the buildup of events, the outcome of which will soon be revealed.

Symbol: Something that suggests or stands for something else without losing its original identity. In literature, symbols combine their literal meaning with the suggestion of an abstract concept. Literary symbols are of two types: those that carry complex associations of meaning no matter what their contexts, and those that derive their suggestive meaning from their functions in specific literary works.

Symbolism: This term has two widely accepted meanings. In historical criticism, it denotes an early modernist literary movement initiated in France during the nineteenth century that reacted against the prevailing standards of realism. Writers in this movement aimed to evoke, indirectly and symbolically, an order of being beyond the material world of the five senses. Poetic expression of personal emotion figured strongly in the movement, typically by means of a private set of symbols uniquely identifiable with the individual poet. The principal aim of the Symbolists was to express in words the highly complex feelings that grew out of everyday contact with the world. In a broader sense, the term "symbolism" refers to the use of one object to represent another.

T

Tall Tale: A humorous tale told in a straightforward, credible tone but relating absolutely impossible events or feats of the characters. Such tales were commonly told of frontier adventures during the settlement of the west in the United States.

Theme: The main point of a work of literature. The term is used interchangeably with thesis.

Thesis: A thesis is both an essay and the point argued in the essay. Thesis novels and thesis plays share the quality of containing a thesis which is supported through the action of the story.

Third Person: See *Point of View*

Tone: The author's attitude toward his or her audience may be deduced from the tone of the work. A formal tone may create distance or convey politeness, while an informal tone may encourage a friendly, intimate, or intrusive feeling in the reader. The author's attitude toward his or her subject matter may also be deduced from the tone of the words he or she uses in discussing it.

Transcendentalism: An American philosophical and religious movement, based in New England from around 1835 until the Civil War. Transcendentalism was a form of American romanticism that had its roots abroad in the works of Thomas Carlyle, Samuel Coleridge, and Johann Wolfgang von Goethe. The Transcendentalists stressed the importance of intuition and subjective experience in communication with God. They rejected religious dogma and texts in favor of mysticism and scientific naturalism. They pursued truths that lie beyond the "colorless" realms perceived by reason and the senses and were active social reformers in public education, women's rights, and the abolition of slavery.

U

Urban Realism: A branch of realist writing that attempts to accurately reflect the often harsh facts of modern urban existence.

Utopia: A fictional perfect place, such as "paradise" or "heaven."

V

Verisimilitude: Literally, the appearance of truth. In literary criticism, the term refers to aspects of a work of literature that seem true to the reader.

Victorian: Refers broadly to the reign of Queen Victoria of England (1837–1901) and to anything with qualities typical of that era. For example, the qualities of smug narrowmindedness, bourgeois materialism, faith in social progress, and priggish morality are often considered Victorian. This stereotype is contradicted by such dramatic intellectual developments as the theories of Charles Darwin, Karl Marx, and Sigmund Freud (which stirred strong debates in England) and the critical attitudes of serious Victorian writers like Charles Dickens and George Eliot. In literature, the Victorian Period was the great age of the English novel, and the latter part of the era saw the rise of movements such as decadence and symbolism. Also known as Victorian Age and Victorian Period.

W

Weltanschauung: A German term referring to a person's worldview or philosophy.

Weltschmerz: A German term meaning "world pain." It describes a sense of anguish about the nature of existence, usually associated with a melancholy, pessimistic attitude.

Z

Zeitgeist: A German term meaning "spirit of the time." It refers to the moral and intellectual trends of a given era.

Cumulative Author/Title Index

Plath, Sylvia
The Bell Jar: V1
The Poisonwood Bible (Kingsolver):
V24
Porter, Katherine Anne
Ship of Fools: V14
The Portrait of a Lady (James): V19
*A Portrait of the Artist as a Young
Man* (Joyce): V7
Potok, Chaim
The Chosen: V4
Power, Susan
The Grass Dancer: V11
A Prayer for Owen Meany (Irving):
V14
Price, Reynolds
A Long and Happy Life: V18
Pride and Prejudice (Austen): V1
The Prime of Miss Jean Brodie
(Spark): V22
The Prince (Machiavelli): V9
Puzo, Mario
The Godfather: V16
Pynchon, Thomas
Gravity's Rainbow: V23

R

Rabbit, Run (Updike): V12
Ragtime (Doctorow): V6
Rand, Ayn
Atlas Shrugged: V10
The Fountainhead: V16
The Razor's Edge (Maugham): V23
Rebecca (du Maurier): V12
The Red Badge of Courage (Crane):
V4
The Red Pony (Steinbeck): V17
The Remains of the Day (Ishiguro):
V13
Remarque, Erich Maria
All Quiet on the Western Front: V4
The Return of the Native (Hardy):
V11
Rhys, Jean
Wide Sargasso Sea: V19
Robinson Crusoe (Defoe): V9
Robinson, Marilynne
Gilead: V24
Rölvaag, O. E.
Giants in the Earth: V5
A Room with a View (Forster): V11
*Roots: The Story of an American
Family* (Haley): V9
Roth, Philip
American Pastoral: V25
Roy, Arundhati
The God of Small Things: V22
Rubyfruit Jungle (Brown): V9
Rumble Fish (Hinton): V15
Rushdie, Salman
Midnight's Children: V23
The Satanic Verses: V22

Russo, Richard
Empire Falls: V25

S

Salinger, J. D.
The Catcher in the Rye: V1
Sartre, Jean-Paul
Nausea: V21
The Satanic Verses (Rushdie): V22
The Scarlet Letter (Hawthorne): V1
Schindler's List (Keneally): V17
Scoop (Waugh): V17
Seize the Day (Bellow): V4
Sense and Sensibility (Austen): V18
A Separate Peace (Knowles): V2
Sewell, Anna
Black Beauty: V22
Shange, Ntozake
Betsey Brown: V11
Shelley, Mary
Frankenstein: V1
Shields, Carol
The Stone Diaries: V23
Ship of Fools (Porter): V14
Shizuko's Daughter (Mori): V15
Shoeless Joe (Kinsella): V15
Shogun: A Novel of Japan (Clavell):
V10
Shute, Nevil
On the Beach: V9
Siddhartha (Hesse): V6
Silas Marner (Eliot): V20
Sinclair, Upton
The Jungle: V6
Sister Carrie (Dreiser): V8
The Slave Dancer (Fox): V12
Slaughterhouse-Five (Vonnegut): V3
Smilla's Sense of Snow (Høeg): V17
Snow Falling on Cedars (Guterson):
V13
Solzhenitsyn, Aleksandr
*One Day in the Life of Ivan
Denisovich:* V6
Song of Solomon (Morrison): V8
Sons and Lovers (Lawrence): V18
Sophie's Choice (Styron): V22
Soul Catcher (Herbert): V17
The Sound and the Fury (Faulkner):
V4
Spark, Muriel
The Prime of Miss Jean Brodie:
V22
Steinbeck, John
East of Eden: V19
The Grapes of Wrath: V7
Of Mice and Men: V1
The Pearl: V5
The Red Pony: V17
Steppenwolf (Hesse): V24
Stevenson, Robert Louis
Dr. Jekyll and Mr. Hyde: V11
Treasure Island: V20

Stoker, Bram
Dracula: V18
The Stone Angel (Laurence): V11
The Stone Diaries (Shields): V23
Stones from the River (Hegi): V25
Stowe, Harriet Beecher
Uncle Tom's Cabin: V6
*The Strange Case of Dr. Jekyll and
Mr. Hyde* (Stevenson): see
Dr. Jekyll and Mr. Hyde
The Stranger (Camus): V6
Styron, William
Sophie's Choice: V22
Sula (Morrison): V14
Summer (Wharton): V20
Summer of My German Soldier
(Greene): V10
The Sun Also Rises (Hemingway):
V5
Surfacing (Atwood): V13
The Sweet Hereafter (Banks): V13
Swift, Graham
Waterland: V18
Swift, Jonathan
Gulliver's Travels: V6

T

A Tale of Two Cities (Dickens): V5
Tambourines to Glory (Hughes):
V21
Tan, Amy
The Joy Luck Club: V1
The Kitchen God's Wife: V13
Ten Little Indians (Christie): V8
Tender Is the Night (Fitzgerald): V19
Tess of the d'Urbervilles (Hardy):
V3
Tex (Hinton): V9
Thackeray, William Makepeace
Vanity Fair: V13
That Was Then, This Is Now
(Hinton): V16
Their Eyes Were Watching God
(Hurston): V3
them (Oates): V8
Things Fall Apart (Achebe): V2
This Side of Paradise (Fitzgerald):
V20
The Three Musketeers (Dumas): V14
The Time Machine (Wells): V17
To Kill a Mockingbird (Lee): V2
To the Lighthouse (Woolf): V8
Tolkien, John Ronald Reuel
The Hobbit: V8
Tolstoy, Leo
War and Peace: V10
Tom Jones (Fielding): V18
Too Late the Phalarope (Paton): V12
Toomer, Jean
Cane: V11
Toward the End of Time (Updike):
V24

Cumulative Nationality/Ethnicity Index

African American

Angelou, Maya
I Know Why the Caged Bird Sings: V2
Baldwin, James
Go Tell It on the Mountain: V4
Butler, Octavia
Kindred: V8
Parable of the Sower: V21
Cleage, Pearl
What Looks Like Crazy on an Ordinary Day: V17
Ellison, Ralph
Invisible Man: V2
Juneteenth: V21
Gaines, Ernest J.
The Autobiography of Miss Jane Pittman: V5
A Gathering of Old Men: V16
A Lesson before Dying: V7
Haley, Alex
Roots: The Story of an American Family: V9
Hughes, Langston
Tambourines to Glory: V21
Hurston, Zora Neale
Their Eyes Were Watching God: V3
Johnson, James Weldon
The Autobiography of an Ex-Coloured Man: V22
Kincaid, Jamaica
Annie John: V3
Morrison, Toni
Beloved: V6
The Bluest Eye: V1
Song of Solomom: V8

Sula: V14
Naylor, Gloria
Mama Day: V7
The Women of Brewster Place: V4
Shange, Ntozake
Betsey Brown: V11
Toomer, Jean
Cane: V11
Walker, Alice
The Color Purple: V5
Wright, Richard
Black Boy: V1

Algerian

Camus, Albert
The Plague: V16
The Stranger: V6

American

Agee, James
A Death in the Family: V22
Alcott, Louisa May
Little Women: V12
Alexie, Sherman
The Lone Ranger and Tonto Fistfight in Heaven: V17
Allison, Dorothy
Bastard Out of Carolina: V11
Alvarez, Julia
How the García Girls Lost Their Accents: V5
Anaya, Rudolfo
Bless Me, Ultima: V12
Anderson, Sherwood
Winesburg, Ohio: V4

Angelou, Maya
I Know Why the Caged Bird Sings: V2
Auel, Jean
The Clan of the Cave Bear: V11
Banks, Russell
The Sweet Hereafter: V13
Baum, L. Frank
The Wonderful Wizard of Oz: V13
Bellamy, Edward
Looking Backward: 2000–1887: V15
Bellow, Saul
Herzog: V14
Blume, Judy
Forever . . .: V24
Borland, Hal
When the Legends Die: V18
Bradbury, Ray
Dandelion Wine: V22
Fahrenheit 451: V1
Bridal, Tessa
The Tree of Red Stars: V17
Brown, Rita Mae
Rubyfruit Jungle: V9
Buck, Pearl S.
The Good Earth: V25
Burdick, Eugene J.
The Ugly American: V23
Butler, Octavia
Kindred: V8
Parable of the Sower: V21
Card, Orson Scott
Ender's Game: V5
Cather, Willa
Death Comes for the Archbishop: V19
My Ántonia: V2

Colombian

García Márquez, Gabriel
  Chronicle of a Death Foretold:
    V10
  Love in the Time of Cholera: V1
  One Hundred Years of Solitude:
    V5

Czechoslovakian

Kundera, Milan
  The Unbearable Lightness of
    Being: V18

Danish

Dinesen, Isak
  Out of Africa: V9
Høeg, Peter
  Smilla's Sense of Snow: V17

Dominican

Alvarez, Julia
  How the García Girls Lost Their
    Accents: V5
  In the Time of Butterflies: V9
Rhys, Jean
  Wide Sargasso Sea: V19

Dutch

Möring, Marcel
  In Babylon: V25

English

Adams, Douglas
  The Hitchhiker's Guide to the
    Galaxy: V7
Adams, Richard
  Watership Down: V11
Austen, Jane
  Emma: V21
  Persuasion: V14
  Pride and Prejudice: V1
  Sense and Sensibility: V18
Ballard, J. G.
  Empire of the Sun: V8
Blair, Eric Arthur
  Animal Farm: V3
Bowen, Elizabeth Dorothea Cole
  The Death of the Heart: V13
Brontë, Charlotte
  Jane Eyre: V4
Brontë, Emily
  Wuthering Heights: V2
Brookner, Anita
  Hotel du Lac: V23
Burgess, Anthony
  A Clockwork Orange: V15

Burney, Fanny
  Evelina: V16
Carroll, Lewis
  Alice's Adventurers in
    Wonderland: V7
Chrisite, Agatha
  Ten Little Indians: V8
Conrad, Joseph
  Heart of Darkness: V2
  Lord Jim: V16
Defoe, Daniel
  Moll Flanders: V13
  Robinson Crusoe: V9
Dickens, Charles
  A Christmas Carol: V10
  David Copperfield: V25
  Great Expectations: V4
  Hard Times: V20
  Oliver Twist: V14
  A Tale of Two Cities: V5
du Maurier, Daphne
  Rebecca: V12
Eliot, George
  Middlemarch: V23
  The Mill on the Floss: V17
  Silas Marner: V20
Fielding, Henry
  Tom Jones: V18
Foden, Giles
  The Last King of Scotland: V15
Forster, E. M.
  A Passage to India: V3
  Howards End: V10
  A Room with a View: V11
Fowles, John
  The French Lieutenant's Woman:
    V21
Golding, William
  Lord of the Flies: V2
Graves, Robert
  I, Claudius: V21
Greene, Graham
  The End of the Affair: V16
Hardy, Thomas
  Far from the Madding Crowd:
    V19
  The Mayor of Casterbridge: V15
  The Return of the Native: V11
  Tess of the d'Urbervilles: V3
Huxley, Aldous
  Brave New World: V6
Ishiguro, Kazuo
  The Remains of the Day: V13
James, Henry
  The Ambassadors: V12
  The Portrait of a Lady: V19
  The Turn of the Screw: V16
Kipling, Rudyard
  Kim: V21
Koestler, Arthur
  Darkness at Noon: V19
Lawrence, D. H.
  Sons and Lovers: V18

Lewis, C. S.
  The Lion, the Witch and the
    Wardrobe: V24
Maugham, W. Somerset
  The Razor's Edge: V23
Orwell, George
  1984: V7
  Animal Farm: V3
Rhys, Jean
  Wide Sargasso Sea: V19
Rushdie, Salman
  The Satanic Verses: V22
Sewell, Anna
  Black Beauty: V22
Shelley, Mary
  Frankenstein: V1
Shute, Nevil
  On the Beach: V9
Spark, Muriel
  The Prime of Miss Jean Brodie:
    V22
Stevenson, Robert Louis
  Dr. Jekyll and Mr. Hyde: V11
Swift, Graham
  Waterland: V18
Swift, Jonathan
  Gulliver's Travels: V6
Thackeray, William Makepeace
  Vanity Fair: V13
Tolkien, J. R. R.
  The Hobbit: V8
Waugh, Evelyn
  Brideshead Revisited: V13
  Scoop: V17
Wells, H. G.
  The Time Machine: V17
  The War of the Worlds: V20
Woolf, Virginia
  Mrs. Dalloway: V12
  To the Lighthouse: V8

European American

Hemingway, Ernest
  The Old Man and the Sea: V6
Stowe, Harriet Beecher
  Uncle Tom's Cabin: V6

French

Camus, Albert
  The Plague: V16
  The Stranger: V6
Dumas, Alexandre
  The Count of Monte Cristo: V19
  The Three Musketeers: V14
Flaubert, Gustave
  Madame Bovary: V14
Gide, André
  The Immoralist: V21
Hugo, Victor
  The Hunchback of Notre Dame:
    V20
  Les Misérables: V5

South African

Coetzee, J. M.
  Dusklands: V21
Gordimer, Nadine
  July's People: V4
Paton, Alan
  Cry, the Beloved Country: V3
  Too Late the Phalarope: V12

Spanish

Saavedra, Miguel de Cervantes
  Don Quixote: V8

Sri Lankan

Ondaatje, Michael
  The English Patient: V23

Swiss

Hesse, Hermann
  Demian: V15
  Siddhartha: V6
  Steppenwolf: V24

Uruguayan

Bridal, Tessa
  The Tree of Red Stars: V17

Vietnamese

Duong Thu Huong
  Paradise of the Blind: V23

West Indian

Kincaid, Jamaica
  Annie John: V3

Subject/Theme Index

*Boldface denotes discussion in
Themes section.

A

Abandonment
David Copperfield: 85–86
The Deerslayer: 114–115, 117
Empire Falls: 138, 147–148
The Good Earth: 186, 188,
190–191

Adulthood
David Copperfield: 83–84, 96

Adventure and Exploration
The Deerslayer: 110, 112, 114,
120–123, 125

Africa
*The Amazing Adventures of
Kavalier & Clay:* 13, 15

Alienation
Stones from the River: 270–271

Ambition
The Deerslayer: 129–133

American Northeast
*The Amazing Adventures of
Kavalier & Clay:* 1–2, 10, 12,
14, 18–20, 26, 28–29
American Pastoral: 32–36,
43–44
The Deerslayer: 110, 112–113,
117, 120–121, 123–124
Empire Falls: 135–136, 141,
148
Independence Day: 209–214,
218–220, 224–225, 227

American Northwest
Stones from the River: 273–274

American South
Cold Mountain: 58–59, 61, 65,
67–69, 73–75, 77–79, 82
Empire Falls: 137, 139–140, 149

Anger
David Copperfield: 104–105, 107
Empire Falls: 138, 141, 145–146,
148–149
The Good Earth: 166, 168–169,
174, 177
No-No Boy: 233, 237
Stones from the River: 253, 262,
264
Waiting: 279–281

Antarctica
*The Amazing Adventures of
Kavalier & Clay:* 5, 10

Anti-Semitism
Stones from the River: 253, 256,
261–265

**Anti-Semitism and
the Catholic Church**
Stones from the River: 261

Apathy
Independence Day: 225, 227–228

Asia
American Pastoral: 35, 43–44
The Good Earth: 164–165,
174–177
In Babylon: 201–202
No-No Boy: 231, 233–234, 237,
239–240, 245–248
Waiting: 276–278, 285–288,
292–295

**Assimilation and
Overcoming Self-Blame**
No-No Boy: 237

Atonement
Empire Falls: 139, 141, 146

Australia
David Copperfield: 89–90, 96

Authoritarianism
*The Amazing Adventures of
Kavalier & Clay:* 2, 4, 10, 14,
16–17, 23–24, 26–31
In Babylon: 196, 199, 201–202
Stones from the River: 250,
253–256, 261, 263–266,
270–271

B

Beauty
The Deerslayer: 110, 112, 114,
116–117, 121–122, 130,
132–133
The Good Earth: 180, 183, 186

Betrayal
The Deerslayer: 115, 120, 123,
129–131, 133

C

Childhood
David Copperfield: 83, 86–87,
94, 96, 103–106, 108
Empire Falls: 137–138, 148–149

Christianity
Stones from the River: 252,
254–255, 261–262, 264–265

City Life
American Pastoral: 52–53

City Versus Country
Waiting: 285